KT-439-452

A GENIUS FOR LIVING

A GENIUS FOR LIVING

A Biography of

Frieda Lawrence

JANET BYRNE

BLOOMSBURY

First published in Great Britain 1995

Bloomsbury Publishing Plc, 2 Soho Square, London W1V 6HB

A CIP catalogue record for this book is
available from the British Library

ISBN 0 7475 1284 1

10 9 8 7 6 5 4 3 2 1

Printed in Great Britain by Clays Ltd, St Ives plc

FOR MY PARENTS,

JAMES J. BYRNE

AND

CELESTA T. BYRNE

CONTENTS

Prologue 1

PART I Germany and England, 1879–1911

1 Mismatches 7
2 The Smell of Invasion 22
3 Ernest Weekley 39
4 Simmering in Nottingham 49
5 "Our Old Mother's Skin" 64

PART II Europe, Asia, Australia, America, 1912–1930

6 Simple Men, Giantesses, and Rabbits 87
7 Over the Alps 114
8 "Mrs. Lawrence" 127
9 "Don't You Know Me? I'm Frieda" 157
10 "She Actually Seemed a Lady" 178
11 *Dies Irae* 194
12 *Heimweh* 219

13 The Queen Bee 230
14 Around the World 255
15 The Lobo 265
16 Golden and Tin Calves 284
17 Angelino Ravagli 299
18 Vence 313

PART III New Mexico, 1931–1956

19 *"Not I, but the Wind . . . "* 343
20 From Hollywood to Laguna Vista 369
21 The Art of Dying 402

Epilogue 415
Notes 417
Selected Bibliography 471
Acknowledgments 477
Index 483

Prologue

Wearing a pale pongee suit wrinkled by two nights in a Pullman sleeper from San Francisco, Frieda Lawrence stepped onto the platform at Lamy, New Mexico, at 5:25 P.M., September 10, 1922.[1] Her eyes were blue-green,[2] flecked with yellow, and her long, wheat-colored hair was looped in a loose twist that fell in thick curls around her neck. She was exhausted after a seven-month trip across four continents, and the vastness of the desert filled her with yearning and a profound abstraction.[3]

D. H. Lawrence, her husband of eight years, giggled nervously as he tried to maneuver their battered double suitcase, two steamer trunks, and a broken-down, hand-painted, five-foot-long panel of a Sicilian cart along the platform. On one side of the panel was a vivid depiction of a medieval jousting scene, on the other a cameo of Saint Geneviève.[4] Next to Frieda, who was fleshy and pink-cheeked and appeared enormously healthy, he looked emaciated in his English schoolmaster's suit of unprocessed wool, his auburn hair brushed strangely forward and down toward his inexpertly groomed Vandyke. Six years younger than Frieda, a day shy of his thirty-seventh birthday, and ill with tuberculosis, he looked by far the smaller, though at five foot nine he was a good four inches taller.

They were a strange couple. She struck one observer as a sturdy stake, not out of place in this desert whistlestop, and Lawrence seemed like a wild, starving animal, tied to her solidity.[5] While he struggled with their luggage, Frieda took in every aspect of the fantasy landscape. Plumes of piñon smoke rose from the chimneys of several hundred low adobe houses, filling the air with a sweet, foreign smell. Past the town's single street, the desert went for miles, interrupted only by the distant dun-and-green foothills of the Sangre de Cristo Mountains. The street, a narrow, dusty strip of dirt rutted by wagon wheels, looked like an oater set. A new hotel in the Harvey House chain, the name El Ortiz written on its facade in florid script, faced the ornate, vaulted brick station house with its Spanish red-tile roof, packhorses idling at the arched door of its stables. It was a Sunday, and a crowd of townspeople, stragglers, and uniformed chambermaids and waitresses—the Harvey girls—milled around a gas pump and two stores: John Pflueger's General Merchandise and a liquor shop. The women's long dresses trailed in the dust. The men wore black hats against the strong sun.[6]

The Taos millionairess Mabel Dodge Sterne and her Pueblo Indian lover, Antonio "Tony" Luhan,[7] waited near Sterne's red Cadillac. Square-shaped, barely five feet, perfectly turned out in a recent bob, a turquoise blue dress, and a dazzling amount of turquoise-and-silver jewelry, she looked impeccable despite the eight-hour drive down from Taos in the Cadillac. Luhan, a hunter and lover of horses, had plucked eyebrows and waist-length hair tied with purple cloths into two string ponytails. Well over six feet tall and two hundred pounds, he wore a blanket over his shoulders in a complicated wrap and a silver belt diagonally across his massive chest. Both had deep brown skin, hers a tan acquired from horseback riding and sunbathing nude on the roof of her sprawling hacienda, which overlooked some seventeen thousand acres of sacred Pueblo land and a *penitente* church specializing in flagellation. The Lawrences, who had never met Sterne, recognized her from a flatteringly out-of-date eight-by-ten she had sent them in Sicily, captioned "Mabel Dodge 5 years ago just come to Taos."[8]

A philanthropist and salon impresario, she had become infatuated with Lawrence after reading *Sons and Lovers* and *Psychoanalysis and the Unconscious*, his book-length rant against Freudians. Her first letter to him had arrived in Sicily almost a year earlier, and she had paid for the

Lawrences' tickets from San Francisco. She disliked Frieda on sight, however, and was unnerved by Lawrence's physical frailty. It seemed clear to her that the two were a poor match. She also imagined that Frieda, seemingly so enchanted by the landscape, was actually envisioning her sex life with Luhan.[9]

Everyone fell silent after an exchange of introductions. Sterne continued to be at a loss for words as they sat on high chairs at the El Ortiz counter with coffee and a snack, and they ate quickly, then climbed into the Cadillac for the trip to Santa Fe, where they planned to spend the night before going on to Sterne's. Several attempts at conversation fell flat, and they passed the seventeen-mile drive in an uncomfortable silence as the clouds threw increasingly long shadows over the foothills, the setting sun turning the mountains the blood red from which they drew their name. Frieda watched the tiny yellow centers of the purple asters and the yellow-and-white Shasta daisies on the side of the road. She had often wondered how she could persuade Lawrence, an incurable wanderer, to stay anywhere. As the immensity of the mesa stretched before her, she felt, as she had known she would, that this was where she belonged.[10]

The quiet was broken suddenly when the engine died and Frieda harangued Lawrence to get out and fix it, though he knew nothing about engines. Luhan, also perplexed, got out and lifted the hood and looked inside, then got back in and pushed the starter button, and the engine roared to life. As they continued the climb to Santa Fe, Luhan, probably thinking about horses, said, "I guess there is some snake around here."[11]

PART I

Germany and England, 1879–1911

I

Mismatches

I

Born Emma Maria Frieda Johanna Baroness (Freiin) von Richthofen, Frieda reached New Mexico after a wandering life in countless borrowed homes and several dozen fourth-class hotels. Her looks were profoundly Teutonic and her temper likened, by admirers and detractors, to that of an Aztec war god, Gypsy, simpleton, fascist, or Bavarian peasant. She saw herself as a nomad, more by default than by choice, and remained by turns oblivious or contemptuous of what others thought of her.

Her story begins in war-weary, starched, petit-bourgeois, and citified circumstances, with the forced germanization of the French city of Metz, in Lorraine, after the Franco-Prussian War in 1870. Between the ages of two and sixteen she lived in the suburb of Sablon, where the family address was 208 Augny West, a large, two-story farmhouse abutting the tin barracks that were home to many of the ten thousand German troops who occupied the city. Mounted cavalrymen in blue capes patrolled the hillsides beyond Sablon and the flatlands between the von Richthofen grange and Metz. The surrounding fields—in more peaceful times bounteous with lilac, roses, poppies, potatoes, asparagus, cabbage, and the Riesling and Sylvaner grapes for Moselle wines—were terraced with *lunettes*, trenchlike fortifications that Frieda's father, Baron Friedrich Ernst Emil Ludwig von Richthofen, had helped construct during the war. They were overgrown with marguerites and lady's slipper, and Frieda, athletic, headstrong, and undisciplinable, loved to play in them, dodging patrolling sentinels, almost always coming home filthy.

The baron was a Silesian-born engineer who, through family connections and no particular effort of his own, had achieved a good position in the Prussian bureaucracy. His great pleasures were hunting, fishing, gambling, and whoring. By day his work, inspecting canals and other civic projects, seems to have brought more titles than responsibilities. At night he lost large sums in the Artillerie Offiziers Casino or, his bankroll not permitting, in the Allgemeines Militär Casino, Metz's gambling house for common soldiers.

The scion of generations of Junkers, Prussian landed aristocracy, he spent much of his life depressed, pining for the gentleman farmer's existence that had been his birthright, but of which his ancestors' lack of foresight, business acumen, and luck had robbed him. The only work that made him happy was horticulture, and he designed a variegated, musky, sprawling garden where Frieda and her sisters, Elisabeth "Else" Helene Amalie Sophie and Helene Johanna Mathilde, spent a great deal of time, following him around while he transplanted wildflowers from the outlying fields, cultivated tulips and iris, and planted an impressive grove of fruit trees, including mirabelles and other plums, strawberries, his own small Riesling grape arbor, and white Argenteuil asparagus with purple tips. A wisteria vine climbed the front of the house.[1] Else, the eldest, was a meticulous and reliable help in the garden. Johanna, nicknamed Nusch, was a beautiful girl with dark skin, "velvety eyes"[2]—at least as Frieda later remembered them—and a tendency to remain aloof from the family, who both adored and neglected her as the youngest. Frieda usually got bored after a few minutes of weeding or planting and wandered off, though she did make great ceremony and drama of seasonal milestones, as when her father got out the asparagus shears for the first cutting every March. Her marching steps behind the baron filled him with pride and a rare sense of domestic happiness.

Returning home from his office, Friedrich usually surveyed his garden extensively before greeting his wife, Baroness Anna Elise Lydia von Richthofen-Marquier; Frieda, waiting in the trees for him, admired the low light catching the gold buttons of the officer's uniform to which his civil service rank then entitled him. Out of the garden, however, he was an unconvincing patriarch. Of his household of Anna, Else, Frieda, Nusch, and four servants, only Frieda, the wild child, could be called an intimate, and from an early age she felt it her duty to compensate for what had gone wrong in his life. Later in life she would describe his temperament, and that of the von Richthofen side of the family, as "mystical," and she spoke appreciatively of "belong[ing] to a family of unusual men."[3] As a child, however, she was convinced that her father "had suffered from inferiors."[4] Hindsight never entirely reversed her precocious conviction that she somehow shared the burden of his sadness, or her immediate, visceral identification with his spectacular flaws and enormous charisma; when she spoke or wrote of him, she often seemed to be describing herself. He *looked*, she felt, as though he had been hurt. People would say the same of her.

On the rare occasions when he was moved to rein in her unruly temperament, she entered his private study with defiance and a blithe and not-unwarranted assumption that she would be forgiven. He nicknamed her Fritzl, the diminutive of his own name, then Fitzli-Putzli—short for the Aztec war god Huitzilopochtli—after an intense reading of William Hickling Prescott's *History of the Conquest of Mexico*. The baron liked to read history. The baroness read French novels and, like Emma Bovary, envied their heroines, "*femmes entretenues* [kept women]," she felt, "who get it all." Otherwise she "took refuge in . . . virtue," as Frieda later wrote, and in "an attitude of superior morality toward [Friedrich]. . . . She thought him immoral, so he would be."[5]

Frieda loved the fact that her mother refused to enter the baron's study—because he let the dogs up on the sofa. Sinking into a happy trance amid the cushions, she would admire his guns, the game heads mounted on plaques on the wall, and the lions and peacocks of the von Richthofen coat of arms, embossed both on the baron's writing paper and on the white handkerchief displayed in the breast pocket of his officer's jacket. It was a vainglorious coat of arms—a black-robed judge on a red chair clutching an eagle-topped gold scepter—and one that the baron and most of his immediate forefathers had little hope of living up to.

2

The crest was originally secured in Berlin in the sixteenth century by a scholar named Paul Schultheiss, a commoner who worked his way into a position as legal adviser to nobility. He latinized his name twice—to Scultetus and, after receiving the juridical coat of arms and a knighthood (signified by the title *Ritter*), to Paulus Praetorius. An adopted son, Samuel Schmidt, continued the family's ascent by becoming mayor of the town of Frankfurt an der Oder, in the province of Brandenburg.[6] His son, Tobias, moved to Silesia (now in Poland) and married a titled woman, Ursula Böhm von Böhmfeldt. Their eldest, Johann, received the Bohemian barony in 1661, during the reign of Frederick the Great, and, appropriately enough, took the family name von Richthofen (which refers to Schultheiss's position).

Five generations separated Johann from Friedrich. Two who ranked high among the more distinguished progeny were sired by distant branches of the family: World War I flying ace Manfred von Richthofen, the "Red Baron" (named for the color he painted his Fokker triplane), and the geographer and explorer Ferdinand von Richthofen, who at twenty-three visited Hunan province for the Wiener Reichsanstalt (Vienna's Imperial Institute). He later traveled to China four more times; to Japan, Formosa, the Philippines, the Celebes, Java, and India; and, like Frieda, climbed the Tirolean Alps and went to Ceylon and the American Southwest.[7]

Friedrich's father, Johann Karl Christian Friedrich Ludwig August Praetorius von Richthofen, came from a line that produced several high-ranking diplomats, among them Emil von Richthofen, an uncle of Friedrich's, who was Prussia's ambassador to Sweden, and his son Oswald, who worked in the Foreign Ministry and later became secretary of state. Johann came of a far less eminent branch of the line, farmers with a vast holding in the Kosel district—southwest of Breslau (Wrocław)—called Raschowa, in Upper Silesia.

"[S]ublime gloom," according to John Quincy Adams, after a tour of the country in 1800–1801, characterized much of Upper Silesia, and extremes of wealth also numbered among its most remarkable features, second only to racial and religious divisiveness.[8] Raschowa was worked by Poles, who in essence functioned as indentured slaves or sharecroppers to the von Richthofens and other Junkers and resented it immensely; Adams's carriage was surrounded by "groups of reapers . . . soliciting our charity" the minute it reached the countryside.[9] Though the von Richthofen clan owned twenty-five estates, Friedrich's family had only a fraction of the property: an estate house he later remembered as resembling a "castle," a small lake, and a forest stocked with game.[10] It was rich with wheat, rye, barley, oats, flax, and beetroot—of great value when, for the brief period of the Napoleonic Wars, the importation of sugar from the British West Indies was embargoed. Johann's father, Ludwig, however, had had no luck with marriage, livestock, or land and crop speculation: He lost three wives; an entire flock of sheep to lightning (or so family legend has it; apparently the flock was small, and sheltering under a tree); and, from the 1820s, when he inherited the estate, much of the family's real property—after the sugar-beet market collapsed. Along with Raschowa he passed the family's bad luck on to Johann, who became further overextended, took only intermittent care of Raschowa, and made an unhappy marriage to Amalie Louise von Laschowski. A proud, regal woman, she was the child of a mixed marriage of Polish and German aristocrats and a rigidly Germanic household. After she bore Johann two sons, Louis and Emil, and a daughter, Helene, Friedrich was born on their eleventh wedding anniversary. Another boy, Paul, followed in 1847.

Life at Raschowa was a bitter disappointment for Amalie, who liked to think of herself as a countess.[11] She returned to her parents' home to deliver Louis, considering it the place she belonged and Raschowa merely an unpleasant stopover, though as time wore on, she became more resigned to the estate and endured her pregnancies there, watching Raschowa go from bad to worse as Johann speculated unsuccessfully. There was very little money to speak of by the time Friedrich came along. Johann, who served as the Kosel district president, left frequently, and Amalie just as frequently put herself into a post chaise for the journey to the industrial county seat of Kosel, where she would stand on the bank of the Oder and weep as she ruminated on her married life to the droning rush of the water and the ax beats of the woodcutters. In the distance ships left the busy inland harbor, carrying coal, lime, grain, and—when it was in demand at all—Raschowa sugar.

• • •

The politically momentous year of 1848 brought a typhoid epidemic and famine to Upper Silesia, killing sixteen thousand people, including Emil, eight, and Paul, just over a year old. *Der Volkerfrühling*, or the Spring of Nations, triggered spasms of nationalism, democratization, and rebellion among the Polish peasants.[12] A band of them massed at Raschowa while Johann was away, and huntsmen and gardeners held them at bay with garden tools and game rifles until two sergeants and ten men arrived from Kosel. One of Friedrich's very few early memories left to posterity is of these soldiers, in particular a Rhineland wheelwright who sat in the drawing room whittling tiny weapons for him.[13] The little boy was clearly destined for the military.

3

By 1862 the militarization—and democratization—of Germany had reached fever pitch. Otto von Bismarck, the Junker who had risen to become the Iron Chancellor of the Second Reich, sided with Kaiser Wilhelm I against the parliamentarists in Berlin. His "iron and blood" speech, one of the great antidemocratic rants of the last century, spurred thousands of young men, both of the cities and the Reich's far-flung provinces, to join the army: "Not by speeches and decisions of majorities," the Iron Chancellor declared in the Reichstag, "will the greatest problems of the time be decided—that was the mistake of 1848–49—but by iron and blood."[14] Friedrich, then seventeen, said goodbye to his father and, with two loaves of bread in his pockets and a glance back at the terraced fields of the moribund estate, set off to join the army. Amalie had died two years before; it is unclear what became of Friedrich's surviving siblings. The ensuing ten years, which led to the unification of Germany, brought a series of wars—against Denmark in 1864, Austria in 1866, and France in 1870. Friedrich, enlisting as a cadet, had qualified for an engineers' regiment by 1869. A fully trained, highly disciplined, and extremely handsome twenty-four-year-old soldier, he had also become well schooled (as his diary attests) in all forms of gambling and debauchery.[15] The Franco-Prussian War was declared by Napoleon III on July 19, 1870, and on August 1, the French marched across German lines. The Germans, armed to the teeth, repulsed them easily and within two and a half weeks had defeated France at Worth, Spicheren, Mars la Tour, and Gravelotte.[16] Friedrich first saw battle on August 21, in a series of skirmishes fought southwest of Strasbourg.

For the next four months of active duty, taken up equally with drinking, gambling, and the building of batteries between Strasbourg and Reims, he helped conquer Champagne, Cognac, and Moselle, one bottle at a time. When the pace of battle required his regiment to throw up hundreds of *lunettes* in several days, he relaxed the following evenings by losing at skat (a three-handed card game) and drinking heavily. Through early September he helped construct eight hundred fortifications under French fire. On September 2 he witnessed thirty men killed and a lieutenant and captain mutilated, but he seems to have become battle hardened: "Rainy weather, our cook is on strike," he wrote in his diary the next day. "In the evening news of Napoleon's surrender." Six days later, near Strasbourg, he saw Napoleon for himself and was unimpressed. War was inconvenient, tedious, and noisy: "French sentinels," he wrote, "shout awfully."[17] On September 27 he spotted the white flag on the Strasbourg Cathedral that signified the surrender of the city.

The following month passed in a haze of grenade explosions, gunfire, and hands of skat, as the Prussians pushed farther into France. Metz capitulated in late October. November brought whist, drunken binges, and two opportunities to use his saber: "In the evening a mad scene at the Horse [a drinking and gambling club]. I beat up an artillery officer with the saber."[18] On the following night, he slapped his orderly, Heinrich, for drinking too much. By the end of November, he was falling asleep dead drunk with his pants on. In late December, in Belfort, thirty miles from the Swiss border, he lay on a battlefield, his right hand smashed by French fire. As he was removed to a hospital, delirious with fever, Friedrich overheard the French doctor treating him predict to his nurse that he would "not see tomorrow."[19] Two days before the New Year, a sergeant arrived to tell him he had been awarded the Iron Cross.

Friedrich emerged from the war a conflicted man: impatient, fierce, controlling, sentimental, and hostile. Discharged with a misshapen and partially paralyzed hand and the rank of Leutnant (the equivalent of a second lieutenant), he became a civil engineer, "a pleasant job," his future wife, Anna Marquier, wrote blithely, "which took him around the beautiful countryside."[20]

4

Like that of the von Richthofens, the family history of Frieda's mother is filled with transience, upward mobility, and failed marriages, and begins with an adoption. Josef Marquier, born in 1749 in Offenburg, Germany, was an eccentric man of French extraction and various professions, among them milliner and merchant. He seems to have had a talent—or mania—for curing the sick, and was constantly being warned by city authorities not to dispense medicine, which he did on an amateur basis. He and his wife, Barbara Stranski, were childless, and some twenty-five years after their marriage, they adopted a son, Franz Josef, born in 1789, the child of Josef Gering, of Neustadt, and his wife, Franziska Willenstein.

At the age of fifteen Franz was forced to assume the familial duties when his adoptive father was locked up for several months in a Karlsruhe penitentiary for his illegal pharmaceutical trade. On his release he was asked to leave Offenburg. He died before being driven out, at the age of fifty-six, leaving Barbara and Franz destitute. She was forced to appeal to the city for rations of firewood during the remaining fourteen years of her life. When Franz reached adulthood, he attempted to become police commissioner, but the city did not look favorably on the application of the son of a man they had had to lock up. Franz became a lawyer instead. He married Walburga Nüble, of Freiburg im Breisgau, on October 20, 1817. Seven months later she gave birth to Josef Adolf, whom they called Adolf, and two years later a girl, Josefa Oktavia. Adolf, Frieda's grandfather, became a lawyer and married Josefa Theresia Walburga Schlosser, apparently a distant cousin. They raised their family in Donaueschingen, thirty miles southeast of Freiburg.[21]

A Catholic village deep in the Black Forest, dotted with shrines, madonnas, and crucifixes, Donaueschingen was essentially an appendage to the court of the Prince von Fürstenburg, whose huge castle dwarfed its tiny, perfect whitewashed houses and small avenues. The town and court functioned separately, but a constant stream of journeymen and royalty, who liked to hunt boar and game birds on the castle's hilly grounds, made for thriving trade and dangled the prospect of upward mobility. Julius, the prince's marksman, kept the villagers up to date on the royal gossip. The Marquiers, like their neighbors, fantasized about life at court, particularly when it became possible to rub elbows with the Fürstenburgs—as in winter, when the gentle slopes were opened for sleigh riding and the village children invited into the castle afterward for cocoa.

Outside court it was a deeply superstitious, bourgeois place, with all the magical beliefs and small-spiritedness of the locales depicted in the Grimm brothers' fairy tales. Hansel and Gretel literally came to life every February, when the story was enacted in the streets and in the surrounding Black Forest. The town eccentric, Fraulein Zepf, was a hermit who kept a chest of money next to her bed and came out to the street only in the evenings, to pump water at the well of the baker, Frau Syfried, and buy her groceries in the gloaming. She crept back home and considered her errands a success if she had managed not to talk to anyone. The regional newspaper arrived nightly by stagecoach—in winter by sleigh. When a bell announced its arrival, the townspeople scrambled through the pines to the posthouse, lighting their way with lanterns. Then the night once again went black, and the night watchman resumed singing on the hour—a lulling rhyme about fire and light and avoiding misfortune.[22]

This was the nightly activity on the working-class Josefstrasse, where Adolf and Josefa lived in a three-family house whose other tenants were an elderly Frenchwoman with pretensions to royalty and a Baroness von Koller, who lived with her two daughters in an elegantly appointed apartment. Anna, Frieda's mother, was born prematurely on July 14, 1851. Despite the summer heat, a fire was lit in the kitchen's porcelain stove and she was put in the stovepipe to warm up. The premature birth and an allergy to milk made her a colicky night terror. "For goodness' sake," Adolf would shout, "throw the crybaby out the window."[23]

Adolf was an ambitious man, a snob, and a domestic tyrant who enjoyed the pomp of outmoded manners harking back, at times, to the seventeenth century. The family's private life was an elaborate rehearsal for a grander existence they would never know, and the strict regimen Adolf enforced at home was at odds with the more freewheeling activities of their neighbors. He aspired to a one-family home and a place in the upper echelon of the professional community, and was inordinately proud that the back of his house fronted the rear of the prince's outbuildings.

Anna grew up associating "cheerfulness" and "love" with their neighbors, and indoors with ostentation and ambition. She became unhappily accustomed to both, and grew up a strange mix of impressionable, pious, judgmental, and extremely devoted to those older neighbors who would have anything to do with her. She loved getting up at seven on freezing mornings to get to church first, and though she described Donaueschingen as a "paradise on earth," where certain behavior was not "tolerated," at heart she hated her parents' mania for discipline and order.[24]

Despite having four siblings, Anna was very lonely. The eldest, Adolf, left for Freiburg when she was still a girl to attend a military institute run by their uncle. A free spirit, Adolf often strayed from the rigors of the academy to wander through the Black Forest with a canary in a cage strapped to his back like a latter-day Papageno. In warm weather Anna and Franz, a younger brother, sat for hours at the source of the Danube.[25] When Anna dropped one of her vast collection of dolls into a chalk pit one day on the way to the river, he immediately jumped in after it. A passerby had to fish out both the doll and her brother, after which Anna led the "victims" home to be dusted off.[26] Anna loved to think of Franz as a victim. He obeyed her slavishly, and she learned to manipulate his affections shamelessly, treating him by turns like a much-valued valet and a plaything, indistinguishable from her dolls. Her favorite doll had eyes that closed when she pulled a hidden wire, to which Anna attached almost mystical significance.

In time Donaueschingen's reliable provincialism and Franz's blind devotion filled Anna with the conviction that she was always right. She demanded beauty, decorum, and ceremony, and she and Franz made daily rounds of Josefstrasse, where her ingratiating good manners and precocious sociability earned them welcome and sweets at almost every door. She had a prodigious appetite. The Leitgab brothers, who ran a grocery store, gave her hard candy, currant bread, and prunes from their cabinets, and taught her aphorisms to memorize and recite by way of thanks. Her home away from home was the Hotel Zum Schützen, where twice a year an itinerant dentist from the spectacular lakeside town of Constance who extracted the teeth of half the Black Forest inhabitants set up shop.

The hotel was run by the Franks, a family of seven. Anna ate freely from their larder and bread bin and spent long hours sitting for Herr Frank, a painter. As an adolescent she looked like a figure from a devotional scene, and Herr Frank used her in his altar pictures. Though she had a gentle underbite, it was not so pronounced as it later became, and her eyes were moody and hooded. Her face was fleshy and oblong, and, with an ostentation out of keeping with her strict toilette and bearing, she wore her dark hair piled in curls above her forehead.

From the time she was twelve, Anna could not bear to be away from the Franks for more than a day. She stretched a rope from her house to the hotel, with a cowbell attached to each end so she could call them. When she contracted measles and had to be quarantined, she hated having to stay home alone with her mother for the required two full weeks and protested so vigorously that she was finally brought to convalesce at the Franks'.

The Marquiers stayed in Donaueschingen long enough to see the first telegraph wire laid. In 1865, when Anna was fourteen, they moved to the nearby village of Villingen, where she entered a convent school and transferred her unanswered daughterly affections to the school organist. In the summer of 1867 they fulfilled one of Adolf's aspirations by moving into a one-family house in Constance, and Anna spent one of her better summers exploring the town with Adolf's canary, which he had bequeathed to her before volunteering for the Bavarian Army. The Bodensee (Lake Constance) carried steamboats across to Austria and Switzerland several times a day, and in the distance stood the alpine range in the Swiss canton of Appenzell. One peak, the Säntis, was usually covered in snow, while in Meersburg, on the northwest arm of the lake, grapevines climbed the hills. A new 250-foot tower in the Gothic style rose from the eleventh-century Romanesque cathedral in the town square, and Anna climbed its interior stairs to look out over the countryside. In the fall she and Franz were shipped off to boarding schools. Franz, forever the family whipping boy, was sent to their uncle's military institute "for stricter discipline."[27] He had developed a passion for brewing beer.[28] Anna, sixteen, went to an extremely progressive girls' school in Freiburg, the Institute Blas.

Anna found Freiburg as pretty as she did Constance, only far more open and learned. Springwater ran down through the gutters of the streets in *Bächle*, narrow streams channeled by exposed troughs. Trains fanning east to the Höllenthal mountains carried amateur climbers in lederhosen and leather ankle boots.[29] The cafés teemed with students her age.

The Institute Blas was in an imposing, ornately decorated building on Kaiserstrasse, several blocks from Freiburg University, one of the most renowned in Germany. The institute had been established in 1864, three years before Anna's arrival, by Julie Blas, a nondescript twenty-four-year-old health and fitness enthusiast who had become a teacher in England at the age of eighteen. She had recruited her first boarder there—a girl who became so smitten she accompanied Blas to Freiburg. Julie's younger sister, Camilla, a painter, furniture decorator, and antique collector, joined the institute shortly after. Neither sister married.

Enormous dedication was typical of most girls who studied with the *Tanten* (aunts), as the Blases liked to be known, and within several years the institute was an international success. Julie often put on a stentorian gray wig for interviews with the parents of prospective pupils to convince them that she was well qualified. She introduced methods of teaching French and English not used before in Germany, and the school dispensed with the typical finishing touches—cooking, sewing, manners, and so forth—in favor of activities like *Stelzen*, walking on stilts.[30] The girls were also taught to beat African drums with authentic rhythms.

The exertions at the Institute Blas gave Anna sturdy muscles, and she developed a solid, curvaceous body. One of nine boarders and a hundred day students, she found the ultimate mother figure in Julie. When the competition from other students proved too much, she could latch on to the Blases' many friends, independent-minded women who, like the *Tanten*, had no interest in marriage. She felt that the "foundation pillars" of her life had been laid: Her "soul and heart opened up for everything beautiful," and when the time came to leave, she cried almost all the way home to her brother Adolf, then stationed in Constance, who had been sent to Freiburg to accompany her on the trip.[31] He replied by spinning impressionistic yarns of the army. She pined for Franz and his devotion, but he had emigrated to the United States, where he planned to become a brewmaster.[32] Apparently she never saw him again.

5

In September 1871 Constance was being readied for the visit of Kaiser Wilhelm I, en route from France to celebrate his victory over Napoleon III. Adolf Marquier was named to a committee of burghers welcoming the kaiser at a fete, and he saw to it that Anna, twenty, was chosen as the "maiden of honor" who would offer the emperor a bouquet of roses.[33]

The Constance Council Hall was packed for the occasion, and all eyes were on Anna, stately and full-figured in an elaborate white dress with several overskirts gathered up in a lace bustle and descending into a multi-tiered train, her hair parted and drawn back severely from her face. She was attended by a dozen younger girls dressed identically in white, who encircled her with a garland of green boughs and pink rosettes that snaked almost around the room. Under the watchful gaze of her father, she strode to the center of the hall. The kaiser accepted the roses, and a cheer went up.

In the crowd Friedrich von Richthofen, in military full dress, decorated with his Iron Cross, a saber at his waist, was riveted by Anna's self-assurance and beauty. They were introduced after the victory ceremony. Anna had never before spoken with a Prussian. Flirtatious and fluent in idiomatic French picked up in the various farmhouses he had occupied during the war, Friedrich seemed charming, worldly, and brave. Like many of his fellow officers flushed with his successes in the war, he conveyed a sense of purpose and mission, though he was by now quite disillusioned about his terminated military career.

Anna considered it an honor to be associated with an officer, and she wanted to get married. If there was any objection within the family to her marrying a Protestant, there is no record of it (there is some indication that she may have converted from Catholicism).[34] Even what she knew of Friedrich's vices seemed noble, as did his nervous tics: She developed a feeling of tenderness for his habit of shaking his wounded right hand "down at his side, as if it hurt."[35] She also appreciated his love of good food and found him beautiful. He ate well but was slight, with a narrow chest. Twenty-six, not very tall, he had a wild beard, a mustache combed and waxed to half-hearted points, in an approximation of the military style of the day, and thick, wavy hair.

He began calling on Anna. A honeymooners' town, Constance was perfect for their idealized if intermittent courtship, conducted between Friedrich's occasional diplomatic junkets and travels for the civil administration of the Reich. They rode the steamboats up the Bodensee and strolled through the marketplace, where a new statue of Winged Victory was being erected. Friedrich told Anna about his childhood in Silesia and reported, selectively, his war experiences in France. They became engaged in March 1872, a year and a half into their courtship, and were married four months later. In the civilian clothing he wore for the wedding, Friedrich was far less impressive, to Anna and her parents, than he had been in uniform.

6

Anna considered her first two years of marriage "pleasant" (the word she had earlier used to describe Friedrich's job) and "nice."[36] She found her own parents' company much more enjoyable than she had before, and her happiest time every day was a walk she and Friedrich took to visit them. They would also stroll to the Council Hall, where a prominent artist was working on a fresco of the kaiser's visit, which featured Anna presenting her bouquet of roses. Adolf was portrayed wearing pointed patent leather shoes, holding a tall silk top hat and reaching for his wine goblet with a thick hand, the unmistakable hauteur of the arriviste on his face. Friedrich was not included.[37]

In 1874 Friedrich was offered the position of minister plenipotentiary and envoy extraordinary to Sweden (*Ausserordentlicher Gesandter und bevollmächtigter Minister für Schweden*), probably through the intercession of his uncle Emil, the ambassador.[38] Inexplicably, the post was to be administered from the proud French town of Château-Salins, in Lorraine, which despised the occupying Prussians. Quite possibly it was diplomatic window dressing and carried few, if any, actual duties; Friedrich eventually made something of a specialty of acquiring such titles. The von Richthofens left Constance in a carriage with their household belongings and clothing, and a small library that included the Marquiers' handwritten family cookbook. Their kitchen maid, Elise, held the cage containing Anna's canary. "In proud spirits to be allowed to work on this German problem, we arrived in Lorraine," Anna wrote, not yet comprehending what awaited them. A French official met them at the district border and instructed them to step into a "most primitive vehicle," its seats elevated to a terrifying height. Elise sat in the back, "where normally the calves were transported for slaughter."[39]

The hostility of the French toward the Prussians quickly became evident, and to Anna the move took on the aspect of a death march, the trip over the rich black earth and green fields making her feel as though "we were going to the end of the world."[40] In Château-Salins they were installed on the first floor of a house filled with French.

When the furniture mover left, Anna and Elise burst into tears. "It is a land with not a word of German, the salad is eaten separately, no lock will close," Elise cried to Anna.

As representatives of the German civil command, they were pariahs, their circle limited to fellow Germans, their greetings snubbed by their neighbors on the second floor. "We did our shopping in Nancy—and were young," Anna wrote.[41] Her loneliness was mitigated somewhat by the birth of Else, a year later, on October 8, 1875, and the family's removal the following year to Saarburg, where they stayed a year and a half. In 1877 Friedrich became county counselor of the privy chamber of the Foreign Office (*Kreisassessor des Geheimen Sekretariats des Auswärtigen Amts*) and was transferred to Metz.[42] In March 1878 they moved again, to Metz.

7

Called "townlet of the gods" by the Romans, Metz was a city of damp stone streets built on small hills, Roman burial mounds, and two thousand years of provincial struggles—Roman and Gallic, Protestant and Catholic, French and German. Still more Roman-seeming than French, its squat stone houses sat like armories, despite the lace curtains that hung in every window, and its dark alleyways were a backward move through history. Even its famous thirteenth-century cathedral seemed tense—clumsy and unbalanced, missing a second tower that had been planned but never built. At dusk ravens croaked themselves to sleep in its ornamental frets.

The von Richthofens moved on March 15, 1878, into rooms let by a Frenchman in a stone house with ten-foot-high shuttered and barricaded windows and a view of the old town walls. The address was 10 Theobaldswall: Under the annexation terms of the Franco-Prussian War, street names had been changed from French to German.[43] The rent apparently being paid by the German civil administration, the apartment also served as Friedrich's office. Frieda was born in the afternoon of August 11, 1879. Anna had hoped for a boy; like the baron, she eventually used the masculine diminutive Fritzl for their second daughter. Amid the litany of her complaints about Theobaldswall is a single reference—"Frieda was born here"—to the events of August 11 and of Frieda's first two years. "Our relations with the house tenants were hostile," she wrote, describing a now-familiar situation; Metz was an "old fortress" that gave her "an unfriendly feeling."[44]

2

The Smell of Invasion

I

Over time many French did become confreres of the Prussians, their attitudes tempered and compromised by the everyday realities of the occupation. Such accommodation was slow in coming, however, and the prevailing mood in the late 1870s was one of contempt and mistrust. Bloated German corpses were occasionally found floating in rivers, French businesses were vandalized, and other crimes of restitution and patriotic passion were rampant. Guy de Maupassant, twenty years old in 1870, when he served as a private in the retreating French Army, later wrote about such an occupation in the story "Boule de Suif." The town, he wrote, had the *smell* of invasion, which "filled the . . . houses and public places, changed the taste of foodstuffs, and made people feel as if they were in a foreign land, far from home, among dangerous savage tribes."[1] In Metz there was a soldier for every two civilians. The streets were filled with the officers of the Blue Hussars, common infantrymen, and civil officials like Friedrich—who in 1880 was designated cultural engineer (*Kulturingenieur*).[2] His entire regiment was also assigned to Metz. Thousands of French had fled the city across the redefined border.

In October 1881, two months after Frieda's second birthday, and with another child on the way, Friedrich and Anna attempted to leave the hostility behind by moving a mile outside the city to Sablon. "Home" had strange connotations for the family of an occupying enemy officer, but in their own fashion Anna and Friedrich did make one, turning the farmhouse into a distinct likeness of the houses in which they had grown up in Donaueschingen and Raschowa. Anna created a bourgeois fantasy of a drawing room in brown and gold, with overstuffed furniture ranged around the walls and heavy brocade drapes hanging in the windows. There Frieda and her sisters were to endure passionate recitations of Goethe, Schiller, and French poetry, delivered in a high-pitched, portentous keen they disliked listening to, though Frieda much later credited her mother with instilling in her a love of the printed word. Anna's expectations constantly foundered, however. She never revised her original opinion of Metz; in fact, her disillusionment grew deeper with the years, as did her pining for Bavaria. "The German spirit did not break through in Lorraine," she wrote.[3] She gave birth to Johanna on June 25, 1882, and determined that this third girl would be her last child.

Despite her appetite, she had no particular gift for cooking, but the rustic kitchen was well stocked, especially on holidays. Christmastime, when the von Richthofens could conjure the closest semblance of happiness, was done in grand Bavarian style, with elaborate, handmade presents, tiny candles on a tree that was hidden for a week behind the closed drawing room doors, set on a side table with a white silk cloth spread beneath it. Anna orchestrated a marzipan evening several days before. The family assembled under a hanging lamp at the round dining room table, where marzipan, made of ground almonds, icing sugar, and rose water, was laid on a butcher block. The girls molded loaves and pears and apples, with cloves for stems; Friedrich, who was dextrous despite his hand, fashioned tiny, complicated animals. A hot poker was used to scorch the finished products, searing and caramelizing them, which added to the flavor. Sausages hung from the ceiling of the larder, and the smell of hot honey and spices filled the air. The girls wore new white cotton dresses on Christmas Eve for the presentation of gifts. The baron gave Frieda poems he had written, likening her "to all the creatures, birds and bees," whose virtues, he felt, she shared.[4] She committed them to memory and in old age could quote them effortlessly.

Elise ran the household, and Anna also retained a washerwoman, Frau Seidel, and a French nurse and a manservant, Wilhelm, who she insisted wear a uniform and white cotton gloves even on sweltering days, when he served lunch in the grape arbor. Anna having lost patience when Else and Frieda were toddlers, the girls went to the servants for all practical matters and in essence grew up under their care. Nusch became passive and undemanding, rarely talked, and had an imaginary grandmother who lived in a *lunette*. "You know I don't really belong to you and this family here. My grandmother lives there," she said to Frieda one day, pointing to distant fields. "I stay with her. She likes me." She stole into the kitchen to dip lumps of sugar in raspberry sauce—"sweets" from her loving grandmother, she told Frieda as she produced them from a pocket.[5] When the French nurse once punished Nusch by locking her in the cellar, Frieda found her there and screamed at the top of her lungs for her to be let out, bringing the whole household to the scene. Nusch was thereafter in awe of Frieda's loud voice and abandon and liked to follow her, clutching a well-worn toy rabbit and staring silently.

She and Nusch shared a bedroom (Else had her own), and they all played on the second floor in a designated "children's room," with pinafores over their dresses. Anna and Friedrich's parental ineptitude and disinterest made the girls by turns competitive for what affection there was or united against one or both parents. Much later Frieda maintained that although Anna and Friedrich had been "wonderful parents," their "war of the sexes" had "broke[n] something that never healed in later life," particularly in Else.[6] Her arguments for the latter are far more convincing. In time the girls made up a forceful if internally combative triumvirate, a configuration Frieda would later re-create in a friendship with her two closest friends in New Mexico.

Her inseparability from her sisters and the indivisibility of their relationship mirrored their circumstances as occupying Germans. Frieda had no close friends other than Else and Nusch and, later, soldiers a decade older. Each girl's traits and talents were identified, constantly referred to, and precisely—somewhat mercilessly—quantified by Anna and Friedrich; well into old age, each sister retained a keen awareness of the advantages of her psychological, physical, and spiritual endowments and how they might be capitalized on. Such self-awareness eventually turned into self-consciousness and, in some sense, self-promotion, and their assets became exaggerated. Nusch, whose early shyness and remove were slowly transformed into a winsome, vaguely self-mocking allure, traded on her looks and charm almost exclusively, occasionally presenting a vulgar, brittle face to the world, as though, Frieda later wrote, she had "drawn a horsehair net of fashion over her very soul."[7] Else's introspection and intelligence imploded at times, and she could seem morose, self-pitying, and self-sacrificing: the very traits Frieda came to dislike in her mother. Frieda's avowed love of the natural world and of those, like her father, who knew how to husband it, her dismissal of and distaste for the pretensions of intellectualism, and her larger-than-life personality eventually brought ridicule down on her, which she spent much of her life rather defensively deflecting or, most often, ignoring.

As a young child she saw herself as coarse compared to her sisters, whose faces were "cameo" and "heart" shaped, while her own was "wild" and "sunburnt."[8] In fact, she had tomboyish good looks, with a beautiful jaw and unruly blond hair that seemed to refuse to grow—a source of great mortification. Else, a precocious intellectual and the "born reformer"[9] of the family, took on the household help as her first cause. When Elise confessed that she was illiterate but wanted to exchange love letters with a local soldier, Else ghostwrote them at the kitchen table. At Christmas she rallied her reluctant sisters to give their old dolls to Frau Seidel's eight children. Frieda, however, envied Frau Seidel in her Hessian boots—amid the soapsuds—"her arms to the elbows in the soft steaming suds, and then hanging up the flapping, snow-white washing in the kitchen yard."[10] She acquired a pair of similar boots, with buttons up the sides, and rarely took them off.

Her favorite servant was Wilhelm, who became her confidant as her mother turned increasingly brusque and unsympathetic. Wilhelm interceded for her when she batted balls through windowpanes, and helped her hide from company. Frieda dreaded introductions to Anna's friends, who arrived heavily perfumed and wearing severe black silk dresses for cultured conversation, afternoon tea, and baba rum cakes. Anna always displayed Nusch first. "[T]hey would exclaim over [Nusch]," Frieda later wrote, "'What a lovely child,' then look at me and say nothing."[11] Frieda would make faces at Nusch, who would giggle uncontrollably until the baroness lost her temper. "You insufferable brats," she shouted, shoving them out the door.[12]

The baroness's fancy rooms did not suit Frieda, who was restless indoors. Occasionally, against orders, she crawled under the drawing room couch to sleep with her dolls in her arms. More often she retreated to the study, nestling with the dogs on the couch, looking at the baron's taxidermic mementos and, lined up in military order on the broad desk she could barely see over, his paperweight, mailing seal, red sealing wax, an onyx bowl, a small piece of a meteorite, and a matched set of ivory-backed hair and clothes brushes.

Outdoors a shed housed the baron's freshly killed game—hare, woodcock, and partridge hung from the rafters; a six-hundred-pound wild boar might be found aging on the floor, tusks and whiskers still attached, a high smell of blood in the air. Frieda watched the seasons change through her father's flowers and kitchen garden:

> After being pent up in the children's room through the winter, looking through the windows and wiping the moisture off them with my apron, spring came. The first event was a crocus, then snowdrops and the blue scylla—all frail and frightened it seemed to venture forth. And then they came in a rush and splendid. The hyacinths, the tulips and parrot tulips, then the bushes burst out, lilac and snowballs and red hawthorn bushes, and the fruit trees in bloom. . . . And the drama of the garden went on. The strawberries came. . . . Then the cherries. Black, big ones, yellow and red. . . . By then I was to be found mostly in the trees.[13]

Munching on fruit in the branches of a cherry tree, she would watch her father return triumphantly from his shooting expeditions with French aristocrats—like a character in Maupassant's "Contes de la bécasse," she wrote.[14] Once every six years Friedrich returned to Silesia for a family reunion and an orgy of stag and boar hunting in the Carpathian Mountains and salmon fishing in the Oder. In fact, he got away whenever he could. One of the baron's most pleasurable visits was to the well-appointed château of a vicomte who lived in a neighboring village. The vicomte was a friend, Friedrich told Frieda, of the world-famous actress Sarah Bernhardt. Friedrich returned home from such visits "full of stories of Sarah," who once tipped the local hairdresser with a priceless ring. Frieda always begged to go along to the vicomte's, but, the baron explained cryptically, at least according to

Frieda's later retelling, "There was the world, and the half-world."[15] The only problem with the story was that Sarah Bernhardt, who detested Germans, lived abroad and in Paris during the years of Frieda's childhood, and her hairdresser was a Parisian. It is unclear whether the embroidery of the facts was Frieda's or her father's.

Though Friedrich apparently enjoyed a life outside his prescribed circle, the friends he brought home were not of the demimonde but men with titles. Frieda enjoyed the company of one of these, a bachelor, Baron Podewils, whom she often found crouching in the raspberry bushes, entertaining the local dogs: "They behave much better than human beings," the baron explained to her, presenting each dog with a sausage.[16]

2

Beyond the garden wall, Metz provided few such happy intimacies. "It was a strange time," Frieda wrote of the feeling of occupation, "I knew that I had nothing in common with most people, an uneasy feeling, I ought to be like them and wasn't."[17] The sense of alienation was exacerbated when she started school, where French schoolmistresses had been replaced literally overnight by German teachers, and French grammar had become a nonsubject. She was defiant and self-righteously superior in the classroom. Schoolmistresses "deadened your wits," she complained to her father, who had delivered Frieda on her first day of school. "We would all love you," said a Miss Myers, "if you were only not so wild and independent, if you would only listen and do as we wish." Frieda found her physically repulsive and told her so, in her imagination: "Your neck is too long and your legs are too short, and there is no love in your water-blue eyes."[18] The only subject that "made sense" to her was mythology, and she identified grandiosely with "Pallas Athene, who jumped out of Jupiter's head with a helmet on and a spear in her hand, and then Venus who came all fresh and lovely out of the sea, and Poseidon who rode the seahorses."[19] Frieda was criticized for not being as clever as Else—who was also conventionally beautiful, with perfect features and a melancholy dignity and eagerness to apply herself that made her the pet of all the teachers—including Miss Myers, whom she idolized. Once at lunch Frieda teased Else for her crush on Miss Myers in front of the other members of the family. Else went upstairs when they had finished eating and hanged Frieda's dolls.

In the afternoons, hidden in her father's trees with her homework undone on her lap, she slumbered, occasionally so deeply that she fell out and tumbled to the ground. Her pinafores got torn from rushing up and down the *lunettes*. She tried but failed to keep pets. A couple of guinea pigs died during an early frost, and she discovered she could not revive them in the oven. She took in a stray dog who arrived with a broken rope around its neck, but the dog bit her, leaving a small scar above her right eye. Mostly she played in huts and foxholes: "I always liked being with the boys and men. Only they gave me the kind of interest I wanted. Women and girls frightened me. My adolescence and youth puzzled me. Pleasure and social stuff left me unsatisfied."[20]

3

The rift between Anna and Friedrich widened as Frieda made her way through school. She consistently felt sympathy for her father, who gambled ever more crazily and began seeing other women. His personal problems did not prevent him from receiving two new titles, construction improvements inspector (*Meliorations-bauinspektor*, *Regierungs und Baurat*) and royal cabinet minister to the German state of Lippe (*Fürstlicher Lippischer Kabinetsminister*).[21] The latter occasionally required him to travel on diplomatic business outside Lorraine. Anna, furious over their mounting bills and shamed by his neglect, withdrew into the parlor with her French novels. She sent Else, who had intellectually outstripped the local schools, to the *Tanten*, with whom she had remained close friends. Frieda, who missed Else terribly the moment she went away and visited her in Freiburg, did not share her mother's devotion to Julie Blas. "You are afraid of her," she taunted Anna.[22] Julie once visited Sablon and was intrigued by the incorrigibility of Frieda, a prospective student, and tried to take her aside several times for private conversations. Frieda slunk away silently, pretending not to understand. When Julie went to the guest bedroom to rest, Frieda stomped overhead with Nusch, bellowing military songs. Her stay at last drew to a close. Anna and the girls escorted her to the station and helped her get settled in her compartment, her bundles arrayed around her. From among them she suddenly produced an African drum and handed it to Frieda, who began to snicker. "If I had such children," Julie said angrily to Anna, once Frieda and Nusch were banished to wait on the platform, "I would drown myself."[23]

The two girls spent much of their time knocking on barracks doors and befriending soldiers, who carved them little wooden dolls, or scampering up the garden wall to hurl rotten fruit at these same soldiers as they drilled. Once they had upset the ranks, they dropped back down into the garden and collapsed with laughter while listening to the commanding officer scream for order. Then they climbed back up to throw more fruit. Frieda's father, who remained (as she later wrote of this period) "perfection on earth"[24] in her eyes, occasionally took her for an afternoon alone. They went to the officers' *Schwimmanstalt*, a swimming club with a beach along the Moselle, restricted to men. Frieda hung on to his neck as he dived from a high board into the river. When she came to shore, the other officers present were surprised to see her girl's swimming costume—the first time. She soon became a fixture there.

Frieda often stared at her father's war-wounded hand, especially one heavily damaged finger, which, she deduced, had something to do with an emotional devastation that paralyzed him and drove him down deeper into a "scattered miserable life" of drinking and gambling.[25] When his former regiment staged a full-scale reenactment of his wounding and the awarding of the Iron Cross, Frieda was overcome. The ceremony took place in a lavish room decorated with military hardware and statues. Friedrich's men spontaneously lifted him to their shoulders afterward and carried him through the hall. "What a hero my father is!" Frieda exclaimed to herself.[26] She lapsed into reveries of a life alone with the baron, imagining "how much better she would be able to handle her father than ever her mother did."[27]

4

From 1892 onward, however, the baron's moments of glory grew fewer and farther between. Else, back from the Institute Blas and teaching school in Metz, occasionally had the humiliating job of obtaining loans from military higher-ups to pay off his debts in town as Friedrich took to his bed after losses at the gambling tables. Her moral rectitude had a considerable influence, and apparently she succeeded, for a time, in imposing some limits on her father's way of life. Her own existence was quickly reduced to a grinding combination of teaching and putting out fires at home as she assumed most of the responsibilities and duties of mother and wife that Anna had renounced. Her best friend from the

Institute Blas, an Austrian Jew named Frieda Schloffer (known to her friends as Friedel), occasionally came to stay, but the baron's behavior discouraged many such visits. Else was effectively put in sole charge of Nusch, who was one of her pupils. On the weekends Else could have serious conversations with no one but the baron: Anna now limited her appearances to dinners and company. She tried to engage him in political debate to keep her mind stimulated, but every conversation ended the same way. "The world," he insisted, "does not change. There always were and there always will be underdogs."[28] Then he and Frieda would go out to the garden and Frieda would watch him catch flies and throw them into the spiderwebs spun over the Riesling vines.

Else left in 1894, at the age of nineteen, to teach in Freiburg, where she met Max Weber. Not yet the world-famous sociologist he was to become, at thirty he was already a prolific writer on social conditions in East Prussia. He had married a cousin, Marianne Schnitger, the year before, and told Marianne that he avoided deep depression through "continual work,"[29] a remark that would have found some resonance with Else. Being away from Metz only sharpened her appetite for more education, and she came under Weber's considerable influence. A dark, brooding Berliner with a mustache, full beard, and a suspicious, haunted expression, the son of a politician who was a domestic bully and a smothering mother of enormous intellect, Weber took to Else immediately. When he told her to study sociology, then a new discipline, she adopted him as her mentor.

With Else gone, Friedrich soon developed the habit of staying out all night and had to be revived and retrieved by Wilhelm in the morning, in time for Frieda to witness her mother shouting viciously at him before she left for school. He whimpered apologies when presented before the baroness, and blamed his behavior on his old regiment. One morning, in the throes of a hangover, he threatened to shoot himself. He insisted that he had been brainwashed and that he suffered an incurable addiction. "I'll blow my brains out and have done with it," he told her, indicating that his weapon of choice would be one of his hunting rifles.

"Blow them out!" she screamed. "That's all you're fit for."[30]

"Like all couples," Frieda later wrote, with the experience of two marriages behind her, "they thought love must drop ready-made from heaven."[31] She gradually came to resent her parents for sacrificing their happiness to the institution of marriage; most often she believed her mother to have been the guiltier (because more willfully passive) party. Her high opinion of her father would survive his moral degeneration through most of her teenage years, principally because she pitied him and because he loved her unconditionally, in spite of her faults, which from an early age she felt were legion, particularly her "almost fanatical" intensity that made her feelings hyper-exaggerated.[32] Her attraction to the baron's sensual aura of failure was the most immediate and aggrandized: She would always require that the men in her life allow her, in some form, to pity them; that they understand her sense of herself as flawed; and that, as in her favorite myths, they give equal play to her attributes and the grandness of her faults.

5

By the time she was fifteen, Frieda's looks and behavior had changed dramatically. Her hair, now dirty blond, had finally grown, and was beautifully thick, with curling tendrils that framed her face. The resemblance to her mother that she would acquire much later in life was nowhere in evidence through her teens, twenties, and thirties, when the mystery, irony, and—as she might have said of her father—"mysticism" of her looks were indisputable, and indisputably those of a von Richthofen. The set of her face was pensive and imperious, with a haughty Prussian abstraction and slightly unbalanced features. Her mouth, in typical von Richthofen fashion, pulled to one side when she broke into a wide and otherwise faultless smile, one small dimple in her right cheek. She had a minuscule cleft in her chin, a pronounced indentation below her lower lip, wide, high cheekbones, and a straight, strong nose. It was the profile of an aristocrat. Her eyes were almond shaped, her body was exceptionally well defined, and long arms, long, shapely legs, and perfect carriage gave her an unmistakable dignity. She was particularly proud of her hands and feet.

Her newfound beauty was apparently noted by one of her teachers: Where and when are unknown, but she seems to have had a "brief, intense" affair with a young schoolmistress. "That's my story," she said some three and a half decades later, after a London viewing of the lesbian cult film *Mädchen in Uniform*, still enjoying the multinational run that preceded its banning in Germany and the United States. The affair was "harmful and destructive," she said—a memory provoked by the film's heroine, Manuela von Meinhardis, a Prussian officer's daughter who contemplates suicide in the throes of a passionate attachment to a teacher.[33]

In the spring of 1894, she developed an enormous crush on a twenty-one-year-old Silesian cousin, Curt von Richthofen, who was attending the Metz officers' school. He belonged to a more entitled branch of the family than Friedrich, and had been well educated. His features were uncannily like Frieda's, with a wide, slightly comical mouth and a jaunty smile "full of splendid teeth."[34] He charmed the whole family. The baroness was thrilled to have such a presentable nephew and invited him over for dinner every Sunday. He came in uniform, his sword slipping over his narrow hips, and when Else visited for weekends he settled himself for long political discussions with her. Frieda began decking herself out in floppy Florentine hats, striped cotton flannel dresses, her mother's jewelry, and white gloves. She went to mass at the garrison church, which Curt attended, and strolled through Metz whenever she thought he might be free to accompany her home. They devised a way of communicating through his friends: As soon as one of them spotted her, they got word to him, and soon he appeared with a landau to drive her home.

The relationship brought Frieda an appreciative audience of Curt's cadet friends, mounted on horseback, and trips to the barracks quickly became invested with eros and passionate sympathy for the soldier's life. Standing in the sunshine of a garden with a corporal one day, Frieda noted the cut and color of his rich blue uniform against the thorny rosebushes he was tying up: "He had a mark over his bed for each day he had still to serve," she wrote. "I looked up at him and understood his suffering."[35] She stood on the bunks in the soldiers' shacks, belting out regional songs in a powerful contralto to assuage their homesickness and listening to the tales of their sexual exploits. A few mentioned the cathedral, where, they said, they consummated their relationships with "town girls" behind the main altar. The unfinished cathedral forever looked to Frieda like a crouching, spreading animal pierced by a finger.[36]

Five years younger than Curt, Frieda had to take the lead. "I am dumb, I am dumb," he lamented his lack of experience. "I don't get the hang of all these tactics I am supposed to understand."[37] On Easter

Sunday night she led him to her father's garden, and among the blooming hyacinths he kissed her for the first time. She "went off like a firecracker," raced back through the garden to her room, got undressed and into bed, and "lay there in an unknown, unbelievable state of bliss."[38]

In the summer they went to the garden more and more often, gorging on white strawberries, a variety she "never saw or tasted again."[39] She passed her sixteenth birthday in August, and Curt was posted elsewhere. As a parting gift he gave her a box of macaroons. She hid them under her bed that night so she would not have to share his memory with her sisters or parents, who, she felt, did not understand the full extent of her sorrow. The following morning, when Nusch got up and went downstairs, Frieda remained in bed, moping. Hunger pangs soon vied with the ache in her heart, however, and, reaching under her bed for the box, she sampled a cookie. Soon there was nothing left in the box, and Frieda was sick to her stomach.

6

In 1896, after Friedrich impregnated one of his mistresses, Selma, she began to demand significant amounts of money from him.[40] With this added drain on his pocketbook, he could not make the mortgage payments on their house and put it up for sale. The family's impending move was kept a secret from Frieda. Else, who was away when the negotiations were under way, was ordered not to confide in Frieda. When packing made further concealment impossible, Frieda became enraged and took it out on Else: "You of course meant well, but I rather expected that you know me better. Don't you think it was much worse just to imagine this, as I of course noticed something, and in any case I did after all find out all about it."[41]

Wilhelm and Frau Seidel were let go, and on July 24, 1896, the family crowded back into a Metz apartment at 49 rue de l'Evêché (Bischofstrasse in its Germanized version), a few blocks from their old apartment on Theobaldswall.[42] Frieda turned seventeen three weeks later, with a new hairstyle: The dismissal of both the servants left only Elise, and the two youngest girls' grooming devolved largely to the baroness, who, with no patience for the knots in her daughters' hair, ordered it cut off.[43]

• • •

In the fall the baroness enrolled Frieda and Nusch briefly at Saint Christiana, a ninety-year-old convent school (called Sainte-Chrétienne by the French) across the street from their new home. Frieda had been extremely restless and high-strung since the loss of the house in Sablon, and she tried the Carmelite nuns' nerves, tearing around all day in her boots: "*Toujours doucement, ma petite Frieda,*" they told her, to no avail.[44] Anna sent her and Nusch to Freiburg.[45]

The Blases had sold their institute two years before, when Julie turned fifty-five,[46] but they still boarded the daughters of friends and old charges and gave language instruction and art training. They had retired to Eichberghaus, a country villa in the Freiburg suburb of Littenweiler. Set off from the town's main street and other houses, it was filled with Camilla's paintings and the furniture she decorated; the back-yard gate led to the Black Forest. Frieda and Nusch spent endless nights in fantasy, acting out *Macbeth* and Schiller's *Die Räuber* in the bedroom they shared, and during the day they wandered through the Black Forest, getting to know the footpaths and enjoying the high altitude. Frieda stayed around the house as little as possible: The *Tanten*, who saved pictures of Anna von Richthofen, Else, and Nusch, had none of Frieda as a seventeen-year-old. She would not sit still long enough to be photographed on the Blases' back-yard bench, which encircled an oak tree. Pictures of herself fascinated but repelled her, and posing made her uncomfortable.

Returning to Metz after a term, she began dating a twenty-four-year-old Prussian lieutenant named Karl von Marbahr. Earnest, fretful, and plodding, Karl saw her only under chaperonage, rarely summoning the courage to stand close enough for them even to touch. One of their sanctioned activities was tennis, a highly orchestrated affair Frieda described as a game for "amusing . . . little wives."[47] One rainy day on the clay courts, she slipped, and Karl castigated himself afterward for not taking the opportunity to kiss her as he broke her fall; a half century later he still regretted the physical reticence.[48]

"Don't imagine that you can marry an officer," Anna continually reminded her daughters. "You have no dowry and a German officer needs a girl with a dowry."[49] She decided to put an end to the relationship by sending Frieda to Berlin for the winter of 1897–98 to "come out" and, she hoped, find a husband. Equipped with a meager allowance, she would stay at the home of her father's cousin Oswald von Richthofen, then serving under Wilhelm II as director of the Colonial Division of the Foreign Ministry. Karl asked her for a photograph before she left, and she went to a studio to have it done. Her face looked lopsided because of her crooked smile, but she gave it to him anyway. Karl saw her off, criticizing himself for his timidity as the train pulled out. "I should have given you a kiss . . . at the station in Metz when you were going away. I still see you at the open window of the car."[50] Some forty years and three husbands later, she addressed a section of her memoirs to Karl.

7

The train from Metz left her at Potsdam Station, and a Russian-style droshky took her through the streets of the city. She had never seen asphalt streets or a city of such ugliness and beauty. The buildings looked absurd to her—the rococo Royal Library resembled a chest of drawers—and the city was unrelievedly flat. Colossal bronze and marble statues lined the broad boulevards and squares, and red lamps shone on the street corners where mail could be delivered by *Rohrpost*—pneumatic tubes. As they approached Oswald's house in the Tiergarten, an exclusive neighborhood adjacent to a six-hundred-acre park, they passed government villas and, on the Unter den Linden, one grand café after another.

Near the southern edge of the Tiergarten, Frieda's carriage drew up at 17 Friedrich Wilhelmstrasse. She was totally unprepared for the cavernous rooms of the house, hung with tents and fitted with Middle Eastern copper lamps and brass pieces. On a table stood a telephone, an instrument she had never used or seen in anyone's home.[51] Earlier in the year Oswald and his wife, Caroline "Lilly" von Hartmann, a beautiful native Berliner, had lived in Alexandria with their sons, Dieprand, Hartmann, and Oswald Jr.—the last now thirteen and the only son still at home. Lilly had contracted cholera and quickly died. Oswald, who had been in Cairo on business, returned to Alexandria to find that for fear of contagion, every servant but one—the family called him by his first name, Achmed—had deserted Lilly as she lay dying. He had brought Achmed back to Berlin with him and built a private monument to Lilly at home, re-creating their years together by draping the interiors in the fabrics and carpets they had accumulated in their travels.[52] Ensconced in a more sober apartment on another floor were two widows in their forties, Anna von Elbe and Elisabeth von Plessen, sisters of Oswald's, both whose husbands had died young.[53] The only person younger than Frieda was Oswald Jr.

Oswald was a lifetime government bureaucrat born in Romania, and his career was solid and unremarkable, distinguished mainly by workmanlike plodding in an age when sycophants and blowhards surrounded the kaiser. A lawyer, indulgent and handsome, he had served under Bismarck until the latter was dismissed in 1890 by Wilhelm II, and now reported to the head of the Foreign Ministry (later chancellor), Prince Bernhard von Bülow. He bored Frieda's father—Friedrich said he was not "hard" enough—who often compared him, as did others, to an industrious bee.[54] At home, however, he was given to irony and grand gestures, and he was amused by Frieda, who called him "Uncle Oswald." He appreciated her boisterous ignorance of big-city convention and teased her about her pretensions: Now eighteen, she was filled with a sense of herself as a von Richthofen, but Oswald was quick to tell her that she "overdid the importance of the Richthofens in a romantic way."[55]

Like her father, Oswald confided in her; unlike Friedrich, however, he allowed her to see the other half of his life. He took her to his former office, where she "waltzed around" Bismarck's old desk[56]—an irreverence Oswald gladly indulged—and he introduced her to the issues being debated in the capital: the kaiser's excesses and the *Realpolitik* of the new German imperialism. Berlin had become an immense showplace for Wilhelm II's love of display. The imperial government met in the Reichstag, but he rarely visited there, because he was adamantly opposed to parliamentarianism and resentful that the building's cupola was bigger than that of the Royal Castle. Ascending the throne in 1888 at the age of thirty-nine, he preferred to devote himself to reviving the "fine old customs and manners of ancient times," including the formal court dress that had gone out of fashion decades before. Nonetheless such modern amenities as electric lamps (almost two thousand) were installed around the palace.[57] He stocked his closets with the uniforms of Austria, Russia, Sweden, England, and Italy; English and German yacht clubs; and every division and regiment of the Prussian Army: helmets, shakos, *schapskas*, epaulettes, swords, and matching cuirasses. When he awoke, he put on riding gear even on days he and his shooting coterie did not canter down the Linden for a hunt in the far reaches of the Tiergarten.

Nowhere was the kaiser's ostentation more evident than at the winter balls he held for up to seven thousand guests. Frieda was invited to one through Oswald's efforts. When the news reached Metz, Anna packed Nusch, now fifteen, off to Berlin, perhaps hoping that her youngest daughter's looks would draw suitors to both the girls. Poised and slender, with a dress model's figure, Nusch was well on her way to becoming a clotheshorse.

The ball included a banquet, which began with a procession through the White Room of court personnel, all in snug tights:

> The Castle is brilliantly lighted from seven o'clock, and up to eight there is a constant stream of arrivals. . . . Besides the officers of the army, there are . . . professors of the University in their violet or red robes, or masters of the great schools of the Academy of Arts, the mayors of the large towns, and the representatives of the urban corporations. . . . Towards half-past eight o'clock the Masters of the Ceremonies knock on the floor with gilt crosses to announce the arrival of the procession of which the Emperor and the Empress form part.[58]

Frieda and Nusch earned a compliment from Wilhelm II: "[V]ery beautiful nieces!" the kaiser told Oswald.[59]

Oswald did not have much time to spend with Frieda. Various military attachés and cousins in uniform chaperoned her, and, all else failing, Frau von Elbe and Frau von Plessen took Frieda to performances of Wagner, Shakespeare, Schiller, and Goethe. There was little exposure to more modern mores: General-Lieutenant Bernhard von Richthofen, a hard-line, right-wing relation and chief of Berlin police, had taken it upon himself to act as censor for the *Kaiserreich*, banning Ibsen and works by Berlin's nascent avant-garde, such as Gerhart Hauptmann's *Die Weber* and Hermann Sudermann's *Sodoms Ende*. "We just don't care for that trend!" he said of the "seditious" dramas he helped expunge from the city.[60] Like Oswald, Bernhard von Richthofen lived in western Berlin, at 35 Linkstrasse, near the Potsdam terminus, but Frieda does not seem to have called on him, or the other six von Richthofens in the city. She was not invited.

Pride prevented her from going out when she did not have the right shoes or gloves, and her small allowance prevented other outings. She could rarely scrape together the money and clothing to go to

Royal Opera subscription balls (twenty marks, or about five dollars) or even to lesser *Levées* and *Couren*—conversation parties.[61] Explaining to Oswald or Frau von Elbe and Frau von Plessen that she had a headache, she would play *Verstecken* (hide-and-seek) with young Oswald: Once, darting out from under the stairs, she just missed knocking over the Grand Duke of Saxe-Weimar, Carl Alexander, on his way in to see the elder von Richthofen.[62] This was the kind of "accident" she increasingly took pleasure in causing. She sent ebullient, pompous letters home, but she was miserable in the big house. It was no longer enough, she concluded, "just to enjoy myself and be a pretty girl. . . . this whole elaborate society was meaningless. . . . What was it all about? It had nothing to do with genuine living." She became preoccupied with her lack of education—"I know so little, and I can do so little. . . . What is going to become of this unknown 'myself'?"[63]—but when Else wrote her that she planned to attend lectures in sociology and economics at Berlin University during the summer and the following academic year, she wrote back defensively: "The notion of being able to become something in Metz is not at all displeasing to me, I do not need to set nearly so high a goal as you!"[64]

3

Ernest Weekley

I

Frieda did not have time to "become something in Metz" when she returned. She was probably home no longer than four months before the family left, in mid-July 1898, for Freiburg. The von Richthofens had begun spending part of each summer with the Blases. Anna orchestrated the trips, signing the Blas guest register when they left with variations on a heroic note of thanks comparing her own, the world's, and her family's disintegration with the Blases' strength.[1]

That summer, as usual, the weather in Freiburg was gorgeous. During the day Frieda, Nusch, Anna, Friedrich, the Blases, and a couple named Schröer—he a professor at Freiburg University—would put on their walking boots and catch the train from Littenweiler up to the Höllenthal to spend a few hours in the mountains among the oak, ash, pine, and beech, walking through last year's brown leaves. Sometimes they went farther: to the Feldberg, the highest mountain in the Black Forest; to the Titisee, a huge glacial lake halfway to Donaueschingen; or to the church tower at Münsingen, at the southern extremity of the Tunisberg, a mountain with a long, low back. Friedrich enjoyed looking at the immense fields of asparagus for which the area was known and down into the plains of Alsace.[2] They ate at little inns, followed the well-marked footpaths, and watched other tourists doing the same things they were doing. Nothing ever happened.

Three weeks before Frieda's nineteenth birthday, the Schröers had a visit from Ernest Weekley, a stylish friend from England who was staying at the Deutscher Kaiser, a guesthouse on the edge of Freiburg. Schröer had hired Weekley to teach at Freiburg the previous spring, a job he had left in November for the position of French lecturer at University College, Nottingham.[3] He had aspired to an Oxford or Cambridge post, but in Nottingham he made 150 pounds a year, and he was able to earn extra money marking papers as an external examiner.[4]

From his seventeenth year Weekley had paid his way through school by teaching on the side and, with a flair for slang and the colloquial (eventually one of his professional specialties), had become fluent in German after one year at the University of Bern. In 1892, already twenty-seven, he obtained his master of arts degree in German and French from London University. He entered Trinity College, Cambridge, the following year, reading medieval and modern languages and earning a First, with distinctions in French and German and a commendation for his pronunciation of German. The Freiburg appointment followed a year at the Sorbonne. This vacation in the Black Forest was the first of his adult life, all free time before having been spent poring over books of Romance and Teutonic philology and writing French textbooks, published in a series called University Tutorial.[5] His greatest regret was that he had no Sanskrit.[6] He also had no wife.

Handsome, with thinning dark blond hair, Weekley had disarming fair eyebrows that could make his eyes appear limpid and sad, a thick walrus mustache, and a full blond beard, grown during this summer trek. He had beautiful clothes and a few dark silk bow ties, and at thirty-three he was already acquiring some of the affectations of professorial success and middle age, including a predictable repertoire of sarcasms, a genius for spotting talent, and a thickening midriff. A good hockey forward in his youth and still a tennis player, he carried himself with the loping grace of a former athlete, resting on the walking stick he liked to carry, a fob watch hanging from his vest pocket, his straw boater or fedora in one hand and a pipe in the other. The Schröers told him about their friends the von Richthofens and proposed introducing him to Frieda.

The von Richthofens must have seemed formidable to a suitor. Friedrich assumed tyrannical poses with Frieda's prospects, and Anna rarely missed an opportunity to foreshadow connubial misery by exposing the unhappiness of her own marriage. Weekley, fourteen years older than Frieda, was no ordinary suitor, however. He expected no von Richthofen dowry and represented a possible future for their daughter.

Weekley was less afraid of them than of Frieda. He was astounded both by her looks and by her quick, natural ripostes to his studied witticisms. A good listener and quick study—from years of practice with soldiers—she had developed a husky and dominant voice. Her speech intrigued him—a curious patois of Bavarian, Alsatian, and Silesian inflections, and a generous sprinkling of French. She called him Ernst, giving the name the German single-syllable, *air* pronunciation. Frieda immediately loved his beard, which was soft and untrimmed (it was the first and last time she would see him with one), and his smile, a slow, self-effacing crinkle that transformed his good looks. When he talked, she enjoyed watching his long, graceful hands.[7]

Days later he sent Frau Professor Schröer with a proposal of marriage. "Carisima!" Frieda wrote Else by the next post. "Take a chair and sit down and then listen: Mama has probably already told you a little about an Englishman. . . . [He] loves me and can and wants to marry me. . . . And I, darling, will say yes, because I am attracted to him as I have never been attracted to anyone before."[8] She was reading a translation of Tennyson when the proposal arrived. "I thought Ernst was Lancelot!" she later said, only half jokingly.[9]

They spent the remaining week in the Black Forest, meeting in the afternoons at a fountain,[10] Weekley reverent and terrified of his passion, handling Frieda like a piece of delicate china as he ennobled her and her character. He felt that she should be an empress rather than the wife of a schoolteacher.[11] His Dickensian childhood, conversely, made Frieda determined to "bring him the bright side of life."[12]

Ernest was the second of nine children of Agnes and Charles Weekley of Hampstead, then an almost entirely rural London suburb. The Weekleys lived in a neighborhood of squatters and the genteel poor. The children were raised in New End House, next to the workhouse. One of Ernest's first childhood memories was running at breakneck speed past a Gypsy encampment down Platt's Lane on his way to school.[13]

Born on April 27, 1865, he had been given the name of a brother of Agnes's who had died, while Agnes was pregnant with Ernest, of tuberculosis—the disease that killed all four of her brothers and would eventually take her eldest son, Montague, at the age of eighteen. Montague's blindness toward the end of his illness haunted Ernest into his old age; the death also loaded him with responsibility as the family's eldest son. Another brother, Charles, died in his thirties, and Ernest grew attached to death's reminders. As a child he had hunted for the ghost of his maternal grandfather, George McCowen, a Scotsman who had been a schoolmaster and parish clerk, in an old passageway of the family home in Uxbridge, Middlesex. Later he developed a fetish for widow's weeds, which he found very sexy.[14]

Since he had spent little time alone with women, his professions of love could be rather stiff. When he bent to kiss Frieda's boots, she thought of how muddy and inelegant they looked. His paralyzed declarations filled her with an uneasy but thrilling sense of power, and she stood back and watched like a cinematographer as their love scenes unfolded in the woods: Wearing a pink-and-white sunhat he particularly loved, she approached the fountain as slowly as possible, to torture him and excite herself.[15] When he felt the strain of his passion, he simply tried to repress his feelings, mistrusting his own happiness.[16] One of the few subjects that came easily to both were the things that had been out of their control as children—death in his case and parental incompatibility in hers—and they spoke of these with irony and sarcasm.

The von Richthofens left for Metz on July 31, briefly seeing Else, who stopped for the day at Eichberghaus en route from Berlin. Else was not entirely taken with Ernest but kept her opinions to herself. She thought him too conventional and a little hysterical.[17] The Blases asked Frieda and Ernest to sign their guest book to commemorate the engagement. "[N]ot poetically endowed, but very happy," Frieda wrote ambiguously.[18] She stayed on alone with the *Tanten* until early August, when Ernest left for Bern to see friends. He missed her terribly and bridged his loneliness by writing to her and to Else, who endured the full measure of his self-castigating joy:

> Lovers are proverbially selfish, and I have often reproached myself for not writing to you sooner. . . . The more I see of [Frieda] the

> more I admire her noble and unspoilt character: may God grant that I may show myself in some measure worthy of such self sacrificing love as she has for me. I only wish, for her sake, that I could offer her a more brilliant future.[19]

2

She and Ernest were reunited in late August. He went to Metz for an engagement party, and from there they sailed to Dover to meet his parents. Frau von Richthofen chaperoned the voyage, for which Frieda wore a sailor dress and cap. It was an unusually sunny crossing. Awkward in the role of mother-in-law, Anna managed to communicate little but grimness to her daughter, a feeling abetted by the seascape as the English Channel heaved green spray up onto the boat. Ernest, Anna felt, "seemed so elderly, so dead."[20]

Ernest's white-haired parents were waiting on the pier. Agnes was a short, overweight woman stuffed into a dark dress, with startling blue eyes and a big forehead. She was fifty-eight but appeared much older. Charles, who was sixty-four, looked to Frieda like Michelangelo's Moses in an English frock coat.[21] Frieda's heart sank as Agnes embraced Ernest and began to chatter, her thick Uxbridge accent, inflected with a hint of a Scottish burr, making her words unintelligible. It was just as well Frieda could not understand; apparently Agnes's first impression of her was of paleness and the lack of a peaches-and-cream complexion.[22] Charles stood silently, then took Frieda's arm, and they proceeded to a nearby hotel for tea. Anna froze when she saw its condition, gleaning from its drabness how low Frieda had contrived to sink with this engagement.[23] Ernest had done nothing to hide his station, but his poise, ambition, and position at Nottingham had distracted Anna from the obvious.

She took the next boat back to Germany. "Don't be a goose," she whispered to Frieda as she departed, seeing that her daughter was near tears.[24] Frieda, feeling "England c[o]me down on the lightness of [my] heart," cried freely on the train to Hampstead with Ernest and his parents.[25] As they rolled over the countryside, which seemed low-lying, monotonous, and too green, she faced out the window: "What a wonderful cow one would make here," she thought, "or a frog."[26]

After thirty-eight years at New End House, the Weekleys now

paid one pound a week for a house almost at the foot of Hampstead Heath, 40 Well Walk, where John Constable had once lived. Ernest's spinster sisters Maude and Kit, who lived with their parents and a brother, George, often saw Constable's ghost, they told Frieda.[27] The rooms were dark, and the family used coal-tar soap, which gave an unmistakable scent to the ground-floor bathroom. An odd set of stairs extended like a platform from the dining room to the dark back yard, a travesty of an English garden.

As relieving officer for the Hampstead Board of Guardians, Charles, an upright, religious man with a mordant wit and sense of moral superiority, administered the Poor Law, finding homes and food for the indigent. In the lower-class accent every sibling but Ernest and his brother Bruce Edward ("Ted") had inherited, he would tell stories of the eccentric alms recipients he had dealt with that day, while the family sat around the fireplace, talking about how quarrelsome and ungrateful these people were. One day Charles, who prided himself on how compatible he and Agnes were after thirty-eight years, visited an elderly married couple he had helped move, after improvements in the Poor Law made it possible for husbands and wives to live together: "'e sits one side of the fire and I sits on the other[,] and the more I looks at 'im the more I 'ates 'im," the disgruntled wife said, forced to live with her spouse after years of happy solitude.[28]

Like Frieda, Agnes had been her father's favorite. Her mother died young, and her eldest sister, Julia, who kept a dame school in Buckinghamshire, raised her. She married Charles when she was twenty, and her hidebound, domineering ways, especially with her four daughters, were much admired, resented, and, by later generations, often mocked. Her daughters grew up catty, conceited, and—with the exception of Maude, a lesbian, who had been partially deaf since childhood—rather plain.[29] The boys were retiring, artless, "good" people, on whom Agnes doted.[30]

The Weekley children had a strange dependency on one another, many of them unable in later life to live with anyone but the family, yet they took vicious swipes at one another, their nastiest reserved for those who got away. These were often asserted indirectly: Charles, "trapped" into wedlock by "a pregnant creature," would suffer the marriage until his untimely death; Gertrude's husband, John Tilley, thirty-six years her senior, was "a lecher"; Ted's wife, Lucy, was "an awful frump of a schoolmistress," and childless. Ernest, horror of horrors, was marrying a German.[31]

Frieda, echoing her mother's assumption about the Weekleys' low status, decided she "had never met people of their stamp before," and found them overreligious, habit-loving, and old-fashioned in their thinking.[32] But she soon developed a fondness for many of them, finding it particularly easy to break through the detachment of her future father-in-law: He was happy to have someone around who was young and considered her "a terrific crasher."[33] He took her to visit three spinster aunts who ran a tobacco shop and still lived in Uxbridge, in an old house "curtained and double-curtained," it seemed to Frieda, "not to let any air in at all." These were strange women, one of whom, Hannah, smoked so heavily that she had a nicotine stain running up the side of her face.[34] Their most joyful possession was a dollhouse built to scale, with infinitesimally small lamps, cradles, and silverware. They talked intimately to Frieda of Queen Victoria, and told her that their father had slept with a loaded gun on the new grave of a dead daughter for weeks because he was afraid of body snatchers.[35]

Frieda made a good impression on Agnes and Maude by eating every scrap of food that was put before her, then returning for seconds. Ernest's childhood deprivations were not in evidence on this trip. Agnes splurged, and the house was warm and cozy, with pies steaming in the pantry and joints of mutton sizzling in the oven. She charmed Frieda by reciting Tennyson from memory as she roamed the kitchen. Charles read a chapter from the Bible every weekday morning. On Sunday morning he put on a top hat and tailcoat with violets in his buttonhole, and the entire family strode behind him down Well Walk into the center of Hampstead, Agnes in a severe silk cape and bonnet trimmed with matching violets.

The engagement trip ended in September, with Ernest heading north to Nottingham and Frieda back to 49 Bischofstrasse in Metz. The apprehension with which she had begun it had been assuaged, largely through the richly persuasive power of the Weekleys' conventionally happy marriage. They had shown their best side, their eccentricities mitigated by a homey personableness and by a regard for one another, however freighted with routine, that the von Richthofens utterly lacked. The "grit," stability, and habituation of English family life seemed "an ideal to strive after," Frieda later wrote;[36] her father's self-destructiveness, Anna's enduring dissatisfaction, and their grandstanding fights were shallow and cynical: "In spite of their vitality, they had failed intrinsically and obstinately" to create an "intimate" family circle.[37] Frieda's worshipful affection for her father was coming to an end. Finally, however, it was the "purity" and uncompromising idealism of Ernest's feelings for her to which Frieda responded.[38] Though she knew he "put [me] on a pedestal and it alarmed" her, she found his "humanity" and simplicity touching and trusted that "soon he would let [me] step off the pedestal . . . and be [my]self."[39]

Almost a year remained until the wedding date, and there is some indication that after all their efforts to marry her off, Frieda's parents now attempted to hinder her leaving Metz. Anna had made clear her lack of sympathy for Ernest and his parents; the baron seems to have reacted even less well to Frieda's choice of fiancé: As the date approached, a look of anxiety crossed his face whenever the subject of the marriage was mentioned, and he "hated her going so far away."[40] Frieda persevered, however, collecting her trousseau and switching from the old German script, which she still often used, to the modern German version so that Ernest could read her letters more easily. On his recommendation she broadened her interest in the English novel, setting aside *Jane Eyre*, which she had read and wept over constantly during her adolescence, for books he sent her. No list of the books remains, and it is unclear whether she was then fluent enough in English to read the language or whether these were German translations—as were, apparently, *Jane Eyre* and the Tennyson that had helped spur her original attraction to Ernest. Apart from one further trip to England the following spring, she seems to have done little else from September 1898 but wait, attempting to "be that sampler of all the virtues [Ernest] thought [her]."[41] It hardly crossed her mind that there was something wrong with his timidity.

3

They were married from the Blases' home on August 29, 1899.[42] Frieda and Else had said their goodbyes in the Black Forest on the twenty-eighth. "I still remember our last walk together, before she was married," Else wrote. "[W]hat a pain it was, that separation!"[43] Else was still happily unmarried. That night the three sisters and their parents slept at Eichberghaus, Frieda and Nusch sharing their old room.

The atmosphere was somewhat funereal: Frieda was suddenly overcome with nostalgia for their performances of *Macbeth* and *Die Räuber*. As though it were the last day of her life, she even managed to remember with fondness every miserable day they had spent in the company of the *Tanten*. At the wedding feast, held in a old inn nearby before the ceremony,[44] the Weekleys and von Richthofens mingled uneasily. After the meal they drove to the neighboring suburb of Wiehre, where Ernest's brother Ted acted as visiting curate. He performed a service at the Anglican Church of Saints George and Boniface, known as the English Church.

Frieda and Ernest left, probably the next day, for Lucerne, a pretty three-hour ride in the red plush of first class, through the sunny apple orchards of Düdingen, Bern, Signau, Langnau, Escholzmatt, Schüpfheim, and Wolhusen. Ernest sat slumped in a corner of the compartment as Frieda waited for "something" that "would make her very happy, happier than she had ever been." Occasionally he reached for her hand. Soon she fell asleep.[45]

She awoke to the nighttime chiaroscuro of the Lake of Lucerne, with its miles of steamboat restaurants. Swans and black waterfowl with white heads clustered near the shore, and gondolas strung with lanterns circled an octagonal turretted building, the Wasserturm, a former prison and torture chamber that had been converted into the town archive. The Alps rose behind the lake. Boarding a droshky, the Weekleys rode slowly beneath rows of quayside chestnut trees and through crooked streets of sixteenth- and seventeenth-century frame houses. The center was less quaint—some ninety hotels, pensions, and inns, an elegant silk shop, an international bookstore, and a shopping street, the Alpenstrasse, where billboards advertised such attractions as a photography studio with Swiss mountain costumes and props, and Stauffer's Museum, featuring lifelike groups of stuffed Alpine animals.[46] Eventually, they made their way to the Hotel Schweizerhof,[47] where they had reserved a room overlooking the lake.

In the best tradition of *fin-de-siècle* honeymoon nights, Ernest killed time, postponing the inevitable with chatter. "[W]e aren't really married yet," he informed Frieda in their room. Sitting on his knee, she could feel his legs tremble beneath her and smell his homespun. "Oh yes," she said matter-of-factly and cheerfully. "I know."[48] Ernest decided to fortify himself with a drink and left the room. Frieda removed her clothing and, noticing an ornate armoire carved "with a stiff Eve and an Adam that looked like the 'missing link,'" she climbed onto it to wait for him. When he finally returned, she leapt into his arms. Mortified, he told her to put on her nightdress, and quickly steered her to the giant bed, fitted like a crypt into a wall recess, where they made love.

Less than two hours later, Ernest was fast asleep, breathing slowly and audibly, and Frieda ventured out to the balcony. Terribly sad, then angry, she wondered why this was all so different from what she had imagined. The lights of the town, reflected on the lake, were "slipping like a scale" on the calm waves as she weighed her chances for a happy marriage before turning in for a fitful night of sleep. "My wedding night," she later wrote cynically. "I wonder if many women have felt my joy!"[49] Within a month she was pregnant.

4

Simmering in Nottingham

I

They arrived in Nottingham three months later, in November 1899, to the kind of cold, stagnant damp only a Midlands factory town in winter can provide. Frieda's first impression of the city was one of unrelenting misery and grayness.[1] The Midland Railway from London, which branched into two lines just outside the city, took them north, up through the heavily industrialized west side. Smoke rose from the chimneys of three hundred bleach works and lace and hosiery factories, and the smell of raw sewage and manufacturing waste in the blighted Leen and Trent Rivers floated on the air, the stench recalling the lines of a contemporary poet singing of the Leen: "Mingling with thee in one stream impure/Make, for half thy course, a common sewer."[2]

Residential neighborhoods were graded by their proximity to the factories and the lowest-paid factory workers' houses; distance from the southernmost slum, the Meadows, with its engineering and boiler works, engine sheds, and cattle market, conferred status. A sixth of the city's population lived in the Meadows: forty thousand people packed four, five, and six families at a time into row houses with no electric lighting, separated by narrow passageways, and reached by unpaved, undrained alleys and roads funneling into pigsties, slaughterhouses, cesspools, communal privies, and ashpits—dirt holes for human waste, covered with ash. The ashpits were lower than the Trent flood level and, until 1875, had flooded each season when the Trent rose, leaching waste into the river. Nightsoil collection men made their rounds in the close yards after dark. Some privies, shared by as many as 125 people, were so badly built they drained back into the houses, leading to outbreaks of intestinal fever, typhus, and cholera.[3] The Weekleys had a vague plan to ascend the scale of Nottingham neighborhoods, which ranged through the large ranks of the middle class up to the near-palatial homes of factory owners, and then leave as soon as Ernest was offered the chair he still fully expected at Oxford, Cambridge, or, failing those, Edinburgh or Liverpool.[4]

The newlyweds got out at Basford Station, in the north, adjacent to an ironworks and a cemetery and mortuary chapels. Chemists' windows were covered with advertisements for cough elixirs, cures for bronchitis, and laudanum, used by women to tranquilize their infants while they "sweated" lacework at home. A fine layer of grit settled over their clothing on the short walk to 92 Nottingham Road,[5] in New Basford, a neighborhood bisected by the tracks of another train line, the Great Central Railway, which was being extended into the center of the city. Surrounding their house were, to the west, a dye and bleach works and a skin yard for removing, curing, dressing, and tanning animal hides, Lovett Mill, and Newcastle Colliery and, to the south, the Forest, a seventeen-acre park.

They broke the news of her pregnancy in mid-December, when Frieda wrote to her parents, Else, and the Weekleys, with whom she and Ernest had decided to spend Christmas. On December 19 she boarded the London train alone for the first of many solitary journeys while Ernest stayed behind to finish the term. He joined her two days later. The air was better in Hampstead than in Nottingham, but Frieda felt maudlin, lonely, and nostalgic for Christmas Eve in Sablon. She resolved to celebrate every Christmas in the German tradition from then on. They spent much of January and February looking for a house, and in the spring moved slightly south, nearer the Forest, to 9

Goldswong Terrace, a fifty-year-old red-brick row house previously inhabited by a dressmaker in a mixed neighborhood of artisans and professionals. The streets smelled of coal-burning stoves, and smoke billowed from chimneypots.

Modern indoor plumbing was a rarity, except in new houses, which were required to have water closets, patented two decades earlier by the Londoner Sir Thomas Crapper.[6] The Weekleys did not have this amenity; the house, though high enough up Woodborough Road to be considered a respectable address, was too high for the waterworks to have reached the neighborhood.[7] Built on a tiny incline, it had a small front garden and a smaller, bricked-over back yard. Terraced houses were made from a mold: The front door opened into a passage that led to the scullery, there were two parlors on the ground floor, and a narrow staircase led up to three bedrooms.[8] Frieda was depressed to discover that the Bohemian glass, old silver, and Persian rugs they had gotten for their wedding looked utterly incongruous. A foul smell of household gas filled the sunless halls.[9]

The darkness and confining boxes of rooms brought out the worst in Frieda and Ernest; the house made them feel small, and Ernest's lovestruck homilies quickly gave way to little poison darts: "I have married an earthquake," he remarked as she ran down the pitched stairs.[10] Such barbs quickly became a staple feature of their marriage. The tiny rooms seemed to amplify every sound, even the "sizz" in Ernest's throat as he drank his nightly pint of stout.[11] He also had little but sarcasm for the lesser gifted of his students at University College, where he became known for his detached air and clever put-downs. "There's a somewhat similar passage in a famous work of literature wholly unknown to you, of course," he would say to his French pupils. "I refer to the Holy Bible."[12]

Frieda left the house as often as possible. Except for a short-lived affiliation with a local singing group, she usually found herself alone; the Midlands accent bedeviled her, and it was not a particularly good time to be a German in England: Germany's support for the Boers had set the two countries against each other, and Frieda, with her heavy accent, was conspicuous. The buildup to the war had incited riots on the London docks and provoked anti-German incidents throughout the country. Eighteen to twenty-eight thousand Boers, mostly women and children, would die in British concentration camps in South Africa from 1900 to late 1901, and Frieda's grief over the casualties was hardly a popular stand in Nottingham—or anywhere in England, for that matter.[13] Her father, afraid she would go over to England's side, regularly sent her German hate articles about England.[14]

She enjoyed the anonymity of the streets, however, where she could court her own isolation and alienation, and often ventured downtown just to have something to do. On clear days the sun slanted between Nottingham's high red-brick factory walls to light up the greasy pools on the old canal, used for freight transport. Like her grandmother weeping by the banks of the Oder, she watched lace, stockings, and machinery being loaded onto barges. Riding the horse trams, which bumped over the closely packed cobblestone streets in the center of the city, she developed a love of corner shops, the strong coffee and rich pastries in the Mikado Café, and Boots Cash Chemists, which had started as a tiny herbalist's on Goose Gate, a street bordering the Lace Market. The lace machinery in the huge factories was steam powered, and she grew to welcome the sound of its hiss and clack. She wandered the construction site of the magnificent new station that was being built for the Central Railway extension, completely anomalous with its glass roof and blinding interior lights, and the Market Place, an open square packed with stalls selling everything from gold to notions to produce. Roaming the produce stalls for hours, calling out for fruit and vegetables and attracting stares of curiosity, she then went on to the Shambles, the local meat market, to buy—observing household budgetary constraints—soup bones.

Back home, she either cooked or surrendered the groceries to Paula, a woman she had hired to help with the household work. According to the local paternalistic custom that dispensed with maids' own last names, this woman was called Paula Weekley.[15] Frieda gave her name the German pronunciation, "Powla."[16] The girl eventually learned enough German to understand Frieda's bilingual instructions and to make sense of the handwritten cookbook Anna had passed on at the wedding, but when Frieda haunted the kitchen or tried to speak to Paula about anything other than dinner or tea, she was rebuffed. An unwritten code discouraged the help from being friendly with the mistress of the house.[17] Frieda also retained a parlormaid, who answered the door, dusted, kept the rooms in order, and likewise could not be her friend, and a "tweeny," for "between" maid.

Her command of English improved, but she discovered she had no patience for her neighbors—the wives of a loan-office proprietor, warehouse manager, schoolmaster, lace-factory machine holder, tea merchant, and pawnbroker.[18] Thursday afternoon became her "at-home," and she attended neighbors' at-homes on the remaining weekdays, but she had little to say to these women. Disregarding the schedule of weekly chores that governed their lives, she feigned ignorance when they tried to tell her the right time to shop, hang out clothes, and call on people. "You did the shopping in the morning, after lunch you paid some calls or somebody called on you, there was the ceremony of tea and then there was dinner."[19] When they tried to advise her about her pregnancy, she ignored them and consulted anatomy and child-rearing books. She forced hyacinths to kill time.

Ernest fed her George Eliot and Thackeray, and she soon moved on to Stendhal and Shakespeare, all but for Stendhal in English. "I think Shakespeare would have liked me," she said to him.

"My God!" he replied. "The megalomania! The folly!"[20]

He taught night classes for workers three times a week, continued to write the stream of French textbooks he had begun years before, and was rarely home.[21] Frieda's resolution to help him see life's lighter side soon fell away under the force of his fierce determination to keep the money coming in. Though they were not exactly unhappy, the strict demarcation of their roles and spheres of interest seemed entirely unnatural to her. Her concerns—fear of childbirth, the spells of absurd happiness and melancholy produced by hormonal changes—seemed amorphous compared to Ernest's: the approval of colleagues, the mounds of paper that covered his desk. She hoped her baby would not be a "nitwit," like her, she wrote Else, but bright, like Ernest.[22] She was thrilled that they never fought.[23]

2

Though their relationship soon devolved largely into one of deft avoidance, both of them hidden at night behind books, at University College functions Frieda was the exotic, attractive foreigner. Her speech was blunt and idiosyncratic, punctuated by hearty belly laughs, she "argued fiercely with the men," and she knew how to draw people out.[24] Though her accent alienated greengrocers, her deep-throated "*Ja!*" facilitated academic conversations and introduced a much-needed worldliness. "Who is that pretty woman over there, with hair like a haystack?" someone asked Ernest, inclining his head in the direction of Frieda, speaking animatedly to a party of professors. "That is my wife," he said proudly.[25]

The Weekleys' closest friend at the college was Frederick Stanley Kipping, who coined the term "silicone" in the course of his research into silicon compounds; much later Ernest befriended the literary scholar Janko Lavrin, professor of Russian.[26] Although Frieda enjoyed most of the men at parties, she tired of their wives, who seemed slavish compared to the wives of German professors. Lily Kipping was one of the few exceptions. Thirteen years older than Frieda, she was outspoken and striking, with bright blue eyes set off by a shock of prematurely white hair. Lily appreciated Frieda's earthiness. "When she comes into the room it's like a Devonshire breeze," she said of her.[27]

After the interminable wet winter, Frieda tried to enjoy the late spring in the last months before the birth. Her father arrived and whisked her off to an English watering hole during an early warm spell. The vacation was ruined for the baron, however, when he found Ernest's brother George at the same seaside resort. George betrayed his uncouthness with overly effusive, friendly overtures to the baron, who promptly snubbed him.[28]

In June, Nusch, then almost eighteen, wrote Frieda that she planned to marry a man twice her age, Max von Schreibershofen, a German General Staff officer and inveterate gambler. The whole family was horrified by the news, and when Anna came to Nottingham shortly afterward for the birth of her first grandchild, it was an unnerving visit, overcast by apprehension over the impending marriage. Although the von Richthofens had long been resigned to Frieda's marriage to an Englishman, Anna's anger splayed out to include Ernest. She told Frieda he was cheap: Shopping for soup bones, Frieda, already a practiced haggler, bargained the butcher down to "threepen'worth," and the baroness left the shop indignantly.[29]

Montague Karl Richthofen Weekley (named for Ernest's dead elder brother) was born on June 15, 1900. Frieda briefly had a nurse but, despite a difficult delivery,[30] felt rejuvenated by the birth and soon began caring for Monty herself. The monotony of Nottingham receded into the distance. Breast-feeding gave her a rare feeling of accomplishment, and she spent hours watching Monty learn to reject his pacifier.[31] Although Ernest was immensely proud of the newborn, he was aloof. Children, he felt, properly belonged to a nanny, a convention Frieda flouted. Her practice of jumping out from behind the parlor curtains to shout endearments and crawling along the floor to amuse the little boy filled Ernest with bewilderment and embarrassment. Monty was bright and serious and learned things quickly. Everyone concluded he must have gotten his brains from his father.

Frieda was unable to travel to Metz for Nusch's wedding, on August 2, celebrated in an ostentatious military ceremony, with Nusch riding at the head of Max's regiment on a horse.[32] Though Else described the event to Frieda as pleasant, Friedrich continued to make no secret of his open dislike of Max. Perhaps he understood him too well.

Once Monty began sleeping through the night, Frieda took to devouring novels on the floor in front of the fire. Ernest would burst in, white with exhaustion from back-to-back lectures, his eyes shining with the pride of accomplishment. Often he could not turn off the stream of lecture: Noticing the novel in Frieda's hand, he would promptly begin lecturing her on its "form."[33] Frieda was more interested in plot, however. She bore the interruption with dismissive grunts and a bare modicum of patience before burying herself again in the pages of her book.

A feeling of restlessness overcame her after eight months. To cure it she often boarded the London commuter train with Monty to visit the only people she knew in England, Ernest's family. At Well Walk she had to endure the inevitable cold Monday roast and Maude's litany of criticisms—she disapproved of Frieda's "strange views of life,"[34] which included her failure to take Monty to church—but her in-laws' was less dispiriting than Nottingham. Sometimes she went to Uxbridge to stay with the three McCowen tobacconists. The eldest wore a black satin dress that brushed the floor as she sold her customers boxes of Players, the new packaged cigarettes manufactured in Nottingham. At night the middle sister read her poetry, which was published in the local paper. Sitting in their double-curtained parlor, Frieda watched as they added furnishings to their elaborate dollhouse. She often returned home more restless than when she had started out.

Besides Lily Kipping, who had a son around the time Monty was born, and a stodgy German woman named Flersheim, Frieda made no further female friends in Nottingham. Her neighbors duly noted her increasingly frequent absences from their at-homes and concluded that she was arrogant. "A household after a time runs all by itself," Frieda wrote Else sardonically, "and now nearly every day, I say, 'What shall I do?' "[35]

She brought Monty to Metz for his first birthday, in June 1901. Nusch, living there with Max, was pregnant with her first child and had become even prettier, but also more exaggerated in her appearance. The effect, in Frieda's eyes, was one of coarseness—so much so that Frieda felt "afraid of" Nusch, she wrote Else, though in all probability envy played a part in her assessment of her younger sister.[36] She blotted out her hard voice and flippancy by conjuring up the old Nusch, with her dreamy eyes and fantasies. Max was grossly extravagant, at least when he was doing well at the gambling tables, and Nusch had an enormous wardrobe. Their first child, a girl named Anita, was born later in the year.

It was hardly a vacation for Frieda. Her parents' static, hopeless relationship filled her with unhappy memories at a time when she needed to escape from the present. Her mother continued to criticize Ernest, and the von Richthofens did not prove to be particularly warm grandparents. Though they were only in their fifties, to Frieda they were beginning to seem very old.[37]

After Frieda's return to Nottingham in the fall, she and Ernest briefly studied Italian together on his rare free evenings.[38] He received his second raise at University College, from £200 to £250, still a fairly paltry sum, and then accepted a series of Saturday lectures at Cambridge, for which he earned less than £4 apiece. Frieda was commissioned by Blackie's, one of Ernest's publishers, to edit a selection of Schiller's ballads for their series of Little German Classics—pocket-size books that were ubiquitous in British classrooms.[39] Using existing translations of the poems, she contributed notes and an uninspired introduction. The work paid £5, and she felt reasonably proud of it, but she denigrated it to Else as a mental exercise for her "rusty brain," which she felt had gone soft from her infatuated absorption with Monty.[40] She regularly reported his baby talk and developments to her sisters and mother. In December she organized their first German Christmas, Sablon-style, baking marzipan, which she scorched with a poker. Pregnant again, nauseated much of the time, Frieda ate the lion's share of the sweets.[41]

Her first trimester proved far more difficult than that of the previous pregnancy, and Ernest seemed never to be at home. The prospect of a second child thrilled her, but she had no one to confide in except Else, whose life seemed so much less dull than hers. Though Germany's universities still did not admit women as full-time matriculated students,[42] Else earned a doctorate in economics at Heidelberg, one of only four women to have done so. She graduated summa cum laude.[43] For a time she was active in Germany's nascent feminist movement. She worked as a factory inspector in Karlsruhe and, through her friendships with Max and Marianne Weber, was rapidly becoming something of a figure in Heidelberg intellectual circles.[44] Max's younger brother, Alfred, a chunky, excitable former art historian who had switched to sociology, fell in love with her, but she did nothing to encourage him. He soon went away to Hawaii and then accepted a three-year teaching position at Prague University; one of his students was Kafka's friend and future literary executor Max Brod.

Else did become engaged, however, to a man identified in surviving correspondence only as "R."[45] Frieda seems to have liked R more than Else did; she described him as "more distinguished" than Nusch's husband, Max, "although without a 'von' and General stripes and bars."[46] R made the engagement trip—alone—from Karlsruhe to the von Richthofens'. Else had described him to her parents in very tentative terms; she also "forgot" to give him their full address. Arriving in Metz, he wandered around the city for some time before finding his way, in a sweat, to the doorstep of 49 Bischofstrasse.[47] Else broke off the engagement shortly thereafter.

The following fall, at the age of twenty-eight, to everyone's surprise, she suddenly decided to marry one of her political economy professors at Heidelberg, Edgar Jaffe, who was thirty-six.[48] When Frieda met Edgar, she was mystified by her sister's choice. Scion of a wealthy Hamburg Jewish merchant family, one of fourteen children, he was a shy, impatient intellectual given to nervous silences and unpredictable nonstop lectures to his friends.[49] His glumness exasperated Frieda. Edgar and Else, however, liked the convenience of the relationship. They were just quiet and melancholy enough not to disrupt each other, and they shared a devotion to Max Weber, with whom Edgar had also studied. They settled on the outskirts of Heidelberg, where Edgar commissioned an architect to build a four-story villa from which he and Else could see the entire city, and where their first child, Friedrich, whom they called Friedel, was born the following year, 1903.[50] Although Else did not love Edgar,[51] she admired him, as she told her friend Friedel Schloffer, also about to get married—to a brilliant psychiatrist, Otto Gross.

With Else's marriage came a final closure to the rather unhappy ménage of the von Richthofens of Metz: "I don't mind who my daughters marry," the baron had once said, "as long as they don't marry a Jew, an Englishman or a gambler."[52] In prompt succession, from eldest to youngest, each had married precisely that way.

3

Frieda gave birth to her second child on the morning of September 13, 1902. "We have definitely decided to christen the little daughter Else Agnes Frieda," Ernest wrote the baron. "What she will later be called depends on her behaviour. If she becomes very learned, she will be called Else; very bold, she will be called Frieda."[53] He repeated the quip to Else: ". . . if impudent, it will be Frieda."[54] They eventually decided on the spelling "Elsa."

Looking for someone to help with the two children, Frieda retained Ida Wilhelmy, a lower-middle-class German teenager with a kind, round face, visionary eyes, and frizzy dark blond hair. She was working for the Flersheims but was not happy there and had gotten very sick. With typical lèse-majesté, Frieda asked her to come to Goldswong Terrace first to recuperate and then, if possible, to take over as the children's nurse.[55] "You must stay with me until you are better," she told Ida, and called in Monty's pediatrician to treat her.[56] For once there was someone in the house Frieda could talk to.

Ida's soft looks belied a decisive, straightforward personality. A strict disciplinarian with the children, she hated gossip, was stolidly loyal to Frieda, and knew her feelings of entrapment and boredom. Although Ida "felt the 'Baroness' very strongly"—by which she presumably meant the effort of subordinating her will to Frieda's—she didn't tell her this until fifty-three years later.[57] She was bossy and devoutly Catholic, and regularly took Monty to see the nuns at the local convent and to masses at the Catholic church, which made Maude Weekley very happy: "It was better that the children should have some religion," she said to Ernest, "even if it was Roman." Ida told the children about God, sin, and heaven, and they said their rosaries and enjoyed themselves immensely.[58] Frieda, by now a confirmed agnostic, nonetheless was tremendously attracted to grand religious symbolism and its use in mythology, literature, and German philosophy, particularly Nietzsche (she later loved Goethe, for much the same reason); a copy of *Thus Spake Zarathustra* seems to have made its way via Else to Goldswong Terrace in late 1902. She had asked her sister for the book after receiving a gift of a calendar, handmade by an old Metz acquaintance whom they both detested but who was devoted to the von Richthofen family, featuring Nietzsche aphorisms.[59]

Frieda became pregnant again, early in 1904, and Ernest decided they needed a bigger house, less for the child than for his books—an enormous library he cataloged by language, with subsections for academic and popular etymology, the latter increasingly occupying more of his time and interest. They left Goldswong Terrace for 8 Vickers Street, near Mapperley Road. Only a few blocks away, it was a far tonier address, on a hill with a good view of the city below. Frieda now had a drawing room, which she outfitted with a piano for practicing Schubert and Brahms (it is not known when or how she learned to play). There were front and back yards; Monty, now three and a half years old, liked playing by himself and began spending most of his time outdoors. He had become a mimic with a precocious sense of the absurd, and, though shy, he disguised it with impersonations of his family and the neighbors in perfect German and English accents. "Policeman, take this boy!" he shouted in German, pounding on a door in imitation of Anna von Richthofen's threat to her disobedient grandchildren.[60]

Frieda was raising the children bilingually, though Monty begged her to use only English in public. "Don't speak German," he would whisper to her on the tram to the Mikado for tea and cakes. "People are looking at us."[61] She adopted Ernest's colloquialisms, which sounded funny with her accent: "I don't give a tuppenny damn," she said of meddlesome neighbors' criticisms of her.[62] On afternoons when Ernest had time to come home briefly between classes for a meal, Monty carried instructions in a mixture of both languages to Paula in the kitchen.[63] He had an enormous vocabulary of real and made-up words and was already giving his father material, combining English and German words to comic effect. "*Schpamm*," Monty said for *Schwamm* (sponge), a neologism Ernest would later cite in a work of popular etymology he had begun plotting out at night. He sat at his father's side for the evening *Times* crosswords and quickly became expert at them. "*Schwesterlein*" was what Monty, inspired by the German fairy tales Frieda read the two children in her bed on Sunday mornings, called his sister, Elsa, a quiet girl with a withering frown.[64]

Frieda's second daughter was born on October 20, 1904. Christened Barbara Joy, she was soon known simply as Barby. Her godfather was a gregarious forty-year-old neighbor, William Enfield Dowson, with whom Frieda and Ernest had become friendly. A machine holder in his family's lace factory, he was also a beachfront real-estate entrepreneur, and drove a car that Frieda later remembered as one of the first in Nottingham, though in fact there were many.[65] His wife, Helena B. Dowson, led one of the city's more conservative contingents of suffragists, the National Union of Women's Suffrage Societies (NUWSS). Made up mostly of families and married women, NUWSS met in a small schoolroom and campaigned for the vote and such causes as state endowment to working mothers. Between 1903 and 1905 they were largely supplanted by Emmeline Pankhurst's militant Women's Social and Political Union (WSPU). The WSPU recruited unmarried upper-middle-class women and took violent measures: They burned mail with tubes of phosphorus and once set fire to the Nottingham Boat Club.[66] The Dowsons lived on Mapperley Road, and Frieda often went to their house in the evening. Sitting in their living room, she tuned out Helena's soapbox rhetoric and declined invitations to suffragette meetings. She got firsthand accounts from Will, who went with Helena but soon tired of the movement—and apparently of Helena.[67] He began taking Frieda for drives in his car. However gauche she was in other things, Frieda proved deft in starting a love affair, and Dowson was ready. She began calling him her "great friend," and much later described the infidelity with euphemisms calculated to obscure: Dowson was the "one great friend" with whom she "felt alive."[68]

He rented out cottages and boats on the Trent, where he also had a little bungalow for himself and his family. In the summer he began inviting Frieda and her children to swim. With Monty on her back, she rode the waves with wild exuberance. Monty, although only four, evidently understood the relationship between his mother and Barby's godfather, to whom he referred in later years, with great irony, as "the great Dowson."[69] Not everyone, however, was as uninhibited as Frieda at the beach. She and her friend Mrs. Flersheim, who had a teenage daughter, brought their children each summer to the resort towns of Chapel St. Leonard, Skegness, and Sutton-on-Sea, on the Lincolnshire coast. Monty once ran naked out of the beach tent, and Mrs. Flersheim rushed to cover the eyes of her daughter, then thirteen.[70]

When not "lustily oar[ing] the waves,"[71] Frieda and Will made love in his car in Sherwood Forest or on a sea of bluebells under ancient oaks on the grounds of Byron's estate, Newstead Abbey; both were an hour's drive from Nottingham. She also relied on him as a confidant and friend. They talked about contemporary novels, he pampered her children, and he made Nottingham seem almost bearable. By then Frieda felt nothing but contempt for the plodding pragmatism of the English; it seemed a hyper-literal and conventional way of looking at and living in the world, and Ernest epitomized it. Still consumed by night lectures and academic piecework, he always returned late and sat with Frieda only for a quick supper of soup, bread, and cheese, his nightly stout, and an exchange of sarcasms before closeting himself in his study, lighting and relighting his pipe as he corrected papers and added to his manuscript of popular etymology. Roaming his study aimlessly the next day, Frieda smelled his tobacco and felt conflicting surges of contentment, familiarity, and rage: "the walls were books, the whole room seemed books, books on the writing-table, books on the floor."[72] His collection now numbered in the thousands.

His passion for Frieda had also become fetishistic. His fantasy, squeezed into the corner of the evening left over after his correcting work was done and his books cataloged, largely centered on depicting her as a virgin.[73] He tried to get her to wear black to arouse him, but she refused.[74] Ernest disliked any mention of sex other than in the bedroom at night: "We don't talk about those things in the daytime," he said to her, calling Frieda his "white snowflower."[75] The metaphor enraged her.

4

Nusch came to see her, stepping from the train in a perfect plaid traveling suit. She thrived on being a garrison wife, entertaining officers in lavish style, in both the drawing room and the bedroom. Nusch pitied Frieda's lack of multiple lovers, nice clothes, glamour, and admirers, and she detested Englishmen, who, she said, were too polite to stare openly and appreciatively. One day she and Frieda entered the Mikado

Café. "I might just as well be the waiter!" she fumed.[76] She left Frieda a couple of snug evening dresses that had to be let out and some parting thoughts about their different ways of life:

> I must have change and the fittings round me and the men. . . . you have no idea how they spoil me. The flowers I get, and the women, how jealous they are of me. Their faces are a study; oh the frumps, the frumps, I don't wonder men are bored to death with the tame cats!

"[Y]our life gives me the creeps, you poor dear," Nusch added.[77]

Frieda found it hard to disagree. She began taking the children each summer to Eichberghaus, where she joined her sisters and her mother, finally growing to understand her mother's attachment to the *Tanten*: They asked no questions and loved children. Ida went along as baby-sitter and spent long afternoons with the children in the Blases' serene garden and cherry orchard under the eaglelike scrutiny of their grandmother, who would occasionally importune the children on their peaceful berrypicking expeditions with her shrill cries of "*Du wirst Bauchweh bekommen!*" (You'll get a tummy ache!) Ida led them out the back-yard gate to conduct elf hunts in the Black Forest, and they left mugs of flowers behind huge trees for the creatures.[78] While the children played, Frieda swapped stories with her sisters. They had both had second children in 1905—Else a girl she named Marianne, after Max Weber's wife, and Nusch a boy, Hadubrand. Else was involved in the editorial work of a journal, *Archiv für Sozialwissenschaft und Sozialpolitik*, which Edgar had bought in 1904 to give to Weber, who was then suffering severe mental breakdowns that prevented him from teaching.[79] Their social world now extended to Munich, where Friedel Schloffer and Otto Gross lived. Frieda listened with fascination to Else's stories of the circle of philosophers, psychiatrists, and anarchists she had met through the Grosses. She was eager to see Munich herself and resolved to visit the city as soon as possible.

In 1906 she again earned some money from Blackie's, annotating six Thuringian folk legends by the nineteenth-century poet-novelist Ludwig Bechstein. The pay for the forty-eight-page pamphlet was another £5.[80] Ernest's salary at University College leapt to £350. He became increasingly overworked and impatient, and his sarcasms more condescending. Frieda suggested brushing up on the colloquial French she had learned in Metz by conversing with a student of his. "My dear Friedl," Ernest replied wearily, "[she] . . . knows far more colloquial French than you do."[81]

She began to imagine running away. After she and Ida had put the children to sleep, she raced up Mapperley Road toward the Dowsons' house—and kept running until she had exhausted herself, then stood and listened to the wind catching in the trees at the top of the plain. When she felt sane again, she turned around and went slowly back home.[82] The Dowsons soon moved from Mapperley Road to Felixtowe, a large house on Clumber Road West in the Park, an exclusive neighborhood of Victorian mansions, ornamental gazebos, and dense gardens, where most of Nottingham's successful businessmen lived.[83]

Frieda made two new friends, Madge and Gladys Bradley, the daughters of a Baptist leather magnate, a Liberal magistrate named Frederick James Bradley. Roughly her age, they were the most free-thinking women she had met, though their repressed childhood had led them to some strange practices, including self-mortification: As little girls, they told Frieda, they had regularly pricked their vaginas with thorns.[84] Gladys was unmarried, intelligent, and attractive, with beautiful gray eyes, a thin, tense mouth, and a voluptuous body, which she liked to show off at the beach. Frieda began inviting her along on family vacations, and Gladys became adroit at winning her confidence and titillating Ernest. "A fine figure in a bathing dress," he remarked of her one day.[85] Frieda suspected that, though he appeared oblivious, he actually harbored feelings for Gladys, and she was irritated that he did not act on them. Frieda blithely confided her affair with Will to her friend, who had an insatiable interest not only in other people's husbands but in their love lives. She kept a pied-à-terre in London, overlooking the Thames, which, out of possible self-interest, she began lending to Frieda.[86]

In the spring of 1907 Frieda set off on a long trip to the Continent that was to change her life irrevocably. Frieda Gross, now separated from her husband, Otto, agreed to put her up in Munich, and she planned to visit Else and Edgar in Heidelberg. She was especially eager to see her sister, who was having an affair with Otto that had drastically altered the tone of her letters. For the first time Frieda was traveling abroad alone.

5

"Our Old Mother's Skin"

I

Frieda awoke to find nothing to eat in Friedel Gross's apartment on Menzingerstrasse, in northern Munich.[1] It had been a decade since she had last seen Else's childhood friend; now twenty-nine, she was a slim and mournfully pretty woman with strawberry blond hair that fell below her waist, a long Roman nose, full lips, and a long-suffering look. Prone to psychosomatic illness, and with a tendency to forget to eat, she was remote and strange and made Frieda feel nervous.[2] "Put your coat on," she told Frieda. "We have breakfast at the *Kaffeehaus*."[3] Frieda was relieved to leave the silent apartment.

They walked through the northeastern loop of the five-hundred-acre Nymphenburg Park, passing its baroque palace and rococo hunting lodge, then made their way into the intellectuals' quarter of Schwabing along dirt roads fanning out to neatly painted clapboard summer houses. After the freezing damp of a north-of-England winter, the mild Bavarian spring was enchanting; wildflowers, still two months off in Nottingham, were beginning to come up in the fields between the houses, and gardeners were putting beds of tulips in the formal Englischer Garten. It was still early when they reached the apartment houses in the center of Schwabing. Wet laundry was strung between the small buildings, and bottles of milk sat on the windowsills. The crooked streets, lined with tiny antique stores, tobacconists, and all-night coffeehouses, were decorated for Carnival, and men in leather breeches and green velvet jackets with carved horn buttons sold fruit out of wheelbarrows. The onion dome of the fifteenth-century Frauenkirche somehow made Frieda's spirit thaw, and she listened with rapture to the distinctive Munich dialect as Friedel led her to the Café Stephanie, Schwabing's Café de Deux Magots.[4] Ordering coffee for them both, Friedel began reading her correspondence and making the day's appointments from a public telephone, while Frieda sat at a table, gawking like a tourist.

Though she had heard a lot about Schwabing from Else, she was overwhelmed by its cast of characters, the furied atmosphere of the Stephanie—also known as the Café Grössenwahn, or Megalomania—and the manic onslaught of ideas. Conversations careened from Jews to expressionism to psychoanalysis, and the conversants, for the first time in Frieda's life, were Jews, expressionists, and analysts. "*Schlawiners*," as the stock Bavarians had nicknamed this bohemian fringe,[5] spoke a patois she hardly recognized. The current fascination, on all lips as Frieda relished her first cup of strong Munich coffee, was the playwright Frank Wedekind's *Frühlings Erwachen* (Awakening of spring), a much-vilified, vicious satire of the middle class that had recently opened in Munich after a run of more than two hundred performances in Berlin. Frieda took in a performance of the play, two of whose teenaged characters die of a botched abortion and a suicide, and became upset: "[T]hat the young," she wrote, "could be so old and unhappy."[6]

Censorship battles and police records were a badge of integrity among the writers, Italian, Swiss, and German anarchists, and art students—among them Leonhard Frank, later one of Munich's most prominent novelists—who crowded the Stephanie's tattered banquettes. Chess players kibbitzed at the corner table of Erich Mühsam, the editor of the journal *Cain*, occasionally breaking with great bravado into one of his revolutionary rhymes. A wealthy Jew from Lübeck, openly bisexual, Mühsam had a long police record in Berlin, and a rather different experience of Wilhelmine society than Frieda's. He later died in a Nazi concentration camp.

Initially charmed, Frieda quickly tired of this type—whom she found "mostly more anxious to talk than to listen"—but not of a twenty-six-year-old Swiss named Ernst Frick, who had one of the thickest dossiers in the Zurich Polizeikommando's file of "Communists, Socialists, Anarchists."[7] Gaunt and aristocratic looking, Frick, unlike the majority of the Stephanie's revolutionaries, was actually a workingman. He arrived one day pushing Otto and Friedel's three-month-old son, Peter, in a baby carriage: Since the Grosses' separation, Friedel had taken Frick as her lover. Struck by the incongruity of this proletarian anarchist behind an expensive pram, Frieda soon took him on as a cause, more in spirit than in any practical sense.[8] A former railway and foundry worker, one of three brothers born in the Zurich suburb of Knonau, Frick had risen through the international anarchists' ranks from what Frieda, with uncharacteristic irony, liked to call the *bessere Leute*.[9] In 1904 he founded a Zurich anarchists' group and the militant workers' journal *Weckruf* (Wake-up call). In 1905, after serving fifteen days for evading compulsory military service, he began to keep two addresses, one of them a cover for *Weckruf* mail and propaganda. After the 1905 uprising in Russia, his circle of thinkers and agitators were joined by the first trickle of Russian revolutionaries who would use Zurich as a stopover until 1917, and the police stepped up their harassment. He had fled to Schwabing when they found papers of "anarchistic content" in his atelier.[10]

Though Schwabing had become a serious alternative for those on the lam (Lenin, living under an alias, had met Rosa Luxemburg there at the turn of the century), there was also much silliness, hedonism, and dilettantism. Countess Franziska "Fanny" zu Reventlow, a Stephanie regular often likened to a Wedekind heroine, straddled both demimondes. A translator, painter, journalist, novelist, and sometime dominatrix, she had a philosophy and history of sexual adventure that resonated with every unspoken thought in Frieda's head. It was also the first time Frieda had seen intellectualism at the service of experimentation. Reventlow, a classic beauty with huge, dark blue, deep-set eyes, an expressive face, and fashionably short blond hair, was the black sheep of an aristocratic family from the small North Sea city of Husum. She called herself a "juggler," a reference not only to the balancing act of mothering her only son and whipping men for a living but to a lifelong wish to join the circus. She once volunteered to tour Siam with Chinese acrobats, as the target of their knife-throwing act.

She never found solace or satisfaction under the big tent, but she compensated by dancing at the masked balls of Carnival in Pierrot costume, playing soubrette parts, and performing as a rope dancer in folk costume at Bavarian country fairs. Though she was constantly broke, when the "Babylon" of Schwabing became commonplace, she always managed to get rich men to pay her way to such places as Constantinople and Corfu. Back in Munich, she changed apartments often, going from ménage to ménage as they became available—and they always did in Schwabing. Her circle was huge: Wedekind, Otto Gross, and lovers who ran the gamut from Rainer Maria Rilke, Else's husband Edgar, and the philosopher Ludwig Klages to a Polish craftsman and glass-painter named Bogdan von Suchocki.[11]

Behind this worldliness lay a provincial aristocratic childhood very much like Frieda's, and though the two women seem to have met only a few times, the effect was hugely revelatory for Frieda. Reventlow's father, like Friedrich von Richthofen, was a more sympathetic and less forbidding figure than her mother, a beautiful, dark woman with a mania for etiquette and feelings of impatience, disgrace, and disgust for her daughter's nascent anarchism. Her marriage in May 1894 to a Hamburg assessor eventually got her to Munich by the age of twenty-three, but he soon divorced her: Her outrageous behavior, he said—as Ernest Weekley would soon be saying of Frieda—was ruining his career and good name. The birth in 1897 of her illegitimate son, Rolf (she kept his father's identity secret, saying she had given herself the child), caused chronic gynecological problems but did not slow her erotic or literary schedule. She kept up her diaries in the Café Bett, the Leopold, and the Simplicissimus, a noisier hangout than the Stephanie, and taught her son in the cafés and at home to save him from the German school system. Her first published works were short sketches for various journals; when one of them was banned for religious slander, she translated the French poets.

Frieda was impressed that Reventlow, despite more than a decade of affairs, "had the face of a very young Madonna."[12] So were a lot of other people. Otto Gross, well known for his spot-psychoanalyses of young women at the Stephanie, told Reventlow he wanted to cure her of, among other compulsions, "forceful self-control,"[13] so that her face would never harden and she would remain a Madonna forever.

2

Otto turned up at the Stephanie one day while Frieda was eating Wiener schnitzel. Unbathed and unchanged (it had been days since he had been to his apartment, in a rural corner of Schwabing), he came through the revolving door into the smoky room looking—at least to Frieda—like a "mountaineer."[14] His body was strong and lithe and full of nervous energy, a strange counterpoint to his utterly ravaged face. A hand-rolled cigarette was set in an elegant seven-inch holder.

Else had not exaggerated his appeal. He was extraordinarily good-looking, with features that had a child's simplicity and perfection and eyes that seemed from moment to moment inspired, haunted, or dazed. He was a cocaine addict, and bloodstains dotted the front of his coat and jacket, leaked from nasal passages that were slowly being laid waste. Like many cult heroes, he had a strange capacity to look different to every person he met. "Reddish hair, most unkempt," read a later warrant for his arrest, ". . . face unclean . . . walks irregularly, almost always looking angrily at the ground."[15] He hid his weak chin with a handlebar mustache and thin beard: "The upper part of his face," wrote his friend Leonhard Frank, "—the pale eyes with their childishly innocent expression, the hooked nose and the full lips, always slightly parted as if he were silently weeping for the world's misery—was at odds with the weak lower part, the chin that was scarcely more than indicated and receded completely out of sight. But nobody, once having seen that fantastic bird's head, ever forgot it."[16] Max Weber equated him with flawed Nietzscheanism; Max Brod portrayed him in his novel *Das grosse Wagnis* (The big venture) as a crazed liberator who becomes a dictator; Freud's future aide and biographer Ernest Jones called him a romantic genius: "Such penetrative powers of divining the inner thoughts of others I was never to see again."[17] Carl Jung, Gross's future analyst, wrote to Freud that he had met his doppelgänger in him. To Frieda he seemed a paradox: awful but wonderful, exaggerated but natural, demoniacal but spiritual.[18] She offered to share her schnitzel with him. "None of your corpses for me," said Otto, a vegetarian, and ordered a plate of spinach and eggs.[19]

Their first conversations, with his repeated exhortations of "*Nichts verdrängen*!" (Repress nothing!) took her entirely off guard.[20] "My real self," she wrote, ". . . shrank from contact like a wild thing."[21] She felt attracted, however, by the intimacy of his dialect—Styrian, from the Austrian Alps, southwest of Vienna—though it was so strong she often missed what he was saying. She had no idea how to answer his loaded questions, much less how to insert herself into his seamless loops of conversation. She began smoking cigarettes.

Though Gross had never formally studied with Freud, he was one of his most avid disciples; Frieda, who had never heard of Freud and his theories, would have none of it at first. "As for Freud's complexes and Karl Marx's labor," she said, "that is all the wrong side of the medal. Call it love and work and it all looks quite different." When Gross, waxing eloquent about Genesis, broached an analysis of Paradise, Frieda simply paraphrased *Pudd'nhead Wilson*: "The Lord can't have been such a bad psychologist as not to have known that Eve would want the apple the minute it was forbidden," she told him. ". . . when they had eaten it, they weren't ashamed of their nakedness at all. 'Look, Adam. There is a pool down by those willows and we will have a swim, and then we'll dry ourselves in the sun. Hurrah! I shall have a small Adam, and then you'll work to get us something to eat while I sing to the baby.' "[22]

She met him often at the Stephanie. Gross, who was writing a paper on personality types, which derived from an earlier book of his, was soon discussing its applications to her, instant production of theory that seemed like fortune-telling—equal parts truth and wish fulfillment. Rather than the loud, "smock ravelled"[23] provincial Frieda felt herself to be, for example, she was a pure example of "narrow," "deep" consciousness—what Jung, borrowing from Gross, later called an "introvert." Like himself, he told her, she had little use or aptitude for facts and information—the "banal." Her emotional life—more to the point—was perfectly realized, with no schism between eros and consciousness. She had a gift for symbolic abstraction and for simplifying the complex, and "a soul kept pure by its genius for insisting upon being itself."[24] Anticipating what a not-dissimilar man would tell her five years later, he said that she had a genius for living.

3

Otto was the son of the magistrate, professor, and eminent criminologist Hans Gross, to whom allusions can be found in the works of Georges Simenon and the American detective and mystery novelist

S. S. Van Dine.[25] Among his contributions to the field was a collection of such real-crime detritus as abortion tools and human bones misshapen by torture, still on display at the Graz Kriminalmuseum.[26] Otto was born in Feldbach, near Graz, on March 17, 1877. His mother, a passive, unworldly woman, was a Protestant; his father a converted Catholic, a huge, bull-necked man who ruled the household like a tyrant. From an early age Otto had a phenomenally retentive memory: When the names of the bones of a prehistoric animal were read to him twice, he could recite the list—and this before he had learned to read. When he did, two books preoccupied him: the Bible, from which he later liked to draw anti-Christian myths to provoke his father, and a book on the natural history of animals, which held so much fascination for him that its pages fell out and had to be taken away and rebound. Frieda recalled going to the Munich Zoo and watching Gross "work up the animals, by merely looking at them, till they nearly went mad."[27]

Hans, who had more refined, "princely"[28] behavior in mind for his only child, felt that Otto identified too closely with the animal kingdom. "Watch out," he warned a guest, "he *bites*."[29] By the age of ten, Otto was far advanced in science, mythology, the old German sagas, Greek, and Latin; but Hans complained that he lacked practicality, a virtue the household elevated above all others.

Otto was sixteen when Hans published his masterwork, *Handbuch für Untersuchungsrichter* (Handbook for examining magistrates), a criminal psychology handbook that appeared under various titles throughout Europe and was eventually adopted as a manual by Scotland Yard.[30] "*Egoism, laziness and conceit are the only human motives on which one may unconditionally depend*"[31] was its central thesis (Hans loved underlining for emphasis), and he maintained that most people are pathological liars. The testimony of witnesses therefore being unreliable, he perfected an objective system for solving crimes—the use of fingerprints, bloodstains, and, later, such detection methods as X rays. One of his subspecialties was criminal jargon: The words "groin," "dick," "fence," "nark," "bent gear" made their first appearance in his work.[32]

He had determined that his son would also pursue the science of crime detection. At the time Otto enrolled in Graz University's Psychiatrisch-Neurologische Klinik—once headed by Hans's former collaborator Richard von Krafft-Ebing and considered the best in the empire after Vienna—Hans thought of psychology as little more than a potentially useful tool for the policeman. Otto had other agendas: He promised to marry several women he met as an undergraduate but reneged on his promises, recoiling "in disappointment or disgust" from each and forcing his parents to intercede and formally reject his various fiancées.[33] He performed brilliantly in examinations and labs but rarely went to class, and once tried to persuade the university's fraternities to close down the local whorehouses, for which he was beaten by fraternity members. As a graduate student he came under the influence of the head of the clinic, the proto-Freudian Gabriel Anton.

In 1897 both father and son left Graz, Hans to teach law at Czernowitz University, on Austria's Russian border, Otto to continue medical studies at the University of Munich. He graduated in 1899 and sailed the coast of South America to Patagonia as a ship's doctor. As he later told Else, he always recalled "standing on the shore at Punta Arenas, looking out over the Pacific, and feeling at the end of everything civilized."[34] On shipboard he became addicted to narcotics. He used cocaine to stay up at night, a habit immortalized by the Schwabing poet Johannes R. Becher in his poem "Café Stephanie": "In Munich it was, in the Café Stephanie, /. . . A thought kept itself awake with cocaine."[35]

Though Gross published his first articles in his father's journal, *Archiv für Kriminalanthropologie und Kriminalistik*, when he returned from South America the two moved worlds apart. Over the next fifteen years, Hans promulgated a bizarre, controlling theory of human nature in papers like "Degeneration and Deportation" and "Castration and Sterilization," which advocated the banishment and mutilation of Gypsies, tramps, and revolutionaries.[36] Psychiatry, for Otto, gradually became neither a criminologist's nor a doctor's practice, but a revolutionary's. He felt that sickness was not to be despised, and he argued from the patient's point of view rather than the doctor's. "Dr. Gross tells me," Jung later wrote Freud, "that he puts a quick stop to the transference by turning people into sexual immoralists. He says the transference to the analyst and its persistent fixation are mere monogamy symbols and as such symptomatic of repression. The truly healthy state for the neurotic is sexual immorality. Hence he associates you with Nietzsche."[37] By 1907 Gross had a considerable history as both doctor and patient to draw on: Starting in 1902 he institutionalized himself fairly regularly for drug-withdrawal cures in Burghölzli, the insane asylum for the canton of Zurich.

He married Frieda Schloffer shortly after his first cure, a move that caused a serious rupture with his father, who disliked her intensely. Frieda had been melancholy since the death of her mother, in Graz, when the little girl was six. Raised by her father, an unsuccessful lawyer who read her the classics at night, in her teens she found surrogates at the Institute Blas. Like Else, she honed her reformer's instinct there, and was unhappy returning to Graz, where life seemed stifled at every turn and she felt unproductive. But for a few nursing lectures, however, she pursued no occupation and waited instead for something unspecified to materialize. That turned out to be Gross, who in 1901–2 was completing his first book, *Die zerebrale Sekundärfunktion* (The secondary function of the brain), in which he had initially proposed his theory of psychological types, albeit in somewhat different form.[38] On their honeymoon they took along *Thus Spake Zarathustra* and a professional psychiatry journal.[39] They vowed to work together forever and, in Munich, to free themselves from the trappings of the upper middle class. Neither seems to have had any awareness of the difficulties awaiting such a life.

Otto's first troubles came quickly, with his first employer, Emil Kraepelin. Kraepelin, then an internationally renowned psychiatrist, had enormous contempt for psychoanalysis. In 1899 he had attempted to formalize and delimit psychiatry by distinguishing between two main groups of diseases, dementia praecox (or schizophrenia) and manic-depressive disorder. In the Nervenklinik der Ludwig-Maximilians-Universität, the two-thousand-patient Munich clinic where Gross worked as an assistant, Kraepelin, its director, forbade his doctors to speak to their patients privately, to keep out any whiff of Freud's new "talking cure." The stress this distance caused Otto was soon complicated by his ongoing narcosis; he eventually became so enraged that he decided to take Kraepelin to court—in essence, for being a non-Freudian—and Ernest Jones had to dissuade him from following through and filing suit. After this professional explosion—and there were others—Gross stopped going to work except at night, when his patients and employer were asleep. He suffered a rather lost, manic period in 1906 and entered Burghölzli again for a short stay. He was having a spurt of productivity in the spring of 1907, when Frieda was visiting Schwabing, and she became a part of it. Their affair evidently started at her instigation: "Do you still remember," he later wrote, ". . . when you chose me in your wonderful aristocratic way?"[40] She was due back in England before the summer, and for all the ground she and Otto covered, their time together was amazingly brief—about two (apparently not sequential) weeks. They stayed in either a pied-à-terre of Edgar Jaffe's or Otto's apartment, Frieda wearing a blue dressing gown that seems to have been shared by several women and may originally have belonged to Otto's wife; he later wrote how it looked on someone else.[41] He worked through the night, fortified by cocaine, while she lay in bed reading his manuscripts: Perhaps inspired by the Stephanie's address, Türkenstrasse, Otto immortalized *her* sexual stamina in the nickname *Türkenpferdl* ("little Turkish horse").[42]

He began calling his paper on personality types their "child," in acknowledgment of her contributions: long, late-night conversations about its Social Darwinist theory of selection, through cultural evolution, of a growing body of individuals with narrow, deep consciousness. He called them people "of the future," by which he meant those who could not cope with modernity or, for that matter, the present. Following Nietzsche's *Twilight of the Idols*, he and Frieda called their age the "Epoch of Decadence," a period of *productive* decadence. He and Frieda, as a couple in love, were personally undergoing one, with infinite possibilities for happiness: "You know my faith," he later wrote her, "that it is always out of *decadence* that a *new harmony* in life creates itself."[43] The new harmony was their evolving relationship: "It is the nature of *our* love that this protracted longing and this great willing should leap into life in an intoxication of the senses."[44] Frieda felt he took too many drugs.[45]

Unlike Nietzsche and Freud, Gross was sure that the hope of the world rested in women—particularly a certain kind of woman: someone "unpolluted by all the things that I hate and fight against . . . free from the code of chastity, from Christianity, from democracy and all that accumulated filth."[46] Along with Freud and Jung, who both analyzed Friedel Gross, he felt that his wife suffered the same "repressions" as he did, and that it was she who had helped him adjust to the world. Now Frieda was helping him see its, and his own, worth,[47] and the effect was a powerful if momentary calm and feeling of synthesis. He had even found a way, in his second book, *Das Freudsche Ideogen-*

itätsmoment und seine Bedeutung im manisch-depressiven Irresein Kraepelins (The Freudian factor of ideogeneity and its significance in Kraepelin's manic-depressive illness), to integrate the utterly incompatible theories of Freud, Gabriel Anton (his old professor from Graz), the Silesian psychiatrist and neuropathologist Carl Wernicke, and Kraepelin.[48] The drama of his presentation, his brilliance and complexity, fascinated Frieda: "[I]t's really the theoretician that I love most of all in you," she later wrote him.[49] Frieda, he felt more with each passing day, seemed entirely free of inhibition—which he defined as sickness.

Although Frieda apparently considered him a "genius at love," their first problems also seem to have centered on bed: "He was a marvelous lover—but I knew it was no good. . . . he talked to you while he was loving you."[50] (His sexual prowess, like everything else about Gross, was a matter of strong opinion: "As a 'lover,'" Else wrote Frieda, "he's incomparable.")[51] He also could not convince Frieda of the pleasures of multiple partners.[52] Often his were patients. Some lived in Schwabing, others in his second home, Ascona, in Switzerland, a place Gross considered the matrix of his people "of the future."

4

Then a village of one thousand olive- and grape-growing peasants, Ascona is nestled in the foothills of the Lepontine Alps, two hundred miles southwest of Munich. Frequented from the 1860s to the turn of the century by Italian political refugees, Eastern European Tolstoyans, and such Russian anarchists as Mikhail Bakunin, it was officially baptized a utopian community in 1902 by seven Belgian, Montenegrin, Austrian, and German intellectuals who, with plans to make themselves self-sufficient, had crossed eight- and ten-thousand-foot mountain passes the year before on foot, wearing sandals and loose muslin dresses or hemp tunics. They quickly disagreed on how to carry out their plans and eventually split up, a few remaining to build a vegetarian sanatorium, Der Berg der Wahrheit, or Monte Verità—Mountain of Truth.[53]

Its opening attracted a good many people, and within two years thirty to sixty philosophers, political refugees, writers, vegetarians, feminists, neopagan mystics, sun worshipers, theosophists, alcoholics (who came for a cure), and occultists (who later held public readings of the poetry of Aleister Crowley) had moved to Ascona. In the following years, visitors included Jung, Isadora Duncan, and Herman Hesse (who originally came for alcohol detoxification). Half the Schwabing regulars shuttled between Munich and Ascona; some of them—Frick, Friedel Gross, Reventlow—eventually moved there permanently.

Frieda loved Ascona. In its religiosity, remoteness, and beauty, the Catholic village reminded her of Donaueschingen. Its hillsides were sprinkled with grottoes, and a tradition of Virgin worship prevailed. Except for a smuggling trade fostered by the close proximity of the Austrian and Italian borders, there was only rudimentary commerce. Fishermen brought their catch each day from the Maggia River and Lake Maggiore, and the protection afforded by the alpine foothills—Corona dei Pinci, Gridone—permitted the kind of vegetation usually found only on an island with fair trade winds: evergreens, palm trees that yielded plump dates, flowering mountain laurel, wild rosebushes, chestnut trees, peach, plum, and fig trees, and a half dozen varieties of berries.

Intellectuals and peasants lived virtually side by side, but the latter made silent oaths and the sign of the cross after passing their scantily clad neighbors in the fields and streets, and they bristled at their flagrant rituals: mud baths and impromptu "burials" of live sanatorium patients in the soil, nude dances under the moon, pagan and occult rites enacted in caves, and bonfires in the evening—to symbolically cleanse the world's air. People lived singly, *à trois*, and in other communal groupings, either in unusual wood cabins they made themselves or in run-down houses abandoned by transient smugglers. Gross designated one such dilapidated barn an orgiastic center.

He came and went freely, though in 1906 a shadow had fallen across his wanderings when he became involved with Lotte Hattemer, one of Ascona's less well-adjusted founders. The daughter of a high-ranking Berlin politician, she had fled her parents' life—if not their money—for one of isolation, devotion, and sexual experimentation at Ascona.[54] An eccentric, religious mystic, and an inveterate walker, Hattemer staked out an abandoned, primitive house and could be found strolling aimlessly around its grounds, her long blond hair brushed straight down over her face, obscuring her view. In 1904 she and a friend, Elly Lenz, a professor's daughter who had previously camped alone in a neighboring chestnut wood, took in Erich Mühsam and his lover, Johann Nohl, the renegade member of a well-off family of academics, who had initiated Mühsam into the science of vagabonding in Berlin. They had come to Ascona by way of a brief stay at the agricultural commune Eden, near Berlin—to which their friend the philosopher Martin Buber also belonged—and were wanted by the police.

Hattemer periodically trekked down the Northern Apennines into Florence, a distance of 220 miles, wearing a crown of fresh flowers like a holy figurine. A visit from her father early in 1906 drove her into a state of nervous tension; she secreted herself in a cave and refused to emerge. A suicide attempt followed, and she was taken in by friends. Gross, her friend and sometime doctor, arrived in Ascona with a large amount of drugs for her, then left for Schwabing. She overdosed the next day, while alone with Nohl. It is not known whether the overdose had been planned by Gross and Hattemer, though it is clear that Gross considered her death a mercy killing. By 1909 the Munich police had connected his and Nohl's names with her death, but neither was ever arrested.

5

Frieda learned that Else was pregnant with Gross's child while visiting at her villa in Heidelberg, and they fought bitterly.[55] She spent a week (still only the second of two) with Gross in Amsterdam on her way back to England, and gave him a ring with the heads of three women in relief—to symbolize herself, Else, and his wife: "[Y]ou won't find 3 people like the 3 of us," she wrote, "on every street-corner."[56] Gross accompanied her on the overnight crossing, bringing along the blue robe. His nights of ecstasy and loneliness in Patagonia, he told Frieda, had predestined their Channel crossing: The Southern Cross above his head in the tropics had prefigured Frieda, the Southern Cross over his life's journey.[57] On the boat he tried to persuade her to leave Ernest, inverting Frieda's objections—particularly her defense of Weekley's good nature—to bolster his own case: "[W]hat do a thousand 'good fellows' with all their being and doing weigh against *one* person who surrenders himself in love to the first impulses of new evolving life from the unknown *future*?" Otto wrote later (he had inherited his father's passion for emphasis), and "You say . . . you do *not* have *the right* to gamble with the existence of a good 'fellow'! You take away from yourself, however, *your own right—nothing* more nor less than *the right to self-determination*."[58] He insisted that being apart from him, and from the primacy of sex with him, would be harmful to her. Nottingham, he said, "with *all* its grey cold *life* . . . *these* are just the kind of damaging surroundings that *don't suit you at all*."[59]

"I go away only in order to return," Frieda told Gross as they parted.[60] The sight of England was grim:

> There was the Dorothy Perkins blooming over a little arbour, and the beds of marguerites and geraniums were flourishing more or less, according to the house. There were the same curtains in the houses, of art linen, the good daddies were wheeling perambulators in the street. . . . Young people were climbing over the stiles. Had it been a Tuesday, washing day, the semi-detacheds would have the washing out.[61]

She boarded the train north, conspicuous in a compartment of businessmen:

> There were bankclerks and small officials and shop assistants. "Hallo, George. Fine day today." And then the whole compartment would be buried behind newspapers. And in the evening . . . George will go home to his little semi-detached in the suburb, to his little wife and a little George, and mow his lawn and, for excitement, collect stamps perhaps. One day George will fall ill and have pneumonia and die, and the other men in the train next morning will say, "Have you heard about poor old George?" And that would be the end, and poor old George had not had much of a show.[62]

In Nottingham, Elsa, five, told Frieda, "You are not our old mother. You have got our old mother's skin on, but you are not our mother that went away."[63]

6

A torrent of letters from Gross—undated, written in pencil, and full of adjectives, superlatives, and triple underscoring—had begun arriving before she got home, mailed under cover of envelopes bearing the Munich return address of Edgar, who urged her to burn the letters.[64] Gross's relationship with Else was the subject of almost every letter. He may have believed in the primacy of the penis, but he wrote only in *Hochdeutsch:*

> Now I am with Else—depths of love, depths of melancholy . . . as never before I have understood her earnestness—she is so great and noble and loves you so warmly and sincerely—so far removed from any possibility of envy—and *yet* she suffers—what cause for *suffering* can there be in the sunny happiness of two people, both of whom you love? . . .
>
> Beloved, these are the days when I *need* the talisman [three-headed ring] that *you* have given me—the days when I must rediscover strength and self-confidence in the *knowledge* that *in you*, Beloved, *my dream of the future* is already *realized*, my ethical ideal already *confirmed as reality*.[65]

"You yourself seem to have no idea what *genius* you have," he wrote in another letter, "how wonderfully and irresistibly power and warmth spring from everything which you inspire with your own life."[66] "I wonder," Frieda wrote back, "if you could write to me in Styrian, High German is all very well for your work—but for myself I'd like your Styrian."[67]

She began reading Plato at Gross's urging, provoking Ernest's chiding remark: "You get your measles late, most people have done with Platos at your age."[68] Even Monty, now eight, was told how silly his mother was for reading Plato "in translation."[69] "You may not think it, Monty," Frieda would say, "but your mother's a clever woman."[70] On Saturdays and Sundays she and he would set off, Frieda with her translation of Plato in her hand, Monty with a schoolbook, for the Mikado Café, where they both gorged on cakes.

She felt very off balance and uncomfortably in the grip of what she later called "a theory of loving men" for the next several months.[71] Ernest's sarcasm about her passionate reading and rereading—of Nietzsche next—reduced her to tears, and she took to the piano for self-expression. Occasionally, as she played a tune, Ernest threw a penny her way. "That's what's so unbearable here," she wrote Gross, "there's not one living person, they're rhinoceros hides, sleepy-heads, geese ducks and I often wish I was a great big kick."[72]

Otto undertook a course of self-imposed drug withdrawal, and discipline and self-control were very much on his mind through the summer: "Dr. Gross says I have lost the trait of forceful self-control and I look much softer," Reventlow wrote in her diary one Sunday in July after an encounter with him in a café.[73] Self-control was easier for him to prescribe, however, than to practice, and he soon found it difficult to express himself without morphine:

> Abstention . . . holds my head and heart in an iron clamp—nothing, nothing of all the things that live and throng within me finds expression—not one wretched half hour in which I might have been able to *express* myself truly, to send you even one greeting in which something of my love would *live*—*Therefore* be indulgent, Beloved: understand, *I am doing* something with this cure which is in general considered pretty well *impossible*—*no-one* has the necessary will-power, so it says in almost all the books, etc. And surely *that* would be *altogether too* horrible if, *in consequence* of seeing it through—if *precisely in consequence of that*, I should find myself *sunk* in your estimation! Look, I *have* enough morphine *in my possession* and need to take only a little of it, *then* this spell breaks and *then* all my capacity for self-expression returns. . . . Beloved, *you* are *not* in *my* position: *you write to me*![74]

Frieda's responses were soothing, and maddening: As the "treatment" progressed, and he began suffering a full-blown persecution mania, she became a beacon of even temper:

> you know perhaps I'm not worth very much, but I wouldn't have been like the 12 apostles, who were so mean as to leave poor Christ in the lurch just when he needed them, as long as he was *giving* them things everything was all right, but as soon as things went badly for him, the wretches, they slunk off. . . . Yesterday I danced around in my room dressed only in a shawl, while the worthy Philistines went to church! I've had a coat made for me in very dark green, like Friedel's blue one.
>
> So whether auf wiedersehen or not
> believe in the unchangeable love
> of your
> Frieda[75]

A few weeks before her twenty-eighth birthday, she and the children went to the Lincolnshire coast with Maude Weekley and Gladys Bradley. Manic letters from Munich about personality types followed, obsessive musings that made the drab simplicity of the spade-and-bucket holiday almost joyous by comparison. "[W]hy, unlucky creature that I am," Frieda replied, "must I be a '*type*', do let me be a living individual and not a dead type *you yourself* are not yet *living* enough, you really are 'sicklied o'er with the pale cast of thought' don't you think so?"[76] She confided her affair to Gladys, whose interest was immediately piqued. In a subsequent letter, Frieda relayed that interest, proposing that he have an affair with Gladys if he visited—"when you come you must *love* her and she you"—and tried to arrange an orgiastic junket to England. "Mühsam, Friedel would be lovely—and perhaps Edgar come to England my friend and I will choose a nice place by the sea and you can all come for 8 or 10 days."[77] Gladys promised Frieda her pied-à-terre for a London rendezvous with Gross, and her sister Madge seems to have offered her fiancé to Frieda in return for some time with Gross: "I hope I will experience something beautiful with him," Frieda wrote Gross.[78]

Gladys had gotten nowhere with Ernest. One day on the beach, she earned Maude's opprobrium by confessing to her that she was in love with a married man. Maude's disapproval would have been all the greater if she had known that Gladys was referring to Ernest.[79]

Frieda had suspected she was pregnant with Gross's child, but now wrote that she was not. Their other "child" was about to be born in Amsterdam, at the First International Congress of Psychiatry, Neurology, Psychology and the Assistance to the Insane.[80] Frieda had made tentative plans to accompany Gross when he presented their heavily worked paper, but she pulled out at the last minute, and Friedel Gross went instead. She and Otto were living together again, and she was soon pregnant with his child.

7

The von Richthofen family was also undergoing strange permutations. Else, now visibly pregnant, ended her affair with Gross to begin a relationship with a doctor whom Gross despised. Else seems to have shared Gross's contempt, but was in the grip of a "shameful" obsession: The man simply bore too powerful a resemblance to Friedrich von Richthofen.[81] "[S]he *cannot say yes at the same time*," Gross insisted, "both to *that man* and *me*."[82] Still fuming about Otto's affair with Frieda, Else also objected to his inconsistency, vagabondage, self-destructiveness, self-absorption, and his reliance on her for practical needs: Their last tryst had ended with Gross asking for twenty-five marks.[83]

In a crazed, incoherent, thirty-four-page letter, he vented his rage over Else's disloyalty and begged Frieda not to be similarly disloyal, all the while raving about the "satanic irony" and "hateful scornful poisonous vampires" ruining his and Else's love. "Things have *not gone well* since that terrible reaction to *our* love: her jealousy had only been driven into her unconscious where, repressed, it now has executed *this revenge*—this is the only possible explanation that tallies with all the details!"[84]

Neither Gross nor Frieda was present when Else gave birth to a boy, Wolfgang Peter, in Heidelberg on December 24, 1907. Like Friedel Gross, she called her son Peter.[85] Edgar legally adopted this son of Gross's.

Gross began a rigorous self-analysis that plunged him into a period of doubt and depression: "Surely," he wrote Frieda, "you still remember how I spoke to you about my love when I was still happy?"[86] He asked her to return to Munich, with or without her children. She sent him a studio photograph of herself instead, and a cheering letter for his wife, who was, he told her, "in a state of profound resignation and skepticism."[87]

In late April 1908 the Grosses attended a psychology congress in Salzburg, though by now her involvement with Frick was paramount. Otto spoke on "cultural perspectives" that, he told Frieda, "lay out the program for my life. . . . suddenly we have a *practical method*, a *technique* of investigation for looking into the essence of the mental life."[88] Freud heard the paper and told Gross that he needed treatment. Gross, who felt he was at the peak of his powers and saw nothing but a clear road ahead for his life "program," was affronted, and reluctant to enter a hospital again, though he insisted his wife seek treatment with Ernest Jones. She eventually acceded, apparently having independently formed a romantic attachment to Jones.[89] The final initiative for Otto's treatment came from Hans, who wrote to Jung, possibly with the ulterior motive of getting his son committed.[90] Jung assumed the case in May at Burghölzli—Gross's third time there.

The treatment progressed quickly from a cure of Gross's "nocturnal light-obsession" to a rigorous analysis of "infantile identification blockages of a specifically homosexual nature."[91] "Whenever I got stuck," Jung wrote Freud of the early sessions, "he analyzed me."[92] By June the analysis had fallen apart, however, and Gross escaped Burghölzli by scaling the garden wall. "There is no development, no psychological yesterday for him," wrote Jung, who seemed puzzled not to have effected a cure in a fortnight or two, "the events of early childhood remain eternally new and operative, so that notwithstanding all the time and all the analysis he reacts to today's events like a 6-year-old boy, for whom the wife is always mother, every friend, everyone who wishes him well or ill always the father, and whose world is a boyish fantasy filled with heaven knows what monstrous possibilities."[93]

Gross continued fathering illegitimate children of his own: A young Swiss analysand, Regina Ullmann, a friend of Frieda and Else's, told him she was pregnant by him, and he cut all ties with her, also leaving her, she told Else, a dose of poison. When she asked Otto's father for financial support, Hans refused, and banished Otto abroad for treatment to evade paying Ullmann. She gave birth to a daughter, converted to Catholicism, and became an inspirational writer and Rilke protégée.[94] Else broke with Otto for good when she learned the news of his behavior: "I at first thought someone must have forced you to give up your relationship to Regina Ullmann—now I see the conflict differently—that relationship, and your (as it must seem to those of us outside it) ruthlessness toward Frieda [Gross], are only symptoms of a development deeply rooted in your nature."[95] Else also tried to convince Frieda that Ernest Weekley, however laboriously, loved her more than Otto did:

> You have to remember the tremendous shadows around the light—can't you see that he's almost destroyed Frieda [Gross]'s life? that he's not able to constrain himself even for a quarter of an hour, whether it be for a person or for an objective value? . . . God, it's useless to say anything. You are under that tremendous power of suggestion which emanates from him and which I myself have felt.[96]

Though Frieda probably suspected Else of being not entirely altruistic, she could see that any hopes of a reasonable life with Gross would soon founder. His chronic instability, his passion for treatments and analyses, and his increasingly disturbing letters were persuasive enough evidence not to rush back to Germany or Switzerland and set up house with him. She seems to have stopped answering him soon after his treatment with Jung failed. By fall he had begun working again, as lecturer in psychopathology at Graz.[97] Frieda's relations with Else normalized in 1909 with the birth of Else's fourth and last child, Hans, fathered in the old style by Edgar.

She and Ernest began looking for a new house. His annual pay increase permitting another move up, they found a new, tall, graceful stone house, Cowley, on Victoria Crescent, Private Road, a curving, hilly, tree-lined street in a very desirable neighborhood near their friends the Kippings. The house was bigger than 8 Vickers Street, with a spacious yard and more rooms, including a sitting room with French windows. None of their curtains fit, and Frieda had red velvet drapes made for them—seemingly her first impulse to decorate in a decade. There was also an indoor toilet, which soon provoked rows with Ernest. He had an almost mystical reverence for the WC, which he used leisurely and very privately, with the lock fastened. He became incensed when Frieda rattled the door to be let in.[98]

Sometime after the move Ernest suffered a near-fatal illness, the nature of which is unknown. Frieda stayed home through much of 1910 to help nurse him back to health. While recuperating he planted a large vegetable and fruit garden, and took particular pleasure in the tomatoes he grew, expounding on their virtues at dinner parties for colleagues. Frieda took refuge in work, a collaboration with Ernst Stahl, a noted translator of Galsworthy whom she had met through Ernest, of a translation of a W. B. Yeats play, *The Land of Heart's Desire*.[99]

In March 1911, Gross provided a new lover, Sophie Benz, with poison to kill herself. She was a professor's daughter who snorted large amounts of cocaine and moved from relationship to relationship (Leonhard Frank was her lover before Gross) in a desperate flight from depression and suicidal tendencies. "Whether the woman willingly or consciously took too much cocaine," wrote the Zurich daily *Tages-Anzeiger*, "or whether she made an error in taking her dosage, is not known." Gross, it was said, in response to her death "had an attack of craziness and needed to be brought . . . to the Mendrisio mental institution."[100] In fact, an Italian doctor and friend had him admitted so that the police would not arrest him.

Friedel Gross moved in with Ernst Frick—whom she had borne a daughter—in Ascona. Frieda visited them in April and, with the full blessings of her first friend in Munich (herself pregnant for the second time by Frick), began an affair with Ernst. In August, Else helped pay for Frick to visit London, where he stayed for three or four weeks in Gladys's apartment, Frieda visiting when she could. Early in the following year, Frick was sentenced to twelve months' imprisonment for the bomb he had set off outside a Zurich police station in 1907; he had also been implicated in a 1908 tram derailment. Frieda tried to send him money to help with his defense;[101] Weekley, busy putting the final touches on his first popular language book, *The Romance of Words*, threatened to kill her for assisting a criminal, and she did not follow through on the initial attempt to aid her former "cause" and lover. It seems that she never saw Otto Gross again. She had had enough love priests in her life—or so she imagined.

PART II

Europe, Asia, Australia, America, 1912–1930

6

Simple Men, Giantesses, and Rabbits

I

On the windy but mild Sunday morning of March 3, 1912,[1] David Herbert Lawrence, a twenty-six-year-old former French student of Ernest's, came to Cowley to talk about a job as a lecturer in the Rhineland. He arrived half an hour early for lunch, and Ernest was out. He was nothing like what Frieda expected. "I've got a real poet," Ernest had told her, a "young genius."[2] To Frieda he seemed "obviously simple."[3] His face was plump after convalescence from a months-long bout with pneumonia, his mustache and thick red hair were assiduously brushed, setting off lucid blue eyes, and he wore a freshly starched wing collar and black patent leather shoes. His walk was quick and birdlike and his shoes clicked and glinted in the sunny hallway. Frieda invited him to the sitting room, where the French windows were open and the red velvet drapes moved slowly in the unseasonably warm air. The staccato tapping of Monty's wooden tops hitting the concrete came from out back. In the front yard Barby and Elsa were pretending to be common, haranguing each other with exaggerated "lower-class" accents.[4]

Lawrence's first words of any length were a tirade against women, which made Frieda peal with laughter. Soon they were immersed in a pretentious conversation about Oedipus—Frieda pronounced the name with slow relish and a long initial "e"—which Lawrence used as a jumping-off point to more denunciations of women.[5] Since the death of his mother, Lydia Beardsall, fifteen months before, he had run through four women: two "fiancées"—a word he used with some license—a "possible fiancée," and a "maîtresse."[6] He was using all four experiences for a *Bildungsroman* with the working title "Paul Morel"—then in its third draft—but he insisted to Frieda that he was "finished" with "attempts at knowing" women.[7]

When Ernest arrived, Paula brought lunch to the table, and the conversation became duller. It seemed to Lawrence that Frieda ignored her husband. Ida saw him before he left and recognized his low birth instantly: "A person like that," she said, "should not wear patent leather shoes."[8]

"You are the most wonderful woman in all England," Lawrence wrote Frieda several days later. He had walked the five hours home to Eastwood, a coal-mining village eight miles northwest of Nottingham, stopping at an ex-fiancée's along the way. "You don't know many women in England," Frieda answered, "how do you know?"[9]

Their next conversations, at Cowley on Sunday mornings, when Ernest was at Cambridge, irked Frieda: Lawrence was convinced that she had "sex in the head" and was a bad wife.[10] That aside, however, she was amazed by his powers of perception—he seemed to look through things and know them from inside, particularly herself. Unlike few Lawrence would ever meet, she welcomed such depth of perception: She had nothing to hide from him. After the degradation of having a husband who had no sooner discovered her real value than forgotten it, and a lover who aggrandized her for a long fortnight into a perfect "type," she was ready to be looked through, and valued. Though the date and circumstances are unknown, they probably made love soon after their first meeting.[11]

2

Bert—as the family called Lawrence—was Lydia's youngest son, born in Eastwood on September 11, 1885. There were four brothers and sisters. The family lived on a commercial street in a small house with an unused storefront, which had formerly been Lydia's haberdashery. The store had failed after some three years, apparently because of a lack of demand and her free hand extending credit, and its loss was bitter to Lydia, whose family had once had a little money and huge aspirations to the middle class. She instilled her upward yearnings in the five children at an early age: They learned to appraise the furniture in friends' houses, to inspect for lace curtains, hung from the obligatory bamboo pole, and to count the oleographs, shiny-surfaced reproductions of well-known masterpieces, which she found elegant. Bert was the only local boy with a new bicycle and a paintbox, and the Lawrences had their own piano.

When the final child, Ada, was born in 1887, the family rented a tall stone row house in a valley on the edge of town. The house had two bedrooms and a meager front yard with rosebushes. Beyond were the railroad tracks and one of Eastwood's countless collieries, where Bert watched trucks and dray horses. The sound of the shunting trucks and immense black elevators and machinery of the mines was constant, as was the smoke. Bert talked to flowers in the surrounding fields and staged plays with girls from the neighborhood, learning early how to assign roles and command obedience and adoration. He was a sickly child, however, and respiratory illnesses often kept him in, sitting before the dusty coal fireplace making up games while his mother worked, wrote verses in a small notebook, or lamented—as was her wont. The house was unpleasant in summer, when the rank smell from the back-lane ashpits was overpowering.

Lawrence's father, Arthur, had started work at the age of seven. He was a garrulous and nature-loving man who was usually asleep, ignored, or out weeding his vegetable garden when home from the mine, where he worked a swing shift. Evenings—at least when the family was together—tended to disintegrate into "carnal, bloody fight[s]" between him and Lydia.[12] When he bought a whole ham, which had to be paid for over time, she complained about it for weeks of paydays.[13] She mimicked his thick Midlands dialect, whose commonness she loathed, and yelled at him for spending money in pubs. Leaving before daybreak or as the children were put to bed, he picked herbs and mushrooms on the roadside out of town to the pit. He was a butty, the man responsible for clearing a section of coal face.

Lydia was a woman of immensely contradictory impulses. Despite her complaints about Arthur she had an intense fear of one day being left alone, and she designated one son after another as her caretaker, though she was determined none would become coal miners and remain in Eastwood. She invested great hopes in Ernest, the eldest, a handsome, enormously intelligent boy who read voraciously, had a talent for poetry and languages, and wound up clerking for lawyers in London. Bert, firmly tied to her apron strings at a young age, was the only one not to challenge the more overbearing of her claims. George, the middle son, was a disappointment: Flippant, ambitionless, and with a strong resemblance to her husband, when he was seventeen he married a girl he had made pregnant, which disgusted Lydia: "*He*," she said, "was never going to leave me."[14] Ernest brought home an attractive stenographer named Louisa "Gipsy" Dennis four years later; though everyone liked her, Lydia concluded that she was aptly nicknamed.

She sent Bert to school just before he was four, but he was given to inexplicable fits of crying and was taken out after six months. His hypersensitivity rattled Lydia, who often placed him on a front-yard stool alone to calm himself. When he was six the family moved uphill to a rented terrace house with bay windows, a view of the valley, and piped-in gas for cooking and heating water. Lydia furnished the parlor in severe mahogany and forbade clutter, by which she meant any personal possessions, giving the room an unpleasant starkness. Bert returned the next year to school—which he later likened to Lowood, the Evangelical charity school in *Jane Eyre*—and managed to stop crying.

By the age of eleven he excelled in art and English; at twelve he won a scholarship to Nottingham High School, where his course work included French and Latin. He rode the train every day and made few friends away from home. A classmate once invited him home to tea, then learned he was a miner's son and snubbed him.[15] The class snobbishness worked both ways: In his school collar and jacket, Bert put on airs at home and during the week worked French idioms, badly, into his letters to Eastwood friends. His reputation was further lowered in March 1900 when an uncle from a neighboring town stabbed his son and was charged with manslaughter, a family crisis that made all the local papers. Now fourteen and acutely sensitive and ambitious, Lawrence was mortified by the scandal.

The following spring, he began going regularly to Haggs Farm, a mile and a half from Eastwood, to visit the Chamberses, a family of seven. Situated at the edge of a reservoir and a thick woods, there were two brooks, an orchard, and a huge stand of fir and spruce trees that filtered out the din and dust of the mines; there was also an old mill in the valley below. The farm was beautiful from spring to mid-July, when the wheat harvest began. Alan, the eldest child, thought that Lawrence, who had never been on a farm, was bizarre. When he was told about "serving the sow" and saw a cow and bull copulating, he was puzzled and then said it was disgusting.

Eventually Alan taught him to milk, chop hay, and pulp turnips, and soon he anticipated the sight of Lawrence, his dark school cravat halfway off, running breathlessly up the Eastwood high road toward the gabled porch of the sprawling two-story farmhouse. Lawrence, who became irresistibly sweet at the farm—he had never known a happy family before—read Virgil to Alan in the fields and sat for hours on a sofa in a recessed kitchen window, reading, peeling onions, and watching the bread come out of the oven. He liked to put on an apron and help with housework, but tore it off if he heard Alan at the doorstep.

His first "fiancée" was Jessie, the second daughter, a sullen girl with a talent for writing, a love of poetry, and a tendency to sink into depression. She read *The Tempest* in a library with Lawrence's sister Ada, huddled over a shared copy. "That's just what I believe," she whispered when they came to Miranda's speeches of womanly modesty and servitude. "I think it's rubbish," Ada replied.[16] Jessie first saw Lawrence at Congregational Sunday School; he stood at the podium to recite a poem and forgot it. His older sister, Emily, giggled uncontrollably in the front row. Lawrence asked for a prompt and then was able to continue.[17] At the farm he was the first to understand and tolerate Jessie's flights of rhapsody and frequent depressions. "*Nil desperandum*," he scrawled for her in chalk on the stable door.[18] She fell in love and began to devote herself to his confessions and passions. He was changeable and didactic, and she followed him with patience and close attention from one day's fulmination to the next day's discourse or literary discovery.

The Chamberses took Jessie out of school at fourteen to work on the farm and as a monitor and assistant teacher of young children at

Underwood National School. Deeply resentful, she became determined to co-opt Lawrence's education. They went to the Mechanics' Institute Library once a week, trudging back up the hill with armloads of Dickens, Fenimore Cooper, Stevenson, Eliot, Thackeray, and the Brontës, whom they read together, discussing the books in the fields until the red tiles on the roofs of the farmhouse and its outbuildings glowed in the sunset. Lacking the language of literary criticism, they recapitulated plots to each other instead. Eventually Lawrence helped Jessie struggle through simple tales in French, and urged her to keep a secret diary in the language, which only he could read.

Lawrence himself was forced to leave school two months before his sixteenth birthday; he began as a clerk in a badly ventilated Nottingham factory that made patients' hospital gowns, staff uniforms, surgical stockings, druggists' supplies, and wooden legs. Shortly after, Ernest died in London of pneumonia and complications from the infectious disease erysipelas, caused by a streptococcus. Lydia and Arthur went to London to bring the body home and were unable to recognize their son's face, swollen with inflammation. Amid her grief Lydia complained about her husband: "Yes, and I had to do everything myself," she told Jessie, "find out about the trains and how to get to Ernest's lodgings. His father was with me but he was no help."[19] The funeral wreath sent by Gipsy was "a large beautiful one," Lydia noted, "but sadly crushed and faded."[20]

Lawrence continued commuting, boarding the train each day with a lunch basket on his arm. He hated the factory, and after Ernest's death became withdrawn and depressed. His colleagues, almost all women, were moved by his sadness and privacy, but also thought he was a pansy—"mardarse" in the local vernacular. Some five months after he began work, a group herded him into a corner on lunch break and tried to strip him. He developed pneumonia a few weeks later and stayed home for nine months with his mother.

Confined to his room and Lydia's kitchen, he endured elaborate confidences of her now-absolute hatred of her husband and an unending catalog of other unhappinesses, offering sympathy or rage when he had the strength. He seems never to have questioned the powerfully manipulative quality of her denigration of Arthur, or her elevation of him as, in effect, her "lover." At night she slept with him in his bed. A growth spurt that followed his recovery brought him to five foot nine, but he did not get rid of a high-pitched, slightly nasal voice—many thought he screeched—and the illness left permanent damage. When he could manage, he went to the Chamberses', sometimes picked up by Jessie's father, who had a milk route. She became his constant companion again, and they were soon considered engaged by local standards, if not Lawrence's: He had begun to think of himself as a ladies' man.

In the autumn of 1902 he became a student teacher in the boys' section of the Albert Street Schools in Eastwood. He both disliked and feared disciplining his hulking students, who had little interest in learning; punishment included caning them. "The sort of boy he was not strong enough to play with," said Jessie's sister May, who taught in the same school, "he was now to try to teach."[21] He escaped the grind several times a week in local art classes and refined a passion for watercolor reproductions of contemporary bucolic paintings, producing one after another at the kitchen table while his mother, Jessie, and neighborhood girls looked on. Lydia grew to dislike Jessie's claim on her son's imagination, but she reveled in the serenity of these afternoons, when her husband was deep down in the mine. "[T]here's safety in numbers," she proclaimed to the girls and to Lawrence, an unmistakable smile of propriety spreading across her face.[22] Lawrence found himself equally loved when he began taking teacher-education classes five half days a week in the nearby town of Ilkeston. Very much in his element among his fellow students—girls, for the most part, and bright, working-class boys trying to stay out of the mines—he became popular for the first time in his life. He began reading poetry from a small red anthology called Palgrave's *Golden Treasury*, but had to hide the book from his sister Emily, who mocked him pitilessly if she caught him at it, and his father, who called poetry "pottery" and disliked the sight of anyone in the family reading anything but a newspaper. Jessie had found a copy of Blake's *Songs of Innocence* and *Songs of Experience*, and he moved on to Swinburne, then began cramming notebooks with his own efforts. "Well, isn't that the very greatest thing?" Jessie said when he confided his ambition. "Ah, *you* say that," Lawrence answered. "But what will the others say? That I'm a fool. A collier's son a poet!"[23]

He was teaching full-time by summer 1905 at the British School in Eastwood, ashamed of the pair of borrowed boots he had to wear each day to class. He returned to Ilkeston every Wednesday afternoon and Saturday to socialize. There he met his second "fiancée," Louie Burrows, a statuesque, earthy sixteen-year-old in front of whom he and Jessie—now also student teaching—would often discuss writers and books. Louie, who was fluent in French and well read, found their disquisitions stiff and ridiculous. They seemed to imagine themselves, she later wrote, as "some character in a poem."[24] She liked Lawrence's eyes, though, their color brought out by a blue serge suit he wore, and he had an unexpectedly silly smile that relieved his terrible seriousness. Jessie disliked Louie's usurpation of her time with Lawrence, but he soon grew expert at juggling the two girls: When he read Verlaine aloud to them, he watched with ruthless amusement as Jessie missed every other word while Louie laughed at his poor accent and pretentious delivery. After the performance he strolled through the woods, Jessie on one arm, Louie on the other.[25]

Though Louie soon became the object of Lawrence's endless fantasizing, he reserved Jessie as his chief reader. He arrived at the Chamberses' over Easter of 1906, clutching the opening pages of "Laetitia," the working title of his first novel, and waited in the fields for her to come home. "We've broken the ice," he said, thrusting the pages into her hands when she arrived.[26] He reappeared periodically with more; though they had agreed to exchange manuscripts, she was intimidated by his singlemindedness and drive and never had any pages to trade. Their conversations narrowed to his work, and he began calling her his "nurse" as he handed over installments at a furious pace.[27]

The heroine of the novel was Lettie Beardsall, a single pregnant woman based loosely on his sister Ada—with his mother's maiden name—whose real first name was Lettice. Jessie encouraged him to continue, though she found Lettie and George Saxton (based on Jessie's brother Alan), a naive farmer who makes Lettie an honest woman, "unreal."[28] Still, it was an amazing work: the glibbest sentimentality and most implausible plot woven effortlessly into the absolute realism and eye for detail of farm incidents that served as a backdrop to the story. His mother, his only other reader, objected to the subject matter: "To think that *my* son should have written such a story."[29]

As summer approached his composition and behavior grew even

more feverish, each delivery of manuscript to Jessie like an erotic assignation. Lawrence was obsessed with masturbation, which he considered shameful.[30] "*Quant à moi, je suis grand animal,*" he wrote across a page of Jessie's diary.[31] One August evening, while walking together on a beach at the Lincolnshire resort town of Mablethorpe, he suddenly screamed that she and her body were "to blame."[32]

In September 1906, when Lawrence and Louie entered University College in Nottingham (Lawrence on a scholarship), Lydia, never a great admirer of Jessie's rustic charms, insisted disingenuously that it was unfair for Bert to string Jessie along without a proposal of marriage. Lawrence prevaricated mightily, reading a bowdlerized version of Schopenhauer's *Metaphysics of Love* aloud to Jessie: "*Qu-en pensez-vous*?" he scribbled in the margin, when they came to a paragraph that exalted sexless friendship.[33] Jessie refused to comprehend. "It comes to this, you know," he finally said bluntly. "You have no sexual attraction at all, none whatsoever."[34] He was now finding all his erotic yearnings in imagined nude studies of and love poetry to Louie, whose papers he also critiqued. Louie was unfazed by his comment on an art essay: "Like most girl writers you are wordy."[35]

3

Ernest Weekley, Lawrence's French professor, tended to dress to the nines, point to the blackboard without rising from his chair, and call his students "Gentlemen" with barely suppressed sarcasm. He was exactly the kind of man Lawrence both envied and dreaded becoming. "He's quite elegant," he wrote Jessie, ". . . too elegant to get on his feet."[36] Lawrence, who usually faced his professors with a sarcasm of his own, spent most of his time in class composing poems or reworking drafts of his novel. He submitted "Study," one of the first poems of his college years, to *The Gong*, the college literary magazine. The poem was immediately rejected:

Close by the wood's edge there's a girl hovers
Looks through the hazel screen out on the meadow
Where, wheeling and screaming the petulant plovers
Wave frightened. Who comes?—A labourer with still tread.
Oh, sunset swims in her eyes' swift pool!
(I curse myself for a studying fool)[37]

Lawrence received his teaching certificate in the summer of 1908, and in late September accepted a job teaching orphans and the poor at Davidson Road School in Croydon, near London; many of his boys came from the Gordon Home for Waifs and Strays. The school was a large new brick building that looked out on a timberyard and two sets of railroad tracks. Still revising his novel, he read Conrad, Tolstoy, and Nietzsche, drafted poems and stories, and befriended a small circle of lesbians, bisexuals, and other Croydon teachers with whom he played cards, read, practiced French and German, and went to London. He roomed with an unhappy couple and was titillated by their marital problems, which he both heard from the wife and overheard as he lay in his room, fantasizing about sex and occasionally writing to female colleagues, asking if they would sleep with him. He began carrying a package of condoms in the pocket of his overcoat. Louie, now teaching in Leicester, kept up a steady stream of letters in English and French, which he unfailingly returned by the next post—husbandly missives filled with forced *joie* and clumsy French. In crisp, passionless letters to Jessie, he also described every crush, flirtation, and missed opportunity in minute detail.

Despite his obvious disinterest, Jessie hung on to her passion for Lawrence. In June 1909, she sent four of his poems to Ford Madox Hueffer (later Ford Madox Ford) at the *English Review*, a new journal that published Hardy, James, Conrad, Tolstoy, and H. G. Wells. Lawrence was vacationing with his parents on the Isle of Wight when Hueffer's reply, inviting him for a meeting in London, arrived at the Chamberses'. He went in September, and found Hueffer a true "gentleman."[38] He was clearly predisposed to think so.

Thirty-six years old, the son of German Catholics from Westphalia who had emigrated to England in the latter half of the nineteenth century, Hueffer was a rotund man with a drooping face and whiskers that made him look like a walrus. Born in London, educated in Bonn, he had a grand, patronizing manner, a boundless imagination, and a healthy appetite for painters' daughters: He married one, Elsie Martindale, and was madly in love with another, the wealthy novelist Violet Hunt, whose Kensington soirees were legendary. He also loved intrigue: His courtship of Martindale had been conducted in code in the personal columns of a newspaper.[39]

Among Hueffer's many affectations was a studied ignorance of the underclasses, and he was overjoyed to have found a working-class writer for his roster. He took Lawrence to lunch with Violet Hunt; to tea with Ernest and Grace Rhys, writer-editors associated with the Everyman series of classics; and to the home of Wells. These adventures provoked Lawrence to write giddy, self-reverential letters to Louie: Wells's "conversation is a continual squirting of thin little jets of weak acid"; Ezra Pound—who introduced Lawrence briefly to Yeats—"is 24, like me,—but his god is beauty, mine, life."[40] Five of Lawrence's poems ran in the November issue of the *Review*, and he gave "Laetitia" (which he had revised and renamed "Nethermere," adding an autobiographical hero, Cyril Mersham) to Hueffer, who was perturbed to find little dialect and no colliers in the seven-hundred-page manuscript. Ever-jovial, he advised his young prodigy to stick to short, less detailed, "workingman" novels, then took Lawrence and Jessie on a round of parties, teas, and at-homes.

Jessie made a strange impression at Hunt's, where she was introduced by the wrong name. Hueffer had no idea what to say to her. He decided that she was probably a bluestocking or "a sort of Socialist" and launched into a speech about suffrage, producing clippings.[41] Ezra Pound, like Lawrence dining out on his literary talent, startled Jessie "by springing to his feet and bowing from the waist with the stiff precision of a mechanical toy."[42] Over the lunch of hot roast beef, potatoes, and Brussels sprouts, served with champagne, Jessie had to ask a serving maid whether to remove her gloves to eat. Pound, equally at home with literary patrons and miners—his father had worked as a registrar of miners' claims—complained about the heavy food and goaded Hueffer, "How would *you* speak to a working man?"[43] Lawrence fared a little better than Jessie in the manners department: Although he had to ask with which knife to cut his asparagus, he atoned by admitting to a passion for Carlyle and Ruskin. "You're the only man I know," Hueffer said, "who really has read all those people."[44] Back in his rooms at Croydon that evening, Lawrence asked Jessie what she wanted to do with her life, and she burst into tears. He changed the subject to sex, and they moved on to his latest effort, *A Collier's Friday Night*, a play written, following Hueffer's advice, largely in dialect. Before the end of the fall, he had finished his first "workingman" short story, "Odour of Chrysanthemums." It was a masterpiece.

Hueffer accepted a short story for publication in the *Review*,

"Goose Fair," which had been co-written by Louie and Lawrence but submitted under his name only. It was the first and last of Lawrence's stories Hueffer saw into print: He was fired as editor amid rumblings of the *Review*'s unprofitability. Before leaving, and despite his objections to "Nethermere" as wordy and unproletarian, he helped arrange for the novel to be published at Heinemann (where it received its final title, *The White Peacock*) via a carefully phrased letter of recommendation in which he described Lawrence's style as a cross between R. D. Blackmore's *Lorna Doone* and William de Morgan, a popular novelist—his books famous for length and copiousness of detail—on the publisher's list. The three-and-a-half-year gestation period and Lawrence's relentless rewriting had resulted in several surprising refinements, among them a Paul Bunyanesque, voyeuristic gamekeeper and an unself-conscious, perfectly realized love scene between Cyril Mersham and George Saxton. Each anticipated the idealized, mythic masculinity and homoeroticism of his later novels; given his penchant for autobiography, they probably also hinted at his own experience with the men of Haggs Farm:

> We [George and Cyril] stood and looked at each other as we rubbed ourselves dry. He was well proportioned, and naturally of handsome physique, heavily limbed. He laughed at me, telling me I was like one of Aubrey Beardsley's long, lean ugly fellows. I referred him to many classic examples of slenderness, declaring myself more exquisite than his grossness, which amused him. . . . laughing he took hold of me and began to rub me briskly, as if I were a child, or rather, a woman he loved and did not fear. I left myself quite limply in his hands, and, to get a better grip of me, he put his arm round me and pressed me against him, and the sweetness of the touch of our naked bodies one against the other was superb. It satisfied in some measure the vague, indecipherable yearning of my soul; and it was the same with him. When he had rubbed me all warm, he let me go, and we looked at each other with eyes of still laughter, and our love was perfect for a moment, more perfect than any love I have known since, either for man or woman.[45]

Lawrence left for Eastwood at Christmas, full of himself and consumed by sexual frustration. A brilliant career had sprung up almost overnight, but at twenty-four he was still a virgin. He visited Jessie and tried to make love to her in the fields. Their long association, he now insisted, was the inevitable buildup to "*une intimité d'amour*." He had loved her all along, he said, but hadn't realized it.[46] He told her that he had condoms. Though she turned down his advances, three months later they began a brief, unhappy affair. Jessie was suspicious of his intentions and simply wanted to marry him.

Lawrence had begun pursuing his maîtresse: a Croydon teacher named Helen Corke, a short, pale, working-class redhead with a pudgy face and a mania for Nietzsche and Wagner. She loved women, she told Lawrence, but was frigid with both sexes. Her recent affair with a married violin teacher had driven the man to suicide, and Corke was recording the affair in a diary of rather gluey prose poems. Lawrence promptly used the story for a second novel, to be called "The Saga of Siegmund," adding to its Wagnerian litany of sexual malaise by incorporating elements of his relationship with Jessie. While composing, he urged Jessie to meet Corke, who fell in love with her, a complication that does not seem to have surprised Lawrence. He wrote its final pages in midsummer and moved back home, breaking off relations with Jessie, to his mother's approval. Only he and Ada had not left home; Emily had married Samuel King, a steam-engine truck driver, and moved out.

Late that summer, Lydia was diagnosed with stomach cancer. Lawrence, devastated, spent the fall nursing her and reading proofs of *The White Peacock*; he shuttled between Eastwood and Croydon, where his flirtation with Corke may or may not have blossomed into an affair. A steady stream of ebullient letters came from Louie, now headmistress at Ratcliffe-on-the-Wreake, a Church of England school in Leicestershire. Each day his father came in from the mine and asked Lawrence and Ada, "Well, an' how is she?" then disappeared.[47] She deteriorated quickly.

Convinced of the waste of his mother's life and of the impossibility of his ever loving another woman as much as her, Lawrence began writing "Paul Morel" as the wet, cold fall set in. Jessie became Miriam, with little adulteration; Louie somehow escaped fictionalization. The mother dominated the early pages, as well as his thoughts when he stopped writing. He and his mother "have loved each other," he wrote a friend, "almost with a husband and wife love. . . . Nobody can have the soul of me. My mother has had it, and nobody can have it again."[48] He was convinced she would not live through the year, and asked his publisher for an advance copy of *The White Peacock*. It arrived at the house December 2 and he presented it to her with the inscription: "To my Mother, with love, D. H. Lawrence." Lydia, who could no longer move and had to be turned over every day, looked at it and said nothing. Lawrence's father leafed through it but could not comprehend it. "And what dun they gi'e thee for that, lad?" he asked. Lawrence replied that he had been paid fifty pounds. "Fifty pound!" Arthur replied incredulously. "An' tha's niver done a day's hard work in thy life."[49]

Lawrence left the house for a few hours the next day to see Louie, and in a quixotic, desperate mood, proposed marriage to her on a train. Her family disliked him, and she understood Lawrence's conviction that he was incapable of loving anyone but his mother, but she accepted. He asked her to copy a new poem of his, "My Love, My Mother," into his notebook. It was later retitled "The Virgin Mother":

And so, my love, Oh mother
I shall always be true to thee
Twice I am born, my mother
As Christ said it should be,
And who can bear me a third time?
—None love—I am true to thee.[50]

On December 8, her tongue and throat caked with a yeast infection, Lydia refused food and water. Lawrence and Ada asked her doctor to give her an overdose of morphine. He refused, and they apparently did it themselves. She died the next day. He paid for the funeral with an advance against royalties of fifteen pounds from Heinemann.[51] Lawrence returned to Croydon before the New Year. *The White Peacock* was published in England and the United States late in January and reviewed widely on both sides of the Atlantic over the next two months. Critics faulted its stilted dialogue, aimless plot, and overall confusion, but Lawrence was praised for his descriptions of nature and his depiction of Lettie. A British reviewer wondered if the author of the book was a woman.[52]

Ambivalence with Louie set in as his work took clearer shape. She had been urging him to save money, and when he splurged on clothes and sent money to Ada in July after receiving a check for ten pounds for "Odour of Chrysanthemums" from Austin Harrison, the new editor of the *English Review*, she became enraged. Lawrence called Louie his "rose." He wanted to deflower her, and when she would not let him, he briefly pursued Helen Corke again before embarking on an affair with Alice Dax, a gangly, married Nottingham woman who was seven years his senior. She had blond hair, a disarming smile, and a dimple in her right cheek. She was considered unattractive: "Since *everyone* said that no man would every marry me," Dax later wrote, "I took the first who offered," a chemist-optician with an Eastwood shop who admired her intelligence.[53] A post office employee, she was a suffragist and had once been "exiled" to a post office on the Isle of Man for her socialist politics. The affair with Lawrence began, said William Hopkin, an Eastwood journalist with a vivid imagination and a love of gossip, one day in her house when Lawrence could not finish a poem. They went upstairs to her bed, made love, and he was able to put the finishing touches on the poem. "I gave Bert sex," Hopkin said he recalled overhearing Dax say. "I had to." Lawrence wrote some sixty poems in 1911, though how many came in the throes of such encounters is unclear: Frieda later dismissed the story out of hand.[54] Dax made her way into later chapters of "Paul Morel," now with the name Clara Dawes and a powerfully jealous husband. One love scene, set on a rocky beach, was among the most powerful Lawrence had written.

Romantic pursuits dimmed in August, when Lawrence received a letter from the eminent book critic, essayist, playwright, and literary scout Edward Garnett, which invited a submission to the American magazine *Century*. As a reader for Gerald Duckworth at the London publishing house of Duckworth and Company, he had considerable literary clout; Lawrence had initiated the correspondence. They had lunch, and Garnett invited Lawrence to his home in Kent, a magnificent house—built to resemble a fifteenth-century farmhouse—called the Cearne, where he lived with his wife, the Russian translator Constance Garnett, and a son, David, who was seven years younger than Lawrence. Garnett, an unorthodox, liberal-minded, and fatherly man with mournful eyes and a tousled bowl haircut, was alone for the night of Lawrence's first visit, a Friday evening in the middle of October, and they sat before the fire, drinking wine. The house had exposed oak beams and a huge country kitchen stocked with earthenware plates and stone beer mugs.

Garnett soon was inviting him for more weekends and acting as his unpaid agent and personal and professional confidant. Lawrence kept him abreast of his love affairs and of his progress on "Paul Morel." When Heinemann expressed interest in late October, Lawrence sent the unfinished manuscript to Jessie and asked her to help him flesh it out, then started to redraft in early November, working from her comments.

He contracted pneumonia not long after. Ada nursed him and acted as his secretary in Croydon, but he was a difficult patient, humiliated by his frailty and furious about the ten-week convalescence. He often lashed out irrationally at his sister, who could not understand his anger and grew to hate his tirades and self-serving manner. Doctors attending Lawrence advised him to curtail his activities, never to teach again, and not to get married—then standard advice to tubercular patients. (Lawrence had tested negative for tuberculosis, as did many who had the disease; such tests were then inadequate.) He had other ideas, but did break the engagement with Louie by letter. "I don't want a home," he also told Jessie. "I want to be free."[55] He saw himself as a wanderer, and began concocting ways of living in Europe.

4

Frieda became Lawrence's reader shortly after the love affair began. He handed her the first chapters of "Paul Morel," several hundred dense pages in impeccable handwriting, which she read in bed, chain-smoking.[56] She was also reading a satire of the British upper class that Will Dowson had recommended—probably *The Patrician*, by John Galsworthy, the popular writer whose affair with the wife of a cousin had caused a public scandal.[57] Next to Lawrence's modernity, Galsworthy's theme of a woman trapped in a loveless marriage seemed patrician and hopelessly grounded in the nineteenth century. "I've met somebody," she told Dowson, "who's going to be much more than Galsworthy.[58]

Frieda told Lawrence about Otto Gross—his hatred of his father, his drug addiction, and his mania for free love—and about Frick, with whom she still corresponded (he wrote from prison) and whom she wanted to help. She suggested they collaborate on a book. Lawrence was aroused and skeptical, and talked with great feeling about his mother. Frieda, who had watched her eleven-year-old Monty grow more aloof, independent, and cynical, was amazed at Lawrence's lingering attachment to his mother, which, she quickly saw, far outstripped hers to her father. "He really loved his mother more than any body, even with his other women," she wrote when she finished reading "Paul Morel"—"real love, sort of Oedipus."[59] Like Jessie, she distrusted the bond, and felt Lawrence's imbalance. Lydia's "fierce and overpowering love," she later wrote, "had harmed the boy who was not strong enough to bear it."[60] Unlike Jessie, however, she knew how to handle it. Lawrence often talked about Jessie, who struck Frieda as sweet but pathetic. She scoffed whenever Lawrence showed up in a pair of pants he had bought with Jessie. She called them "Miriam's trousers."

Frieda had plenty of opportunities to leave the house; Ernest, intensely preoccupied with the publication of his *The Romance of Words*, was rarely home. Jessie's sister May lent them her small cottage when the family was out, a setting Lawrence used for two erotic poems. He was terrified they would get caught together. They went to a performance of George Bernard Shaw's *Man and Superman* at Nottingham's Royal Theatre, which he worked obliquely into his novel, but he preferred meeting at out-of-the-way train stations. Frieda brought Elsa and Barby, in pink-and-white-striped Viyella dresses, along on one tryst. Lawrence was waiting in a country lane, pale, tense, and unsmiling. He made a bad impression on Barby: "I didn't like him," she later said, "children don't like that sort of young man, they like somebody genial, like a doctor, and some of the professors at the University College that we knew."[61] They walked to a brook, and he bent down and lit matches to float in paper boats. "[T]his is the Spanish Armada, and you don't know what that was," he said. "Yes we do," Elsa replied.[62] Frieda invited him back to Cowley on April 7, Easter Sunday. Paula and the parlor maid were off, and Ernest was not there. She went into the kitchen to make tea but could not figure out how to turn on the gas. Lawrence was appalled at how removed she was from the daily workings of the house and happy to find a chink in the armor of her "Godalmightiness."[63] Now four weeks into their love affair, she still called him "Mr. Lawrence," as a sexual taunt. On another Sunday, which also passed with no sign of Ernest, Frieda proposed he stay the night. Lawrence declined and insisted she tell Ernest they were in love. She refused.

Gladys gave them carte blanche to her London apartment, and Lawrence got them invited to the Cearne: "[S]he is the daughter of Baron von Richthofen," he wrote Garnett, "of the ancient and famous house of Richthofen—but she's splendid, she is really. . . . perfectly unconventional, but really good—in the best sense."[64] They made plans to spend a week in Germany early in May—it was the fiftieth anniversary of the baron's army service, and Frieda intended to stay in Europe through the summer. Lawrence was by now entertaining the idea of living abroad with her—in some versions of his plans, this included Monty, Elsa, and Barby—and he urged her to effect a complete break with the pretense and dishonesty of an affair. She ventured into Ernest's study one day, intending to say something—she did not know what—about Lawrence, but only managed to tell him, apparently not too cleverly, about Otto Gross and Frick (in some versions of the story, Frick and Dowson). He seemed not to understand and dismissed her from the room. She left in tears, and they lived in uneasy silence for the following three days.

Early in the morning of Friday, May 3, Frieda packed a small bag for herself and dressed Elsa and Barby for the train to London. "Monty," Frieda called back, "aren't you coming to kiss me goodbye?"[65] He was utterly absorbed in a game of tops and appeared, briefly and reluctantly, before Frieda and the girls left. In London she dropped them off at the Weekleys' in Hampstead. At two o'clock she went to Charing Cross Station and met Lawrence at the ladies' room door.

They sailed across the Channel to Ostend in a murky drizzle, resting on a thick coil of rope on deck and talking about their pasts as England disappeared behind them in the rain. Frieda had known Lawrence for a total of eight weeks.

5

They boarded the Metz train and arrived just after six on a foggy morning. The baron and Else waited on the platform to meet them. Frieda and Lawrence left the train separately. "I've brought somebody along with me," she whispered to Else."[66] Lawrence checked in to a hotel, and Frieda, her sister, and her father crossed the tracks to Montigny, the suburb where her parents now lived. The streets were filled with the sound of workmen hammering together booths for the May Exhibition, the city's annual spring fair.

Despite the early hour, there was bedlam at the von Richthofens'. It was a new house, with a balcony overlooking fortifications. Relatives, soldiers, and children roamed the rooms, and Anna, who had grown very fat, raced from wing to wing in a black silk dress, catering to the whims of elderly relatives and giving orders to the kitchen help. Nusch, now thirty, came with a supply of elegant accessories to share with Frieda and Else for the weekend. Else, who had never warmed to Ernest, met Lawrence at a café. He struck her as frail, shy, and self-possessed. "I had the impression that it was a very serious relationship," she later said, and "in some way good for Frieda."[67]

Later in the day the baron escorted his daughters proudly to the fair, following several paces behind them in the crush of people. At his seigneurial best, he greeted friends as they glided slowly past women in colored tights, contortionists, and candy booths with names like Turkish Delight. Lawrence appeared around a corner, wearing an old raincoat and holding a rain cap in his hand, and for a moment Frieda was terrified that Nusch would despise him. He was stunned by their collective beauty, and immediately attracted to Nusch. He spoke to each briefly, then disappeared into the crowd and went back to his hotel: As the day wore on he drank three pints of beer, wrote a nervous postcard to Jessie's sister, and began mentally drafting a letter of confession to Ernest Weekley. "You can go with him," Nusch surprised Frieda by saying. "You can trust him."[68]

Various rendezvous, including one in Lawrence's hotel room that was interrupted by the manager, were all Frieda could manage for the next couple of days. Panicked telegrams and letters began arriving from Ernest, at least a half dozen to Anna and Friedrich, asking them to intercede for him. On the Friday after Frieda left, he and Monty had to confront the empty house once the maids had gone for the night, and her confession of infidelity suddenly struck like "*ein Blitz aus klaren Himmel*" (a bolt from the blue).[69] "I was insane for ten days," Ernest wrote the baron.[70] Frieda's parents were enraged that she had been stupid and indiscreet enough to get caught. According to the code of behavior that governed affairs among their class in Germany and, by now, in the family as a whole (with the possible exception of

Anna), Frieda had made an unbelievable blunder. For Friedrich, such lapses among his daughters invariably now provoked self-loathing and strong shows of the long-dormant paternal imperative. His replies to Ernest do not survive, but it is clear from Ernest's own letters that they were copious, indignant, immensely welcome in Nottingham, and contained no hint of the moral double standard Friedrich's disapproval of Frieda betrayed.

It poured on the morning of the baron's jubilee celebration. Lawrence was not invited, and Frieda failed to show up for a morning appointment with him. Angry and sullen, he delivered a letter to her house and, following the Moselle River, walked out past rows of tin barracks to the surrounding countryside. He saw no beauty in the hillsides of empty grapevines—they just looked like fields of bristling sticks, merging into one huge hedgehog. He was also wary of the cavalrymen who galloped over the hills. Hiking out to the Moselle Valley, he found lilac, poppies, and some early roses in bloom but could not escape a feeling of menace in conversations with village shopkeepers. He stopped to have his hair cut and to buy a bar of soap. "This is French soap," the barber explained in French, "this is German." When Lawrence asked the difference, the barber quickly said, "The French, of course, is better. The German . . . cheaper." In the afternoon he watched dark-haired schoolboys run home in their starched pinafores, screaming happily to one another in French. A soldier approached them on horseback to ask a question, and they immediately switched to German. At a café back in town, he asked for cigarettes. "The French, of course," a waitress advised, "are better."[71]

The next day Frieda took him to the *lunettes* of her childhood. He was fascinated by a square emerald ring she wore, and turned it absent-mindedly as they lay in the grass talking, relaxed for the first time in days. A soldier wearing a tall helmet accosted them, however, with a torrent of German, of which Lawrence understood only the word "*verboten*." He had been trying to eavesdrop on their conversation and suspected Lawrence of being an English spy. Frieda protested and he released them, after threatening to contact the baron.

Lawrence and Friedrich met over tea in Montigny almost immediately after. Offering a German cigarette, the baron asked him—at least as Lawrence wrote in his later, thinly fictionalized novel *Mr. Noon*—what he thought of Bavaria. Lawrence had never been there, and tried to summon his rusty French while balancing a delicate china teacup. "*[L]a peuple*," he answered, "*est très intéressante*." "Le *peuple*" corrected the baron, and the conversation and the tea ground to a halt.[72] Later he took Frieda into his study. "My child," he said, "what are you doing? I always thought you had so much sense. I know the world." Furious, she answered, "Yes, that may be, but you never knew the best."[73] That night she dreamed that her father and Lawrence fought and that Lawrence won.

6

On May 7 Lawrence sent Ernest the confession he had been formulating for four days:

> You will know by now the extent of the trouble. Don't curse my impudence in writing to you. In this hour we are only simple men, and Mrs. Weekley will have told you everything, but you do not suffer alone. It is really torture to me in this position. There are three of us, though I do not compare my sufferings with what yours must be, and I am here as a distant friend, and you can imagine the thousand baffling lies it all entails. Mrs. Weekley hates it, but it has had to be. I love your wife and she loves me. I am not frivolous or impertinent. Mrs. Weekley is afraid of being stunted and not allowed to grow, and so she must live her own life. All women in their nature are like giantesses. They will break through everything and go on with their own lives. The position is one of torture for us all. Do not think I am a student of your class—a young cripple. In this matter are we not simple men?[74]

The baron demanded that Lawrence leave, and Frieda saw him off, giving him seventy marks, borrowed from Nusch, to pay for a hotel in the town of Trier, two hours away. She promised to meet him there alone in a few days with the things she would need to stay with him indefinitely. He waited for her in a hotel full of businessmen, dreaming of Ernest's and the baron's anger, Frieda's lineage, and her regal profile: "I seem to love you," he wrote her, "because you've got such a nice chin."[75]

Nusch went back to her own home in Metz shortly after, Else and her children to Wolfratshausen, a village near Munich, and Frieda was left alone with her parents. She immediately slept with a titled German soldier, Udo von Henning. The liaison horrified Lawrence when she wrote him about it, but he reacted with sophisticated distaste, recalling the Maupassant story in which a French wet nurse whose breasts are painfully full suckles a hungry Italian man on a train.[76] He retaliated by flirting with a German cousin of his, a woman close to Frieda's age, who had recently gotten married.

Ernest, who had not yet received Lawrence's letter, wired Frieda in Montigny to ask if she had been unfaithful "recently"; he meant with Lawrence, whom he now suspected. If she had been unfaithful, he said, she should wire "*ganz* recent" to distinguish this "very recent" infidelity from her previous affairs.[77] Telegram in hand, Frieda set off for a day in Trier—with no luggage, and with Anna and Nusch as chaperones: The baron had forbidden her to go alone. According to Lawrence's depiction in *Mr. Noon*, the three women stepped from the train in elaborate traveling suits and huge hats, a sight that infuriated Lawrence. He particularly disliked the tall pink Viennese hat of Nusch's that Frieda wore.[78]

Anna settled herself at an outdoor café table and lectured Lawrence in a thin, piercing voice, her hat tipping to one side as she spoke. Frieda sat next to her mother and ate everyone's pastries. "[Y]ou see," the baroness explained, switching from German to English and back, "her father can't allow it. He can't allow his daughter to go off this way. . . . Her father is a gentleman and an officer."[79] Lawrence said little or nothing.

To give him and Frieda some time alone, the baroness instructed a taxi driver to take her and Nusch on a tour of the city. They watched the baroness's ample rump disappear into the car and then went to the telegraph office. Her parents' objections only enforced Frieda's resolve. "*Ganz* recent," she wired Ernest, but her confession was late. Ernest had received Lawrence's letter the same day. "*Keine Möglichkeit*," he wired back: "No possibility" of a reconciliation.[80]

Lily Kipping saw Ernest wandering up and down the rows of his vegetable garden the day Lawrence's letter arrived. He looked haggard and strangely diminished. Feeling uneasy, she told her husband, "I am going out to see Professor Weekley."[81] She took her son with her and they were admitted by the parlor maid. Ernest sent the boys out to play with their tops in the back yard. "Frieda has left me," he said without preamble, bursting into tears as he and Lily stood at the kitchen window, watching the boys. He retreated to his study later in the day to reply to Lawrence, but could not bring himself to address him and wrote to Frieda instead, with no salutation.

> I did not mean to write again, but I must. I had a letter from Lawrence this morning. I bear him no ill-will and hope you will be happy with him. But have some pity on me. Do you want to drive me to suicide to simplify things? I will not do it. I shall write to or see the Hampstead people [his parents] today. I am quite clear what to do, but you ought to help me. The children will never come back to Nottingham. I shall take a house somewhere outside London—get the old people and Maude to move to it—they will do this for me—and I shall live between there and Nottingham. . . . The children will go to school in London and form new friendships and there will be a family home. It is the best thing. All compromises are unthinkable. We are not rabbits. Do not let all generosity be on my side. Have some remorse for all your deception of a loving man. Let me know at once that you agree to a divorce. The thing can be managed very quietly, but unless you help by an admission, this will be difficult. And then it might cost me my post here and our children could starve. You loved me once—help me now—but quickly.[82]

Frieda asked Lawrence to return to Metz for moral support. He refused, and she packed, left, and went to Else's home in Wolfratshausen, where she stayed in bed for two days. Apparently she suspected she was pregnant, a possibility that made her extremely nervous but which Lawrence—experiencing, he wrote Frieda, his first paternal urges—relished: "I want you to have children to me. . . . I never thought I should have that definite desire."[83] It was not a wish destined for fulfillment. Frieda evidently got her period sometime after this letter, and thereafter, for reasons unknown, there were no pregnancies.

She met Lawrence in Munich on May 24, the day after publication of *The Trespasser*, the novel begun as "The Saga of Siegmund," which Garnett had helped place at Duckworth. In her bag were Otto Gross's letters and a copy of Friedel Gross's silk dressing gown, made for her by a dressmaker in Nottingham. They spent a night in Schwabing, then took a bus south to Beuerberg, a remote, thinly populated village of Bavarian farmhouses with white gables and black balconies, carpeted in fields of bluebells and surrounded by the foothills of the Alps. Posing as a married couple, they checked in to an inn and were given a big, bare room with a gruesome religious oil painting above two beds pushed together.

Their first nights were awkward and full of struggle. Lawrence "was no very wonderful experience" for Frieda, he wrote in *Mr. Noon*, "though she was a wonderful experience to him."[84] They had their worst hours after falling asleep. Guilty dreams of Ernest and money concerns plagued them, and he occasionally suffered the residual effects of pneumonia: night sweats, restlessness, and fever. The poems he wrote during his first months with Frieda are among his most mature and honest:

The night was a failure
but why not—?

In the darkness
with the pale dawn seething at the window through the black frame
I could not be free,
not free myself from the past, those others—
and our love was a confusion,
there was a horror,
you recoiled away from me.[85]

Frieda often woke in the middle of the night, terrified of the consequences of leaving Nottingham. Smoking a cigarette by the window, she would stand motionless in her dressing gown, lost in thought about her family, until Lawrence awakened. His grandiose, impractical condolences about the children rarely helped: "Don't be sad," he told her, "I'll make a new heaven and earth for them, don't cry, you see if I don't."[86] He disliked prolonged scenes, and Frieda's crying spells frightened and infuriated him. "You don't care a damn about those brats really," he once said, "and they don't care about you."[87] He soon became competitive at any mention of them. Else forwarded mail from Ernest, with its frequent threats that he would never let Frieda see the children again and that her behavior would kill his mother. One day Frieda lay down and banged her head on the floor in distress. "If that's how you feel," Lawrence said flatly, "you must go back to them."[88]

Letters from relatives and neighbors were full of melodrama. Maude compared Frieda to the iceberg that sank the *Titanic*.[89] Lily Kipping invoked a past catastrophe: "Don't you remember," she wrote, "when E[rnest] was so ill and you thought you would never see him again?"[90] Friedrich von Richthofen was more succinct: "You travel about the world like a barmaid."[91]

After a week in Beuerberg, Else offered them an apartment one stop down the local train line. It belonged to Alfred Weber, whom after years of ambivalence Else had taken as her lover. Small and tidy, the apartment was on the second floor of a house situated just above the village of Icking, twenty miles from Munich. A tiny balcony looked out over the Alps, the Isar River, fields of pastel flowers, a dark beechwood forest, and the white village square below. Living on the equivalent of fifteen shillings a week, borrowed, variously, from Else or Nusch, she and Lawrence laid their breakfast table with dark red wild roses they collected along the Isar, fresh eggs, dense black bread, raspberries, and wild strawberries and milk left each morning by Frau Leitner, a fat shopkeeper who ran a store on the ground floor. At midday Lawrence went down to drink schnapps and buy sausage and bacon from her while her husband sat by, his mustache dripping with homemade beer.

Occasionally Frieda longed for more comfort. Alone one day in Munich, she splurged on cambric handkerchiefs embossed with the letter "F" and a coronet. "Now I'll draw *my* coat of arms," Lawrence said when she showed them to him, and drew a pickaxe, blackboard, fountain pen, and two lions.[92] Undressing for a swim in the Isar one afternoon, she broke the heel of a shoe and threw the pair in. When Lawrence upbraided her, she said, "Things are there for me and not I for them, so when they are a nuisance I throw them away."[93] She mocked his reverence for order—he liked to segregate undergarments by fabric in the chest of drawers—and the love letters from old girlfriends that came regularly. Helen Corke, to whom Lawrence's publisher had sent a copy of *The Trespasser*, was effusive with praise: "We are such stuff as dreams are made on—but aye we make fair dreams, what matter!"[94] Frieda tore up the letter.

His ongoing oedipal drama provoked more serious fights, as did the unevenness and emotional detritus of their lovemaking. Lawrence veered from torturous indirection, furtiveness, and hostility to a childlike thrill; feelings after sex tended to subjection or elation, and there seemed little in between. One day Frieda found "My Love, My Mother," in Louie's handwriting. She defaced it:

> Good God!!!!! I hate it Yes, worse luck—what a poem to write. . . . I have tried I have fought, I have nearly killed myself in the battle to get you into connection with myself and other people, sadly I proved to my self that *I* can love, but *never* you—Now I will leave you for some days and I will see if being alone will help you to see me as I am, I will heal again by myself, you cannot help me, you are a sad thing, I know your secret and your despair, I have seen you are ashamed—I have made you better, that is my reward.[95]

Shortly after this or some similar blowup she dived into the Isar, swam across, and, it is said, had sex with a local woodcutter on the other side.[96]

Lawrence was mystified by both her libido and her anger. He read Otto Gross's letters, which Frieda, who urged Lawrence to go to Ascona, kept for instruction, reference, and emotional ballast. Lawrence scoffed at Gross's theorizing, but absorbed more than he realized from the letters: In a quiet moment he told Frieda, "You have a genius for living," and did not seem to know whom he was paraphrasing.[97]

When the anger and intensity of their fights subsided, very little else seemed to matter. The candor of their conversations and the depth of his interest in the machinations of her inner life still came as a complete revelation to Frieda, and despite her uncertainty she felt utterly challenged. She was showing him how to enjoy life, and he reveled in her body:

> *When she rises in the morning*
> *I linger to watch her;*
> *She spreads the bath-cloth underneath the window*
> *And the sunbeams catch her*
> *Glistening white on the shoulders:*
> *While down her sides the mellow*
> *Golden shadow glows as*
> *She stoops to the sponge, and her swung breasts*
> *Sway like full-blown yellow*
> *Gloire de Dijon roses.*[98]

"Frieda is awfully good-looking," he wrote Garnett, who had cautioned him that sexual passion could not sustain a relationship. ". . . She's got a figure like a fine Rubens woman, but her face is almost Greek. . . . I am *awfully* well—you should see me."[99]

It also helped that critical reaction to *The Trespasser* was fairly good; besides the occasional sisterly stipend, they would have to rely entirely on his writing for money. Lawrence abandoned his idea of a German lectureship and sent "Paul Morel" to Heinemann. He confided his worries to Else, who visited often. "Ach money!" she was apparently given to saying. "Money will come!"[100] He loved Germany because it was not England, and he loved Frieda because she stood up to him like a force of nature: "a bitch," as his hero reflects in *Mr. Noon*, trading snarl for snarl."[101] In late June, a friend wrote to tell Lawrence that the London *Daily News* had written he had the makings of an artist if only he could "burn with an intenser vision."[102] The phrase made Frieda shriek with laughter.[103]

7

Over the Alps

I

On August 2 Frieda and Lawrence lay naked in bed listening to the late-afternoon rain as a Munich-bound local pulled in to the Icking station. A stocky figure stepped from the train, wearing a black silk coat and matching skirt that brushed the ground and a tall, black, boat-shaped hat. She put up a large black umbrella and made her way slowly toward their building, a long, laborious walk for her, up and down a few small hills. Something brought Frieda out of bed and she was standing naked at the window when she suddenly recognized the woman as her mother.

The baroness had not been invited. Frieda and Lawrence scrambled to dress as she approached the house, rummaging through stockings, garters, a chemise, knickers, French stays, and a petticoat, all strewn on the floor with his tweed jacket and trousers. Anna rested for a moment with Frau Leitner, whom she knew from previous visits to Else; then they heard her struggling up the stairs. She entered without ceremony, looking unhappy and nervous, lowered herself into a chair, and without preamble directed a stream of invective and rhetorical questions at Lawrence in a relentless, haughty warble broken by the occasional sarcastic "*Ja*." Who *was* he, she asked, that Frieda, the daughter of a high-born and highly cultured gentleman, should clean his boots and empty his slops? And how could a gentleman with any decency expect the wife of a clever professor to share his poverty? Lawrence had heard the speech before, but it had a terrible ring now, and the baroness's sudden appearance, old-world elegance, and nastiness shocked him into submission. He shrank further and further into his chair while Frieda stood her ground in a corner, occasionally shouting back objections, which her mother ignored. Then Anna left, as suddenly as she had come. Lawrence accompanied her to the station, still cowed, and making small talk along the way.[1]

As she watched her mother's figure recede up the final hill, Frieda reflected on how clumsy and ungraceful she had become. She reserved her real disgust for Lawrence, however. His silence during her mother's harangue enraged her. When he returned, she crawled under a chair in imitation of a frightened dog, shrieking with derisive laughter.[2] They fought for the rest of the night.

The baroness, exhausted but morally relieved, rode the remaining twenty minutes into Munich. Else met her and they talked about Lawrence: a lovable and trustworthy man, Anna told her.[3]

Three days later Frieda and Lawrence awoke in the dark at about 4:30 A.M. Two matching Burberry raincoats and German knapsacks were ready at the door. Alfred Weber needed his apartment back, and, with no place else to go, they were going to walk across the mountains to Italy. Lawrence's knapsack was stocked with notebooks; he planned to draft poems and short sketches to earn money. They left at five in a heavy mist. The beech and chestnut trees dripped onto their raincoats and soaked a Panama hat Frieda wore. They headed down the Isar Valley through the Austrian Tirol. "[W]e were happy in our adventure," Frieda wrote, "free, going to unknown parts."[4] Neither had ever been to Italy.

They averaged ten miles a day, sometimes in heavy rainfall. The scent of wild thyme rose from the roadsides, which were also lined with purple pansies. Occasionally they had to move to the side to get out of the way of wooden wagons, drawn by bulls. High above them snow gleamed on the mountaintops. Like a good Englishman, Lawrence made tea every afternoon on a portable stove. Dinners consisted of cheese, sausage, and fruit from the villages they walked through. On their second night out, they avoided the rain for a few hours in a wooden chapel filled with ex-voto pictures and candles. Lawrence lit them all and scribbled notes amid the smell of burning wax. Frieda wandered ahead and found a hay hut, where they spent the night. The crucifixes in the mountain passes haunted Lawrence; when he looked at them, he saw the face of Ernest Weekley:

One moment the hate leaps at me standing there,
One moment I see the stillness of agony,
Something frozen in silence, that dare not be
Loosed; one moment the darkness frightens me.

Then among the averted pansies, beneath the high
White peaks of snow, at the foot of the sunken Christ
I stood in a chill of anguish, trying to say
The joy I bought was not too highly priced.[5]

Various footpaths, local buses, and trains brought them to the cheese-making village of Mayrhofen, twenty miles southeast of Innsbruck. It was August 10; midnight brought Frieda's thirty-third birthday.

2

It had been a strange summer. A month before, in early July, Frieda wrote Ernest that she was never coming back to him. The announcement brought waves of unwelcome letters and visits from various von Richthofens, and letters from Nottingham that provoked tears and loud arguments in the small apartment in Icking. Ernest wrote incessantly, often twice a day. He was living alone at Cowley with Monty, who was attending the summer term at Nottingham High School.[6] The girls had never left their grandparents' since Frieda had dropped them off three months before. *The Romance of Words* had become a critical success and a bestseller, and was reprinted in June. Frieda, Ernest told Monty, had "gone away and was ill."[7] Monty had stopped eating normally—his appetite would not improve until mid-autumn—and in later years his main memory of the aftermath of Frieda's departure was of stomach cramps and frequent nausea. To cheer the boy up, Ernest took him to the Mikado Café, which made Monty bilious. Ernest's letters veered from vituperation to pledges of love, and included suicide threats, proclamations of his will to live despite Frieda's cruelty, and dire predictions: Lawrence, he warned her, would get violent with her someday.[8] He threatened that Frieda would never see Monty, Elsa, and Barby again and offered her an apartment of her own in London. She proposed a visitation agreement—she would see the children at Christmas and Easter—but Ernest prevaricated: A friend told him that Lawrence was tubercular and might not last long.[9] He hoped that Lawrence's death might solve many of their problems. Lawrence, still shocked by his success in liberating Frieda, was immensely interested in Ernest's erratic behavior, his discomfort, and his past. He also apparently liked hearing about his sexual appetite.[10]

Frieda found it difficult to take Ernest seriously: The bullying, whining letters now irritated her intensely. She seems to have been unaware that she had no rights under English marriage law, and that Ernest could easily make good on his threats. Under coverture, the legal status of a woman that lay at the basis of English marriage law, the children belonged to him. According to the child custody laws she could lose all rights to see them if he filed for divorce and a charge of adultery was proved.[11] She felt Ernest deserved Gladys Bradley, who was pursuing him with a vengeance and who, after facilitating each of Frieda's affairs, joined the sizable number of neighbors who condemned her. They never spoke again. "He is in love with Gladys Bradley," she declared angrily, "now he can marry her."[12] Ernest, who considered his own celibacy a rebuke to Frieda, put Cowley on the market early in August, took Monty out of Nottingham High School,[13] and moved in with his parents. Ida had left several months before Frieda, to train in London as a nurse.[14]

Ernest's resolve stiffened as Frieda moved farther away. In mid-August he hired detectives to trace her movements. The household at Well Walk now numbered nine: Ernest's parents, Monty, Elsa, Barby, his brother George, and his sisters Kit (a nurse) and Maude, whom Ernest told the children to call "Mama." The mood there was grim, and everyone felt stifled in the small space. United in their hatred of her, Ernest's parents coddled him and treated him like an invalid. He still had not told the girls anything. "Where is Mama?" they asked him at breakfast one morning. "You girls musn't ask about Mama just now," Agnes replied, as Ernest blanched and left the room. "Papa is worried."[15] Everyone evaded their questions, and they cried themselves to sleep at night. Although they were used to Frieda's trips abroad, they were baffled by her long absence and silence and by their father's peculiar behavior.

Before school started a surgeon bought Cowley, and Ernest went to Nottingham to break up the household. Furniture, kitchen implements, and linens were brought to Hampstead and stuffed in wherever there was space. Ernest rented a bed-sit from a German spinster for weeknights in Nottingham. Commuting to Nottingham every Sunday and back to London on Friday, he allowed himself the luxury of a first-class ticket. He used the extra space to spread out and grade examination papers.[16] Sunday nights immediately became a torture for Monty, who cried inconsolably when Ernest packed his briefcase and walked out the door to the Hampstead underground station. He was convinced that each time his father left, the departure would be permanent.[17]

Ernest charged Agnes and Maude with stamping out traces of nascent "Bohemianism" in the children during his constant absences.[18] Maude brought them to the local Anglican church, and they were soon indoctrinated into the family's rigidly puritanical moral code, whose cardinal virtues were respectability and thrift. Agnes set the tone: When a former maid brought her child with her from Camden one Sunday to borrow a pound, Agnes remarked to eight-year-old Barby, "If she had left the baby behind, she could have walked and saved the second tram fare." It was a round-trip distance of more than ten miles, mostly uphill.[19] Agnes, who deeply resented the sudden influx of children, relished the homely incidents that gave rise to such lessons.

Ernest's sister Gert, who lived in the large, immaculate London suburb of Chiswick in an ugly house with a monkey puzzle tree outside, suggested that they look for a place near her. West of Hammersmith, northeast of Kew and Richmond, and five miles from Hyde Park Corner, Chiswick had the advantage of being a pleasant three-mile walk, largely along the Thames, from Saint Paul's, a tony ecumenical public school with high standards, in which Ernest enrolled Monty. Its disadvantage was the family's dislike of Gert's husband, John Tilley, who had a puce complexion and was badly overweight and twice her age.[20] Ernest, however, liked the anonymity, and the cheerless nonidentity of the neighborhood accommodated his feeling of being in limbo. He found a Victorian house with a large garden and a cavernous study with rows of windows on either end and enough room for all his books finally to be displayed at once. All nine members of the family moved in. Ernest hoped to live in neutral, hardworking silence, but an atmosphere of secrecy and grief immediately permeated the house, which was decorated with a confusing array of Weekley family heirlooms and furnishings from Cowley. Hung in the drawing room windows at the front of the house, the red velvet drapes from Frieda's sitting room seemed completely out of place. "Poor Papa!" the children whispered to one another as they tiptoed past him on weekends to avoid breaking his concentration.[21]

Alarmed at the now-huge weekly food budget, Agnes hired a cook named Alice; her staple was bread pudding with bottled almond flavoring, a dessert that was stretched to last for days. Agnes frequently managed to insult Alice, and, with broad anti-German innuendo now common among the Weekley elders, Frieda in absentia: "She'll poison us," she complained when the dish was served, "with 'prussic' acid!" Monty quickly perfected imitations of the Weekleys' speech patterns and invented derogatory nicknames: Agnes was "Gadabout," after a poem called "Grandpapa Gadabout." Hiding behind furniture, he pantomimed her wooden recitations of Tennyson's poem "The Grandmother," a family favorite. Ernest took to reciting melancholy biblical aphorisms in German ("All wrongdoing is avenged on earth," he would tell the children). He also became a target of his son's mockery. Monty, who called him "P.," for Papa, would say, "P. divides men into three categories like this," mimicking Ernest's arch cadences: "An accursed Jew; a pretentious ass; a very common fellow." The main target of Monty's ridicule, however, was Maude, who worshiped Charles and frequently held forth on the moral virtues of marriage. "Given the right man, and the right woman . . . ," she would begin, until Monty's expert mimicry stopped her, occasionally reducing her to tears. Maude resented being put in charge of the children, and developed a streak of sadistic humor and vengeful storytelling to relieve her frustrations, including a series of tales of "the Chief" and her "boys"—with herself as the former.[22] She indulged Monty but hated Barby, who resembled her. Delicate and fine boned, with sharp, pretty features, Barby had an irreverence that infuriated Maude and a gift for well-placed bons mots. She was afraid of Maude's sudden bursts of temper and relied on Elsa for protection.

The most obedient and well-behaved of the three, Elsa, nine, had her own fierce moral code, which she lost no time applying to her relatives: "How conceited Uncle George is," she complained when her uncle preened at the hall mirror. One night when the Tilleys came to dinner, John guzzled and nearly choked to death. Kit, with a cool indifference that belied her profession, sat by, stonily silent. "Fetch a basin!" Agnes screamed, while Gert whacked her husband's back. Finally he was led to the drawing room sofa. When he recovered he asked for dessert. Barby fled to the attic. When the incident was over, Elsa went to find her. "How selfish Aunt Kit is," she said.[23]

The girls had a brief respite when Ernest sent them at summer's end to their Uncle Ted Weekley's new parish in Essex for a vacation with Ted and his wife, Lucy, whom Maude disliked. When Maude and Ernest arrived to collect the girls, Ted took Maude on a tour of his new home. "Just the sort of house," she said pointedly, "for a man with a large family." Ted was unfazed. "Yes," he replied. "Unfortunately that isn't so in our case." The couple's childlessness was the subject of frequent family discussion. "That's not *Ted*'s fault!" Agnes once exclaimed in exasperation to Lucy herself. Before leaving, Ernest asked his brother to take snapshots of Elsa and Barby. Whether by chance or Ernest's design, they struck forlorn poses. Back in Chiswick he wrote Frieda, "I will be a father and a mother to them," and enclosed one of the pictures.[24]

3

Frieda and Lawrence rented a farmhouse in Mayrhofen. From the windows they watched the life of the village go by. Mules in caravans tied together with tasseled red rope descended from the mountains each day loaded with wheels of Emmenthal and Gruyère. An oleander flowered at their doorstep, and a stream rushed down from the mountains. Confused about the direction "Paul Morel" should take, Lawrence worked only sporadically. They enjoyed the countryside too much to stay indoors. Hiking up the valleys past cows and fields of flowers, they cooled themselves off in fresh streams. Frieda sunbathed nude while Lawrence, who was self-conscious about his white body and thin chest despite protests to the contrary,[25] sat by, watching her, writing, gathering flowers along the roadsides, or chatting in broken Italian with peasants who passed by. An incurable gossip, he soon learned the status of every local love affair. Wardrobe exigencies drove Frieda, who was running out of clothes, to buy a couple of yards of red cotton crepe for a "peasant sack."[26] She liked it better than the shapeless muslin frocks and tight Victorian dresses with their complicated, buttressing petticoats she had had in Nottingham. Lawrence, who disapproved of her French lace underwear, sewed her several pairs of calico and cambric bloomers.

On August 26 they sent their trunks on to Italy by train and left Mayrhofen with Edward Garnett's son, David, and a friend of David's named Harold Hobson, who planned to hike with them for two days. Tall, virile, outgoing, and voluble, the son of a prominent British social economist, Hobson was on his way home to England from an excursion to Moscow. He and Frieda liked each other immediately. Lawrence was annoyed by their constant chatter and split off with David whenever he could.

They hiked south toward the higher reaches and raw grandeur of the mountains that ascended to the Brenner Pass, at an elevation of four and a half thousand feet. Guides with sprigs of edelweiss in their hat brims used picks and ropes to clear away the ice and snow from paths cut through the mountains, and tiny, brightly colored alpine flowers grew all over. David, an amateur botanist, dawdled at the roadsides and made extra forays up the sides of mountains with Lawrence, pulling up hundreds of specimens for his herbarium at home, while Frieda and Harold walked alone happily, talking nonstop. On their second evening, the two flower pickers went off alone for a last haul. Frieda and Harold stayed behind at a roadside hay hut and made love before Lawrence and David returned.[27] The two young men left the next day. Frieda said nothing to Lawrence about what had happened.

They still faced days of strenuous walking, much of it in the cold. When their strength flagged, they took trains. The weather turned hotter when they climbed down the mountainsides into small villages, where black grapes hung over the lintels and bundles of tobacco stalks lay drying. Other towns were less picturesque, with filthy lavatories and bug-infested rooms. Frieda's hat got crushed, its red velvet ribbon ran onto the straw, and her crepe dress became so shabby with small rips that she had to keep her raincoat on when they tried to find rooms. Trient (Trento) was particularly grim, and Frieda's sudden confession of her interlude with Harold did not improve the atmosphere. Boarding a train, they arrived in Riva, on the north shore of Lake Garda, on September 4. It was the first pleasant place they had seen in a couple of days. Pretending to be married, they checked into a *pensione*.

They attracted a lot of attention in the village. Frieda had received four gold-embroidered silk hats and an elegant evening dress in the mail from Nusch; after letting out the seams, she started wearing the dress in the daytime. Her outfits made a strange contrast to the faded cotton dresses and head kerchiefs of the Austro-Italian lakeside villagers. Lawrence, who still wore his customary English tweed suit, had overcome his aversion to her big hats and enjoyed modeling the new ones, nude, in their bedroom.[28] The locals, who soon called him "Lorenzo," assumed that they were wealthy eccentrics. The misconception was reinforced when royalties on *The Trespasser* arrived, a windfall of fifty pounds. Lawrence began leaving huge tips in local restaurants, which were usually someone's kitchen, and happily ordered liters of Asti Spumante.

Each day they strolled around the lake in their strange clothes to hunt for an apartment. Frieda remembered little or no Italian from her nighttime classes with Ernest but occasionally summoned the courage to approach a stranger with some faltering question. Trips to the post office were a major event. To avoid expensive postal charges, they asked favors of people in England: Elsa's tenth birthday was on September 13, and they told David Garnett to send her a book. He put Lawrence's name on the return address. Ernest returned it with an indignant letter.

Late in September they met a Bavarian hotel proprietor named Maria Samuelli, who recommended a vacant house, the Villa Igea, in the tiny village of Gargnano. It was accessible only by steamer and rented for eighty lire a month. They packed their bags September 27 and caught the boat; before going Frieda wrapped up Gross's letters and sent them to Ernest by way of explaining her motivation to find a better life, and, by inference, the reasons for the failure of their marriage and how much she had changed. Her own letters to him had proved entirely ineffective in conveying such messages, serving only to gratify his sense of having been wounded, and postponing the divorce she now felt was inevitable. His anger, in her eyes, was as self-referential as she had come to believe his passion had once been, and she evidently intended Gross's unmistakable, highly specific passion to be instructive. The letters devastated him. Lacking Frieda's new address, he wrote a letter of sad outrage to her mother.

The baroness, whom Ernest addressed as "Mama," was unimpressed. Like everyone in the family by now, she felt Frieda's immovability, and she was also beginning to derive a vague, vicarious excitement and satisfaction from her daughter's affair, which may have answered a need of her own for amorous restitution. Anna, Lawrence wrote Garnett approvingly, was "utterly non-moral."[29] It is unclear whether the baron likewise had begun to reverse his low opinion of Lawrence. Despite future amicable letters[30] from Anna to Chiswick, however, the tide of von Richthofen family sentiment never turned again in Ernest's favor.

4

Surrounded by olive, chestnut, and fig trees and terraced grapevines that shone red and yellow in the sun, Gargnano was a winemaking village and a center for the Bersaglieri, the sharpshooting branch of the Italian Army, known as much for their marksmanship and agility as for their highly decorated uniforms and plumed helmets. "I lie with joy out of a window, that looks on the road and watch the Italians," Frieda wrote. "They are beautiful creatures. The men so loose and soldiers with *such* hats, a foam of cockfeathers on them I long for one, a hat not a soldier."[31]

They had a floor of the Igea, which was near the village square, where the Nebbiolo grapes for the local red Lombardy wine were pressed. There were two bedrooms, a dining room, an immense kitchen stocked with polished copper pots, and a garden filled with oranges, peaches, persimmons, and bamboo trees. The acrid smell of crushed grapes and fermenting wine wafted up to them through numerous windows, along with the sounds of the villagers' stomping feet and even—so they imagined—the squish of grapes. They had a view of Lake Garda. It was almost always sunny in Gargnano, but when it rained, the lake, normally a clear purplish green, turned a magnificent dark blue, with brilliant whitecaps. Lawrence intended to finish revising "Paul Morel." They desperately needed the money. Frieda felt that the oedipal drama, buried under strained metaphors, purple prose, undigested Schopenhauer, and an implausible love story between Paul and Miriam, had to be teased out of the manuscript. She coolly outlined the problem of its revision to Edward Garnett: "I think L. quite missed the point. . . . he is so often beside the point 'but "I'll learn him to be a toad" as the boy said as he stamped on the toad.' "[32]

Lawrence's commitment to his novel was passionate. For the next month and a half, he woke early and sat at the kitchen table, writing at the phenomenal pace of seven pages a day.[33] Frieda learned how to cook, and how to wash sheets in a small tin pail. Arguments between them about the novel's language, the motivation of Miriam (a largely faithful depiction of Jessie), and the intention of Mrs. Morel were constant and exhausting. Occasionally Frieda wrote passages for him. "What do you think my mother felt like then?" he would ask, handing her a sheet of clean paper and a sheaf of manuscript with a scene that stumped him.[34] She line-edited as she went along: "hoyty-toyty," she wrote above overblown phrases.[35] She was also obsessively poring over *Anna Karenina*, which she had first read in Nottingham, but which had now suddenly acquired new meaning. She concluded that Anna had ruined two marriages instead of just one: "She made a mess of hers and Vronsky's marriage because she could not take the social condemnation. I decided I would not let that happen to me."[36] A letter from Will Dowson came one day during the period of her fascination with Tolstoy's heroine. "If you had to elope," he wrote, "why not with me?"[37] She slipped the letter between the pages of *Anna Karenina*. Shortly after, she sent Ernest the book, presumably with a letter of analysis—it has not come down for posterity—of Anna's dilemma and wrongful choice and the moral Frieda drew from them. After a brief silence following Ernest's receipt of Gross's love declarations, letters had begun arriving from him again, and Frieda probably hoped to bring the weight of literary history to bear on his intractableness. Vengefulness may also have been a motive: Dowson's letter was still inside when the book arrived. Ernest examined it, then mailed it to Lawrence without comment. "That's the free-masonry," Frieda said, echoing a comment of Lawrence's shortly after his letter of confession to Ernest Weekley had crossed in the mail with the barrage from Nottingham, "that exists among men."[38]

Tolstoy's novel spurred Frieda's understanding of the Miriam character, whom she increasingly felt was too passive—more a sacrificial victim and a relic of the nineteenth-century novel than a harbinger of the twentieth century. In October and early November, Lawrence threw away at least one of four old Miriam chapters; the new pages contained some sections written or drafted by Frieda. The changes made Miriam's nature uglier and grasping. Control and possession, rather than love, became the basis of her attraction to Paul and provided the motivation for Paul's break with her, which now acquired an edge of real cruelty. Lawrence next killed off Mrs. Morel, drawing heavily on the death of his mother. He relied on Frieda for emotional vetting as he completed the chore of expelling Mother and Jessie from his system.[39] The work took its toll on both of them: Frieda even grew accustomed to eerie "sightings" of Lydia Lawrence lookalikes in Gargnano,[40] and they both got sick when Lawrence wrote Mrs. Morel's death scene.[41] The novel often irritated them both, and occasionally Lawrence took a break to write poems "heaps nicer," Frieda wrote Edward Garnett, ". . . than those 'baby ones.' "[42]

Lawrence entertained himself by reading Ernest's letters. After one argument with Frieda, he copied out passages that struck him as particularly ludicrous, for use as dialogue in *The Fight for Barbara*, a comic play he wrote in a burst of inspiration and spleen over three days. The heroine was a Frieda variant named Barbara Tressider, a prevaricating aristocrat who is chased across Italy by her parents and her starchy, melodramatic husband, Frederick, after eloping with Jimmy Wesson, a lower-class Englishman. Lawrence made Barbara childless and gave Anna von Richthofen (now Lady Charlcote) a scene in which she barges in to scream at Wesson.[43] Frieda, "fed up [with] all this 'house of Atreus' feeling," got back at Lawrence with a parody of "Paul Morel" entitled *Paul Morel, or His Mother's Darling*. "This kind of thing isn't called a skit," Lawrence said tersely after reading her play.[44] It soon disappeared.

"Paul Morel" became *Sons and Lovers* one day in October after Lawrence made slight revisions to a passage in which Mr. Morel interrupts a kiss between Paul and his mother. He finished the final hundred pages in the first weeks of November and sent it to Duckworth. Frieda wrote a defense of the novel to Garnett, who had criticized the formlessness of earlier drafts. She instinctively grasped the importance of individual perception and the modernist brilliance of the book:

> I dont think he has "no form"; I used to. But now I think anybody must see in Paul Morel the hang of it. The mother is really the thread, the domineering note, I think the honesty, the vividness of a book suffers if you subject it to "form." I have heard so much about "form" with Ernst, why are you English so keen on it, their own form wants smashing in almost any direction, but they cant come out of their snail house. . . . any new thing must find a shape, then afterwards one can call it "art." I hate art, it seems like grammar, wants to make a language all grammar, language was first and then they abstracted grammar; I quite firmly believe that L is quite great in spite of his "gaps." Look at the vividness of his stuff, it knocks you down I think. It is perhaps too "intimate" comes too close, but I believe that is youth. . . . I am sure he is a real artist, the way things pour out of him, *he* seems only in the pen, and isnt that how it ought to be? We *all* go for things, look at them with preconceived notions, things must have a "precedence." We have lost the faculty of seeing things unprejudiced, live off our own bat, think off our own free mind.[45]

Garnett accepted the manuscript but blue-penciled some kinky passages, breasts (belonging to Clara Dawes, now an amalgam of Alice Dax and Frieda), and oedipal excesses (much of Paul's older brother). The cuts amounted to a tenth of the manuscript.[46] Lawrence did not mind, because Duckworth paid him. The advance was one hundred pounds.

They spent a peculiar Christmas. All of a sudden there was no more *Sons and Lovers* around, and no more mail from Ernest, who denied Frieda's request to see the children. Lawrence caught a cold and spent Christmas Day in bed, eating *torrone*, the sticky nougat candy they both loved. Harold Hobson, who came and overstayed three weeks, was a strangely manic presence. The New Year passed dolefully and uneventfully, and on February 11, 1913, Ernest filed a petition for divorce on grounds of adultery.

8

"Mrs. Lawrence"

I

Starved for books at the Igea, Frieda read the Bible. Unlike Lawrence's guilty visions of Ernest in the wooden Jesuses of the Tirol, she did not see her husband in Christ's image. "I rather like Christ," she told Lawrence, a sentence that would probably have earned a snort of condescension from Ernest.[1] Lawrence was intrigued by the reference and her easygoing ardor: Inspired by the Gospel of John, and further guided by a desire to exercise in his writing more of the passion that he felt Frieda and most women exhibited on a daily basis ("men daren't allow it"), he wrote a long foreword to *Sons and Lovers* and impulsively sent it off to Garnett.[2] His passionate intentions turned involuted and self-conscious rather quickly, but he hoped, he wrote Garnett, that it would "amuse" him:[3]

> John, the beloved disciple, says, "The Word was made Flesh." But why should he turn things round? The women simply go on bearing talkative sons, as an answer. "The Flesh was made Word."
>
> . . . And so it was written: "The Word was made Flesh," then, as corollary, "And of the Flesh was made Flesh-of-the-Flesh, woman." This is again backward. . . . The woman is the Flesh.

It went on, with rambling passages suggestive of the Book of Revelation, a flower-and-bee metaphor that stretched for several pages, a disquisition on the function of the queen bee—one of Lawrence's terms of endearment for Frieda—and concluded with a single oblique reference to the novel: "The old son-lover was Oedipus. The name of the new one is legion."[4] Frieda had qualms: "We fought over it," she wrote Garnett, who was simply baffled. Lawrence retracted it with a red face: "I would die of shame if that Foreword were printed," he wrote Garnett soon after. The barely contained sexual braggadocio evidently embarrassed Lawrence, and all agreed that the foreword was pedantic, but its style and narrative form presaged later novels, notably *The Rainbow* and *Women in Love*. The search for some entirely new, more passionate, and more philosophic form of narrative—"deeper than" *Sons and Lovers*—was clearly consuming him.[5]

He cultivated an equally anomalous botanical metaphor in a review, for the London literary journal *Rhythm*, of *Georgian Poetry 1911–1912*, an anthology published in December that included his poem "Snap-Dragon." The anthology was compiled and edited by Edward Marsh, a writer, former and future private secretary to Winston Churchill, and patron of *Rhythm* and, later, of Lawrence. Unlike Frieda and Garnett, *Rhythm*'s editors—the New Zealand short-story writer Katherine Mansfield and John Middleton Murry, a free-lance editor and critic—were not disturbed by Lawrence's free-form poetics and tendency to stray from the subject at hand: After comparing life to a flowering orange tree, which, somehow, the Georgians evoked for him, the review segued into a happy paean to his love for Frieda.[6] As in the *Sons and Lovers* foreword, it was clearly an excuse to write about his fascination and sexual satisfaction with her. An air of magnificence, she later wrote, seemed to surround them during these months, adding luster even to mundane events, and for Lawrence the effect translated directly into his work. Frieda's foreignness, and the workings of her imagination on his own, were yielding as much fruit as he had hoped—often entirely more than she was willing to give up: "You use me," she complained, "as a scientist his 'dissecting rabbit,' I am your 'Versuchs Kaninchen.' "[7]

With no book going and their cash dwindling, Lawrence, desperate for an overarching theme for his next novel, began preaching to friends, correspondents, and admirers—who were beginning to accrue.

"My great religion," he wrote to one Ernest Collings, a British painter and illustrator he had never met, "is a belief in the blood, the flesh, as being wiser than the intellect. . . . The intellect is only a bit and a bridle."[8] To an old friend in Eastwood, an ardent women's rights advocate, he predicted that his work would liberate women "better than the suffrage."[9]

Three projects dead-ended in Eastwood, which he could not seem to stop writing about. "My mother made a failure of her life," began "Elsa Culverwell," a novel (drawn from discarded "Paul Morel" material) that he abandoned after twenty pages—to begin work on "The Insurrection of Miss Houghton," a pre-feminist novel set in a variant of Eastwood.[10] Under prevailing decency standards, the book, whose heroine takes an Italian lover, would never have made it, as the contemporary phrase went, "to the lending libraries," but the thrill of impropriety filled Lawrence with "venomous" satisfaction, and he raced through two hundred pages, hardly blotting a word and often drafting five pages a day.[11] A fictionalized book about the Scottish poet Robert Burns, whose life he likewise thought about transplanting to the Midlands, also failed to pan out. His *Love Poems and Others*, a selection from the previous six years, was published in February. Lawrence had high hopes, but the book sold fewer than one hundred copies in the three months following publication.[12] His old maîtresse Helen Corke was a recurring presence, with a rather stiff and shallow bow to Edgar Allan Poe:

> *Helen, you let my kisses stream*
> *Wasteful into the night's black nostrils; drink*
> *Me up, I pray; oh you, who are Night's bacchante,*
> *How can you from my bowl of kisses shrink?*[13]

Of the twenty-seven poems included, only one had been composed since meeting Frieda. The love poems to her, which he wrote feverishly, were brilliant and direct:

> *Between her breasts is my home, between her breasts.*
> *Three sides set on me space and fear, but the fourth side rests,*
> *Warm in a city of strength, between her breasts.*

All day long I am busy and happy at my work
I need not glance over my shoulder in fear of the terrors that lurk
Behind. I am fortified, I am glad at my work.

I need not look after my soul; beguile my fear
With prayer, I need only come home each night to find the dear
Door on the latch, and shut myself in, shut out fear.

I need only come home each night and lay
My face between her breasts;
And what of good I have given the day, my peace attests.

And what I have failed in, what I have wronged
Comes up unnamed from her body and surely
Silent tongued I am ashamed.

And I hope to spend an eternity
With my face down-buried between her breasts
And my still heart full of security
And my still hands full of her breasts.[14]

2

In the loneliness and isolation of the villa, Lawrence's fixation on work—"a writing machine," Frieda called him—was unnerving.[15] He was given to inexplicable rages and days of utter exhaustion, and he often wrote himself sick. Each time Frieda nursed him with a patience and resolve she was seldom able to give the pages of his abortive novels. "Often he was ill when his consciousness tried to penetrate into deeper strata," she later wrote, "it was an interplay of body and soul. . . . He demanded so much of me and I *had* to be there for him so completely."[16]

She was terrified that a serious illness might force her to postpone going to England for Easter, which fell on March 23. Elsa and Barby, who attended Miss Dollman's, a dame school in northeast Chiswick, had a week's vacation, Monty had the same days off from Saint Paul's, and she had been counting on seeing them since Ernest's refusal of a visit at Christmas.[17] She considered her chances good: Though he had not written, he had not flatly refused, and Frieda doubtlessly both overestimated her lingering appeal to the man she had abandoned and underestimated the staying power of his rage. Probably the silence between them engendered fantasies. Divorce law forbade him from contacting her, and she could not get in touch, or even write him in care of Goldberg, Barrett & Newell (the firm in Finsbury Circus representing him), but he *could* send a message through Else or Anna.[18] He did still correspond regularly with her mother, but the letters, forwarded to Frieda, veered only from condemnatory sentences to lachrymose apologies for the outbursts after Frieda had left him, without once mentioning the children.

On February 10 her old neighbor Lily Kipping forwarded a letter from Ernest's lawyers: "We should advise Professor Weekley to refer Mrs Weekley to the Court, pending the divorce proceedings. Any request she has to make concerning the children, should be made to the Court."[19] Frieda did not know "what court or anything," and ignored the letter.[20] The British attitude to divorce as quasi criminal and morally reprehensible was as inconsequential to her as the petitions, citations, affidavits, notices, and orders the bureaucratic machinery of divorce was churning out. Her remove was typical of the Continent in the early twentieth century—both in attitude and statute: "Divorce is release from misfortune and not a crime," read a fairly representative contemporary codicil from the laws of Norway, which, like German law, did not penalize and marginalize the guilty party in divorces.[21] In England very little had changed since the Norman Conquest: "Outside the family married women had the same legal status as children and lunatics."[22] The idea of jurisprudence superseding maternity particularly galled Frieda,[23] and the child custody rules of British common law were even more draconian than divorce law. If Ernest would not cooperate, she was determined to see the children "on the sly."[24]

The divorce papers were served at the Igea on March 4, a sunny day. Frieda and Lawrence were alone when a "mangy old gentleman" came through the garden gate, bowing gracefully and smiling. "I am the English Consul," he announced, then asked for "the Signor Lavrenchy." Invited in, he executed more bows and turns as he produced a long sheet of paper for Lawrence and gave Frieda a similar sheet: "*per la signora*." Lawrence, named as co-respondent, was riveted by the phrase "habitually committed adultery together." He looked up and saw the consul standing absently. "[T]here is no need to reply?" he asked, to break the silence. "*No, signore—credo no.*"[25]

Two weeks before Easter, Frieda finally sought legal advice—from Edward Garnett's brother, Robert, a senior partner in the London firm of Darley, Cumberland and Co.[26] She did not know how they would pay him. Lawrence had his own problems. Immersed in proofs of *Sons and Lovers* for several weeks, he was thoroughly sick of them, and felt apprehensive about what Jessie, with whom he had not corresponded in eight months, might think. On March 13 he mailed an extra set to the rooms she had rented after a falling out with her family.[27] Included was a strange invitation: "Frieda and I discuss you endlessly. We should like you to come out to us some time." He added that he and Frieda were to marry as soon as the divorce came through.[28] Jessie considered the book a blasphemous travesty of their friendship. She was absorbed in her own account, a novel that Garnett was encouraging her to complete, and was furious at the intrusion. After reading the proofs, she redirected the package to Ada and sat by the fire for a day, unable to eat, and "shiver[ing] as if I had ague fits."[29] She returned his letter, and they never communicated with each other again.

Lawrence was standing at an easel late the same afternoon his package arrived at Jessie's, drawing a local scene of cypresses, olive trees, and a vaulting bridge. He tried to rouse Frieda from a book she was reading on a couch nearby—for an opinion of the sketch—but she was depressed to have heard nothing from either Robert Garnett or Ernest, and rose from the couch only to stare absently out the row of large windows looking onto Lake Garda. A fleet of tiny sailboats moved slowly in a calm wind. "Come and look," Lawrence begged. "Not quite soft and misty enough for me," she said blankly, "but the bridge is a joy." He was rubbing a soft eraser across the spots she disliked when she heard the postman's familiar deep basso from beyond the garden gate and went out to meet him. "*Buona sera, signora,*" he said, and held out an envelope addressed in Ernest's neat, distinctive hand. It was an unusually short letter: "I have done with you, I want to forget you and you must be dead to the children. You know the law is on my side."[30]

"The law!" she screamed at Lawrence. "Can they undo the fact that those children are mine?"

"It's no good, going on like that," he yelled, striking a table with his bony fist, angry at the disturbance to his watercoloring and frightened by her fury.[31]

Frieda said little or nothing for the next two days. She spent her time staring at the lake from the window and mechanically cleaning the house. Her ability to disappear into herself, leaving a vagueness and abstraction, befuddled Lawrence, who had seen this side before and knew that weeks could pass before she could be coaxed out. He took to his bed on the third day and began "The Sisters," an attempt at a "pot-boiler."[32] It rained for most of the following week, and he wrote forty-six pages.

Easter passed with Lawrence still in bed, now infuriated by Frieda's chilly despair. As much as he hated this reserve, he was also trying to capture something of it in Ella—later renamed Ursula—one of the two sisters he was sketching out, taking as inspiration both Frieda's isolating mechanism and the Venus de Milo.[33] A third character, Birkin, made his way into the novel, a thinly disguised version of Lawrence, evidently philosophizing at great length about love and female frailty, enabling Lawrence to draft without the slightest self-consciousness. Frieda invited Else, to relieve the foul mood of the house, and Lawrence finally got out of bed—using the opportunity to put something of Else (with a nod to Nusch) into the pages of his book. Both were grafted onto the characters of Ella and her sister, Gudrun. Else thought that they had been alone too long, and invited them along on a trip to Rome and Verona.[34] Frieda very much wanted to see Florence.

They left the Igea shortly after and went to stay in a neighboring farmhouse with a Swedish watercolorist, Antonia Almgren, whom the Garnetts had recommended as a houseguest a month before. (Frieda, who disliked the prospect of living with a complete stranger, especially an unattached woman with emotional problems, had squelched the idea.) Lawrence was intrigued that Antonia had once lived in Lapland and, sensing a future subject, quickly became versed in the details of her love life, which she enumerated each night over dinner: Two years younger than Frieda, she had run away from her husband, John, a prominent sculptor whose patrons included the Swedish crown prince.[35] Convinced that he was mentally unstable and would be arriving any day to force her to come home, she had taken the pseudonym "Mrs. Anthony." After a couple of nights in the farmhouse hearing about this enraged, deserted man, Frieda was despondent and livid. Florence, she decided, was completely out of the question, and what she wanted was to get back home—if only back to Germany. Antonia's selfish prattle disgusted her:

> I *do* feel sorry for John, he must have taken her seriously and she is cold to give one shivers. . . . I had a pang of jealousy because of her, but the bubble's pricked, L approaches all people (women specially) as if they were Gothic cathedrals, then he finds that they are little houses and hates them for it! . . . could'nt anybody tell John, that he is a blithering, blighted imbecile, duffer and idiot to want her back? She is a sensationalist, loves all this chasing game, would'nt, could'nt do without it now! He *must* leave her, with an effort of will get rid of her inside or he will be quite done for soon![36]

Lawrence later wrote a travel sketch, "The Dance," that featured a veiled but unmistakable likeness of Antonia. Garnett, fearing for his friend's anonymity, insisted it be modified.[37]

Traveling as "Mr and Mrs Lawrence," they spent several nights in a cheap hotel in Verona, where they saw Else, and left Italy by train on April 14, their luggage readdressed from Florence—which they had decided to bypass—to Munich. Lawrence had written 110 pages of "The Sisters." The potboiler he had begun quickly and painlessly "for the 'jeunes filles'" had become "an earnest and painful work" that nagged at him day and night.[38]

3

They were soon installed in a small, new, self-consciously rustic summer house at the edge of a forest of fir trees in the Bavarian village of Irschenhausen, fifteen miles from Munich. It belonged to Edgar Jaffe and was situated on a hilly meadow, carpeted in blue gentians and yellow and purple primroses. Deer and hare fed on the property, and the Tirolean Alps, twenty miles to the southeast, changed from green to blue-black in the late light. It was a tidy forest community with an odd air of lonely industry and almost fanatical privacy. An ancient-looking ox plodded up and down the hill from the immaculate village, carrying food and baggage to neighboring log cabins, visible through the trees. "*Grüss Gott*," the local peasants and vacationing Munich hikers said to one another on the manicured paths that cut through the firs. There was not much to do, and it rained a lot.

Frieda and Lawrence felt hemmed in[39] after the warmth, early fruit harvests, and abundant wine of Italy, and missed Lake Garda, the unkempt bustle of Gargnano, and the chance to speak Italian, whose rudiments they had slowly mastered. Occasionally they went to the Wolfratshausen market to pick through the umbrellas, suspenders, and gingerbread on sale,[40] and from time to time they had a visit from Edgar, who had become a professor of economics at the Technical College of Munich University in 1910. Sitting by the green tile dining room stove that shone dully in the light of an oil lamp, his feet resting on a Persian rug, original Dürer engravings and indigenous pottery ranged behind him on wooden shelves,[41] Edgar held a stone mug filled with brown beer and eagerly repeated his lectures on capitalism.

Lawrence resumed work on "The Sisters," but it seemed vague to him, an abstract discourse on the nature of female sexuality, now that they had settled in the forest. It stymied him at every turn, and he blamed Frieda's preoccupation with her children: "I could not get my soul into it," he later told Garnett. "That was because of the struggle and the resistance between Frieda and me."[42] Else, who had gotten them Edgar's cottage rent-free, often visited from her own cottage in Wolfratshausen. "[S]he is a person who arranges other folk's affairs," Lawrence complained to Garnett.[43] Though he was irritated at her intervention, she had a subtle and calming influence, and her sublime indifference to her husband Edgar was convenient for his novel. Probably with Else in mind, Lawrence had added, among other characters, Gudrun's two lovers, the mining industrialist Gerald, whose profound belief in capitalism may owe something to Edgar, and the sculptor Loerke, a man with the iconoclastic personality of Otto Gross and a repugnant physiognomy that seems to have been a product either of Lawrence's invention or of jealousy. He appreciated Else's respect for his work, and other, more practical help: When the *English Review* asked for a three-thousand-word article on German poetry, he decided (though he had already published two reviews on the subject) that he needed Else:

> It is the modern, new stuff they want to hear about—say that which is published in the last ten years—such people as [Richard] Dehmel,

> and [Detlev von] Liliencron [*sic*], Stefan George, Ricarda Huch, Elsa Laska Schule [*sic*]. Haven't you got a strong opinion about modern German poetry. . . . It would be rather a cute idea to write about:
>
> "The Woman-Poets of the Germany of Today"
>
> . . . I should love doing it myself, if I knew enough about it.[44]

"What cheek," Frieda wrote in the margin, "he doesn't know *anything.*"

Lawrence envied and admired the unshakable loyalty between Frieda and Else, and struggled to get something of it into "The Sisters." He reached page 145 by April 23, and admitted he did not understand what he was writing about.[45] More than the expense of a trip to London, of which Frieda talked endlessly, and fear of and annoyance at her divided loyalties, he worried about the upset of another move.

While they vacillated and fought, Frieda hatched a plan with her mother that would obviate the need to travel to England. Anna and Friedrich had recently moved to Ländli, a Baden-Baden spa, fulfilling Anna's fervent desire, since her consignment to Metz thirty-five years before, to return to Germany proper.[46] If Ernest would send the children there over the Whitsun school holiday of May 10–12, she could see them under her supervision. The plan fell through, the holiday passed, and they whiled away the time reading Jessie Chambers's novel about Lawrence, sent by Garnett. Frieda found it lovable and sad, but it threw Lawrence into a depression.[47] Tired of being cooped up with him, she set off for Baden-Baden alone.

She found her mother in euphoric spirits and the baron declining visibly. Symptoms of a degenerative neurological disease had begun to show up shortly before the von Richthofens' departure from Montigny, and, despite occasional periods of lucidity, his condition had worsened once they were installed at Ländli. The onset of the disease had coincided with his retirement. Often when he opened his mouth to speak, he became confused and nothing came out, but at other times he directed a torrent of confessional lamentations at Frieda, telling her of the thousand marks he owed his former mistress Selma. He could enjoy neither the Baden spas nor the countryside, now in full spring bloom, and his memory was failing badly. "I don't understand the world any more," he told Frieda, who was shattered by the experience of seeing him so diminished.[48]

Anna talked more openly to Frieda than she ever had before, and Frieda, for one of the first times she could remember, felt neither removed from nor resentful of her mother, who, at sixty-two, seemed at last to have found her parental metier. She cautioned Frieda, entirely unself-consciously and apparently with little awareness of what she was betraying about herself, that she was taking too hard a line with Lawrence on the subject of her children and would have to accede to Ernest's sovereignty. She told her, in essence, that the parental bond had a life of its own and would or would not survive her separation from Monty, Elsa, and Barby no matter what she did. Not a message Frieda was prepared to bow to, it nevertheless bespoke the dispassionate thought of a lawyer's daughter, and the baroness's now-unquestioning acceptance of her changed circumstances meant a lot to Frieda. Over the years their relationship was slowly transforming from one of mistrust, misunderstanding, and resentment to a rather soulful, if never entirely easy, dependency, a belated enactment of the mother-daughter relationship that had gone largely uncultivated in Metz.

It was a change provoked in part by Frieda's realization that, despite their differences, their temperamental similarities were obvious and inevitable: Each of them, she saw on this trip, fell back on devices of inscrutability and deflection despite their newfound candor. Her mother also knew her better than anyone, with the possible exception of Lawrence. As perhaps befitting a woman who had subjected her maternal responsibility to her love of nineteenth-century novels, Anna's chief understanding of Frieda in later years would come largely through Lawrence's increasingly modernist novels. With the ambivalence that characterized almost all her relations with Frieda, she told her that she was a throwback to an earlier time—an "atavismus."[49] She did not explain precisely what she meant—presumably an elementalness that made Frieda seemed etched out of the Roman walls and paving stones of Metz—but Frieda, who evidently saw some truth to the remark and had a weakness for Latin conceits, repeated it to friends throughout her life, seeming to consider it a compliment. Her atavism, in fact, was summed up in her looks, which seemed, by turns, timeless and utterly out of time, as though she had been born into the wrong century, a quality that later made her much sought after by sculptors and painters. Each of them, from a student of Aristide Maillot to Barby, failed to capture her entirely accurately, prevented as much by their own limitations as by Frieda's immense guardedness under close scrutiny.

When Frieda returned to Irschenhausen, Lawrence was still depressed, and in the state of nervous near-collapse he tended to descend into whenever she left him. "When I went away," she later wrote, "it was always terrible. He hated me."[50] She resolved once more to depart for England, and waited in nervous anticipation for him to put the final touches on "The Sisters."

He was discouraged in his efforts by Garnett, who, after a reading of the first half of the manuscript, decided that both heroines were "remarkable females" rather than flesh-and-blood characters, and apparently suggested a serious overhaul. Lawrence, who preferred to start over again rather than to rewrite, rushed through the draft, evidently blurring his heroines: Frieda recognized herself in both of them, and agreed with Garnett:

> We roared over the "remarkable females" you just hit them! The worst, it's like his impudence, they are *me*, these beastly, superior arrogant females! Lawrence *hated* me just over the children, I daresay *I* was'nt all I might have been, so he wrote this! I know now why Göthe wrote *Iphigenie* so superb she is, but I ll be hanged if any man wants to love her, as well be married to the tablets of the ten commandments, though mind you a man looks for that in a woman too! The book will be all right in the end, you trust me for my own sake, they will have to be women and not superior flounders.[51]

He edged toward page 300 by the first week of June. As was his wont, he talked out almost every twist and turn to Frieda, and they fought constantly. Neither Else nor Edgar had been around for some time, and they had seen no one else. One day, they were washing and drying the dishes, and Lawrence began fulminating about relations between the sexes, a diatribe that became more and more irrational and insistent. Frieda, wiping an earthenware plate, felt disgusted as she listened to his "philosophy." Women had no souls, he said. When he added that they could not love, Frieda smashed his head with the plate and walked out.[52]

She arrived within an hour at Else's cottage, a walk of several miles through the woods. Else's son Friedel, ten years old, listened with rapt attention as Frieda told Else what had happened. He knew of Frieda's impending divorce from his Uncle Ernst and was distressed to see her upset with Lawrence, to whom he had developed a fierce attraction during long walks in the woods, listening to him talk about flowers and hunting for mushrooms. "Tante Frieda," he interrupted, "now you will get tired of this man and three uncles from one aunt are too much!"[53] She stayed at Else's for two days, reading in bed, and taking *Luftbäder*—"air baths" through the woods in their striped bathing suits—with Friedel and Marianne, eight; Hans, four; and Peter, Otto Gross's son, an ethereal-looking boy with a sweet, piping voice who, at five, bore a strong resemblance to his father.

She returned to find Lawrence absorbed in two short stories of German military life. "Honour and Arms," which Garnett later retitled "The Prussian Officer," was a strange tale of violence and latent homosexuality between an overbearing, aristocratic infantry captain and his orderly. Its power haunted Frieda: "He wrote it before the war," she later remembered,

> but as if he sensed it. The unhappy, conscious man, the superior in authority envying the other man his simple, satisfied nature. I felt as if he himself was both these people. . . . It is a queer story and it frightened me at the time of the dark corners of Lawrence's soul, the human soul altogether.[54]

In "Vin Ordinaire"—later called "The Thorn in the Flesh"—a common soldier on maneuvers knocks a sergeant over fortifications into a moat, and hides at the home of a baron whose servant he has an affair with. Both were masterful accomplishments: the vividness of nineteenth-century scene painting combined with enormous psychological depth, conjured in a few pages.

He was now ready to accompany Frieda back to England. "[W]e are L and I such good friends," Frieda wrote Garnett soon after, announcing their imminent arrival at his house. "I will wear a fragment of that plate, in a locket round my neck."[55] Garnett had been told the details of the violence. They assumed his and other friends' interest and were rarely mistaken.

4

They arrived in Holland by train in a thunderstorm, and sailed to Harwich. At 8:30 in the morning of Thursday, June 19, after more than a year abroad, they pulled in to Paddington Station and boarded a train for the Cearne.

Though Frieda went into London to see Robert Garnett on Monday, when the ensuing week brought no overtures from Ernest, she decided to take matters into her own hands: On June 30, a Monday, she stood outside Colet House, an ivy-covered brick building in a quadrant of Saint Paul's, a rose fastened in the lapel of a light summer coat. Thirteen-year-old boys in gray wool pants and blue blazers streamed from the building for the midday break; Monty came running headlong through the dark passageway, several inches taller than when she had last seen him in the back yard at Cowley. He did not recognize her until he had almost bumped into her. "You, you," he stammered, and stopped short, his gray eyes clouded with disbelief.[56] Uncertain what to do, he looked beyond her and saw Lawrence standing uncomfortably at a distance.[57]

Monty was not supposed to leave the grounds alone, and Frieda asked him to tell one of his teachers that his Aunt Maude had come to take him out for half an hour. With Lawrence trailing, they went to a suburban teashop. Frieda ordered a bowl of strawberries and cream, and wept. Monty, sitting sideways to avoid looking straight at her, pulled a large, soiled handkerchief from his pocket and put it in her hand. Searching for conversation, he asked how she made a living. Frieda, probably thinking of *Sons and Lovers*, answered, "I wrote a novel." Monty lit up for the first time. "You know it's a bad lookout," he smiled impishly, with a hint of sarcasm, sounding every inch his father, who had doubtlessly warned his son that bestsellers did not come easily, "you don't make much money by writing." Frieda asked him to meet her the next day on Turnham Green, a seven-acre square in central Chiswick, and to bring Elsa and Barby. "You know I couldn't stand Nottingham and the life any more," she said, bringing the tea to a close. "[Y]ou can't understand things now, but you will later on. I want to be able to see you." Monty was absorbed in drawing her a picture of Colet House. "Shall I ask Papa?" he asked, and began to cry.

She walked him back to Saint Paul's and they toured the grounds.

Frieda gave him half a crown and a letter to read on the way back home, and told him not to tell anyone he had seen her. She left him at the electric tram, which went along the High Road. As she disappeared down the platform, he cried freely and read her letter, carefully putting it out of sight before opening the door of 49 Harvard Road.[58]

5

On clear days the most pleasant way to Saint Paul's from Harvard Road was down Barrowgate Road and Hogarth Lane to the Thames, along the riverside walk to Hammersmith, and up Queen Street and Great Church Lane. The girls walked in the opposite direction to Miss Dollman's, northeast to Bedford Park, a bland, fashionable neighborhood of unpaved roads, immaculate Queen Anne style houses, and spacious, recently planted lawns perfect for croquet, tennis, and lawn bowling.[59] The three children showed up as planned at Turnham Green the following day, July 1, under the shadow of the spire of Christ Church. "Mama, you are back," they cried as they "danced around me in complete delight"—at least as Frieda later remembered it—and asked when she was coming home.

"I can't come back," Frieda said, "you must come to me. We shall have to wait."[60]

Her answer perplexed Elsa and Barby, who still had not been told why she no longer lived with them. When all three children arrived home from school later in the day, disconsolate and agitated, Maude took Monty aside and questioned him sternly. Frightened of her wrath, and upset by Frieda's sudden reappearance, he told her what had happened.[61] Maude waited in silent fury for Ernest to return from Nottingham at the end of the week. On Friday, climbing the stairs to the second floor of the house, she found the letter Frieda had given Monty lying on a step. After carrying it with him since Monday, he had left or dropped it in plain view. When Ernest got back that evening, she presented it to him, and he apparently threatened to shoot Frieda: A letter to Frieda from a woman, perhaps Maude or Lily Kipping, was left on the Garnetts' lawn shortly after, containing an ominous suggestion of "Ernst and pistols," as Lawrence later related to Constance.[62] In any case, it discouraged Frieda from further forays to London for secret meetings with the children, for the time being.

• • •

She roamed the Cearne, fighting with Lawrence. They were loud, taunting arguments whose vehemence shocked Katharine Clayton, Constance's younger sister, who was visiting. Between spats, Lawrence, who had begun to look unwell almost as soon as they had arrived in England, harassed the entire household with the minutiae of assembling stories (many later included in his first collection, *The Prussian Officer and Other Stories*), putting Katharine and her nineteen-year-old son to work typing the manuscripts. David Garnett, home for a weekend, found Lawrence's heartless attitude toward Frieda's children shocking, and took her side. He and Frieda spent long hours talking, daydreaming, and sharing confidences in the surrounding woods; one hot afternoon, she propositioned him, but nothing came of it. Lawrence shared his own confidences with David, complaining to him of Frieda's tryst the year before with Harold Hobson. "Harold is no gentleman," Lawrence remonstrated, a comment that sounded to David as though it had come straight out of a letter of Ernest Weekley's. Roaming the house, he found one of Frieda's cambric handkerchiefs balled up on the floor outside their bedroom door. The coronet was smeared with arterial blood that Lawrence had spat, a sign, David was later to realize, of tuberculosis.[63] On July 9, Frieda and Lawrence set off for Broadstairs, a seaside resort at the tip of Kent.

They stopped in London for less than a day, Lawrence racing from office to office: He spoke with Garnett about engaging J. B. Pinker, a literary agent who had taken an interest in his work; Gerald Duckworth; and Norman Douglas, an Austrian-born writer and former zoologist who was assistant editor of the *English Review*. In the past five and a half weeks *Sons and Lovers* had been reviewed, largely favorably, in the *Standard*, the *Westminster Gazette*, the *Daily Chronicle*, the *Saturday Review*, and elsewhere, and Lawrence was now sought after.[64] It was around noon when he and Frieda, wearing large straw hats, dropped off a review of the German edition of Thomas Mann's *Death in Venice* at 57 Chancery Lane, the office of *Rhythm*—rechristened the *Blue Review* by Mansfield and Murry, because of credit problems. Lawrence's mastery of German literary nuance was, at best, incomplete, and his criticism of Mann's over-reliance on "form" contained strong echoes of Frieda's letter to Garnett just prior to his acceptance of *Sons and Lovers*, suggesting it may have been she, not Lawrence, who read the novella and provided the theme of the review. "The

Soiled Rose" (later retitled "Shades of Spring"), a short story based largely on his relationship with Jessie that he wrote in December 1911, had appeared in the May issue of the *Blue Review*, coinciding with publication of *Sons and Lovers*.

Mansfield, a thin, dark-haired woman with small, pretty features, unflinching, flirtatious "gu-gu" eyes, as Frieda and Lawrence were soon calling them, and an enigmatic smile, sat on the floor beside a huge goldfish bowl in which the fish swam among shells and plants. Thick poufs were strewn on the floor, and there was little, if any, furniture, though the office also served as Mansfield and Murry's apartment. Frieda, relieved to find a reprieve from the usual London man of letters, immediately liked Mansfield's delicacy, wit, glamour, spontaneity, and sense of interior design.[65] Twenty-four years old, the daughter of a wealthy New Zealand businessman, educated in Wellington and at Queen's College, London, she was married, though not to Murry: At twenty, wearing a black suit, she had walked through a ceremony with a shy, polite singing teacher named George Bowden, then left him on their wedding night without consummating the relationship. Three months later, in the fifth month of a pregnancy from a previous lover, she miscarried after being packed off to Germany by her mother, who believed in the purgative power of extended continental tours. In Bad Wörishofen, she met Floryan Sobieniowski, a Polish translator, who gave her translations of Chekhov, which included the story "*Spat' khochetsia*" (Sleepyhead or Sleepy). Her "The-Child-Who-Was-Tired," a brazen theft, was published in the political weekly *New Age*, and made her a literary name at the age of twenty-one. (It was included in her first collection, *In a German Pension*, in December 1911.)[66]

She suffered from incurable gonorrhea, contracted from Sobieniowski. Before meeting Murry, she had had a triangular affair with a schoolteacher and his girlfriend and a brief affair with a Viennese journalist. Her relations with Murry, a ponderous, handsome, ambitious Oxford man whose father was a petty civil servant, were largely asexual. He had contracted gonorrhea separately, in a brothel, but had been cured immediately. He did not know the cause of the chronic dental, arthritic, and other pains Mansfield endured, side effects of the disease.

There were a lot of things he did not know about Mansfield, who was a compulsive liar. He did not know that she had a "wife," as Mansfield called her, Ida Baker, whom she had met at Queen's College.[67] It was a "Boston marriage," asexual, but Ida was devoted to Mansfield and found her life interrupted by the unending slew of Mansfield's medical, financial, and emotional breakdowns. A doctor's daughter, she was now reduced to work as a hair brusher in a beauty salon, partially because of the sums of money she handed out to Mansfield.

Lawrence instantly made a cause of Murry, whom he found boyish and likable: "only a lad of 23. He came of the common people in Peckham," he wrote Constance Garnett.[68] Murry had been living and working with Mansfield since April 1912, when she took him in as a paying boarder at a previous London apartment. The two couples took a bus to Soho for lunch, where they evidently exchanged stories of marital complications. Mansfield was indignant that Ernest refused to let his children see Frieda, and offered to carry messages to them while they were away in Broadstairs.

"The Lawrences," under which name they continued to travel, were anomalous at the seashore. Amid children, striped beach tents, and what Lawrence described as "fat fatherly Jews and their motor-cars," they read novels and kept to themselves.[69] Garnett forwarded more reviews of *Sons and Lovers*, including one from the *Nation*, complaining of the unevenness of the novel—the reviewer did not like the second half—and the tedium of Paul's affairs.[70] Edward Marsh sent Lawrence a check for three pounds for his contribution to *Georgian Poetry* and announced he would be nearby, visiting his friend Herbert Asquith, son of the prime minister. He arrived on Sunday morning, July 20, an unassuming man who looked far more Edwardian than the aesthete his anthology presaged, and took Lawrence and Frieda to tea at the Asquiths', an idiosyncratic house made of old ship's timbers. Lawrence, introducing Frieda as his wife, was immediately attracted to Herbert's wife, Cynthia, granddaughter of the earl of Wemyss, a beautiful woman with flawless, porcelain skin, a soothing smile, and a calm, unhurried approach to life and love: "to be at [my] best with one man," she told a friend, "[I] must see a great many others."[71] Her chubby two-year-old son, John, clung to her loose, heavily embroidered silk clothing.

It was an atmosphere of wealth and privilege to which Frieda, who struck Marsh as animated, robust, and very much the German aristocrat, had no trouble adapting. Lawrence, he thought, looked "terribly ill" beside her. Probably exasperated by Lawrence's fawning attitude to Cynthia, Frieda turned to Marsh and insulted him: She couldn't connect a love of poetry, she told him, with his appearance. Marsh thought the afternoon a "tremendous success."[72]

The "Lawrences" had expected the "Murrys"—as they called them—to show up for tea. "I suppose they hadn't the money for the railway tickets," Marsh suggested when they did not arrive.[73] They had, in fact, bankrupted themselves publishing the final issue of the *Blue Review*, with Lawrence's review of *Death in Venice*. Lawrence, who could be generous to a fault when money came his way, offered the loan of a pound, coaxing them out the following weekend. They took the train with Gordon Campbell, an Irish lawyer with a London practice whose brogue and melancholy dignity appealed to Frieda. At a party on the beach that night, everyone stripped for a swim in the darkness, followed by a supper of beef and tomatoes they roasted in the coals of a campfire. Mansfield told Frieda of chasing Monty all over Saint Paul's the week before to give him notes and money from her, exertions that seem to have inspired a letter from Ernest, invoking the image of Frieda's dead, rotting body. Revolted, Frieda dashed off a letter to Else:

> Ernst's "decayed corpse" still lies in my bones! But there is something to that—For him love is dead and unpleasantly dead . . . I am still like something that whizzes through "Nothingness" . . . outwardly I'm doing well—L, after being *thoroughly* miserable the days here, is recovering—Much to-do is being made over him . . . I too am a "success"—God, it makes so little difference to one, if at the same time one is glad to get away from oneself a little, and luckily we von Richthofens possess the gift of being able to lose ourselves in others. When I compare L. with the others, I see that he possesses his own, inner, independent activity; he is so much more than one at first thinks—But now inwardly to tear myself loose from the children is horrible—the daily contact, it is as when living pieces of flesh are torn from one, luckily I think the children do not feel it *so* much. . . . Enjoy your children thoroughly . . . such love, one accepts it so matter-of-factly, and doesn't realise the value.[74]

Since leaving Nottingham, Frieda had fielded far blacker outpourings from Lawrence than Ernest's invectives, and she detested them equally; but the moral battlefield with Lawrence was clearly, to her, on a higher ground. Lawrence, whatever his failings, had helped her hone a sense of self, and she could not forget the purposelessness and tedium of her years with Ernest: "If you have lived with an artist," she later told a friend, "other men are so *boring*!"[75] It was a justification she invoked throughout her life, with a finality that never quite concealed the pain—even remorse, a feeling she despised—from which it had arisen.

The beach party broke up on Monday morning, and on the train back to London Mansfield began a copy of *Sons and Lovers* that Lawrence had handed out as a parting gift. She was so bowled over that she wrote a thirty-eight-page précis of an intensely autobiographical, thirty-five-chapter *Bildungsroman* the following Saturday.[76] She returned to Saint Paul's, but Monty, who spotted her from inside Colet House, dispatched a schoolmate with a message: "He was not to talk to people who came to the school to see him."[77] On July 28, Ernest, armed with an affidavit sworn by Maude, in which she testified to Frieda's tea with Monty and the meeting with the children on Turnham Green, obtained custody and a restraining order that prevented Frieda from "interfering or attempting to interfere" with the children.[78]

After a brief sweep with Lawrence through London to make connections and sell more of his work,[79] she returned alone to Germany the following week. Lawrence's sister Ada was getting married to a tailor, William Clarke, in Eastwood on August 4, but Frieda could not attend: Lawrence had still not gotten up the courage to tell his elder sister, Emily, about Frieda. He joined Frieda four days later at Jaffe's cottage, which Else had managed to secure for them again. On August 11, her thirty-fourth birthday, Frieda's niece and two nephews surprised her by arriving from Else's through the woods dressed in white, bedecked with flowers, and carrying baskets of apricots, peaches, candy, perfume, and a gift of a harmonica. The children changed into their bathing suits for *Luftbäder*, Peter recited a poem, and Frieda, wearing a Bavarian peasant dress, stood on the veranda and tried playing the harmonica.[80]

Lawrence began an entirely new draft of "The Sisters," and as he built up to a pace of three pages a day, he seemed happy to be relieved of the burden of his manuscript's rocky past, and was full of apologies to Frieda for his treatment of her through the first draft. Garnett had criticized his heroine's abrupt plunge into maturity, and Lawrence, evidently also inspired by Thomas Mann's family saga *Buddenbrooks*, which he had apparently read with Frieda in preparation for his *Blue Review* piece on *Death in Venice*, decided to give Ursula a past—in essence, Frieda's. She spent the second week of September at Else's, and on the seventeenth—the publication day of *Sons and Lovers* in the United States, by a publisher of mixed repute named Mitchell Kennerly—she and Lawrence, who had completed a hundred pages, parted for nine days. Frieda visited her parents and may have gone to Ascona. She seems to have urged Lawrence to accompany her there, but the plans fell apart. Instead he took a steamer across Lake Constance, traveled down the Rhine to Schaffhausen, a city of beer breweries, and walked across Switzerland by himself. In a villa on the Lake of Lucerne, with thoughts of Frieda's Ascona friends evidently on his mind, he pretended to be Otto Gross while having tea with two old ladies and their invalid dog:

> I said I was from Graz; that my father was a doctor in Graz, and that I was walking for my pleasure through the countries of Europe.
>
> I said this because I knew a doctor from Graz who was always wandering about, and because I did not want to be myself, an Englishman. . . . I wanted to be something else.[81]

6

Gross, from whom Frieda had not heard since the spate of letters four years earlier, was being hunted by his father. He now divided his time between Berlin and Ascona, where he was trying to found an open university. He also wanted to launch a monthly journal, *Sigyn*, devoted to psychoanalysis, culture, and the economy, and was publishing essays in the Berlin weekly *Die Aktion*, in which he contended, among other things, that the state was run on a principle of "secondary homosexuality" (as distinguished from primary, or healthy, homosexuality).[82]

His essays enraged Hans, who disinherited Otto in a will largely devoted to proving he was insane: It included affidavits sworn by psychiatrists, and stipulated that Otto should be locked up when Hans died. However, Hans had a change of heart shortly after the will was executed, and, armed with similar affidavits, convinced the Berlin Polizeikommando that his son was a psychopath and had to be institutionalized instantly. Otto was with Richard Oehring, a Berlin writer and Dadaist, when, on November 9, a small cadre of police officers showed up to arrest him. Otto, never at a loss for words, greeted them with the friendly outpouring of a welcome speech and was transported under guard over the border to Troppau, an Austrian insane asylum. An enormous public campaign in Vienna, Berlin, and Munich, which also spread to Paris, led to his release: "Free Otto Gross," read ten thousand leaflets distributed by the Viennese Akademischer Verband für Literatur und Musik (academic society for literature and music); countless journals Otto had influenced or been associated with editorialized against Hans, as did Vienna's liberal newspaper *Neue Freie Presse*. "[D]enounce the unworthy actions of a narrow-minded father (all our fathers are narrow-minded)," wrote the surrealist Blaise Cendrars in an issue of the Munich journal *Revolution* devoted to Otto's cause, "who does not hesitate to shatter the life work of this brilliant son"; Apollinaire denounced Hans in his regular column in *Mercure de France*, calling Otto "the founder of psychoanalysis."[83] The campaign worked, and Otto began analysis with Wilhelm Stekel, a condition of his release. Stekel diagnosed and treated him for neurosis and recommended Otto, strangely enough, to a children's hospital, where he worked briefly until accepting employment at a hospital for epidemic diseases in the town of Vinkovci, eighty-five miles northwest of Belgrade.

After Hans's death in 1915, Otto resumed a way of life described by his friend Franz Jung as "conventional"[84] and was taken up briefly by Kafka, who vividly remembered his law classes at Prague University under Hans. Kafka, who began *The Trial* shortly after reading Otto's *Aktion* essays, rode a train one night from Budapest to Vienna with him and Anton Kuh, a voluble Viennese journalist, and liked Gross immediately, although he—not surprisingly—could not get a word in edgewise. At a party at Max Brod's later in the month, Otto held forth on a new magazine project, *Blätter zur Bekämpfung des Machtwillens* (Journal for the suppression of the will to power). It never got off the ground, and Otto subsequently threw off the shackles of "convention" once again. Like many others, he was finally ruined by the Great War: Found starving in an abandoned Berlin factory warehouse in 1920, he was taken by friends to a sanatorium in Pankow, north of the city. He died on March 13 and was buried in a suburban Jewish cemetery, apparently on the mistaken assumption that his last name indicated he was of Jewish birth. In her memoirs fifteen years later Frieda wrote of him:

> He had been a doctor in the World War, and had died. How he must have suffered! He, who had dreamed of a glorious coming day for all men, saw before him the torn bodies and broken spirits of the young that he had dreamed his dream of happiness for! No wonder he had died, as so many had died with their hopes denied and broken.[85]

7

Rejuvenated by the separation from Lawrence, Frieda waited for him in Milan on Friday, September 26, 1913, with some new clothes and a stack of stationery bearing the von Richthofen coat of arms, which her mother had given her in Baden-Baden. Edgar Jaffe, vacationing in Italy, had promised to scout out a house on the Bay of Lerici, sixty miles southeast of Genoa, where, he may have told Frieda, Fanny Reventlow had vacationed the year before. They took a train to La Spezia, crossed the bay on the local *vaporino*, and were met by Jaffe and his mistress—he and Else had long since dispensed with any pretense of monogamy—in a rowboat. The two couples rounded the headlands to a village called Fiascherino, where Edgar deposited them on the shore and directed them uphill for their first look at a small pink fisherman's house almost hidden by a grove of olive trees. Six days later they moved in. They began seeing a lot of Edgar, who monopolized Frieda, as she wrote Else, with hand-wringing stories of various sums of money being exchanged within the family, and of Selma, who was still dunning Friedrich (the baron's illegitimate son was now a teenager):

> Edgar is here with quite a charming creature, Model von Keller, very nice inwardly, but *why* he gives himself the agony is quite incomprehensible to me—she bores him stiff, because he gives so little of him-

> self; I think she interests me more than him. . . . Please tell me exactly *how much* Papa still has to pay—he told me *1000 M*, if only he wouldn't live so vilely! One doesn't believe him, and Edgar thinks that somehow Selma is behind it and in some way is putting pressure on him—or is it the 16-year-old son. . . . It's a *mess*—and then he pretends that quite undeservedly and without *his* having done anything, the heavens are tormenting him for all his virtues with a Selma! I know you feel sorry for him, but don't let it bother you and if Edgar *has to pay*, that shouldn't matter, he gives you and the children little enough. As soon as I see how things go, I will give you the 200 M which Alfred loaned us. Of course you don't give me another sou.[86]

They were an hour's walk from where Shelley had drowned in his sailboat, "but our position," wrote Lawrence, who also acquired a boat, "is a million times prettier."[87] Frieda, conscious of both his poor swimming and lack of strength, watched from the shore as he paddled out into the choppy water. "If you can't be a real poet," she screamed over the surf, "you'll drown like one, anyhow."[88] Mitchell Kennerley sent a copy of the American edition of *Sons and Lovers* and a piece from the *New York Times Book Review* that praised its "rare excellence."[89] They hired a maid and ordered twenty-five liters of Ligurian wine—stout bottles wrapped in rush—and, after much negotiation and confusion, a piano, which arrived by rowboat. Lawrence apologized for the crested stationery in letters to friends through the fall.

8

On October 18, Sir Samuel Thomas Evans convened a preliminary divorce hearing at the Royal Courts of Justice on the Strand in London. Ernest gave evidence, which included Lawrence's letter of the previous May, and Sir Samuel pronounced a decree nisi, an effective, though not final, end to the marriage. Neither Frieda nor Lawrence was represented. Ernest, who had made every effort to keep the story out of the papers, was mortified to discover Lawrence's letter, reprinted in full, on the front page of three widely circulated London newspapers, among them the penny *News of the World.* TO LIVE HER OWN LIFE. LADY LEAVES HER HUSBAND AND JOINS AUTHOR, read the Sunday morning special edition of October 19, which noted: "Petitioner tried to get his wife to return to him, but failed."[90] The Sunday

Times reduced the story to a modest paragraph in its Law Courts columns.[91] ARE WE NOT SIMPLE MEN? queried the *Daily Mail* the following Monday, in a quarter-column explication of the case, which ran between stories of a street brawl between a produce man and a bus driver, and a destitute woman whose son stole hotel bedsheets for her to sell.[92] Lawrence, still not a household name despite the reviews of *Sons and Lovers*—the book was not in wide circulation because many librarians and booksellers objected to its content—was identified as "Mr. B.[*sic*] H. Lawrence, described as being an author."[93] In November he was charged with Ernest's divorce costs, just over £144.[94] Lacking the money, he ignored the bill. "We live like princes," Frieda wrote Cynthia Asquith, "on £8 a month!"[95] They had a little over £50 in the bank.

Intensely happy to be back in Italy, they became social for the first time and, in their best clothes—Lawrence in a black broadcloth suit and black patent leather boots—attended a local wedding the morning of November 29. It was a daylong feast that began with an immense breakfast after a 7:30 A.M. religious service interrupted by the constant clacking of *zoccoli*—homemade wooden children's sandals—on the floor of the church. The wedding party, sweating in the heat, walked several miles up paths littered with goat droppings and down into the village of Ameglia for a civil ceremony, at which Lawrence served as witness, then back to the village of Tellaro—a six-hour round-trip. A swarm of children followed the bride, who, despite the terrain, was dressed in a flowing silk gown and tossed them candy from an immense bag.

Lawrence and Frieda were enjoying themselves thoroughly when four foppish-looking Englishmen arrived. They were three of the Georgian poets he had written about in *Rhythm*, accompanied by a neighboring Sunday painter and expatriate, Aubrey Waterfield, who presided with his wife, Lina Waterfield, a journalist, in a rented castle near the marble quarries of Carrara, ten miles inland. Lawrence, swilling Ligurian wine and mentally taking notes, was unhappy to break ranks from the feast—freshly killed fowl and octopus with arms half a yard long, brought in from the sea by Ezechiele Azzarini, the groom—to rub elbows with the poets.[96] He was also depressed that Ezechiele did not live up to his ideas of romance: "Yes—it's expected! What can you do?" he replied, when Lawrence took him aside for a man-to-man talk to learn his feelings about marriage.[97] Aubrey Waterfield invited him and Frieda to the castle for a visit.

They spent a weekend there shortly before Christmas. The Waterfields were a high-minded couple with an aesthetic dislike of the "filth" of Tellaro, and had once watched in amazed disgust as villagers stuffed a new mattress with horsehair in the piazza. Lina, finally unable to stomach the sight, had picked up her skirts and raced down a narrow street to wait for Aubrey. She was startled by the embroidered crepe blouse and peasant dress in which Frieda arrived (buttoned at the bodice, it "showed off her buxom figure to full advantage") and the pair of suede lace-up boots she sported over white woolen tights—Bavarian folk dress. Aubrey took Frieda aside, and they talked at length about temperament, character, her children, and Lawrence. Frieda boasted that she was "as responsible for his writing as he is himself"—a comment that left Aubrey at a loss for words, though he found an interpretation later: "[S]he only does it to blind herself for deserting the children."[98]

The conclusion that Frieda gave up her children only to mother Lawrence was one that friends, acquaintances, and even those who had never met them could not seem to resist drawing. Further advanced in England by the advent of British psychoanalysis, it still had little meaning for Frieda, who, not surprisingly, mistrusted the neatness of this particular intellectual conceit. Lawrence "needed" her, she was given to saying, but the need, at least during this period of their romance, was secondary to the vividness and spontaneity of their love. The romance of being emotional outlaws also allowed no concessions either to such reductions or to conventional morality, whatever the cost.

For Christmas she invited their maid and her family of fifteen, and they stood around the piano and sang folk songs. Frieda, suffering the perennial longing for the marzipan evenings of her childhood, also mourned the loss of her children:

> It got me from time to time like an illness. We had trespassed the laws of men, if not God, and you have to pay. Lawrence and I paid in full. . . . it's an eternal human law: too much happiness isn't allowed us mere mortals. And I and Lawrence seemed at times to surpass the measure of human bliss. He could be so deeply and richly happy, that young Lawrence that I have known.[99]

Donaueschingen, Germany (circa 1850), birthplace of Frieda's mother, Anna Marquier. *(Fürstlich Fürstenbergisches Archiv/Georg Goerlipp)*

Artist's rendering of Anna presenting a bouquet of roses to Kaiser Wilhelm I at Council Hall, Constance, Germany, 1871. *(Pressebild-Archiv [Constance]/Heinz Finke)*

Second lieutenant Friedrich von Richthofen, early 1871. To Frieda as a child, he was "perfection on earth." *(Ian Weekley)*

Studio portrait, with painted backdrop, of Frieda (*left*, with doll carriage) and her older sister, Else. The deep-set, almost Slavic eyes and wide cheekbones that made her a beauty in her teens and twenties are just visible beneath the baby fat. *(Photography Collection, Harry Ransom Humanities Research Center, University of Texas at Austin [HRC])*

Frieda at fifteen. After marrying D. H. Lawrence, on the back of the photo she wrote, "*Rainbow*. Ursula," indicating her role as Lawrence's model for the character in his novel. *(W. Schneider/H. Reuther & Cie Nachf.; HRC)*

Julie *(left)* and Camilla Blas, sisters and the friends and former teachers of Anna von Richthofen. Gifted educators with an international reputation, they found Frieda's incorrigibility a challenge. *Right:* Eichberghaus, the Blases' home in the Freiburg suburb of Littenweiler, where Frieda lived in the fall and winter of 1896–97. *(Marianne Pitsch, Fritz Schaffer)*

Johanna von Richthofen, Frieda's younger sister, "Nusch" to the family, dressed for a ball at the Royal Castle, Berlin, 1898. *(E. Bieber/HRC)*

Frieda as a teenager. *(HRC)*

Frieda *(center)*, Else *(left)*, and Nusch. Frieda later reconfigured the triumvirate with her two closest friends in New Mexico. *(Used with the permission of Barbara Barr)*

Studio portrait, *right to left:* Frieda; her first husband, Ernest Weekley, a British linguist and French teacher; and his parents, Agnes and Charles, at the time of Frieda's engagement trip to London. *(Killick & Abbot Rosslyn Hill Studios, Hampstead/Nottingham County Library)*

The Mikado Café *(right)* became (along with Sherwood Forest) one of Frieda's refuges during her marriage to Ernest. *(Nottingham County Library)*

Frieda at twenty-eight, shortly after the beginning of a brief but passionate affair in Munich with Otto Gross, an Austrian psychoanalyst and free-love advocate. "Restless . . . ," she wrote on the back when she sent Gross this studio portrait. *(L. Peudy, F.R.S.P., Nottingham/HRC)*

Otto Gross *(second from left)* and friends, 1914 or 1915. *(Courtesy Harald Szeeman and Martin Green)*

Fiftieth wedding anniversary of Agnes and Charles Weekley, 1911. The following year, Frieda made her first trip to Europe with Lawrence; she never returned to her family. Her daughters are seated, front: Elsa, nine *(right)*, and Barby, seven *(center)*, with their brother, Monty, 11 *(left)*. *Middle row, left to right:* Maude Weekley, the children's surrogate mother after Frieda's departure; Agnes; Charles; Norah, a cousin of the Weekley children; the cigarette-loving Hannah McCowen, "Aunt Daisy." *Back row:* Gert, Ted, Lucy, Ernest, Frieda, Marjorie (Norah's sister), George, and Kit Weekley. *(Courtesy of Barbara Barr)*

Ida Wilhelmy, the Weekleys' German nanny, with *(left to right)* Barby, Monty, and Elsa, in 1908 or 1909. *(University of Nottingham Library)*

Lawrence in a photo taken sometime within a year of his meeting Frieda. *(University of Nottingham Library)*

Frieda and Lawrence's wedding day, July 13, 1914, with witnesses Katherine Mansfield and John Middleton Murry. *(HRC)*

Barby and Ernest, years after he divorced Frieda. *(British Library)*

9

Lawrence struggled with "The Sisters"—now renamed "The Wedding Ring"—through the remainder of the winter. Frieda took to sitting on a hammock in the yard, and invited Else to visit. "Sometimes in the night," she confided to her sister, "I go out and lie down here, in the open air, because I feel I am so awfully sad, and there is such a horrible feeling in my inside, I just feel as if I should burst."[100]

Lawrence's novel became very long, and the character of Ella grew into an unsuccessful amalgam of Frieda and Louie. He delivered 340 pages, the first part, to Garnett, who told him that, among other problems, it was unbelievable and did not have enough vivid scenes. Lawrence bluntly answered that he was bored with writing about the lower middle classes, and that "manners and circumstances and scenes dont interest me any more."[101] The only thing he and Garnett could agree about was that Frieda's inattention was partially to blame for the manuscript's failure, which Garnett expressed in a letter to Frieda. "If he denies my life and suffering," she replied, with a rare succinctness that summed up much of their eternal quarrel, "I deny his art."[102]

She and Lawrence were also beginning to suspect that Garnett was too old fashioned, steeped in the realism of the nineteenth century, and trying to pigeonhole Lawrence into writing another *Sons and Lovers*, which, Frieda told Garnett, she did not even like that much any more. "Miriam and Clara and Pauls love affairs," she had decided, shortly after the American edition had been published, "weren't worth writing about."[103] Now she went further:

> ["The Wedding Ring"] is a failure but you must feel something at the back of it struggling, trying to come out—You see I dont really believe in *Sons and Lovers* it feels as if there were nothing *behind* all those happenings as if there were no "Hinterland der Seele" only intensely felt fugitive things—I who am a believer though I dont know in what, to me it seems an irreligious book—It does not seem the deepest and last thing said, if for instance a man loves in a book the pretty curl in the neck of "her," if he loves it ever so intensely and beautifully, there is something behind that curl, *more* than that curl, there is *she*, the living, striving *she*. . . . I am going to throw my self into the novel now and you will see what a "gioia" it will be.[104]

She plunged in and, possibly thinking of Plato or W. H. Davies, the Welsh poet they had been reading, soon renamed it *The Rainbow*.[105]

The divorce became final on April 27, 1914, when the High Court pronounced a decree absolute,[106] leaving Frieda free to remarry. She was ambivalent, but Lawrence believed firmly in the institution. Ernest had not conceded anything on the issue of children's visits, and, free to write her, "plays marionette Moses," as Lawrence confided to Middleton Murry, "then John Halifax Gentleman, then Othello, then a Maupassant hero tracking down his victims, one stock piece after another with amazing energy."[107] He and Frieda made plans to marry in London in June.[108]

In late March the British novelist Ivy Low, the twenty-four-year-old daughter of London intellectuals and the niece of Barbara Low, a Freudian analyst, wrote Lawrence one of his first truly ecstatic fan letters. She had found *Sons and Lovers* in her mother's library earlier that month and read it in one sitting. "This is a book about the Oedipus complex!" she exclaimed to a friend afterward, overcome by Lawrence's treatment of its theme, and outraged by a two-part piece in the *Times Literary Supplement* by Henry James, who had described Lawrence as "[hanging] in the dusty rear" of "The Younger Generation," among whom James included Conrad, Galsworthy, Wells, and Arnold Bennett.[109] Lawrence invited her to Italy on von Richthofen family paper: "Don't let the crest upset you," he wrote in April, drawing a line through it, "my wife's father was a baron, and we're just using up old note paper."[110] She arrived several weeks later. Expecting to dress for dinner, she had borrowed a tailored wardrobe and an embroidered peasant blouse current among London intellectuals, which got on Frieda's nerves. Lawrence, thrilled to have a vivacious, straightforward Englishwoman around the house, flirted with her relentlessly, then began finding her faults "one by one, and quite a few that no one else ever discovered," as she later remembered.[111] His vehement disapproval and Frieda's impatience soon pervaded the house. Ivy left for London in mid-June thoroughly demoralized. She did not publish a novel again for more than fifteen years.

Frieda and Lawrence left Italy soon after, on June 8, she stopping off to see her parents; Lawrence took the long way, walking back over Switzerland with a British engineer. They met in Heidelberg in the middle of the month, and stayed a week with Alfred Weber, captive audience to his compulsive monologues on political economics.[112] They arrived in London June 25 and moved in to their Irish friend Gordon Campbell's apartment, and the next day Frieda headed for Chiswick. Ernest had concealed their address from her, and she walked the streets until she saw the red drapes from Cowley hanging in the front window of 49 Harvard Road, let herself in the back door, which was unlocked, and walked upstairs to the nursery.

The children were eating dinner with Maude and their grandmother. A brief stunned silence followed until Maude, pale and livid, ordered Frieda to leave. She refused, and Agnes stormed her and pushed her out the door, screaming for her to get out. The children, caught up in the frenzy, joined in, shouting at her to go away. "[T]he bond we had with our mother had completely withered," Barby later recalled. "She was an unreal woman to us by then. Something rather strange and even a little horrifying."[113] Frieda, shocked and humiliated, left the house.[114] It had been just under a year since the meeting on Turnham Green. Sometime during the following three weeks, when she had gotten over the sting of the encounter, she waited outside Miss Dollman's one morning and managed to talk with Elsa and Barby for a few minutes before their first class. "When are you coming back?" Barby asked her.

"No more," Frieda replied.[115] The girls still did not understand. When they got home they told Maude that they had seen their mother. They knew it would enrage her but were not sure why. Maude told them they were never to walk to school alone any more. She dispatched their Aunt Kit to accompany them, and told them to run in the other direction if they saw Frieda again. On July 13 Frieda and Lawrence, wearing their straw hats, Lawrence in a three-piece summer-wool suit, Frieda in a long, loose dress and a waist-length jacket held together at the waist with a scarf, took a cab to the Kensington Registry Office with Campbell, Mansfield, and Murry early in the morning. On the way Lawrence stopped the car and ran into a jewelry store to buy a wedding ring. Frieda, who still wore her old wedding ring, took it off and gave it to Mansfield.[116] It was a short, impersonal ceremony, with their friends as witnesses. They took snapshots afterward in Campbell's back yard, his wet towels hanging from a clothesline above their heads.

The next day Frieda went to Bedford Park to intercept Elsa and Barby on their way to Miss Dollman's. She was standing in front of the building, smiling uncertainly, when they arrived with Kit. Like the rest of the adults in the family, including Ernest, Kit was afraid of Maude, and never hesitated to obey her orders. Frieda's implacable figure and smile also filled her with a desire to avenge her brother. "Run, children, run!" she shrieked to the girls at the top of her thin voice. Elsa and Barby scampered obediently toward the building, clutching their hats and schoolbags in their hands, Kit laboring behind them. Barby could not resist looking back, and saw Frieda's face transformed by bewilderment, but the smile still in place, as though, Barby later recalled, she did not want to leave them with a bad memory.[117]

9

"Don't You Know Me? I'm Frieda"

I

Frieda and Lawrence were flattered and irked by the reputation that had preceded them to London. Ivy Low, on her return from Italy, had been telling friends, family, and a widening circle of fashionable and aspiring writers about the intimidating volatility of this odd relationship—Lawrence's genius, Frieda's peasant clothes, the carnival atmosphere of their love for each other. He was becoming famous, and they were fun to be with and in great demand, but few had any real idea of what to expect, or just how trying they could be. Lawrence was usually spared; Frieda became the butt of gossip among a coterie of litterateurs determined to keep Lawrence to themselves. Catherine Jackson, a Scottish divorcée who had reviewed *The White Peacock* for the *Glasgow Herald* three years before, invited them to tea in Hampstead late in June and had one of the milder reactions to Frieda. Expecting a Junker in a dirndl skirt and embroidered bodice, she was disappointed by her large formal hat, stern checked suit, and straightforward vigor. "[S]he struck me," Jackson wrote, "as being a typical German *Frau*." Lawrence was unlike anyone she had ever met:

hair the color of dust, a sweet mouth, a brisk, fussy manner, and a stream of speech with which he directed conversations like a schoolmaster following a rigid syllabus.[1]

The Murrys were not doing well. Living in rooms they had taken after losing the *Blue Review* office the previous year and enduring an unsuccessful stay in Paris, both had suffered attacks of pleurisy, Mansfield's exacerbated by an accelerated heartbeat. They recovered lying on a single mattress on the floor. Mansfield was mortified by the dirty staircase Frieda and Lawrence had to ascend to get to the apartment, and there were not enough chairs to go around for a dinner party. A happy presence in the dumpy lodgings at first, the Lawrences quickly became a source of friction. Frieda had gotten her divorce, for one thing—Mansfield's husband had gone to America without granting one—and in a single week, Lawrence realized the success that had eluded them since Mansfield's entrée into the literary world more than five years earlier: He engaged J. B. Pinker as his literary agent, accepted an offer of three hundred pounds for *The Rainbow* from the publishing house of Methuen (which had not seen the manuscript), and was commissioned by the small house of James Nisbet and Co. to write a short study of Thomas Hardy. Murry was working on *Still Life*, a novel that was going nowhere, and existed largely on Mansfield's monthly allowance of ten pounds, supplemented very occasionally with his small checks for free-lance art criticism from the *Westminster Gazette*. She had been auditioning for work as an actress. Embarrassed into a screaming fight after the Lawrences left one evening, they moved again. Their new apartment in Chelsea was bug-infested, and they found themselves fighting a losing battle, relying on a homemade repellent of paraffin and sulfur that made the place stink.[2]

With money advanced out of pocket by Pinker, the Lawrences bought new clothes and began accepting formal dinner invitations. Over a meal at H. G. Wells's, Murry, a fussy dresser, was outraged by the awkwardness with which Lawrence's dress suit hung on his thin frame, and inwardly cursed Frieda for the breach in taste and etiquette. Prematurely balding, and secretly relying on a snake-oil remedy for hair growth, he was unaware that he was himself regarded as something of a "book reviewer" and hack journalist by the upper strata at such soirees, many of whom vastly preferred Mansfield's company and talents to his.

Frieda was not invited to a large, poets-only dinner thrown by the millionaire American poet Amy Lowell for Lawrence, Hueffer, Pound, the sculptor Henri Gaudier-Brzeska, and the American poet H. D. and her husband, Richard Aldington; everyone but Lawrence had been represented in *Des Imagistes*, an anthology published on both sides of the Atlantic earlier in the year.[3] Lowell, who had sailed to London shortly before with a custom-made maroon limousine on board, lived in a capacious suite at the Berkeley Hotel, with casement windows opening onto Piccadilly and Green Park. The rooms were graced by long mirrors of etched, beveled glass, but, self-conscious about her weight, Lowell had them all draped in fabric. Lawrence made something of an entrance, casting a momentary pall with news he had gotten over lunch from Edward Marsh (soon to be Sir Edward Marsh)—probably secondhand from Winston Churchill: England was on the brink of entering the war, precipitated two days earlier by the assassination in Sarajevo of Austria's Archduke Franz Ferdinand. Such subjects as European alliances and neutrality treaties were quickly pushed aside, however, for readings of French poetry and a debate about imagism, which quickly gave way to some acid repartee between Pound and Lowell. They despised each other (Pound loved to refer to imagism as "Amygism") and were vying for Lawrence, whom both considered one of the great contemporary poets. Lawrence, still newly enough arrived back in London to appreciate such literary waftings, took it all in with great interest, though his suspicion of literary trends, manifestos, and backstabbings kept him from taking sides. He was very much taken with H. D., a tall, stooping, beautiful bisexual and former girlfriend of Pound's, who was achieving her first success. The daughter of an eccentric astronomer, she had never been outside the Pennsylvania cities of Bethlehem and Upper Darby until her move to London three years earlier, at the age of twenty-five. She was pregnant but not yet aware of it. "Mrs. Aldington has a few good poems," Lawrence wrote the next day to Harriet Monroe, the American editor of the journal *Poetry*, who had recently accepted six of his poems.[4] "He liked her flower poems," H. D. wrote in *Bid Me to Live*, a *roman à clef* begun six years later:

> He had particularly liked the blue iris-poem. . . . Matrix to jewel, he had flamed around her, he was red-hot lava; then somehow he

> seemed to have projected her out, so that she was cool, cold, seated there. He was burnt out too, and white, but there was no dark flame now, none of his dark-god, unless he were Dis of the under-world, the husband of Persephone. Yes, he was her husband.[5]

Lawrence was more friendly to the vorticism of Wyndham Lewis, to whom Pound introduced him.[6] The two poets had just published the first issue of *Blast*, a boldly designed, oversize journal that jibed with Lawrence's appreciation for Emilio Marinetti and the other Italian futurists, in whom he found something akin to the anti-realist, anti-intellectual spirit of *The Rainbow*. Lawrence's novel, despite the concessions to Garnett, in some respects strayed further than ever, in its present form, from Garnett's suggestion that he create recognizable, traditional scenes, dialogue, and characters; increasingly, it reflected his and Frieda's inner lives. Frieda's impatience with the intellectual bias and machinery of the love affairs of *Sons and Lovers*, and with the book's accretions of realistic detail, were having an effect on Lawrence. "I like [futurism] because it is the applying to emotions of the purging of the old forms and sentimentalities," he wrote to a friend. Lawrence's dictum for artistic revivification, however, was "to make it more the joint work of man and woman. I think *the* one thing to do, is for men to have courage to draw nearer to women, expose themselves to them, and be altered by them."[7]

For the moment, though, he left Frieda behind in London to deal with her children while he set off for the lakes and moors of Westmorland in the Lake District. Among his three male companions was a Russian Jew named Samuel Solomonovich Koteliansky, a morose, hopelessly romantic political refugee and translator who had come to England four years before on an economics scholarship from Kiev University. Lawrence liked his orderliness, impeccable manners, love of ceremony over tea, white shirts with colorfully embroidered neckbands, and frizzy hair, which rose a good three inches straight up. Kot, as friends called him, had a sturdy ego and an aptitude for difficult people, and gave Lawrence a feeling of timelessness, well-being, and unself-consciousness. As they hiked past fields of gorse, he sang a version of Psalm 33 in Hebrew, "*Ranenu Sadekim b'Adonai*"[8] (Rejoice in the Lord, O ye righteous); Lawrence made a crown of lilies from a pond on a hill, danced in the rain, which fell almost continually, and dreamed of founding a communal utopian community, which he called Rananim, after the song.

His epiphany was shattered when he descended to the industrial town of Barrow-in-Furness on August 5. England had declared war on Germany the day before, following the German invasion of Luxembourg and Belgium, a violation of neutrality laws. "When you get at 'em, Clem, let 'em have it," he overheard a woman shout to her doughboy boyfriend at the Barrow station, as a line of cars marked "War" pulled out.[9] There were few trains available to civilians, and Lawrence began walking down the coast to Frieda, eventually hitching a ride in a fishing boat.

2

War came as a great inconvenience to the Lawrences. Accustomed to traveling and borrowing at will, they soon found themselves unable to leave the country, and they could get no help from Nusch, Else, Edgar, Alfred Weber, or Frieda's mother, who had also begun supplying them with occasional gifts of cash, apparently not long after Frieda had first visited her in Baden-Baden.[10] It quickly became difficult to get any mail at all through to her family, and they were forced to communicate through a safe address in Switzerland, probably Friedel Gross's in Ascona. Else had a different view of the war than did Frieda and Edgar, both pacifists. In her living room hung a large photograph of Paul von Hindenburg, the German field marshal and future president, and she lamented that neither of her sons was old enough to fight.[11] Frieda annoyed their more militaristic friends with her exultations that Monty was only fourteen.

On August 8 *The Rainbow* was rejected by Methuen (which, nevertheless, would eventually publish the book) with a euphemistic reference to its erotic passages and aimlessness. Pinker delivered the bad news, which precipitated an abrupt reconsideration of finances and a plan to rent a cheap cottage in the country. London was too expensive, even if they were not paying rent, and Gordon Campbell's wife, Beatrice, who had gone to Ireland for the summer to deliver her first baby, was soon returning, which meant they could not stay in his house much longer.

Frieda's Germanness also made London an uncomfortable proposition. The Home Office had been amassing a file on her, apparently dating from before her marriage to Lawrence, and she soon found herself treated by many of his friends less as a nuisance than as a foreign enemy. "I felt helpless and an outcast," she later wrote, "and only a burden and a difficulty for Lawrence. I, the Hunwife in a foreign country!"[12] At a dinner party at Edward Garnett's London pied-à-terre, a tiny apartment reached by a narrow staircase, Frieda complained of the hypocrisy of their friends to H. G. Newth, a zoology lecturer at the Imperial College of Science, where David was working toward a botany degree. As she and Lawrence were descending the stairs at midnight, Newth, probably drunk and spoiling for provocation, shouted "*Auf wiedersehen, gnädige Baronin* [Goodbye, gracious baroness]" in a hyper-exaggerated accent. The downstairs tenants reported Garnett to the police, who showed up several days later, entered without a search warrant, asked how many Germans lived in the apartment, and returned twice during the next two weeks.[13]

Lawrence was still attracting patrons, among them Lady Ottoline Morrell, half-sister of the sixth duke of Portland and daughter of Lieutenant General Arthur Cavendish-Bentinck and his second wife, Lady Bolsover. Raised in Welbeck Abbey in Nottinghamshire, she came of a long line of statesmen, scientists, and politicians, but she found their milieu, tastes, and colonial politics—if not their money—repugnant. In defiance she married a Liberal member of parliament, Philip Morrell, and moved to bohemian splendor in a large Bloomsbury house, where her parties and Thursday at-homes became legendary. It was a passionless marriage, however, and her generosity was largely mocked by her guests. Given to wearing antique dresses of satin and silk and eighteenth-century shepherdess's shawls, she was well known in the neighborhood: On a walk with Virginia and Leonard Woolf, shepherding her many Pekingese on separate leashes in every color of the rainbow, a group of laborers once whooped and whistled uncontrollably when she drew into sight.[14]

She had had two friends and Bertrand Russell, the eminent Cambridge mathematician, to dinner one night in the spring of 1911. The other guests departed early, and Russell, whom she had entertained before but did not know well, suddenly told her that he loved her, demanded that she end her marriage, and explained that he was going to leave his wife, Alys, who had maintained a frigid sexual abstinence for nine years running. Despite a history of affairs, Ottoline was repulsed by sex (*volupté*, she called it) and neither physically attracted to Russell nor prepared to leave Philip. Russell's mind intrigued her powerfully, however, and only her reluctance and a persistent gum infection of Russell's prevented a tryst.

He left for Paris soon after, and a succession of urgent love letters arrived. The affair began in earnest after a few false starts; within six months Alys had agreed to a quiet separation. Russell, equipped with his bicycle, books, a desk, a table, linens, and some silverware Alys consented to let him have, rented a small, badly lit apartment two minutes' walk from the Morrells'. Ottoline, put off by its dinginess, refurbished it with a few runs through Chelsea antique shops. Their earliest rendezvous followed a complicated schedule, based largely on Philip's immutable habit of walking the dogs just after dinner each evening, but this pretense was dropped when, eventually, Philip condoned the affair. "My life before 1910 and my life after 1914 were as sharply separated as Faust's life before and after he met Mephistopheles," Russell later wrote. "I underwent a process of rejuvenation, inaugurated by Ottoline Morrell."[15]

Ottoline heard from David Garnett that Lawrence and Frieda were in London, and invited them in mid-August. It was a hot, humid day, and her hallway was saturated with the smell of musk, potpourri, incense, orris root, and rotting oranges stuck with cloves. In the foyer the Pekingese wheezed and clicked their nails across the floor. Ottoline was tall, big boned, and enormously attractive, with reddish hair (much later, hennaed so heavily it turned purple) and penetrating eyes, though she also tended to over-apply makeup, which accentuated her long face and prominent features. Suffering from chronic rheumatism, arthritis, and fatigue, she had a drawn-out way of talking and a stilted gait, which Frieda and her other guests assumed were affectations.

"Oh dear," Frieda later wrote, "we were asked to lunch by a few lion huntresses and the human being in me felt only insulted. You were fed more or less well, you sat next to somebody whose name had also been printed in the papers, the hostess didn't know who or what you were, thought you were somebody else, and wanted to shoo you away after you were fed like chickens that had become a nuisance."[16]

3

In between dinners and teas the Lawrences and Murrys stood in London train stations, watching soldiers depart. Frieda wept openly, shocked into childhood garrison memories by the sight of wives and girlfriends seeing them off. "Nationality was just an accident and here was grief," she later wrote. "Lawrence was ashamed of my tears. He himself was bewildered and lost, became abstract and mental, and couldn't feel any more. I, who had been brought up with all the 'big-drumming' of German militarism, I was scared."[17] Before the end of August, both couples had fled London, the Murrys for their annual *ferragosto*, to Cornwall, the Lawrences to a former farm laborer's cottage near Chesham, a Buckinghamshire village an hour outside London. The rent for the house was six shillings a week. It was situated beside a grove of apple and elm trees, had no water closet, and was a walk of three and a half miles from the train station. "Out of sheer rage" about their reduced situation and the war, Lawrence wrote Pinker, "I've begun my book about Thomas Hardy."[18] The only people they knew within walking distance were the novelist Gilbert Cannan, whom Henry James had also ranked above Lawrence in appraising the younger generation, and his wife, Mary Ansell, an out-of-work actress and the former wife of James Barrie. Cannan, who religiously wrote exactly a thousand words each morning, was working on a *roman à clef*, *Mendel*, that soon featured a Frieda-like character named Nelly Oliver, a pushy, stupid artist's mistress everyone learns to hate.

> Mendel disliked her, though he tried hard to persuade himself that she was charming. He was baffled by the solemnity with which Logan [Lawrence] was taking her, for she seemed to him the type made for occasional solace and not for companionship. Exploring her with his mind and instinct, she seemed to him soft and pulpy, not unlike an orange, and if she and Logan were to set up a common life, then he would be like a pip indeed. . . . How could he explain to her the nature of genius? Can you explain the night to an insect that lives but an hour in the morning? . . . She . . . was loud and shrill and triumphant, continually setting Mendel's teeth on edge, for the purity of his instinct was disgusted by the blurring and swamping of life by any emotion, and the quality of hers was not such as to win indulgence.[19]

The character of Mendel was based on the Cannans' longtime houseguest Mark Gertler, a young painter from the prestigious Slade School of Art, who was using this time in the country to recover from an unrequited love for a fellow painter. Raised among Jewish immigrants in London's East End, he was boyish, talented, and compelling. The Lawrences immediately liked his disheveled good looks and brilliant conversation. Frieda, with great relish and an exaggerated roll of the *r*, called him "Gairrrtler."[20] Only thirty-five, she had already begun a lifelong habit of "collecting" young people, particularly young men, on whose opinions and careers she invariably lavished huge generosity of spirit.

Gertler was a friend of Marsh, who supported the war and believed that an innate hatred, not nationalistic aims, polarized Germany and the Allies. After hearing this from Gertler, Frieda dashed off a letter, of a sort that was to become typical for her, and which made her few friends:

> This abstract hate of a fairytale German ogre (they used of Napoleon to say that he ate little children for breakfast,) it's mostly an artificial thing—Also in the Boer war they used to my horror tell ghastly stories of British cruelty in Germany. . . . I hate the glorification of war . . . I used to think war so glorious my father such a hero with his iron cross and his hand that a bullet had torn—But I know now, that there are finer and truer things to live and die for—I do think *my* lot the sinners—But they will learn their lesson—So will the English, they will have to alter their stiffness in attitude as we our mechanical ideal—You *are* not to hate the Germans.[21]

Marsh never replied.

Buckinghamshire was a lonely, hostile place after London. Frieda was suspected by local authorities: A policeman popped up from behind a hedge one day when she and Lawrence were picking blackberries for jam, and they were accused of poisoning the crop. Frieda began translating *The Widowing of Mrs. Holroyd*, a dialect play, based loosely on the life of a Midlands aunt, that Lawrence had begun in 1909 and revised in 1913,[22] then withdrew into a book on Christian symbolism. Houseguests were too few and short-lived to relieve the tedium much. Amy Lowell arrived in her limousine with a uniformed driver, was distressed by the dampness and poverty, and left the same day.

Lawrence developed bronchitis and cultivated his first beard, which grew in a brighter shade of red than his hair. He liked its warmth, he said, and the fact that it concealed his face, which had a tendency to become dramatically thin and hollow with every fresh pulmonary illness. He seemed to suffer ailments and symptoms, from pneumonia to spitting of small amounts of blood, with increasing regularity, though "I have had bronchitis," as he was later to say, "since I was a fortnight old."[23] The contrast with Frieda, whose robust health manifested itself with an extra inch at the waistline per annum, was striking. His study of Hardy, which he wrote quickly, contained only two chapters on the novels; the rest was devoted to Lawrence's own philosophy, with chapter-length digressions on anarchy, individualism, and the nature of women and men. Bertram Christian, the director of James Nisbet and Co., rejected it as not being about its subject.

The Murrys, wandering aimlessly from Cornwall to Kent and elsewhere, visited in mid-October, and Lawrence and Frieda, by now desperate for friends, persuaded them to stay. While Frieda and Mansfield shared confidences (Mansfield, in an unusually loquacious mood, seems to have offered Frieda the details of her history of lesbian affairs), Murry rode his bicycle around the countryside house hunting—he had halfheartedly tried to enlist in the war by joining a bicycle corps in September, then reconsidered and got a doctor's dispensation. He found a cottage three miles away, across stinking cabbage fields, and he and Lawrence began painting and plastering, Murry at a sluggish pace that infuriated Lawrence. "Get it *done*!" he screamed shrilly at him one day, grabbing the paintbrush out of his hand.[24] His manner with Murry veered from utter impatience—he lectured him about manliness and Oedipus—to solicitude and confessional complaints about his sex life with Frieda. She disliked sodomy, he bemoaned one day, and they were forced to endure a "dual 'mortification' "—it is not clear what was meant by that—when she did not want to have sex. Such confessions aroused the sympathy of Murry, who had begun actively to dislike Frieda:

> F. accuses him of taking her "as a dog does a bitch." . . . Sincerely I do not believe she loves *him* at all. She is in love with the idea of him

> as a famous and brilliant novelist—and that's all. And the idea that she should have been allowed to tyrannize over him with her damnably false "love" for her children is utterly repulsive to me. . . . She is stupid in any case, and stupid assertiveness is hard enough to bear.[25]

Murry, who limited his own confidences to oblique references to a lack of sex with Mansfield, was advised by Lawrence to grow up, take charge, and be more of a man. Back at home, Murry told Mansfield he wanted a dominant woman who would "keep him."[26] By the time the Murrys had made their cottage habitable, the shifting alliances between the two couples had become unpredictable, with frequent nasty exchanges. Two days after the Murrys had arrived, Lawrence had received fifty pounds from the Royal Literary Fund, a charitable organization that sponsored writers. The grant was made on the strength of letters of endorsement from Marsh, Cannan, and others; an application that cited "The War" as his cause of financial distress; and his growing oeuvre: *Sons and Lovers* and the two previous novels, *Love Poems and Others*, and *The Widowing of Mrs. Holroyd*.[27] Although Lawrence angrily laughed in the face of the "tame thin-gutted charity" from "the stodgy, stomachy authors,"[28] it whetted competition between himself and the Murrys. Lawrence expertly parlayed the gift into more charity: Smaller sums trickled in from friends and supporters. Amy Lowell, recently returned to Brookline, Massachusetts, shipped a used typewriter, and he and Frieda began embroidering small pieces of fabric and painting plates and boxes to sell at a consignment shop in Hampstead. The shop turned them away, and they took to peddling them privately to friends.

Kot, with whom Lawrence had entered into a lively, intimate correspondence since their walking tour, visited on a rainy weekend and took an instant dislike to Frieda. Despondent about her children, she talked about them until he grew livid and dogmatic. "[Y]ou have left your children to marry Lawrence," he told her. "You must choose either your children or Lawrence—and if you choose Lawrence, you must stop complaining about the children." She left the house and walked the three miles to the Murrys', arriving in tears. Mansfield, who took her side in the argument, and who was eager for the chance to meet Kot, walked over in the rain to deliver a familiar message to

Lawrence, hitching her skirt to ford a flooded duckpond between the two houses. She arrived sopping wet, kept her skirt well hiked for Kot's benefit, and told Lawrence that Frieda was not coming back. "Damn the woman," he screamed, "tell her I never want to see her again."[29] Mansfield disappeared into the rain without answering. Murry, forced to remain alone with Frieda, had to "prevent myself from being actively insolent to her."[30]

In London for dental work one cold day late in November, Frieda waited outside 49 Harvard Road for a glimpse of the children. It was pouring, and she crouched behind a hedge near the house, her Panama hat dripping and bending in the rain. The futility and embarrassment of hiding from her own children struck her, and she began to weep before they appeared. She had chosen a bad vantage point, the rain was coming down in sheets, and she was overcome with tears and could hardly make them out as they scurried in their front door. Sobbing convulsively, she made her way to the Campbells' house in South Kensington, probably the only people she could think of who lived remotely nearby. It was a distance of several miles. The rain did not let up, and her hair, which had come undone and hung from her hat in strands, was plastered to her cheeks. She knocked on the door, and Beatrice appeared and looked at her blankly. "Don't you know me?" she bawled. "I'm Frieda." Beatrice, who had not been in London when the Lawrences had stayed there, had in fact never met Frieda.[31] She took her in to dry her off and sent her on her way.

Convinced that nothing would be resolved unless she confronted Ernest, Frieda decided to accompany Lawrence to Derbyshire on a visit to his sister Ada, from where she could continue on to Nottingham. Lawrence, who often criticized Frieda for acting too aristocratic with the working class, had never introduced her to his family. They spent a couple of days, and despite Lawrence's fears, Ada felt relaxed enough with Frieda to reminisce about their childhood: how they had pretended to have at-homes by perching in a wheelbarrow, where Ada presided as a socialite named Mrs. Lawson. Frieda was charmed, and her huge whiskey laugh filled the house. She was determined to find Ernest outside Nottingham College, but she miscalculated the time of his departure and was forced to go to his bed-sit.

It was in a small, undistinguished brick house a few blocks southwest of the college, past an institute for the blind. She announced herself to Ryker Behrendt, Ernest's landlady, as Mrs. Lawson, the first name that came to mind. Ernest appeared and began yelling at Frieda. The two and a half years since she had left Cowley had taken their toll on both, and Frieda submitted to his anger with little more than monosyllables. Lawrence later re-created much of the conversation to a friend, setting Ernest contemptuously in the past with a Latinism, *quondam* (sometime), that derided both the man's loss and his effete love of language:

> Quondam Husband: And what are you doing in *this* town.
> Frieda: I came to see you about the children.
> Quondam Husband: Aren't you ashamed to show your face where you are known? Isn't the commonest prostitute better than you?
> Frieda: Oh no.
> Quon. Husb.: Do you want to drive me off the face of the earth, Woman? Is there no place where I can have peace?
> Frieda: You see I must speak to you about the children.
> Quon. Husb.: You shall *not* have them—they don't want to see you. . . . *If* you had to go away, why didn't you go away with a *gentleman*?
> Frieda: He is a *great* man.
> . . . Q. Husb.: Don't you know you are the vilest creature on earth?[32]

"[I]f I *were* a prostitute," Frieda later reflected, "the children would be *mine* and a man would be obliged to pay me."[33]

4

Lawrence was thrilled by Frieda's indifferent response to Ernest's chastisement, which he considered a reaffirmation of her love for him. He resumed work on *The Rainbow* the moment they returned to Buckinghamshire, writing more than a thousand words a day, sending off hundred-page installments to Pinker throughout the winter. The rendition of Ursula's genealogy that he had begun after Garnett's requests to flesh her out with a past was increasingly modeled, and with remarkable emotional accuracy, on the von Richthofen lineage. He gave Ursula a grandmother, Lydia Lensky, a German Pole with the dolorous temperament and depressions of Friedrich's mother, Amalie von Laschowski, the self-styled countess who wept by the banks of the

Oder. Lydia's daughter, Anna, like Friedrich born during a European revolution, is left fatherless by a man who—like many of the von Richthofen men in Frieda's branch of the family—is an exemplary public figure and domestic failure. They move to Yorkshire and Lydia marries Tom Brangwen, a member of a local, indifferently successful farming family. Anna's childhood and personality became, increasingly, Frieda's:

> She was always uneasy in the world. . . . "What do *I* care about that lot of girls?" she would say to her father, contemptuously; "they are nobody. . . . They're bagatelle." . . . She had a curious shrinking from commonplace people, and particularly from the young lady of her day. She would not go into company because of the ill-at-ease feeling other people brought upon her. And she never could decide whether it were her fault or theirs. . . . At school, or in the world, she was usually at fault, she felt usually that she ought to be slinking in disgrace. She never was quite sure, in herself, whether she were wrong, or whether the others were wrong. She had not done her lessons: well, she did not see any reason why she *should* do her lessons, if she did not want to. Was there some occult reason why she should? Were these people, schoolmistresses, representatives of some mystic Right, some Higher Good? They seemed to think so themselves. But she could not for her life see why a woman should bully and insult her because she did not know thirty lines of *As You Like It*. . . . she despised inwardly the coarsely working nature of the mistress. Therefore she was always at outs with authority. From constant telling, she came almost to believe in her own badness, her own intrinsic inferiority.[34]

Anna's first love, for her cousin Will Brangwen, was modeled on Frieda's for her cousin Curt, a love that unleashes her sexuality and effects her independence from her father. As in *Buddenbrooks*, in which the narrative thread of one domineering female character dictates the course of a family saga, Anna soon dominated half of Lawrence's novel, which he began to refer to as his "Brangwensaga."

In subsequent chapters, which give way to another generation of Brangwens, Lawrence dwelled on Frieda's memories of her father:

> He was very fond of swimming, and in warm weather would take her down to the canal, to a silent place, or to a big pond or reservoir, to

> bathe. He would take her on his back as he went swimming, and she clung close, feeling his strong movement under her, so strong, as if it would uphold all the world. . . . He said, would she ride on his back whilst he jumped off the canal bridge down into the water beneath. . . . He loved to feel the naked child clinging to his shoulders. There was a curious fight between their two wills. . . . They were clinging to each other, and making up to each other for the strange blow that had been struck at them. . . . his eyes were full of the blackness of death, it was as if death had cut between their two lives, and separated them.
>
> Still they were not separate. There was this curious taunting intimacy between them.[35]

For his portrait of Will and Anna's marriage, Lawrence occasionally drew on Frieda's recollections of life with Ernest: Will is disturbed to find Anna, pregnant with Ursula, dancing nude in their bedroom, as Frieda did on Sundays while the rest of the city went to church. More often, particularly for scenes of desultory lovemaking and romantic agony, Lawrence drew on his own marriage: "Why, if Anna left him for even a week, did he seem to be clinging like a madman to the edge of reality, and slipping surely, surely into the flood of unreality that would drown him."[36] Because of the huge emphasis on characters based on Frieda, the novel quickly became too bulky, and Lawrence was forced to separate it into two. The stories of Ursula, Gudrun, and their lovers, with which he had started the book almost two years before, were saved for use in a future novel, not yet thought through.

5

Despite the trove of Frieda material, Lawrence often regretted that he lived with a German and, with calculated disloyalty, intimated that her nationality jeopardized his success. Gilbert Cannan brought his friend Compton Mackenzie, who had just published a novel, *Sinister Street*, to great popular acclaim, to meet Lawrence, whom they found crouched next to a pail of soapy water, scrubbing the floor with a hard brush. Mackenzie was struck by how personally Lawrence took the war, which he denounced with an enraged air of persecution, explaining how his problems were exacerbated by Frieda's Germanness. "I can't face the depressing view of these flat English fields," ventured

Mackenzie, eager to change the subject, "surrounded by their melancholy elms without leaves." Lawrence immediately yelled out Frieda's name. She appeared at the top of the stairs in a pair of boldly striped wool stockings, at which the two men tried not to stare as she began to make her descent. Before her head and shoulders had emerged from the landing, Lawrence shouted at her to "shut that bloody door" at the top of the stairs. She complied, greeted their guests, and faced him placidly.

"Frieda!" he shouted.

"What is it, Lorenzo?"

"We can't stay in this cottage with these elms. We must get down somewhere to the sea."[37] Mackenzie assured him that the war would end in a few months, offered them a house he had in Capri, and left, astonished.

They spent Christmas with the Murrys, Gertler, Kot, and the Cannans, getting drunk on Chianti Kot had brought from London and punch Lawrence made on a Primus stove in the attic. Throughout several days of parties, Lawrence talked at great length of Rananim, to which, he said, they could all retreat. Its motto, he explained to Kot, would be "*fier*"—proud—and its symbol, fast becoming a personal icon, the phoenix rising from its own ashes. In the following weeks he told everyone he met about Rananim, though no one—including Frieda—was very interested. The holiday without her children had produced the usual melancholy, and she was not interested in much of anything. Retreating from time to time to her bedroom and a box of family photos carried from Nottingham, she would lie on the bed with a cigarette dangling from her lips, staring for hours at the pictures spread before her. Lawrence despised her inertness, and even Mansfield, still always ready to actively help Frieda undermine Ernest's resistance, silently cursed her gloom and sloth.

Shortly after the New Year, they packed their belongings, not bothering to throw away scraps of faded mistletoe and other garbage, as Mansfield noted with disgust. Lawrence, usually a meticulous housekeeper, felt no need to clean or make repairs to places they were about to leave (though he often guiltily compiled lengthy lists of broken items for their furious landlords); Frieda did not notice or care. They were moving to a remote cottage in Sussex, and parted unemotionally with the Murrys. It now required an extraordinary amount of effort at politeness for Murry not to explode at Frieda or, for that matter, for the four of them to get along, and no one had the strength to pretend.

A former cattle shed, the Sussex cottage reminded Frieda of a cloister.[38] Amenities included indoor plumbing and running hot water; they were to have use of the grounds: It was set on the eighty-acre estate of a large, eccentric literary family, the Meynells, who lived in various houses spaced widely over the acreage. The cottage was free, loaned by Viola Meynell, a novelist to whom Catherine Jackson, Lawrence's Scottish reviewer, had introduced them in London. Plain, assertive, and rabidly acquisitive of reality for her novels' sake, she saw a potential subject in almost everyone she met, and carried a copybook for notes toward her latest work in progress.[39] The father, Wilfred, *chef de ménage*, was an eccentric Catholic magazine editor who liked to lead his essayist/poet wife, Alice, across the lawn in a slow procession: To Frieda they looked like an apparition of Dante and Beatrice.[40] The centerpiece of the property was an old farmhouse Wilfred had furnished incongruously with Italian bric-a-brac and William Morris wallpaper.[41] When the Lawrences showed up for meals, they often found the living room darkened and Alice lying on a large, overstuffed couch.

Frieda disliked the subdued, self-conscious religiosity of the estate, and in later years could not dissociate its gloom from a letter she received from her mother shortly after they moved in. The baron, Anna wrote, had been apathetic and restless through the late fall, and had not noticed the passage of Christmas. Anna had hired a friar to help nurse him. "His interest in war news vanished completely," she wrote Frieda, "and it was tragic when he tried to write and couldn't get a word together." On January 3, when she had him driven to a hospital in the town of Illenau for tests, he thought they were setting out for the Blases for their summer vacation. "That is the old Römerstrasse," he suddenly said en route, transported forty-five years back to the Franco-Prussian War, "which led here from Strasbourg." While being examined medically, he ate crumbs from his pocket, entirely unaware of his surroundings. Two days later, he suffered a stroke and was paralyzed. He lapsed into incoherence until Else arrived. "*Kinder* [children]," he said to her, then fell back into a state of confusion.[42] He died just before midnight on January 29, 1915, and was buried in Baden-Baden. Frieda, overcome with grief, did not tell Lawrence.

6

Though deeply immersed in finishing *The Rainbow*, Lawrence occasionally went to London with Frieda. Introduced to E. M. Forster at one of Ottoline's Thursdays, he talked incessantly about Rananim. Forster was hardly interested in having his way of life dictated on some remote island, then Lawrence's choice of site, but he was taken with Lawrence, who struck him as "a sandy haired passionate Nibelung."[43] A correspondence began. "I am tired of class, and humanity, and personal salvation," Lawrence wrote in a long letter that rambled from thoughts of resurrection, "love of a woman," angels, and devils to the class difference between them.[44] Frieda, who had found Forster a sympathetic listener, appended a note, saying she liked *Where Angels Fear to Tread*. Forster took offense at being written to by two people on the same piece of paper, and told them he would not "have dealings with a firm."[45] "Three cheers for the 'firm,'" Frieda replied, and invited him for a weekend.[46] He arrived with news of a rumor that the lending libraries would soon be withdrawing *The Prussian Officer* from circulation: Published by Duckworth on November 26, 1914, to mixed reviews, the book was perceived as unpatriotic by some and "disgusting" by others.[47] Lawrence was furious. He grew incensed when the subject turned obliquely to homosexuality—which Forster seems to have made implicitly clear he had no intention of renouncing for the greater fulfillment of the wedded state—and they were soon quarreling endlessly. Lawrence tried lecturing him on world revolution, and was inconsolably depressed by the time Forster left. Frieda tried to mend fences:

> No, you don't do L. or his work justice. God knows he is a fool, and undeveloped, but he is so genuine, a genuine force, inhuman like one also—and such a strain; but you ought to help him, he is really very inarticulate and *unformed*. . . . I . . . enjoyed your stay awfully and you ought to have enjoyed it more! . . . you are not to be suspicious— . . . L. is in London, so this is not a joint letter—I am *not* going to ask you to come again, you will have to come of your own free will—You are *not* to mind L's "customs beastly, manners none"; think, *I* have to put up with them, and they have improved! I think you are both vile with each other, it was all the time on the brink of quarreling—

> watching each other like two tomcats! And there is the spring coming, and I feel bruised and battered and I do so want to enjoy him (the spring) to the full![48]

The friendship, which eventually petered out amicably, unnerved Lawrence and inaugurated a period of soul-searching, sexual ambivalence, and confused declarations of homophobia.

He was soon confiding his thoughts and worries to Bertrand Russell, whom Ottoline brought to Sussex. Ottoline had begun supplying Lawrence with books, advice, invitations, and offers to read his manuscripts, and they had entered into a mutually flattering correspondence with soulful, sympathetic tones and coy flirtations. "One tries hard to stick to ones ideal of one man–one woman, in love," Lawrence mused in one letter, "but probably you are right, and one should go to different persons to get companionship for the different sides of ones nature."[49] The correspondence offended and gradually sickened Frieda, who seems to have been envious of Lady Ottoline's title, which ranked higher than hers.

Lawrence had been initially nervous about meeting Russell, but within an hour he talked freely about sexual relations, state revolution, the nationalization of industry, and a world without money. Russell came away astounded by Lawrence's charisma and powers of perception, if not his grasp of economics. "He is amazing," he said to Ottoline, when they had said goodbye and the Lawrences were out of earshot. "He sees through and through one."[50] Lawrence wrote him a lengthy letter, devoted largely to sodomy, masturbation, and Forster.[51] Frieda, left alone with Ottoline through much of the afternoon, had made use of the time by confiding her deadlock with Ernest and asking her to intercede. Ernest, she told Ottoline, would not be able to resist her charm and position in society. Lawrence, certain that Frieda had overstepped an invisible boundary, was furious and upbraided her hysterically. He then turned around and, certain he would be able to handle the matter more tactfully, put the same request to Ottoline himself. "Don't abrogate one jot or title of your high birth," he advised her.[52] Nothing came of the idea.

Murry, with the still-incomplete manuscript of *Still Life*, arrived on their doorstep in the third week of February, ill, and heartsick over a recent abandonment by Mansfield: Three days before, she had lied her way past French army officials to a village near Dijon for an assignation with Francis Carco, a poet-journalist and former French correspondent for *Rhythm*, now serving as a mail carrier with a bakery unit along the Saône. Murry put himself in Lawrence's hands, steering as clear as possible of Frieda, and the two discussed *Still Life*. Unlike almost everyone who read it, Lawrence found it a powerful novel with enormous potential. The two men shared every waking hour, and within three days Lawrence came down with a bad cold, which he passed on to Frieda. Murry stayed on for a week, an interlude of extraordinary cheerfulness for Lawrence. "He is one of the men of the future—you will see," he wrote Ottoline. "He is with me for the Revolution. . . . he is my partner—the only man who quite simply is with me—One day he'll be ahead of me. Because he'll build up the temple if I carve out the way."[53] Frieda could not wait for him to leave. When he did, she broke the news of her father's death, now a month old. "You didn't expect," Lawrence said, "to keep your father all your life?"[54] She had grown used to his stinging, unfeeling remarks, which she attributed to the war. "Naturally, I came in for all Lawrence's tortured, irritable moods," she wrote later. "His sweetness had disappeared and he turned against me as well as the rest for the time being. It all made him ill."[55]

Murry derided Frieda, the "bitch," in whining letters throughout the spring to Mansfield, who continued to spend time away from him in Carco's Paris apartment while humoring and cajoling him in their correspondence.[56] "What a great fat *sod* she is," she obligingly replied, when Murry described a dinner to which Frieda had arrived late, only to eat the lion's share of the cold meats he served, "I should like to send a pig to kill her—a real filthy pig. Lawrence has got queer blind places, hasn't he?"[57] Murry was soon hatching a plan to take Lawrence on a short summer vacation, during which, he informed Mansfield, he would persuade him to leave Frieda. "I have an idea," he wrote, "that he might be happy were he away with me for a bit, because he would know that I was loving him."[58]

"Fancy GIVING YOURSELF UP to LOVING someone for a fortnight," Mansfield shot back in the next post.[59] The plan was never mentioned again.

7

Lawrence laid the manuscript of *The Rainbow* to rest at six hundred pages on March 2. Final additions included Anna and Will Brangwen's "shameful, natural and unnatural acts of sensual voluptuousness. . . . Shame, what was it?" Lawrence and Frieda came down with influenza nearly on the day he put the final pen stroke on the last page. He engaged Viola Meynell as typist, and tried his hand again at philosophy, inspired by Russell and the war. Russell invited him to Cambridge for a weekend, and Lawrence became upset at the number of Russell's homosexual colleagues, among them John Maynard Keynes, who arrived for Sunday breakfast at 11:00 A.M. in a pair of pajamas, looking as if he had just woken up. Lawrence could hardly wait to return to Frieda. The following month David Garnett brought a homosexual friend along on a visit, and Lawrence suffered nightmares about beetles.

While he was away at Cambridge, Ford Madox Hueffer, Violet Hunt, and H. G. Wells's wife, Jane, surprised Frieda by turning up at the cottage. Hueffer, who had been threatened in January with expulsion from his house in West Sussex by local authorities suspicious of his Germanness, was making various attempts to keep himself in the good graces of the authorities; he now worked as a writer for Wellington House, the propaganda arm of the British war machine. Frieda, who not seen him for years, apparently suspected that he had come in the guise of friendship to dredge up unflattering information in order to please his new employers. He might well have been: He seems to have offered no better explanation for the visit than to intimate that he had come in order to prevent Lawrence from being hounded by the authorities, which probably made Frieda even more suspicious. "Are you a German too?" she boomed ironically, in German. Hueffer was embarrassed and scandalized by her lapse. "That made him squirm and he hummed and hawed," she later wrote. ". . . So I did not think much of him." She served tea and hoped they would leave, but the conversation dragged on, turning to the German occupation of Belgium, the subject of a popular, sentimental poem, *Antwerp*, that Hueffer had just published. Hunt, who disliked Frieda, later used considerable poetic license in an account of the afternoon: "Dirty Belgians! Who cares for them?" she had Frieda shouting, a dialogue that was entered as incriminating evidence in Frieda's burgeoning Home Office file—perhaps by Hueffer. In his autobiography, published long after he had anglicized his last name to Ford, Hueffer claimed altruism as his motive for coming unannounced.[60]

10

"She Actually Seemed a Lady"

I

Viola Meynell finished typing Lawrence's manuscript in April, and he resubmitted it to Methuen, only to be told that, though they now considered the manuscript basically publishable, its gratuitous sex was objectionable. Lawrence, afraid they would refuse to pay him the balance of the advance, agreed to omit sentences and phrases but not to make wholesale deletions, and set to work on the typescript.[1] Money problems pressed harder. Ernest's solicitors, Goldberg, Newell, who had been sending letters dunning for divorce costs, had Lawrence summoned to the Probate, Divorce and Admiralty Division of the High Court to be examined for bankruptcy, this following an unanswered order from two months before to declare his capacity to pay these costs. Robert Garnett represented him on May 3, and he was ordered to account for all the money owing him from publishers, including the balance of the advance for *The Rainbow*. "I wouldn't pay them if I were a millionaire," Lawrence wrote Russell. "I would rather go to prison. Messrs Goldberg Newall and Co, beasts, bugs, leeches, shall not have a penny from me if I can help it."[2] A month later he apparently made a partial settlement, lamenting to Pinker, "This money for the *Rainbow* is all I have to look forward to at all—and Mrs Lawrence can't get any money from Germany now."[3]

Though he was now able to publish poems and short stories in publications ranging from the *Manchester Guardian* to *The Egoist*—a literary journal co-edited by James Joyce's later patron, Harriet Shaw Weaver—they were for small sums, which came irregularly. Their difficulties were exacerbated by the May 7 sinking of the Cunard liner *Lusitania* by a German submarine, which led to some angry preaching. "I am mad with rage," Lawrence wrote Ottoline, ". . . I would like to kill a million Germans—two million."[4] His letters to intimates were a watered-down version of his rantings to Frieda, who decided to get an apartment by herself in London. She hoped to find and furnish it before the coming fall.

To various friends these fits of Lawrence's—astounding in their ferocity, and unnerving to have to witness—were either evidence of his genius or indications of a series of breakdowns. Frieda never bothered to differentiate. "I simply must be by myself sometimes," she wrote Ottoline, "L is very wearing and also I will see the children on their way to school, that they dont get used to *not* seeing me." Lawrence ascribed Frieda's desire to be alone to chronic dissatisfaction and "female perversity": when "a woman has got her children, she doesn't care about them," he complained in a postscript, "and if she has a man, she doesn't care about him, she only wants her children."[5] While she was away apartment hunting, Lawrence fantasized about the Germans dropping a bomb and killing her. "[I]t is the kind of fate," he wrote Forster, "she is cut out for."[6] He thought she should forget about the children, wait until they became older, and then let them decide for themselves if they wanted to have anything to do with her.

2

Frieda, Lawrence, and Gordon Campbell were Ottoline's first overnight guests at Garsington, a Tudor mansion on five hundred acres near Oxford that she hoped would be a haven for conscientious objectors, writers, painters, homosexuals, lesbians, bisexuals, and various friends and hangers-on. Among the household staff was Maria Nys, a Belgian teenager who had emigrated to England when the Germans invaded the year before. Ottoline had given her a room in her Bloomsbury home, and—the gossip ran—had begun a halfhearted romance with her. Maria was passionately attached and became upset whenever Ottoline went away or threatened to dismiss her "for her own good."[7] She was still recovering from a suicide attempt—she had swallowed sleeping pills after one such threatened abandonment—when, on Saturday, June 12, Lawrence and Frieda arrived to spend the week.

Half hidden on a hill, the great house was surrounded by outbuildings that had been stylishly refurbished, an immense garden, and a swimming pond cloistered by rows of yew trees and classical plaster statues. Peacocks strolled on the lawn; indoors the Lawrences were greeted by Ottoline's breathless dogs and the familiar scent of musk. It was a dark, hushed interior cordoned off from the verdant grounds by yards of heavy silk drapes, thick Persian rugs, walls paneled in oak, whose grain had been obscured by layers of lurid paint—bright reds and peacock green—and several large works by Augustus John, of which one bold, dark, flattering portrait of Ottoline was given pride of place. Some of the rooms were unfinished, and Lawrence put on overalls and helped Ottoline and her nine-year-old daughter, Julian, apply gold leaf to the sitting room's molding. Frieda, perched on a table, laughed loudly. "I am just as remarkable and important as Lorenzo," she shouted.[8] Everyone ignored her.

It was a strained visit, with impromptu performances of skits, directed by Lawrence, and stilted encounters with Philip Morrell, who affected riding breeches, double-breasted waistcoats, and various other gentleman-farmer accessories.[9] Frieda confided to him she would prefer an out-and-out affair between Lawrence and Ottoline to "all this soul-mush."[10] On Tuesday, three days after they had arrived, she and Lawrence began fighting. The following morning—it was Ottoline's forty-second birthday—Frieda threatened to leave without him. They stood in the hall together, Lawrence paralyzed by indecision, Frieda furious at his wishy-washiness, before she finally stormed off. "I felt," she later wrote, ". . . Perhaps I ought to leave Lawrence to her influence; what might they not do together for England? I am powerless, and a Hun, and a nobody."[11]

Philip took Lawrence under wing and told him in no uncertain terms to "assert himself and leave" Frieda. "[A]fter a frenzy of angry barks" throughout the course of the day, however, he eventually got on a train himself and followed her. "[H]e turns with drooping tail and seeks refuge in Frieda," Ottoline wrote, "his 'dark abode.'"[12] She was convinced, she wrote Russell, that Frieda was a raging egotist, and she hoped she would either die or run away with a sadist.[13] Four days later Ottoline dispatched Russell to pay a call on them. Lawrence waxed eloquent about Ottoline, who, he told Russell, was a goddess. Overcome with enthusiasm, he composed a long letter to her, but Frieda tore it up.

Herbert and Lady Asquith—she had acquired the title the year before, when her father succeeded her grandfather as earl of Weymss—showed up in the middle of Russell's visit. Herbert, just back from a tour of duty as an artillery officer, was suffering shell shock and a sore mouth, from which three teeth had been knocked out. Cynthia, two of whose lovers were to die in the war, was depressed by her husband's obliviousness of her, and invited the Lawrences to their house in Littlehampton, along the coast. Russell departed, having decided he liked Frieda more than he had thought. "I mind her much more," he wrote Ottoline, "when you are about."[14]

They drove to Littlehampton in a car the Asquiths had borrowed for the trip from 10 Downing Street, and Frieda and Cynthia went to the beach to talk. Cynthia, overcome with her own unhappiness, had little patience for Frieda's complaints about Ottoline, who, Frieda said, insisted on "treating her as an appendage and explaining her husband to her as being dropped straight from the sky." Her patience grew even thinner when they rejoined their husbands and began discussing the war. Frieda declared that the Germans had no sense of English notions of fair play. Lawrence, jumping into the breach, maintained that if everyone acted exactly like the "filthy" but "logical" Germans, "some conclusion might at least be arrived at, which with the present lunatic compromise between utter barbarism and half-hearted humanitarianism, could never be."[15]

3

Friends found the Lawrences more and more intolerable as the war ground on. In July, Lawrence visited Russell in London and discussed forming an activist religious society, as well as a collaboration on a series of lectures on ethics. He excitedly proclaimed a "Blutbruderschaft," a clunky German term he soon began to invoke with male friends, for some reason always omitting the umlaut over the second *u*.[16] The visit tried Russell's nerves, as he confided to Ottoline:

> the day Lawrence was with me was horrid. I got filled with despair, and just counting the moments till it was ended. . . . Lawrence is very like Shelley—just as fine, but with a similar impatience of fact. The revolution he hopes for is just like Shelley's prophecy of banded anarchs fleeing while the people celebrate a feast of love. His psychology of people is amazingly good up to a point, but at a certain point he gets misled by love of violent colouring.[17]

Frieda, forced to sit through hours of hotheaded dialogue between the two men, realized they were talking less about "revolution" than about themselves: "I had listened to talk on politics at my uncle Oswald Richthofen's in Berlin . . . and what Lawrence and Bertie discussed did not seem like politics to me. I thought they were both off their tracks [and] out of their elements."[18] She tried to temper Lawrence's overeagerness with stories of Ascona, which made an indelible impression on Russell, whose affair with Ottoline, as he was now fond of explaining to friends, mistresses, and anyone else who would listen, had freed him from the constraints of monogamy, marriage, and prudishness. He later concluded, however, that Ascona had bred fascism in Frieda:

> Lawrence, though most people did not realize it, was his wife's mouthpiece. He had the eloquence, but she had the ideas. She used to spend part of every summer in a colony of Austrian Freudians at a time when psychoanalysis was little known in England. Somehow, she imbibed prematurely the ideas afterwards developed by Mussolini and Hitler, and these ideas she transmitted to Lawrence, shall we say, by blood-consciousness. Lawrence was an essentially timid man who tried to conceal his timidity by bluster. His wife was not timid, and her denunciations have the character of thunder, not of bluster. Under her wing he felt comparatively safe.[19]

Ironically Russell inadvertently provided the inspiration for several years' worth of proto-fascist rants: Before they parted he presented Lawrence with an anthology of the pre-Socratics that included the

Heraclitean fragments, fleshed out and annotated by the contemporary Greek scholar John Burnet. The notion of the "Counsel of one" and the belief that the masses lacked the brains and moral fiber to govern themselves inspired a sudden philosophical turnaround in Lawrence.[20] "I *don't* believe in the democratic electorate," he wrote Ottoline soon after. "The working man is not fit to elect the ultimate government of the country. And the holding of office *shall not* rest upon the Choice of the mob: it shall be almost immune from them. . . . The war is resolving itself into a war between Labour and Capital."[21] He predicted a civil war on the order of the French Revolution if the right leader—a kaiser, like Germany's, or "an elected King, something like Julius Caesar," as he explained to Russell[22]—were not found.

4

While Lawrence developed his philosophy, Frieda at last found an apartment, the bottom floor of a small, semi-detached house in the Vale of Health, an enclave on the edge of Hampstead Heath. Lawrence, however, had no real intention of letting Frieda go without him. They left for London together in August, after a year out of the city. Lawrence had received £132 from Methuen, which seemed to assure their rent—three pounds a month—indefinitely.

Frieda stepped up her efforts to see the children as soon as they arrived. Apparently through sheer persistence, she finally broke Ernest's resolve, or perhaps, for reasons unknown, he had finally decided it was time. The previous September he had transferred Elsa, now twelve years old, to Saint Paul's Girls' School, where she was in the fourth form; before the summer term had ended, a week before, he had enrolled Barby in the lower fourth form.[23] Frieda wanted to see them before the fall 1915 term began on September 15.

Ernest had finally told the children that he and Frieda were divorced, a concept neither Barby nor Elsa entirely understood. Its reality was blurred by the years of being in the dark about why their mother had disappeared. "Would you like to see Mama?" he asked Barby one day. They were resting in a churchyard after a long walk. "Not very much," she replied, apprehensive and confused.[24] Evidently Elsa and Monty were more enthusiastic. He allowed Frieda to meet with the children in his lawyers' offices for half an hour on her thirty-sixth birthday.

Carrying a gift box of candy she had opened and sampled on the way from Hampstead, she arrived at 2 West Street in Finsbury Circus on the morning of August 11, her face animated and streaked with tears. Elsa and Barby were rather thin and drawn, the result of wartime food rationing: Maude hoarded the meat coupons for their grandfather, and with cheese in short supply, they had little protein in their diet. They subsisted on tiny portions of rissole, plus the cook's heavily flavored rice pudding and large teas given by a well-off neighbor, who was appalled by the unfair apportioning of food in the house.[25] None of the deprivations came to light in the meeting, however; the two girls stared nervously and said next to nothing. Monty chatted cheerfully, and helped keep the conversation going until a clerk entered and said the time was over.

She was soon allowed to see the children outside the office, subject to Ernest's approval. He made one provision: Lawrence could not be with her.[26] During the four months they lasted in Hampstead, she saw them when visits could be arranged, usually for tea. One afternoon Mansfield joined them all in a tearoom adjoining the Baron's Court Underground station. On another visit Frieda took them to Gertler's studio on Rudall Crescent in Hampstead—a side of the neighborhood they had never seen in their years at their grandparents'—and the smell of turpentine and bold, thickly painted canvases greatly impressed Barby, who had started to draw and paint. She was about to turn eleven, and was an indifferent student. Recently she had presented her father, whose penchant for morbidity she appreciated, with a sobering illustration of Schiller's "Death and the Maiden," the maiden modeled on herself.[27] Monty perfected a sidesplitting imitation of Frieda's pronunciation of Gertler's name,[28] with which he tormented his sisters when Frieda was not around.

Frieda loved the visits and the distance they provided from Lawrence's fulminations and inflammatory political pronouncements, which London seemed to add fuel to. "There must be King and Queen," he wrote Cynthia Asquith, whose father-in-law now headed the coalition cabinet, "and Lords and Ladies, and burghers and burgesses, and servants: but not King George and Queen Mary [the reigning monarchs], not Lord Kitchener [secretary of state for war] or Earl Grey [Sir Edward Grey, foreign secretary] or Mr Asquith or Lloyd George [minister of munitions]."[29] He proposed moving to

South America, where the adherents of Rananim could travel on horseback and eke out a subsistence life. To Russell and others he suggested Florida as an alternative site. Frieda mentioned sailing to Australia. "I hear you make an income of fifty thousand a year," she greeted J. M. Barrie, who had sent Lawrence an appreciative letter in Italy. "Why shouldn't you give Lorenzo enough money to pay for our passage?" She "could never understand any embarrassment about money," Cynthia Asquith, who had made the introductions to Barrie, later wrote, "or see any reason why it should not be transferred from a well-filled to an empty pocket—had the full purse been her own, her views would have been the same."[30] Barrie never asked them back.

5

Caught up in a big crowd on Hampstead Heath one night in mid-September, Frieda and Lawrence watched a German airship float overhead. "In that Zeppelin," Frieda thought, "are perhaps men I have danced with when I was a girl, boys I have played with, and here they come to bring destruction and death."[31] At least one intimate friend, her onetime lover Udo von Henning, had been killed—on September 7, in the Battle of Charleroi in Belgium. Her shy cousin Manfred, a graduate of the German Cadet Corps, had joined the army at nineteen. Awarded the Iron Cross for service as a border cavalryman, he had recently gone through training with the air force and emerged as a pilot. Though normally fairly reticent in his personal affect, he had, "for no particular reason," as he later wrote, ". . . got the idea of painting my crate glowing red."[32] He became an instant folk hero. "[I]f this dark crowd knew I was a German," Frieda wrote, "they would tear me to pieces in their fear."[33]

She did not feel much protected by Lawrence, who had begun expending his much-dwindled store of sexual tenderness on H. D., also living in Hampstead. The poet had suffered a miscarriage, which she attributed to the abruptness with which she had been told of the sinking of the *Lusitania*.[34] The loss and Aldington's simultaneous affair with Brigit Patmore, the wife of the poet Coventry Patmore, had effectively ended their marriage; Lawrence began visiting when Aldington was not there. Readings of each other's manuscripts gave way to silences during which Lawrence, enormously attracted by H. D.'s unhappiness, watched her cut up fruit at the kitchen table. Threatened by Frieda's renewed bonds with her children, the abstract problem of the death of H. D.'s unborn child was easier, and far more reconcilable with his vehement, contradictory feelings about mother love.

Mansfield and Murry were also in London, and Lawrence soon coaxed them and Kot into helping him put out a journal devoted partially to his political philosophy. Lawrence paid for an office, Murry came up with a name, *The Signature*, which, he said, implied a lack of editorial agreement: Only the person who signed an article was responsible for its content. They printed subscription forms, which Lawrence sent to everyone he knew. Ernest Jones, then heading the London Psycho-Analytical Society, received one. Lawrence seems to have acquired a letter strongly urging his medical exemption from the war from Jones, who may or may not have known Frieda by reputation via his previous treatment of Gross's wife. He found her "charming," a view not altered when she entered his treatment room one night, apparently without an appointment, and frantically told him that she was afraid Lawrence intended to kill her. In an impromptu session Jones suggested to Frieda that she mistreated Lawrence, and did not charge her for his opinion.[35]

As checks for *The Signature* trickled in—Jones's evidently was one—Lawrence solicited work from friends, among them Russell, who sent an article urging a negotiated end to the war, arguing that it was undermining civilization. Lawrence, who now believed that the war had been inevitable and should be carried to its bloody extreme, was enraged, and fired off a letter attacking not only Russell's politics—he accused him of hypocrisy and "perverted, mental blood-lust"—but his character, which, he wrote, was "repressed."[36] Russell was so unnerved by the letter, and evidently also at such a low ebb in his emotional life, that he briefly contemplated suicide. Lawrence later tried to soften the blow by explaining he had been analyzing himself as much as Russell.

6

The Rainbow was published on September 30, with a dust jacket, whose literalness Lawrence disliked, depicting a couple locked in a passionate embrace. The dedication was to Else, an acknowledgment of her financial help during the early drafting and of material he had drawn from her adolescence. Lawrence trusted Frieda's gossip and instant character appraisals: He drew heavily on Else's passionate attachment to her teachers, notably Miss Myers, whose watery eyes and long neck Frieda had hated in Sablon. That crush, and Frieda's affair with her schoolmistress, made their way into the book (in a chapter depicting Gudrun's fixation on and seduction by her teacher, Winifred Unger) via a seamless conflation with Mansfield's sexual history, as she had confided it to Frieda in Buckinghamshire.[37] Lawrence, with characteristic ambivalence, entitled the chapter "Shame."

The chapter became a favorite target of reviews, frequently politically minded, which moved from individual disgust to universal condemnation to calls for a nationwide ban. One exception was a favorable review by Catherine Jackson in the *Glasgow Herald*, and she got fired for writing it. Few friends liked the book: "I don't think his Female Psychology is really good," wrote Ottoline, who had trouble differentiating among the women. " . . . It is always his wife."[38] Cynthia Asquith found it difficult to get beyond her dislike of Lawrence's repetition of the word "belly," and appealed to him for an explanation of the book's "message."[39] Lawrence, too dispirited to reply, delegated that chore to Frieda, who, just as weary of the impatience and obtuseness of Lawrence's so-called literary friends, was reduced to thematic, incoherent generalities:

> I think that the idea in *The Rainbow* is: *Love the ideal* as a background to these marriages which are really all failures to some extent. Hence the Rainbow between the ideal and these partial failures, because they are not *complete* failures. In the end the man fails Ursula because he has no ideal beyond the old existing state, it does not satisfy her nor him. For perfect love you don't only have two people, it must include a bigger, universal connection. An *idea*, something outside themselves, and it is really against individualism.[40]

Such rendering of his ideas tended to provoke laughter behind Frieda's back. On other occasions her ability to convey the gist of a work in progress with a sentence or two elicited admiration and envy—that one's spouse "lived in one's characters so vividly."[41] The vividness was especially notable when the characters had sprung, directly or indirectly, from Frieda's own circle of experience. A brush with court-martial by the baron and a fellow soldier during the

Franco-Prussian War was one of a growing list of anecdotes that made their way first into her conversation, later into Lawrence's oeuvre:

> One winter night [my father and his friend] brought two girls back to their room. Of course it was forbidden, but how irresistible *that* is! . . . can you imagine their horror—these two young men, when they got back [from a dawn march], the girls were dead! Suffocated by fumes from the stove![42]

The story became, with little alteration, "The Mortal Coil"—"one of my purest creations," Lawrence said.[43]

Despite or because of such contributions (and the resentment they engendered), Frieda came in for a full share of Lawrence's irrational outbursts and free-floating fury, which the war continued to make more frequent and acute—"the whipping-lass for all society," as Brigit Patmore recalled, "[offering] herself to his wrath with her gay gibes and wilfulness."[44]

Lawrence's compulsion to blame her for their problems and to find fault opened the door for others' spite, much of it rooted in the conviction that Frieda did not deserve him: As Murry and Kot, in particular, were now often heard to repeat, she was simply too dumb. Few dared venture this opinion in the presence of Lawrence, who maintained a high respect for Frieda's intelligence despite increasingly prolonged periods of disaffection, and would not tolerate such denigration. Her boisterous spirits, lack of obsequiousness, and impatience with the more belabored unwritten rules of British politesse, however, were, he felt, legitimate grounds for friends' poor opinions.

The first issue of *The Signature* was published on the heels of the novel. It featured an installment of Lawrence's philosophy, "The Crown," which drew on Heraclitus's principles of flux and dialectic; the Austrian sexual theorist Otto Weininger, a Nietzschean and anti-Semite (and Jew) whose revolutionary virulence had begun to inform Lawrence's ideas—all, seemingly, in the service of advocating dictatorship and free love. This strange piece evidently went unread by many subscribers, and most of those who did read it were either angry or baffled. Mansfield and Murry soon bowed out as contributors, and the magazine died two issues later.

Lawrence, frustrated by his efforts to be heard in England, continued to fantasize about going to the United States. He now hoped to bring Murry, and perhaps Mansfield, along. On October 22 he went to the Foreign Office to apply for a passport; Frieda filled out her application form a week later. The Murrys made no attempt to get the requisite papers in order.

In its October issue the *English Review* published a brilliant antiwar story of Lawrence's, entirely out of keeping with his aggressive "philosophy," called "England, My England," an account of a passionate couple (modeled on their Sussex hostess Viola Meynell's sister Madeline and her husband, Percy Lucas) who discover they are unsuited to one another. Their relationship devolves into nagging and passivity until he finds his calling as a soldier. Wounded by a shell, in a final, futile encounter with the enemy he kills three Germans point-blank with a revolver, then is killed and has his face mutilated by a fourth. "In nearly all men, now, the great desire is *not* to fight for house and home," Lawrence later explained his motive in writing the story:

> They will prove to themselves, by fighting, that their greater desire, on the whole, was *not* to fight for their nation, or sea-power, but to know a new value: to recognize a new, stronger desire in themselves, more spiritual and gladdening. Or else they will die. But many will die falsely. *All* Greece died. It must not be so again, we must have more sense. It is cruelly sad to see men caught in the clutches of the past, working automatically in the spell of an authorised desire, that is a desire no longer. That *should not be*.[45]

When Lucas, Lawrence's model, was killed in the Battle of the Somme nine months later, Lawrence felt aggrieved to have appropriated the facts of his friends' lives. He maintained, however, that the story vindicated his views on the falseness of patriotism and the ambiguity of machismo.

The death toll among their friends and relatives increased steadily. On October 19, Cynthia Asquith's brother, a soldier for three weeks, died in battle; Mansfield's brother was killed before even seeing action: A grenade went off in his hand as he was teaching recruits. The casualty list of von Richthofen family friends was even lengthier, and on October 9 Frieda's seven-year-old nephew Peter, Otto and Else's son, died suddenly, of an unknown cause. Else had celebrated her fortieth birthday with her four children and the baroness and put him to bed because he felt ill. He was too weak to get up the next morning and did not last until the afternoon. Anna was sent for, and arrived to find the hearse at the door. Edgar, who had been in Brussels since August, serving in the German administration headquartered in occupied Belgium, arrived just in time for the funeral.[46]

On November 5, with help from a friend of a friend in the Foreign Office, the Lawrences received their passports. The possibility of an actual departure and the realization of his plans for Rananim spooked Lawrence, but his apprehension seemed insignificant in the face of news an acquaintance, the novelist W. L. George, told him the same day: Scotland Yard, acting under a little-used, fifty-eight-year-old obscenity law, had seized all copies of *The Rainbow*.

Before the full spiral of implications of the police action had unwound in Lawrence's mind, he found himself and Frieda guests of honor at a party given by the Honorable Dorothy Eugenie Brett, daughter of Reginald Baliol Brett, second Viscount Esher. Brett, as she had taken to calling herself while still a student at the Slade, was a friend of Gertler's and Ottoline's. An aspiring painter, she was kept comfortable in London by her father, who paid the rent on her duplex-cum-studio on Earl's Court Road. Intensely solitary, she had taken an immediate liking to Lawrence when they met a few weeks before, and had planned the party when he was busily telling everyone he and Frieda would soon be leaving for the United States. Frieda spent most of the night dancing with a man whose name no one later remembered—Lawrence did not like to dance. She also drew the attention of the future memoirist Lytton Strachey. "I was surprised to find that I liked her looks very much," wrote Strachey, whom Ottoline had prepared for someone vulgar. "She actually seemed (there's no other word for it) a lady." Lawrence appeared ill and "devoured by internal distresses."[47] He was also one of the few people who was not visibly drunk. The party fell apart when a game of romantic charades—which some guests had turned into an opportunity for mate-swapping—was interrupted by a group of loud, similarly drunk gate-crashers. Brett, whose skills as a hostess were eccentric, decided that these unruly people needed to be entertained. Undeterred by the fact that she was partially deaf and carried an ear trumpet the size of a small Victrola, she improvised on her pianola until everyone either left or collapsed on the floor.

7

In the following weeks Lawrence oscillated between outrage and hopelessness. Eventually he decided on a sequel, which would draw on the voluminous material unused in *The Rainbow*. It seemed a self-destructive impulse: Apart from a flurry of ineffectual concern in Bloomsbury, there was very little public outcry at *The Rainbow*'s suppression. The Incorporated Society of Authors, Playwrights and Composers, a London organization led by Thomas Hardy, expressed interest in some kind of defense, but nothing more came of it than an exchange of letters among the society's secretary, Pinker, and Lawrence. On November 13 an obscenity trial was held in Magistrates Court; Lawrence, Pinker, and Algernon Methuen (the director of the publishing house, who had pleaded guilty in advance, claiming that one of his readers had misled him) did not attend. On November 18 Philip Morrell raised the issue in debate in the House of Commons, asking if the home secretary knew of the police action and if Lawrence could answer the charge. The home secretary dismissed the questions by replying that Home Office approval was unnecessary to prosecute the book and that not Lawrence but Methuen was responsible for its defense. A follow-up question submitted by Morrell on December 1 brought similarly unsatisfactory results.

Lawrence began writing to friends to say he and Frieda had decided to sail to the United States. He solicited money for passage and expenses from Ottoline, Marsh, and others. A week later he changed his mind, just as publicly, in the meantime collecting new adherents for Rananim. Included were Aldous Huxley, who came to tea in mid-December with an introduction from Ottoline; a twenty-year-old Bulgarian aspiring writer, Dikran Kouyoumdjian (the future bestselling novelist Michael Arlen); the Oxford undergraduate Philip Heseltine (later the composer Peter Warlock), who suffered from manic-depressive disorder; a poet, Robert Nichols, who was confined to a hospital due to shell shock; and Dorothy Warren, a niece of Philip Morrell's. Lawrence, worried that Nichols might be homosexual, suggested he marry Warren. If Nichols would not marry Warren, then he hoped Heseltine could.

The prospect of settling in Florida gained credence when it was learned that a friend of Heseltine's, the composer Frederick Delius, had an overgrown orange grove near Jacksonville. An American acquaintance suggested Fort Myers, and Lawrence began studying a map of Florida: "a little town on *West* of peninsula," he wrote the Murrys, who had moved to France, "5,000 people, many niggers—9 miles from sea, on a big river one mile wide: many fish, and quails, and wild turkeys: land flat, covered with orange groves and pine trees: climate perfect."[48]

Lawrence prepared himself for immersion in the new novel by reading James Frazer's *The Golden Bough* and *Totemism and Exogamy*, which, somehow, led back to the "blood-consciousness" that had occupied him in Italy before he began *The Rainbow*. Italy and the spring of 1914 seemed so far off he misremembered his infatuation with blood-consciousness as having occurred "when I was about twenty"—rather than eighteen months before, when he was twenty-eight. He was soon sharing his ideas with Russell, some remnant of their friendship having survived the previous exchange:

> When I take a woman . . . [t]here is a transmission, I don't know of what, between her blood and mine, in the act of connection. So that afterwards, even if she goes away, the blood-consciousness persists between us, when the mental consciousness is suspended. . . . All living things, even plants, have a blood-being. If a lizard falls on the breast of a pregnant woman, then the blood-being of the lizard passes with a shock into the blood-being of the woman, and is transferred to the foetus, probably without intervention either of nerve or brain consciousness. And this is the origin of totem: and for this reason some tribes no doubt really *were* kangaroos: they contained the blood-knowledge of the kangaroo.[49]

An expurgated version of *The Rainbow* was printed in the United States by J. B. Huebsch, a small, independent firm,[50] inevitably renewing Lawrence's hope in the idea of moving to Florida. Huebsch, however, assumed that the New York Society for the Suppression of Vice would likewise try to suppress it, and made no effort to actually distribute or sell copies until the war was over. Lawrence received no royalty checks over the next four years.

His plan to move to Florida collapsed on December 11, the

national deadline for war-service registration. Required to undergo a physical examination (though his health made exemption certain), he was enraged and humiliated at the prospect of having to take his clothes off in front of two recruiting sergeants and a group of strange men. He stood in line at a recruiting center for two hours, then, before reaching the head of the line, stalked off and returned home. His fit of pique made it highly impractical, if not impossible, for them to obtain the exit visas needed for travel to the United States for the duration of the war.

Toward the end of December he and Frieda gave up the Hampstead apartment. They went to his sister Ada's for Christmas, then on to a borrowed, furnished house in Cornwall, loaned by the novelist and architect J. D. Beresford and his wife, Beatrice. "This is the first move to Florida," said Lawrence, apparently in the grip of some fantasy.[51] He continued to refer to their imminent emigration, though not a single friend or recruit was willing to book passage, and Kot and Murry openly challenged him. "He didn't like the Vale of Heath [*sic*]," Frieda later wrote of their stay in London, which had lasted just under five months, "and he didn't like the little flat and he didn't like me or anybody else."[52]

11

Dies Irae

I

The Cornwall house, which the Lawrences shared with the Beresfords' housekeeper-cook and her illegitimate six-year-old daughter, was on a windy, muddy hill with a view of the Atlantic. Insulated from the violent midwinter coastal storms by granite walls several feet thick, it seemed sturdy and timeless—"Celtic," Lawrence called it—and in its clean, open rooms, they were briefly restored to their prewar euphoria. "We *love* being here," he wrote to the Beresfords and at least eight other friends.[1] Less than two weeks after they had settled in, however, rage over the censorship and prosecution of *The Rainbow* welled up, tied in with hatred of the war. He suffered a massive tubercular attack, which he euphemistically called a cold, though his left hand felt paralyzed, a constant pain traveled down his right side, and his right arm and leg went numb.

Unable to hold a pen, he lashed out at Frieda. She was alarmed by their sudden loss of happiness and Lawrence's outbursts and mood swings, and began writing to his friends, asking for visits and presents. She did not hesitate to suggest cash: Amy Lowell, to whom she eventually put a blunt request, sent sixty pounds from Brookline, and continued to provide large amounts through the end of the war. Lawrence protested to Frieda but did nothing to stop the stream of plaintive letters. However shamed and furious the charity made him, he shared her unshakable belief in his genius and agreed that they could use the money as well as or better than the person sending it.

The messianic character of Shatov in Dostoyevsky's *The Possessed* provided the pretext for an appeal to Kot for a favorite liqueur of Lawrence's:

> I have been thinking of you lately reading Dostojewsky. . . . I thought Shatov (do you remember him?) was like you. Am I wrong? . . . the people are all so cruel and Dostojewsky brings it home. But Lawrence got very cross with me and says Dostojewsky is a liar. . . . I don't like D.'s women, they really are quite off their chumps and stupid. . . . Lawrence loved your "Kümmel" and if you can afford it *really*, send him one. . . . I hope you will come and see us soon.[2]

Kot immediately complied, also enclosing cigarettes for Frieda. In the meantime she had fired off a panicky confession to Bertrand Russell:

> I really don't know what to do. If you have a few days to spare it really would be kind of you if you came down. I know he would very much enjoy seeing you, and to me it would be a help. I feel it such a responsibility, it's too much for me. He might just die because everything is too much for him. But he simply mustn't die. It's not as if it concerned me alone. I know you are not extra cheerful yourself, but then at present who could be? . . . Lawrence is full of ideas to write and is very seedy and can't. Do come, it might do you good and I would be very glad. There are so few people Lawrence can bear the sight of.[3]

Russell had recently returned to London from Devon, where he had spent several days with T. S. Eliot's wife, Vivienne, contemplating an affair while attempting to nurse her through influenza and a nervous collapse that prefigured years of instability.[4] Immersed in reading Havelock Ellis[5] and busy with lectures on social democracy and the philosophy of politics (the ethics series Lawrence had planned to collaborate on), he did not reply until a month later, in a letter that dwelled on his own depression.

Lawrence, who tended to use such correspondence as nose rags, complained of the letter to Ottoline, whose own relationship with Russell now consisted largely of epistolary angst and malice: "very miserable. He doesn't know why he lives at all: mere obstinacy and pride, he says, keep him alive." Lawrence could not conceal his resentment: "His lectures are all right in themselves, but their *effect* is negligible. They are a financial success. But all the people who matter are too busy doing other things to come to listen. He lives only for fussy trivialities, and for nothing else."[6] Frieda shared the sour grapes: "You told me to say to Lawrence that you loved him," she wrote Russell. "Yet I dont *feel* that you care for him—I dont think you care for any body or if you do it is in a most unsatisfying way—And your belief in your social democratic ideal is *not* vital to you, it seems mostly obstinacy. It is a stale old bun even to you."[7] The lectures, published in November as *Principles of Social Reconstruction*, made Russell famous. He fell in love with a young, married actress-pacifist (Lady Constance Malleson, whom he called Colette, her stage name) the following year, and the Lawrences never heard from him again.

Ottoline, unasked, kept Lawrence supplied with books, hand-embroidered woolens, food, and alternative medicines—bark and root extracts and a powdered-milk protein substitute called Plasmon. He was promised a permanent home at Garsington, as well as a special Paris edition of *The Rainbow*, via her friend Prince Antoine Bibesco, but nothing came of either overture. The indictment of Frieda in this constant solicitude was clear if unspoken, though Ottoline was more direct with mutual friends. Lawrence, she was often heard to say, despised Frieda and should leave her. Frieda was responsible for his bad health, whereas her own wide-ranging influence was necessary to rescue his reputation. Two confidants were Heseltine and Kouyoumdjian, who visited in December—despite the fact that Ottoline found the two young men uncouth—and were lavished with good food, mediocre one-act dramas, and slurs on Frieda's fourteenth-rate nobility. The hospitality did not inspire loyalty: Invited down to Cornwall, Heseltine and Kouyoumdjian repeated everything.

Frieda was furious that Ottoline, no longer content to mock her (she had suspected that for months), was now predicting the imminent collapse of her marriage. Her next letter to Ottoline, which she felt she had to write, was notably mild and characterless, however. Perhaps she felt cowed by Ottoline's condescension; perhaps they simply needed the money and packages. "You have been very unfair to me, I think, you have tried to put me down as of no account—I could understand that as you must have had to put up with some terrible artists' wives. . . . I do think it's our real desire to be friends!"[8] Ottoline forwarded the letter to Russell. "Isn't Frieda a mad woman!!" she wrote. "She would send me mad too."[9]

2

Though Lawrence had suspected that he was tubercular at least since spitting blood at the Cearne, two and a half years before, he did not want to hear a diagnosis or see a doctor he did not know. Frieda arranged for him to be examined by Maitland Radford, the writer-physician son of a poet they had met at the Meynells' estate in Sussex, and apparently made it clear to the doctor beforehand that Lawrence was on edge. Radford said he found nothing organically wrong apart from unhealthy bronchial mucus and nervous exhaustion. He recommended bed rest, a diagnosis and cure Lawrence was prepared to accept.[10]

He spent much of January and February of 1916 indoors, for the first and last time in his life making peace with the difficulty of working in the face of serious illness—even if he had arranged to keep its nature a mystery. "The day must come when work is not so deathly to us," he counseled Gertler, who had written gloomily about a painting he was absorbed in finishing. ". . . It used to be, as it is with you, a pure process of self-destruction. But that gets better. I can only work now when I feel well."[11] He found time to sew a brown velvet dress with an embroidered collar for their housekeeper's elder daughter, who boarded with her grandparents,[12] and to correct proofs of *Twilight in Italy*, a brilliant collection of acerbic travel essays. Its publication brought him little satisfaction: The book was not well received—the *Times Literary Supplement* called it stylish but "perverse"—and it sold badly in the United States.[13]

When he began to show signs of recovery, he embarked on two exhausting projects, both failures. "Goats and Compasses," an incomprehensible tract on idealized heterosexual and homosexual love, comprised "the first, the destructive half of my philosophy," he wrote to Ottoline, who promptly told Russell that it was unworthy rubbish, attributable to Frieda.[14] The second project was more ambitious: Rainbow Books and Music, a private press, à la Virginia and Leonard Woolf's Hogarth Press, through which he would issue a subscription edition of *The Rainbow*. Heseltine wrote a pompous advertising prospectus and printed a thousand copies, which only annoyed Lawrence's friends, particularly Murry, whose now-completed novel was piggybacked on in some versions, without his permission. (Published later in the year by Constable, *Still Life* flopped.)

Lawrence did little better when he tried to sell a book of poems, *Amores*. It was a strange, disparate collection: five to his mother (including "The Virgin Mother"); leftover verses to Helen Corke and Louie Burrows; rhyming poems dating from his early twenties; even "Study," which had been rejected by the literary magazine of University College. Beresford tried to interest his own publisher, Sidgwick and Jackson, but they rejected the manuscript with an insulting letter that attempted to instruct Lawrence "as to how to write poetry."[15]

He and Frieda also had to relinquish the Beresfords' house. Frieda was badly in need of winter clothes and bundled up for house-hunting excursions down thirty-five miles of the Cornish coast in an assortment of summer outfits and a pair of bright red wool stockings. Lawrence's wardrobe was threadbare; even his underwear was patched. Wearing a slouch hat, brown corduroy suit, wing collar, and an old tie, he startled locals with his appearance and high, defiant voice. He was infuriated at the rents, of three to five pounds per week, that these "greedy," "selfish" people were charging. Nothing turned up, and they took rooms in a small inn in Zennor, a mining village ten miles from Land's End that had fallen into desuetude. Lawrence, in a parting letter to Beresford, recommended the extermination of all Cornishmen, whom he likened to insects.[16]

3

They had never felt farther from London and the war or more marginalized and dependent on each other. There were no prospects for money in sight, and they did not want to squander what they did have on the inn much longer than a week. Each morning they set out along the footpaths connecting the farms between Zennor and the neighboring fishing village of Saint Ives, which had seven houses and one church.

One evening early in March, wandering on to a wheat and dairy property outside Zennor called Tregerthen, they met a sixteen-year-old boy named Stanley Hocking, whose family had been tenant-farming the place for generations. They struck the boy as "a rather odd-looking pair." He pointed to a clump of disused two- and three-story stone cottages that had been vacant for years except for occasional squatters and "dubious characters."[17] The smallest, which Lawrence immediately took to, was surrounded by black boulders and half-frozen gorse bushes. It was damp, leaky, and had no running water, but there was a footpath leading a hundred yards uphill to a clear spring. Across a narrow lane were three other cottages that had been inexpertly joined to make a continuous large building topped by an incongruous tower that looked out on the Atlantic. The rent for the small cottage was five pounds a year.

Lawrence set to work sewing bright yellow kitchen curtains, which he painstakingly appliquéd in green. Mixing their own paint, they coated the kitchen walls pink and the cabinets bright blue, and built shelves for a set of heavy earthenware plates they had brought from Germany. When it rained, which it did incessantly, water gushed through the front door. "As usual," Frieda later wrote, "we made it out of a granite hole into a livable place."[18] They sent to London for housewares inherited and accumulated over four years on the road, most of which were stored in Gertler's bathtub: a set of brass candlesticks that had belonged to Lawrence's mother, a Persian rug, blankets, an eiderdown, china, an enamel bowl for washing dishes, a mirror, a fireplace fender, saucepan, folding cot, mattress, pillows, and a kitchen table and chair set. Some of the heavier things arrived by train, and they had to lug them from the station to the cottage.

Lawrence, writing vividly to the Murrys about the sunshine and pleasant prospect of their "little monastery" and the moors that buttressed it, persuaded them to leave a villa they had found in the south of France and rent the turreted house across the lane. "Let it be agreed for ever," he wrote, "I am Blutbruder: a Blutbruderschaft between us all."[19] He described the tower in great detail, and told Mansfield it would be an ideal place for her to write. After months of frustration, she was plowing through a long story, with the working title "The Aloe," that would become one of her masterpieces.[20]

Although sickness had left Lawrence gaunt, he offered to supervise the structural work and decorating and negotiated with the landlord to move an unsightly outhouse he knew would offend Mansfield. His generosity mystified Frieda: "Lawrence has already quite settled you there," she wrote her. "[I]n fact he seemed *more* anxious to make you happy there with all you can wish for than that we should have all we want." After Buckinghamshire she was wary of living so near the Murrys: "I am so anxious now to *live* without any more soulharrassing . . . Lawrence has had a bad time . . . Some of the wonder of the world has gone for him."[21]

The Murrys arrived early in April and, to Mansfield's chagrin, were forced to stay at the inn in Zennor for almost two weeks while they scrubbed, stained the floors, painted, and furnished. Murry varnished all their chairs black. "Look," Mansfield said to Frieda, "at the funeral procession of chairs."[22] Her deadpan expression and meaningful sidelong glances at Murry's expense captivated Frieda, who had begun responding in kind to Murry's pointed dismissals of her. "I had a hard time," she wrote, "not to laugh and be rude"; in Murry's version, the joke was on Frieda.[23] She spent overcast mornings in bed reading Shelley and Dostoyevsky. When the clouds parted, she roused herself and boiled sheets and heavy clothing on the tiny, single-burner oil stove in the scullery, then dragged the heavy, steaming piles outside to scrub in soapy water. Mansfield, fatigued by the work of renovating, and beginning to realize the utter unsuitability of the Cornish coast, became infuriated at the spectacle of Frieda, her arms plunged into the suds, perspiration beading on her forehead, cheeks pink with exertion as she proudly spread the gleaming wash on the grass to bleach and dry in the sun.

Frieda had gotten wind, possibly through Mansfield, of more backbiting from Ottoline and sent another letter:

> Steadily and persistently you have treated me with arrogance and insolence! . . . Your last letter to me was again cheap and vulgar . . . you have tried to separate Lawrence and me because you wanted some sort of unwholesome relation with him—All the time you felt good and holy! . . . Either you treat me with ordinary courtesy and respect or I wish neither to hear from you or see you again! . . . Someday it may dawn on you what a good thing you have rejected in my genuine friendship, that I offered you; but I know when you get

> this letter you will feel as you always do, that an injury has been done to you, while all your feelings and actions have been good and blameless! *That* is so hopeless about you and that *I* am the unreasonable person![24]

Ottoline, doubtless reveling in Frieda's faulty syntax, sent the letter on to Murry, who had been borrowing money since Christmas and repaying obeisance with gossip. The recirculated letter arrived at the Lawrences' cottage, where the Murrys were still receiving mail until they could move in. "O. sent you Frieda's letter," Lawrence immediately guessed.[25] Murry could hardly wait to get back to the inn to inform Ottoline of the interception of her forwarded mail. Frieda was ransacking their correspondence, he told Ottoline, because she hated herself for leaving Ernest Weekley and the luxuries of Nottingham (he cited the loss of her cook, tweeny, and parlor maid). "F. is *monstrum, horrendum, informe, ingens* [a horrible, deformed, huge monster]," he added, quoting Virgil. Lawrence, he felt, was washed up as a novelist.[26]

4

Actually Murry felt that Lawrence was passing the torch, a "kindly gardener," he later opined, who cultivated him like a seedling: "His off-hand, half-schoolmastery way of imparting his amazing range of country lore suited me perfectly."[27] He listened raptly to Lawrence's strongly felt opinions of the life span of farm animals, the symbology of sex, and Dostoyevsky (Lawrence offered to help him write a study of Dostoyevsky he had embarked on, if he could not manage to do it himself).

The two were soon filling their knapsacks with books and lunch for days in the fields, where Lawrence, unaware of Murry's two-facedness and struggling with a powerful attraction to him, suggested they consummate their "Blutbruderschaft" with a "blood-rite in keeping with the primeval rocks about us." Murry, who apparently had been sodomized as a boy, later claimed to be baffled by Lawrence's intensity:

> His relation with Frieda left room, and perhaps need, for a relation with a man of something of the kind and quality of my relation with Katherine; and he wanted this relation with me. It was possible only if it left my relation with Katherine intact, and indeed were based on

> that relation: for I was I only in that relation; or at any rate, only in that relation was I a man who had anything to give to Lawrence.[28]

Murry, whom Lawrence always seemed to reduce to a jellyfish, tried out various holding patterns, depending on the mood and demands of the particular day: He reacted like a disapproving older brother, as though Lawrence were fooling around with the wrong sort of women; played the role of good student and sycophant, conceding the inadequacies of marriage and the need to supplement it with a relationship with a man; hinted at a crippling dependence on Mansfield, for which he sought Lawrence's advice. Lawrence eventually saw through each avoidance tactic and denounced it, at which point Murry discarded it and went on to the next. He could always complain to Ottoline.

Mansfield had hired a maid to free her to concentrate on "The Aloe." Her writing dried up, however, and she spent long mornings and afternoons on a couch in the tower, writing letters to friends and sending away for Murry's hair-growth potion. She was easily enraged: at Frieda's cheerfulness and health, the high winds that ruined their occasional treks into Zennor to buy food, Murry's daylong absences, Lawrence's unpredictability. "[H]e has gone a little bit out of his mind," she wrote Kot. She resented his fixation on Murry, and felt helpless when his rages weakened him so much he had to go to bed. Normal conversations degenerated into shouting matches. "[Y]ou have gone wrong in your sex and belong to an obscene spirit," he said when Mansfield did not agree with him.[29] He argued that the Murrys, who liked to think of themselves as teenagers and had a private language of nicknames, euphemisms, and elaborate explanations for their abstention from sex, had perverted their relationship. He was disgusted by their penchant for bathing together.[30]

Their presence was conducive to his writing, however: He had begun his sequel to *The Rainbow* within days of their moving in, working with enthusiasm, speed, and a singlemindedness he had not known since composing the final version of *Sons and Lovers* in Italy. Once intended (in its original incarnation as "The Sisters") as a book to do more for women than universal suffrage, it quickly became a novel built around homosexuality. The character of Rupert Birkin, still Lawrence's mouthpiece, had a pale, ill-looking body; Gerald Critch, Gudrun's lover, had Murry's "hard-limbed" body and plodding intelligence. The first chapter was a forthright confession of Lawrence's newly activated love for Murry:

> All the time, he [Birkin] recognized that, although he was always drawn to women, feeling more at home with a woman than with a man, yet it was for men that he felt the hot, flushing, roused attraction which a man is supposed to feel for the other sex. Although nearly all his living interchange went on with one woman or another, although he was terribly intimate with at least one woman, and practically never intimate with a man, yet the male physique had a fascination for him, and for the female physique he felt only a fondness, a sort of sacred love, as for a sister.[31]

The attraction was complicated by similar feelings for Stanley Hocking's older brother William Henry, a languid, unself-conscious man about Lawrence's age who had left school at the age of thirteen to take over Tregerthen. He soon made his appearance in the novel:

> There would come into a restaurant a strange Cornish type of man, with dark eyes like holes in his head, or like the eyes of a rat, and with dark, fine, rather stiff hair, and full, heavy, softly-strong limbs. Then again Birkin would feel the desire spring up in him, the desire to know this man, to have him, as it were to eat him, to take the very substance of him. And watching the strange, rather furtive, rabbit-like way in which the strong, softly-built man ate, Birkin would feel the rousedness burning in his own breast, as if this were what he wanted, as if the satisfaction of his desire lay in the body of the young, strong man opposite.[32]

5

Within five weeks of the Murrys' arrival, the fantasy of a communal life had evaporated. Mansfield was furious about having relocated from the South of France, where writing had gone well and she and Murry had pursued their own ravenous symbiosis happily and successfully. Frieda confronted Lawrence about his pursuit of Murry and about their own sex life, which had all but dissolved, and got little but self-justifying vituperation. Rowboat rides along the coast and junk shopping in the town of Penzance for old wooden furniture discarded by fishermen were safe excursions, but almost anytime they were indoors Lawrence exploded. Murry began looking for another house.

One afternoon at tea Mansfield brought up Shelley. "Ode to a Skylark," Frieda announced, "was false." Lawrence, who loved the poem, accused her of ignorance and showing off, and Frieda ordered him to leave the house. "I'll give you a dab on the cheek to quiet you, you dirty hussy," he yelled back, while Mansfield slipped out the door. The argument was still raging at dinnertime, when Frieda emerged from the moonless night into the Murrys' kitchen. "I have finally done with him. It is all over for ever," she told Mansfield, and went back outside, where she walked circles around their house. Lawrence came running out and lunged at her, screaming in a falsetto as he punched her and pulled at her hair. She escaped his clutches into the Murrys' kitchen, sobbing, Lawrence chasing behind. In the glare of the kitchen lanterns, his skin was greenish white and he looked seriously ill. "[H]e just hit," Mansfield later wrote Kot, "thumped the big soft woman." While Murry looked on squeamishly, Frieda let Lawrence strike until he was spent and then collapsed in one of the black chairs. Lawrence, slumped over, bit his nails. Fifteen minutes passed, then he abruptly asked a question about French literature. Frieda poured herself a cup of coffee and they began to reminisce about a meal of "very rich but very good macaroni cheese" they had once enjoyed.

Late the following morning, he made a great show of bringing her breakfast in bed, and they sang songs through the afternoon. "I don't know which disgusts one worse," Mansfield wrote. "[W]hen they are very loving and playing with each other or when they are roaring at each other and he is pulling out Frieda's hair and saying 'I'll cut your bloody throat, you bitch.'"[33] She recapitulated the events to Ottoline, with a few embellishments: "Saucepans and frying pans hurtled through the air." Frieda took "Awful Relish" in being beaten, and dressed up and prattled afterward. Lawrence was "lost, like a little gold ring in that immense german christmas pudding which is Frieda. . . . One simply looks and waits for someone to come with a knife and cut her up into the smallest pieces that L. may see the light and shine again. . . . I could not write like this to anyone but you."[34] Other correspondents received similar letters.

One night in June, Murry heard Lawrence scream out his nickname: "Jack is killing me." He decided to reassure Lawrence, but he chose his words—an unconvincing profession of love—badly. "I hate your love, I hate it," Lawrence railed. "You're an obscene bug, sucking my life away."[35] Murry intensified the search for another house and soon found one thirty miles away on the Channel coast. They moved in the middle of the month. "The north side was too rugged for them," Lawrence explained to a mutual friend.[36]

In their two months as neighbors, he had finished most of his novel, which Frieda, probably in a furious moment, suggested he call "*Dies Irae*," day of wrath, from the funeral dirge.[37] Lawrence took over payments on the Murrys' lease, and he and Frieda often retreated to separate houses to sleep.

6

Thirty-five years after the fact, Frieda attributed Lawrence's homosexual drives to temporary unhappiness. She felt far less equanimity when the experiments were under way, and by her own account bitterly "fought him and won."[38] The real nature of their arguments and of her "victory," and the question of whether Lawrence ever consummated a homosexual relationship in his years with her, will probably always be a mystery. What is clear is that Frieda felt some contempt for and impatience with his sexual ambivalence, and was humiliated and hurt by what she later called his unfaithfulness.

His inclinations consumed much of their remaining fourteen months in Cornwall. With Murry gone she had to contend with William Henry Hocking. Lawrence was soon spending an inordinate amount of time with him, trying to interest him in modern poetry and Rananim, writing to friends in London to put him up and make introductions. In the evenings he often slipped down to the Hockings', where he gave Stanley French lessons and taught him to play chess. Frieda came to get him one night in a heavy rainstorm. "Lorenzo, Lorenzo," she shouted, "where are you? Why do you leave me alone on such a night as this?" Lawrence packed up his French books and took her home.[39]

Despite his clumsiness with a pitchfork and ill health, which made him unable to withstand the long hours, he volunteered to help William Henry with the wheat harvest in July.[40] Frieda, who had no illusions of a return to the land, joined him in the fields, perhaps to keep an eye on him, perhaps to assuage the loneliness she felt when he left her alone in the house. She enjoyed *croust*—the afternoon Cornish tea, served al fresco—but otherwise limited her conversation to occasional, often irrational small talk and condemnation of the war. Lawrence kept up a running commentary on everything from Rananim to the futility of birth; when he became agitated, his voice pierced the silence of the fields. "Where in the hell did she find him?" a workman asked one day, when the Lawrences were out of earshot. "I should think that she must have found him in a Lucky Bag," one of the halfpenny sacks of candy sold locally, which came with a toy that squeaked.[41] Tregerthen made its way into Lawrence's 1923 novel *Kangaroo*; the farm became Trendrinnan, and Lawrence became Richard Somers, one of the key hands in the harvest: "'He'd never have got his hay in but for Mr. Somers,' they said. . . . Work went like steam when he was on Trendrinnan farm."[42] William Henry became John Thomas, slang for penis.

Lawrence's infatuation waned as the harvest drew to a close: "I think William Henry was thinking that the whole thing [Rananim] was nonsense," Stanley later recalled, "and he wasn't having anything to do with it. After all, you can't leave a farm. You can't pack up and leave your animals and relatives and go somewhere to an imaginary place."[43] With his immense capacity for sublimation, Lawrence went back to work immediately. "I and the type writer," he wrote a friend a month later, "have sworn a Blutbruderschaft."[44]

7

Lawrence had started typing his novel when the Murrys left, struggling with carbon paper and ribbons that never seemed to fit, rewriting liberally as he typed. He had retracted the homosexual chapter, or "suppressed Prologue," as it was later to be known, somewhere along the way. The new first chapter featured a conversation between Ursula and Gudrun about the inanity of marriage. Ottoline, whom Lawrence had written into the Prologue as Hermione Roddice, Rupert's former lover, had become Ursula's bête noire. A meddler, she constantly comes between Ursula and Birkin. Lawrence gave free rein to satire: Hermione's antique clothes are soiled and torn, and her speech is so affected she slurs. He took special zest in scenes pitting Hermione and Ursula against each other:

> The two women looked at each other. Ursula resented Hermione's long, grave, downward-looking face. There was something of the stupidity and the unenlightened self-esteem of a horse in it. "She's got a horse-face," Ursula said to herself, "she runs between blinkers."[45]

His friendship with Ottoline had outlived its usefulness, and he quietly exacted revenge in other ways: His poems *Amores*, which Pinker had finally placed, had included a lugubrious dedication in the American edition: "To Ottoline Morrell in Tribute to Her Noble and Independent Sympathy and Her Generous Understanding These Poems are Gratefully Dedicated."[46] He shortened it for the British edition: "To Ottoline Morrell."[47]

The novel acquired a final title, *Women in Love*, and there were few interruptions over the latter part of the summer except for a summons Lawrence received to be examined for the military. The British cabinet had instituted compulsory service in late December; legislation passed in May and the start of general conscription in June led to the call-up. Although he was once again diagnosed as tubercular and received an exemption, the point-blank summation of his condition and the experience of bedding down in a drafty barracks with hundreds of men he did not know and having his genitals and anus touched by examining officials made him frightened and angry. He developed a phobia of leaving the neighborhood and a dread of talking to strangers.

In mid-August Frieda wrote Ernest for permission to see the children before the Saint Paul's fall term,[48] and Lawrence retreated further. When he spotted a man in a pair of white flannel pants on a field path—the sign of a day tripper taking a stroll, inevitably with his wife and children—he wanted to hide behind bushes, and fantasized about shaking an immense box of powdered insect repellant from the sky to "exterminate" such families. "[T]hey creep in," he wrote Kot, "the obstructions, the people, like bugs they creep invidiously in." There were too many of them, he explained, to crush underfoot.[49] "I am too much afraid of the world to go out," he wrote another friend, a week and a half before Frieda left.[50]

The first days of September passed with no reply from Ernest. Lawrence kept recommending that Frieda wait until the children were consenting adults: "Then, if there *is* love," he wrote a friend, "if there *is* a connection, it is undeniable: if there *be* no active love, nothing can create it."[51] Undeterred, she arranged for an apartment in Hampstead, and sometime during the second week of September, Ernest yielded.

Early on the afternoon of September 16, a Saturday, Monty, Elsa, and Barby took the Underground to Paddington Station to meet her train. Monty, an erect, aloof sixteen-year-old with little of the volubility Frieda remembered, was mortified by the apple blossom branches she brought from Cornwall and held in her arms. His misgivings evaporated at a Covent Garden matinee later in the afternoon, however, watching Sir Thomas Beecham conduct Mozart's *The Marriage of Figaro*. None of the children, whose knowledge of music was limited largely to Frieda's playing Schubert and Brahms on the piano at Cowley, had ever seen or heard an orchestra, and they were transfixed by the performances of Frederic Ranalow, a popular *Beggar's Opera* star, who played Figaro, and Désirée Ellinger as Susanna.[52] Frieda took them to tea at Lyon's afterward and gave them each ten shillings. Clutching the money, the girls went off to the bathroom together. "We mustn't like Mama," Elsa instructed Barby, "now that we've got ten shillings."[53]

On her return Frieda found Lawrence ill, depressed, and itching to accept an invitation to the Murrys', whom they had not seen for almost two months. No one had a very good time, and almost as soon as she and Lawrence got back home, they fought at dinner. Lawrence, singing a song with a seemingly endless refrain, retreated to the scullery to wash the dishes. His back was to her, and their stoneware thudded against the enamel dishwashing pot, the noise drowning out any further argument. Creeping up behind him, Frieda hit him over the head with a dinner plate. "That," he screamed, reeling around to face her, "was like a woman!" and added that since she was a woman, she was "right." He was relieved, he said, that the plate had not killed him.[54]

"I think Frieda and I are really at peace with each other, for ever," he wrote Mansfield shortly after.[55] "It is a fight one has to fight—the old Adam to be killed in me, the old Eve in her—then a new Adam and a new Eve," he elaborated to Murry, in an allusion to "New Eve and Old Adam," an autobiographical story of romantic failure he had written three months after meeting Frieda. "Till the fight is finished, it is only honorable to fight. But oh dear, it is very horrible and agonising."[56]

Frieda was less certain that the worst was over. "What would you do," she asked Catherine Carswell (their friend Catherine Jackson, recently remarried), who came to stay for a week, "if you had a man like that to deal with?" Carswell, who had a history of involvement with emotionally unstable men, carefully said that she would consider herself lucky if someone of Lawrence's intelligence thought it worth arguing with her. When Frieda confided her fear that Lawrence "was mad and that she would have to leave him," Carswell reassured her that Lawrence was a visionary.[57]

By the end of October the manuscript of *Women in Love* had grown to 666 pages, and Lawrence sent it to Pinker to be retyped. Though there was still a powerful undercurrent of homosexual yearning, the novel was now largely about ambivalent heterosexual love. Frieda's affair with the Nottingham lacemaker Will Dowson, transposed into an affair between Ursula and Rupert, made its way into a chapter called "Excurse," complete with a coitus on a carpet of bluebells in Sherwood Forest. Their lovemaking becomes more unsatisfactory, and Ursula eventually submits to anal sex, recalling Frieda's complaints as recorded by Murry. Gerald no longer resembled Murry much, though an erotic nude wrestling match with Rupert brought that aspect of both the novel and the friendship to a climax of sorts. Friends who had caused offense or failed to remain loyal through the first two years of the war came under attack, particularly Heseltine (Halliday in the book), who had fallen into disfavor after a nasty correspondence involving Frieda and a woman he eventually married.

One of the few to escape was Mansfield, recognizable as Gudrun, cautious, brittle, self-consciously intelligent, often disgusted with her lover Gerald. At novel's end Gerald dies improbably in a snowdrift. A final conversation between Ursula and Birkin reflected the state of the Lawrences' marriage and captured his homoerotic yearning with a straightforwardness he was rarely capable of in life:

> "Did you need Gerald?" she asked one evening.
>
> "Yes," he said.
>
> "Aren't I enough for you?"
>
> "No," he said. "You are enough for me, as far as a woman is concerned. You are all women to me. But I wanted a man friend, as eternal as you and I are eternal."
>
> "Why aren't I enough?" she said. "You are enough for me. I don't want anybody else but you. Why isn't it the same with you?"

"Having you, I can live all my life without anybody else, any other sheer intimacy. But to make it complete, really happy, I wanted eternal union with a man too: another kind of love," he said.

"I don't believe it," she said. "It's an obstinacy, a theory, a perversity."

"Well——" he said.

"You can't have two kinds of love. Why should you!"

"It seems as if I can't," he said. "Yet I wanted it."

"You can't have it, because it's false, impossible," she said.

"I don't believe that," he answered.[58]

The completed manuscript came back to Lawrence in November. Frieda hand-corrected one copy, and he began circulating it among friends. He was nervous about its being read by anyone who had anything to do with Garsington, and withheld it from Ottoline for as long as possible, though friends such as Murry were quick to inform her she was the book's villainess. She finally got her hands on the copy with Frieda's corrections. "[I]t is of course Frieda's revenge," she insisted to Russell, never doubting Frieda had written the most scurrilous parts.[59] She threatened libel if the manuscript were to be published in its current condition. Publication in any form soon proved to be a moot issue: Pinker, assiduously submitting the novel to one publisher after another, received nothing but rejections.

8

The Lawrences spent a rainy Christmas Eve entertaining Esther Andrews and Robert Mountsier, New Yorkers who had arrived on their doorstep in November and become long-term houseguests. She was a commercial artist, he a newspaper editor and aspiring literary agent who wanted to represent Lawrence in the United States. In the middle of dinner a policeman who had struggled through the mud on a bicycle from Saint Ives appeared at the door and began questioning their reasons for being in Cornwall. It was the beginning of a clumsy harassment campaign, instigated in part by a local vicar's daughter, who objected to Frieda's Germanness and Lawrence's failure to serve in the war, and spurred by the proliferation of U-boats along the coast through the winter. The Germans declared unrestricted submarine warfare on the last day of January 1917, and Frieda and Lawrence were widely suspected of signaling U-boats with scarves and coded messages flashed with lanterns. The accusations reached fever pitch when three British ships were sunk in the Bristol Channel and washed up at Land's End and Saint Ives. "Local people in Zennor knew that Frieda was a German," their landlord's son later recalled, "and they immediately called her a German spy."[60] Her relation to the Red Baron, who logged his fiftieth air kill in April, was undoubtedly a subject of discussion in the village. Nor did it help that she continued to receive a stream of letters from her family via the safe address in Switzerland, and subscribed to the *Berliner Tageblatt*. The local mail carrier, a notorious jingo, kept their neighbors and the village authorities abreast of each delivery, and some of their mail was apparently censored in London well before it reached the village. A policeman was detailed to crouch below the windows of the cottage to eavesdrop.

Routine searches became commonplace: Returning from Zennor with a loaf of bread one day, Frieda had to empty her knapsack for a policeman who suspected she was concealing a camera. Lawrence was thought to be German, impersonating an Englishman: "There was an unfortunate policeman from St. Ives," Frieda later wrote, who "had to trot up so many times to our cottage to look over and over again Lawrence's papers, to see if he were really an Englishman and his father without a doubt an Englishman, and if his mother was English."[61] In February, their applications for passport renewal were refused by London military authorities.

Lawrence reapplied, dreaming again about Rananim, which he had relocated to, among other places, the Marquesas (in the South Pacific) in the course of the war. Mountsier, who had left shortly after the New Year, promised to set him and Frieda up in New York, which quickly became Lawrence's new mecca. Esther Andrews had stayed on at the cottage, and developed a crush on Lawrence. He was smitten as well, called her Hadaffah, an approximation of her Hebrew name, and encouraged her to stay as long as she liked. She bought fabric and made patterns for Russian blouses based on Frieda's Bavarian blouses, showing up each day to sew until Frieda could no longer stand her. "I try my best to bring them both to reason—Frieda and Hadaf—but in vain," Lawrence wrote Mountsier. "It is a duel without pistols for all of us."[62] She left in mid-January and returned several months later, when Frieda was in bed with colitis after a trip to London that had again left her infuriated with Ernest. He had begun dating their old neighbor Gladys Bradley. Frieda raged to Kot:

> I was *disgusted* to find that Ernst who poses as the tragic figure to the children, takes Gladys (she is a handsome, coarse girl) out to dinner, flirts with her, but keeps of course the last respectability—Lord, I was so furious—but then he *is* both things, but the children are different, thank God![63]

Andrews propositioned Lawrence one day when Frieda, still bedridden, was safely out of reach. They seem to have attempted to make love, and failed. Frieda confronted them and, perhaps more humiliated for Lawrence's sake than for her own, evicted Andrews.[64] By then the United States had declared war on Germany, and Lawrence had sworn off the New World. "America is a stink-pot in my nostrils," he wrote Kot, "after having been the land of the future for me."[65] Privately telling friends he hoped he would never write another novel, he turned his attention to old poems charting the early months of his affair with Frieda, to which he had added several decidedly more ambivalent poems over the past year. He was nervous about releasing them but made no effort to disguise the overtly autobiographical nature of the manuscript, *Look! We Have Come Through!*, which he prefaced with a three-sentence précis of their flight from London. Chatto and Windus offered an advance of twenty-one pounds, provided he delete "Meeting among the Mountains," about Ernest Weekley, and "Song of a Man Who Is Loved"—both objected to on grounds of indecency, despite their having already appeared elsewhere. (They were reinstated in the American edition.) Laced with references to Frieda, the collection was moving to any who knew their story and did not despise her origins or Germanness:

> *She said as well to me:*
> *. . . "When I was a child, I loved my father's*
> *riding-whip*
> *that he used so often.*
> *I loved to handle it, it seemed like a near part*
> *of him.*
> *So I did his pens, and the jasper seal on his*
> *desk.*

Something seemed to surge through me when I
touched them."[66]

Such poems as "Mutilation" were an admission of a dependence Lawrence was loath to admit:

It aches in me.
What is England or France, far off,
But a name she might take?
I don't mind this continent stretching, the sea
far away;
It aches in me for her
Like the agony of limbs cut off and aching;
Not even longing,
It is only agony.

A cripple!
Oh God, to be mutilated!
To be a cripple
And if I never see her again?

I think, if they told me so
I could convulse the heavens with my horror.
I think I could alter the frame of things in
my agony.
I think I could break the System with my
heart.[67]

The title came from "Song of a Man Who Has Come Through," one of Frieda's favorites:

Not I, not I, but the wind that blows through me!
A fine wind is blowing the new direction of Time.
If only I let it bear me, carry me, if only it carry
me!
If only I am sensitive, subtle, oh, delicate, a winged
gift!

If only, most lovely of all, I yield myself and am
borrowed
By the fine, fine wind that takes its course through
the chaos of the world.[68]

9

Apart from the twenty-one pounds and a trickle of handouts, money dried up almost entirely through 1917 and 1918. Lawrence remained determined to sell his philosophical essays. The *English Review* published the first four essays of a series, "The Reality of Peace" (in which he made use of bug imagery and expressed a preference for war in marriage over impersonal world war), but rejected the final three. Other metaphysical essays went the rounds of the journals. Frieda had grown to hate the incomprehensibility of these writings, and disliked watching him make a fool of himself by submitting them over and over. After one rejection she confiscated a manuscript and threw it into the fireplace. "There you are, Lorenzo," she yelled. "[T]hey've all come back again. They are all philosophy," she shouted as the paper blazed, "and nobody wants them!"[69]

The gloom followed Lawrence to the fields when the late spring brought warm weather. "It's all very well to see the dear little lambs playing and gamboling," he said to Stanley Hocking as they watched them running up and down the rocks one day, "but what are they born for? Only for the cruel butcher's knife. Futile it all is. . . . Every birth means a death. Therefore all life is futile."[70] He was preoccupied with the war's mounting death toll and with another call-up for the military, but he need not have worried: On June 23 he was pronounced exempt a third time.

He plunged himself into scrubbing and furnishing a tinner's cottage several miles west of Tregerthen for Cecil Gray, a twenty-two-year-old Scotsman and former roommate of Heseltine. Lawrence had never met him, and knew only that he had completed an exhaustive study of the folk music of the Hebrides and had obtained a medical exemption from active service in the war because of a bad heart. The cottage was on the grounds of a ruined castle perched on a cliff looking out to the sea. Gray, who had an independent family income, imperiously directed Lawrence's purchases—eight chairs, three tables, lamps, a mirror, a chest of drawers, and pillows—by letter. He arrived in midsummer and was hardly what Lawrence had expected. Ironic, fastidious, urbane, and sophisticated, an avowed heterosexual with a love of good whiskey, he had come to write, he told the Lawrences, a cantata based on Flaubert's *La Tentation de Saint Antoine*, which had been translated in 1910. Lawrence thought it the work of a dilettante, but he was soon spending much of his time with Gray, immersed in long disquisitions on homosexuality. One afternoon Gray heard a knock and found Lawrence at the door. "[H]ow long have you been in love with me?" Lawrence asked.[71]

Frieda was left to fend for herself when they paired off for long days together. She had come to like being alone in the daytime, and spent the time making embroidered caps out of old, often stained, blouses, which she sent as gifts to such people as Lady Asquith. Years later a friend to whom she sent one as a baby gift recalled an underarm perspiration stain in the white lace.[72]

After dark, when she was by herself, the possibility of the police turning up at the doorstep frightened her. Trips to the outhouse became a terrifying prospect after a policeman stopped her one night to ask why she had left the house. Eventually she began suffering aural hallucinations: Wounded soldiers, she thought, were calling out to her from the fields.

By the wheat harvest Lawrence had lost enthusiasm for Gray, who in turn had grown sick of Lawrence's "bombastic, pseudo-mystical, psycho-philosophical" obsession with theories of ideal male love.[73] When the baling began Lawrence stayed closer to Tregerthen, disappearing into the fields with William Henry. The renewal of his infatuation provoked bitter fights with Frieda through the summer. Left to eat by herself when work lasted through dinnertime, she was often furious when he finally came home, and screaming matches occasionally drove him back to the Hockings' for most of the night. She discovered that if she went over to Gray's in the afternoon, stayed for supper, and did not arrive back home until the light was fading, she could kill most of her free hours fairly pleasantly. She and Gray sat at his piano, chatting about music and singing Hebridean folk songs, and she was soon talking freely about her frustration with Lawrence, conversations that later led Gray to describe Lawrence as "not very far removed from" impotence.[74] By late summer or early fall, he and

Frieda had evidently begun an affair, despite a neuritis of the leg that kept her in bed for some six weeks.

What little is known of their relationship suggests that it was more comforting than passionate. He was the only person other than Mansfield with whom she had had anything resembling an intimate conversation since moving to Cornwall, and she seems to have kept most of what happened from Lawrence. His interest in William Henry had again run its course by the end of the harvest, and he occasionally joined Frieda and Gray for dinner and impromptu piano concerts and evenings of German folk songs. Local authorities soon suspected a full-fledged spy ring, spearheaded by Gray. Twelve men armed with rifles burst in on one such evening late in August, interrogated the three, and then searched the house. Gray, who often neglected to shield his windows at night with the required blackout fabric, was later fined under the Defence of the Realm regulations for having an exposed light.

One evening six weeks later, Frieda returned from a trip to Gray's to find their cottage ransacked. The sergeant of the Saint Ives police arrived the next morning with an army officer and, while two detectives resumed the house search, informed the Lawrences that they were being expelled from Cornwall. "This is your English liberty," Frieda shouted. "Here we live and don't do anybody any harm, and these creatures have the right to come here and touch our private things."

"Be quiet," Lawrence told her. He and Frieda left for London three days later.[75]

10

H. D., with whom Lawrence had been corresponding regularly and pruriently, offered a small duplex pied-à-terre she and Aldington kept in Bloomsbury. They moved in on October 20, followed shortly by detectives, who tailed them relentlessly and eavesdropped at the apartment door. Air raids were constant, requiring the tenants to take cover in the cellar. Lawrence usually refused to make the trip downstairs, and Frieda would run up, fruitlessly trying to persuade him. Her Germanness greatly upset the Aldingtons' elderly landlady, and Lawrence appeased her with empty compliments on her collections of jewelry and imported glassware.

H. D. was shocked by the changes Lawrence had undergone. In addition to weight loss and a strange fire in his eyes, he was pent up, nervous, and afraid to be alone with her in a room unless he was writing and she simply sat by, quietly watching his pen move across the page of a German diary or English butcher's ledger. Occasionally they found themselves simultaneously engaged in the same silent pursuit: Motionless on opposite sides of the sitting room, which was painted apricot and lit by candles, they composed poems with elaborate conceits, often inspired by Attic tragedians whom she was translating. He seemed to her utterly dependent on and dwarfed by Frieda, with whom he constantly bickered. "[S]hut-up, shut-up, shut-up, you damn Prussian," he would yell, at least as H. D. later rendered his rebukes in *Bid Me to Live*, "I don't want to hear anything you can tell me."[76] H. D. felt attracted, but her tentative overtures fell flat: He insisted on an emotional triangle.[77]

Frieda had evidently chosen her moment to tell Lawrence about the affair with Gray, and now talked freely about him. Letters flew between Gray and Lawrence filled with veiled accusations and defenses, though in fact Lawrence was largely unfazed. Gray had heard about Lawrence's uncertain flirtation with H. D. and criticized him for preferring a foot-washing "Magdalen" to Frieda. Lawrence replied:

> [T]he pure understanding between the Magdalen and Jesus went deeper than the understanding between the disciples and Jesus, or Jesus and the Bethany women. . . . you and Frieda need to go one world deeper in knowledge. . . . I don't mind being told where I am wrong—not by you or anybody I respect. Only you don't seem to be going for me in anything where I am really wrong: a bit Pharisaic, both you and Frieda: external. . . . my "women", Esther Andrews, Hilda Aldington etc, represent, in an impure and unproud, subservient, cringing, bad fashion, I admit,—but represent none the less the threshold of a new world, or underworld, of knowledge and being. . . . You want an emotional sensuous underworld, like Frieda and the Hebrideans: my "women" want an ecstatic subtly-intellectual underworld, like Greeks—Orphicism—like Magdalen.[78]

H. D. began to wonder if Lawrence found her repugnant, and spoke to Frieda, whose frankness she admired. Accustomed to

Lawrence's thwarted passions for such women (she called them his "spiritual brides," a term he borrowed for *Women in Love*), Frieda confided that she considered his homosexuality a stronger threat: "Lawrence does not really care for women. He only cares for men," she assured her. "Hilda, *you have no idea of what he is like*."[79]

Advance copies of *Look! We Have Come Through!* brought little appreciation. H. D., who had read the poems in manuscript and thought them too body obsessed and literal, had not changed her mind. The *Times Literary Supplement* criticized his verbosity and overexcitability. Gray, whose working understanding of the degree to which the Lawrences had or had not come through was informed by Frieda's confidences, told him the book was a lie. Ottoline handed her copy across the breakfast table to Bertrand Russell one morning, their friendship having survived the demise of their affair. "They may have come through," Russell said, "but I don't see why I should look."[80]

12

Heimweh

1

In mid-December, after a last-ditch attempt to enjoy London in a borrowed apartment that Lawrence found too middle class, they left the city for a friend's empty cottage in Berkshire. It was tiny, barely furnished, and equipped with little more than a few saucepans. Though soon bedridden with bronchitis, Lawrence worked in fits and starts on a book of critical essays he had begun in Cornwall on the transcendental in American literature. (It was later published as *Studies in Classic American Literature*.)[1] Despite protestations that he had given up writing novels, he began what would eventually become *Aaron's Rod*, full of the occupants of H. D.'s apartment. By turns peevish and soul searching, it featured a grotesquerie of Cecil Gray (Cyril Scott), pale, fat, and sporting a pince-nez, and the vaguely demonic, conflicted, and autobiographicized flutist, Aaron Sisson, whose relationship to his wife and his flute (rod) is decidedly double edged.

Frieda, singularly absent from its initial pages, considered the novel a welcome change from Lawrence's obscure and unreadable philosophy. (She eventually appeared as Tanny Lilly, the blunt-speaking wife of a second Lawrence-like character, Rawdon Lilly.) After what felt like "several lifetimes" lived through during the writing of *Women in Love*,[2] she was happy to be alone with him again, though their lack of funds was a huge strain. They began soliciting gifts of cash from patrons and the few friends, like Kot, who had not dropped them. Almost everyone else kept their distance. Murry spent a protracted recuperation at Garsington—from exhaustion brought on by working as a translator in the War Office—but the Lawrences were never invited, though it was only twenty miles north of Berkshire. When Murry and Mansfield married later in the year, Frieda and Lawrence were not on the guest list.

Police continued to stalk them: at the cottage and on the road, interrupting their long, regular walks through the pine woods and thick hazel copses, spent searching for dandelions, which they fermented; at night they were occasionally awakened by corks popping out of the bottles of homemade wine. In the village, people remarked on their eccentric clothing and were amazed to see his breathless sprints to catch the mail carrier's bike taking away the last post, Frieda plodding nonchalantly behind. Lawrence made picture hats for her that could be spotted hundreds of yards off, "bobbing up and down like a lid on a boiling saucepan."[3] He also sewed her an odd short jacket of blue linen to match one of his, and augmented his own meager spring wardrobe with unusual accessories: a scarlet tie and a floppy white cotton hat that looked like a toddler's. He found modern tailoring preposterous and unmanly, and wore such clothes, he told a neighbor, because "I like people to look at me."[4] The local children, taught that Christ's hair was ginger colored, trailed behind him, shouting "Walking Jesus."[5] He made selections for two slim collections of poetry. A miscellany of old work brought an advance of just six pounds, five shillings from the publisher Martin Secker, who had admired Lawrence's work since 1911; Secker titled it *New Poems* in a vain effort to increase its salability. Issued in paperback in October, it was Lawrence's sole publication of any length that year. He sold the other collection, *Bay*, to a disorganized Charing Cross Road bookseller, balletomane, and sometime author who ran a hand press; eighteen months after delivery of the manuscript, the book finally appeared, full of typographical errors. He also earned small sums of money from stories published in the *English Review* and two anthologized poems, but the drying up of even these negligible sources would remain a constant, major preoccupation throughout 1918, keeping him and Frieda largely confined to the countryside.

Frieda did manage at least two trips to London to see her children. In April she startled Monty, seventeen and proud of his Officers' Training Corps uniform, by referring to the carnage of "this stupid war." Horrified at the prospect of him fighting his own relatives, she offered, apparently in all sincerity, to hide him "somewhere in a cave or in a wood."[6] Several days later her cousin the Red Baron was shot down over Amiens and killed.

2

Their immediate neighbors in Berkshire were Violet Monk and Cecily Lambert, cousins in their early twenties who ran a farm they had inherited from their grandfather. Monk was a neurotic recluse and hypochondriac with a form of dyspepsia so severe she could not eat in public. Raised in luxury, she worked the plow and shovel in costumes more appropriate to dressage than to a dirt farm: shirt, tie, and laced calfskin boots from a tony West End clothier. The two women were trudging up the meadow to the farmhouse one evening after milking their goats and feeding the pigs and hens when Lawrence, whom they had seen but never met, suddenly sped toward them and introduced himself. Frieda, disheveled and out of breath, a wide-brimmed straw hat partially obscuring her face, trailed several yards behind in a full, loud blue-and-white checked skirt.

Monk, recently jilted by a man she loved, was impatient with guests, but the Lawrences were invited in. He proceeded to interview them for an hour over tea, bread, and jam, while Lambert, her skirts caked with mud, wondered what these strange people wanted. His intense curiosity left her with the entirely accurate feeling that he wanted "to obtain copy."[7] Monk simply felt ill, and incensed that a stranger was taking up so much of their time. She said next to nothing and allowed her cousin to do the serving.

He also began visiting the nearby cottage of a literary family named Farjeon, whom he and Frieda had first met in 1915, or possibly before the war. He offered Joan Farjeon, the daughter of Sir Hamo Thornycroft, a Royal Academician and well-known sculptor, a huge bouquet of wildflowers picked from the high road and fields he had passed through on the first visit, painted her a wooden bowl, sewed a linen jacket for her husband, Herbert, a drama critic, and gave their children botanical lectures on every visit. Their three-year-old daughter refused to believe he was real until she touched him. Lawrence still preferred to keep his precarious health a secret, and insisted Frieda also stalwartly deny it. "Lawrence must have sunshine," she explained to Joan, on one of the rare times she accompanied him to the house. "But it isn't tuberculosis, it *isn't*!"[8]

By May they were utterly destitute, and left Berkshire for a furnished Midlands cottage with a backyard croquet lawn that his sister Ada found for them. She offered to pay the rent for a year, a kindness Lawrence accepted, though humiliation soon drove him to apply to the Royal Literary Fund, which awarded him fifty pounds in July. Desperate to keep the cash flowing, he also accepted a commission of fifty pounds, originally offered several years before by Oxford University Press, to write a textbook of European history for children. The money was payable on completion of the manuscript, and he dashed off three chapters in a few hot weeks in July. He soon became disgusted and set the project aside to work on three short stories—among them "The Fox," about Lambert and Monk, whom he cast as clingy, dependent lesbians—as well as an unsuccessful Eastwood-derived drama and *Women in Love* offshoot, *Touch and Go*, which featured a subplot with partial portraits of himself and Mansfield. He sent the play to Mansfield, who had suffered serious health setbacks over the last year: a diagnosis of tuberculosis (an infection she may have caught from Lawrence in Cornwall), followed by an attack of pleurisy. She disliked the play, and, unable to humor Lawrence, pronounced it "*black* with miners."[9]

3

Lawrence's own health was steadily deteriorating, but he was reclassified C3—fit for light, menial work, such as scrubbing public bathrooms—two weeks after a third examination for the military on September 11, his thirty-third birthday. He fired off angry letters to friends like Cynthia Asquith, Catherine Carswell, and Mark Gertler, in which he fretted about the possibility of finding a job that would exempt him from service. Reminding Asquith that he had been a schoolmaster, he asked her to pull strings in the Board of Education: "I need a start—and I'm not going to be an under-servant to anybody:

no, I'm not."[10] It was one of the few times he was forced to contemplate earning money at anything other than his writing. Six weeks later he was saved from either fate by the Armistice. He and Frieda went to London for a week of parties.

Though the promise of peace brought prospects of an end to their wartime penury, ostracism, misery, and enforced residence in England, Frieda hardly felt like celebrating the defeat of Germany. Lawrence, unable to enjoy England's victory or Germany's defeat, silenced an animated group of David Garnett's friends at a Bloomsbury party with somber reflections about how the world was now even worse off.

> Very soon war will break out again and overwhelm you. It makes me sick to see you rejoicing like a butterfly in the last rays of the sun before the winter. The crowd outside thinks that Germany is crushed forever. But the Germans will soon rise again. Europe is done for: England most of all the countries. The war isn't over. Even if the fighting should stop, the evil will be worse because the hate will be dammed up in men's hearts and will show itself in all sorts of ways.[11]

He spent much of the rest of the week in London complaining to Mansfield: about Frieda (she "wants me to become a german and I'm *not* a german"), Murry, and the Murrys' marriage.[12] She had let Murry turn her into a devouring mother, he told her, making their union incestuous. She perpetuated this, he insisted, because it simultaneously fascinated and repelled her.

This strange new take came from Jung's *The Unconscious*, published the year before, which Lawrence had borrowed from Kot and was reading with horror and fascination, finding himself, Frieda, and their friends on every page. Despite *Sons and Lovers*, he had only begun reading twentieth-century psychology during the war, his entire previous knowledge having come indirectly from Frieda (via Gross) and, later, analyst-friends such as Barbara Low and her brother-in-law, David Eder. Mansfield, who despised the science, was relieved when he decided to leave for the Midlands.

Frieda remained in the city, no longer quite so suspected, ridiculed, or reviled as she had been in the worst days of the war. Mansfield, for one, had a change of heart and considered her infinitely more reasonable than Lawrence. "Perhaps his whole trouble," she wrote to Ottoline, "is that he has not a real sense of humour. He takes himself dreadfully seriously nowadays: I mean he sees himself as a symbolic figure—a prophet—the voice in the wilderness crying 'woe'."[13]

Still under the spell of Jung, and beginning to contemplate a book of his own on psychology, Lawrence wrote to Mansfield after settling back into the Midlands:

> [T]his Mother-incest idea can become an obsession. But it seems to me there is this much truth in it: that at certain periods the man has a desire and a tendency to return unto the woman, make her his goal and end, find his justification in her. In this way he casts himself as it were into her womb, and she, the Magna Mater, receives him with gratification. This is a kind of incest. . . . I have done it, and now struggle all my might to get out. In a way, Frieda is the devouring mother.—It is awfully hard, once the sex relation has gone this way, to recover. If we don't recover, we die. . . . I do think a woman must yield some sort of precedence to a man, and he must take this precedence. I do think men must go absolutely in front of their women. Consequently the women must follow as it were unquestioning. I can't help it, I believe this. Frieda doesn't. Hence our fight.[14]

4

Frieda stayed in London a month, arranging for food packages to be sent to her mother. The baroness had also spent four years wandering from one borrowed home to another, and was now back in Baden-Baden. Frantic letters decrying the lack of basic foodstuffs arrived regularly, filled with lists of relatives and friends who had died in the war. The terms of the Armistice (which included the return to the French of Metz and the rest of Alsace-Lorraine that had been annexed) were insufferable to her:

> To us who had taken part in the 1870 war, it sounded like a death-knell in our souls. Alsace-Lorraine lost—to whose flourishing we felt as if we had personally contributed! How many a monument of German diligence and excellence remain there. Papa's complete life's work in enemy hands! Thank goodness he did not live to see the

break-up! We old ones will find it difficult to learn to understand the world.[15]

Frieda found it hard to sympathize with her mother's loss of status, but her sad, hysterical tone made her long to be of some help, and the visions of hunger and destitution the letters conjured up kept her in a state of anxiety. She thought of little else but going to Germany. It was still impossible to travel, however, and there was nothing she could do but wait out the end of the war. When she returned to the Midlands, even Lawrence's dire predictions about the future of civilization could not distract her from her preoccupation with her family.

He finished his children's history textbook, later published pseudonymously (Lawrence H. Davison) as *Movements in European History*, and succumbed to a two-month, near-fatal attack of influenza. Ada invited him to recuperate in her house, and though her nursing eventually helped him to recover, it caused Lawrence an unpleasant flashback to the tubercular attack he had endured under her care in his twenties. Frieda fitted in effortlessly, helping with the baking and sewing dresses for his older sister Emily's ten-year-old daughter. He was convinced that her cheerfulness masked maleficent intentions: Even her hands on him, he wrote, felt evil. Her plans to leave for Germany enraged him.

The loss of friends and the plunge his reputation had taken during the war had made him more reliant on Frieda, and more determined to do without her. He began thinking again about Rananim, now locating it somewhere in Palestine or Zululand. Frieda had more or less ceased to give the idea any credence, and he retaliated by making melodrama of her preparations, distorting her wish to see her family into grand, operatic "*Heimweh*"—homesickness—for the "Fatherland."[16] The slightest show of independence irked him; even letters from Mansfield to her became a cause of friction. Despite a series of rapprochements with the Murrys, Lawrence felt a basic mistrust, and when Murry wrote to invite submissions to the *Athenaeum*, a prestigious journal he had recently begun editing, Lawrence, at first flattered, was soon excoriating him in bitter letters to Kot and others. In a confessional letter to Kot he connected his health to an unwillingness to contemplate Germany:

> I am not going to be left to Frieda's tender mercies until I am well again. She really is a devil—and I feel as if I would part from her for ever—let her go alone to Germany, while I take another road. For it is true, I have been bullied by her long enough. I really could leave her now, without a pang, I believe. The time comes, to make an end, one way or another. If this illness hasn't been a lesson to her, it has to me.[17]

Nothing came of his threats, and when he felt well enough and the Berkshire cottage they had used the year before was again offered, they returned, with Ada in tow for several weeks. He resumed work on *Aaron's Rod* and continued to resist Frieda's trip abroad. The signing of the Treaty of Versailles in early July seemed to guarantee her imminent departure, but she soon learned that she could not leave the country until peace was ratified. Lawrence's anger often erupted out of some commonplace. At a dinner party at the cottage, he served Monk, Lambert, and several others a delicacy of wild mushrooms and potatoes swimming in butter. Frieda had prepared a dessert of baked sugared prunes but failed to presoak them. One by one the guests palmed the rock-hard fruits into their handkerchiefs and Lawrence, mortified, began screaming. The party came to a standstill until finally he decided that the outburst, just as suddenly as it had begun, was over.

The nuisance of occasionally having to give up their borrowed cottage to its rightful owner also sent Lawrence into a tailspin. She asked them to leave for half the summer, and they shifted to the house of Rosalind Baynes, Joan Farjeon's sister and the wife of a friend and admirer of Lawrence's, Godwin Baynes, a doctor. Baynes worked in a hospital near Cambridge and was rarely around, and his marriage was disintegrating. Lawrence seems to have quickly developed a crush on Rosalind, an empathic, gentle woman with a pre-Raphaelite face. A letter to Godwin strongly echoed his "simple men" confession to Ernest:

> Why bother about divorce? The publicity is hateful and there isn't much to gain. One has to learn that love is a secondary thing in life. . . . I believe if you would both come off the personal, emotional, insistent plane, and would be each of you self sufficient and to a degree indifferent or reckless, you and Rosalind would keep a lasting relationship. Its an ignominious thing, either exacting or chasing

> after love. Love isn't all that important: one's own free soul is first.
>
> Excuse this impertinence.[18]

He concluded by advising Godwin, whose extramarital flirtations, hetero- and homosexual, were the subject of much gossip,[19] to read Whitman's "Calamus. A Song," paying special attention to its homosexual content: "I believe in what he calls 'manly love', the real implicit reliance of one man on another: as sacred a unison as marriage."[20]

He was soon proposing to Herbert Farjeon that they collaborate on a play about his sister-in-law, and also briefly considered using the Bayneses' unhappiness as the centerpiece of a novel. As with Helen Corke and "The Saga of Siegmund," there was ample background material from which to draw: Rosalind's unconventional childhood and coming-of-age had culminated in her marriage to and rather public estrangement from Godwin.[21] Farjeon was unwilling to exploit the family material and convinced Lawrence not to; instead Lawrence collaborated with Kot by mail on a book of ironic epigrams by the fin-de-siècle Russian philosopher-critic Leo Shestov. Rosalind, who had never seen a man do housework, was impressed by the relish with which Lawrence did the chores, "illuminating with a super-rational quality the most menial thing."[22] She was a supremely tactful woman who managed never to upset him: They had long conversations about central Italy's mild, sunny climate; he charmed her three daughters, aged five, three, and one; and she offered an introduction to Orazio Cervi, an artist's model for her father and other British sculptors, who had retired on his earnings to a house in the Abruzzi mountain village of Picinisco, fifty miles south of Rome.

Though the war was effectively over, Frieda was repeatedly denied a passport and a required Dutch visa; the bureaucratic impediments seemed to grow with each follow-up inquiry. When letters from her mother and sisters provoked tears over the delay, Lawrence complained, "[S]he still insists on 'feeling' her trials."[23] Their cottage had not yet been vacated by early September, and they moved in with Lambert and Monk. Frustrated, and angry about the constant uprooting and probably about Lawrence's obvious interest in Baynes, Frieda staked out a room for herself almost immediately after arriving at the farmhouse and went to bed. Lawrence furiously carried down her full chamber pots for two days, tossing the contents into the flowerbeds with an audible splash. Lambert began to find it extremely difficult to field his conversation. "Prostitutey," he declared of some old crepe de chine she routed out of a cupboard one night to make underclothing.[24] When Frieda finally emerged, she confided to Lambert that she wanted a child of Lawrence's; anticipating a prolonged stay, Lambert asked Frieda if she would move into Lawrence's bedroom. Frieda said that sharing a room would make her feel "too much married."[25]

She sat at Monk's sewing machine and accidentally jammed it. Lawrence, enraged at her carelessness, ordered her to scour the brick kitchen floor on her hands and knees. Crying bitterly, she instantly complied. As she worked her way around the room, the tears subsided and she began yelling at Lawrence. When she had finished the job, she walked to their cottage, where the owner was still in residence, and asked to be taken in, "like an unhappy hen," Lawrence wrote a friend, who "flutters from roost to roost."[26] He remained with Lambert and Monk, holed up in a room alone, adding to *Aaron's Rod*, until the cottage soon became free again.

Their constant moving throughout the war had convinced Frieda of the need of a fixed home, and of the impossibility of finding it in England. Lawrence's strenuous objections to permanence, she knew, derived largely from the wholesale rejection by the British of his work and of them. They had found their greatest happiness in Italy, and she felt certain that if she made the first step to the Continent he would follow her. A policeman showed up on September 22 to verify her travel application, now more than a month old; two weeks later her passport arrived, without the Dutch visa. Unwilling to wait any longer, she went to London with Lawrence, managed to obtain the visa in person the next day, and immediately booked passage. On October 15, 1919, Lawrence, still without a travel plan of his own, accompanied her to Liverpool Street Station and helped her board the Harwich–Hook of Holland express. Having eloped from a train station and separated and reunited in one or another at least ten times since, these were charged locales, suggestive of guilt, desire, acrimonious leavetakings, and betrayals, real and imagined. "She had a look of almost vindictive triumph," Lawrence later wrote in a thinly fictionalized account of their leavetaking in *Kangaroo*, "and almost malignant love as the train pulled out."[27]

Frieda's new passport told a different story: Wearing a tailored linen suit and cheap, out-of-season straw hat with a wide, halfheartedly decorated brim, in her photograph she has a tired and forbearing smile; the nearly empty pages were soon to be crammed with visas and entry and exit stamps. The past five years had produced a new stolidity, and the heavy, impassive set of her shoulders and chest made her look older than her forty years and far more like her mother than ever, but her face, tanned like a Gypsy's, was unmistakably that of a wanderer.

13

The Queen Bee

I

Lawrence caught a cold and weathered it alone. To pass the time in bed in Berkshire and at Ada's, he sewed sheepskin coats for Rosalind Baynes's two elder daughters. The United States, Palestine, and Zululand seemed strange and remote, and he pursued a lead on an Italian cargo vessel, keeping Baynes, who was preparing to move to Italy with her children, abreast of the details of the search. He hoped, he wrote Catherine Carswell, to live and work on a Neapolitan farm.

There had been a vague plan to meet in Italy in the event of such a change of heart, and he waited for a letter from Frieda. None came; two telegrams informed him of the loss of some of her belongings in Holland and of her arrival in Baden-Baden. He sold most of his books in Reading and took a train to London, where he stayed at Kot's, emptied his bank account, and gave Carswell his frayed complete works of Thomas De Quincey, the only books acquired during the war that had meaning for him: De Quincey's debunking of Plato's and Goethe's "classic ideal of human balance" filled him with malevolent cheer.[1] Carefully monitoring the shifting value of the lira, he changed a small number of pounds at a good rate.

The passage to Naples failed to materialize, and he booked a train to Florence, then one of the cheapest cities in Italy. He was impatient to leave. The intellectual preoccupations and rarefied talk of London left him bored or disgusted, and the city felt inhuman, cold, and filthy. Hunched over a modern gas fireplace in the apartment of an American acquaintance one evening, shivering, he spoke of his wife almost obsessively, and entirely disparagingly. "He told us that Frieda had gone to visit her relatives in Germany," wrote Richard Aldington, who later walked the streets with him, "and seemed not to care if he never saw her again."[2]

Most other friends were unavailable or unwanted. H. D. had given birth in March to a daughter, Perdita (the father was Cecil Gray), boarded her at a nursery in South Kensington, and left for several months in the Scilly Islands with her lover Bryher, the daughter of a shipping magnate. On her return to London, distraught and confused about motherhood, Bryher, and her poetry, she began an analysis and love affair with Havelock Ellis. "[T]he Fountain of life," as Ellis later referred to her in his autobiography of the same name, urinated on him while he lay between her legs.[3] Lawrence had not written to her since learning of the pregnancy.

On November 14 at Charing Cross he boarded a train to Paris, the first leg of his journey. Carswell saw him off; nervous about his unhealthy appearance and the chill of the second-class compartment, she bundled him in a worn camel-hair coat lining and a huge black-and-white shepherd's shawl inherited from her grandmother. He could not afford a sleeper, and spent the journey of more than fifty hours sitting up. The deep suspicion of "incest" in his own and the Murrys' marriages was fueling his interest in his psychology book, which he hoped to write quickly and sell in installments to an American magazine. Frustrated by the constant stalling of the trains, however, he was unable to get much done and instead wrote Baynes a lengthy letter on the mechanics of postwar travel.

In Turin the hospitality of wealthy expatriates, Lady Delphine Therese Becker and Sir Walter Frederick Becker, a recently knighted former shipowner, provoked a letter to Lady Asquith, who almost always heard from Lawrence when he met nobility:

> Knight, K.C.B. OBM or OB something—parvenu etc—great luxury—rather nice people really—but my stomach, my stomach, it has

> a bad habit of turning a complete somersault when it finds itself in the wrong element, like a dolphin in the air. . . . He is going to die—moi non. He knows that, the impotent old wolf, so he is ready in one half to murder me.[4]

He left their villa after two days with enough material for two chapters of *Aaron's Rod*. Another, hopefully nostalgic, stop proved similarly joyless: Getting off in La Spezia, across the bay from the house in which he had written the early drafts of *The Rainbow*, he passed a lonely, aimless two days, then boarded a train again.

No one was waiting to meet him in Florence. It was cold, and the city seemed a variant of London—unfeeling and coated with a film of psychic dirt by the war. He had sent a note ahead to Norman Douglas, the Scotsman, now a novelist, whom he had met at the *English Review* in 1911–12, and found a reply waiting at a travel office directing him to the Pension Balestra, on the Lungarno. He ran into Douglas before he could get there: Undeterred by the chill, he was out for a walk with Maurice Magnus, an American expatriate and former stage manager for Isadora Duncan, more recently a deserter from the French Foreign Legion. Sporting a pair of identical small black hats with curled brims, the two men seemed to Lawrence to share some secret and to be determinedly at home in this city he knew little or nothing about. Douglas, middle-aged and well-fed-looking, with chapped skin and thick, curling eyebrows, had a certain unctuous poise and called to mind a down-at-the-heels intellectual on vacation. Magnus, chubby and inscrutable, with a mincing, patronizing voice, wore impeccable grays that only seemed to advertise an inherent emotional shabbiness, and evoked a picture of a small bird wearing the mask of another, at least to Lawrence: "a sparrow painted to resemble a tom-tit."[5] Carrying his own hand luggage, his thick tangle of beard untrimmed since Berkshire—he could not bring himself to go to strange barbers—Lawrence felt unkempt, self-conscious, and condescended to.

The Balestra, where Douglas and Magnus were also staying, was a dimly lit stone building furnished in dirty plush and peeling gilt. Douglas had reserved him an immense room overlooking the river, and the view was magnificent, but he had no one to call on but friends of friends. Lilian Trench, wife of the Irish playwright and poet Frederic Trench, whom Kot knew, was living in nearby Settignano and introduced him to Gertrude Stein's brother, Leo, who had photographs and stories from a vacation in Taos, New Mexico, that whetted Lawrence's appetite for the United States again. He spent the rest of his time with Douglas and Magnus, quickly developing a headlong homoerotic attachment to Magnus, who was a leech. With no steady income and a taste for good champagne, heavy brocade dressing gowns, and traveling first class, he cadged small but regular amounts, which Lawrence could not seem to refuse, even after losing four hundred francs himself to a pickpocket on a train. After one such handout Magnus, suddenly in desperate need of evading creditors and the service, booked a first-class seat on the midnight train to Rome. Lawrence was scandalized by the extravagance but could not help admiring his nerve. The next he heard of him, he had become an oblate at the sixteenth-century monastery at Monte Cassino.

2

One of the disjunctions in Frieda's life as she endlessly crisscrossed Europe and England after her divorce was her occasional oblivious proximity to her children. This happened with Elsa, as Frieda came down from Baden-Baden via Basel, to meet Lawrence. Seventeen and "a bit more solid" after seven months on the Continent, Elsa was auditing college classes in Switzerland with a friend from Saint Paul's and three Dutch girls, under whose influence she had begun to wear her hair up. Barby wrote Frieda about Elsa's studies in a long letter, but it came four months too late, and Frieda missed the only chance to see her eldest daughter outside England in her teens, free of the restrictions Ernest had imposed.

She was preoccupied, as she traveled south, with the food shortages and firewood lines she had left behind in Germany, and with her mother's solitude. Faced with the prospect of living alone or continuing to wander, Anna had taken a suite in the Ludwig-Wilhelm-Stift, a once-grand home for widows, where the hierarchies of breeding, titles, and the careers of late husbands were still observed with haughty precision. Located on a wide road winding out of town to the Black Forest, its huge northern windows framed a rock outcropping that rose with imposing menace to the monumental Altes Schloss. Seated in her bedroom, with a view of the castle, Anna had seemed dwarfed by her surroundings. The baron's death, the war, and advancing years had softened her bullying personality to a teasing, ironic magnanimity, and she had become something of an enigma to Frieda. Framed by long, coiled, silver hair that looked like thistledown, her face was inscrutable, her voice lowered to a slow, plangent evenness, and she seemed subdued by the constant reminders of death all around her. She rarely spoke of her husband or her embattled marriage, at least to Frieda.

It had been a relief when Nusch arrived, and the two sisters acted as though they were back in Sablon: "We had to be on our best behavior, except in my mother's beautiful rooms, where all the wildness of our childhood came back."[6] Else had also come, and Frieda and Nusch, continually laughing at the slightest provocation, drowned out her anxious conversations with Anna about the Weimar government and her children's futures. Else's moroseness had intensified with the burden of caring for Edgar, who had suffered a nervous breakdown after serving as minister of finance in the short-lived Bavarian republic established in Munich in November 1918. The remainder of her affection and attention went to Max Weber, with whom she had resumed relations in 1917 after a rift caused by the repercussions of her affair with his brother Alfred. Nusch had spent much of the war at the bedsides of dying boyfriends. The baroness could no longer trouble about her daughters' romantic complications, and simply made it clear their husbands were as welcome at the Stift as their lovers.

Indefatigably cheerful, with the efficiency of a nurse and a natural elegant tenderness, Nusch treated her mother with a cool, sweet solicitude Anna loved: "*Goldfasanchen,*" she called her—"my little golden pheasant."[7] Frieda was charmed, and relieved of having to display such tenderness herself. She was incapable of it with her mother. Their relationship was formal and subdued: Quoting Goethe to each other and discussing Lawrence's novels, they made a strange tableau on their way to the dining room, the baroness in a dark, ancient-looking, floor-length dress, a fox-fur scarf across her chest, Frieda in a red-and-green cinched peasant skirt. Anna had been reading Lawrence's books avidly, then hiding them—his reputation had preceded him to Germany, and she was terrified the other residents would wonder why she was reading the works of a pornographer. "But it's always you in Lorenzo's books, all his women are you," she said, in a tone that managed to convey disapproval and pride at the same time.[8]

Frieda reached Florence at four in the morning on December 3, exhausted by the twenty-four-hour trip. Because of the hour and the fog, the descent into the hollow of the Arno Valley from the central Apennines was not as beautiful as it normally was, but Florence was a gorgeous blur of indistinction, and Lawrence was waiting for her in the Piazza Santa Maria Novella. They had been apart six and a half weeks. He noticed her weight loss, which he mentioned to half a dozen correspondents over the next three months.[9] As always, the long separation fostered the absorbing fiction that they were strangers.

This reunion was particularly romantic. Though Lawrence detested scenes of spontaneous joy, he suggested that they ride through the streets in an open horsedrawn carriage. "We went along the Lungarno," Frieda wrote, ". . . in that moonlight night, and ever since Florence is the most beautiful town to me . . . delicate and flowery." Beneath the arches of the Uffizi they could see the lights of distant houses beyond the Arno come on, and to the west, the expanse of the Carrara Mountains looked purple:

> I saw the pale crouching Duomo and in the thick moonmist the Giotto tower disappeared at the top into the sky. The Palazzo Vecchio with Michelangelo's *David* and all the statues of men, we passed. "This is a men's town," I said, "not like Paris, where all statues are women."[10]

Trade started before dawn, and mule- and horsedrawn commercial carts crossed the Ponte Vecchio next to theirs, the tradesmen shielded from the rain by big green umbrellas, the animals' heads covered by ludicrously tiny gray bonnets.

The revelry of enchantment fell apart at the Balestra. Douglas had stayed on, and his friendship with Lawrence made Frieda feel as though she were trapped in a male version of the gossipy Victorian serial novel *Cranford*.[11] The two had established a private conversational repertoire and a rather snide rapport based on spite, gossip, literature, religion, and Magnus, about whom Lawrence could not seem to stop talking. Frieda, practiced at recognizing the ambivalence of such preoccupations, was irked at the thought of his sharing their money with a man who had no intention of repaying, and she detested Magnus without having met him. Douglas she was able to handle with long conversations in German, in which he was not only fluent but funny.

Her time alone with Lawrence was in the morning. They were so close to the Ponte Vecchio they could practically count its red roof tiles, and they lingered at the window over breakfast, lost in historical abstraction as the scene at the bridge unfolded. Frieda's stomach had shrunk in Germany, and she became ill from immense meals and too much Balestra wine.

On December 6 a windfall of fifty pounds arrived from New York, an advance for American rights to *Women in Love* from Thomas Seltzer. A Russian Jew who had emigrated at the age of twelve, he worked briefly for Boni and Liveright and formed his own small house in 1918. He and Lawrence had begun negotiating in September, setting off an argument with Benjamin Huebsch, who had kept *The Rainbow* in print (if not publicly available) in the United States through the war, and published *The Trespasser*, *Amores*, *The Prussian Officer*, *Twilight in Italy*, and *Look! We Have Come Through!*

Huebsch informed Lawrence that Pinker had never submitted *Women in Love*, and that he wanted to publish it. After years of doubting whether this much-rejected work would ever see print, the scramble left Lawrence cold and imperious. "Pinker, publishers, everybody," he wrote Huebsch, "even you, previously—treated me with such vagueness and evasiveness, as if I were an aimiable [*sic*] imbecile, and left me to contrive on sixpence—no, basta!"[12] It was not only Huebsch's manner and his failure to provide for him that infuriated Lawrence: He was nursing an anti-Semitic paranoia, fostered during the war years. "I hear Huebsch is a Jew," he had written an American editor in 1917. "Are you a Jew also? The best of Jews is, that they *know* truth from untruth. The worst of them is, that they are rather slave-like, and that almost inevitably, in action, they betray the truth they know. . . . they cringe their buttocks to the fetish of Mammon, peeping over their shoulders to see if the truth is watching them."[13]

Frieda was silent, at least in her letters, on the subject of Lawrence's anti-Semitism; much later in her life, in response to two letters from Richard Aldington, she uttered the only such remarks she herself is known to have made: "[T]he Jews" and "the Jewish element" in publishing, she concurred, prevented Lawrence's books from being more widely distributed.[14]

The money from Seltzer was somehow not tainted, however; Lawrence later attributed his agreeing to do business with him to the small scale and independence of the company and Seltzer's willingness to take risks. He deposited part of the advance in a newly opened Florentine bank account, and on December 10 he and Frieda left for Rome, where they were turned away from a *pensione* because of her Germanness. After staying briefly as guests in an apartment near the Villa Borghese, where Lawrence had five hundred lire stolen, they pushed on to Orazio Cervi's house in Picinisco. "We are in the wilds here I tell you," Frieda wrote, "men like brigands, fine women in bright peasant get-ups, and the most heavenly sun and clear mountain air."[15] Picinisco was a little too "staggeringly primitive," though, Lawrence reported to Baynes, and they left at 5:30 in the morning several days later, arriving—after a five-mile walk with their baggage, a mail-bus ride, the train from Cassino to Naples, and a boat trip—on the island of Capri.[16] Compton Mackenzie, who had been nonplussed by Frieda's striped stockings and Lawrence's attitude to the war in Buckinghamshire, was living there, and Lawrence, remembering his offer of a house, had written ahead.

3

The house turned out not to be free. On Christmas Day 1919 they moved into a noisy apartment above a popular café that had panoramic views of Vesuvius and the Mediterranean and access to the roof, where they hung clothes to dry. It came with a maid, Liberata, who wore Frieda's jewelry and clothing when they went out. Lawrence's sisters kept them in English tea. Another friend from Buckinghamshire, Mary Cannan, whose husband's unappetizing portrayal of Frieda in *Mendel* had been conveniently forgotten, also lived on the island. Frieda bought a thin, drooping fir tree and invited her for the holidays.

Island life was confining. Quickly bored with each other and their small circle, which included the popular novelist Francis Brett Young and his wife, Jessica, they began fighting. They took their marital problems to Mackenzie, an extravagant presence with his pastel suits, kilts, and hats from an exclusive Bond Street shop that Lawrence, typically, decided were effeminate. Frieda found him easy to talk to. "But why won't Lorenzo let me have lace on my underclothes, Mackenzie? . . . Look at what he makes me wear," she lamented, hiking her skirt and showing a pair of the calico bloomers Lawrence still made for her. Lawrence in turn confided that he had been troubled for some time by his and Frieda's failure to have simultaneous orgasms. Later, pointing his index finger at his fly, he told Mackenzie that he wanted to discover a race of people who thought through their genitals.[17] Mackenzie was not much help: Basically, he told Lawrence, he considered sex comical. Years after leaving Capri, Lawrence was still angry about this irreverent attitude, and satirized him as a vapid rich man with bizarre sartorial tastes in the short story "The Man Who Loved Islands."

Winter storms and postal strikes often kept the mail in a steamer at nearby Castellammare di Stabia for up to a week. The waits made Lawrence anxious, and he sent abrupt letters to friends and business associates, including one to Pinker, firing him. His agenting had been basically satisfactory, but Lawrence could not help associating him with the wartime stagnation of his career. He was also a Jew. The change soon began to seem propitious: He had an offer from Martin Secker to publish *Women in Love* and reissue *The Rainbow* in England (an advance of one hundred pounds was eventually paid for the former; the latter failed to appear in print until 1926); Seltzer finalized their agreement to publish *Women in Love* in the States; and in New York he hired Robert Mountsier, the journalist who had visited Cornwall asking to be his agent. Mountsier's unqualified admiration, seemingly malleable nature, and relative lack of experience perfectly fitted an old-fashioned instinct of Lawrence's—intensified by publishers' avoidance of him during the war—to negotiate on his own behalf.

Business out of the way, he began toying with advertising in the *Nairobi Herald*: He wanted to "help a man make some sort of a farm in Africa," but nothing came of it.[18] He and Frieda left the island for three days on the Amalfi coast. She now knew such stabs at an alternative lifestyle to be harbingers of an acute viral infection or tubercular attack. Another warning sign of sickness—sometimes it came with the onset of illness—was a venomous attack on a friend or herself, as with Lawrence's resistance to her trip to Baden-Baden.

This time both happened. Lawrence wrote an abusive letter to Murry when several manuscripts he had submitted over the past month for publication in the *Athenaeum*—a reversal of an earlier decision not to have anything to do with Murry's magazine—were turned down. "I received your letter and also the returned articles," he wrote. ". . . I have no doubt you 'didn't like them'. . . . But as a matter of fact, what it amounts to is that you are a dirty little worm."[19] A week later, he was in bed with the flu but found the strength to write to Mansfield, who was spending a week in a French nursing home: "I loathe you, you revolt me stewing in your consumption."[20] When Frieda, who owned two diamond rings, had one stolen from their apartment and Lawrence received several checks from the United States, they decided to leave Capri for good.[21]

He had begun corresponding with Magnus and was reluctant to go without first seeing him. Sending five pounds ahead, which provoked a scene with Frieda, he made the journey to Monte Cassino alone. His stay in the monastery was unpleasant, filling him with sexual anxiety: Unable to get warm in a coat borrowed from the monks, reading "Dregs: Experiences of an American in the Foreign Legion," an autobiographical manuscript replete with sodomitic detail that Magnus had recently completed and wanted help selling, he felt oppressed by the antiquity and, so he perceived, latent homosexuality of the place and what he took to be the mindless, money-grubbing habits of the peasants who worked the fields below. Conversation ranged from Magnus's mother, of whom he carried an extravagant photograph (a copy of a portrait in a Rome art gallery—though Magnus did not tell Lawrence, and despite Magnus's American citizenship, she was apparently Hedwigis Rosamunda Liebeträu Magnus, half-sister of Wilhelm II), to the third-century B.C. Greek poet Theocritus, who had lived in Sicily. Magnus said the island had been waiting for Lawrence since then. A week later he was house hunting in Sicily with the Brett Youngs. Fontana Vecchia, a pink stucco farmhouse on a terraced hill near Taormina, seventy miles north of Syracuse and fifteen from Mount Etna, cost him and Frieda the equivalent of $175 a year for two floors. They moved in on March 8, in the middle of a sirocco. "Living in Sicily after the war years was like coming to life again," Frieda wrote.[22] They looked out on the Ionian Sea and Greece from balconies on both floors. There were pools of green water, and lemon and orange trees grew in the chalky soil.

The ground floor of the house was occupied by relatives of their landlord, Francesco "Ciccio" Cacopardo, a bachelor and professional chef. The Cacopardos in residence spanned several generations.

Grazia, the matriarch, shared her olives, corn, spinach, and beans from the garden, which was spotted with the crumbled remains of a Greek temple, and there were grapes from a private vineyard. Ciccio's brother, Carmelo, grew grain that the family hand-threshed, tossing it into the air and letting the wind winnow the chaff, and Grazia baked bread in an oven so big it was "more like a cowshed," putting in a loaf for them twice a week.[23] The fresh ingredients inspired a new proficiency in the kitchen: Each Sunday morning Frieda used Grazia's oven to bake cakes, tarts, and meat pies, which she cooled on the dining-room sideboard. They drew drinking water from a spring a hundred yards away and carried it to the house in terra cotta jugs. There was no plumbing.

After removing a pair of heavy, dark red drapes, they began waking up early with the sun, which shone directly into their bedroom. They hiked before the scorching summer heat set in. "The early almond blossoms pink and white, the asphodels, the wild narcissi and anemones, all these we found during our walks, nothing new would escape Lawrence and we never got tired of finding new treasures," Frieda wrote.[24] A dirt road led to the hills above Taormina, where goatherds played reed pipes to their animals. Neighboring villagers got around on donkeys; Frieda's reputed delight with one such man, Pepina d'Allura, an illiterate twenty-four-year-old mule driver from Castelmola, about three miles away, later found its way into *I Peccati e gli Amori di Taormina* (The sins and loves of Taormina), a rather fanciful, possibly apocryphal book by an Italian journalist that purports to recount their liaison. Frieda is described as an ex-dancer with "beautiful ivory legs." Their first tryst was in a rainstorm, according to the author; thereafter d'Allura "transformed a grove of palm trees into an alcove and a whole vineyard into a sort of nudist camp in the spirit of eros."[25]

Though the Lawrences extolled the virtues of living among peasants, their involvement as a childless couple in this family-centered village was marginal and voyeuristic: When people asked Frieda if she had children, she answered no, "like a Judas," as she wrote Else.[26] A letter to Monty, who had been admitted to Oxford on scholarship and was already a success at rugby and running (he earned a medal as a miler), provoked a curt reply. Frieda's relations with him were still badly fractured, and he did not want a wayward mother to confuse the image he was carefully developing. He was busy trying to erase traces of both parents: Lanky and handsome, he underwent a rhinoplasty to change the slightly hooked Weekley nose.[27] Frieda tried two letters to Barby, then settled in for a long wait: Overseas letters often languished three to four weeks before leaving the island.

Lawrence became fascinated when Ciccio began courting a Venetian refugee, Emma Motta, displaced with her parents and nine siblings when Austria invaded northern Italy during the war.[28] The locals, who felt Ciccio should marry one of them, became furious when the plans were announced. The romance and its complications inspired a return to "The Insurrection of Miss Houghton," the Eastwood-based manuscript he had abandoned in 1913 at page 200 before beginning "The Sisters." Conflating Taormina and what he had seen of Picinisco and heard from Baynes of Orazio Cervi, he renamed it *The Lost Girl* and started over; Ciccio became Cicio, the lover of Lawrence's heroine, Alvina Houghton; Cervi became Pancrazio; Magnus was May, an unscrupulous theater manager.

Magnus himself appeared early one morning during the final week of the novel's composition: There was a commotion on the stairs leading from the lower balcony to the garden, and Lawrence looked out to find him ascending to the landing. Police, he said, had come to the monastery to arrest him, and he had escaped with "Dregs," run down the mountain, and boarded a train to Naples, hiding in the bathroom most of the trip. Arriving in Taormina a few days before, he had checked into the most expensive local hotel. Frieda's worst fears about Magnus were confirmed the instant she saw him.[29]

"To Lawrence's logical puritanical mind Magnus presented a problem of human relations," she later wrote, referring both to Magnus's freeloading and Lawrence's sexual confusion. ". . . To me it was no problem. Had I been fond of Magnus, had he any meaning, or purpose—but no, he seemed only anti-social, a poor devil without any pride, and he didn't seem to matter anyhow."[30] She refused to let him stay in their house, and was soon fighting with Lawrence, bitter shouting matches that astounded Jan Juta, a temporary houseguest. An Afrikaner from Cape Town who had gone to Oxford, he was studying at the British School in Rome. "I could kill him," Lawrence fumed about Magnus to Juta, whom, judging from later letters, Lawrence also found attractive, "he makes my bowels boil with fury." When Juta asked him why he bothered, Lawrence replied, "I don't know, except that I suppose I am a fool and fall for all his sob stuff."[31] Like many onlookers Juta was shocked by the volatility of the marriage, which Magnus's visit intensified. Frieda, he wrote, refused to allow Lawrence to "elude" her. "They were amazingly happy," Juta marveled, ". . . welded in a way most people could not understand." Lawrence's "unwillingness to compromise or break faith with the truth of himself," however, Juta wrote euphemistically, provoked Frieda's jealousy.[32]

Magnus checked out of his hotel and headed for Malta, leaving behind a bill Lawrence felt compelled to pay. Two weeks later he followed him, with Frieda in tow, justifying the trip with the explanation that Mary Cannan had always wanted to see Malta, "lured" him and Frieda, and paid their fare.[33] Traveling second class on the steamer from Palermo, they ran into Magnus, installed on the first-class deck, "a jewel," Lawrence wrote Juta, ". . . in a white suit, floating in whiskies and soda. . . . He has taken a small house at Città Vecchia, and is going to sit elegantly on Malta till he bursts again.—No, I don't like him—shall not bother with him any more." He nonetheless became thoroughly involved in his complicated business affairs, sending off a letter on his behalf to Douglas Goldring, a British playwright with German connections who had helped bring Lawrence to the attention of Insel-Verlag, a publisher interested in translating his books. Magnus, Lawrence wrote, had translated several contemporary German, Austrian, Russian, and Norwegian plays, owned the performance rights, and wanted to get them produced. Over drinks in Magnus's room (one of the island's more exclusive, for which Magnus did not intend to pay), Lawrence evidently also confided that he was bisexual, and searching for fellow bisexual partners.[34] He paid this other outstanding hotel bill of Magnus's, and had a silk suit made for himself before he and Frieda departed.

The letter from Barby telling Frieda of Elsa's whereabouts was waiting in Taormina. Expelled from Saint Paul's for sketching nudes in her math book, Barby had spent the Easter holiday with relatives while Ernest vacationed with Elsa in Switzerland. She was trying to persuade her father to let her enroll in the Slade; he applauded her talent but said that an artistic career would not mix with marriage.[35] Amid self-deprecation and family gossip, Barby made it clear that her loyalties now lay with Frieda:

> Thank you for your letters which came one on top of the other. I had a terrible fear that perhaps my letter would reach you too late. I mean that you would have plucked us from your heart and buried us forever!
>
> Please don't worry about my health. I am very healthy and getting quite fat—not a bit aneamic, I mean anaemic or aenemic. . . . I have written to Monty and [Elsa] and told them I wrote to you and have sent Elsa your address. . . . I am sorry Monty wrote you a nasty letter, but it wasn't from his inside. He is nasty, though. I expect he'll swear at me for writing to you but I don't care.[36]

Frieda decided to return to Baden-Baden for an extended stay. She tried to persuade Lawrence to come, but the prospect depressed him, as he explained to the baroness, whom he now affectionately addressed as "*Meine liebe Schwiegermutter.*" He and Anna had begun corresponding, straightforward, generous letters that rarely raised his hackles, and she was soon acting as a conduit to Insel-Verlag.

Frieda departed in mid-August; Lawrence saw her off in Milan and remained to tour Italy. A detour to Magnus, who had returned to Monte Cassino, was short and disillusioning, and he never saw the monastery again: Magnus, heavily in debt, tracked down by detectives who tried to serve him with extradition papers, killed himself in Malta the following year by swallowing hydrocyanic acid. Lawrence, guilt-ridden, and devastated by the senselessness of the act, later helped get "Dregs" published (as *Memoirs of the Foreign Legion*), contributing an introduction to improve its salability. It included a brief mention of Magnus's lineage—Lawrence had learned after the suicide that he was said to have been the illegitimate product of German royal stock[37]—and an inspired description of the monastery, which was destroyed early in 1944 by Allied bombardment, after it had been occupied by the Wehrmacht.

Lawrence ended his travels in San Gervasio, outside Florence, in a villa found for him by Baynes, who was living in Fiesole. Its windows had been shattered by a nearby ammunition-dump explosion a couple of weeks before, but he was undaunted by the mess. He walked to

Baynes's almost every day or gave luncheon and tea parties at his own villa "to elegant people," he wrote a friend, "mostly American."[38] On the night of his thirty-fifth birthday, after a dinner consisting mainly of mortadella and marsala, he and Baynes took a long walk through a field of wild thyme and marjoram, and after a conversation about her recent sexual abstinence, he said, "I don't see why you and I should not have a sex time together," cautioning that love was impersonal and god-like. "[T]here must be understanding of the god *together*," he added, and suggested that they consummate the relationship immediately. She declined, "though I longed to dash into his arms," and he walked her home, kissed her in her hallway, and returned two days later. After dinner, followed by a dessert of sorb apples and several hours spent on the terrace, holding hands in the dark, they went to bed.[39]

A series of highly charged poems—he called them "Fruit Studies"—emerged, apparently over the next two days, which he spent alone. Among them were "Pomegranate," "Peach," "Medlars and Sorb-Apples," and "Figs"; themes of animal copulation, animal and human reproduction, and women's sexual fulfillment proliferated, as did images of masturbation, crucifixion, and overripeness, which Lawrence always seemed to compare to female genitalia. He sent the poems to Mountsier and began going to Baynes's again; two were later published in the *New Republic*, which paid twenty dollars apiece.[40] They eventually made their way into a collection entitled *Birds, Beasts and Flowers*. It was Lawrence's first extramarital affair with a woman, and he kept it a secret: "All feels very fizzy and bubbly," he wrote Amy Lowell, safely distant in the United States, "but don't suppose anything big will happen—though it just might."[41]

Letters from Frieda began to arrive, with invitations to join her in Germany that provoked white lies to the baroness: "I feel, it is so late in the year, and the autumn with the leaves falling would be sad," he wrote her. "I would much rather come in spring. I should love to come next April, when we leave Taormina, and perhaps we could spend a whole summer together, you and F and me."[42] Finally Frieda suggested meeting him in Venice. Baynes seems to have accompanied him to the train station, and he ate the *panforte* she apparently gave him for the ride with great relish, and drank "*mediocre* white wine," as he wrote her, in a letter from Venice in which he also complained, "F . . . writes tiresomely from Germany."[43]

4

Germany was far less diminished than just after the war, or so it seemed from the confines of the Stift. Meat was available again, and the shortage of necessities, still evident in most cities, was simply not spoken of. Else and Nusch joined Frieda for part of the fall. Else's rekindled affair with Max Weber had become bogged down in mutual guilt and, for Weber, depression: Marianne, his wife, was also Else's best friend. Absorbed in his great essays on the sociology of religion, he had become increasingly obsessed with death, his conversation filled with rambling nostalgia, remorse for his lost childhood, and images of ruin and defeat. A cold early in the summer had progressed to a systemic disease, and periods of sustained delirium had set in. Marianne and Else had taken turns nursing him, and he had repeatedly called out for one or the other—if the wrong one came, he shouted her away. He had also suffered paranoid fantasies about Alfred, whose affair with Else he could not forgive: "Give it to me quickly," he said, reaching for a glass of milk at his bedside, "or Alfred will suck it away."[44] He died on June 14, 1920, leaving Else the manuscripts of three volumes of *Religionssoziologie*, which she saw through to publication shortly after. Frieda stayed for five weeks, attempting to rouse Else from bouts of intense self-blame, plumbing Nusch's wardrobe for castoffs, and immersing herself in Lawrence's editorial/business affairs. To bypass the Italian mail she had brought along copies of *Sons and Lovers*, *The Rainbow*, and the published poetry, and sent them to Dr. Anton Kippenberg, the director of Insel-Verlag. The house was considering Else as translator, and before long almost the entire family was involved, with cordial letters passing back and forth between Kippenberg and the baroness. Frieda, enjoying her first such involvement since her letters to Garnett about the early failure of *The Rainbow*, worked the grapevine and managed to learn through Gross's former lover Regina Ullmann, who had had dealings with Insel-Verlag, that they paid notoriously slowly. Lawrence—also considering losses that would be suffered in the exchange—specified that his royalties be sent directly to Anna, for her support. Before leaving, Frieda traveled to Munich and evidently visited Ascona: ". . . return to innocent barefooted dance under heaven," Lawrence wrote Compton Mackenzie, "one of the reactions into sentimental naïveté, I presume."[45]

She met Lawrence in Venice on October 7 after a series of passport difficulties and delays. They picnicked on the deserted Lido in the pale blue light of a chilly afternoon with a bottle of *spumante* Lawrence bought with a check from Edward Marsh for *Georgian Poetry* royalties. "We are glad to be together again," Frieda wrote to friends.[46] The world, Lawrence wrote Marsh, felt "magical."[47] They returned to Fontana Vecchia via Florence and Rome in the middle of the month. Huge, dramatic thunderstorms brought out the vivid colors of late-flowering roses, creeping vines, and cyclamens, prompting more poems for *Birds, Beasts and Flowers*.

Their happiness was soon compromised and complicated by a resurgence of the sexual anxiety he had confided to Mackenzie, and by his vehement resistance to the spring visit he had promised the baroness, for which Frieda was agitating. Stories of the dewy beauty of the Black Forest enraged him; he told her she was naive for failing to realize the world was still a political tinderbox, waiting to go up in flames. Their arguments became hopelessly confused with differences of opinion about his work. She found *Birds, Beasts and Flowers*, whose provenance she must have suspected, heavy-handed and depressing. "Frieda hates it," he wrote Amy Lowell of the collection, which grew quickly. "I like it."[48]

She preferred to bask in the pending German sale of the earlier novels and poems and large advance sales of *The Lost Girl*—thirteen hundred copies; the novel earned Lawrence his first and only literary award, the one-hundred-pound James Tait Black Memorial Prize. Her casual, impatient attitude toward publishers and editors had not changed. "I have *not* heard from that Insel-Verlag whether he has the books that I sent," she wrote Else on All Soul's Day. ". . . One should not behave as if one is so happy if one is printed, which I in my stupidity did!"[49] Three days later, Lawrence received a letter from Kippenberg, forwarded by Frieda's mother, with a firm offer of thirty-five pounds per book for exclusive rights to titles published through 1924.

A year after the end of the war, Lawrençe's career was beginning a modest renaissance, his will to write had returned in force, and he had shed some of the self-aggrandizing idealism that had alienated almost everyone. The month of November alone was an astonishing prelude to years of solid, almost frenetic work. He sent off the nearly completed manuscript of *Birds, Beasts and Flowers* to be typed; unable to end *Aaron's Rod*, he refused to agonize, and simply set it aside to begin *Mr. Noon*, its Midlands hero modeled, before the later transformation into someone much like Lawrence, on a classmate at Nottingham High School. *Women in Love* was published in a deluxe, fifteen-dollar limited edition in the United States. Baynes and the time in Fiesole became a huge, active part of his imaginative life; they corresponded, intermittently and somewhat wistfully, until some time before her remarriage in 1926, Frieda occasionally adding postscripts; and Lawrence later borrowed the outlines of the Thornycroft family history—and of Baynes's character and those of her father and sister Joan—for his last novel, *Lady Chatterley's Lover*.[50]

5

By early January, anticipating the annual Taormina tourist season, the Lawrences went northwest to Sardinia. A steamer left Palermo every other Wednesday for the island. They arrived on a Tuesday, and Frieda, who loved open-air markets, headed for the Via Maqueda, a dense commercial street clogged with produce and fabric stalls, women pushing baby strollers, and horsedrawn carriages. She carried their portable stove, thermos, and a basket of half-eaten, homemade scrambled-egg-and-bacon sandwiches. Lawrence, trailing behind with their knapsack, which looked huge on his thin back, attracted the attention of three teenage girls, who found the "*sacco militare*" ridiculous. They howled at the sound of his voice, raised in fury against Frieda's plowing through bolts of cheap curtain material labeled "*fantasia*." He had been losing his hearing over the last few years and, unable to discriminate sound in a crowd, was oblivious of the girls, trailing and taunting him. Frieda, humiliated, screamed at them in execrable Italian while he stood by silently. He hated Frieda's Italian, which he called "sledge-hammer."

"[T]he English are fools," Frieda said to him. "They always put up with this Italian impudence."[51]

Sea and Sardinia, Lawrence's brilliant record of the eight-day trip, came easily in the weeks following their return. The queen bee, long a staple metaphor in his nature lexicon and still a preferred endearment for Frieda, acquired a decidedly more loaded meaning: Frieda, identified on the first pages as the queen bee, later shortened to "q-b," is conspicuous not only for her innate naturalness but for her almost annihilative, enfeebling power. A Sardinian village they lunched in provoked a discourse on a male peasant enclave, with Frieda in its midst, of a kind that had become typical of Lawrence's idealization of men who were not like him:

> [T]he *essential* courtesy in all of them was quite perfect, so manly and utterly simple. Just the same with the q-b. They treated her with a sensitive, manly simplicity, which one could not but be thankful for. They made none of the odious politenesses which are detestable in well-brought-up people. They made no advances and did none of the hateful homage of the adulating male. They were quiet, and kind, and sensitive to the natural flow of life, and quite without airs. I liked them extremely. Men who can be quietly kind and simple to a woman, without wanting to show off to make an impression, they are men still.[52]

Lawrence, passively outside the action, gauges his reactions through Frieda. He really no longer trusted anyone but her; as his dependence increased, her feelings became correspondingly more compassionate and pitying, and less passionate, as she was to write Murry thirty years later:

> I believe my deepest feeling for L. was a profound compassion. He wanted so much that he could never have with his intensity. I felt so terribly sorry for him or I could never have stood it all. Sometimes he went over the edge of sanity. I was many times frightened but never the last bit of me. Once, I remember he had worked himself up and his hands were on my throat and he was pressing me against the wall and ground out: "I am the master, I am the master." I said: "Is that all? You can be master as much as you like, I don't care." His hands dropped away, he looked at me in astonishment and was all right.[53]

Lawrence finished the manuscript on February 22. Nine days later Frieda received an urgent telegram from Else informing her that the baroness was ill. Lawrence accused her of fabricating the communication in order to get him to Germany, and though she begged him to accompany her, he refused, saying he wanted to sail to America instead. He went with her as far as Palermo, where he "looked at ships," as he told Mountsier, "and started enquiries going in the port."[54] He was soon embarrassed into contrite letters to Anna, who had suffered a heart attack. Frieda had to travel to Rome because of passport technicalities, and did not reach Baden-Baden until mid-March. Though Anna was out of danger by then, she resolved to spend most of the remainder of 1921 with her mother, and was soon taking her on careful walks through the fields of spring flowers surrounding the Stift, waiting for Lawrence to arrive: Lonely and bored without her, he had changed his mind. "I sit in Fontana Vecchia," he wrote Anna, "and feel the house very empty without F."[55]

Else, fatigued by months of caring for Edgar in Munich—his breakdown had led to pneumonia—summoned Frieda to help. She found her brother-in-law a virtual invalid[56] and Else struggling to maintain his elaborate network of correspondence. Lawrence, still stalling in Taormina, insisted on putting his English publishing affairs in order before making the trip. He hired Albert Curtis Brown, a non-Jew, as his new British agent. *Birds, Beasts and Flowers*, for which he had had high hopes, was not generating much response on either side of the Atlantic; even Amy Lowell had not replied to an advance copy. "The bitch is probably jealous," Lawrence wrote Mountsier before setting off.[57]

He arrived on April 26, and he and Frieda, who had returned, took separate bedrooms at the Hôtel Krone, an inn three miles out of town, frequented largely by itinerant peasants. Two days later Edgar died. Frieda took a train to Munich, and Lawrence lost no time getting down to work, staking out a patch of undergrowth in the woods behind the Altes Schloss, to which he returned every morning. Sitting against an immense pine, he picked up where he had left off with *Aaron's Rod*. "I was glad Edgar died," he wrote Else, "better death than ignominious living on. Life had no place for him after the war."[58] Kot, who read of the death in the London papers, wrote to ask Lawrence if they were related. "Yes, Edgar Jaffe was my brother in law," he answered. "But he had gone cracked after being Bolshevist Minister of finance for Bavaria."[59]

They tried to socialize when Frieda settled back in, but, despite a wealth of local asparagus, Rhine wine, pork, and freshly killed game and fowl, cooking and entertaining in the no-frills setting were failures: Geese, goats, and a pet pig wandered the common rooms, and one evening a chicken flew into the soup tureen. Anna invited them for large teas of pumpernickel bread, *Trüffelleberwurst*, fresh cream, and strawberries, at which Lawrence was addressed by the honorific "*Herr Doktor*." The thick growth of trees to the north and east brought early dusks, and the gas lights were turned up, illuminating the genteel shabbiness into which the Stift, with no money for upkeep or improvements, was descending. Lawrence admired Anna's cheerful bossiness with the other residents, and she treated him alternately like a suitor and the son she had never had. "It's strange," she told Frieda, "that an old woman can still be as fond of a man as I am of that Lorenzo." Occasionally Lawrence, feeling he had won a tremendous victory over her, was lulled into taking her into his confidence with complaints of Frieda's stubbornness, impossible personality, and disorder. "I know her longer than you," she rebuffed him, enjoying the chance to throw him off guard.[60] He slowly gained weight trying to match her appetite, still tremendous despite her failing health. She and Frieda urged him to stay through the summer. Though he protested that postwar Germany was not an environment conducive to work, he finished *Aaron's Rod* in less than a month, and immediately began a sequel to *Psychoanalysis and the Unconscious*, provisionally entitled "The Child and the Unconscious."

Nusch, whose twenty-one-year marriage had all but disintegrated, arrived for a visit with Emil Krug, a Berlin banker with whom she had been having a long-standing affair, and charmed Lawrence with her fractured English and enormous sex appeal. "Lorenzo," she said, leaping onto his knee, "you are so nice, I like your red beard." He and Krug discussed parceling out his German royalties to Nusch and Else's children as well as the baroness, but Lawrence far preferred to join Nusch and Frieda for "long female talks."[61] Nusch invited them to Zell-am-See, an Austrian village on a small lake where she and her husband kept a chalet, and they spent much of July and August there, joined by Else and her children. Frieda, ensconced in a room with a balcony one floor above Lawrence's, loved visiting the nearby glaciers, and argued bitterly with him when he announced that he felt restless and wanted to take advantage of the offer of a free apartment in Florence.

She capitulated, and they spent almost a month; if he saw Baynes, the visits have not been recorded for posterity.[62] He and Frieda continued on to Capri, where they stayed for a week with Earl and Achsah Brewster, wealthy New England painters with a passion for non-Christian religions, South and East Asian culture, and wearing burnooses. The Brewsters urged them to visit Ceylon, where they were headed in the fall. Frieda, put off by Achsah's "Pictures of huge St. Francis's and unbirdy birds and white chiffon clouds of garments round her solid flesh," had no interest in sailing halfway around the world to live with them, but Lawrence was soon fantasizing about the East.[63] The impotence of Christianity and the soul-crushing effects of machinery, he said, were driving him off the Continent, though he cautioned Earl that he had no intention of worshiping Buddha.

Waiting for them when they reached Taormina was a single review of the first British edition of *Women in Love*, entitled "A Book the Police Should Ban."[64] The book was generating little but accusations of obscenity from the conservative press. There was scant response among the literati other than Bloomsbury gossip, though Rebecca West, who regularly reviewed Lawrence's work and whom he had met in Florence in the spring, had devoted three columns to it in a July issue of the *New Statesman*.[65] Virginia Woolf, rushing though a borrowed copy so she could pass it on to her sister, Vanessa Bell, complained about its length and enigmatic symbolism but confessed a malicious interest in the parts about Ottoline:

> She has just smashed L's head open with a ball of lapus [*sic*] lazuli—but then balls are smashed on every other page—cats—cattle—even the fish and the water lilies are at it all day long. There is no suspense or mystery: water is all semen: I get a little bored, and make out the riddles too easily. Only this puzzles me: what does it mean when a woman does eurythmics in front of a head of Highland cattle?[66]

Murry, later claiming not to have understood Gerald was modeled on him, pronounced the book constipated and disgusting in an *Athenaeum* review. Philip Heseltine objected to his likeness as Halliday and hired a solicitor to threaten that he would bring libel charges. "Heseltine ought to be flushed down a sewer," Lawrence fumed to Secker, "for he is a simple shit."[67] The suit was forestalled when Heseltine agreed to settle for textual changes in the second printing and a lump-sum payment from Secker of a little over sixty pounds.

Lawrence weathered the bad press and conspicuous silences through work and fantasy. Insel-Verlag had engaged Else for the *Rainbow* translation, and proofs began arriving in batches to be corrected. "[G]ood and solid," Lawrence pronounced her version of his novel. "[P]erhaps a bit heavy: but then it is very hard for me to get used to myself in another language."[68] (The book was eventually translated by someone else.) In between, he completed "The Child and the Unconscious," which he had retitled *Fantasia of the Unconscious*, and several remarkable stories, among them "The Captain's Doll," whose protagonist was loosely based on Nusch; "The Ladybird"; a revised version of "The Fox," his portrait of their Berkshire farmer friends Violet Monk and Cecily Lambert; and other work eventually collected in *The Captain's Doll* and *England, My England*.[69] He began telling friends that if Ceylon did not work out, he planned to "find a ship that would carry me around the world and land me somewhere in the West—New Mexico or California—and I could have a little house and two goats, somewhere away by myself in the Rocky Mountains."[70] In some versions the topology of the mountain retreat sounded suspiciously like what he had insisted on leaving behind in Austria. At other times, a seething, inexpressible anger took over, and he could not even fantasize: "I feel my summer travels didn't do much more than put me in a perfect fury with everything," he wrote Monk. "But then that's the effect most things have on me. The older I get, the angrier I become."[71]

Frieda, negotiating with Ernest for a Christmas visit, gave vent to her own fantasies, fears, self-recriminations, and confusion to Else early in November:

> I can only say that this way or that, life can hardly be endured; this evening I am thinking that Ernst is ill—nevertheless, Lawrence and I still, and more so, have a strong feeling that a not-being-together is no longer conceivable. . . . of course I am not angry with E. and I also know how well he means. . . . still one has to fight one's way through and great shreds of the soul remain behind, whether they will ever grow again, one can only hope. . . . How I will get through Christmas is a dread—otherwise we are so united.[72]

Three days later a letter to Lawrence—prompted by two installments in the *Dial* of *Sea and Sardinia*—arrived, from an unknown New York–Florentine socialite named Mabel Dodge Sterne. She admired the book's evocation of place, she wrote, and wanted his help in similarly evoking Taos (where she had relocated), "bring[ing] together the two ends of humanity, our own thin end, and the last dark strand from the previous, pre-white era."[73] Enclosed were a few sprigs of sagebrush and a medicinal herb that tasted like licorice.

Sterne's earlier reading of *Sons and Lovers* and *Psychoanalysis and the Unconscious*—published in New York in May 1921, to reviews that ranged from puzzled to outright scornful—had sent her hunting for clues to Lawrence's personal life: She submitted *Sons and Lovers* to the prominent American Freudian Smith Ely Jelliffe, a friend, and he informed her the author was suffering a "severe homosexual fixation."[74] Frieda, sensing a burgeoning flirtation, began her own correspondence with Sterne less than a week later, announcing herself in no uncertain terms as "Frieda Lawrence geb. [born] von Richthofen"—she often preferred this fulsome sign-off when writing to people she had not met.[75] Sterne was soon enlisting Leo Stein's help in encouraging the move to Taos. Stein wrote, describing Sterne as the "all but perfect hostess," but enraged Lawrence with a mocking criticism of *Psychoanalysis and the Unconscious*.[76] Lawrence, as roused as if he were back in England, fighting with the Murrys and Lady Ottoline, passed Stein's letter on to Sterne. As she had perhaps hoped, his appetite for epistolary intrigue had been whetted. Frieda quickly assembled a cruise wardrobe: three suit-dresses made from local linens and silks in light-colored checked patterns. "She says to tell you the chequered materials are not very chequered, and she does *not* look fat in them," Lawrence wrote the baroness, in a newsy, happy letter.[77]

January brought illness and a change of plans. Downed by the flu, Lawrence mailed away for berths on the RMS *Osterley* to Ceylon, paying with *Lost Girl* prize money. The sailing was scheduled for February 26, 1922. "At the eleventh hour I couldnt simply face America," he later explained, "the magnetism shoved me away."[78] They left for Palermo on February 20 and stayed in a hotel for three nights with Ruth Wheelock, a secretary in the American Consulate whom Lawrence had hired to type *Sea and Sardinia* and *Mr. Noon*, now a considerably longer and more sexually explicit novel. There were references to Otto Gross and instantly recognizable likenesses of Frieda, Else, Edgar, and the baroness. Convinced it would never be accepted for publication, he had set it aside.

As a parting gift Wheelock gave Frieda a five-foot panel from a painted Sicilian cart later described by a friend of the Lawrences' as depicting two scenes referring, somehow, to the life of the fourteenth-century Milanese general Marco Visconti: a joust and Saint Geneviève. Though Lawrence protested that they could not manage it—they were carrying two steamer trunks weighted with household items and books, a double suitcase, a hatbox, and four pieces of hand luggage—Frieda prevailed. They sailed to Naples and boarded the *Osterley*. "In my mind I have already lived in Taos," Frieda wrote Mabel, "and suddenly when it was all fixed, our going to Taos, Lawrence sprang Ceylon onto me."[79]

14

Around the World

I

It was a lulling, sixteen-day voyage. Lawrence worked on a translation of *Mastro-don Gesualdo*, a novel by the Sicilian writer Giovanni Verga, which he had begun in Taormina, staved off seasickness with a succession of pills and foul-tasting liquid medicines, and wrote the baroness long, ungrammatical letters in German, which Frieda corrected. She was hooking an immense rug and lounged on a deck chair, yarn bulging from a sewing bag. They befriended a group of Australians, among them Anna Jenkins, a socialite and patroness of the arts who offered a free apartment in Perth. There were huge meals and frequent snacks, including a midday one of Bovril or, once they had sailed past the Sahara, ice cream. Dolphins leapt by the side of the ship in the Indian Ocean, and silvery flying fish the size of butterflies sparkled against an unfailingly blue sky. Earl Brewster, conspicuous in huge, flowing whites, was waiting on the Colombo wharf to take them to his bungalow, as he called it, near Kandy, fifty miles inland, in the up-country.

The dubiousness of visiting the tropics in the spring was soon evident. April, the hottest month of the year, was two weeks away, and the incessant sun made Lawrence dizzy and nauseated, or, as he began writing friends, unmanned. The usual benefits of the up-country, higher elevation and cooler temperature, were canceled out by the design of the bungalow—actually a small estate on sprawling grounds overgrown with coconut and other palms—which had glass skylights that gave it the feeling of a terrarium. From its wide verandas, they could see the lake in the center of Kandy, a mile and a half distant, reachable on foot or by rickshaw, and, in the other direction, the Mahaweli River.

They had not packed properly for the climate. Achsah distributed white clothing and pith helmets—topees, she called them. She used indigenous or colonial terms for every object in the house and kinship terms for her servants, with an obvious delight in the language and a crude approximation of a Sinhalese accent; so it was that the Lawrences were given tiffin rather than the late-morning lunch, which was prepared by the *appu* (head cook). Her housekeeping and furnishings were idiosyncratic. Apart from a replica of Big Ben on the mantel and several huge plaster statues of parrots and Christian saints, she maintained a Zen-like simplicity, modeled on the local Temple of the Tooth, the monastery where Earl studied Buddhism and Pali, its theological language. There were meditation mats, but virtually no other furniture except rattan beds that sagged like hammocks. Such flourishes, which had seemed innocuous in Capri, now struck Lawrence as utterly pretentious. He felt confined and at the Brewsters' mercy, and began bluntly enumerating their "faults" for them, telling them he did not believe in holding anything back.[1] Frieda had little or nothing to say to Achsah, and could not remember how to spell her name.

The Brewsters' nine-year-old daughter, Harwood, followed her *ayah* sluggishly around the house, pulling a homemade wooden carriage shaped like a hearse, its uneven wheels rumbling along the floors. In it sat a porcelain doll with a scarred face; it had been smashed and replaced with a silk stocking on which Achsah had painted a face. Frieda and Achsah took turns reading her *The Swiss Family Robinson* at bedtime.

Lawrence spent long hours indoors, sick to his stomach despite a daily spoonful of cod-liver oil, which Frieda now carried on all their trips in a small flask hand-labeled "liver mixture."[2] At some point he developed a mild malarial infection. He finished the *Mastro-don Gesualdo* translation and started on Verga's shorter works, and a visit by the future duke of Windsor to Kandy inspired a poem, "Elephant"; otherwise he felt too ill, distracted, or annoyed to write. The white temples that proliferated in the lush landscape, overgrown with fragrant, yellow-flowering champac trees, looked like "decked up pigsties."[3] Wildcats bounded over the skylights each night, terrifying him, and he was convinced that snakes would slip under the doors, despite the vigilance of the armed night watchman the Brewsters had hired. One night rats made a nest in his topee. He was awakened by the chanting of the servants, who, during *poya*, the full moon, sat cross-legged on the floor after making *puja* to a painting of the Buddha, and by the sounds of the jungle: "[B]irds shriek and pop and cackle," he wrote Mary Cannan, ". . . creatures jerk and bounce about."[4] He detested the smell of the local fruits, except pineapple, which he could not digest: "[My] inside has never hurt me so much in all my 36 years."[5] The persistent scent of coconut oil, he wrote Mabel Dodge Sterne, made him think of blood and sweat.

On April 3 he cabled Mountsier in New York, instructing him to transfer a thousand dollars to a bank in Kandy. Over the past year he had banked a fair portion of his American earnings, which included a five-hundred-dollar *Lost Girl* advance and *Women in Love* royalties on the fifteen-dollar edition, both paid by Seltzer. When the money arrived he booked berths for himself and Frieda on the RMS *Orsova* to Western Australia. He also bought Frieda seven sapphires, which went into a flower-shaped brooch, and a box of moonstones from a Kandy jewelry store in which she spent much of her time, rummaging through worn leather bags filled with precious stones.

The sailing was April 24. Frieda breathed a sigh of relief to Sterne, with whom she was still trying to get on a friendly footing: "Ashsah [*sic*] Brewster was quite simple and nice, but a kind of New England 'culture' was very irritating; if she had only been content to be her simple self instead of all her flights!"[6] They were met by Jenkins, their friend from the Naples-Ceylon sailing, who had arranged introductions and an appearance at the Booklovers, a famous Perth bookshop. Before the day was out, Lawrence had booked the first available passage to Sydney, two weeks later.

He was fantasizing about their next destination—Tahiti—and his nervous plans and persistent dissatisfaction worried and exhausted Frieda, who made him agree to rent a house for at least three months when they reached Sydney. Jenkins booked rooms for them at a nearby guest house/nursing home. She explained to Mollie Skinner, the nurse and writer who helped run it, that she was bringing "an author D. H. Lawrence," whom she described as "a restless nostalgic, arrogant person who would not stay in Perth," and "his wife a German Countess."[7] Lawrence's presence was publicized in the local paper, and letters and calling cards trickled in from writers of mediocre talent, eager to meet the notorious author of banned literature. Among them were the poet William Siebenhaar, a transplanted Dutchman in his late fifties, and Katharine Susannah Prichard, a novelist and daughter-in-law of the Australian prime minister, who was so excited at the prospect of meeting him she gave birth prematurely.

He preferred Jenkins and her matronly friends, who rented cars and took him out into the bush. The spare beauty amazed and spooked him, particularly at night, when he often slipped away alone to watch the moon. He hoped to "recreate" himself in Australia by writing a novel, but felt effaced by the immensity of the landscape and mystified by the gregarious, unpretentious people he had met so far, whom he despaired of being able to capture.[8]

He began to change his mind when he read an unpublished manuscript of Skinner's. The author of a midwifery textbook, written after completing nurse's training in the slums of London, and a pseudonymous World War I novel based on her experiences as a nurse in India and Burma, she had a talent, Lawrence thought, for evoking the country and for "the borderline where probability merges into magic."[9] They eventually collaborated on a manuscript that she drafted and he partially rewrote, *The Boy in the Bush*, an effort marred by disagreements and conflicting claims of ownership.

He and Frieda left for Sydney on May 18. As a farewell gift Siebenhaar gave them *Dorothea, A Lyrical Romance in Verse*, a twelve-year-old book of his poems, and *Sentimental Sonnets*, which he had written with another man. Lawrence threw the books into the Southern Ocean after leaving the port. Tired of strangers, he kept to himself for much of the nine-day trip, except for some conversations with a former Australian army officer, who apparently offered the address of Major William Rendal Scott, an influential Sydney businessman and Freemason.[10] The rest of the time he wrote to friends, whom he told he would soon be in the United States. Though he did not have enough money for the sailing, it was becoming clear that he might actually be able to earn a living there. Indeed, American sales in the coming months outstripped the British more than three times, with books like *Aaron's Rod* (which had been published in April). *Women in Love*, seemingly all but forgotten by Secker, would become a New York cause célèbre when Seltzer capitalized on an unsuccessful prosecution by the Society for the Suppression of Vice with a new, $2.00 edition that sold ten thousand copies before the end of 1922, earning Lawrence $2,000.00 in royalties. Additional royalties came from Huebsch and, with sales to American magazines, his U.S. earnings for the year totaled $5,439.67; on average, he estimated, he earned £120.00 annually in British royalties, a tenth of the American amount.[11] Frieda made friends with Nottingham hosiery mechanics who were relocating to an industrial suburb of Sydney, and kept their wives in stitches telling stories sprinkled with butchered Sinhalese.

Sydney turned out to be unaffordable, and Lawrence disapproved of the people. Every woman aspired to silk stockings, he wrote Else after Frieda bought a pair, and the men were similarly materialistic, their manner crude and overly familiar. Frieda, whose desire for a house had become almost as obsessive as Lawrence's need to keep pushing on, was not prepared to go much farther. They boarded a train down the coast and, according to Frieda's later memory, picked the first place from the window that looked acceptable, Thirroul, a new, nondescript township with streets of sand, which catered to vacationers. It may also have been recommended by Major Scott, whom Lawrence had apparently met and become intrigued by: He was affiliated with the King and Empire Alliance, a right-wing political organization that was also a front for a secret army/"police" force, mobilized to take over in the event of a Labour party victory (in fact Labour lost the 1922 state elections, held in December). Alfred and Lucy Callcott, local real-estate agents, found them a three-bedroom bungalow, called Wyewurk by its pun-loving owners. Recently vacated by a family of fourteen, it was filthy, the yard and porch littered with trash, but the living room was immense, the jarrah floors were beautiful, and Frieda felt soothed by the crashing surf of the South Pacific, several hundred yards from the back doorstep. They dragged a huge, dusty, soiled rug outside to beat and scrub, and she spent the next few days scouring the furnishings and her hair, which had become infested with lice on the boat. The dressers and kitchen table soon were covered with Italian and Sinhalese fabric remnants, and embroidered silk panels hung on the living room wall next to a decorative black Greek handbag—a gift from the Brewsters—filled with knickknacks and ornaments picked up on their travels. "Frieda is so happy with her new house," Lawrence wrote the baroness, "she makes all so lovely."[12]

He was less so. The coastline reminded him of Cornwall, bringing unpleasant memories of the police interrogations during the war, and the discovery that there were coal mines nearby evoked Eastwood a bit too familiarly. Overcome with nostalgia "for Europe, for Sicily, for old civilisation," he became convinced he and Frieda had been fools to leave Taormina, and concluded that Australians, unlike Italians, lacked an inner self and any interest in cultivating one.[13] "I am so weary of these utterly à terre democratic peoples. Probably America will be as bad," he complained to Sterne on June 3.[14] The same day, he started *Kangaroo*, its hero a thin, bearded, disaffected British essayist (Richard Lovat Somers) recently arrived in Sydney with his wife (Harriet), a radiantly healthy, middle-aged woman with European good looks:

> Somers for the first time felt himself immersed in real democracy—in spite of all disparity in wealth. The instinct of the place was absolutely and flatly democratic, *à terre* democratic. . . . And this was what Richard Lovat Somers could not stand. You may be the most liberal Liberal Englishman, and yet you cannot fail to see the categorical difference between the responsible and the irresponsible classes. You cannot fail to admit the necessity for *rule*.[15]

He targeted August as the date of completion, and booked passage to San Francisco. "This is the most democratic place I have *ever* been in," he wrote Else on June 13, after completing about two hundred pages. "And the more I see of democracy the more I dislike it. It just brings everything down to the mere vulgar level of wages and prices, electric light and water closets. . . . You *never* knew anything so nothing, Nichts, Nullus, niente."[16]

Sterne kept him supplied with photographs and notes of Taos, and lists of the prospective books on which she wanted him to collaborate, including her life story. Her letters grew increasingly intimate, proprietary, indiscreet, and long; one, on a roll of parchment, measured seven feet. She provided an elaborate history of her love interests and sexual motivation. Her present partner, Tony Luhan, was a married Taos Pueblo Indian; she pacified his wife, Candelaria, with a monthly stipend, since having had what she described to Lawrence as a "Fight" with the woman.[17] Frieda passed the details on to Else. "As dernier cri she has a real Indian as a friend—she enticed him from his faithful wife 'Candelabra.'"[18] Gifts were frequent, and calculated to appeal to Lawrence's abiding belief in blood consciousness, love of preindustrial society, and *nostalgie de la boue*. Among them was a pseudo-psychological tract, *The Glands Regulating Personality*, a strangely timed revival of medieval physiology; its author maintained that lymphatic and pituitary secretions determined personality type, and recommended megadoses of Pituitrin and Adrenalin to improve the species.[19] Gifts to Frieda were less frequent and appealed to baser instincts; a necklace, "charmed" to lure them to Taos, never arrived. She was explicitly excluded from the intellectual side of the correspondence, but, accustomed to such condescension, simply ignored it. "We are reading the Gland book in turns," she wrote Sterne, ". . . it always is funny when a man sees salvation in 'glands.'"[20] Anticipating gossip, she tried to stem its tide: "I am frightened of people's spite and vulgarity. . . . If you can only keep it dark for a little while that we are coming! let's have our meeting without the spiteful comments of New York on *all* of us."[21] She was clearly searching for the right note to strike with her, trying, among other things, to appeal to her reputed sense of beauty and place:

> We are sitting here perched on the Pacific, lovely for that and the air and space but the tin cans and newspapers *flying* over the *ugly* little town behind are not to be thought of—And quite a nice statue of an "Anzac" [World War I Australian or New Zealand soldier] stands at the corner, just like a forgotten milk can, no grass round it or *anything*, only filthy paper flying and a tin cinema show near—I *can not* bear it. . . . By the way *dont give* us too little a place to live in, we are much too quarrelsome—it's quite fatal—We can afford it nowdays, I mean we are'nt as poor as we used to be—but we must'nt be too much on top of each other or we get on each other's nerves.

She reported Lawrence's progress on *Kangaroo*: "gone it full tilt at page 305—but has come to a stop and kicks."[22]

2

Named for one of its central characters, Benjamin ("Kangaroo") Cooley, the novel is one of Lawrence's clunkier and more polemical, based in part on political news gleaned from *Corriere della Sera*, which he had read avidly in Taormina, and the *Sydney Bulletin*. Its argument, that fascism has a tremendous appeal not only to the uneducated but to people of refinement, is occasionally redeemed by long passages of truth and real beauty, though these are usually reserved for Lawrence's deep hatred of England and are unrelated to the main action.

Kangaroo, a fascist agitator with a "long and lean and pendulous" face, tremendous muscularity, and a strange lope, is also improbably Jewish, apparently based loosely on Kot; David Eder; and Sir Charles Rosenthal, an Australian architect and leader of the King and Empire Alliance. Cooley heads the Diggers (probably based on the self-styled King and Empire Alliance army, and possibly also on the then-extant Returned Servicemen's League), homoerotically inclined World War I veterans hoping to overthrow democracy in Australia.[23] Richard's attempts to infiltrate the Diggers in order to gather material for an essay result in a fleeting fascination with their politics, and several torpid *Blutbrüderschaft* scenes with, among others, Richard and Harriet Somerses' next-door neighbor, Jack Callcott. Though the name belonged to the Lawrences' realtors, the prototypes for the character seem to have been Major Scott and a man who lived, as in the book, next door to Wyewurk (which became, in the novel, Torestin). Callcott's bulging thighs, ambiguous masculinity, and naïveté arouse and disgust Richard. In a scene of political violence, Callcott kills three men and exults, "Having a woman's something, isn't it? But it's a flea-bite, nothing, compared to killing your man when your blood comes up." Kangaroo, mortally wounded by a bullet to the abdomen the same day, begs Richard to declare his love: "'Was ever woman so coy and hard to please!' he said, in a warm, soft voice. 'Why don't you want to love me, you stiff-necked and uncircumcised Philistine?'"[24]

Harriet, one of Lawrence's most transparent likenesses of Frieda, is disgusted with Richard's efforts to find an Australian "mate": "Wives are *supposed* to have to take their husbands back a little damaged and repentant from their *love affairs* with other women. I'll be hanged if it wouldn't be more fun than this business of seeing you come back once more fooled from your attempts with *men*." Richard agonizes over the choice between her and "the pure male activity," and fantasizes in a dream that she is slowly metamorphosing into his mother. In "Harriet and Lovat at Sea in Marriage," a chapter thick with sexual innuendo, Lawrence casts marriage in lordship and bondage terms: "[H]e'd got into his head this idea of being lord and master, and Harriet's acknowledging him as such. Not just verbally." Frieda and Lawrence's own fights were much talked about in Thirroul (in *Kangaroo* it became Mullumbimby); when the boy from the local greengrocer heard screams, he refused to deliver. Cornwall found its way into a long chapter, "The Nightmare," that ranged from the humiliation of being examined for military duty to Lawrence's relationship with William Henry Hocking: "He was very thick with John Thomas. . . . Harriet was a great deal alone."[25] Mountsier, whom Lawrence kept abreast of his quick progress, made an appearance as Monsell, and the Christmas Eve interrogation by Cornish police was faithfully reproduced. Though Mountsier and Frieda eventually questioned the wisdom of including this utterly anomalous English material, Lawrence, rightly judging that it was one of the most compelling chapters in the book, refused to take it out.

He mailed off the manuscript on July 20, and, with almost three weeks still to go before they departed for the United States, and a surprise gift of eight pounds from Achsah Brewster, they rented a car and driver to tour the coast with the two Nottingham couples Frieda had regaled with travel stories on the sailing from Ceylon. Lawrence had borrowed money from one of them shortly after settling in Thirroul, and wanted to repay the loan. They arrived on a Saturday at Wyewurk, and on Sunday they drove from Bulli Pass Summit, which had a panoramic view of the South Pacific, to Fitzroy Falls, where they had a picnic. Frieda, noticeably heavier than on the sailing, did most of the talking, occasionally interrupted by detailed botanical lectures by Lawrence, who characteristically had acquired an encyclopedic knowledge of Australian flora and fauna.[26]

Nothing was said about leaving Australia, but almost as soon as their guests left, Lawrence got out the trunks with the special relish he reserved for leavetakings, and, as usual, his anticipation was clouded by last-minute misgivings. Word came from Mountsier that *Hearst's International* had paid a thousand dollars for "The Captain's Doll," the story based on Nusch—his second largest sale to date. Australia would be a good place to settle down, he reasoned, if he were complacent and had nothing left to accomplish, but "there is still some fight to fight," he wrote Achsah Brewster. He explained his restlessness in messianic terms, like a man preoccupied with his own mortality: His conscience impelled him to hurry to see America and make some sense of it by writing about it.[27] At times his arguments must have seemed convincing—Frieda later inexplicably claimed to have wanted to settle down in Australia for good—but indecision was anathema to her, and she had come to detest the gray gum trees and parched countryside. "The nicest and most elegant object in Thirroul is a beautiful German cannon!" she wrote Else. She told Lawrence she was "determined to have a little farm in America."[28] They boarded the RMS *Tahiti* on August 11. A brief stop in Wellington, New Zealand, Mansfield's birthplace, convinced Lawrence he understood something about her he had never known before, and inspired a nostalgic, one-word postcard, "*Ricordi* [memories]."[29]

Their first brush with the New World was in Papeete, Tahiti, where the ship took on the cast and crew of *Lost and Found on a South Sea Island*, a Raoul Walsh film about an American sea captain's rescue of his daughter from feuding Samoans in Pago Pago. "They seemed to sleep all day and looked white and tired in the evening," Frieda later wrote of the stars. "Cases of empty champagne bottles stood outside their cabin in the morning."[30] Lawrence pronounced them "common" and "shop-girls," and was even less impressed with the Tahitians: "If you are thinking of coming here don't," he warned Compton Mackenzie. "The people are brown and soft."[31]

In San Francisco they were surprised that the electric lights of the city obscured the moonlight, and confused by cafeteria protocol: "We . . . did not know how to behave," Frieda later wrote, "how to take our plates and food."[32] The Palace Hotel, where they stayed, was "a great building with post and shops in it, like a little town in itself: costs very much," Lawrence wrote the baroness. ". . . Everybody is very nice, everything very *comfortable*. . . . I really hate this mechanical *comfort*."[33] They had spent virtually all their cash on board and at ports of call, and had to cable Mountsier for several hundred dollars. Lawrence immediately sent thirty to Frieda's mother. Sterne, taking no chances, cabled first-class train tickets to Lamy, New Mexico, seventeen miles southeast of Santa Fe, and told them to expect her on the platform.

15

The Lobo

I

Sterne, who prided herself on her intuition and clairvoyance, had envisioned a different couple, more cosmopolitan and handsome. They looked like refugees, stoic but out of place. Frieda's pongee outfit, probably one of the Taormina suits she and Lawrence had assured the baroness complemented her figure, was snug from the weight she had gained in Australia and looked pathetically formal in the desert; two days' travel (they had boarded the Grand Canyon Limited in San Francisco on Friday night, September 8) had not improved its appearance. Lawrence's thick three-piece wool suit, bought in heavier and healthier times, was a source of deep embarrassment, hanging awkwardly on his narrowing frame. They did not wait to be helped. The hand baggage, which included packages wrapped in brown paper and tied with string, looked weightless in Frieda's strong, shapely arms. She hauled them carelessly down the platform while Lawrence struggled with the book- and crockery-filled steamer trunks and the painted Sicilian panel.

An industrial magnate's daughter who had probably never picked up a suitcase in her forty-three years, Sterne was slightly horrified. "I had an impression of his slim fragility beside Frieda's solidity," she later wrote, "of a red beard that was somehow too old for him, and of a nervous incompetence."[1] Tony Luhan maintained an unnerving silence beside her, providing none of the "redskin welcome" Lawrence had anticipated.[2] They were an undeniably handsome couple, with their turquoise-and-silver ensembles and burnished skin, and seemed very much part of the landscape. Her Cadillac, one of several she kept in Taos, was covered with a thin film of reddish road dust; its gray side curtains were down, the doors were ajar, awaiting the Lawrences' hand luggage, and the expensive leather upholstery inside augured a privileged world.

Frieda's eyes were bleary and unfocused as she tried to adjust to the strong, slanting, late-afternoon light. She smiled ingenuously, and Sterne cringed:

> . . . her half-open mouth with the lower jaw pulled a little sideways. Frieda always had a mouth rather like a gunman. . . . [She] was over-expansive, vociferous, with a kind of forced, false bonhomie. . . . I made out, in the twinkling of an eye, that Frieda immediately saw Tony and me sexually, visualizing our relationship. I experienced her swift, female measurement of him, and how the shock of acceptance made her blink.

Lawrence shared Frieda's carnal thoughts, according to Sterne, because he had no choice: He had sublimated his instincts to hers—she was his "medium"—a dependence that mortified him.[3] Already beginning to regret her epistolary confidences of the past year, Sterne led them silently through the crowd. Frieda later remembered thinking, "She has eyes one can trust."[4]

2

Something of a medium herself—a *Kulturträger*, or culture carrier, Lawrence was soon calling her—Mabel had arrived in Taos in 1917 with her third husband, Maurice Sterne, a Russian-born sculptor, and a sixteen-year-old son born during her first marriage, John Evans. The boy's paternity was in question: His father may have been Mabel's former gynecologist. Raised in Buffalo, New York, she had lived in Paris, Florence, and Greenwich Village; in each city, she had suffered nervous breakdowns and had made suicide attempts, diagnosed much later as symptoms of manic-depressive disorder. Extremely acquisitive, she dabbled with great success in art (from Venetian glass to architectural ornaments), social activism (the Industrial Workers of the World's 1913 Paterson Strike Pageant for silk-factory employees was her brainchild), journalism, and famous people. Despite her protestations to Lawrence that she needed his help in conjuring Taos, her writing talent was considerable. However, she suffered bouts of illness, ran through a host of cures, from psychoanalysis and a steady diet of Nietzsche to Christian Science healing, theosophy, and astrology. An annual income of $13,750 (interest on her inheritance) and frequent large cash gifts from her mother enabled her to indulge lavishly in each: She went to Mary Baker Eddy protégée Emma Curtis Hopkins for thrice-weekly Christian Science sessions; her analyst was A. A. Brill, Freud's American translator and popularizer.[5] When nothing else worked, she moved.

She was best known as a salonist. Married at twenty-one to a steamship owner's son who died in a hunting accident two and a half years later, she had moved to Europe with her son and married another American, Edwin Dodge, a Bostonian trained in architecture at the École des Beaux-Arts. Their first house, the Villa Curonia, a fifteenth-century Medici villa outside Florence, was the setting of her first salon (guests included André Gide, Gertrude Stein, and Eleonora Duse) and two suicide efforts. In the first she ate figs with glass shards; in the second she drank a bottle of laudanum. Both were occasioned by a thwarted liaison with her chauffeur, one of several romances that foundered on her or her partner's frigidity or ambivalence. Other potential lovers were a Florentine homosexual, her son's American tutor, and Stein, who wrote an elliptical "Portrait of Mabel Dodge at the Villa Curonia." Ostensibly an homage, its three pages were given almost entirely to a cubist cataloging of the riches of an empty house; the title contains the only reference to Mabel, who nevertheless was flattered, and greatly impressed by Stein's nonlinear style.[6] She had it published in a limited edition of three hundred, with covers fashioned of Florentine wallpaper.

When the Dodges left Florence in November 1912 to move to New York City, the "Portrait" became Mabel's *carte de visite*, distributed liberally in literary, psychoanalytic, labor, and political circles, often with invitations to the salon she established in her new home, at

23 Fifth Avenue. People were soon coming in droves of a hundred or more to her Wednesdays and Thursdays, which lasted through the following year, a period coinciding with the end of her marriage to Dodge. (To ward off a breakdown she suspected he was about to bring on, she exiled him to the Brevoort Hotel and never summoned him back.) Among the more famous were Brill; Emma Goldman, "Big Bill" Haywood, and John Reed, with whom she lived while writing articles and short stories for *The Masses* and serving on its advisory board; Carl Van Vechten, also her lover; William English Walling, the co-founder of the National Association for the Advancement of Colored People; Alfred Stieglitz and the painter Andrew Dasburg; Margaret Sanger, Lincoln Steffens, Walter Lippmann, and Max Eastman. Upton Sinclair, a regular, recalled a time she sold her dining room chairs to bail several socialists out of jail.[7]

World War I, and an unhappy, dragged-out break-up with Reed, helped bring about the end of the salon, and eventually she moved to 23 Washington Square, an opulent apartment with rustic wood beams (later frequently misidentified as the site of her salon).[8] In the two and a half years between the breakup and her marriage to Maurice Sterne, she became a nationally syndicated advice columnist for the Hearst chain; her pieces covered such topics as Walt Whitman, adoption, the Industrial Revolution (which, like Lawrence, she mistrusted and condemned), and psychoanalysis, distilled for "shop girls and clerks": "For the mature woman there is no father," she wrote. "There is no master. There is only herself."[9]

In Taos she and Sterne originally rented rooms from Arthur Manby, an eccentric, wealthy Englishman. Accusations that the newlyweds were German spies (he had a slight Russian-Yiddish accent) turned Mabel against the town, whose drab stores, dusty plaza, and endless succession of filthy, transient covered wagons she found sloppy and unattractive. She loved the ancient Tiwa culture of the Pueblo, however, the seventeen thousand acres of unspoiled land two miles north. The Tiwa lived in windowless, eleventh-century adobe houses and according to customs of similar vintage, despite incursions by the Spanish, Christian missionaries, and, during the war with Mexico, the American army. Mabel admired their aloof self-sufficiency and semi-agrarian existence, and what she mistakenly perceived as an absence of stress among the women, who seemed impervious to the personal and domestic misfortunes she had endured. She cut her long, dark-brown hair, which she had previously worn in two buns, like earmuffs, began wearing shawls draped over her shoulders, and sat for hours each day with the women, learning how to speak, walk, and act like them. When she discovered that modern medical care was largely nonexistent, she paid for supplies and drugs, including arsenic for syphilis, which raged at the rate of about 12 percent. Occasionally she brought Maurice and her son, John, along, though Maurice thought the Tiwa were unsanitary and idle.[10]

The Sternes met Tony and his wife Candelaria in January 1918. Candelaria, stunning in red and white, happened to see them wandering through the Pueblo and invited them in. Tony was bent over a drum, which he continued to beat, saying nothing, but the attraction to Mabel was instantaneous. She invited him to her house to play the drum, and he learned to drive; they were soon taking long trips through the countryside in her Cadillacs. In June, acting on his advice, she bought a small house and twelve acres of land abutting the Pueblo for fifteen hundred dollars.[11] Tony erected a tepee out in front, and each night drummed from within until she joined him. He had syphilis, which Mabel eventually contracted. Maurice acquired a shotgun, intending to drive Luhan out of his tepee and off the property, but the gun terrified him and he had to content himself with insulting Mabel and her sexual relations. She threw him out, and he moved back East, where he received monthly one-hundred-dollar support checks from her until their divorce, four years later.

3

Sterne and the Lawrences arrived in Santa Fe by eight o'clock. The poet-memoirist Harold "Hal" Witter Bynner, new to New Mexico via Brooklyn, Harvard, California, and China, put them up for the night. He was a middle-aged man with a modest private income supplemented by lecturing and teaching; a three-room house; and decidedly mixed feelings about granting favors to Sterne, whom he had known for seven months. Relations with her tended to be feudal, dictated by her patronage and power. An avid gossip, though, Bynner had read most of the letters from the Lawrences (despite Frieda's request not to broadcast their arrival, Sterne had distributed them freely to friends) and was looking forward to meeting the famous writer and his much-discussed wife.

The letters and Sterne's hostile predisposition to Frieda had made for voyeuristic talk about the viability of the Lawrences' marriage among a small circle in Santa Fe, Taos, and New York, where Frieda's reputed stupidity and possessiveness and Lawrence's poverty had become a matter of legend. These were also "issues" in Boston, where Amy Lowell, whom Bynner knew from the poetry circuit, was still providing firsthand accounts of the terrible apartments and borrowed houses during the war. Though Bynner had an intense dislike of Lowell and her poetry, anti-Frieda sentiment seemed universal, and he was half expecting the worst: a dull, grasping wife "beneath her husband's stature." A reading of Lawrence's two psychology books had left an impression of "a sort of Freudian prig," however, and his mind was open.[12] Tall, handsome, and balding, with owlish good looks, horn-rimmed glasses, and an amused, thoughtful expression, he was hopefully watering the sage when Luhan steered the Cadillac into his tiny yard, dropped off his passengers and their hand luggage, and began trying to park. Lawrence held on to the Sicilian panel, one end of which rested on the ground. Luhan, still trying to park, backed into it and split it in two with a loud crack, sending Lawrence flying. "It's your fault, Frieda!" Lawrence screamed. "You've made me carry that vile thing around the world, but I'm done with it. Take it, Mr. Bynner, keep it, it's yours! Put it out of my sight!"

Bynner was amused by Frieda's broad smile and her steady stream of reassuring noises and loud "*Ja*"s to Lawrence, who turned to Luhan when he was finished with her: "You're a fool, Tony!"[13] They were the first words he had spoken to him directly since they had met. Mabel, deeply satisfied by the contretemps, smiled and began introductions. Frieda insisted the accident was nothing, told Bynner she still wanted the panel, and soon had everyone on her side. "I knew," Bynner later wrote, "that the reports I had heard as to Mrs. Lawrence being . . . something of an incubus, were either malicious or stupidly mistaken."[14] He was to become one of her true American friends.

Despite the late hour, he assembled more people for dinner: the painter William Penhallow Henderson, his wife, the poet Alice Corbin, and their teenage daughter, also named Alice. Lawrence helped Bynner's maid prepare the food while Frieda chain-smoked and kept up a running commentary on Lawrence's kitchen skills and her own clumsiness: eggs never "drooled," she said, when Lorenzo cracked them, and objects perilously close to the edges of sideboards never tumbled.[15] Willard "Spud" Johnson, Bynner's lover and secretary, arrived from seeing a Tom Mix movie with his watch on his ankle—his wrists were too slender to hold it[16]—completing the party of nine. Twenty-five and refined-looking, with a taste for velveteen pants and silk neckerchiefs, he was an itinerant journalist whose work eventually spanned the country, from the *Denver Post* to *The New Yorker*. He was co-editing *Laughing Horse*, a satirical magazine published by the University of California, where he had been Bynner's student three years before.

Lawrence dominated the dinner talk, everything from Lowell and the local gossip to his mirthful, precise impersonations of Murry, Norman Douglas, Bertrand Russell, British evangelists, and commoners on the London double-deckers in the rain. When the party broke up—Sterne had arranged a more comfortable place for herself and Luhan to sleep and promised to return in the morning to drive them to Taos—the Lawrences stayed up late talking, a brilliant, celebrity-filled conversation that left Bynner exhausted, exhilarated, and charmed by their marriage, which seemed rock-solid.[17]

4

A massive storm broke as they drove through Taos Canyon, a harrowing ride along a winding, rutted ledge interrupted by boulders, with sheer six-hundred-foot drops to the Rio Grande. Lesser vehicles than Sterne's often failed to make it up the one-lane grades and had to descend in reverse. When someone came from the other direction, the northbound driver hugged the canyon wall and waited for the Santa Fe–bound car to pass. As they approached the village of Ranchos, the rain stopped, the driving became less treacherous, and Taos Valley opened before them—"an unforgettable experience," Frieda later wrote, "with all the deep mountains sitting mysteriously around in a ring, and so much sky."[18] Huge white clouds cast shadows over Lobo peak, seventeen miles in the distance, Taos Mountain, and, bordering the vast fields of sage and red dirt, the Sangre de Cristos, which looked soft, iridescent, and unreal. Thickly draped with Ponderosa pine, aspen, and cottonwoods, the mountains seemed to be wearing green flannel pajamas. The green was broken up by thin gold stripes: the leaves of aspens, which had begun turning early—"the mountains put[ting] on their bobcatcoats," as Frieda later wrote Bynner.[19] She grew to love the New Mexican fall, thereafter linked irrevocably in her mind with the certainty that, after years of impermanence and not belonging, she had finally found a home. The purple asters glowed in the after-storm brilliance. It was late afternoon, September 11, Lawrence's thirty-seventh birthday.

Sterne and Luhan lived together on her twelve-acre property, in a sprawling house they had designed and grafted onto the original tiny building. The Big House, as it was usually called (or Los Gallos, after the ceramic Mexican chickens she placed on the roof), was filled with possessions accumulated in Italy and New York: grand furniture, artworks, and objects that mingled—strangely but sometimes successfully—with rough-hewn local Spanish pieces and Indian artifacts. Low-ceilinged, with a dark, soothing interior, small windows, endless rooms, and handsome *vigas* (dark-stained round beams running the width of most of the rooms), the house reminded Lawrence of the "nasty little" temples of Ceylon, as he was quick to tell Sterne.[20] The sunroof of Luhan's bedroom faced the Pueblo, where Candelaria still lived (rather well, on her monthly subsidy from Sterne). Some nights Tony walked to the Pueblo and slept over, returning to Los Gallos the following morning, a practice that infuriated Mabel but over which she had no control.[21]

Surrounding the Big House were one-room adobe cottages for guests. Over the summer Mabel had commissioned the building of a "Pink House" for the Lawrences, its thick outer mud walls the color of a baby's receiving blanket. Some two hundred yards beyond her root cellar, a patio with Adirondack chairs and a swinging bench, and a footbridge over a tiny brook, the house was furnished with Indian blankets; paintings of animals and Pueblo dances hung on the walls. Their "front yard," like Mabel's, was the entire southern brink of the Pueblo. They had Lawrence's birthday meal by candlelight at the long wooden table in the Big House dining room. Luhan sat customarily silent while Sterne, who "wanted Lawrence to get into the Indian thing *soon*," discussed plans for Luhan to drive a small party two days later 120 miles across the desert to the Jicarilla reservation, where the Apaches were dancing.[22] Frieda would stay home with her.

The elevation (6,965 feet) made Lawrence dizzy, tired, and vague.[23]

Dogs barked, farther out the coyotes howled, and in the morning, magpies called monotonously to each other. There were letters from Germany, two from the baroness and one from Else.[24] Frieda set up clothes- and dishwashing stations on the porch, and they drove to the Pueblo, whose imminent despoiling by whites Sterne spent the better part of the trip lamenting. "*[B]uy* it," Frieda urged her, "and keep it like this forever!"

"Don't be vulgar," Lawrence said.[25]

5

Sterne was not oblivious to the power Frieda's spontaneity had with Lawrence, and took her aside whenever she got the chance. They talked for hours, largely about sex, Sterne inspired by Jelliffe's analysis of the latent homosexuality of *Sons and Lovers*, Frieda getting in a few blunt complaints on the subject. Sterne followed up with notes, delivered across the two hundred yards by Tiwa servants, and was rewarded with more confidences (all recorded by Mabel, with varying degrees of accuracy and goodwill, many years later):

> I have suffered tortures sometimes when Lawrence talked to people, when they drew him out just to "see his goods" and then jeered at him. . . . And for all that you will detest Lawrence sometimes and sometimes he talks bosh—but that is so human in him that he isn't "superbo." It's a joy to me that Tony wants to go with him—but tell Tony that he is frail, he can't stand so very much!

Quizzed about Cornwall, she confessed to "two times Lawrence had evaded her" for a farmer. Questions about their love life, Frieda's influence over the novels, poems, and stories, and their time in London provoked boasts and admissions of long-standing literary grudges:

> [H]e gets his books from me. . . . Nobody knows that. Why, I have done pages of his books for him. In *Sons and Lovers* I actually wrote pages into it. Oh, it was terrible when he was writing that one! I thought it would kill him. That mother. . . . Everyone thinks Lawrence is so wonderful. Well, I am something in myself, too. The Kot thinks I am not good enough for him! . . . He thinks I should just be willing to scrub the floor for Lorenzo.[26]

The grilling continued for the five days Lawrence was away on the Jicarilla reservation: "I answered truthfully," Frieda later wrote, "giving the show away completely as usual."[27] When Lawrence returned, Frieda repeated the conversations to him. Irritated more than angered by her disloyalty, he made plans with Sterne to get started immediately on a novel of her life in Taos. They agreed to meet on her roof the following day.

When he arrived for the session, Sterne was sunning herself while she watched her pigeons mate in the multistoried dovecote bordering the southwestern edge of the patio, wearing only a white cashmere burnoose and moccasins. Lawrence, momentarily repulsed, remained fully clothed in the strong sun, complaining about Frieda's "obtuseness" and "north German psyche."[28] The talk turned to menopause, which Sterne, forty-three (Frieda's age), was beginning to undergo; she argued that the absence of regular periods made her a better catalyst than Frieda for his writing.[29] "The burden of consciousness is too great for a woman to carry," Lawrence conceded, several hours later, before descending to the first floor so she could dress and walk him back home. "She has enough to bear with her ever-recurring menstruation."[30] Walking to the Pink House they spotted Frieda, hanging bedsheets in the sun. Lawrence lowered his head and began giggling into his beard when she turned to face them, disgust and aggravation darkening her face. He had been gone the whole morning. Arms akimbo and looking far more like a "gunman" than she had a couple of weeks before at Lamy, she stared down Sterne, who walked home without saying hello. It is not known what passed between Frieda and Lawrence that afternoon, but by evening he informed Sterne that the collaboration could not continue unless they worked at the Pink House under Frieda's supervision. "I had always regarded Lawrence's genius as given to me," Frieda later wrote, a claim to which he appeared to have no answer.[31] Sterne refused to agree to Frieda's terms.

At the Pueblo Lawrence acquired the nicknames "Red Wolf" (according to some, "Red Fox") and—shades of Berkshire—"Creeping Jesus."[32] Though fundamentally skeptical of the Tiwa's spirituality, he could not help admiring the agelessness of their ceremonies, particularly the predawn footraces of the yearly harvest festival, San Geronimo, held at the end of September:

> The young men, even the boys, run naked, smeared with white earth and stuck with bits of eagle fluff for the swiftness of the heavens, and

> the old men brush them with eagle feathers, to give them power. And they run in the strange hurling fashion of the primitive world, hurled forward.[33]

Sterne accompanied them to San Geronimo but stayed away from the Pink House for awhile, rationalizing Lawrence's betrayal as the symptom of a bad, solipsistic marriage: Frieda, she decided, felt compelled to provoke him when he ignored her; Lawrence hated her chronic need for attention but could not stand to be without her:

> At the end of an evening when he had not particularly noticed her, she would begin insulting him. He would almost dance with rage before her where she sat stolid and composed, but with a glare in her green eyes, as she puffed her cigarette into his face or—leaving it drooping in the corner of her mouth, a sight he always detested—mouthed some vulgar criticism up at him, one eye closed against the smoke, her head cocked: a perfectly disgusting picture, when she did so!
>
> "Take that dirty cigarette out of your mouth! And stop sticking out that fat belly of yours!" he yelled once, shaking his finger in her face.
>
> "You'd better stop that talk or I'll tell about *your* things," she taunted.[34]

Occasionally such scenes ended at the Pink House in violent, frustrated lovemaking that degenerated into tears and fistfights, leaving bruises. These were painfully obvious to Sterne when she and Frieda, who continued to confide in her, bathed with Luhan and Lawrence at a radium spring in the Rio Grande Gorge, a narrow chasm in the vast grassy tableland that descended vertiginously for hundreds of feet. From the bottom the sky was just a thin blue line specked every now and then by an almost invisible eagle. Called Manby Hot Springs after Sterne's former landlord (who had tried to make a tourist attraction of it), the spot became one of their favorite haunts during the fall. Driving and then hiking down with picnic baskets, towels, blankets, cooking supplies, and empty gallon bottles for spring water strapped to their backs, they would split off into groups divided by sex, Lawrence, Luhan, and occasionally Bynner bathing first, followed by Frieda and Sterne. A stone changing room near the outdoor spring led to the larger pool and rock basin. "I saw the big, voluptuous woman standing naked in the dim stone room," Sterne later recalled, "... and there were often great black and blue bruises on her blond flesh." One morning she arrived at the Pink House unexpectedly and found Frieda

> in the kitchen, spent and old from too many tears. I asked her what was the matter and she, still undone with misery and discouragement, broke out again in sobs.
>
> "I cannot stand it," she wept. "He tears me to pieces. Last night he was so loving and so tender with me, and this morning he hates me. He hit me—and said he would not be any woman's servant. Sometimes I believe he is mad."[35]

Lawrence openly advocated marital force—to Sterne's son, John, for example, who was planning to marry Alice Henderson, the teenager they had met at Bynner's. He believed it was the most expedient way to settle arguments. Frieda had learned, as far back as Cornwall, that the fights ended quickest when she did not respond. Like a savvy prizefighter, she usually let him spend his anger until he became physically exhausted. "[T]he bond of hate," Lawrence told Sterne, "can be stronger than the bond of love."[36] For Frieda passing years brought less resentment than equanimity, colored by a defensiveness she never lost: "What does it amount to that he hit out at me in a rage, when I exasperated him, or mostly when the life around him drove him to the end of his patience? I didn't care very much. ... Battles must be. If he had sulked or borne me a grudge, how tedious!"[37]

6

Sterne soon agreed to work at the Pink House, but the first session was unproductive. Frieda sang and swept the floor with a vengeance, and Sterne left with little or nothing to show. Lawrence came down with a cold and took to his bed. So far, all he had been able to write was an ironic, seven-page scene, "The Wilful Woman," based on Sterne's memory of arriving in New Mexico in the middle of the night five years before. Lawrence did not show Sterne the manuscript, which he kept hidden from everyone but Frieda, explaining to Sterne, "it will spoil your view."[38] He found that having separate sets of secrets from each of them was profoundly titillating. The pages open—like "Odour of Chrysanthemums," one of his first commercial successes—with a train. Unlike the powerful black machine lumbering past Midlands fields, collieries, and people, however, Sterne's train never arrives. Perhaps he had read Stein's portrait; the story is atypically mystical and modernist: a parable in which Sterne (Sybil Monde), ridiculous and self-defeating, psychically impedes the train's progress.

Frieda took great delight in the story, though she was probably aware that it was as metaphorical of Lawrence's life as of Sterne's, its irony deriving as much from Lawrence's identification with the heroine as from his contempt for Sterne's suffocating patronage and Americanness, of which he complained in a letter to Else:

> Well here we are in the Land of the Free and the Home of the Brave. But both freedom and bravery need defining. . . . Mabel Sterne is very nice to us—though I hate living on somebody else's property and accepting their kindnesses. . . . Everything in America goes by *will*. A great negative *will* seems to be turned against all spontaneous life—there seems to be no *feeling* at all. . . . how can one write about it, save analytically. Frieda, like you, always secretly hankered after America and its freedoms. . . . But now she is just beginning to taste the iron ugliness of what it means.[39]

When Sterne was called away to Santa Fe for a few days after more unsuccessful sessions at the Pink House, Lawrence, at a loss for where to go next, gave her written instructions specifying what he wanted notes on, among them her affairs with Maurice and Luhan, and the "Fight with Tony's wife."[40] The atmosphere at the Pink House improved hugely in her absence; Frieda wrote glibly to Mountsier, who had written enclosing photos of her mother: "I *love* the land and like Mabel D—L. was just on the defensive. . . . Lawr has actually begun a novel about here and Mabel D—It's *very* clever the beginning, it will be rather sardonic!"[41] Mountsier's letter complained about *Kangaroo*, which Lawrence had sent from Australia in late July for typing. Mountsier did not particularly like the book, and asked for changes and an additional chapter at the end. Lawrence, engrossed with the idea of female domination that informed "The Wilful Woman," plugged it into *Kangaroo*. It made for a strange finale: "You won't give in, Mr. Somers, will you?" asks Jaz, a Labor sympathizer introduced earlier in the novel, who reappears as the Somerses are leaving for the States. "You won't give in to the women. . . . Well, now, what will you do? Will you give in to America, do you think? . . . Why, Mr. Somers! . . . seems to me you just go round the world looking for things you're not going to give in to."[42] Frieda pronounced the chapter "shallow," a judgment that Lawrence, whose faith in her opinions of his work rarely wavered, passed on to Mountsier when he mailed the revised manuscript in. Perhaps he hoped that Mountsier would stake a claim by disagreeing with Frieda; the man was not turning out to be the unconditionally approving agent he had expected, however, and he was furious with him and Frieda for their criticism.

It was clear to Sterne on her return that Frieda, with her amazing self-assurance where Lawrence's work was concerned, had now entirely gained the advantage. Her opposition to the collaboration was becoming thorough and unstoppable; besides resenting Sterne's demands on Lawrence's time, she simply didn't think the project was worth the effort. "The Wilful Woman" was largely forgotten while Lawrence turned to other work: a poem, "Eagle in New Mexico," whose bloody imagery probably owed something to Sterne's continuing discussions of menopause (and perhaps to her own poems on the subject), and an article condemning the Bursum Land Bill (federal legislation designed to give Spanish and Anglo New Mexicans the advantage over Indians in land disputes), which Sterne encouraged him to write. Probably with Sterne's intercession, it was published on Christmas Eve in the *New York Times*. He also wrote a *Laughing Horse* review of *Fantazius Mallare*, a Ben Hecht satire of *Fantasia of the Unconscious*. His power to provoke banishment proved transatlantic: The putatively obscene content of the review got Spud Johnson's co-publisher, Roy Chanslor, an undergraduate, suspended from the University of California.

Sterne resumed writing Lawrence the kind of long, intimate letters she had sent him before his arrival in New Mexico. He showed them all to Frieda, explaining, "It's your business to see that other women don't come too close to me."[43] Her replies to Sterne ranged from friendly to hysterical:

> You didn't want a *relationship* with either Lawrence or me, you only want people in your *power*—the game that you play with him *bores* me in both of you. . . . I despise it—it's the same man-hunt, the female on the hunt—lo taliho! The hunt is up![44]

Sterne told Frieda she was the wrong woman for Lawrence. "Try it yourself, living with a genius," Frieda replied, "see what it is like and how easy it is, take him if you can."[45] Lawrence occasionally took up the cudgels for Frieda; she conformed, for example (this after years of disagreement between them), to his sartorial ideal—as he hoped Sterne one day would:

> I have always thought that the kind of clothes my mother wore were the most lovely pattern any woman could have: a long, full skirt and her little waist buttoned snugly down the front over her breast! I always make Frieda wear that kind of dress, though sometimes she longs to be *chic*! . . .
>
> No, nice full skirts, with maybe a ribbon around the waist—and white stockings—that's the correct dress for a *woman*![46]

As with H. D., Murry, and Hocking, though, he sometimes just seemed to want to have both of them. Picking apples in Sterne's orchard one day, he leapt from a tree, crawled over to a patch of grass where Frieda and Sterne were locked in conversation, and threw himself at them, crying in mock agony, "O *implacable* Aphrodite!"[47]

7

As the fall wore on, Sterne busied herself with the "mother complexes" of several new Big House guests. The painter and former Fifth Avenue salon habitué Andrew Dasburg, who arrived from New York for an extended stay, suffered one so serious that he "couldn't hardly swallow his food at the table"; another man had "a family complex and two mother complexes."[48] Between these mealtime mass analyses, her guests struck up friendships and talked about her behind her back: Lawrence recommended to Dasburg that they tar and feather her and run her out of town.[49] Sterne suffered their ingratitude, and worried about her son John, who, she wrote Leo Stein, was "very jealous of all my friends except Tony." John began telling people that his mother was "tired of those Lawrences who sponge on her."[50] The rumor reached them, and they began thinking of a way to move. One possible site they looked at briefly—abandoned cabins on 160 acres on the Lobo—did not take them far enough from Sterne, who had bought the land for John. It began to snow heavily in November, and midway into the month they were offered Del Monte, an unused ranch less than two miles from John's place. Alfred and Lucy Hawk, its owners, were away in California for the winter; the Lawrences would pay one hundred dollars a month to their son and daughter-in-law, William and Rachel Hawk, for use of the property's two cabins. They were a five-minute walk from the house of the younger couple, who arranged for milk and meat to be provided to the Lawrences from their own 125 head of cattle and the pigs they raised. The provisions would be included in the rental price. They spent a week clearing out rat, squirrel, and chipmunk nests and droppings, fumigating, and replacing broken windows. Knud Merrild and Kai Götzsche, Danish painters in their twenties who had a car, decided to spend the winter in the second cabin, and the four moved in early in December: "I think you will find everything in the house," Lawrence wrote Sterne on the morning he and Frieda left Los Gallos, "except a dish and a plate, smashed."[51]

"Dear mère," Frieda wrote the baroness a week later:

> Here we sit high up, so splendid in our wooden house, we have worked hard and made it nice—Lawrence and [Merrild and Götzsche] chopped down a metre-thick tree—Everything is so good and unadulterated, thick cream on the milk and from calf and from pig as much as you want.[52]

They acquired a terrier, Pips, and Lawrence hung a copy he had drawn of Piero di Cosimo's *Death of Procris* above the mantel.[53] Frieda decorated a huge Ponderosa pine outside in anticipation of Christmas, the one holiday ritual she continued to observe with childlike reverence; when Lawrence sent the baroness cash, Frieda specified that some of it be put toward the traditional von Richthofen venison roast, this time for the Stift.[54]

A woman at the Pueblo tanned five skunk hides to use as a rug, and friends visited, notably Bynner, who brought his mother, on vacation from New York. It was a drive of more than five hours from Santa Fe to the ranch, and they found Lawrence in a bad mood, irked by Frieda's smoking and other, unnamed sources of despair. Standing at the stove, frying their lunch in a skillet, he tried to knock a Lucky Strike out of her mouth with the pan, but she managed to hold on to it. "She should have hit back," Mrs. Bynner told her son later. "What's the matter with her? She looks strong. He's an odd duck, but he's worth hitting back at."[55] Frieda befriended Rachel Hawk, who was two decades younger and had an enormous circle of town friends who came up every Sunday to ride. She and Lawrence had learned to ride in town, and rented horses to take up into the surrounding hills. Lawrence made an occasion of the trips, preparing food, homemade bread, and pies, which he packed carefully in saddlebags. In a leather shirt, a bright blue homemade sweater that matched his eyes, blue overalls, and puttees and high boots from Gusdorf's, the Taos general store, he hardly resembled the man on the platform at Lamy. There was color in his cheeks, and the rough outdoor life satisfied and strengthened him. Frieda dressed with a strange flair, in clothes acquired around the globe:

> One day she had on a lettuce-green China silk dress, long to her ankles, which was—she was a little plump—very tight in the middle, and she had a lace bertha on around the top, a capelike thing; and it was that lovely yellow that's on the inside of lettuce. And her face—her cheeks were always bright red. Lawrence looked at her and he said, "My God, you look just like a salad." We kind of laughed—she *did* look like a salad. And her hair was the mayonnaise on top of the salad.[56]

Apart from Merrild, Götzsche, "the Bynners" (as Lawrence nicknamed Bynner and Johnson), and the Hawks, they lived alone. The Lobo was too remote to attract any but the most serious of Lawrence's devotees, and for awhile they enjoyed the isolation, though the *Taos Valley News and El Crepusculo*, the town paper, kept tabs on them: "DH Lawrance and wife K Merrild [*sic*] . . . who have been in town for some time have gone to the Hawk Ranch to spend the winter."[57] Visits from Mountsier and Seltzer over Christmas were strained. The two men differed on every significant publishing decision, and Lawrence could not get used to Seltzer, though his undivided loyalty easily withstood the demands that Lawrence—who fully realized the leverage his steadily increasing American sales gave him in negotiation—constantly made. Mountsier's dislike of *Kangaroo* still rankled, and his manner irritated Seltzer. By the time Seltzer left, he had made it clear to Lawrence that he would not work with Mountsier. "[S]uch a nice tiny

Jew," Lawrence wrote a friend, "but nice, one of the *believing* sort."[58] Mountsier, made to feel unwelcome, moved down to Taos for the duration of his stay.

Shortly after, Lawrence learned via a letter from Murry that Mansfield had died of tuberculosis after an attempted cure with the Greek-Armenian guru George Gurdjieff at the Institute for the Harmonious Development of Man, in Fontainebleau. The news spooked him—"As if worse were coming," he wrote Murry—and seemed to go to the heart of his resolve with Mountsier: a heightening sense of his own mortality that banished any lingering sentiment for his agent.[59] He fired him the day after the correspondence with Murry. As Frieda wrote Seltzer's wife, Adele,

> On the very last day after Lawrence had told him, he wanted him to go—*I* was left alone with him for lunch—Lawr took some sandwiches and went off—Mountsier very sad. . . . Our poor Catherine [*sic*] Mansfield is buried—near Paris, it was so sad and again so inevitable that she had to die—She chose a death road and *dare* not face reality![60]

Lawrence's attitude to Mansfield's death was sympathetic but almost entirely self-referential. He had never countenanced her cures, treatments, or stays in sanatoriums (by undertaking them, he felt she had somehow allowed her tuberculosis to consume her). It was a view Frieda now shared, along with his conviction that the fewer concessions made to the vagaries of Lawrence's health, the freer they would remain of the inevitability of a terminal attack.

Though it was February and Lawrence had so far avoided the usual winter illness, the thought of colds, flu, and bronchitis was never far off. Complaints about the hard work and frigid nights up on the Lobo crept into his letters, and he was soon talking about going to Mexico. He had written little or nothing since arriving in San Francisco, and was still casting around for a subject for an American novel, which he now believed he ought to write south of the border. Frieda did not want to leave Taos, but part of their pact to ignore Lawrence's physical frailty was an assumption of his complete freedom and capability of movement. Neither of them knew the extent of malarial infection in Mexico.

Lawrence grew restless, and his agitation came in irrational outbursts, most directed toward Frieda or their dog, whom Lawrence kicked while she was in heat. Frieda relied on Knud Merrild, entrusting him with cartons of Lucky Strikes she hid from Lawrence and with letters to her children she did not want to chance Lawrence's seeing in the mailbox at the end of the road—an old packing box hung from a tree by leather straps. Merrild gave the letters directly to the mailman, who came each day from the nearby village of San Cristobal on horseback. Incoming letters from the Weekley children—infrequent as they were—also infuriated Lawrence, provoking "endless quarrels."[61] She hid out in Rachel's house whenever Lawrence's anger became particularly violent and sustained. "First he would start on a horse," Rachel later recalled. "If there was no horse around he'd tie up the dog and beat on it. If there was no dog or horse he'd beat on Frieda." Cooking became a risky adventure: "Once she cooked some meat and it wasn't done all the way, and Lawrence jumped from the table, yelling that if he wanted something done right he'd have to do it himself."[62]

Mexico soon seemed like the answer to all his problems. America was poisoned with obstinacy, he said; "the wildness and woolliness and westernity and motor-cars and art and sage and savage are so mixed up, so incongruous, that it is a farce."[63] On March 19 they left for Santa Fe to spend the night with Bynner and Johnson, who had agreed to follow them to Mexico City. Over breakfast the next morning, Lawrence, an organized, fussy traveler, lectured Frieda on the necessity of keeping track of their luggage and belongings. "Your only outlook, Frieda," he cautioned, "is the umbrellas."[64] Bynner and Johnson drove them to the Santa Fe station to catch the train to El Paso; when they returned home they found the umbrellas, still strapped together in the hall. On March 21 the Lawrences crossed the frontier into Mexico, where the skies were clear.

16

Golden and Tin Calves

I

They arrived in Mexico City on March 24, 1923. Frieda spent five days combing the Thieves' Market and a government pawnshop for fabric, shawls, throws, serapes, and cheap pottery to decorate their four-peso-a-night room, in an Italian-run *pensione*. Bynner and Johnson joined them for the Easter weekend and stayed for the duration of the trip. *The Passion of Christ*, a silent film with live marimba accompaniment, was showing on Holy Saturday; the band broke into the 1922 number one hit, Paul Whiteman's "Three O'Clock in the Morning," for the rather hyper-real crucifixion scene, and Frieda doubled up in the aisle.[1] It threw Lawrence into a quarrelsome funk: "Low" culture and Frieda's appreciation of kitsch irritated him, and he found the religious impulse south of the border to be wrong-headed. He recognized the country's natural flair for paganism and sadism, but felt that the pleasure in Christ's suffering should be replaced by a revival of Aztec and Mayan beliefs, "which used to let them kill *ad lib*."[2]

"One moment they're groveling in the churches," he told Bynner. "You would think they were agonized by the old tragedy. The next moment they're gadding in the streets, full of gaiety and pulque, as though they had never heard of Jesus."[3] Beneath the Nietzschean lay a closet parishioner who believed that it was sacrilege to allow Catholicism in a country so ancient and steeped in violence. His diatribe, interrupted by ineffectual protestations from Bynner, Johnson, and Frieda, continued into the night. Tempers were still running high when they attended a bullfight on Easter Sunday. The crowd started pelting Bynner's bald spot with blood oranges, and Lawrence advised him to put his hat on. He became nauseated when a mammoth white bull gored a blindfolded horse, and started screeching at the crowd in broken Spanish and accusing Bynner and Johnson of bloodthirstiness. He bolted from his seat and fled the arena, Frieda following.

He was soon processing the bullfight and his regard for Mexicans into a novel he had failed to begin in the United States. Unable to concentrate, however, he committed little or nothing to paper. Instead, they went sightseeing—by car with two chauffeurs to San Juan, where they saw the Teotihuacán pyramids and the Temple of Quetzalcoatl, and to Puebla, Xochimilco, Cuernavaca, Tehuacán, Orizaba, Cholulo, and Atlixco. In Mexico City, they socialized with British and American expatriates, many of whom found Lawrence a trying man: The incessant heat and the difficulty of getting clean water and food played havoc with his nerves and brought more than the usual explosions of anger—at them or Frieda, sometimes both.

His public denunciations of his wife were becoming mean and unpredictable. Lawrence was getting sicker, and Frieda's exuberance and overweight galled and embarrassed him; riding on rented horses through Mexican villages on day trips, she seemed huge and conspicuous—like a bear, he later wrote.[4] Her long-standing habits—chain-smoking, and sitting with her legs apart, like a "slut," though often long skirts concealed all but her ankles—were also frequent targets. ("[N]o decent women in England," he told her, would have "anything to do with" her.)[5] His vitriol left him sapped, and Frieda humiliated or at a loss: "If I answer him," she told Bynner, "it's worse. If I don't answer him, that's bad too but it's the best I can do. So I sit and stare at him like a silly dummy and people think that what he says is true or that I have no feelings, that I'm just a dumb beast as some of them say."[6] When even silence failed to stanch a tirade, she went to Sanborn's, a local teahouse, for strawberry shortcake.

Beyond the constant anxiety over his health, Lawrence could not shake a nagging certainty that they should live elsewhere; that they would soon be assaulted; that Mexico was full of bandits, thieves, and cheats. This conviction grew into an acute paranoia about revolutions as he began looking for a rental property in the countryside, finding only haciendas trashed and looted several years earlier in raids by Pancho Villa: "there's Bolshevism and Fascism and . . . all such," he wrote the baroness. ". . . And the Indians are always outside. . . . like black water, over which go our dirty motor-ships with stink and noise, the black water is dirtied, but not really changed."[7] For a man whose politics had been confined almost exclusively to his novels and to personal calamity, it seemed a strangely heated reaction (some suggest he feared reprisals for the views espoused in *Kangaroo*, then being typeset);[8] five months after the Lawrences left Mexico, however, a bloody revolution brought on much of what he had anticipated.

Early in May he rented a house with beautiful tiled floors and a pistol-toting night watchman; he had traveled some two hundred miles northwest of Mexico City to find the property, in Chapala, two hours from Guadalajara. With the immaculate waters of twenty-mile-wide Lake Chapala just outside an ornate gate, and banana and oleander trees surrounding a sweeping veranda, it promised "paradise," he wired Frieda, who lugged their house-worth of possessions to the train.[9] A day later, laying the new-bought serapes down as rugs on the cool, clay tiles, she hoped that their isolation—they were the only English-speaking people for dozens of miles—would help restore domestic tranquillity. Lawrence was soon fighting with the servants over the proper interval between tile scrubbings, however. And he was wondering about a return to England. "Don't I change from day to day about staying here?" he asked Seltzer. "Wonder what ails me," he wrote Murry.[10]

The renewal of correspondence with Murry had begun with solicitation of a chapter of *Fantasia of the Unconscious* for the premiere issue of *Adelphi*, a journal Murry planned to launch in June, with Kot as business manager.[11] Both had written in February, asking Lawrence to join them on the project and move to London. Murry had acquired considerable critical influence, and though Lawrence had refused, he could not entirely dismiss the convenience of access to a powerful venue run by two men who had once been his closest friends. A profound ambivalence toward Murry vied with lingering love, envy, competition, and patronization, and Murry's confusion was as great: His reviews of Lawrence's novels ranged from negative to scathing—some almost as nasty as his priggish panning of *Women in Love*—but he was covetous of Lawrence's stature. He wrote frequently, letters filled with abject apologies for past differences and references to Lawrence as co-editor. He insisted that his participation was crucial to the *Adelphi*'s success, and implied that a quota of its pages would be devoted to him.

In fact, Murry's agenda for the journal centered around Mansfield, whose talent, career, and reputation he was now heard to compare with Lawrence's, often to the latter's disadvantage. Mansfield had left conflicting directions to Murry in a letter and last will, urging him both to use what he wanted of her papers and to burn them, instructions he took as license to mine each notebook, unpublished manuscript, and letter for possible publication. He found a vast supply, which he was preparing for gradual release, with sweeping claims to their greatness. (*The Doves' Nest and Other Stories*, mostly fragments, came out in June; in ensuing years he published poems, other short fiction, and sanitized versions of letters and journals, eventually making a career of her unfinished oeuvre.)

Lawrence's objections to such garbage picking, as he called it, were made up in equal parts of righteous defense of his fellow consumptive, bitterness over his own persecution and literary neglect, and disgust at Murry's misunderstanding and neglect of his wife while she was alive. In the three years before her death, his loyalty had been spotty. At best, his praise of her work had been hyperbolic, which had infuriated Mansfield; at worst, he had been dismissive, rejecting at least one of her stories for the *Athenaeum* as unworthy. His husbandly attentions had been even more erratic, with attempts at affairs with Dorothy Brett, then one of Mansfield's closest friends, and Lady Cynthia Asquith's sister-in-law the Princess Bibesco. A writer, the princess had submitted a story that Murry passed for an opinion to Mansfield (whom he also employed as a reviewer), offering her five pounds to read it. Mansfield refused the assignment (which Murry himself then evidently took on, praising the story to its author as "clever)";[12] Mansfield later wrote the princess directly, castigating her for pursuing a married man. She also quit her reviewing work, for which Murry often failed to pay her. When she died, Murry "forgot" to pay funeral costs, causing her remains to be disinterred and removed to a pauper's grave until her father and a brother-in-law paid for a permanent plot.[13]

An advance copy of the first number of the *Adelphi* arrived in Chapala in mid-June, featuring the excerpt from *Fantasia* (with no mention of the book), a Mansfield fragment, and an editorial in which Murry professed he neither deserved nor wanted to be editor. "Oh God," Lawrence wrote Seltzer. "Am I going back to Europe to that?"[14]

2

It was, temporarily, a moot question; after months of writer's block in Taos and Mexico City and several false starts in Chapala, his "American" novel (now set in Mexico) was taking shape, at the rate of thirteen or more pages a day. It was inspired by the cult of the gods Huitzilopochtli (source of the baron's old nickname for Frieda), Texcatlipoca, and the two-headed Quetzalcoatl, Lawrence having gleaned the essentials of Aztec religious myth from copious sources, including a fin-de-siècle textbook by Zelia Nuttall, a California-born archaeologist and one of the few Mexico City expatriates he had not alienated. (One of the heads of Quetzalcoatl provided the novel's eventual title, *The Plumed Serpent*.)

Despite the heavy influence of mythology—distilled with Revelation symbology, theosophy, fantasy, even some Midlands folklore—Lawrence, always able to turn personal failure into prophetic literature, was transforming the more painful aspects of marital disillusionment for its pages, sounding the battle themes of his own home in grandiloquent terms. Marriage was now posited as cosmic duality, a fascination first planted in his mind while he watched Tiwa ceremonies in New Mexico and reinforced by Nuttall's book. It had an irresistible resonance for him: As he was to write of the hero and heroine of *St. Mawr*, the brilliant novella in which, a year later, he achieved the *Plumed Serpent*'s premises in more direct, unalloyed terms:

> Lou and Rico had a curious exhausting effect on one another: neither knew why. They were fond of one another. Some inscrutable bond held them together. But it was a strange vibration of the nerves, rather than of the blood. A nervous attachment, rather than a sexual love. A curious tension of will, rather than a spontaneous passion.

> Each was curiously under the domination of the other. They were a pair—they had to be together. Yet quite soon they shrank from one another. This attachment of the will and the nerves was destructive.[15]

In the larger novel he initially dispensed with the carnal dynamic almost altogether, collapsing his and Frieda's temperaments and voices into a single heroine, Kate Leslie, an Irish widow who marries an Indian, Don Cipriano; he was undoubtedly also thinking of Mabel Sterne, who, they heard through the gossip mill, had married Tony Luhan. The Easter bullfight took up the first chapter; the second was devoted largely to a grudgingly admiring portrait of Nuttall ("Mrs. Norris"). Bynner and Johnson, who had joined the Lawrences in Chapala, staying at a nearby hotel, became minor American characters: Owen Rhys, an idle, apathetic socialist, and Bud Villiers, a frail, effeminate young aesthete with superhuman calm. To type the manuscript, Lawrence hired Johnson, who was also typing Bynner's memoirs. He often took long walks with Johnson in the afternoon while Frieda relaxed on her veranda, chatting with Bynner. Lawrence resented their intimacy: "Bynner thinks he's a liberal, but isn't," he was fond of telling Johnson. "He talks about Socialism but lives on capital. . . . He's a Playboy of the Western World, playing the rôle of patron of the arts."[16] Bynner was angered by these frequent put-downs and Lawrence's utter lack of remorse after bouts with Frieda, and devoted his mornings to some rather catty journal pages about the great man. At night he and Johnson brought their poetry for him to critique; Lawrence never mentioned his own novel.

One night Bynner arrived alone and found Frieda asleep in a chair and Lawrence fuming over a letter from Murry, who, he told Bynner, thrusting the letter into his hands, was a "shit-head," at least as Bynner later wrote: More likely he said "shit-bag," fast becoming Lawrence's term for Frieda in moments of extreme rage.[17] His shouts awakened her, and she tried to change the subject by interesting Bynner in the box of family photographs she still transported from country to country. Lawrence buried himself behind a newspaper; when Frieda began talking about her children, he leapt up, grabbed the pictures, tore several in half, and stamped on the pieces. Once such tantrums started, urges to control his anger usually failed, and he directed a stream of invective Frieda's way. She hated the term "shit-bag."

Bynner urged her to take the offensive: Whenever she saw signs of an outburst, he said, she should immediately scream at Lawrence, stunning him. She tried it for awhile, sometimes with success, then took to waiting out the rages in Bynner's hotel room, smoking from the packs of Mexican cigarettes, Elegantes, that they kept for her. "Bynner and Mrs. Lawrence would discuss the outlandishness of a husband," Johnson wrote, "as only a bachelor and a married woman can."[18] By the end of such sessions, she was usually reconciled to the idea of returning to Lawrence. "There are two bonds," she told Bynner, unconsciously presaging the above-quoted passage from *St. Mawr*. "One of love, one of strangeness. In our hearts, it is well."[19] Despite their differences, Lawrence relied solely on Frieda for approval of his novel, and she acquired more than a passing familiarity with Nuttall and various clunky history and adventure books, including Prescott's *Conquest of Mexico*, her father's old favorite. Though she occasionally felt smothered by Lawrence's obsessions—"those Aztec ideas," she would sigh—she was thrilled to see him working, and reported every few hundred pages to the Seltzers, describing the book to Adele Seltzer as "the most splendid thing he ever did."[20] Her remarks on the prose itself, which she read nightly, provided rich material: Lawrence often transferred their conversations to the next day's writing with only slight modifications. "I can't be so dumb," she lamented to Bynner after an argument, repeating a refrain that seemed to stretch across her lifetime,"when he quotes me all the time."[21]

Within two months, Lawrence had arrived at his novel's overarching theme, the final banishment of Catholicism and capitalism by primeval ritual, and had finished well over four hundred pages, enough to make him at once secure and restless. Frieda had begun lobbying to get to London before the summer was out—for the usual reason, her children—and with an eye to the *Adelphi* (Lawrence followed it closely despite his dislike of the premiere issue), he orchestrated a plan to get there by way of New York, which they had never seen. Proofs of three forthcoming books—*Kangaroo*, *Birds, Beasts and Flowers*, and *Mastro-don Gesualdo*, the Verga novel—were waiting at Seltzer's office to be proofread.

By the third week of July (via trains to Laredo, Texas, and New Orleans, and a boat to New York), they were installed in a borrowed cottage in Morris Plains, New Jersey. Though Lawrence took a fancy to the Battery, "where the rag-tag lie on the grass," the few New York parties and meetings they attended—with, among others, the editors of the *Nation*—were unpleasant or unmemorable, inevitably reminding him of London.[22] He also found unbearable Frieda's anticipation of her first visit with her children in four years, and by early August had decided to stay in the United States. "I wish you'd look after her a bit: would it be a nuisance?" he wrote Murry, whose ongoing overtures he could not seem to ignore. ". . . you know, wrong or not, I can't stomach the chasing of those Weekley children."[23]

Furious to have come so far only to have him change his mind, Frieda booked herself passage on the *Orbita*, a Royal Mail steam packet sailing for England on August 18. The day arrived with no change of heart on Lawrence's part. He helped her on with her hand luggage, and shortly before the *Orbita* weighed anchor, she impulsively begged him not to disembark, provoking a bitter fight. The abandonment, coupled with months of public humiliation and unstinting attention to his novel, filled her with weltschmerz. "Here I am," she wrote Bynner:

> . . . "all by mineself" on such a dull boat. Chapala seems a dream, an impossible dream. I was not happy in New York or New Jersey. It may have been partly the Seltzers, they are very nice, but I don't know what it was, I felt such a poor little night light, hateful.
>
> I met a few, very few, people. The nice ones all knew you, but everybody seems so tired. I am sure all those layers of people put away in their apartments on top of each other like boxes of gloves or hankies make the air dead. It makes me feel drugged. Lawrence you *knew* wouldn't like it.
>
> . . . I do hope my journey won't be useless, especially as far as my children go. Lawrence wouldn't come, he is going to wander. Where we meet again, I don't know.[24]

3

She arrived in Southampton ten days later, took a train to London, and shuttled between borrowed apartments before finding a Hampstead bed-sit. Her presence set off a ripple of excitement and revulsion among Lawrence's friends; others besides Murry had begun receiving letters from him asking them to look after her. (In those Lawrence wrote after Frieda's sailing, his resolve not to go to England wavered, and he hinted at an appearance in London by October.) Cordial visits were followed by backbiting, tête-à-têtes, and furious correspondence. Gertler, renting a room in the same house as Frieda, wrote Ottoline at Garsington every few days:

> Since she has come I have seen her only three times. She is quite alright only somehow very uncomfortable to be with and also somewhat of a bore. She is worse than she might be because she apes Lawrence and his ideas coming out of her large German body sound silly and vulgar.[25]

Kot, who, as Frieda had confided in Mabel, regarded Frieda as more fit to be Lawrence's servant than wife, urged her, with a great show of concern, to wait for Lawrence in Germany, where she would be happier; when she announced plans to go to Baden-Baden at the end of September, he bragged to Gertler of his success in having manipulated her. "Everybody is very nice," she wrote Adele Seltzer obliviously. Murry, she told her, "said how he realised that Lawrence was a greater man than he was and how bitter it was for him to come to that conclusion, and how he has hated L—but now he had for ever accepted him, no matter what Lawr did."[26]

Murry had consummated the relationship with Brett in April, three and a half months after Mansfield's death, and was living with her in the house she now rented on Pond Street, infamous for its filth (she disliked housekeeping), beautifully painted rooms, and her Thursdays, usually attended only by men. She did not have many female friends, and was desperate for a confidante: Her only other such outlet was a journal, addressed to Mansfield, toward whom she felt, not surprisingly, a tremendous sense of guilt. She quickly latched on to Frieda and poured out her anxieties, which veered from the danger of pregnancy (there were two false alarms) to questions of Murry's fidelity. Frieda suggested she marry him, and confronted Murry directly.

"Couldn't you love Brett?" she asked him.

"God forgive me," he replied. "She [is] dirty."[27]

"I go to Germany on the 28, Murry goes to Switzerland, we travel together via Paris," Frieda wrote Adele.[28] Murry explained his impending absence to Brett as a business trip; he had to visit Sierre, he told her, a Swiss town where Mansfield had stored manuscripts. To others he talked about consulting a Freiburg psychiatric specialist for Vivienne Eliot, who was still fighting mental illness. He and Frieda set off together, and a day or two into the trip, she made a pass at him, which he rejected, pleading fear, loyalty to Lawrence, and, evidently, a vow of "chastity."[29] Whether her interest was genuine or a gambit to induce Lawrence to come to England sooner is impossible to know. She and Murry seem to have parted at Freiburg, Frieda traveling on to Baden-Baden. By October 3 Murry was regretting the missed opportunity, and wrote Brett to end their affair, explaining (with massive circumlocution) that he wanted to play the field and would move out of Pond Street when he returned. Another letter with similar news followed on October 5. He arrived shortly after, and bedded down with her for a couple of nights before effecting the move. Less than seven months later he married Violet le Maistre, an *Adelphi* assistant. (She died of tuberculosis in 1931, leaving two children, Katherine and John Middleton Murry II.)

4

Lawrence, after a desultory trek through California, had returned to Mexico with Götzsche, who was writing panicked letters to Merrild:

> I am avoiding L. as much as possible at present because, considering all things, he is really insane when he is as now. . . . You know his ways, and how he bends his head far down, till his beard is resting on his chest and he says (not laughing) "Hee, hee, hee" every time one talks to him. . . . it would be too difficult to live with a man like L. in the long run. Frieda is at least an absolute necessity as quencher. I have sometimes the feeling that he is afraid she will run away from him now, and he cannot bear to be alone.[30]

Lawrence rarely heard from Frieda and was reduced to tracing her whereabouts secondhand, through mail from Murry or the Seltzers. To assuage his loneliness and occupy his time, he had renewed correspondence with the Australian nurse Mollie Skinner and embarked on their disputed collaboration, *The Boy in the Bush*, a *Bildungsroman* based on the life of her brother. He was also trying his hand at *Adelphi* submissions, the first on Catholicism, in which he now claimed to believe. It was an anomalous essay for someone who had just finished expelling the religion from Mexico in *The Plumed Serpent*, and seems to have elicited consternation and some derision from Murry and Kot. When Frieda returned to London from Germany, where she had finally written Lawrence two long, glum letters attempting to sort out their marriage, she jumped into the fray with a defense of her husband, in the form of a letter to Kot, also intended for Murry's eyes:

> Why did Lawrence write that article? Because I told him he was the golden calf round which he danced and wanted me to dance too. And I was sick of it. And so are you all, all golden calves or even "tin ones" round which you dance. If you were *really* religious men, if the Lord were above you and you weren't little gods yourselves, you would also know that man was meant to have a woman; I am supposed to be impressed by your chastities: I am not, it's male conceit. How little you must understand of Lawrence's books, Kot, when you can say that I am the "Porter" in the firm! Why, my faith has been the heart of it! And as far as being a man, I know to my sorrow, that I am six times the "man" that any of you are! Now call me all the names you like, I don't care! . . . And I think you all treat that generous Brett *vilely*! Especially Jack [Murry]! And you make me feel a sneak when I come to the "Adelphi," nobody can have an open and free relationship with you. You make me feel as if I wanted to rob the safe or play the temptation of St. Antony. No, there is no fun in temptation, one can't play the game for two! Why can't you simply treat me as a human being?[31]

The following day Kot and Murry, tormented by guilt and probably spoiling for a showdown, solemnly urged her to summon Lawrence to England by cable. She wrote the single word "Come" on the telegraph office form (mistakenly relayed in New York as "cone"), and instantly felt she had made a mistake.[32]

It was the message Lawrence had been waiting for. The remainder of his time in Mexico was given over to a search for the right ship and haranguing, piteous letters to Frieda, her mother, and anyone else who would listen: Frieda's letters from Baden-Baden had not arrived until ten days after the "cone" telegram, and were ambivalent. "F. must always think and write and say and ponder *how* she loves me," he wrote the baroness. "It's stupidity. I am after all no Christ lying on his mother's lap, I go my way through the world, and if F. finds it very hard work to love me, then, dear God, let her give her love a rest."[33] To Frieda he wrote stiffly, "I am glad if you have a good time with your flat and your children," and offered her an independent income, to be deposited from his earnings into a bank account she had opened on arrival in London.[34]

The separation, now almost three months long, had sucked the life out of him. Consumed by grandiose delusions, thoughts of his mother, and theories of mother love that Frieda had always despised, he turned to the baroness:

> Oh Schwiegermutter, you are nice and old and understand again as the first virgin understands, that a man must be more than nice and good, and that heroes have more value than saints. Frieda doesn't understand that today a man needs to be a hero, and more than a husband. Husband yes, also. But more. . . . the courageous old one understands me better than the young one: or some of me. . . . Oh Schwiegermutter Schwiegermutter, you understand, as my mother finally understood, that the man does not need, does not ask for love from his wife, but strength, strength, strength. It is fighting, fighting, fighting and still fighting. And one needs strength and courage and weapons. And the stupid woman always sings love! love! love!—and the rights of love! the rights of woman's love! To the devil with love. Give me strength, only battle-strength, weapon-strength, fighting-strength.[35]

"*Why* can't he say he will be glad to see me?" Frieda wrote Kot. "Always a misery and pain! It makes me *sick*!"[36]

Murry's amorous feelings for Frieda, insidiously kindled by her disgust with his cowardice and backstabbing, were very much in evidence on December 12, when Frieda, accompanied by him and Kot, met Lawrence at Paddington. Exhausted from having sailed direct from Veracruz to Plymouth, and revolted by Frieda and Murry's obvious rapport, he turned green—at least according to Murry—and muttered, "I can't bear it."[37]

5

His broader response to their "[c]humminess" (for which he seemed to blame only Murry) was slow in coming, confined at first to criticism of the *Adelphi* and Murry's handling of Mansfield's literary remains.[38] Despite Frieda's showing off in the first flush of the romance—"Murry is Somebody!" she declared to Carswell, "[a]nd the *Adelphi* is Something!!"—Lawrence's relief at being reunited with her was profound, and he did his best to be agreeable, even consenting to a meeting with her daughters. Murry was also invited.[39] Monty, twenty-three, an assistant to the director of the Victoria and Albert Museum (he had briefly worked in the advertising department of Yardley's Cosmetics after graduating from Oxford) and very much his father's son, with a love of crossword puzzles and nineteenth-century French literary criticism, stonily declined all invitations. "[A]t least Monty doesn't reveal any fearful tendencies to vice," Ernest said, though he never mentioned Frieda by name.[40]

Stories "that the Lawrences threw saucepans or plates at each other" had embarrassed and thrilled the three children, but there was no sign of discord when Barby and Elsa arrived.[41] Lawrence made an indelible impression on Barby, not unlike the one he had made on Frieda twelve years before:

> I had not seen anyone like him before; nor have I since. He was tall and fragile—a queer, unearthly creature. He had a high-pitched voice, a slight Midlands accent, and a mocking, but spirited and brilliant manner. I liked his eyes. They were blue, wide apart, in cave-like sockets, under a fine brow. . . . He had high cheekbones, a clubby "Midlands" nose, and a well-shaped jaw. . . . He seemed beyond being human and ordinary, and I felt at once that he was more like an element—say a rock or rushing water.[42]

They talked about the Slade, in which she had at last persuaded Ernest to let her enroll. Lawrence warned her that she would get little or nothing out of the school, which, he said, was overacademic. Turning to Elsa, he simply said, "Barby is not the stuff of which artists are made."[43] Elsa, sensible, conventional, and given to stoic silences, did not reply. "A cad," she later said of Lawrence.[44]

• • •

As Christmas 1923 approached, the Lawrences turned their sights to New Mexico, where they planned to return in the spring. Lawrence inexplicably urged Murry to come along and, hoping for additional recruits, hosted a small party at the Café Royal, a London restaurant whose habitués he had satirized in *Women in Love*. He invited, among others, Kot, Carswell, and Brett. It was his first meeting with Brett since just after the war. She held her brass hearing trumpet, which she called Toby, under his mouth, and Lawrence, who found her prehensile charm and goofy simplicity touching, teased her about "the impossibility of making love into" the hearing aid/amplifier she had also begun carrying, with its glowing glass electron tubes.[45] Later, drunk on claret and port, he formally invited everyone present to join him and Frieda in Taos, where, he said, Mabel Dodge Luhan would feed and house them. Silence gave way to a shouting match and demurrals. Confessions of disloyalty from Murry followed, and in the course of a speech Kot broke every wineglass within reach. Lawrence keeled over and threw up.

Everyone declined the offer but Brett, whom Lawrence was soon writing into the last chapter of *The Boy in the Bush*, as a young deaf woman who agrees to join the protagonist's confused marital ménage. He spent much of January with her, helping her fill out the papers she needed to go abroad. They booked three berths for March 5, 1924, aboard the huge Cunard liner *Aquitania*, and Lawrence took to offering Brett advice about her painting. Though he considered her dedication to her work unfeminine, he admired unflagging persistence in anything, and occasionally "helped" by picking up a paintbrush and amending her canvases. Brett returned his attention with bawdy tales of Murry and utter devotion—"like a God," Lawrence seemed to her, "the Lord of us all, the light streaming down on [his] dark, gold hair."[46]

In late January, Lawrence and Frieda went to Paris, where he drafted three stories, "The Border Line," "Jimmy and the Desperate Woman," and "The Last Laugh," in each casting Murry as a baffled aesthete-libertine who is occasionally also impotent. In the first, as a journalist married to a German baroness, he is cuckolded and killed off from beyond the grave by the ghost of her dead first husband, a superb lover; in the second, as a divorced magazine editor, he attempts to bed a poetess and is haunted by her miner husband; in the third he abandons a deaf woman and is suddenly killed by Pan—a figure with whom Lawrence (who appears in the story as himself, "Lorenzo," a red-bearded "satyr") had begun to feel a profound identification. Lawrence took time out to wander the streets with Frieda, who had several elegant dresses made that she almost immediately regretted as out of character, and they called on Sylvia Beach, the publisher of *Ulysses*, at Shakespeare and Company. Lawrence, who may have plagiarized James Joyce years before in a story entitled "The Shadow in the Rose Garden," counted himself among those who could not read the great novel—"so like a schoolmaster with dirt and stuff in his head: sometimes good, though: but too mental," he had written Seltzer in November 1922, after perusing a borrowed copy.[47] He enjoyed Beach's company, however, and asked Seltzer to send her a photo of himself for the walls of the "famous modern little library" on the rue de l'Odéon.[48]

He and Frieda continued on to Germany to visit the baroness. "I don't care what you think of me," Lawrence wrote Murry from Baden-Baden, "I don't care what you say of me, I don't even care what you do against me, as a writer. . . . You haven't any genuine [emotions], except a certain anger."[49]

They returned to London a week before the sailing, and spent their last nights in England with Brett, Kot, Gertler—and Murry. Lawrence, ever the center of attention, held forth on subjects Frieda had heard too much of, and she sat in the background, knitting, though she did interrupt him one evening. Denouncing her in the Midlands-accented "thees" and "thas" to which he still resorted in moments of blinding anger, he broke an entire tea set with a fireplace poker while their friends looked on. "Beware, Frieda!" he screamed, finally dropping the dialect. "If ever you talk to me like that again, it will not be the tea things I smash, but your head. Oh, yes. I'll kill you. So beware!" The anger at Murry had finally come crashing through, and everyone present seemed to understand, including Lawrence. "Frieda should not make me so angry," he chuckled mirthlessly, reaching for Brett's hand as Frieda swept up the broken crockery.[50] After a while Brett learned to turn her hearing aid off when the fights began.

17

Angelino Ravagli

I

They sailed into New York in a blizzard, and were met by Seltzer. His business was floundering, and he was seriously in debt to Lawrence, who was forced to engage an Englishman in the New York office of Curtis Brown slowly to extract more than three thousand dollars in the previous year's royalties for *The Captain's Doll*, *Studies in Classic American Literature*, *Kangaroo*, *Mastro-don Gesualdo*, and *Birds, Beasts and Flowers*, among others.

Lawrence had had seven books published in the United States during 1923, more than during any year to date, and was much in demand, particularly in the magazine world: Frank Crowninshield, the editor of *Vanity Fair*, took him out to lunch. Willa Cather, who had been to Taos in 1912, and her lover, Edith Lewis, a college roommate of Achsah Brewster's, gave them tea at their Bank Street apartment, but the conversation failed when Lawrence dismissed "literature and literary people" with an unsuccessful mixture of humor and patronization.[1] (He later arranged to have copies of his books sent to Cather, one of the few living writers he did not denounce, possibly because he had not read her.) "New York jeers at us all," he wrote Murry self-consciously.[2] There was little to show for the literary outpouring in

Lawrence's New York account, where he liked to maintain a minimum balance of two thousand dollars. He had hoped to draw freely on his earnings to go West; as it was, after withdrawing what he thought they would need, only thirty dollars remained until Seltzer replenished the pot in October.[3]

By March 22 they arrived in Taos at Mabel Luhan's, which had become the haven of a handful of Harvard graduates, East Coast poets and painters, and, on occasion, Mary Austin, an eccentric writer who suffered from multiple-personality disorder, and Jaime de Angulo, a Paris-born expatriate doctor, anthropologist, onetime cowboy, and linguist of Spanish parentage who had just come by way of, among other places, Tegucigalpa (Honduras) and Zurich (where he had worked with Jung; he was largely responsible for Jung's only visit to Taos, in the winter of 1924–25). They settled into a two-story house on the property, and Frieda began making friends: Clarence Thompson, a screenwriter and new figure in Taos's burgeoning homosexual community, and Swinburne Hale, a tall, swashbuckling womanizer who had covered the walls of his house, a log cabin several miles out on the west mesa, in coyote skins. Lawrence detested most of these poseurs and would-be artists, as he thought them, though he soon developed an erotic attachment to Thompson, as had Mabel.

Her health and mental well-being had suffered since they had last seen her; she was less invested in probing the depths of their marriage, and Frieda found it somewhat easier to get along with her than she had in 1922. Lawrence, of course, could not resist the urge to provoke her, referring to her behind her back as a "small bison with the crudeness of a sixteen-year-old."[4] Mabel realized it was unlikely they would remain in Taos long if she could not resolve her differences with him, and again offered her son John's 160-acre ranch, this time with a deed. He accepted, with one caveat: He disliked possessions, he told her, and wanted Frieda named sole owner. Frieda wrote to Else for the original manuscript of *Sons and Lovers*, and gave it to Mabel in exchange. The manuscript, Hale informed her grandiosely, was worth at least fifty thousand dollars. (In fact, thirteen years later, another, incomplete *Sons and Lovers* manuscript was appraised at only fifteen hundred dollars; the ranch was worth five thousand, according to a 1928 estimate of Lawrence's.)[5] That the manuscript had other than sentimental value interested Frieda equally as a vindication of her belief in Lawrence's genius and as a portent of market value. Ownership of a home, with the attendant prospect of settling down, interested her more.

The ranch's three log-and-adobe cabins, the first real property they had owned in ten years of marriage, were virtual ruins, untouched since they had inspected them in 1922. From the highest point on the grounds, up a trail of sage, pine, and cedar to an elevation of almost nine thousand feet, they saw snow on the Rocky Mountains. Below lay San Cristobal and, more than a thousand feet away, the desert, blue and liquid-looking. The spectacular surroundings appeared almost immediately in Lawrence's work, inspiring some of his most lyrical, grounded prose since *Sons and Lovers*. "Her cabin faced the slow down-slope of the clearing, the alfalfa field," he wrote in *St. Mawr*, which he started in June, "her long, low cabin, crouching under the great pine-tree that threw up its trunk sheer in front. . . . beyond and below . . . hummocks of mountains rising like wet rock from a vast strand."[6] They called it Lobo Ranch, after the mountain on which it stood, but later in the summer changed the name to Kiowa, after a nonindigenous Indian tribe.

It took five weeks, $463,[7] and a crew of a dozen men from Taos Pueblo and elsewhere to rebuild and outfit the houses and clear and reroute an irrigation ditch fed by the Gallina, a stream that flowed down from a canyon. Brett took the smallest house. The Lawrences had separate bedrooms, for which beds were hewn from trees cut on the property. For bread making they repaired a conical outdoor oven that accommodated twenty loaves. Lawrence carved a writing chair out of a block of wood with a penknife and built a cupboard for his manuscripts. Working with the hired help, they relaxed by riding horses, their only form of transportation. Mabel gave Frieda a divided khaki skirt, and Frieda acquired a gray horse, Azul, and a silver-studded saddle. "Oh, it's wonderful," she shouted to Lawrence one evening, riding to their old friends the Hawks, three miles below, "wonderful to feel his great thighs moving, to feel his powerful legs!"

"Rubbish, Frieda!" he replied. "Don't talk like that. You have been reading my books; you don't feel anything of the sort!"[8]

She became engrossed in reading a Bible, borrowed from Mabel or left by the previous owners (farmers with six hundred goats, whose voluminous droppings they still had to shovel and dispose of by the truckload). It brought back her enjoyment of the New Testament at the Villa Igea a decade earlier, and became her favorite book, which she reread dozens of times over the following decades and forced on friends. She preferred to read it in German, and acquired a copy that became something of a personal talisman.

Entertainment was scarce or nonexistent. Occasionally they were picked up by Tony in one of Mabel's Cadillacs for a weekend back in the two-story house at Los Gallos. At a party in the Big House in June, Lawrence, drunk on brandy, broke his usual ban on dancing when Frieda and Thompson danced together. Frieda had heard, via Mabel, that Lawrence had propositioned Thompson, with whom he wanted to ride away on horseback, and the dance was Frieda's retaliation. Lawrence, furious at the sight of them cheek to cheek, invited Mabel onto the dance floor and, using her as a "battering ram," began slamming them.[9] Frieda and Thompson departed arm in arm.

Word of the jealous episode spread to Spud Johnson, probably via Mabel, who was trying to hire Johnson away from Bynner as secretary (a job he eventually took). When Johnson wrote Lawrence to ask his opinion of the career move, Lawrence, denouncing "triangles vicious or otherwise," advised him to think seriously before entering her employ.[10] Mabel, enraged by Lawrence's meddling, accused him, perhaps not without justification, of having seduced Thompson: When Friedel Jaffe, the twenty-one-year-old son of Frieda's sister Else, arrived in New York later in the summer, Lawrence dispatched Thompson, then visiting the city, to "tell him about Taos (not beneath the surface)," presumably a reference to the homosexual community.[11] He was soon writing "The Woman Who Rode Away," whose heroine, a woman with Mabel's nature, his own self-loathing, and Frieda's coloring, is offered as a human sacrifice by Indians.

As his relations with Mabel deteriorated, Frieda's continued to improve; Mabel's devotion to Lawrence now seemed mild compared to Brett's. Several of Brett's studies for paintings featured Lawrence as Christ; in 1926, she would produce a crucifixion scene, with Lawrence both nailed to the cross and dancing, Pan-like, before it. Lawrence had hired her to type, and a day rarely passed without a visit from her and a fight with Frieda, who (Brett told Lawrence) was lazy, stupid, and the wrong woman for him.

Their ongoing disputes fascinated and tired Lawrence, who was also worn out by the rough life in the woods and by a feverish writing pace. In addition to *St. Mawr*, "The Woman Who Rode Away," and lesser pieces, he traveled the state, gathering material for essays on Indian dances, eventually published in the *New York Times Magazine* and elsewhere.[12] Declining visibly by early August, he collapsed and spat blood for two days, and was diagnosed as tubercular by a local doctor. The news of his father's death in September at the age of seventy-eight[13] may have set him back further, though he had little reaction other than brief letters to his sisters, with a gift of cash for funeral and burial costs. (Frieda's first—perhaps only—meeting with Arthur Lawrence had been in Derbyshire in 1918: He had come away baffled that his thin son had married a woman twice his size and with a voice louder and deeper than his.)[14] In any case Lawrence took no break to digest the news, continuing to travel and write—notably "The Princess," a story of sexual violation whose heroine, based on Brett, is raped by a Mexican guide. Good with the rod and reel and an excellent fly fisherman, Brett often wandered the mountainside alone on her horse in oversized men's corduroys, an enormous blouse, and a sombrero into which she stuffed her thick, short hair. Celibate but for her short affair with Murry, she had an acute fear of being attacked on her solitary expeditions, and carried a foot-long stiletto next to her right calf inside a knee-high cowboy boot. (The knife was also good for skinning the day's catch.) The princess in the story is helpless in the face of her attack, then suffers a nervous breakdown.

"What do you think of *The Boy in the Bush*?" Lawrence asked Brett one day. Copies of the novel, published in late August, had recently arrived, with a dust jacket by Lawrence of a man and a kangaroo that borrowed from a collaborative drawing by him and Brett. She replied that she would have preferred its hero—who barely recovers after a concussion, fever, and blood loss from a finger cut off by a rival—to die. "That is how I wrote it first," Lawrence answered. "I made him die—only Frieda made me change it."

"I couldn't stand the superiority of the man, always the same self-importance," Frieda, absorbed in embroidery, explained to Brett. "'Let him become ordinary,' I said. Always this superiority and death."[15] Brett insisted that the ending had ruined the story, Lawrence glumly agreed, and it became a running argument, one of many that festered through the fall.

Against Frieda's wishes the three left for Mexico in late October.

They stayed briefly in Mexico City, where efforts to lionize Lawrence were, as on the first trip to New York, miserable failures. His youthful eagerness for literary fame had changed to self-conscious mistrust, and he harbored enormous contempt for hangers-on. At a PEN dinner in his honor he delivered a speech on manliness that fell "completely flat."[16] It was the first and last public speech of his career.

They had lunch at Nuttall's with Somerset Maugham, whose 1919 *Moon and Sixpence*, loosely based on Gauguin's time in Tahiti, Lawrence had read in 1920 and criticized as "forcé."[17] Frieda, seated beside Maugham for the meal, asked what he thought of Mexico. "Do you want me to admire men in big hats?" he said archly.

"I don't care what you admire," she replied.[18]

Lawrence took an immediate dislike to the man: "A bit rancid," he wrote Curtis Brown.[19]

They eventually settled in Oaxaca, about two hundred miles southeast of Mexico City, renting half of a house owned by Edward Arden Rickards, a Mexican-born Scottish priest. Lawrence worked on essays, eventually collected in the travel book *Mornings in Mexico*, and struggled with a second draft of *The Plumed Serpent*, adding or refining material that would later draw charges of sadomasochism and misogyny, as well as criticism of his use of religion in the service of sex (and vice versa) and both in the service of female subjugation.[20] The final chapters feature a bloody (and, at least to some, fascistic) ritual and an interrupted coitus. Interpretations of the latter have ranged from Lawrence's wish to deny women orgasm to, at the other end of the scale, his preference for drawn-out sex, but it is the former of these that has followed him more conspicuously into posterity.[21] Frieda offered reasons other than the marital battleground for the novel's cynicism: "[T]he end is muffed," she wrote Bynner, "the religious part is'nt religious, but dessicated swelled head"[22]—a rare *jeu de mots* (given the novel's endless paganism) in her otherwise unremittingly straightforward approach to literary criticism.

Brett, as ubiquitous as at the ranch and, with little or no Spanish, more dependent, photographed them incessantly as they toured—trips to the nearby Mitla ruins and elsewhere that often left Lawrence drained. "Like the eye of the Lord, she was," Frieda wrote, "when I washed, when I lay under a bush with a book, her eyes seemed to be there, only I hope the eye of the Lord looks on me more kindly."[23] She finally gave Brett a written ultimatum: The "spinster and curate" relationship between her and Lawrence was unnatural, and they should "make love to each other" or Brett should leave.[24] Lawrence seconded the suggestion she leave in a follow-up letter, omitting the injunction to have sex. Brett went to Mexico City, then traveled on to New Mexico.

Shortly after her departure, Lawrence and Frieda moved to a hotel and came down with the flu; his was followed by typhoid and malaria. Confined to bed under hot sandbags—his preferred treatment for keeping warm, weighted, and immobile—he predicted to Frieda that she would have to bury him in the Jalatlaco River *camposanto*, the local cemetery. "No, no," she shot back, laughing, "it's such an ugly cemetery, don't you think of it."

"But if I die," he persisted, "nothing has mattered but you, nothing at all."[25]

2

Frieda appreciated the natural helpfulness, or *Selbsverständlichkeit*, as she put it, of a handful of expatriates who called to monitor Lawrence's progress, providing food, encouragement, and comic relief.[26] Norman and Geraldine Taylor, Protestant missionaries, befriended them. He was a former Royal Canadian Air Force pilot, and when Frieda mentioned that she was a cousin of Manfred von Richthofen, he told her—or so her memoirs recount—that he had been present in the village east of Amiens when the Red Baron was shot down by a Canadian pilot with the Royal British Air Force in 1918. Frieda, who had an unquenchable fascination with her illustrious cousin (in the 1940s she saw movies about him repeatedly), seems to have made this up, however. Geraldine arrived with soup for Lawrence on one of his worst days. Before it was served, she knelt at the foot of his bed and prayed assiduously. Frieda, stir-crazy after weeks of nursing Lawrence, and genuinely afraid for his life, began to cry. The prayers dragged on, Lawrence said nothing, and Frieda, anticipating a rebuke for having allowed the woman in, was so relieved when he finally uttered something innocuous that she giggled uncontrollably as the tears continued to fall and the soup was served.

By late February 1925, he had recovered sufficiently to travel, and they boarded a train for Mexico City. Halfway through the journey, he had to be taken off, and they spent the night in a hotel. "He will never be quite well again," thought Frieda. "[H]e is ill, he is doomed. All my love, all my strength, will never make him whole again." Overwhelmed by the strain, she burst into sobs "like a maniac the whole night. And he disliked me for it."[27] They continued on to Mexico City, where a doctor took blood and sputum tests and pronounced Lawrence tubercular in the third degree, a terminal stage, predicting that he would live "[a] year or two at the most."[28] Seriously underweight, he often coughed through the night and talked of sailing to England. He was advised not to undertake the long trip, and Frieda encouraged him to return to the ranch.

She had become expert at shouting down immigration officials, who constantly subjected their heavily stamped passports and, of late, Lawrence himself—because of his sickly pallor—to intense scrutiny. They got past El Paso with a coat of rouge applied to his cheeks, but not before being stopped by health inspectors, despite Frieda's attempts to brush them aside (Lawrence evidently was required to remove his clothing); in some versions of the story they were detained twice, the second time in Laredo. Frieda's own appearance had changed drastically in Mexico. She had gained at least twenty pounds in the last six months, most of the weight settled in a wide paunch that Lawrence alternately vilified and compared appreciatively to a freshly baked loaf of bread. Her hair had been cut short to just below her chin, parted on the left and interrupted by what looked like self-inflicted bangs, a style either influenced by Brett or dictated by the lice and the difficulty of caring for long hair in the Oaxacan tropics. She bore a remarkable resemblance to herself as a child; next to Lawrence, she looked larger than life.

Back at the Lobo, Lawrence acquired a cow, Susan, which he milked with some difficulty. He followed her wanderings with a pair of opera glasses, a gift from the baroness that was hand-delivered by Friedel Jaffe, who came for most of the summer. Lawrence, declaring he was sick of "personal" works "about a woman,"[29] wrote a biblical play, *David*, lying on an outdoor porch in the sun; Frieda spent her days translating it into German. The work, accomplished in their first weeks back, in almost complete isolation, was therapeutic for both.

> I had been reading the old testament again in German and the puzzling figure of "David" with his so personal relationship to the Lord would send me to Lawrence asking him "How was it?"
>
> . . . He freed himself in writing this play in voicing Saul's madness and despair, and Samuel's struggle to transfer his allegiance from Saul, whom he had loved to David at the Lord's command. Lawrence was these people while he wrote, and writing he escaped his own shadows and wrote himself back to health.[30]

She had sent a letter ahead to Brett from Mexico, asking her not to be on their property when they returned, and Brett had complied, moving to a cabin below on the Hawks' land. (Years later, she dismantled it, moved it up the mountainside back toward Kiowa, and named it Tower Beyond Tragedy.) She could not resist resuming daily visits, however, once the Lawrences had settled in. Arriving late each day after fishing, she typed and helped with chores. "Brett," Frieda said to her, "I detest your adoration for Lawrence, only one thing I would detest more, and that is if you adored me."[31]

Lawrence's health had stabilized again by mid-September, and he and Frieda returned to London, leaving Brett to look after the ranch. They went via New York. Seltzer, nearing bankruptcy, now owed Lawrence almost five thousand dollars in royalties, for old books and his sole 1925 Lawrence title—*Little Novels of Sicily*, Verga translations. He had been avoiding him or concealing increasingly severe financial difficulties over the past year with clumsy excuses, which made Lawrence furious but also gave him an out: He regarded the silences and obfuscations as a breach of trust, and had few compunctions about abandoning a sinking ship. *The Plumed Serpent* was already promised to Alfred A. Knopf, who had brought out *St. Mawr* in June (and, eight months before, in October 1924, *Memoirs of the Foreign Legion*, with Lawrence's introduction).

Lawrence had first met Knopf in 1923; he renewed his acquaintance with him and met his wife and business partner, Blanche. Though Centaur—a small Philadelphia bookshop/press that had released a bibliography of Lawrence's works in June—issued his next U.S. book, *Reflections on the Death of a Porcupine and Other Essays*, Knopf thereafter became his main publisher, bringing out *The Plumed Serpent* in February 1926 and *David* in April 1926.

A visit to Lawrence's sisters in the Midlands and Derbyshire, shortly after they arrived in London, ended with him confined to bed with a bad cold. Emily and Ada nursed him, rather pointedly leaving Frieda little or nothing to do. She invited Barby, who was staying with a Nottingham colleague of Ernest's. Lawrence, holding forth from his sickbed, advised Barby to break off an engagement with an Irishman some years her senior (she eventually did). As evening approached she was invited to stay the night, and phoned her host. He abruptly ordered her back, pointing out that Ernest would not approve. "These mean, dirty little insults your mother has had to put up with all these years!" Lawrence screamed as Barby left, dejected and humiliated.[32]

They stayed in borrowed rooms back in London, where Lawrence's meetings with the literati opened old wounds. Dorothy Richardson, the novelist whom Virginia Woolf had credited with introducing stream-of-consciousness in *Pointed Roofs*, the first of a twelve-book work-in-progress entitled *Pilgrimage*, caused an outburst over tea by unwittingly committing some minor impropriety, though a few days later Lawrence accompanied her and H. D.—now redeemed in his eyes—on a round of visits to friends' homes. William Gerhardie, a thirty-year-old, Russian-born British novelist and protégé of newspaper magnate Lord Beaverbrook, came to dinner. Lawrence, perhaps thinking of poor reviews of his novels in Beaverbrook's papers or of their jingoism and anti-German hate articles, told him that his patron was a bloodsucker. Frieda chimed in, denouncing the man, whom neither had met. "Not so much intensity, Frieda," Lawrence cautioned.

"If I want to be intense I'll be intense," she replied, "and you go to hell!" Gerhardie confided that Bertrand Russell had told him Lawrence had "no mind."

"Have you ever seen him in a bathing-dress?" Lawrence answered. "Poor Bertie Russell! He is all Disembodied Mind!"[33]

They continued on to Baden-Baden, where Frieda got a permanent wave that made her look "a little Jane Austenish," as she wrote Brett, who was exploring hypnosis as a cure for her deafness and making plans to follow them to whichever country they settled in.[34] Lawrence wrote every week: "I can't stand Frieda's children. They have a sort of suburban bounce and *suffisance* which puts me off. . . . The boy kept his loftiness to the Vic and Albert Museum, and soon, very probably, will sit in one of the glass cases, as a specimen of the perfect young Englishman."[35]

3

By mid-November, anticipating the winter, they had checked into a hotel in Spotorno, a sparsely populated fishing village sixty miles down the Italian Riviera from Genoa. The village had been recommended by the Genoese wife of Lawrence's London publisher, Rina Secker, who had family there. It was dull and well off the tourist map, and the Lawrences, with the reverse snobbism that a decade of low-end rentals had engendered, approved it as safely free of Englishmen. Rina found a vacant four-story pink stucco villa, the Bernarda, and Frieda and Lawrence arranged for its rental with the caretaker, a peasant named Giovanni Rossi, who lived in separate quarters in the basement.

The house was owned by Ina Serafina Ravagli, known as Serafina, an Italian language and history teacher at the Istituto Magistrale Superiore in Savona, ten miles to the north; there was a wine and oil cellar, a vineyard garden, and a balconied bedroom, with a commanding view of a ruined castle and the sea, which Lawrence chose as his own. Rossi asked for several days to prepare it, and they spent the mornings walking the beach and village in their best clothes, Frieda in an immense picture hat and the Parisian dresses she had come to despise, Lawrence in a somber brown suit, overcoat, and a homburg he had acquired in London. In the afternoons they relaxed at the Albergo Ligure, a local inn.

Apart from Secker's in-laws they knew no one. Frieda invited Barby and Elsa for Christmas and to stay through the spring. To her surprise, Ernest granted permission, with the stipulation that they not stay under Lawrence's roof but take rooms twenty-five miles away at a pensione in Alassio, a mini-colony for retired Anglo-Indian civil servants and British military officers, drawn by favorable exchange rates and united in bemused condescension toward the locals.

Word of the English *autore* and his well-dressed baroness wife traveled quickly, and Serafina's husband, Angelo Nunzio Gaspero, a Bersaglieri lieutenant with a well-known penchant for foreign women, arrived at the Ligure to collect the rent. He came dressed for the occasion, in gray-green trousers and jacket with stiff epaulettes and a cobalt blue silk sash that stretched diagonally across his broad chest, a black hat sporting the glossy black feathers of the *cedrone*, a rooster imported from China, and the Cross of War; he had been wounded twice in World War I—once, like Frieda's father, in his hand. He had narrowly avoided having a finger amputated. Just over five feet six inches tall, he was built like a jockey, with brown eyes, a disarming smile, and sleek dark hair pomaded back from a low brow. He found only Lawrence, whose spoken Italian was rusty (and largely limited to the kitchen and market), and had a hard time making himself understood. Astonished by Ravagli's appearance and courtly behavior, he went to get Frieda. "You must come look at him," he said. "[H]e is so smart."[36]

No doubt reminded of the Bersaglieri she had watched from the window in Gargnano while Lawrence rewrote "Paul Morel," Frieda marveled in broken, "sledge-hammer" Italian over the elaborate beauty of his clothes. In a low, seductive voice that friends later described as a cross between Maurice Chevalier's and Charles Boyer's, he replied glibly that officers were required to wear full dress on the birthday of Queen Elena, duchess of Aosta, the Montenegrin wife of King Vittorio Emmanuele III. The Queen's birthday was actually months off, though Ravagli was celebrating his own thirty-fourth birthday the following week.[37] Lawrence paid him in British currency, twenty-five pounds for five months.

Ravagli began visiting Frieda once a week, in uniform, occasionally taking English lessons from Lawrence, though "Lawrence was always busy," he later recalled, "mostly doing housework."[38] One day he found him in the kitchen, gasping for air and shouting expletives at the wood- and coal-burning stove, which was spewing black smoke. Changing from his regimentals to a pair of overalls, Ravagli disconnected and cleaned the stovepipe, which had become packed at the joint with soot, jogged out to the garden, selected and wrapped a rock in a rag attached to a rope, then climbed to the roof and cleared the four-story chimney with the rock. Lawrence, holding a bucket to catch the dirt, remarked to Frieda, "That is a man who would be useful to have at the Kiowa Ranch."[39]

Serafina, six years older than Angelo, occasionally came with their two children, Magda (Carla), three, and Stefanino, five, who loved the homemade candy and cakes and the rich laughter of the big, pretty German woman.[40] Lawrence labored over small gifts for Serafina, whose soft-spoken intelligence, openness, and self-effacing manner he found touching: "Sometimes I found Lawrence busy painting decorative designs on silk material or on handkerchiefs," Angelo later remembered, "in indelible inks, extremely well executed, one of which he gave as a present to my wife."[41] The two men had little or nothing to say to each other, though Lawrence admired Angelo's gait, quick from fifteen years of running into battle in perfect formation, for which the Bersaglieri are famous. More often, while the children played and Lawrence and Serafina talked (usually in French, in which she was fluent), Angelo took Frieda aside and told her about his boyhood and career, the aimlessness he had felt since the war ended, and his intense boredom with Italy. One of nine children, born 180 miles away to impoverished peasants in Tredozio, he had sold eggplant, peppers, and tomatoes at a homemade wooden roadside stand along the village's only road before joining the army to earn a living. He had married Serafina six years before, on September 4, 1919, not long after being released—in some versions of the story he escaped—from a German prisoner-of-war camp near Ellwangen. He had been taken to the camp, via two others near Mannheim and Baden-Baden, after the Italian retreat from Caporetto (now Kobarid), a village on the Isonzo River, northeast of Udine.[42] On returning from the camp he had been treated not as a hero but with the suspicion accorded deserters—who numbered high on the list of huge Italian losses at Caporetto—but still his eyes shone with pride and a strange romance: "At . . . best, he seemed to have stepped across the centuries right out of the *Iliad*," wrote Frieda, who affectionately called him Angelino, "an Achilles or Menelaus." He told her that "Once you have known war, everything else seems dull."[43]

She found his ingenuousness refreshing, and his impish sense of humor was a welcome distraction from Lawrence's intensity. His straightforward sexuality was equally welcomed, and gave her a feeling of being desired she had not had in years. They began an affair sometime after their first meeting alone, either almost immediately or about two years later, in 1928, in either case probably with Lawrence's knowledge. Frieda may have hoped to win back Lawrence's carnal interest, and Lawrence may have shared her hope. Their sex life, long a byproduct of his helpless tubercular rages, had become erratic or nonexistent since the disease had reached its terminal stage. Neither fully understood the debilitating effects of tuberculosis on sexual appetite—depressed desire and impotence—and in their ignorance they simply continued to make sex a subject of fierce argument.

"We have a nice little Bersaglieri officer to whom the villa belongs I am thrilled by his cockfeathers he is almost as nice as the feathers!" Frieda wrote to Brett, who had followed them as far as Capri by early December.[44] Barby had also arrived, with Elsa to follow in February.

4

The Lawrences made the trip to Alassio, which they found odious. Frieda wanted Barby to come to Spotorno with them immediately. When she suggested the idea to the lesbian proprietors of Barby's *pensione*, a colonial archbishop's niece and an Englishwoman who reminded Barby of one of her Weekley uncles, they lectured Frieda on the importance of her daughter's mixing "in the *best* set."[45] Frieda left without her. "I get so scared," she wrote Brett, "as if they could pull me in and out of their 'sets'! Barby bewildered I think she is scared of L and me, God knows why—All I want of them is to learn to get something out of life, I dont care what they *feel* about me."[46]

Flouting Ernest's orders, Barby arrived at the Bernarda two Sundays later. Frieda gave her a room on the first floor. Early next morning, Barby was awakened by scuffling noises overhead and rushed upstairs. "He has been horrid," Frieda said, explaining that they had fought about her.[47] There were fingernail marks raked across her neck. She seemed resigned and trapped, "'a bird in the gilded cage'—of D.H.L.'s genius." An inbred "German reverence for the artist" and deference to Lawrence's enormous talent, Barby later wrote, was justification for accepting his blows.[48] Lawrence brooded on the edge of the bed. Beating Frieda, he had once told Brett, was a humiliation to him.

The rest of the day passed uneventfully. Frieda, inspired by Barby, worked on a small painting while Lawrence hovered, offering advice. By dinnertime, however, he was on the rampage again. "Don't you imagine your mother loves you," he warned Barby, hurling a glass of Chianti at Frieda, "she doesn't love anybody, look at her false face."[49]

"She's too good for you," Barby shouted, outraged at the sight of the red wine trickling down her mother's cheeks, "it's casting pearls before swine!" Frieda left the room in tears, and Barby asked Lawrence, "Do you care for her?"

"It's indecent to ask," he said. "Look what I've done for your mother! Haven't I just helped her with her rotten painting?"[50]

18

Vence

I

Frieda had a huge investment in making a success of Christmas, the first in fourteen years under the same roof as Barby. She was in an uneasy, ambiguous position, something between a mother and an acquaintance, and made too great an effort at festivity, full of a mannered bluster that wore poorly. Nothing she did could induce the domestic set piece she had in mind, and nothing could stop her from trying. Her self-consciousness was exacerbated by Lawrence, who seemed to be watching her every move, looking for missteps or signs of disloyalty. He still harbored fears of a shift of allegiance to her children, and rarely lost a chance to snipe at her aptitude for mothering or to denigrate Barby as Ernest's child—characterless, vapid, unworldly, spoiled. To others he complained that Barby flirted with him. His appetite for manipulating the family dynamic and for controlling and distorting his own impulses was insatiable—he actually liked the girl quite a bit—and the insults, unkindnesses, and obfuscations sent Frieda into embarrassed rages that she alternately tried to conceal from or explain to Barby. She had hoped to teach her something about reality and about love but was hardly in a position to be doing so.

More often than not, she disappeared for solitary walks, returning when she felt prepared to face the ménage again.

Barby could not quite wrap her mouth around the word "Mother" and called Frieda "Mrs. L.," later warming to "Ma." Like many children of divorce, she had the gift of being invisible or charismatically present as circumstance dictated, and found her way, often creatively, through the confusion and the endless fights. The volatile, unstructured household seemed "like a draught of life," and painting came easily for the first time.[1] Lawrence, who felt some wistfulness, if not real regret, over his and Frieda's lack of children, told Barby that a childhood case of mumps had left him sterile (which may or may not have been true), and supervised her work with unstinting energy, often plunging in to add scale figures to landscapes—indispensable, he said, to good art. Among their collaborations was the first picture she sold, a pastoral house-building scene.

His attention was flattering, and she was fascinated by the contradictions in his character: an old-worldly, bossy gallantry mixed with an almost hysterical rigidity. His own penchant for flirting soon came through, and at times their rapport seemed uncannily like his and Frieda's in the early years. On seaside walks he talked about his mother, who, as he had long been telling people, had been given undue moral leverage in *Sons and Lovers*, at the expense of his father. Without segue he would lecture Barby about thrift, tidiness, and her lack of regard for convention, which would prevent her from attracting a husband. In turn she told him stories of life at 49 Harvard Road under Maude and Agnes Weekley, and she had a novelist's eye for detail.

Barby returned to Alassio before New Year's and Lawrence began *The Virgin and the Gipsy*, a short, satirical novel of an English family shamed by the unspeakable irresponsibility of a German woman who has married into it, run away, and left two daughters. The family suffers further moral decline when the younger daughter has an affair with a Gypsy, and is eventually punished by a flood of biblical proportions. The two matriarchs, now called Aunt Cissie and Granny, were sketched with a rancor rivaled only by that with which Lawrence drew Ernest's character, a rector who "cracked sarcastic little jokes all the time."[2] The book was done in less than a month, in time for Barby's next visit. He had used verbatim many of the conversations she remembered from childhood, occasionally introducing slight modifications: "Granny did *not* say 'At least we don't come of half-depraved stock' but 'At least we're not *German*.'"[3] He submitted it to Secker for use in a three-novella book, but the collection never materialized.

On February 5 he came down with flu. He was in bed, spitting blood, when his sister Ada and a friend, Lizzie Booth, arrived on the tenth, for what Lawrence had billed as a relaxed visit to the Bernarda, to be followed by a French seaside vacation. Actually he had invited them in a panic, as ballast for Barby and Elsa, who was due the following day with her future mother-in-law, Eileen Seaman; she had recently become engaged to Bernal Edward "Teddy" De Martelly Seaman, an officer in the Royal Navy. The plan quickly backfired. He had not bargained on Ada's asserting herself with real force against Frieda, whom she accused of shabby nursing and poor cooking and edged out of the kitchen. She was not fit, Ada maintained, to take care of "Our Bert," a childhood endearment the family had not dropped. Frieda hated seeing Lawrence babied and catered to but avoided joining the fight—the first night. By the time Elsa showed up with Mrs. Seaman, however, Frieda was on the rampage, and Lawrence felt besieged and overrun by women. Elsa and Mrs. Seaman had flown from London to Paris, and he announced his hatred of the modernity of air travel to Barby: "I can't stand those artificial sensations."[4] The girls and Mrs. Seaman checked into the Albergo Ligure, and the house settled into a routine seething between Frieda and Ada.

Ravagli's weekly visit brought the volume back up: Lawrence invited his sister to his bedroom and complained of Frieda, and probably of Ravagli; Frieda overheard from the balcony and tried to effect a reconciliation, sharing Lawrence's bed that night. By morning she was convinced that "all was well between them," though she was shortly disabused of the notion. Ada, who had watched the bedroom comings and goings, felt sure that her brother was being manipulated. "I hate you," she told Frieda, intercepting her in the kitchen, "from the bottom of my heart." The next night Lawrence locked Frieda out of his bedroom and gave Ada the key, which Frieda found intolerable: "It was the only time he had really hurt me."[5] She packed a bag and joined her daughters at the hotel. She knew she didn't stand a chance against the Lawrences' will to fight, complicate, exclude, and draw lines of moral rectitude, and found she had little taste for the struggle, her own energies bent on the reunion with her daughters.

When communication became necessary Barby was sent to the Bernarda with messages. She delivered them with the chilly reserve of a butler, and Lawrence knew he had pushed Frieda too far. If there was a final showdown, neither wrote about it for posterity. Frieda later worked hard and occasionally lied freely to leave an impression of a largely happy, if intensely pugilistic, marriage, and suggested in this instance that she had been right and that Lawrence's relationship with his sister soured as a result of the confrontation—a victory for their marriage.[6] In fact, the evidence suggests that at this point they were utterly estranged.

Undoubtedly Frieda loved Lawrence, even if he drained her emotional reserves or failed to fulfill her needs. The marriage had become her life's work, and its disappointments were inevitable: "I believe I had what few women have," she later wrote, "a real destiny. Destinies are not mathematics and they don't come out like two and two make four."[7] Clearly the marriage was also Lawrence's life's work, though, as was so often the case, he acted under an entirely different, if not altogether exclusive, set of mandates: a belief in the sanctity, worth, and permanance of the institution, in which he had not wavered since 1912, and a feeling approximating the Oriental belief in the rescuer's (his) responsibility for the rescued (Frieda) that probably derived partly from a cuckolder's lingering guilt. Divorce was putrid, as he had occasionally counseled friends, and out of the question. Henceforth, though, separations came frequently.

He, Ada, and Lizzie left for an excruciatingly dull vacation in Monte Carlo and Nice, and Mrs. Seaman, Elsa, Barby, and Frieda moved back into the empty villa. In the week on the Riviera, Lawrence dashed off one of his most anthologized stories, "The Rocking-Horse Winner," for a ghost-story collection edited by Lady Cynthia Asquith, who had rejected an earlier Lawrence submission.[8] A parable of failed marriage, false wealth, and childhood misery, based ostensibly on Asquith's autistic son but with plenty of autobiographical resonance, it was accepted by his former patroness, who clearly did not see the reference.

2

Lawrence continued on, almost aimlessly, to Capri, where the Brewsters, in the midst of closing their villa in preparation for a trip, fed and housed him. He probably had some vague notion of a liaison with Brett, who had taken up a long residence in a nearby hotel. She arrived punctually at mealtimes and got a strong dose of Lawrence's marital complaints. In the evenings they foraged through the Brewsters' half-packed trunks for charades props and spent hours applying pancake makeup; Lawrence loved taking the role of an aging, androgynous schoolmaster with rouged cheeks, and once remained in character through dinner.

The Brewsters left two weeks later, and, with no one else to call on, Lawrence invited Brett to join him on the mainland. They settled into a two-bedroom cottage rented by an overbooked hotelier in the small village of Ravello, north of Amalfi, spending the days outdoors and the nights playing bezique. She fantasized about a life with him, and he talked about buying a sailboat and island-hopping in Greece; their only obstacle, he lamented, was a lack of money. He was probably just passing the time; Brett, however, took it all very seriously. An English magazine called *Eve: The Ladies Pictorial* had run a photograph of the two with the Brewsters in Capri, and journalists sought him out for interviews, but Brett and the hotel desk fended off most curiosity seekers: He disliked seeing photos of himself in the papers, which tended to overemphasize his bearded, unsmiling, "dark" side.

She completed the crucifixion painting she had begun studies for in New Mexico: Her Christ, she explained, was a composite of Lawrence and John the Baptist. It looked exactly like him, as did the Pan with the red Vandyke, marbled goat legs, and lily-of-the-valley loincloth that sat on a boulder before the cross. On the third night, he came to her bedroom in his nightshirt. "I do not believe in a relationship unless there is a physical relationship as well," he said, echoing Frieda's letter to Brett in Oaxaca.[9] He kissed her, and she was surprised to discover his beard was soft. Thrilled and terrified, she lay motionless. "It's no good," Lawrence said, and left the room. The following day neither spoke of the incident, but he came back that night for another attempt. "I tried to be warm and loving and female," Brett wrote. "[H]e was I think struggling to be successfully male; it was a horrible failure." Lawrence became enraged. "Your pubes are wrong," he told her, and stalked out.[10] Humiliated, she departed for Capri the next day. Lawrence went with her as far as the Amalfi port and helped her board the steamer. A series of letters followed in the next three years, ranging in tone from cruel to chatty to chiding to outright embarrassing—hers were unabashedly lovestruck, with no trace of anger or disappointment—but the two never saw each other again.

3

Elsa and Barby did not particularly like Ravagli, who, in Lawrence's absence, developed a frank admiration for "Frieda's two beautiful daughters."[11] They strongly urged her to make up with Lawrence, and may have helped compose a conciliatory letter she sent him a day or two after Brett had left. Her three weeks with Barby and Elsa, she wrote, had made her see the wisdom of living "more with other people," and she proposed a family trip to Germany.[12] Lawrence began making his way north, taunting her en route with a postcard depicting Jonah and the whale that he captioned: "Who is going to swallow whom?" It annoyed her immensely and made her regret her overture. "Mrs. L.," Elsa and Barby told her, laughing. "[B]e reasonable, you have married him, now you must stick to him."[13] They persuaded her to dress up to meet his train on Easter Sunday, a gesture that thrilled Lawrence. "I'm back!" he wrote the baroness. ". . . For the moment I am the Easter Lamb."[14]

Angelino was conveniently called away to Tredozio, where his mother lay dying for much of the month. The time alone with Elsa and Barby had restored Frieda's self-confidence, and her happiness was infectious. Lawrence scoffed at suggestions of his own growing fondness for the young women, but he could not conceal his pleasure when the peasants of Spotorno mistook the two, who were long-legged and thin, for his daughters. "They are nice girls really," he wrote Else. "[I]t is Frieda who, in a sense, has made a bad use of them."[15] Elsa's autocratic bearing, straitlaced manner, and disgust for open fighting helped to discourage arguments. When they did erupt she put a stop to them, once by reprimanding her mother for reducing Lawrence to tears. "F's daughters are really very funny: they sit on their mother with ferocity, simply won't stand her cheek, and fly at her very much in her own style," Lawrence wrote Kot with obvious pleasure. "It leaves her a bit flabbergasted, and it's very good for her."[16] They likewise knew the effect it had on Lawrence, and probably played the scenes out for his benefit, manipulating his volatile temper.

On occasion he still attempted to dispense fatherly advice, lecturing Elsa, for example, on the insignificance of human life compared to the magnitude of outer space. That night she happened to drink heavily during dinner and, taking up where his lecture had left off, began to babble, arguing forcibly and nonsensically with him. Frieda and Barby, who had never seen her drunk, laughed high-spiritedly. "The contrast from her usual self is too sharp," Lawrence cautioned. "It frightens me."[17]

They gave up the villa on April 20 and traveled together via Pisa to Florence. Elsa and Barby met the Lawrences' "eccentric" friends, as Barby called their homosexual Florentine circle: Norman Douglas; Reginald Turner, a writer and friend of Oscar Wilde; and Giuseppe "Pino" Orioli, a former Charing Cross book dealer who sold antiquarian volumes out of a cluttered shop on the Lungarno Corsini and published the work of friends, among them Douglas.[18] The son of a northern Italian sausage maker and an emotionally disturbed mother who had delivered him in her sickbed at the lunatic asylum in a village in Romagna, he was small, chubby, and well spoken, with a debonair manner and a gift for profanity and long, involved stories. "[L]ike Boccaccio," as Frieda put it.[19] She and Orioli had a tremendous natural affinity. "Lawrence was a homosexual gone wrong," he wrote much later, in a reminiscence translated (and possibly doctored in Lawrence's disfavor) by Douglas, "repressed in childhood by a puritan environment. That is the key to his life and his writings."[20] The assumption, and Orioli's appreciation of Frieda's earthy glamour, created a classic emotional triangle. Her appeal to Lawrence's openly homosexual friends was familiar from the relationship with Bynner, and she now played the role of one of the points of the triangle—one of the few "conventional" wifely roles she did play in the marriage, in the time-honored tradition of vociferously heterosexual wives and their sexually conflicted husbands—with rueful humor and, many felt, a grace out of keeping with the forthright anger of earlier years.

4

The plan to go to Germany was forgotten; Lawrence begged off, and Elsa and Barby vastly preferred Italy to *Grossmama* (grandmother), whom they had not seen for fifteen years. They remembered her penchant for scolding, and Lawrence's stories of her gustatory habits helped evoke a caricaturish childhood memory of an obese, strange woman. She reminded him, he said, of the hungry Germans in Anita Loos's *Gentleman Prefer Blondes*, the previous year's bestseller, which he had just read. "Two hours after supper she has a few snails," he told them. "Then at bedtime some honey-cake, with Schnapps."[21] Frieda did not have the heart to insist on the trip.

The girls returned to England, and she and Lawrence moved to the upper floor of the Villa Mirenda, seven miles outside Florence; at twenty-five pounds a year it was less than half what Serafina Ravagli charged, and they quickly stocked its kitchen at the Quarant'Otto, or, as they liked to call it, "the '48,'" Florence's Woolworth's.[22] Apart from three peasant families and the expatriate members of a British traveling puppet show, there was no one within miles. Frieda hankered for home ground, and she and Lawrence both loved Florence, albeit occasionally for very different reasons. For the first time there was money to rent a house as a permanent base, and they kept the Mirenda for two years, with several months-long absences. They hired a maid, who occasionally also did errands, but for the most part they were self-sufficient. A tram into the city left from the hamlet of Vingone, a mile and a half away, and Lawrence often went in for meals and drinks with "the boys," as he called Orioli, Douglas, and Turner.[23]

His friendships with them were uneven. Douglas's relentless contempt for the conventions of the London literary world stoked Lawrence's cynicism, and he felt the pleasure of acceptance in their clique, depending heavily on Orioli's goodwill and bookshop, which he used as a business office and conduit to international publishing gossip. The men often made the trip to the Mirenda, where Lawrence lavished exquisite care on the service of tea and occasionally ruined the afternoon with his overly poisonous tongue. At such times he criticized everything: their rejection of sexual convention (Douglas's attraction to young boys particularly disgusted him), the late hours they kept, their excessive drinking, and their fellow well-known homosexual expatriates. When they brought Charles Scott-Moncrieff and Harold Acton to the Mirenda one day, Acton's show of "refinement" made Lawrence cringe, and he endured the visit in almost complete silence. What bothered him most, strangely, was Acton's slight of Mabel (whom he had known in Florence)—a whimsical reference to Tony Luhan's coming "to dinner in his war-paint."[24] The talk turned to Henry James, whom Acton claimed as a favorite author. Lawrence, probably remembering James's 1914 low ranking of him in the *Times Literary Supplement*, bitterly denounced him. Douglas took Lawrence's side, and the argument degenerated into a broadside against James's Americanness.

Though Frieda claimed to relish the quiet and isolation of Tuscany, she was lonely, and Lawrence's nervous idleness weighed on her, as did his bouts of illness, which came regularly. Friends now spoke freely and admiringly of her ability to "raise Lawrence from the dead," simply by walking into his sickroom. Just as freely they condemned her failure to insist that he see doctors regularly, but she had come to share Lawrence's sense of the inability of the medical establishment to treat tuberculosis and doubted the value of spas, seaside convalescent homes, and other such "magic mountains." Lawrence struggled against his much-diminished energy and a new feeling of loathing that the idea of writing brought, and he relished the restfulness of inactivity, though lack of a project posed as much of a problem as did hard work. He and Frieda had never known each other or a married life without a novel, and to a great extent their happiness depended on the very productivity that was liable to run him into the ground:

> I think the greatest pleasure and satisfaction for a woman is to live with a creative man, when he goes ahead and fights—I found it so. Always when he was in the middle of a novel or writing I felt happy as if something were happening, there was a new thing coming into the world. Often before he conceived a new idea he was irritable and disagreeable, but when it had come, the new vision, he could go ahead, and was eager and absorbed.[25]

Secker offered Frieda a translation assignment—a small German book of correspondence between Richard Strauss and Hugo von Hofmannsthal—but, turning the project down, she rented a piano and often sat alone in their huge, unfurnished *salotta*, singing *Lied des Gefangenen Jägers*, about an imprisoned hunter, set to Schubert.[26] "Aunt Else told me that whenever she heard her sing it she felt sad," recalled Barby, who was soon back for a visit, "because there was a sound in Frieda's voice of a being also imprisoned."[27] Ravagli sent letters and a gift of sheet music from Porto Maurizio, a town south of

Savona to which he had been transferred, making no effort to conceal his unhappiness over the separation from Frieda. If she answered, she does not seem to have told Lawrence, who described Ravagli's sentimentality to Secker with great irony and disgust, but always sent along his own, unfailingly polite replies.

5

The years of globetrotting had come to an end. Though they talked about returning to the Lobo, Lawrence's health forbade the crossing of oceans, and Frieda did not want to live with Brett, whom she herself had invited to settle at the ranch. She had wanted to remove Brett from their lives, and perhaps to help put her and Lawrence as far away as possible from the Ravello debacle, though she knew very little of what had happened there. It was a generous, if backhanded, offer, and a fortuitous move for Brett, who stayed rent-free, built her own life, and never again returned to the Continent. She had much to tell Mabel about the Lawrences, however, and was of the opinion that he wanted only to get away from Frieda. Mabel passed the sentiment on to Frieda, and a vicious, intermittent correspondence filled the following decade, not abating in the slightest even after Lawrence's death.

They spent part of the summer and fall of 1926 in England. It would be Lawrence's last trip home. Frieda had two criteria for gauging their London stays—the ease and frequency of visits to her children, and signs of Lawrence's increasing popularity—and this one was a resounding success. Lawrence had been embraced wholeheartedly by a passionate group of new readers, mostly boys in their late teens and early twenties. A new interpretation of his handling of their marriage in his novels gave their relationship a public allure, and the improved climate may have figured in Monty's finally agreeing to come and meet Lawrence; he had also read *Sea and Sardinia*, which he felt captured his mother's manner and speech perfectly. He broke the ice by extending his hand before Frieda had a chance to make introductions. The gesture took her entirely by surprise, and she sat in dazed appreciation as Lawrence and her son talked about John Singer Sargent, who had died the year before. Monty could not help noticing that Lawrence hardly spoke the King's English, and was soon imitating his accent for his sisters: "Sargent, sooch a bad pēynter."[28] The reconciliation between her two men was nonetheless a supreme vindication. She made Monty a part of their social life, introducing him to their London circle, but Lawrence had little stomach for Frieda's *Muttertier* mode, and arranged to visit friends in Scotland. Frieda used the time alone to socialize. A reconciliation was effected with Kot, to whom she spoke with pride of invitations to her son's "bachelor place": "Of course this is what I have always longed for."[29]

Lawrence stopped in Nottingham on the way down from Scotland. The sight of picketing miners and the cheap soap and hats and wilting groceries in the store windows of Eastwood left him with an expatriate's relief, disgust, and guilt, and after a couple of days he was back in London. It was clear to most old friends that he had suffered miserably since his last trip to England, the previous fall; some, like Catherine Carswell, were horrified by his weight loss (between fifteen and twenty pounds), which made his clothes hang pathetically large; on the streets of Hampstead, she said, he looked like the prow of a tall, narrow sailboat and Frieda a crisp, massive sail.[30]

Apart from overweight Frieda had not aged much; her hair was turning gray, a condition she began to cover sometime after her fifty-first birthday by rinsing it with saffron.[31] Forced to monitor Lawrence's exertions, she tried not to seem too nursely. To Richard Aldington and his girlfriend, Dorothy (Arabella) Yorke, whom they had met at H. D.'s during the war, she talked uneasily of Lawrence's frailty and bluntly informed them that he was impotent.[32] During a visit from Rolf Gardiner, a passionate young fan with whom Lawrence had been corresponding for two years, she hovered after serving a meal of chops and ale while the two talked about "the approaching doom of civilisation," German politics, and ethnic dance. Gardiner, a Cambridge graduate and back-to-the-land idealist who later founded international work camps for the unemployed, had hoped to enlist Lawrence actively in his various causes, which included a proto-fascist, ex-Scouts' group called Kibbo Kift, the Woodcraft Kindred. Despite Bertrand Russell's conviction of the Lawrences' fascist leanings, Gardiner left with the distinct impression of an iconoclast who would not be joining any clubs soon, fascist or otherwise. Lawrence's opinion of Benito Mussolini, whom they discussed intermittently in later correspondence, was essentially one of amused condescension, with an occasional concession to his talent for "leadership." Nothing had changed or matured appreciably in Lawrence's very private political universe since World War I. The visit came to an end when, wearing a pair of bedroom slippers, he leapt up to demonstrate the steps of Sinhalese devil dancers, the Tiwa, and Mexican Indians. Frieda was alarmed, and tried to get him to stop. "You look so pale," she said, "won't you go and lie down, my Lorenzo?"[33]

6

The trip to England reactivated several friendships, among them with Aldous Huxley, now a successful novelist, and his wife, Maria. They arrived at the Mirenda on October 22 in a 61,000-lire, custom-made Bugatti. The Lawrences had known Maria (*née* Nys) since the teenage infatuation with Lady Ottoline that had driven her to attempt suicide, and were fond of her; young enough to be one of Frieda's daughters, with the poise of a much older woman, she was delicate and self-effacing with Lawrence, never arriving without a huge bouquet of fresh, hand-picked lotus blossoms or other rare flowers.

The Huxleys had a well-bred disregard for the ordinary, and considered themselves heirs to the Lawrences' unconventional lifestyle. Their easy, Socratic deference had a tonic effect: "A new man's ideas are not so easy to grasp right away and it makes people hostile," Frieda later wrote. "There were a few like Aldous and Maria Huxley who patiently listened."[34] They had married shortly after the war, an open relationship that would last several decades and allow her affairs with, among others, Mercedes De Acosta, an Argentine poet and lover of Greta Garbo. Occasionally, she seduced women for Huxley. The laissez-faire marriage and world-weary modernity intrigued Lawrence, and the fascination was mutual, even to the point of taking up each other's cudgels. In his 1936 novel *Eyeless in Gaza*, Huxley based the character of a sarcastic sociologist at least in part on Ernest Weekley; his 1955 *roman à clef The Genius and the Goddess* featured Frieda as Katy Maartens, an indefatigable adultress and artistic catalyst.[35]

The age difference between the two couples prevented much of the open peer jealousy and backbiting that had plagued the foursome with the Murrys. The friendship did suffer reversals, third-party complaints, and gossip, however. Maria invited Barby to their apartment in London shortly after returning from the Mirenda, and spent the visit discussing the Lawrences. Like most people who accepted their hospitality, she could not resist talking about them. Barby confessed she did not understand the marriage. Calling it a "great passion," Maria said patronizingly: "Frieda is silly. She is like a child, but Lawrence likes her *because* she is a child."[36]

The Huxleys had been winding up the rental of a house in the Dolomites after a trip around the world, and had found several used canvases while packing up; Maria, possibly remembering Lawrence's love of copying masterpieces when he was younger, had left them at the Mirenda. It was the beginning of an avocational obsession that would occupy Lawrence's last years almost as much as his writing. Frieda, who disliked the barrenness of the Mirenda's high-ceilinged rooms—vaulted like a church spire's and freshly whitewashed with a vine-sprayer by the neighboring peasants—suggested that Lawrence begin painting immediately to brighten the big spaces. The canvases were larger than any he had attempted before, but he seized on the idea, making paint by mixing pigment and oil left over from a lacquering of the door- and window frames and slapping it on with a large housepainting brush. The activity had something of the self-mortifying, cathartic effect of being in the confessional; Lawrence's resentment, and perhaps his appreciation, of Frieda's sexual appetite figured prominently. A seminude *Holy Family*, his first effort, signed "Lorenzo," was hung in the *salotta*, Mary's breasts bared to the viewer though everyone else is rather primly and fully clothed. Above the Christ Child's halo is a shaft of light in the shape of a penis. "The phallic" had become a thematic preoccupation—used, for example, to explain the driving force behind *Anna Karenina*, in the previous year's essay "The Novel"—and he vowed to include the symbol in all future paintings:

> I . . . put a phallus . . . in each one of my pictures somewhere. And I paint no picture that wont shock people's castrated social spirituality. . . . the phallus is a great sacred image: it represents a deep, deep life which has been denied in us, and still is denied. Women deny it horribly, with a grinning travesty of sex.[37]

The Mirenda had the sour smell of fermentation after the autumn grape harvest. Every morning he went outdoors with a notebook, in which he was beginning a new story; when he grew tired of it, he painted, stocking up in Florence on more canvases, brushes, oil, pigments, and, eventually, watercolors. The preparation of lunch—usually winepress-fed pigeons, which tasted and smelled of the dregs—was often interrupted when he called Frieda away to "hold out an arm or a leg for him to draw, or tell him what I thought of his painting."[38] After years of Lawrence preparing the meals, she had assumed most of the cooking duties, and, with a chef's self-absorption and pride in her offerings, often summoned him to the table with the nickname "Little Pigeon."[39] Lawrence claimed no formal painterly inspiration other than a subject borrowed from *The Decameron*, and called his work "more modern even than these artistic anarchists [futurists and cubists]."[40] In *Boccaccio Story*, three nuns scamper past tilled fields and a slumbering naked peasant with thick thighs (a portrait of one of their neighbors); the perspective was strangely skewed by two overlarge dogs, evidently originally intended to be in the background. In the 4½ x 3½-foot *Flight Back into Paradise*, a Rubenesque, red-haired Eve, seemingly a conflation of himself and Frieda, flees a burning industrial town; a black-haired Adam, demonic and potbellied, stands beside her, the Archangel Michael blocking their way at the gate to Paradise. He told Frieda that he was thinking of giving up writing to become an artist, a career he found less taxing and expensive, but the story he had begun came in huge batches, about fourteen pages a day, and was clearly on its way to becoming a novel. She read what he had written after lunch each afternoon, awed by his speed and absorption and moved by its precision, misery, and muted irony; the story was of an aristocrat paralyzed and rendered impotent by a World War I wound, and of a love affair consummated in the woods by his well-born wife and their gamekeeper. "Lawrence goes into the woods to write," Frieda wrote to Monty, "he is writing a short long story, always breaking new ground, the curious class feeling this time or rather the soul against the body, no I dont explain it well, the *animal* part."[41]

Three weeks into the project, Ravagli, who had been promoted to captain and posted to Gradisca, a village northwest of Trieste, wired to announce that he was taking a trip to Florence. He explained that he had to testify as a witness in the court-martial of a soldier who had gone AWOL. They met him at a restaurant for what Ravagli later described as "a very gay lunch," but Lawrence's suspicions were aroused when he told them the court-martial had been postponed indefinitely.[42] His attentions to Frieda throughout the meal and complaints of the loneliness of Gradisca further irritated Lawrence. "[H]e is so miserable there," he wrote Secker several days later, "and descended on me with such a dense fog of that peculiar inert Italian misery, dreariness, that I am only just recovering."[43] Ravagli showed up again two weeks later, arriving unexpectedly at the Mirenda. The court-martial was finally under way, he said. Lawrence, who was beginning to think the trial was a pretext for Ravagli's seeing Frieda, demanded to see his travel pass, and he produced a document stating the date on which he was required to return to Gradisca. He stayed for tea, and never came back.

Lawrence completed a draft of his novel almost to the day of Ravagli's departure. He had been at work for five weeks. The manuscript was sprinkled with variations on the word "fuck," used by the gamekeeper to describe his proclivities in lovemaking. Yet it was the novel's uncanny Puritanism that mainly impressed Frieda, as she later wrote:

> Other races have marriage too, but the Mediterraneans seem to have Homer's ancient pattern still of the faithful Penelope at home, but the man wanders off after Circe and Calypsos—to come home again to his Penelope when he has wandered enough; she is always there for him. The French have *l'amour*, the Americans their easy and quick divorces and so on, but only the English have this special brand of marriage. It is not the bonds of interests, or comrade-ship or even children, but the God-given unity of marriage. England's greatness was largely based on her profound conception of marriage, and that is part of Puritanism. . . . [Lawrence] wanted to emphasize what he wanted to put across. This idea was if you put a thing square and fair and above-board, there is no more room for unwholesome mystery. He wanted to do away with the nasty thrill of dirty stories.[44]

Lawrence began a second draft with little or no break, now occasionally adding the word "penis," spoken by the gamekeeper—Parkin in this version, as he had been in the first, but soon to be renamed Mellors. By early February 1927 it had acquired the title *Lady Chatterley's Lover*.

7

He knew that the content and language would infuriate his publishers and agent, and, as if to defer the onslaught of criticism, secreted finished portions in a bureau he had lacquered yellow and decorated with painted pink roses. He and Frieda debated the merits of publication versus the vilification the book was certain to encounter: "You have written it, you believe in it," she said, "all right, then publish it."[45] He completed the second draft, some ninety thousand words, in less than four months, but the passage of time did not assuage his fears, and he put the notebooks away.

Looking for a distraction and hoping to find material for a travel book, he went with Earl Brewster to the Etruscan tombs in the villages of Tarquinia, Cerveteri, Volterra, Maremma, Vulci, and Chiusi. The three-week trip gave him material for *Etruscan Essays* and prompted a biblical novella, *The Escaped Cock*—a title suggested by a mechanical rooster cracking through an egg he saw in a toystore window; its themes of resurrection and sexual failure inform *Lady Chatterley's Lover*. While he wandered Frieda went to Baden-Baden, a dispiriting trip that left her with a bad cold and a longing for Lawrence. Her failure to bring Elsa and Barby saddened the baroness. "Now you are alone again," Frieda wrote her on returning to the Mirenda. "But in the summer I'm really coming with *both* [girls], they *would* like to come to you, terribly!"[46]

Barby continued to prefer Italy, arriving on Frieda's heels for her second extended stay. She was taken with the amateurish power of Lawrence's paintings, so shiny from hand-applied paint that they resembled oleographic reproductions of themselves. Filled with pudgy nudes, many resembling Frieda, they covered the walls of the Mirenda; interspersed were small watercolors of Frieda's, including a series featuring their Kiowa Ranch chickens, with captions such as "There is a rooster, a tough old bird."[47] She gave one of the chicken watercolors to Barby to carry back for Elsa, and the two put it up on the mantelpiece at Harvard Road. It became a favorite of Ernest's, who was not told who the artist was.

Work on *The Escaped Cock* and *Etruscan Places* went quickly; they saw almost no one over the spring apart from Edith Sitwell and her brother, Osbert, who returned a visit the Lawrences had paid their parents the previous spring. The elder Sitwells, Sir George and Lady Ida, lived an hour's drive from the Mirenda in a castle furnished with antiques, among them four-poster Venetian beds. Frieda had toured the bedrooms with Sir George and, playing the part of the Bavarian yokel she sometimes affected with British aristocrats, bounded onto each bed to test the horsehair mattresses while Lawrence pointed out the uselessness of having chairs that could not be sat in. "[A] funny little petit-maître [fop]," Lady Ida wrote of him when they left. Osbert, who thought Lawrence had "the face of a genius," later accused him of using himself and his family as models for the Chatterleys.[48] He joined a growing list: Among proposed models for the character of Connie Chatterley were most of the well-bred women Lawrence knew; besides the similarities to Rosalind Baynes noted by her sister, they included Lady Cynthia Asquith, Brett, a Mrs. Griggs of Zennor, Cornwall (a woman descended from Scottish aristocrats), and Lady Ottoline Morrell. (Lady Ottoline had begun an affair in the summer of 1920 with the Garsington handyman and groundskeeper; her mother, Lady Bolsover, was immensely fond of the Welbeck Abbey gamekeeper.)[49] Frieda, who may or may not have seen traces of herself and Else in Connie and her sister (or in a portrait, introduced much later, of the gamekeeper's sexually voracious wife), made no direct claim: "My feeble contribution" to the novel, she was to write Mabel, was its thesis of the sacredness of sex—"this religious (if you can call it so) approach to physical love."[50] Elsewhere, Mabel, with or without justification, gave Frieda more credit; Frieda had told her, she wrote a friend (in a letter that purported to record one of their conversations verbatim), that Lawrence "got" the book "intuitively" from her and Angelino.[51]

It was a hot, dry summer. The peach harvest peaked in early July. On the sixth, Lawrence, picking fruit in the garden, became exhausted by the glare of the sun and the parched air and went to his bedroom to rest. Several minutes later he called out to Frieda in a choked voice; blood was coming from his mouth in a steady stream.[52] He was forced to stay in bed for six weeks, under daily attendance by a doctor; every morning at 4:00, the maid made the short trip to Vingone in a horse-drawn wagon and continued on to Florence for milk, then thought to help diseased lungs. On the ride back she kept it from spoiling with a chunk of ice wrapped in a kerchief, resting on a bed of sawdust.

It was his most serious hemorrhage since Mexico and, even after bed rest, required months of recuperation, some spent in Villach, an Austrian resort where Nusch was staying. She had divorced her first husband and married Emil Krug, the banker the Lawrences had met in Austria in 1921. They all celebrated Frieda's forty-eighth birthday with a swim on August 11, except for Lawrence, for whom such exertions were now forbidden. Frieda was dismayed by the rolls of fat on nude sunbathers and avoided cake at teatime.

They moved on to the Jaffe summer house in Irschenhausen, where they had lived in 1913, when he was struggling with "The Sisters." Spring water, daily doses of malt beer and chalk, and a diet of local vegetables, freshly killed game birds, and huge trout brought some superficial improvements in his health. Their food was prepared by a maid who bought the best ingredients at various shops in Munich, setting off each day with a basket on her arm. Walking was difficult for Lawrence; to fill the hours Frieda read Goethe and Lawrence played patience and translated more Verga—*Cavalleria Rusticana*. She arranged with her sister to have Lawrence examined by Hans Carossa, a Munich writer-doctor who specialized in tuberculosis. He arrived at the house with Franz Schoenberner, the editor of *Jugend* and a friend of Else, whom he had once employed as a translator. Carossa made a great show of discussing possible cures; Lawrence listened intently, then changed the subject to their animals in New Mexico. "An average man with those lungs would have died long ago," Carossa confided to Schoenberner on the walk to the station. "But with a real artist no normal prognosis is ever sure. There are other forces involved. Maybe Lawrence can live two or even three years more. But no medical treatment can really save him."[53]

They returned to the Mirenda in October by way of Baden-Baden and Milan, and in December he began a third version of *Lady Chatterley's Lover*, contracting for self-publication through Orioli, who agreed to take only 10 percent of profits, as he had done with other authors, including Douglas—virtually a reverse of most such splits in traditional publishing. It removed the necessity of arguing with editors and publishers demanding cuts, and the manuscript became more explicit. Lawrence introduced the word "cunt," scenes of sodomy, and the character of Michaelis (an Irish playwright and lover of Connie's who precedes the gamekeeper) after renewing his acquaintance (and infatuation) with Dikran Kouyjoumdjian, who had effected the name change to Michael Arlen and become a bestselling Mayfair novelist, documenting the pecadilloes of London society. The character became a mouthpiece for several of Lawrence's own sexual complaints; he faults Connie's failure to "go off at the same time as a man" and her habit of postcoital masturbation to come to orgasm after him.[54] Eventually all the male characters began to resemble Lawrence.

He worked faster than ever before, producing as many as seventeen pages a day. By January 8, 1928, he had completed 724 pages. He packed his notebooks, and they set off on the twentieth for Les Diablerets, Switzerland, where the Huxleys had taken a house for the ski season with Aldous's brother Julian and his wife, Juliette. They remained for about two months, much of it taken up with preparation of the typescript. Half was being done in England by Carswell and others; Lawrence instructed Maria, who undertook the second half, not to utter any of the four-letter words. Frieda, the only wife not typing (Juliette was working on the manuscript of *The Science of Life*, her husband's collaboration with H. G. and G. P. Wells), found she had no aptitude for skiing, and lay in bed chain-smoking Gold Leaf cigarettes and reading *Corydon*, André Gide's defense of homosexuality. The book's arguments for sexual tolerance, running the gamut from the Greeks and Darwin to zoology and Whitman, had incited the French intellectual community to blistering debates that would culminate the following year in an exchange of letters in the *Nouvelle Revue Française*. Lawrence disliked the book, particularly its "scientific" aspects: "A damp little production," he called it, while making his "personal distrust of evolution" clear to Julian.[55] Frieda's unfettered enthusiasm for contemporary books of ideas was always a sore point. "Shut up, woman!" he shouted routinely when she went on too long or vehemently.[56] They left Les Diablerets with a nearly completed typescript.

Printing, by the Tipografia Giuntina, a Florentine shop with limited supplies, took almost six months; the book was published in July and deemed obscene by, among others, postal authorities, not long after delivery of the first copies. Orioli, who acted as distributor, delivered copies circuitously: in brown wrappers, or with plain covers bearing a false title. Reviews were almost uniformly condemnatory until an appreciation by Edmund Wilson in the *New Republic* a year after publication. Unprotected by copyright, it was widely pirated. Friends in

America and such longtime admirers as Alfred Stieglitz, who hoped to capitalize on the publicity surrounding the book with an exhibition of Lawrence's paintings in New York (it never materialized), tried to help track down the pirates, usually to no avail. Though Lawrence had attempted to establish copyright by getting Secker and Knopf to publish editions, they had rejected even an expurgated version, "John Thomas and Lady Jane," the second half of the title coined from British slang for the vagina. Following in Joyce's footsteps, he approached Sylvia Beach about a Paris paperback; she declined, though the book was eventually issued by another French bookseller, Edward Titus, husband of the makeup millionairess Helena Rubenstein, who offset from the Florence edition.

The headaches of publication were mitigated by the financial success of the book. Of the thousand Florentine hardcovers, some eight hundred copies were sold at £2 ($10 in America) within eight months of publication, netting Lawrence just over £1,239, far exceeding initial earnings from any previous book.[57] The Paris edition, first printed in May 1929, would sell 11,000 copies in roughly two years (Lawrence split both the cost of printing and royalties with Titus); a German edition sold 4,500 within a few months of publication. The novel made Lawrence a household name: Widely traded, its resale value in New York was as high as $50. When Orioli learned this, he bought up the last two hundred copies himself and conducted his own "resale" operation from Florence, charging $21 per copy.

8

The notoriety brought a spate of assignments from such lowbrow London papers as the *Sunday Dispatch*, the *Evening News*, and the *Daily Express*, which paid £10 to £25 for two-thousand-word pieces (on such subjects as pornography, henpecking, sex, nagging, aspirations to wealth) that usually took Lawrence less than two hours to write. He placed fifteen in as many months during 1928 and 1929. The sudden influx of cash, combined with the Florence royalties, allowed him to repay debts (£50 to his sister Ada for the Midlands rental she had paid in 1918–19). It also helped end the Mirenda tenancy. He could no longer bear Tuscany or the house, which, Frieda later wrote, he associated irrevocably with his last hemorrhage, and he thought that higher altitudes and the sea might help.

They could afford the best hotels, and against Frieda's wishes began wandering, mostly in France and Switzerland, but the proprietors of a hotel in Saint Nizier-de-Pariset, near Grenoble, asked them to leave when it became apparent that Lawrence was tubercular, and after a brief stay in Chexbres-sur-Vevey, near Lausanne, he agreed it would be better to have another house. They rented a chalet above Gsteig, and occasionally made the trip into nearby Gstaad by mailbus. Frieda shed weight through long walks and a berry-juice diet. It was the closest they had come to idyllic, mountain isolation since their Bavarian honeymoon, and Lawrence wrote cozily to his family and publishers of "we two alone,"[58] though the Brewsters, who were staying in the village, took tea with them almost daily. Else arrived to celebrate Frieda's forty-ninth birthday, and Lawrence's sister Emily came for two weeks with her daughter Peggy, now nineteen. He had urged them to make the trip, and Emily had arrived hopefully, laden with a quilt for her brother and wool-and-silk stockings and thick handwoven undershirts for Frieda, for whom Lawrence no longer hand-sewed undergarments, but the visit unnerved him: He felt he had to hide his copy of *Lady Chatterley's Lover*, Emily's awkward conversation irritated him, and he became ill and took to his bed, guilty, in the end, over his relief at her departure.

His strength and mood at a low ebb, he and Frieda continued on to Baden-Baden, where he developed a cold. The unrelenting illnesses made him fussy and distraught, and he decided, suddenly, that they should try the south of France. Frieda, dispatched to get the last of their belongings still stored at the Mirenda, detoured either to Gradisca, where Ravagli was still stationed, or Spotorno, to meet him at the Villa Bernarda; a previous visit to one of the two places had taken place in the spring. She arrived several days late for a rendezvous with Lawrence on the Côte d'Azur, where he had been waiting with Else, her daughter Marianne, and Alfred Weber. They stayed for a month with Aldington on the offshore island of Port Cros, then checked into a hotel in Bandol, ten miles west of Toulon, where they would remain for four months.

The seashore did not have the hoped-for effect, and Lawrence was unwell much of the time, but he managed to begin *Pansies*, a collection of mostly light verse that he preferred to describe as "*pensées*" rather than poems. He was apparently unaware of the slang meaning of pansy, and disbelieved it when told by the visiting Welsh novelist Rhys Davies, whose fare to Bandol he apparently had paid after the exchange of a few letters. "[D]oggerel," Frieda called the work, her laughter filling the room when he read it out loud from his sickbed, a small straw African cap on his head, which, he explained to Davies, "keeps my brain warm."[59] His concentration was failing, there were days when he was too exhausted to walk to the corner, and his testiness and feelings of persecution were pronounced. Davies, who later supported such unconventional writers as Anna Kavan, liked Frieda's opulent good nature, and they spent long afternoons in cafés along the Riviera, discussing Lawrence's standing in London. He told her that the strongest following was among the younger generation, and she urged him to repeat the compliment to Lawrence: "It will please him so much. Because he feels they *all* hate him."[60]

Davies did so, and Lawrence, who refused to believe him, was soon excoriating him and his peers. Denials gave way to grandiose claims—"All you young writers," he told him, "have me to thank for what freedom you enjoy."[61] The unpredictability of his outbursts infuriated Davies, but he could not resist the sheer force of Lawrence's personality, and kept returning. One night he joined the Lawrences for dinner, and Frieda talked excitedly about a German book on Rasputin, sent by Aldous Huxley—probably *Rasputin, the Holy Devil*, by Rene Fülöp-Miller, a belletrist whose oeuvre included editions of the diary of Dostoyevsky's wife and of Isadora Duncan's memoirs, treatises on Russian and American theater, and a book on the Jesuits that Frieda later partially translated.[62] Over the soup course, Lawrence threatened to slap her.

She was left alone to entertain visitors he did not have the strength to see. With an unstinting sincerity that astonished those who had come, unlike Davies, without invitations or letters of introduction, half expecting to be turned away, she told stories of the early years in Italy, listened to problems, and read and praised manuscripts. Most were young, solipsistic, narcissistic, charming, and naive, and absorbed her energy wholesale, seeming, as she had once said of Lawrence, to need her. A void was opening in the face of his death, which now seemed inevitable, and made her crave their interest. It was the beginning of a quarter century-career of encouraging and inspiring Lawrence acolytes.

• • •

Lawrence now had several new like-minded friends, mentors, and patrons, among them Harry and Caresse Crosby, jet-setting American publishers whose *outré* glamour and snob appeal might once have seemed calculated to offend his more stringent tastes. Their Black Sun Press imprint, devoted to a cluster of handpicked Europeans and Americans, catered to an intellectual elite that could afford limited, fine-press editions of work that had often been published months before at a fraction of the cost. They had bought an unexpurgated version of Lawrence's previously published story *Sun* with illegal gold pieces concealed in a gold snuff box; *The Escaped Cock*, which Lawrence had added to after its original publication (in a New York journal called *Forum*), was their next project. They lived in Henri Rousseau's former home, an old mill in Ermenonville, north of Paris, and invited the Lawrences for Easter weekend. Caresse had met Frieda in Paris and disliked her; on this trip, she made her dislike known, taking Lawrence out in a donkey cart each day to hunt for dandelions and leaving her behind. Frieda stayed indoors with Harry, playing the gramophone, and thinking of Elsa, whose marriage to Teddy Seaman was scheduled for the following weekend. Propriety had eliminated her being invited.

The Crosbys' music library included a Columbia 78-rpm recording of Bessie Smith's "Empty Bed Blues, Part 1 and Part 2," whose trombone accompaniment and tongue-in-cheek lyrics Frieda liked, and she played it over and over. Returning from the fields one evening, Lawrence became disgusted, and broke it over her head while the Crosbys looked on, then cracked the entire collection in the same way, at least according to Caresse, who claimed Frieda retaliated by smashing several plates. Frieda later denied the story: "They must have been relieved when we left. . . . So much crockery I must have smashed through the years!! I did it only once! When L. told me women had no souls and couldn't love!"[63] Harry sent her a gramophone of her own not long after. Lawrence, who disliked recorded music, wanted to bequeath it to Orioli, but Frieda prevailed.

From Ermenonville they returned to a Paris hotel Lawrence had stayed in while Frieda was away in Baden-Baden, but the city did not appeal to either of them, and they decided to go south. She had always fantasized about living in Mallorca, and they spent two months in Palma hotels; the climate reactivated Lawrence's Mexican malaria, and a broken ankle, sustained while swimming, temporarily immobilized Frieda:

> I looked around and saw a Spanish officer on a splendid horse, looking out towards the sea; I was disturbed in my loneliness and wanted to dash to my bathing cloak and go away. I sprang on to a heap of seaweeds that had a hole underneath it and rocks. Like a gunshot my ankle snapped, I collapsed sick with pain. The officer rode up and offered me his horse that danced about. I thought: what a waste of a romantic situation; the ankle hurts so much, I can't get on to a prancing horse.[64]

She decided to have it looked at by a Park Lane specialist and, saying goodbye to Lawrence somewhere in Spain or France, returned to Paris by train, reaching London on June 22. The trip was actually something of a combined errand: An exhibition of sixteen oil paintings and nine watercolors of Lawrence's had opened at a prominent Mayfair gallery the previous week, and he was eager for a firsthand report. The gallery was run by Dorothy Warren, the niece of Philip Morrell's whom Lawrence had tried to marry off to various Rananim invitees during the war. Now married to Philip Trotter—a former Welsh Guardsman she also employed as secretary and administrator—she was a friend of Barby, who had helped secure the show.

Negative reviews in the first week, most of them criticizing the works' "filth," were attracting capacity crowds. For a party in her honor on July 4, Frieda helped Philip Trotter make *Erdbeerbowle* with wild strawberries he had insisted on having flown in from France, and argued with him over his refusal to stretch this champagne punch with soda water, which he called "an unwarrantable adulteration," reminding her he had "come of age in the Black Forest."[65] A self-styled aesthete with rigid tastes, an expertise in Styrian jade, and a lack of concern and aptitude for selling the gallery's work, he was amazed by Frieda's innate sense of salesmanship. Like a canny shopkeeper, she noted the number of copies of Lawrence's novels in bookshop windows or in people's hands on the Underground. "All this fuss means lots more money for Lawr's work," she wrote a Mallorcan acquaintance, "I am determined about it!"[66] She helped the Trotters make their first sale, to a Cambridge undergraduate for fifty-two pounds, of

Finding of Moses—a midsize oil Lawrence had once described to Else as "my pictures of five negresses . . . or, if the Schwiegermutter had to name it, Ein fürchterliches Schauerstück [a terrible horror play]."[67] The party was an immense success: Frieda arrived before the crowd, wearing bright red shoes and a dress of her own design, cut out and stitched together on her bed at the Kingsley Hotel.[68] In her arms was a bouquet of lilies, a "pure" response, she said, to charges of indecency and calls for the pictures' removal, which now ran almost daily in the papers. Hobbling around on her swollen ankle—the bone had been set improperly by the specialist—she held court with a group of their London friends, publishers, potential buyers, her children, and Ada, who had made the trip from the Midlands. The arguments at the Villa Bernarda had been forgiven and forgotten. Two provisional offers, for *Boccaccio Story* and *Leda*, a watercolor, were made before night's end.

Frieda was not at the gallery the following afternoon when two plainclothes detectives and two uniformed constables arrived with orders to impound offending paintings—about half the work. They cited the Obscene Publications Act of 1857, under which copies of *The Rainbow* had been destroyed thirteen and a half years before. Armed police waited outside, forming a cordon around the gallery and holding open the doors of a police van, awaiting the contraband. *Contadini*, a male nude and popular favorite, was removed first, turned backward, and leaned against the wall, exposing the stretchers. It was followed by *Dance-Sketch*, a Pan study set in the woods, which contained no nudes. As the raid got into full swing, the Aga Khan arrived, creating a stir among celebrity spotters, the detectives, and the Trotters: As every London artist and gallery owner knew, he was a phenomenally wealthy man and a generous patron. Fresh from a party at Buckingham Palace, in formal evening clothes, carrying a black silk top hat and a heavily jeweled cane, he stared intently at *Boccaccio Story*, while, as Philip later wrote, a short, "shabby" man from Nottingham strode over to *Contadini* and began twirling the canvas in his hands, apparently daring someone to stop him. He was shooed away by the police. The Aga Khan pointed to the back of *Contadini*, ordered one of the detectives to turn it around, and, with the detective serving as an easel, invited "the little man" to view it with him, an egalitarian tableau much remarked on by Philip, who nonetheless failed to effect a sale. "This gracious incident," he later wrote portentously, ". . . contribut[ed] one of the few moments of comic relief to an essentially tragic chapter in our social history."[69] At closing time, seven oils, five watercolors, and all remaining copies of a full-color catalogue with a manifesto by Lawrence (priced at upwards of fifty pounds) had been confiscated. Among the banned works were *Boccaccio Story* and *Leda*, whose prospective buyers quickly canceled their offers.

Four days and several fêtes later, Frieda received a panicked wire from Orioli, informing her that Lawrence was seriously ill in Florence. Orioli was nursing him at his own apartment, where Lawrence had arrived, exhausted, after a trip to Marseilles and a week in Forte dei Marmi, several miles south of Carrara. She wired back her imminent arrival and set off, causing further injury to her ankle, now badly misshapen and throbbing, on a Milan train platform. Exhausted, thirsty, and sick with worry, she found Lawrence sitting up in bed, peaches from the recent harvest set out on a table, and a notebook of new poems, *Nettles*, in progess. Though he looked ill, it was obvious that his condition must have stabilized somewhat. A look of relief and gratitude filled his eyes, and she decided to keep her anxiety to herself. "What lovely peaches," she said, and devoured them one by one.[70]

9

They left for Germany, where the coolness, they hoped, would help revive him. He lost more weight in Baden-Baden, and wrote and spoke resentfully to friends and Frieda of the baroness's longevity, declaring that she would outlive him. They moved on to a rental in Rottach-am-Tegernsee, near Oberbayern, where he underwent arsenic treatments, which, not surprisingly, weakened him further. Frieda kept huge bunches of blue gentians on the floor for him to see when he woke before dawn each morning—a hacking cough and labored breathing prevented him from sleeping much—and they soon appeared in "Bavarian Gentians," a brilliant meditation on mortality and, with "Ship of Death," one of his last great poems. Before they left in September, she had her ankle set by a veterinarian, who rebroke the bone and splinted it perfectly. It never troubled her again.

Returning to Bandol, they rented the Villa Beau-Soleil, a sunny, six-room bungalow with central heating and running hot and cold water, for a thousand francs a month. The climate seemed ideal, but Lawrence's resistance had been severely undermined, and he developed bronchitis. It was a dreadful summer for both of them. The strain of caring for him and his frequent rebukes for small blunders or the wrong overture made Frieda feel unsettled, and she sent for Else and Barby. "He was falling away from life and me," she later wrote, "and with all my strength I was helpless."[71] She tried to interest him in the New Testament by comparing the pleasure she got from it to the excitement of galloping across the Taos mesa on her horse, but he had always preferred the Old Testament, and put it down after a few attempts to read it aloud, irritated, he said, by the complexity of the symbolism. His weight had dropped to ninety-seven pounds.

In February he reluctantly submitted to an examination by a British doctor, who ordered bed rest in a sanatorium in Vence, fifteen miles away in the Maritime Alps. Frieda and Earl Brewster helped transport him by train and car, and she checked into a hotel. Visitors began arriving from England, among them H. G. Wells, who informed him that his problem was hysteria, and the Aga Khan, who proposed another show of the paintings and hinted that he might like to buy them. (Frieda, reluctant to part with them, later quoted a price of twenty thousand pounds, and the offer was withdrawn.) "The English kill all their poets off by the time they are forty," said Lawrence, who had celebrated his forty-fourth birthday in Rottach-am-Tegernsee six months before.[72]

A month of camphorated oil injections brought little or no relief. "Your mother does not care for me any more," he told Barby. "[T]he death in me is repellent to her."[73] Other days he insisted to Barby that Frieda return to Ernest: "That's what she really wants to do."[74] Frieda took to camping out in his room on a cane chair until, one morning, he told her that her presence exasperated him. She left and returned later in the morning with red eyes. "Don't mind," he said contritely. "You know I want nothing but you, but sometimes something is stronger in me."[75]

She decided to move him, and rented the Villa Robermond, a house a short distance away, hiring a British nurse and a doctor—a Corsican named Maestracci whose manner Lawrence liked—to pay visits every couple of days. Lawrence did not have the strength to put on his shoes for the taxi ride. The following day, Sunday, March 2, 1930, he got out of bed, washed, and brushed his teeth, but the exertions sapped his strength, and he got back under the covers to read a

Vence library copy of a biography of Christopher Columbus. By evening he developed a high fever. His head was pounding, and he slipped in and out of delirium. "Give me the thermometer," he ordered Frieda, a look of sharp pain crossing his face, and she burst into tears. He pleaded with her not to cry, and she sat at the foot of the bed, one hand under the covers, holding his emaciated left ankle. "I don't know where I am, I don't know where my hands are," he told her.[76] He saw his body, he said, lying on the table across the room. In a moment of consciousness, he asked for morphine. Barby was sent to get Maestracci. She put her arm around Lawrence before leaving. "Put your arm round me like Barby did," he said firmly to Frieda. "It made me feel better."[77] In the driveway Barby ran into the Huxleys, arriving in their Bugatti, and she directed them to Lawrence's room. She returned with the nursing home superintendent, bearing a syringe of morphine, and found Maria cradling Lawrence's head in her hands. It soothed him, he explained, because her hands were exactly the size and shape of his mother's.

The injection calmed him but could not reduce his fever. He said he longed to be able to sweat, and Barby and Aldous departed a second time to try to get Maestracci. When they returned Frieda and Maria were in the kitchen. Barby quickly explained that they had not been able to find the doctor. "It doesn't matter," Frieda said softly.[78]

PART III

New Mexico, 1931–1956

19

"Not I, but the Wind . . . "

I

At 9:00 A.M. on Monday, May 18, 1931, the SS *Conte Grande* docked at Pier 95, at the foot of West Fifty-fifth Street in New York City.[1] Angelino Ravagli walked quickly down the ramp, comb marks still visible in his rich brown hair, his skin dark from the ten-day sailing from Genoa. On a six-month leave from the Bersaglieri, never before out of Europe, he wore his white flannels, silk shirt, and matching ascot with a mixture of aplomb and the career soldier's unease in civilian clothing. Frieda walked beside him, her hair, strawberry blond from a recent saffron rinse, covered by a tall, wide-brimmed homemade hat. They had spent much of the crossing in bed. "[Y]ou'll be glad to know that life is wonderful for me, quite newly so," Frieda had written the day before to Martha Gordon Crotch, a British expatriate she had befriended in Vence in the fourteen months since Lawrence's death. "[A]fter all, I'm a lucky bitch."[2] A press cadre she had half expected to mount a "grand reception" was not waiting; she and Angelino were greeted only by a Lawrence enthusiast, a "Mr. Philips," to whom Crotch had written.[3] She had told him Frieda would be traveling alone, but he picked them out of the crowd nonetheless, probably from a description sent by Crotch and a seven-year-old photo of the Lawrences' last departure from the United States. If Frieda was self-conscious about the white lie she did not betray it, and Mr. Philips's tact instantly put her at ease. "It's such a *vonerful* country," as Mabel Dodge Luhan later rendered her appreciation, introducing a "Germanic" mispronunciation Frieda had long since lost or never suffered from, "where you arrive with a man & nobody says a *vord*."[4]

Mr. Philips was possibly Harry Irving "Hi" Phillips, a *New York Sun* columnist and Hearst syndicate writer.[5] He accompanied them to the Prince George, a hotel on East Twenty-eighth Street, and may have had a hand in an unsigned interview that appeared in the *Sun* two days later, headlined: WIFE TO DEFEND MEMORY OF POET; MRS. D.H. LAWRENCE TO WRITE ANSWER TO MURRY'S STORY. Murry had published a memoir of Lawrence, *Son of Woman*, the previous week, liberally wielding textual analysis and a Freudian scalpel to prove that Lawrence had suffered emasculating mother love; Frieda was referred to throughout as "the wife." She denounced the book as "the lies of a man who was dominated by a stronger personality and resented it," and called Murry a "queer, divided fish," announcing her intention to write her own memoir by way of rebuttal. Her quotes made good copy and were picked up by the syndicate, and a rash of longer interviews appeared in the next days. "In New Mexico Mrs. Lawrence hopes to bake bread, do washing, milk cows and saddle horses and so live simply," the *Evening Post* concluded, "but with a hint of misgivings she suggested that 'it may be too simple, all alone' "—a remark that quickly generated marriage proposals.[6]

Meetings on Lawrence's work took up most of the remainder of her time in New York. Royalties were long overdue on several books, and she was in the midst of ongoing litigation, initiated on behalf of Lawrence three years before by Benjamin Stern, a New York publishing lawyer, to reverse copyrights on some ten titles published originally by Seltzer, whose business had gone under not long after Lawrence had shifted his allegiance to Knopf in the mid-1920s. Seltzer had assigned the rights to his nephews, the firm of Albert and Charles Boni, and they were not having much more luck than their uncle. By the end of the week, the negotiations had begun to try Frieda's nerves,

Lawrence in the 1920s. *(HRC)*

Train station, Lamy, New Mexico, circa 1919; the Lawrences arrived on the Grand Canyon Limited from San Francisco on September 10, 1922. *(Wesley Bradfield/Museum of New Mexico, Santa Fe)*

Willard "Spud" Johnson, Harold "Hal" Witter Bynner, and Lawrence, early 1920s. *(Frieda Lawrence/HRC)*

The Lawrences, Chapala, Mexico, 1923. *(Witter Bynner/Courtesy of Clark Kimball)*

Atlixco, 1923. *(Witter Bynner/Courtesy of Clark Kimball)*

Passport obtained October 6, 1919; partly because Frieda was suspected of spying for Germany, the Lawrences were denied passports throughout the war. *(HRC)*

Angelo Ravagli, who became Frieda's third husband. *(Courtesy of Saki Karavas)*

Frieda in Italy, about the time she met Angelino, as she called Ravagli. *(HRC)*

Baroness Anna von Richthofen, in old age. *(HRC; Klinik fur Orthopädie, Handchirurgie, Baden-Baden)*

Taos Plaza as it appeared when Frieda returned with Ravagli (after Lawrence's death in Vence, France, in 1930) to live at a ranch seventeen miles out of town that she had acquired by trading the manuscript of *Sons and Lovers*. *(Harwood Foundation, Taos)*

Frieda (*center*; with cigarette), Mabel Dodge Luhan (*left*), and Dorothy Brett (with transistor hearing aid) on Frieda's porch. *(Cady Wells/Harwood Foundation)*

Left to right: Angelino, Spud Johnson, Frieda, and Cady Wells on the mesa near Los Pinos, the house that Frieda bought in El Prado, six miles outside Taos, in 1938. *(Alexander Böker)*

Frieda (*right*) and her friend Millicent Rogers on the mesa. Rogers, Standard Oil heiress, *Vogue* model, Taos patroness, and goldsmith, was voted the second-best-dressed woman in America in 1948. *(Millicent Rogers Museum, Taos)*

Frieda and Angelino in Texas, en route to Laguna Vista, a Gulf Coast township where, in 1947, she bought a third house. *(Harwood Foundation)*

Angelino and Charley Goldtrap, back from duck hunting, Laguna Vista. *(Bunny Smirch)*

Dorothy Horgan, Frieda's only real rival for Angelino's affection, shown sometime in the 1940s. *(William Hughes)*

Frieda and Nusch, during the latter's 1949 trip to Taos, shown in front of a "glitter" painting by Brett that Frieda owned. *(HRC)*

Frieda in 1952, wearing the jewelry, some made by Millicent Rogers, that she was rarely without in her final years. *(Sanford Roth/Courtesy of Suzette Hausner)*

and she felt "bullied" by a volley of telegrams from Laurence Pollinger, now Lawrence's Curtis Brown–London agent, urging her to pay more attention to British contracts.[7] She had hoped that Angelino would be able to help with the American negotiations, but his command of English was limited, his capacity for the Byzantine clauses of publishing contracts nonexistent, and as her boyfriend he was not welcomed by Stern, the Bonis, or Lawrence's Curtis Brown–New York agent, Edwin Rich, who did their best to hide smirks and insinuations under a veneer of professionalism. He indulged a love of cooking by roaming the efficiency kitchens of the offices and apartments they visited, inspecting rotary can openers and other culinary gadgets he had never seen: "*Viva l'America*," he said over and over again, with an approving smile and an eye to outfitting their own kitchen.[8]

Angelino's childlike excitement by turns charmed and infuriated Frieda. It was reassuring to be with someone whose grounding in the day-to-day was unshakable, but they had little of substance to talk about but the ranch, his lack of interest in anything beyond the most prosaic details seemed willfully passive, and at times she felt quite alone. Despite the reckless bravura of the affair, she missed Lawrence, and moments of happiness gave way to crying jags. As they wandered around Lower Manhattan, taking in the sights and browsing through Woolworth's, she worried that she had made a huge mistake in inviting him to live with her.

The week came to a close, and, stymieing Curtis Brown–New York's efforts to coordinate with the London office, she had done nothing about the telegrams from Pollinger. As was becoming her practice with business she disliked, she ignored them. Apart from the meetings with Stern, the Bonis, and Rich, she had seen almost no one, avoiding "the 'useful' swanks" in favor of the Automats, where they had meals with Phillips and his friends.[9] By way of thanks Frieda gave him one of two printing plates made from a drawing by Lawrence of a phoenix rising from its ashes. The gift helped lighten their load—among other baggage, they were traveling with her gramophone. They boarded The Twentieth-Century Limited on Sunday, the twenty-fourth, reached Taos on June 2, and headed straight to Mabel's.

The two had not seen each other since 1924, and Mabel scrutinized Frieda with a practiced, unforgiving eye. Frieda now wore reading glasses, a gold-rimmed pair whose formality made her seem "ages older," and she looked "all crumpled up," but at fifty-one her vitality was overwhelming. Flush with the strange freedom of widowhood, her affection for Angelino, whom Frieda called "the Capitano," as Lawrence always had, was manifest and touching.[10] Laughing and sobbing freely, she talked excitedly about a Lawrence "temple" she wanted Angelino to build on the Lobo, an idea inspired by a visit to the Egyptian wing of the British Museum. It was an emotional reunion, and, for Mabel, timely: She had contracted with Knopf for *Lorenzo in Taos*, a highly impressionistic, vaguely defamatory memoir completed within a month of his death, and she needed Frieda's permission to publish it. Frieda had read and disliked the manuscript, which she thought made not only herself and Lawrence but Mabel look foolish, and she had asked her to rewrite it. Mabel had chosen her moment well, however, and Frieda gave her assent readily, asking only that Mabel dedicate the book to Tony rather than the California poet Robinson Jeffers—a friend and Lawrence surrogate to whom it was "addressed" through the device of apostrophe. Ecstatic, Mabel called in two business telegrams to Knopf, then a rather catty one to Jeffers's wife, Una, about the book and about Angelino, whose presence flummoxed her. "Ole Cap' " Patchen, the telegraph operator and stationmaster at Taos Junction, spread word throughout the county, and Ravagli was known almost instantly as "Il Capitano," Mabel's epithet for him.[11]

Lunch was served, and the conversation, now apparently in Italian, turned to a man Angelino claimed to love "better than his son"—Benito Mussolini—"the flower of the world."[12] Frieda, who did not share his feelings, finally shouted him down and—at least according to Mabel—attacked him with her knife and fork. She could not wait to get to the ranch, and impulsively offered to buy a blue La Salle that Mabel had given Tony several years before, though she did not know how to operate a car. The two couples set out in separate cars, women in one, Angelino and Tony in the La Salle, stopping in the plaza to buy a new mattress.

Angelino loved to drive. He earned Tony's silent respect by negotiating the twisting, rutted road with expertise, borne of years of alpine motorbiking with the Bersaglieri, and after the silent contempt of the New York literati, the bonding seemed a positive augury. His spirits sank when he saw the house, however. Though Brett, there to greet them, had scrubbed the floors, it had had no structural repairs since 1924, and Frieda had not told him there was no running water, indoor toilet, or electricity. While he paced the small rooms in silence, knocking on walls and staring at the dust-caked *vigas*, Frieda lit a Lucky Strike, and Tony, Mabel, and Brett stood by awkwardly, all three convinced that they saw the spirit of Lawrence in the rooms. Angelino, who did not believe in ghosts, unpacked his razor and shaving brush, built a fire, and began clearing sludge from the irrigation ditch. He donned Lawrence's old blue work shirt and corduroy work pants, still hanging on a peg in his former bedroom, but they were at least a size too small, could not be buttoned, and had to be held up with his belt. Brett confided to Mabel that, after seeing Angelino, she was sorry she had not actually slept with Lawrence—in her then-current revisionist history of their nights in Ravello, Lawrence's rejection of her was forgotten. Mabel and Tony drove back to Taos, where she wrote a long letter to Una: "He is the muscle & brawn kind, very determined & self willed unshakeable! . . . They seem to adore each other & he is the Boss & gets his own way in everything!"[13]

Brett composed a blow-by-blow account of the homecoming for Alfred Stieglitz, with whom she had embarked on a long, intimate correspondence. The intimacy was one-sided (she had failed to engage him as her artist's representative several years before), but the letters, with their frequent, confessional references to Lawrence and ruminations on everything from painting to suicide, helped lessen the loneliness that often overcame her on the Lobo:

> The lifelong struggle to keep Frieda from what [Lawrence] called "pulling up her skirts at every man" ends in a lusty Roman and I feel chilled to the bone. . . . Lawrence could not, I know, sexually satisfy a woman like Frieda, he had not the physical strength, this lusty Italian keeps her nerves quiet, keeps her satisfied but Lawrence couldn't fulfil his excitement . . . and whenever she forced him to it, he beat her up afterwards.[14]

The only way Frieda would be able to entice Angelino to remain, Brett wrote later in the summer, would be with the gold that was rumored (briefly and, as it turned out, falsely) to have been unearthed on the Lobo.

Brett was living, still rent-free, in the expanded Tower Beyond Tragedy, several hundred yards down the mountain, having moved off the main part of the ranch the previous June after an unsuccessful bid to mortgage the entire property from Frieda. There had been a row over manuscripts, the Lawrences unjustly accusing her of having sold several, presumably left at the ranch but later found in Germany. Some time after the move down to the Tower, Frieda had learned the details of the attempted affair in Ravello from friends in London and Florence, and she had considered asking her to leave altogether, particularly when Brett began firing off letters to Mabel, Una, Stieglitz, and even Frieda declaring that Frieda, not tuberculosis, had caused Lawrence's death. The years of friendship had forged an unbreakable bond, however, and Brett, Frieda knew, had no money to live elsewhere.

With indefatigable obliviousness—a perennial good faith that was half blindness, half a kind of Pascalian wager that dictated a belief in her friends' essential goodwill—Frieda retired for the night secure in the belief that "Mabel and Brett are lovely with me now that Lorenzo is dead."[15] She cared far less about their intrigues, stocktaking, and telegrams now, and far more about Angelino, who clearly did not share her delight in bathing in a tin tub before the fireplace with water carried in buckets from the irrigation ditch. The sound of pack rats scurrying under the floorboards and up and down the walls made his skin crawl, and the pitch black and near-absolute silence of the property spooked him. He woke early the following morning and immediately began sweeping, tossing away papers, and breaking up old furniture and pictures. Within two days he had assembled an immense pile, which he ordered two young Tiwa, sent by Mabel to help with the cleanup, to burn. Shouting at them in the voice he normally reserved for uncooperative Bersaglieri, he kept them at work till dark, and was still convinced that they were not feeding the bonfire fast enough. They quit the next day, and he had to finish the job himself. Frieda salvaged Lawrence's writing table and the chair he had carved with his penknife.

Mabel made the trip to the ranch several times a week, ostensibly to bring groceries and the mail, which poured in, largely in response to the New York interviews. Her conversations with Frieda, which ranged from their children to an ongoing plan to make the spare cabin on the property available to visiting writers, found their way directly to Una:

> So they are going to flock! I was up there the day before yesterday & took her mail—one mail—& in it she had 5 offers proper & improper from unknown gents. . . . One was from a french one who described himself as being "encore assez agréable et distingué, et capable à satisfaire les goûts les plus raffinés d'une femme!" Two others besides from women—one who said she was highstrung & couldn't stand the ordinary life of people, another quite obviously Lesbian! Frieda, dressed in a filthy torn old cotton dress with her feet & ankles *black* with grime showing in the sandals read them . . . looking scared. "Really—its—quite—frightinng [*sic*]!"[16]

The first visiting writer, an eighteen-year-old named Parke whom Frieda had met in New York, arrived late in June and took an instant dislike to Angelino, whose Old World habit of dressing for lunch he disapproved of. Disgusted by Angelino's silk shirt and white flannels, one day he came to the table naked, as a show of protest, and Frieda threw him out of the house.

She burned *Son of Woman* at the foot of the immense Ponderosa pine she usually decorated for Christmas, to which Brett had affixed a painting on tin of a phoenix rising, and sent the ashes to Murry in a cardboard box: "Love's Labor Lost!" she wrote, in a letter accusing him of profiteering and of failing, as in life, to understand Lawrence, his intentions, and his work.[17] To mark the site of the burning, she had Angelino set up a pickle jar in which she placed a candle, later lit for special occasions.

That candle and dozens of homemade paper lanterns in the *tricolore* of the Italian flag illuminated a party on July 1 for seventeen Taoseños to bless the newly reconfigured household and celebrate Frieda's return to the United States. UNA NOCE [*sic*] IN VENEZIA! read a banner mounted by Angelino, who, like most visitors to the ranch, was struck by its watery vistas.[18] He made huge pots of spaghetti, and the gramophone was placed on the edge of a rectangle of grass scythed to a perfectly flat dance floor. All the women danced with him—he had a rather balletic sense of step and an even smoother facility with his hands, which groped freely. It was an unseasonably cold evening, and

Frieda, in a calf-length white buckskin dress fringed with small bells, her permed hair frizzed and luminescent in the stiff wind, sat on a picnic bench with Mabel and Brett, watching her guests with a big smile. "Here we are!" she yelled above the gramophone, a cigarette dangling from the side of her mouth. "We three! Wouldn't Lawrence be *astonished* if he could see the ranch tonight!"[19]

2

Frieda had never doubted she would return to the Lobo, and the relative lack of generosity of certain segments of the British press after Lawrence's death had been one of several deciding factors. Though there had been accolades, and sober, accurate assessments of his work that assayed his lasting reputation, few matched her own, far more exalted view. An impulse to caricature ran high in some quarters, and Lawrence was occasionally vilified, many of the pieces filed by Nice stringers who had made no effort to visit the Villa Robermond or interview anyone in Vence. Instead they had congregated in an Anglo-American bar on the Riviera, where at least one well-thumbed copy of *Lady Chatterley's Lover* was making the rounds to sniggers and sarcasm.

There had been no reporters present when Lawrence was buried on March 4. Frieda had spent the night of his death alone with the body, singing his favorite German lieder, English hymns, and Hebridean folk tunes. For the funeral procession, eschewing widow's weeds, she had worn scarlet and gold silk, following behind two "wild-looking" honorary pallbearers who maneuvered the oak casket down a slippery hill in a horsedrawn hearse to Vence's only cemetery.[20] The boldness and youthful pattern of the dress had shocked some ("If you were a year or two younger," Lawrence had apparently once said of the garment, "it would suit you better"[21]), as did Barby's dancing on the terrace to the gramophone each morning—in some versions, Frieda joined her—in the week after his death.[22] Frieda believed Lawrence had passed joyously through "the door" to "'the other side,' " becoming "of the elements again,"[23] and she had declined a British chaplain's offer to pray over the grave, watching in silence with Barby and several friends—among them the Huxleys and Achsah Brewster—as he was lowered into the ground. "Good-bye Lorenzo," she said at the last minute, tossing in huge handfuls of mimosa.[24] "We had a simple, cheap funeral," she wrote Bynner, "he would have liked it cheap . . . "[25]

Skimping was not entirely a matter of choice, however. Lawrence had died intestate, and by contemporary British law, without a will or proof of his intention to leave everything to Frieda, his royalties were not hers, though the interest on the estate was, as well as a nominal cash payment (£1,000) and his manuscripts and material property—what there was of it. In the event of her death, Lawrence's siblings would receive all. His effects were estimated at £2,438[26]—about $12,200 in 1930 currency. Lawrence's brother George and his sister Emily believed that Frieda was entitled to the income from the estate until her death but that the copyrights should revert to them thereafter. To prove her entitlement to both the income and the disposition of copyrights, Frieda cited what she said were Lawrence's intentions: Three days before the move to the sanatorium, he had suggested redrafting a will, written jointly with Murry in 1914 in Buckinghamshire and subsequently lost, in which he would leave everything to her; she had brushed aside the idea because of the state of his health. Ada sided with Frieda: "I don't really like her," she told Crotch, on a visit with her sixteen-year-old son Jack, ". . . but the way she stuck to him was wonderful. He would drag her off on one of his sudden journeys without hardly giving her time to pack, perhaps when they had only just settled somewhere and got fairly comfortable, but on she would go, and, if only for this, I say whatever Bert left she is entitled to."[27]

Lawrence's manuscripts were potentially invaluable, as he himself had long realized. A rush to acquire was already under way among collectors and dealers, and publishers were frantically searching for usable material. A request by Caresse Crosby for unpublished stories provoked a bitter quarrel: Frieda asked her to return Lawrence's *Escaped Cock* because of its sentimental value, and received a rather cold, queenly reply explaining that Lawrence had given the manuscript to Harry.[28] Lawrence, who had not forgotten Murry's bounty hunt through Mansfield's papers, had tried to avert similar scenarios by contracting through Pollinger and Orioli for his last complete works. Among them were editions of *Nettles* and *The Virgin and the Gipsy*, which now stood to sell briskly.

The copyrights, however, clearly had the most lasting value, as everyone concerned seemed to realize. Frieda received advice from all quarters, often conflicting and almost always unbidden. She could not help noticing how tailored the helpfulness was to the party offering it, as Barby explained to the couple Signe Toksvig and Francis Hackett, writers who visited the Robermond:

> Her affairs go on slowly of course her employees don't have the brilliance in business that Lawrence had about other things and that pains her, specially as they are so Jehovah telling her what to do. There is a strong feeling (also on Orioli's part) that the M.S.S. should not be given up to the Estate, or the pictures. Monty is getting very cross with anybody who isn't ready to obey the law at once and Ma says laws are always being changed by people with a little, I mean a few, guts.[29]

Frieda's immediate concern was cash. Apart from earnings she received directly from Titus for the Paris edition of *Lady Chatterley's Lover*, ten thousand francs every few months, there was not much available with the estate still in probate. She and Titus had begun a correspondence a month before Lawrence's death, when he had become too ill to write long business letters, and the letters flowed easily until he began making clear his hope for first claim on manuscripts, a raft of letters that ranged in tone from gallant to hectoring to petulant. Frieda came to resent his obvious sense of entitlement and let the correspondence lapse—in between urgent requests for money. Doing business became largely a matter of personal taste and instinct: "[O]ther brains I haven't got," she liked to say.[30] Like Lawrence, she favored Orioli, who preferred verbal agreements—sealed during languorous, drunken picnics in the Tuscan countryside—to contracts, signatures, and deadlines. The most valuable manuscripts, the three versions of *Lady Chatterley's Lover*, were in his safekeeping, and to further reward his loyalty Frieda simply gave him Lawrence's final poems—written in the months before his death and eventually titled *Last Poems*—and the manuscript of *Apocalypse*, his last significant work of nonfiction, on the Book of Revelation. The decision infuriated Titus, and probably Pollinger, but Orioli's irreverence appealed to her. Anyone who evinced too great an interest in Lawrence's literary leavings was given the cold shoulder or shown a ludicrous price tag. Approached by the renowned Philadelphia collector Abraham Simon Wolfe "Abe" Rosenbach, who expressed interest in buying all extant manuscripts, she blurted out a price of £25,000. It was a prescient, even modest, estimate of their eventual worth, but the figure was considered laughable by the standards of the day, and Rosenbach bowed out. It "may not be *practical* business," Frieda wrote Titus, "but it's *big*, imaginative business and I know in my bones what Lorenzo's things are worth—You know it too."[31]

3

On the day of Lawrence's funeral, Angelino Ravagli boarded a train in Gradisca to spend a month's furlough with his family in Savona. He was being transferred again, to Pieve di Teco, a godforsaken village near the city of Ormea, but the assignment came as a great relief: The village was some twenty-five miles from Savona, and he would be able to see more of his infant son, to whom Serafina had given birth six months before. They had named him Federico, after Frieda, his godmother.

It was a dull journey of nearly two hundred miles, and he alighted at Voghera, near Genoa, to buy a copy of *Corriere della Sera*. He had little patience for reading, and had nearly finished scanning the headlines when he noticed the quarter-column obituary on page 8:

> David Herbert Lawrence, the famous English novelist, playwright, and painter, died of tuberculosis at the age of 45 in a small village in the Maritime Alps (Vence). His wife, of German descent, was with him until his death.
>
> David Herbert Lawrence was one of the most representative and original of the modern English writers. . . . An ideologue steeped in Freudianism, realist almost to the point of indecency, he brought an almost hallucinatory vision of life to his numerous works. . . . Some could not be published in his homeland, so offensive were they to the conservative tendency of Great Britain. His best-known works are "Sons and Lovers," "Women in Love," "Fantasia of the Unconscious," and "The Boy in the Bush": all of them permeated by a paradoxical and heated eroticism which is perhaps the writer's most characteristic element. Lawrence was also a painter, though his work was controversial. Just last year the authorities were forced to close a one-man show of his works in London, due to the excessive realism of some of his paintings.[32]

The news of Lawrence's death was "a great shock," Angelino wrote later; he had "lost track of the Lawrences" in 1927, he added, falsely.[33] A few months earlier, he had vetoed a rendezvous with Frieda, on the grounds that Lawrence, on his way to the sanatorium, was near death and Frieda should not risk being away.[34] When he reached Savona, he wired her, offering his sympathy and inviting her to the family home.

Frieda arrived soon after, evidently welcomed by Serafina. Angelino "[gave] himself," Frieda later wrote, ". . . with a man's silent sympathy," possibly during sidetrips to the Villa Bernarda, which had evidently been empty since the Lawrences' tenancy.[35] To relieve Serafina of the burden of child care, they sometimes brought Federico along. Within seven days Angelino accepted the invitation to America, a decision that ironically had Lawrence's unwitting imprimatur: "I was to help her on the Kiowa Ranch . . . as Lawrence had predicted several years before."[36] From the start the journey was couched in euphemisms, which became more elaborate as the idea took shape over the following year. Though Serafina, accustomed to not seeing her husband for months at a time, was apparently miserable at the prospect of an ocean separating them, she—and Angelino—may have suspected practical advantages to the association with Frieda. In their eyes she was a wealthy woman.[37] Frieda offered several explanations for her half of it, among them, roughly in order of importance and significance: companionship, a love uncomplicated by the violence and emotional turmoil of her marriage to Lawrence, the sexual fulfillment she felt was due her after years of dissatisfaction, and the chance to offer Angelino a new life out of the military, which depressed him. She clearly also had a sense of herself, as in the marriage to Lawrence, taking up fate's gauntlet. Fate, in her case, seemingly included a dictate to repeat variations on her past. "Of course Angie *was* Professor Weekley, in a way," Barby would later say, recalling Lawrence's remark that Frieda should return to Weekley after Lawrence's death. "[She was] reconciling herself to Ernest, I think, partly—that and her father, and a few other things thrown in."[38] The equation seems more than anomalous, but as Frieda was to write, in a rare caveat to (and self-absolution from) her otherwise firm conviction and blind trust in fate's blessings and curses: "Our deepest selves are buried so very deep down and we don't let them come up to the surface. We think we know so much and we don't really and maybe about ourselves least of all."[39]

4

Murry came to Vence shortly after Frieda left Savona. He had not been heard from for some five years—in a letter Frieda had found hateful and thrown away before Lawrence could see it—but he spoke passionately of Lawrence now, quoting liberally from his own flattering obituary, which had appeared in the London *Times* two weeks earlier.[40] He also read aloud from *The Rainbow*, which choked Frieda up, and then asked her to bed, at least according to a later account by Mabel, who may have had her own reasons for thus shaping the story. Frieda, as the account continues, agreed, and regretted it almost immediately. Murry, much to her disgust, loved to be "scolded," and assumed a little boy's sheepishness, which he hoped she would find stimulating. Within a week she had him out of the house, in time for Easter, which she wanted to spend alone. For Murry it was a deeply satisfying affair, the first in which he felt truly sated, he confessed sixteen years later, in letters that all but asked for assurances that she valued it as deeply; glossing and sidestepping, she would tell him warmly that his friendship had been immensely important.

Orioli arrived for a visit after Easter, and Frieda suggested that he and Barby accompany her to Pieve di Teco. Barby was not doing well, having spent much of Frieda's stay in Savona in bed, convinced Lawrence's ghost was moving in and out of the Robermond. Signe Toksvig had left a copy of her first novel, *The Last Devil*, on witchcraft, and Barby was proving immensely suggestible.[41] She had also gleaned or been told directly the upshot of the visit from Murry, who reminded her of the food at Harvard Road, insubstantial and overflavored with almond extract.[42] Frieda's affair with Angelino was, in its way, equally unsettling, but she agreed to the trip. He met them in uniform at the Ormea train station and went to a café with Orioli, leaving the women to settle into what Barby later remembered as a "seedy little hovel."[43] Orioli, according to Barby, returned from the café several hours later with the strong impression, which he shared with both women, that Angelino had cold feet about the affair and, presumably, the trip to New Mexico. Frieda would have none of it, and insisted Orioli did not understand Ravagli, whom she likened to a hummingbird. In her hands, she said, he would be "a second Lawrence,"[44] apparently referring to an as-yet unmanifested artistic talent. Barby was unnerved, and left with Orioli to spend a week in Florence.

Frieda had it out with Angelino, and a reconciliation was effected, a scenario they would replay over the next two and a half years until they settled permanently at the ranch. Frustration with his intellectual limits was already giving her pause:

> I felt thoroughly humiliated. . . . Once I was beaten, when in my conceit I thought I could give Lawrence *complete* health, I fought so hard—This time I am beaten trying to give a *mind* to a man, who hasn't got one—But he is honest and charming and gentle.[45]

He "says he is terrified of the freedom life with me offers him," she explained, writing from Heidelberg, where she soon went to visit Else.[46] It was an unhappy trip—she and Else had long since learned the impossibility of their seeing eye to eye in affairs of the heart. Else had invited Alfred Weber to live with her, and was helping him with *Kulturgeschichte als Kultursoziologie*, a heavily theoretical, implicitly anti-Nazi tome that looked longingly to the days when an aristocratic, cultured elite ruled Germany and the world. Frieda seems to have written no one about her country's burgeoning fascism, and it is not known if she even noticed, though it would have been out of character for Weber not to have talked copiously about his work. She left Heidelberg, however, with a feeling of loathing:

> I met so many "important" people in Heidelberg, living "only" with a Lawrence for 18 years, I had forgotten how "important" people are—And the women don't know that there ever was or will be—a *man*—give me 3 months in Heidelberg and I'd be roasted alive in the marketplace.[47]

In Baden-Baden, she found the baroness consumed by grief over Lawrence's death. Frieda was in the odd position of having to cheer *her* up and, feeling unequal to the task, sent for Orioli. Anna, now almost seventy-nine, was suffering from emphysema; largely confined to her room, she had begun an impassioned reading of the works of Shakespeare. She revived somewhat when Orioli arrived, bringing Douglas, and she joined them in the common rooms for huge meals, accompanied by immense amounts of *Bowle*. Douglas's impeccable German charmed her, and she impressed them with her knowledge and love of literature and indulged them in her grand, eighteenth-century manner, but depression overcame her when the men left.

Effectively alone again, Frieda read over Lawrence's first fourteen letters to her—they had been left in the baroness's room at the Stift—and broke down. She summoned Barby, who had become ill in Vence with what was initially diagnosed as tuberculosis. The baroness, despite decades of exhortations to bring the girls, discovered she had little taste for Barby, however. It took Nusch (similarly summoned by Frieda, she had made the trip from Austria) to stem the tide of morbidity. The four had several meals together, Barby gamely trying to keep up with her grandmother's appetite, but Anna was soon criticizing her for not speaking German, like her mother. "My mother left me," Barby replied.[48] She departed not long after, with a case of bronchitis brought on, she felt, by the incessant Black Forest rain. She reached Vence in a state of feverish delirium. Crotch wired Frieda, who immediately left for Vence.

An elderly local doctor pronounced a condition of "*grande hystérie*" and recommended bed rest.[49] He seemed at a loss for further treatment, and his uncertainty and vagueness made Frieda feel panicked. Eventually it was decided—apparently by the two of them—that Barby needed not only medical attention but the companionship and intimacy of a man. A Calabrian stonemason, from whom Frieda had commissioned a multicolored stone phoenix mosaic for Lawrence's grave, was petitioned to nurse and then seduce Barby, and they evidently made love several times. The sessions stopped when Maestracci, Lawrence's former doctor, was called in. Though Barby was showing classic signs of a nervous breakdown—depression, weight loss, enormous depletion of energy, and brief, uncontrollable rages and tantrums, usually directed at Frieda—there was evidently a serious organic component to the illness, for which Maestracci summoned a Nice specialist.[50] "My lovely daughter Barby is very ill & the horror of it, it's her *brain*," Frieda wrote Bynner.[51] Mabel Luhan later wrote two letters in which she offered an elaborate diagnosis of syphilis, contracted prior to the interlude with the stonemason, and claimed that Frieda told her the story. The baroness, Mabel added, had suspected Barby might be syphilitic, and Lawrence had as well.[52] Her account has never been corroborated; according to Barby herself, the disease was a form of meningitis.[53]

Barby languished at the Villa Robermond for the summer, during which Monty and Elsa occasionally spelled Frieda in caring for her, with mixed success. Though Barby was Monty's favorite sister—they had friends in common, and had spent much of their nightlife during the late twenties together, dancing at the Savoy[54]—her impulses and loyalties were skewed, and she occasionally lashed out at him. He was awkward and terrified, not recognizing the girl who lay in bed (and, according to Mabel, attacked him sexually) as his beautiful, witty sister.[55] Elsa seems to have escaped Barby's wrath, and looked after her when Frieda was called to London in late July for persistent legal problems, now being handled by a prominent estate lawyer, C. D. Medley: The British courts had ruled on June 5 that the estate be coadministered with Lawrence's brother George, whom Frieda had come to mistrust. Ada, also represented by Medley, still backed Frieda's claim to the copyrights, much to the chagrin of George and Emily, who had hired their own lawyer. Barby's sickness had diminished Frieda's taste for fighting, however, and, with little accomplished, she returned to Vence to assume her watch.

By fall Barby was at last permitted to travel. Accompanied by a nurse she referred to as her French "gaoler,"[56] she crossed the Channel for a stay with her uncle Ted and aunt Lucy in Great Maplestead. The familiar childhood getaway had a salubrious effect, and she made a more or less complete recovery, though nervous depression periodically overcame her in the next decades. She eventually married, much as her mother had, a miner's son turned writer, named Stuart Barr.[57]

The experience left Frieda depleted, and she cleared her belongings out of the Robermond and rented a villa called Les Aspras. "There is no mother instinct in me strong enough to stand another dose," she told Crotch, with whom she lived while Les Aspras was being readied.[58] Crotch had problems of her own—a British doctor had left a five-inch forceps in her abdomen, eventually removed at great emotional, medical, and legal cost to her—and she was distracted and cheered by Frieda, who, like a one-man band, punctuated sentences with a smack of her hand on a brass table that rattled a set of ashtrays kept for her constant use; her voice, raspy from years of cigarette smoke, rose and fell dramatically, spontaneously activating the strings of Crotch's piano.[59] Frieda had retrieved Lawrence's paintings from London after their release by the police, and Crotch exhibited them in a tearoom she ran, drawing tourists, scholars, and customers eager to buy the Paris edition of *Lady Chatterley's Lover*, which was sold at a front table. The work dwarfed the small room, but Frieda loved the intimacy of the setting—an improvement over the Trotters' London gallery, she felt—and such visitors as the widow of Frank Harris (who had died in Nice) were pleased to find her holding court.

The peaceful interlude was broken by an urgent summons to Baden-Baden on November 20. Frieda took the first train, and was met at the front door of the Stift on the morning of the twenty-first by a staff nurse, who informed her that "*Die Baronin*" was dead.[60] It is not known when the funeral was held, or who, apart from Else and Nusch, attended; there was no published obituary. Anna was buried in a local cemetery next to Friedrich.

5

Determined not to spend her first Christmas alone in Vence, Frieda invited herself and Crotch to Florence in a "Teutonically sentimental" letter to Orioli, which, with semi-malicious glee, he was soon showing mutual friends. Among those who had read it by the time they arrived was Douglas, who diagnosed Frieda's unhappiness as unanswered maternal longing and offered her "a boy of fourteen" he was then seeing: "I prefer them younger, would you like to take him over?" Frieda was flabbergasted, probably for one of the first times in her life, and could think of no reply other than "I have children of my own."[61] She never saw him again.

Richard Aldington, whom Orioli had also shown her letter, joined them for Christmas Eve, which they spent wandering from one church to another with Orioli, who got thoroughly drunk. Aldington introduced Frieda to A. S. Frere Reeves, an editor at Heinemann, whom she may or may not have gone to bed with and with whom she was to find common ground in marital violence: He and his first wife, he would tell her, "smashed five suites of bedroom furniture."[62] They negotiated the first major publishing and distribution contract for Lawrence's books shortly after. The deal had Pollinger fuming, but like most business decisions Frieda was to make over the next quarter century, it proved to be entirely sound: Besides backing up Orioli's fine-press editions of *Apocalypse*, *The Virgin and the Gipsy*, and *Last Poems* with large simultaneous London editions, Heinemann published a selection, edited by Huxley, of Lawrence's letters, and eventually assumed almost the entire backlist. A similar arrangement, orchestrated by Curtis Brown, was reached in New York with Viking, but Frieda had no friends there, the publisher foolishly did not court her, and she disliked their bureaucratic efficiency and had a low opinion of them for years: "I know they dont think much of Lawrence and ought to sell cheese, not books."[63]

The arrangement with Heinemann was formalized after the New Year in London, where, Orioli in tow, she also began prosecuting the battle over the estate with tremendous vigor. There was little time left over for much else; Monty had married Vera Edith Ross, an aspiring painter who had been at the Slade with Barby, but if Frieda saw them the visit was brief; it would be some twenty years before she would get to know her.[64] Their first child, a son, Ian, was born the following May.

Frieda spent the remainder of the winter and early spring of 1931 at Les Aspras, visited by, among others, Serafina and her children, who arrived shortly before the *Conte Grande* sailing. It was a fiasco from the start: A trunk holding Federico's diapers and the entire family's clothing would not open, and Frieda left to meet Angelino and prepare for the departure for the United States before Serafina's visit was over, asking Crotch to look in on them every day (she was the only person besides Frieda whom they knew there). Crotch thought Angelino, whom she had never met, would soon join the family and relieve her. When he did not appear, a question provoked sly winks from Stefanino, now almost eleven, in whom Angelino had confided, and a tearful explanation from Serafina: Her husband was on his way to Taos, she said, to help "Madame Lawrence on the '*ferme*.'"[65] By trip's end the children had ruined the upholstery in the garishly decorated salon, bringing threats of a lawsuit and a fine of five thousand francs from the owner, who claimed it had been reduced to a "*poulailler*," a henhouse.[66]

6

Frieda spent much of her time at the Lobo trying to coax memories of Lawrence onto paper. It never occurred to her to write in anything but English. Though the act of composition filled her with self-consciousness—"Can't you hear him jeer at me as the 'famous author's wife'?" she wrote Mabel[67]—it also gave her a new appreciation both of the solitary nature of the enterprise and, to some degree, of the soundness of her contention to Edward Garnett, as Lawrence made the transition from *Sons and Lovers* to *The Rainbow*, that form and intellect mattered far less than writerly passion. Frieda had written English "Germanically" almost on principle for decades, and she had no intention of (and less facility for) producing a grammatically sanitized, King's English memoir that would be above intellectual reproach. She also did not want to write in the "Lawrencian" manner. Brett, assiduously composing her own memoir, confided to Frieda that it was being "dictated" by Lawrence from beyond the grave. Frieda read the manuscript, which bore the unmistakable hand of Brett. "We all write our own books, dear," she said.[68]

She had never learned to type, and to avoid the Taos gossip mill sent batches to Crotch, in whom she had freely confided the best and the worst of life with Lawrence with a candor that was not to be repeated in her book. For all Frieda's bluntness, the writing of her memoir proved an exercise in selective memory. Thousands of small omissions, euphemisms, and elisions produced a story of immense optimism, with just enough of the underbelly of the marriage for a satisfying verisimilitude. "I . . . could not help feeling it was not the same Frieda I knew," Crotch later wrote, ". . . but someone who must have been 'born again.' "[69] She decided to call the book *"Not I, but the Wind . . . ,"* from the first line of one of the poems in which Lawrence had celebrated their love and interdependence: Implicit was the notion of each having been the other's source of happiness, reification, and fulfillment, as well as the destined quality of the relationship, with all its blemishes. Occasionally she passed along pages of her manuscript for Mabel to read, but she seems to have relied primarily on Angelino, who, by the time they left the Lobo, in late November 1931, had channeled his dissatisfaction with the rough charms of the house Lawrence had built into plans to build another, larger one, impervious to pack rats, on their next trip to New Mexico. The funds that enabled them to undertake the building, as well as the next few years of traveling, came largely through Frieda's successful claim to the estate exactly a year later.

After six months in London at the Kingsley Hotel, much of it taken up by an expensive legal proceeding against George Lawrence, she entered London's Divorce, Probate and Admiralty Division of the High Court of Justice on the morning of November 3, 1932, while a divorce suit was in progress. George Lawrence was outraged by her attire and, at least according to his son's later recollection, by her refusal to extinguish the Woodbines she chain-smoked.[70] Her chances for winning the case seemed to her to diminish as the minutes ticked by, and her gaze turned to the different wigs worn by the judge, Lord Merrivale (curly) and several barristers (straight). Her confidence had been steadily eroded in recent conversations with Aldous Huxley and other friends of Lawrence's, who, on visits to her rooms at the Kingsley, had made it clear they opposed not only her claim but her forthright pursuit of it. "[T]he stupid woman," Huxley had written a friend in mid-October. ". . . Her diplomatic methods consist in calling everyone a liar, a swine and a lousy swindler, and then in the next letter being charming—then she's surprised that people don't succumb to the charm."[71]

Huxley's was one of the milder reactions, and it was backed with real affection; others viewed Frieda as little but a menace or a curiosity. "D.H.L.'s Frieda," wrote E. M. Forster, "seen last week after an interval of 15 years, still uttered the old war cries . . . but her manner was nervous, almost propititory. . . . There was something both pretentious and rotten about her, as in his pictures. . . . Very proud of having no friends, equally so of her apparatus for collecting and compelling them."[72] Beatrice Campbell, now known as Lady Glenavy (her husband, Gordon, had succeeded to a barony the year before), came to tea with Kot, who stared Frieda down as she lavished hospitality, serving large cream cakes and eating several herself. Kot's visits to the hotel had become a weekly ritual, but he still could not abide Frieda. The cream spread to her cheeks, and he was filled with disgust. "Lawrence wanted me to be happy," she said, holding back tears. "Lawrence always wanted me to be happy."[73]

Merrivale began the estate proceedings with praise for Lawrence's "distinguished" reputation and, to Frieda's surprise, "treated *me* with such respect." Called to the witness box, "I pulled all my force together . . . just went ahead, felt I could convince crocodiles that Lawrence wanted me to have his inheritance."[74] Murry testified that he and Lawrence had made wills witnessed by Mansfield and Frieda. His own, introduced into evidence, was dated November 9, 1914.

Medley's summation depicted the Lawrences' happiness and inseparability in glowing terms. ("Oh, but no! That's not true! We fought like hell!" Frieda was later said to have protested—an apocryphal story that survived decades of retelling.)[75] "He and his wife were a couple most devoted to each other all their married life," wrote the London *Times*, in an account of the proceedings attributing the lost will to the peripatetic lifestyle of the Lawrences, "*citoyens du monde.*"[76] Frieda offered five hundred pounds apiece and a couple of Lawrence's paintings to Emily and George and the same to Ada, who had gone over to her siblings' side in the case. Only George and Emily accepted the settlement; Ada, to whom she had proffered the seminude *Holy Family*, refused, and was never again reconciled to Frieda. In the Public Record Office of the Family Division of the High Court, the following, apparently a replica of the document Murry produced, is now offered as Lawrence's will, dated November 9, 1914: "I, the undersigned do hereby give and bequeath unto my wife Frieda Lawrence all those things real and personal of which I die possessed."

They returned to the ranch six months after the hearing, on May 2, 1933. Frieda began paying Angelino a salary of $100 a month (later raised to $120), a supplement to his army pension, which, as a reservist, he continued receiving in absentia. The salary apparently went to his family,[77] though it has also been suggested—there is no proof—that Frieda had in fact bought him out of the army and paid the family, much as Mabel had been paying Candelaria Luhan all those years. Frieda, who tended to live frugally, occasionally added an extra fifty dollars to Angelino's allowance, but she was just as likely to refuse requests for more money, and she retained complete control over the purse strings: They did not have a joint bank account. She invested the lion's share of proceeds from the estate in real estate, travel, and blue-chip stocks; Lawrence had begun dabbling in the stock market before he died. Among her larger holdings were shares in American Agricultural Chemical Co., General Motors, Massachusetts Guaranteed Housing, American Telephone and Telegraph, Molybdenum Corporation of America, Standard Oil, and U.S. Rubber.

They laid the stone-and-cement foundation for the new log house on the Lobo almost immediately. Angelino and a Swedish carpenter designed the modern second-story bathroom (which had running cold water but lacked a water heater), and Frieda commissioned a Colorado sculptor to fashion the likenesses of herself and Angelino that still grace the mantelpiece. In the south cornerstone they embedded, as Angelino recorded in a diary:

> a glass bottle with a list of the names of Mrs. Frieda Lawrence—Captain Angelo Ravagli and the one of the workmen with this note:
>
> "This house is wanted by Frieda Lawrence and Cpt. Angelo Ravagli in its simple style and modest apperance to reppresent unity of intent and construction that comes from the finest sentiment of friendship. . . . On the bottle we add Mrs Frieda Lawrence and Cpt. Ravagli's Photographs in uniform of the Italian Army, some coins of American, French and Germany money, plus a piece of coral and two molar of Ravagli's teeth."[78]

7

With construction under way, Frieda, holed up in the old house, put the finishing touches on "*Not I, but the Wind . . .* " Although she had struggled with it, off and on, for two years, she finally overcame both her self-consciousness and the strong feeling that it was Lawrence and not her that people wanted to hear. She did so in the form of letters, largely to her mother: Of the book's fifty thousand words, half are his.

Despite her contempt for Viking, she had decided to keep all publishing interests consolidated there; following Lawrence's example, however, she had a special edition of a thousand printed. Signed, numbered, hand bound, with a phoenix on the spine and a Knud Merrild caricature of Lawrence on the jacket, they were printed on Worthy's Dacian, a heavy, creamy stock, and published by Rydal, a Santa Fe fine press, selling for twice as much as the Viking edition. Though Frieda now retained her own agent, Alan Collins, of Curtis Brown, Angelino nominally handled most of the business matters connected with the publication. She gradually consigned most of the estate paperwork to him as well, but his interest in Lawrence, whose books he never read, was limited, and Frieda's influence showed clearly in every major decision.

"*Not I, but the Wind . . .* " was published in October 1934. The Rydal edition sold briskly, and Viking reprinted several times, the first within a month. The book generated an enormous amount of fan mail, particularly from married women who warmed to Frieda's depiction of marriage as imperfect. Alice Dax, the Nottingham suffragette with whom Lawrence had gone to bed, wrote glowingly to her of the book's fresh style and treatment of Lawrence. It was widely reviewed, with frequent, goading references to the intrigues perpetrated by Mabel and Brett's memoirs, which had preceded hers by two years and eighteen months, respectively.[79] Reviewers uniformly singled out the unusually close relationship between Lawrence and the baroness—"surely one of the rare instances of a notable correspondence between son and mother-in-law in the history of biography"[80]—and unanimously rated Frieda's as the best of the spate of Lawrence books (seventeen, according to a count by *Newsweek*, which mocked Frieda's use of English) that had been published since his death.

March 2, 1935, was the fifth anniversary of Lawrence's death. The previous summer, an unfounded rumor about the grave's never having been paid for, apparently started by a disgruntled petty official in Vence, had circulated in the European press, leading to a widely published letter from Huxley (who had in fact paid the cost of the grave in 1930). The sensationalism and untruth of the story made Frieda determined to have Lawrence returned to American shores. From a hospital bed in Albuquerque, where she was confined for more than a month by double pneumonia, she dispatched Angelino to Vence to have the body exhumed and cremated, and the ashes—he called them "hashes"[81]—returned to the Lobo.

On the evening of March 11, Angelino arrived at Crotch's home in Vence and explained to her in broken English that he had come to bring Lawrence back to the ranch. Crotch was struck by his quiet manner and sincere face, and agreed to meet him in the cemetery at daylight. She arrived with a friend, and watched with the caretaker and a *garde champêtre* as the earth was turned. A casket, lined with zinc, was gradually filled by the gravediggers with "a few spadefuls of unrecognisable matter, but among it a hairbrush appeared intact and horridly fresh looking."[82] As Crotch was leaving, Angelino rushed up and breathlessly explained that the personnel at the hotel in which he had been staying had failed to awaken him.

She received a letter a week later from Savona, which Angelino visited at least once each year:

> The ashes of Lawrence is all ready. I can take it any time. But yesterday I am going to the Vice Consulate in Genoa and I having not found the Vice Consulate, the Consulate General dont want to give me a answer, and I must wait till thursday when come back from Venetia the Vice Consul.
>
> In the meantime I have send telegram to Frieda because she intersting the American Consulate at gives me the visa for make the special and delicate mission.
>
> Barbara [Weekley] tell me know that she can do anything because the American Consulate from London he must have confirmation from Genoa.
>
> My trip it was good my family send thanks very much for your good help.[83]

Nineteen days and several official contretemps later, visa and ashes in hand (the remains had been cremated in Marseilles), Angelino sailed on the *Conte di Savoia* from Villefranche. Alfred Stieglitz helped him get through Customs in New York, and later wrote, enigmatically, that some odd fate—he never specified—had befallen the ashes. The urn—in some versions of the story it is a sealed copper box—was left behind on the Lamy platform, where Angelino was met by Frieda, fully recovered. According to one source the ashes were eaten by Bynner in Santa Fe—in a cup of chili and/or stirred into a pot of tea—then replaced with common fireplace ashes; others, notably a Baron Prosper de Haulleville, a relative of Maria Huxley, later maintained that Lawrence's ashes never departed France to begin with. The urn was left behind again in Taos, at the home of Nikolai Fechin, a renowned Russian artist and a leading figure among local émigrés. Fechin's eccentric wife, Tinka, a friend of Frieda's, kept it on the living room mantel, surrounded by icons and candles, until Frieda returned for it a week later.[84]

The Lawrence memorial, a squat white concrete building on the crest of a hill several hundred feet above Frieda and Angelino's new house, had been completed several weeks before Angelino's departure for Savona. It was a magnificent choice of site. The structure itself, however, was not exactly the resting place Frieda had envisioned in the British Museum. Though to some she favorably compared it to a temple of Isis that Lawrence had described in *The Escaped Cock* (which had been retitled *The Man Who Died* by a publisher), to others she complained of its earthbound appearance and lack of architectural distinction. "Now we have it and everybody knows about it," she would tell a visitor in 1939, likening it to a crypt, "so it is too late to do anything."[85] Perched on the peak of the pitched roof was a phoenix, fashioned by Paul Keith, a Texas oilman turned sculptor.

At dusk on September 15, four days after what would have been Lawrence's fiftieth birthday, he was laid to rest. Barby was present at the ceremony, officiated by her husband; they were spending the summer, a vacation spoiled by Barby's irritation at Angelino's flirtations with local women and her suspicion, stoked by Mabel, that he was angling for Frieda's money: During an argument one night, taking a cue from Lawrence, she apparently hurled a glass at him.[86] Frieda invited several Pueblo dancers, who performed in paint and feathers. Miriam Golden, a former Shakespearean actress living in the Taos neighborhood of Ranchitos, presided in a black lace dress, declaiming several of Lawrence's poems.[87] The Italian flag, which Angelino had raised on a pole beside the old house, snapped in a strong breeze that preceded a thunderstorm. (Angelino later added Lawrence's typewriter to the tomb's interior tableau. He had tried to use the machine and found it jammed, then "repaired" it by boiling it, which ruined the rubber keys and wood platen.)[88] The ceremony was boycotted by, among others, Mabel, who disapproved of a public memorial and felt Lawrence would instead have wished to be scattered to the winds—a wish she insisted he had expressed. Her objection was so heartfelt that she had conspired with Brett, who shared her reservations (the "Mausoleum look[s] like a station toilet," Brett complained to Una Jeffers[89]), to help steal the ashes. Some say they succeeded, and that Frieda was forced to reclaim them. Hoping to make Lawrence inviolable, she and Angelino reportedly mixed them into a lime-and-water solution that partially comprised a concrete altar within the building; the altar was decorated in large, sweeping letters with Lawrence's initials. Others insist that the ashes—actually ashes and pieces of bone—went behind a huge, removable cinderblock sealed with mortar. Brett watched the proceedings from behind a distant tree. A dancing party followed, to the music of a local Mexican orchestra hired by Frieda, and a bonfire was lit. The guests—some were strangers who had arrived in response to an open notice placed by Frieda in a Santa Fe paper—feasted on hot dogs and homemade red wine, poured from a spigoted barrel kept in the larder.

The story of the ashes was widely publicized some fifty years later after the airing of a freely fictionalized adaptation of the events on the popular television show "Ripley's Believe It or Not," hosted by actor Jack Palance; the "Lawrence shrine," as it quickly became known, was visited by a constant stream of people from around the world, who braved the steep incline and several cattle guards to sign a guest register and view cremation documents, issued in Marseilles, which Frieda had framed and mounted on the wall to the left of the altar.

Frieda maintained that the ashes were in the cement, and her recitation of the tale of how they got there was received with appreciation and incredulity at a round of parties in Cambridge and Boston the following year. Invited to lecture on Lawrence at Harvard in connection with an exhibition of his manuscripts, she and Angelino were staying at the Concord home of Harry K. Wells, an aspiring Lawrence biographer, and his wife, Jenny. They were easygoing guests, Angelino making gnocchi and bread after one failed attempt (the dough, which he left on the radiator to rise before dawn, swelled to six times its size and stuck to the wall when the heat came on). The Wellses, in their twenties, had amassed a Lawrenciana trove the year before; among other material it included 160 letters Orioli had sold them for a thousand dollars (he had freely removed them from a trunk Frieda had left in his safekeeping) and letters from Lawrence to Kot and Bertrand Russell. Frieda loved their unqualified enthusiasm for Lawrence, and relied on Jenny for dress protocol: Told she would need at least one formal gown at Harvard, she ordered several yards of gold lamé from the Montgomery Ward catalog, cut a hole for the neck, and trimmed the hem with brown velvet, an outfit that, worn with sneakers and an elaborate turquoise necklace, got a lot of use. At a "cosmopolitan week end" given by the poet Merrill Moore, she described the theft of the ashes to Louis Untermeyer, whom she and Lawrence had met in London in 1926. "It weighs over a ton," she said of the altar. "A dozen men could not lift it."[90]

20

From Hollywood to Laguna Vista

I

In Hollywood for a break from the cold and snowdrifts on the Lobo in March 1936, Frieda found a man she trusted to broker Lawrence's manuscripts. It was a choice only she could have made: Jacob Israel Zeitlin, a Texas poet, journalist, and former hobo and bakery supply salesman who ran a bookstore on West Sixth Street in Los Angeles. She was introduced to Zeitlin by a new friend, Galka Scheyer, a German émigré and American agent for the painters known as "*die blaue Vier*"—Wassily Kandinsky, Paul Klee, Alexei Jawlensky, and Lyonel Feininger. The rising tide of German anti-Semitism was making Frieda nervous about Else and Alfred Weber in Heidelberg: Though Alfred was not Jewish, many, if not most, in their circle were, and the "taint" of his work and of Else's former marriage to the deceased Edgar Jaffe apparently, so Frieda seems to have thought, made them both suspect. (Else's view of Hitler during this period is not known; a Hitler postcard from her to Frieda survives, whose preprinted greeting, from "Our Führer," can be read as ironic or—seemingly less likely, given Else's collaboration with Alfred on *Kulturgeschichte als*

Kultursoziologie—rapt.)[1] Frieda was determined to pay their passage to the United States by selling *The Rainbow*, which bore the dedication to her sister.

Zeitlin could hardly believe his good luck, the first in nine years. The depression, a string of bad business decisions, and a yearlong bout with tuberculosis had kept him insolvent through much of the late twenties and early thirties. The store, which specialized in rare and out-of-print books and first editions, was his third location. One had been several doors down, in a building so narrow its number was followed by "½," the other the foyer of a larger bookstore, for which he had had to invent a mailing address. He was an extremely likable man with exalted standards, little or no capital, laconic good manners, and an unaffected love of literature that continued to draw regular customers. Most were students, however, looking for used books; during frequent dry periods he and his wife, Jean, lived largely on her salary. She worked for Frank J. Hogan, an attorney who had successfully defended the California oilman Edward L. Doheny in the Teapot Dome scandal against bribery charges brought by the government. Zeitlin had met Doheny in 1925, as the prosecution was winding down; new to California, he had cut Doheny's lawn and watered his flowers, and the job had paid unexpected dividends—Doheny had a passion for Shakespeare folio editions. He introduced Zeitlin to like-minded friends, among them Abe Rosenbach, the Philadelphian to whom Frieda had once quoted a price of £25,000 for Lawrence's manuscripts, but Doheny remained only one of Zeitlin's two high-rolling customers; the other was Elmer Belt, a neighboring physician with a thriving urology practice.[2]

A man's man, Zeitlin did not expect much of Frieda herself. She surprised him by launching into a conversation about wrestling. Though she had initially felt a revulsion for the sport, it had become one of her great passions; years later, when she and Angelino bought a TV, she liked watching "[t]he young handsome ones, so quick and dancing," as she wrote Bynner, "and the old tough ones too."[3] Talk of wrestling continued over lunch the next time they met. Zeitlin brought his "secretary," Lawrence Clark Powell, a perennial student and future UCLA dean with a doctorate in literature from the University of Dijon, earned for a thesis on Robinson Jeffers. Frieda kept the two men and Scheyer entertained for four hours with stories of the

Jefferses, Mabel, Mansfield, Murry, and, of course, Lawrence, all the while savoring Zeitlin's unhurried approach and restraint: Nothing was said about terms until Scheyer interposed to ask whether Jake, as everyone called Zeitlin, was definitely interested. "Does a cat like cream?" he said—exactly the kind of repartee Frieda loved.[4] A nine-month, renewable letter of agreement was drafted, authorizing him as sole agent for *The Rainbow*, which Frieda priced at $7,500, offering a commission of 15 percent. A separate clause extended authorization to the entire oeuvre. They agreed to meet in three days for Japanese food and good seats at that evening's matches.

Scheyer, from a family with a canning factory in Braunschweig, was a woman whose style was exactly the kind to win Frieda's trust, if only because she was something of a kindred spirit. She had striking dyed-red hair and a pronounced accent, tempered by the *Schlawiner* jargon; like Frieda, she had gravitated to Schwabing between 1907 and 1912, and in 1927 had left Germany for Los Angeles, arriving by way of several years in New York and San Francisco. Her collection of contemporary art was one of the most important in the United States; besides those of *die blaue Vier*, it included works by Oskar Kokoschka, Picasso, and Diego Rivera, later a major bequest to the Pasadena Art Institute.[5] Frieda enjoyed fingering the priceless Japanese textiles Scheyer owned, and depended on her for practical help in business: Early in February, not long after they had met, Scheyer had arranged for an exhibition at the prominent Los Angeles gallery Stendhal of Lawrence's paintings, which had been in Serafina Ravagli's care since leaving Crotch's tearoom. She also found studio space for Angelino, who had decided to take up painting: His first two works were under way, the first a strange rendering of a pub in Tredozio, the second an Arizona mining town they had passed through in the La Salle on their way to Hollywood. They were miserable failures, though his flair for flat detail and his naive, colorful palette, somewhere between those of Lawrence and Grandma Moses, were later put to better use in ceramics, for which he had some talent.

References to Angelino as a "gigolo," "gold digger," "fanny pincher," or "Frieda's chauffeur" were soon making the rounds in Hollywood, usually tempered by an appreciation of the good-natured practicality with which he managed her everyday affairs.[6] He could hardly be faulted for indifference to Frieda, though the attention he paid her was increasingly less tender than familial. Frieda, who—as she was later to write—desired little more than health and a man "with courage" whom "she could believe in,"[7] gradually came to accept Angelino's vigilance in attending to the machinery of their lives as a substitute for the romance of their early years. For Angelino the role, essentially that of a well-trusted factotum, brought with it a share of humiliations, though pride—and a mistrust of others' claims on Frieda's time, attention, and fortune, which became more acute as the years went by—often brought out his imperious side.

Despite night classes in English three times a week at a local high school, he was self-conscious about his lack of language, and sat in silence during Frieda's conversations with such friends as the screenwriter Dudley Nichols, whom he simply could not follow. Nichols's speech was sprinkled with abstractions and aphorisms from Montaigne and Plutarch's *Lives*, editions of which he pressed on Frieda. She treated him like a son, praising his integrity and urging him not to work too hard; since winning an Academy Award the previous year for John Ford's *The Informer*, he had been deluged with offers he felt he could not turn down. Other friends, like the dress designer Adrian, Mabel's couturier since her abandonment of Southwest fashion the previous year, tolerated Angelino for Frieda's sake only, as did Mabel herself, whose own Hollywood circle—she spent the winter in Carmel, where the Jefferses lived—now included Thornton Wilder, Greta Garbo, and Leopold Stokowski. Mabel had become somewhat intolerant of all but the moneyed, titled, and famous, or the writers, like Jean Toomer, who still accepted her hospitality. She went out of her way to let Angelino know he was not welcome at her parties.

He began going to dance halls, a different young woman on his arm each night, Zeitlin usually providing the introductions. He found some of his dates not warmhearted enough—"could," as he later wrote Zeitlin—but also "very beautiful,"[8] and he confided to most of them that it was a "contract" or "agreement" with Frieda that had brought him to the United States, words with which he had placated his wife; now they were expressions of independence from Frieda, and the beginning of what was to become rather massive infidelity. To others the words were used defiantly, bitterly, or with wounded pride, often in letters composed seemingly only by way of practicing his English, which he had been advised to do as frequently as possible in night school. The addressees extended to Frieda's daughters. Stories of the past summer's fights with Barby were making the rounds of the family, and he tried to present his side to Elsa. "Last summer it was not so happy realy. . . . But now the past is past and the best is to not to speak of it any more."[9] Elsa was not disposed to sympathy: *The Virgin and the Gipsy* had infuriated the entire Weekley family, who clearly recognized both themselves and Barby's influence: "Your name is mud, my girl," Elsa had said to her after reading the book.[10]

Having started her own family—her first child, a son, Geoffrey, was born in the spring of 1933—Elsa no longer wanted much to do with Frieda's ménage; letters were rare, and she never visited the United States. When Angelino got no reply, his attempt at damage control continued in a letter to Else's son Friedel Jaffe:

> I think is not necessary telling to you that the harmony with us—Barby and Stuart it was not so good . . . because they would have told you every detail about it. Perhaps it was my fault, but I dont believe it because I was here before them and naturally I cant give to any body the permission to inquiry and to calumniate me—
>
> Until a contrary proof I am a man in all extension of the word—and not a marionette to do what every people like—I do what I want according to Friedas agreement—and nothing else—[11]

Frieda usually explained Angelino's wanderings as a twist of fate, inevitable and beyond her control, and she made a virtue of their "companionability," a word that recurs unfailingly in interviews with their friends. Any bitterness she might have felt was never expressed; perhaps she truthfully felt none. Angelino's presence *had* become very convenient to her, particularly on the Lobo; the upkeep of the ranch, where fields of alfalfa were planted and horses, a small flock of sheep, and a Jersey cow grazed, was well beyond her capacity, as were raising and slaughtering lambs and pigs; he, for his part, infinitely preferred life with her to a return to Savona and the army. To one neighbor he seemed to be "really taking care of Frieda with full knowledge of what his reward was. . . . She accepted that, lived with it, and was not ashamed of loving him."[12] His reward, as she made clear to him, was to be a substantial share of the estate. As long as his interest in other women was fleeting, she gave him free rein "to have his flings,"[13] insisting that, at fifty-seven, she was old and preferred to read at night. "The California women are the most attractive women in the world," she maintained, and she made no effort to compete. Unlike Mabel's Adrian creations, her wardrobe remained homemade and out of date. "If I try to be stylish," she wrote Bynner, "it is pitiful only."[14]

2

Hoping for a preemptive offer on *The Rainbow*, Zeitlin sent Hogan a lofty, rather ineffectual sales pitch, explaining the sentimental value of the manuscript to Frieda and Else. Hogan was not interested, however, and when the manuscript proved otherwise unsalable for the designated price, Zeitlin arranged for an exhibition at Stanford University to help attract buyers. Frieda and Angelino returned to the ranch, Lawrence's paintings tied to the roof of the La Salle after the closing of the Stendhal show. Not a single canvas had been sold. "I dont think about anything except the lambs and pintos and pigs and radishes and alfalfa," Frieda wrote Zeitlin, "and Angelino is building a beautiful room for L's pictures."[15]

Else and Alfred, it turned out, had no intention of resettling their family in New Mexico. Frieda persuaded her sister—free, it seems, to travel, though the Nazis did not permit everyone to do so—to visit Taos alone in October 1937, a trip probably financed by proceeds from *Nur der Wind*, the German edition of her memoir. The book was published in Berlin in a very free translation by Else, who eliminated the names of several prominent friends of the Lawrences as well as the more spontaneous asides—on the pointless nature of war, for example, and Frieda's distaste for the military. The changes were made largely to appease Nazi censors, but Else also seized the opportunity to improve her sister's syntax, paragraph structure, and overall organization.[16] Apart from helping to assure Frieda that she would be safe in Heidelberg, her visit to Taos was not much of a success: like almost everyone from Frieda's former life, she had little use for Angelino. Half a century later, Taoseños still spoke of her penchant for correcting their pronunciation of English, which she spoke flawlessly, with hardly a trace of a German accent.[17]

Sale of *The Rainbow* was largely forgotten. When inquiries did trickle in, Frieda was less interested in the size of the offers than in whether a potential buyer was a "nice person"; selling manuscripts to strangers simply for profit disturbed her, at least in principle: "If I were rich, then I would have a huge fire of all his Mss, that's what he would have liked, you know he hated the personal touch. But I daresay he wanted me to have the money."[18] She also believed, correctly, that the value of the collection was rising, and that ultimately it would benefit her to retain and keep together the most highly prized manuscripts.

She had kept drafts of some minor works for herself and enjoyed showing them to scholars, students, and visiting writers, who arrived at the Lobo by the carload, often meeting such Hollywood celebrities as Lillian Gish on the way down. On occasion people she admired or whose artistry she appreciated—Charlie Chaplin was one—were surprised to receive manuscripts as gifts, forwarded by Zeitlin with a polite note. Those she disliked found prickly letters in their mailboxes; among them was William York Tindall, author of *D. H. Lawrence & Susan His Cow*, a scathing, semi-humorous condemnation of Lawrence's lack of originality, based largely on letters from Frieda about Lawrence's source material. Frieda especially detested his analysis of *Women in Love*:

> It made me laugh when you cannot explain by "fashion or reason" that Ursula wears red or green stockings. Can't you imagine that she did it for fun and that red stockings might look attractive in the snow?
>
> Was not the purpose of your book to show that Lawrence was a fool and you much too smart to swallow him? . . . I am old and alone now but the glow of his world makes one feel rich, richer than ever your wife will be with all your cleverness.[19]

Tindall later retracted some of his claims and championed Lawrence.

Frieda was less successful with others: A friend of Murry named Edward Gilbert, a Cambridge scholar with a love of mysticism, church history, and antiquated verb forms ("shew"), reserved his highest praise for Lydia Lawrence, "the woman I most respected and admired"; his first letter to Frieda, probably sent with Murry's blessing, was filled with philosophic circumlocution, references to Lawrence's "pagan" creed, leading questions about their love life, and several pious asides about his own wife.[20] Frieda had read too many such letters from litterateurs projecting erotic fantasy onto her, among them some of

Murry's. In her first reply she managed both to conceal her impatience and deflect his prurience:

> Since Lawrence died, all these donkey's years already, he has grown and grown for me. . . . To me his relationship, his bond with everything in creation was so amazing, no preconceived ideas, just a meeting between him and a creature, a tree, a cloud, anything. I called it love, but it was something else—*Bejahung* in German, "saying yes." . . . I believe my chief merit, as I see it, was that to me not too much mattered, except that he should come off, do what he wanted and had to do.
>
> I think a real relationship only begins where the all too personal leaves off, and we fought like nothing on earth ever fought, being both possessive and jealous.
>
> Wives are not respectful, but he was so real to me. I don't think "respect" matters to women. I didn't apply "principles" to him . . .
>
> Murry and he had no "love affair." But Lawrence did not disbelieve in homosexuality.
>
> If you could make posterity see him as he was, that would be great. Your wife sounds a lovely person.[21]

Gilbert persisted, taking another tack: "An order existed wherein Lawrence was predominantly valued *as a man*," but "humanly and theoretically" his life had been a "failure." Frieda had had enough, and sent an angry rejoinder, from which Gilbert could only surmise that she had failed to comprehend the intricacies of his argument. The correspondence took some strange turns, then got nasty; his final reward was the full force of Frieda's fury—exactly what Lawrence had endured, he concluded hopefully: "I got a good idea of what the famous quarrels were like, from Lawrence's point of view."[22] Frieda got rid of the bad taste the correspondence left in an essay, one of several completed in her lifetime and never published, entitled "D.H. Lawrence, the Failure," in which she concluded, essentially, that if Lawrence's life amounted to nothing, she would eat her hat.[23]

3

Aldous Huxley, ending a U.S. lecture tour, spent the summer of 1937 at the ranch with Maria and their teenage son, Matthew. Their friendship, with its reminders of the past, meant a lot to Frieda, and she lavished hospitality. Still, the Huxleys were initially put off by the lack of amenities and fresh produce. Though Aldous's 1932 bestseller *Brave New World* was set in New Mexico, much of the material had come from books of ethnography borrowed from the Smithsonian Institution,[24] and they were unprepared for the Lobo's homespun flavor. Maria, whose vegetarian tastes bordered on the fanatical, was repulsed by the offer of raw bacon for breakfast: Angelino cured his own—inexpertly, according to neighbors who received gifts of it, undepilated.[25] He "is so Italian," Maria wrote a friend in London, Baron Edward Sackville-West, "that of course we have to humour him a bit." Frieda began making them pumpkin-blossom omelets instead.

Maria was also unnerved by the vats of cow's milk in various stages of curdling on the kitchen table—Frieda churned her own butter and made sour cream and yogurt—and brought along a pair of rubber gloves to do the washing when they were invited for dinner: Among the night's earthenware and china in the washing tin was the vessel from which Frieda's pet pig, who wandered the kitchen, ate:

> there are . . . the pig-bowl and the cat-bowl and the dog-bowl; many things to horrify me and shock me; yet [Frieda] is essentially clean if you can imagine that; perhaps because she is a blonde. . . . Meanwhile there she sits, talking of Montaigne or Buddha or Mabel Dodge and making us all feel happy and at home. . . . My compromise is to keep my toes nicely painted because my finger-nails have had to go with so many other things.[26]

Aldous, a staunch pacifist, had fled England, discouraged by his failure to help stem the tide of World War II. Short of cash, he had decided to try his luck as a screenwriter, spurred by letters from fellow exiles writing for the movies and a visit from Zeitlin, whom Huxley, on Frieda's advice, hired to sell film rights to his novels. As August approached he raced to finish *Ends and Means*, a collection of antiwar essays, often working straight through the night without lighting even an oil lamp; his eyesight had been severely defective since an episode in his adolescence of sudden near-blindness, and the darkness made little or no difference to him.

Lawrence's manuscripts moved on from Stanford to the exhibition at Harvard, which had expressed tentative interest in buying them. Frieda asked $25,000, a fifth of what she had quoted Rosenbach, and considered their counteroffer of $10,000 to be "stingy."[27] The manuscripts were transferred to the Los Angeles Public Library late in 1937, by which time Zeitlin had managed to get out a sales catalog, with money from Dr. Belt, the urologist. Notably missing from its pages, however, were *Sons and Lovers* and *Lady Chatterley's Lover*, the most requested Lawrence manuscripts. Getting hold of *Sons and Lovers* proved impossible: Mabel had bartered the manuscript when a close friend—in some versions of the story it is she herself—was presented with a treatment bill from Brill that the friend or Mabel could not afford to pay.[28] (The manuscript remained in the Brill family until 1963, when the University of California bought it for $17,000.) The three *Lady Chatterley* manuscripts were still with Orioli in Florence. Frieda had written him the previous winter, offering a percentage of their sale by way of repaying him for having acted as a way station for the property. Orioli, who clearly felt that he deserved to be compensated more handsomely, ignored the letter. Over the summer Frieda had dispatched Marianne von Eckardt, Else's daughter, now married and living in Italy, to Florence with a letter of authorization; Orioli informed von Eckardt that he would not entrust them to her and that at least one of the manuscripts was rightfully his. His freedom in selling Lawrence's letters to the Wellses had already irritated Frieda, and his refusal to cooperate with von Eckardt, whom she had informally designated her "agent," provoked Frieda to a rare outburst of anger at her old friend.

Angelino wrote to his wife's stepfather, Stefano Manara, an elderly lawyer in practice with a Florentine firm, asking if they had any legal recourse. Manara and a colleague explained that they could sue Orioli for embezzlement, but Frieda, convinced that he would buckle under less pressure, suggested they simply arrive at his doorstep and ask for the manuscripts back. They showed up one morning in October, so early that they probably awakened Orioli, and served him with a power of attorney; Orioli conceded on a return visit several hours later. MANUSCRIPTS RECOVERED, Manara wired Frieda.[29] Angelino picked them up on his annual visit to Savona. It was to be one of his longest, about five months, lasting through the spring of 1938.

4

Frieda spent much of his absence with friends in Albuquerque, working on a second book, conceived during the recuperation from pneumonia in 1935. Encouraged by the warm reception to the memoir form of *"Not I, but the Wind . . ."*—several publishers, among them Viking, Macmillan, and Putnam, had asked for more autobiographical material—she organized her thoughts around a rather unsuccessful six-week trip to South America four years before, a visit to a sister and brother of Angelino's who lived in a Buenos Aires slum. The picaresque form the manuscript eventually took was prefigured by the days before the journey, spent trying to contain a legal fiasco brought on by Angelino's having persuaded Frieda to lend a thousand dollars to a fellow Italian expatriate, Nick Luciani, who speculated in California grapes. The grapes were destroyed in a truck accident, Frieda sued to get her money back, Luciani counter-sued (among the charges was Frieda's putative theft of an additional thousand dollars), and she and Angelino were briefly arrested.

First drafts of the manuscript consisted largely of unadulterated notes, taken as she and Angelino (he fleeing a warrant for a second arrest) drove through Colorado to New Orleans before boarding the ship to Buenos Aires. "On the walls are 'texts,'" she wrote of a café: "'If your wife can't cook don't abuse her—eat here and keep her for a pet.'"[30] Such ramblings eventually were merged with reminiscences of Metz, Sablon, Otto Gross, Weekley, Lawrence, and her parents and friends, for whom she used pseudonyms. The working title, "What's the Big Idea," was changed to "And the Fullness Thereof," from the first verse of Psalm 24: "The earth is the Lord's, and the fullness thereof; the world, and they that dwell therein." The manuscript grew to a hundred pages (four devoted to Luciani, or "B—"), and consumed her mornings and afternoons; in the evenings she socialized with friends, among them the writers Paul Horgan and Erna Fergusson. Before going to sleep, she worked on long weekly letters to Angelino, whom she addressed as "one" or "No. 1!": They moved artlessly from endearments, the day's events, and questions about his family to news of Zeitlin's first two Lawrence customers—a British collector and T. E. "Ed" Hanley, an oil and brickmaking baron and notorious cheapskate whose manuscripts, first editions, and Impressionist paintings, all bought on an idiosyncratic installment plan, were stored unceremoniously in a drafty Victorian house in Bradford, Pennsylvania.[31] Serafina often added notes and family snapshots to Angelino's replies.

With the first installments from Hanley, Frieda went on a check-writing spree over Christmas. The recipients included neighbors and friends (some also received bottles of whiskey, decorated with cotton-bearded Santas); two checks, each in the amount of fifty dollars, were sent to a sister of Angelino's who had fallen ill in Tredozio. Angelino—for whom Frieda was also financing a months-long apprenticeship with a Savona ceramist, a trade she hoped he might parlay into a small business back in Taos that would help make him self-sufficient—chided her spendthrift habits, and asked for a raise:

> You think I ought to give you more money. If I were rich, yes, but I am not and I don't think it is reasonable. I know there is only the 120 every month, but think of the money we spend. Going to South America and Boston and Hollywood. We spend quite a lot of money, but you don't think of that. Now I pay you for five months when you are away *and* the journey *and* some money for this time. Many times you work hard, but also many times you just paint and *I* do all the work. You never think of money, except when you think of Italy. But I hope that now that you are in Italy you realise what a good life you have in America. I *don't* want you to be grateful, but just to know that you have a better and freer life than most men. So there![32]

In fact, she was marshaling her money with an eye to Angelino's interests: In February she bought a second house, in the neighboring village of El Prado, with two outbuildings, one designated a guest house, the other large enough to hold a kiln, transported for Angelino from Denver. The months in Albuquerque, where daily life was appreciably easier than at the ranch, prompted the decision; she called the house Los Pinos. Previously owned by a Baron von Maltzahn, an Austrian and, some say, a raging Nazi,[33] it was surrounded by three hundred acres of alfalfa, timothy hay, and sagebrush, and extended toward the western boundary of the Pueblo, from which drumming and singing were audible through the hayfields; on occasion, Frieda "saw a flying saucer above the house."[34] To the east and southeast was Taos. "Maltzahn has left for Austria. . . . I fear that instead of having done him a good turn by buying his place I may have done him a bad one," Frieda, who had visited Santa Fe the previous summer with von Maltzahn and the Huxleys, wrote Bynner. "I would'nt put my head in the Nazinooze [Nazi noose]."[35] They had all been subjected to a torrent of the baron's racial hatreds, and Frieda was relieved to see him go.

Angelino arrived in May—via Santa Fe, where he deposited the three *Lady Chatterley* manuscripts in Bynner's safe—to find the lion's share of the furnishing already completed and the immediate property cleared of the semi-domesticated animals von Maltzahn had kept, among them an owl and a large pack of dogs. Trips to the Montaner Dance Hall, Mike's Night Club, and La Fonda, a hotel in Taos Plaza, could now be made conveniently every night; Saki Karavas, the son of the hotel's Greek owners, an engaging, handsome globetrotter and self-styled "playboy," became Angelino's best friend, one of the few people in Taos who appreciated him on his own merits.[36] Ensconced in the lower ranch, as the property became known to distinguish it from Kiowa, Angelino was soon making buttons, fish platters, and crockery sets, initialed AR with a flourish. Young women with an interest in learning to spin pots made their way to him: Many were newcomers to town, greeted by Angelino as they stepped off the Greyhound bus at the south end of Taos.

The lower ranch was also an ideal rental property; Charles Du Tant, a book collector and publisher of the *Taos Star*, one of the few rivals to the *Taos Valley News and El Crepusculo*, now shortened to *El Crepusculo* and edited by Spud Johnson, spent the summer of 1939 there with his wife while Frieda and Angelino moved back to Kiowa, a pattern they would keep to for the next decade and a half. Their neighbors, J. J. and Juanita Montoya, acted as caretakers when the property was empty. The spring cleaning of the ranch included ousting the pack rats, which had survived the cement foundation Angelino had poured, and it was one of the few tasks Frieda helped Juanita with. She spent the rest in play with the Montoyas' daughter, Lillian, for whom she deconstructed outgrown Bavarian blouses for an elaborate wardrobe of doll clothes.

Her affection for and dependence on the Montoyas posed a considerable threat to Angelino, who, as in the first weeks at Kiowa seven years before, asserted his authority with commands more appropriate to the battlefield than "the rim," as Taoseños call the mesa of which El

Prado forms a part. J. J., who had built a dining room table and custom-made wooden beds for the separate rooms Frieda and Angelino now kept, came in for his full share of Angelino's resentment; Angelino had instructed Frieda to buy a set of iron bedsteads, similar to the ones he had gradually replaced their Kiowa set with, but, as she had explained in a letter to Savona, "I don't like those ugly beds."[37] Lillian, to whom Angelino believed Frieda might impulsively leave a large inheritance, learned to run home across the fields at the first sound of the La Salle's engine, signaling Angelino's approach. "He shielded Frieda from everyone," she recalled three and a half decades later. "I was just a child and not interested in her will."[38] J. J., born to one of Taos's more eminent families, was not so easily dismissed or talked down to: "I told him not to talk to me the way he'd been doing," and Angelino's gruffness eventually abated, though he did try stinting on wages. Frieda, who had delegated the job of paying their employees to him, got wind of it: "That's *my* money!" she said to him, within earshot of J. J., and the "mistake" was never repeated.[39] Over time Angelino did his best to make friendship with J. J. seem casual and effortless, at least during the twice-annual transfer of "chattels," as Frieda called their household belongings. The animals were transported, one by one, in the back seat of the La Salle.

The guest houses at Kiowa, in addition to housing writers, gradually became a revolving door for Frieda's friends: Georgia O'Keeffe; Millicent Rogers, a Standard Oil heiress, jeweler, *Vogue* model, and Taos patroness; and the painter Rebecca James, secretary of the town's only museum, the Harwood Foundation, spent long weekends.[40] The friendship with Rogers slowly supplanted Frieda's with Mabel; Rogers eventually also usurped Mabel's role as the town's preeminent hostess and, some say, conducted an affair with Tony Luhan, as did O'Keeffe.[41] O'Keeffe, who collected erotica, loved the display of Lawrence's paintings, which filled the walls of the room Angelino had built for the purpose; with Frieda and Zeitlin's help, she added to a valuable collection of Lawrence first editions started by Stieglitz. "I can remember very clearly the first time I ever saw her," she recalled of Frieda, "standing in a doorway, with her hair all frizzed out, wearing a cheap red calico dress that looked as though she'd just wiped out the frying pan with it. She was not thin, and not young, but there was something radiant and wonderful about her."[42] O'Keeffe once lay under Frieda's favorite pine for several days; the result was *The Lawrence Tree*, one of her most anomalous and successful works.

Frieda decorated the upper ranch houses in the style of the Bavarian summer houses she and Lawrence had borrowed during their courtship, though Angelino's influence was unmistakable: Arrayed on kitchen shelves were plates recycled from red-clay tiles that had once lined a short-lived swimming pool, ruined when one of their horses fell in. Small-scale tables and chairs had been cut to fit by the Swedish carpenter who had helped with the log house's construction, and framed embroidery and artifacts from Bynner's travels through China adorned the walls. In contrast to such homes as Rogers's, a vast adobe with sweeping bay windows, where dinner parties were opulent, imported, and, one memorable Thanksgiving, served by black butlers transported from Virginia for the night,[43] Frieda's tastes were understated and egalitarian—aggressively and, some felt, self-consciously so. Hot dogs and pots of chili preceded hand-cranked ice cream, and artists rubbed elbows with the titled and high-ranking—among them Baron Phillipe de Rothschild, Count (and *Corriere della Sera* correspondent) and Countess Guido di Piovine of Milan, and the future German ambassador Alexander Böker—and millionaires. "I had a lovely man here," Frieda wrote Bynner, ". . . Carl Weeks, he is 'Armand' cosmetics, has made millions and given a milliondollar place to Des Moines. He gave us some smoked trout and made a saladdresing and was a real American interested in art and trout and cocktails, just everything."[44]

More often her friends were largely unknown outside northern New Mexico: the Santa Fe writer Raymond Otis; Willard Hougland, a Harwood Foundation board member whom she briefly engaged as agent; Ruth Fish, active in the Taos Chamber of Commerce; Ruth Swayne, a businesswoman who ran a dude ranch; Eve Young-Hunter, the wife of the prominent local artist John Young-Hunter; Mabel Degen, a painter; Gisella Loeffler, a Viennese-born folk artist; Cady Wells, a painter and photographer; Eleanora Kissel, Velma Shultis, Jo Cameron. They were often treated by Frieda to lunch at La Doña Luz, a Taos restaurant with a huge cellar of Alsatian wines.[45]

Monty came in July 1939 and spent more than a month. The only one of her children to have matured entirely without her supervision, he impressed her with his effortless manner with her friends. His second child, Julia, four, brought to four the number of Frieda's British grandchildren, none of whom she had met: Barby had given birth to her only child, Ursula, two years before. Her conversations with Monty were largely about them, literature, estate business, and England's imminent entry into the war, and he told her of her condemnation by the Weekley family as he had grown up. When the time for his departure approached, Frieda presented him with a silver cigarette case inscribed in her handwriting, a gift he treasured, according to a companion, long after he had quit smoking.[46] It was the first dispassionate view he had had of his mother, and for the rest of his life he spoke of her in fond, semi-historical terms; criticism was impersonal, grounded in the context of turn-of-the-century mores or such abstractions as class and personality predisposition:

> It must be admitted, in the atmosphere of those days, that Frieda was, as ever, a cake eater and haver. . . . whatever you say about the rights and wrongs of the thing, that always looms large at any stage. . . . She wanted everything and didn't see why she shouldn't get it. No difficulty about it at all.
>
> . . . [She] absolutely reject[ed] any kind of mental discipline. That was very much brought home to me when . . . I met her sister Elsa . . . again, and the contrast was fantastic. Here was a sort of Oxford Museum official, and Aunt *Ilsa*, and we were so much on all fours as I can't describe it. The very first time we met, the contrast with Frieda was overwhelming. Her English was extraordinary. She spoke it with a much better accent then, living in Germany, than Frieda ever acquired. Most curious. But the main thing was the immediate rapport. We'd both been brought up in the same nursery.[47]

He was forced to take a leave of absence from the Victoria and Albert for wartime service in the Ministry of Supply shortly after his return to London. Frieda wrote him on August 22:

> If you have any influence work for the simplification of things. These governments have become too ponderous and choked. I believe a great deal of the unholy success of Hitler and Mussolini lay in their simplifying things. You can also learn from the devil.

> A young Viennese came to see me who had been in a concentration camp for nine months, horrible, just horrible. Young boys, 17 and 18, stormtroopers trained to beat men of 60 with whips. What a crime. I feel like turning into one of those awful propaganda women to help save what can be saved of decency in the world.[48]

Ten days later Germany invaded Poland. For the next five years Frieda became known to the Weekley grandchildren by her daughters' old name for her, Mrs. L., the "strange semi-American being," as her grandson Ian later recalled, "from whom we received regular and very welcome food parcels" and Indian headdresses.[49]

W. H. Auden arrived with his lover, Chester Kallman, a day or two after Monty's departure: Word of Frieda's generosity with her property had spread to New York, and Auden, then sharing an apartment with Christopher Isherwood, had written ahead, receiving directions to Los Pinos and a request to confirm his arrival in New Mexico by way of reply. The latter was ignored or forgotten when Auden was offered another, larger house. They had crossed the country by Greyhound and were picked up at the Taos station by Frieda's friend Rudolph Kieve, an aspiring novelist and chief psychiatrist at the state insane asylum in Las Vegas, New Mexico, some sixty miles away. He drove them to the promised house, which was in ruins, home to only a family of hens. They continued on to El Prado, but Frieda, assuming that Auden was not coming, had rented the lower ranch to two New York painters, Margaret Lefranc and Annette Stevens. A shouting match with the two women was followed by a conciliatory dinner, and the next day Kieve drove Auden and Kallman to the Lobo and helped finesse an invitation to remain in one of the guest houses for a month. The first stop, before settling in, was a brief visit to Lawrence's grave: The "chapel . . . is rather creepy," Auden wrote a friend. "Cars of women pilgrims go up every day to stand reverently there and wonder what it would have been like to sleep with him."[50] They both liked Frieda enormously—"Marvelous woman"[51]—and appreciated her laissez-faire hospitality: Once installed they took advantage of her huge lunches, served at one. Kallman, whose health was poor, thrived despite a nosebleed, a common reaction to the altitude.

The mountain reaches also shocked Tennessee Williams's system: Arriving in Auden and Kallman's wake, he suffered appendicitis en route to Taos from Santa Fe, was hospitalized, and later wrote a heavily embroidered account of his release and journey to the Lobo. He put Frieda, who still had not learned to drive, at the wheel of the La Salle:

> We . . . stopped at a cantina along the road and purchased a big jug of wine and we drank and laughed as we went up the mountain and then all at once I found myself breathless. "Please stop the car, I can't breathe!" I got out. . . . We commenced a wild race down. It was like something out of a chase scene in the movies. Frieda drove that car like a firetruck.[52]

Ten years later Frieda would record that "a Leonard Bernstein came, a musician"; thirty years old, he wanted a quiet place in which to finish his symphony *The Age of Anxiety*.[53] The cross-country drive, undertaken with his teenage brother, Burton, and Stephen Spender, whom Bernstein had met at Tanglewood, was memorable for the number of blowouts their convertible sustained. Spender stayed in El Prado and Bernstein went to Kiowa, where Frieda had an old upright piano of uncertain origin on which she liked to play "Onward, Christian Soldiers" for visitors as they ascended the incline to Lawrence's grave.[54] It was hopelessly out of tune—perhaps one reason why Bernstein left within a week.

5

The constant stream of visitors aroused the jealousy of Rachel Hawk's brother Harold, a failed writer whose house, on the property below Kiowa, had to be passed on the ascent. Unlike the rest of his family, he disliked Frieda, despite a show of friendship: He had brought her mail, which included letters from Else and friends in Germany, during the previous winter in Albuquerque. Well educated and living on a modest pension, he apparently also worked as an informer for the Federal Bureau of Investigation (FBI), to whom he reported Frieda's German correspondence, suggesting a "relationship to the Nazi Party with whom she was regularly in correspondence."[55] The FBI could find no reason to prosecute, however, and turned the investigation over to the Immigration and Naturalization Service (INS), which was still smarting from a "vicious" letter of complaint Lawrence had written after the return trip from Mexico to the ranch in March 1925.[56]

Late in July an INS officer interviewed Frieda and Angelino for several hours, concentrating almost exclusively on the nature of their relationship. "He is my lover," Frieda readily confessed,[57] and was stunned when a charge of moral turpitude and another, unspecified charge were announced and their passports seized. Angelino, still an Italian citizen and, though it would be more than two years before Italy declared war against the United States, effectively an enemy alien, was threatened with deportation. Frieda appealed to Mabel, who, setting aside her disregard for Angelino, enlisted the help of several well-placed friends—among them Frances Perkins, the secretary of labor, who vacationed in Taos—to retrieve the passports and halt the investigation. Francis Biddle, a prominent lawyer—Frieda occasionally modeled for his brother George, a painter and sculptor with an international reputation—added his support on assuming the position of U.S. solicitor general (he later became U.S. attorney general). "Francis Biddle sent me a message that he was the boss now and I could 'sin' as much as I liked," Frieda wrote Bynner. "I told him my sinning days were over, every dog had his day and every bitch hers, but I thanked him all the same."[58] There were no more visits—at least for the time being.

The exigencies of exile were by no means unfamiliar to Frieda—it had been a condition of her life since her childhood in postwar Metz—and she tried to put the incident behind her. An article in the *New Mexico Quarterly*,[59] the first of many to find in such novels as *Kangaroo* and *The Plumed Serpent* a subtext for Lawrence's flirtation with fascism, did not help, though in fact his works were attacked from both sides in the groundswell of World War II: On February 9, 1935, Munich police had confiscated and banned *Sons and Lovers* and *Lady Chatterley's Lover*, described as "dangerous to Nazi Germany."[60]

Among such Taos intellectuals as Henry A. Sauerwein, Jr., a former Office of Strategic Services employee, Frieda's lifelong defense of Lawrence's politics earned her a reputation for being "of the fascist mindset," a step away from the active right-wing politics that found a breeding ground in Taos in the late 1940s and early 1950s.[61] The charge, in Frieda's case, is difficult, if not impossible, to prove, both because of her lack of interest in politics and because she is amply on record, from at least 1937 onward, as detesting Hitler and—much earlier—Italian Fascism.[62]

The charge of fascist leanings (never put to her while she was alive) was fomented partly by her short acquaintance with Baron von Maltzahn and by public speeches in which she debunked Lawrence's detractors. The first, in July 1940, was delivered at the University of New Mexico in Albuquerque. As Frank Waters, a friend and well-known Southwest writer, recalled, she preceded him at the podium:

> I drove her down to Albuquerque to give the talk. On the way down there, I was telling her about a paper I had written on *The Plumed Serpent*, published in one of my books. I said *The Plumed Serpent* was a horrible, horrible prophesy: a rejuvenation of the old Aztec cults, which came true in Germany—a horrible bloodbath. . . . it's a wonderful book, probably the best book he ever wrote. But I think his philosophy all wrong. . . . Frieda said, "Frank, you ought to publish that . . ."—which was very nice. But of course when she got [up] to talk, in a nice way without mentioning my piece of this idea, she copied it—completely. She wanted to lay the groundwork. I thought this was very clever.[63]

Frieda's thoughts reached a wider audience in the *Virginia Quarterly Review*:

> As for [Lawrence's] being a Fascist, that is bunk. He was neither a Fascist nor a Communist nor any other "ist." His belief in the blood was a very different affair from the Nazi "Aryan" theory, for instance. It was the very opposite. It was not a theory, but a living experience with Lawrence—an experience that made him love, not hate.[64]

The reference to Hitler's Aryan ideal was by no means idle; in a notebook of Frieda's is the following passage, translated from a German book she had been perusing:

> Then at last came a damp cold night in Flanders, through which we marched silently, and when the day began to emerge from the fog, suddenly an iron salute came whizzing over our heads towards us and with a sharp report the small bullets struck between our rows, whipping up the wet earth; but before the small cloud had dispersed, out of two hundred throats the first hurrah roared a welcome to the first

> messenger of death, but then it began to crackle and to roar, to sing and howl, and with feverish eyes each one of us was drawn forward faster and faster over burnt fields and hedges till suddenly the fight began, the fight of man against man. But from the distance the sounds of a song met our ears, coming nearer and nearer, passing from company to company, and then while death plunged his hand busily into our rows, the song also reached us, and now we passed it on: Deutschland Deutschland *"über alles, über alles in der Welt!*["]
>
> After 4 days we came back. Even our step had become different. Boys of seventeen now resembled men.

The book was *Mein Kampf*: "People said it was badly written, they said it was boring. Others said it was crazy and insignificant. But for all that it has been effective in its ideology." The translated passage was, she added, "good writing": "It said what it wanted to say quite clearly."[65]

The notebook from which the passage is drawn probably dates from the late 1930s or early 1940s, judging from Frieda's handwriting and what is explicit and implicit in her remarks: that Hitler had been deemed "crazy" and was reviled. It is impossible to draw the supposition, given the weight of evidence to the contrary, that Frieda supported Hitler early in his rise to power, as did many Germans who later despised him.[66] Fascination with *Mein Kampf* was widespread in the United States by the early 1940s, and her interest in the propaganda and "literary" power of the book may have been spurred in part by her friend Francis Hackett, who had visited Vence with Signe Toksvig after Lawrence's death. The contribution of Hackett, a left-wing journalist, to the anti-Hitler literature, *What "Mein Kampf" Means to America*, was published in New York in 1941.

Certain friends, Bynner among them, disputed the wisdom of Frieda's loyalty to her husband, maintaining that Lawrence's belief in the rule of the elite, first expressed during World War I, translated indirectly into a propensity for, if not fascism, then autocracy. Bynner, for one, believed that Lawrence stopped short of fascism: "Of one thing we may be sure, viz: that Lorenzo would not have cared for such heroes as Hitler or Mussolini—unless say I, with slight malice, he might have happened to be one of them himself," he wrote Frieda in August 1942, presaging Bertrand Russell's later, famous remark that Lawrence (via Frieda, as Russell later elaborated) "developed the whole philosophy of fascism before the politicians had thought of it."[67] By the time of Bynner's letter, Pearl Harbor, the American entry into World War II, and a rapid rise in anti-German sentiment in the United States underscored the insecurity of her position, and she and Angie, as he was now called by Frieda and most friends in New Mexico, had decided to seek citizenship.

6

The American internment of the West Coast Japanese and Japanese Americans and the mood of political conservatism in California discouraged them from making the annual trip to Hollywood in 1943 and 1944—since meeting Zeitlin in 1936 they had returned there most winters—and in November 1944 they set out in the La Salle for the home of Johnnie Griffin, a friend in Brownsville, Texas; a copy of the Constitution, which they had been sent to memorize, was packed in their luggage. Griffin, who spent summers in New Mexico, had described the idyllic fishing and privacy of the Gulf Coast, and Angie, an avid fisherman, was intrigued. Frieda had other reasons for wanting to get away. Over the summer Angie had met Dorothy Horgan, a New Yorker half Frieda's age. Engaging and self-deprecating, with a love of pleasure, she had the added appeal of a total distinterest in the ongoing intrigues of the Lawrence milieu, whose glamour its more arriviste members, in particular, had a large investment in perpetuating. The cult of sexual freedom that had grown up around Lawrence, who himself had spent a total of only nineteen months in New Mexico, pivoted on widespread revisionist readings (in some cases misreadings) of the novels, particularly *Lady Chatterley's Lover*; Angie was often referred to around town as "the real Lady Chatterley's Lover," an avatar of manly promiscuity who appealed equally to both sexes. Among many—for example, in Bynner's inner circle, a Southwest who's who with distinctly international accents—such literalism was regarded with great irony. Bynner himself, whose appeal to women was powerful and lifelong (he had once been engaged to Edna St. Vincent Millay),[68] needed no justification for his own homosexuality, and observed from the sidelines with detached amusement. England, too, was undergoing its own Lawrence revival: "Lawrence," as Barby was later to write, "without any intention at all spawned a generation of moral imbeciles. We women ran round looking for a gamekeeper and the men fancied themselves the conceited fools in the role."[69] In Taos another appropriation, particularly by those who had arrived too late to meet Lawrence, was the use of his work and life as a literary rationale and springboard for the prevalent tradition of *mariage blanc* and other nontraditional marital arrangements. By extension Frieda and Angie's relationship was a subject for close scrutiny, emulation, and, for some, opprobrium or ridicule.

Among certain echelons of the town's elaborate social hierarchies, based largely on race, sexual orientation, longevity of residence, and an elaborate set of intangible standards disguised as a kind of Western egalitarianism, the prevailing perception of Angie as a Lawrence mascot/cuckolder made him something of a laughingstock, much as Frieda had been, in relation to Lawrence. In turn, some in Taos had little use for Dorothy Horgan's East Coast pedigree. Unlike Mabel's relatively old money, Horgan's was distinctly nouveau, particularly as filtered through and embellished by Taos hearsay (said to be the heiress to the Kroger chain store fortune, she was only a distant relative of its founders), and she had a contempt for intellectual pretension. Like Angie, she also had little interest in Lawrence's novels. And she loved the way Angie danced.

Dorothy and her husband of twelve years, Ralph, a voluble, outspoken Irishman who managed a Ford dealership in New York, had an open relationship, and the affair with Angie started almost immediately after he and Dorothy were introduced, at a picnic at Twining (now Taos Ski Valley) by a relative of hers, Marie Korn, who lived in Dallas and spent summers in New Mexico. Dorothy had an immense, fully staffed Park Avenue apartment in which she raised her teenage daughter, Barbara; for this first summer in New Mexico, they were roughing it at Estes Es, an expensive dude ranch, while Ralph endured marine boot camp. Dorothy's meeting with Frieda came shortly after the picnic at Twining, which Frieda had not attended: Barbara, dispatched to Los Pinos with instructions to invite her to lunch, left the message with a woman she took to be "the cook," stout and ruddy and up to her wrists in bread dough, her full-length apron covered with cigarette ash and flour.[70]

It was the only affair of any duration or real seriousness since Angie and Frieda had met, and the first, Frieda felt, to threaten her primacy. Angie's ardor for Dorothy was overwhelming, and unrealistic.

Convinced that she would leave Ralph for him, he pursued her tirelessly, unaware both of the subtle slights and innuendos of many of her friends, whose loyalty to Ralph took precedence, and of Dorothy's own ambivalence: Though she was enormously fond of Angie, she regarded the relationship with a great deal of distance and good humor. Frieda was nonetheless very grateful for Griffin's invitation to Brownsville.

They stayed from late November through April, and Frieda found escape in "And the Fullness Thereof" and letters—most apparently never intended to be sent—to Karl von Marbahr, the childhood sweetheart from whom she had received her first kiss in her father's garden in Sablon. They had corresponded intermittently in the early years of her marriage to Lawrence. Now working in German film as a scout and censor, von Marbahr had read *Lady Chatterley's Lover* before the war and, convinced "your Lawrence" must have been its author, had tracked her down, probably through Else; Connie Chatterley, he wrote Frieda, seemed an utterly faithful representation of the girl he remembered. Though the war had temporarily ended the exchange of letters, she was so flattered that she replaced the existing opening to her book, the trip with Angie to Buenos Aires, with an invocation of Marbahr—"I want to hear from you so much. I want to know where you are, what you are doing and how you are."[71]

Dorothy and Barbara arrived in Taos for their second summer, and Angie was soon looking for pretexts to make the trip into town. Probably for the first time, Frieda keenly felt the loss of her ability to inspire passion in him, a failure their much-vaunted friendship seemed powerless to assuage. As he complained to a neighbor, the contrast with Dorothy soon proved too great for him to bear; "repulsed by Frieda physically, . . . he'd go in and he'd lock his door. And Frieda came pounding at it."[72] Before long, however, the futility of challenging him was clear to Frieda, her desire to do so fell away, and she and Horgan independently developed some semblance of a workable friendship. In time Frieda appreciated, if not the woman herself, her impeccable sense of style: On a visit to the spectacular walled adobe house Horgan built several miles southeast of Taos, its interior graced by Angie's handmade tiles, she often rummaged with childlike appreciation through the silks and taffetas transported from Park Avenue. "When the skies fall," Frieda took to saying, "get on with the washing." She lived the adage literally and to extremes, even scrubbing the wool throw rugs in their new house on the Lobo at five every morning "to let off steam," as she told the wife of her Santa Fe physician, Eric Peter Hausner.[73] An Austrian-Czech émigré who had studied under Freud, Hausner often talked at length to Frieda after physical examinations, which became more regular when, in 1947, her blood-sugar levels showed the onset of diabetes. Angie's infidelities, which she likened to the capers of an errant schoolboy, were, she suggested to him, minor compared to the years of sexual incompatibility with Lawrence.

For Frieda's family the affair confirmed Angie's indifference and opportunism, though not everyone restricted the blame to him. The wife of Frieda's nephew Friedel, Marianne Riezler Jeffrey (the Anglicization of Jaffe they had assumed, after emigrating to the United States before World War II), arrived for a visit and indignantly endured several weeks' worth of Angie's flirtations, the nickname "Marianina," which he bestowed on her, ringing in her ears. His advances disgusted Riezler, a woman solidly reared in the German bourgeoisie, but she considered Frieda's failure to wear hairpins and a bra just as deplorable. At the bottom of her intense dislike of Frieda was the latter's abandonment of her children: "I was a young, devoted mother, and I said to Frieda, 'I can't understand how you could have left them.' Frieda couldn't forgive *me* for saying it."[74] The feud, like most in the family, was soon being relayed to Germany and England. Barby, by now firmly established as her mother's apologist, was later to provide an indirect reply:

> I have always felt that [my parents'] divorce was a turning point, serving to bring about a change in the attitude towards women in my mother's position. I believe she was right to act as she did; all the boring women who have told me "I could never leave my children" have helped to convince me.[75]

For the moment, Frieda retaliated, according to Riezler, by consigning her to scrub the floor at Kiowa after a raucous party co-hosted by Bynner, with whom Frieda shared a birthday. Forty-nine years after her stay, Riezler still recalled the stench; Bynner had been sick and passed out.

When Friedel's American employer, a Mr. Frohnknecht, vacationed at the ranch in the fall of 1945, he received a full account from Angie of his headlong attraction to Horgan. Frieda wrote to Friedel, trying to stem the gossip:

> [Frohnknecht] will have told you about Angelino's love affair—I dont let it disturb me—
>
> Angelino has made it possible for me, to live the way I want to live—all these years—
>
> We have seen a lot together, but if he wants to leave me, then that is that.[76]

Ralph Horgan, who, after his tour with the marines, kept visits to New Mexico to a maximum of two weeks (he was intensely bored by the Southwest), accepted Angie's presence in their lives with grim humor. "Well, Dorothy's going to have her wop with us tonight," he would announce to guests, a remark that, depending on who was present, was greeted with silence or polite laughter.[77]

7

Ironically, close to the onset of the affair, Frieda was commissioned to write a foreword to the first version of *Lady Chatterley's Lover*. The book's precepts, including that of love across class lines, as well as their embodiment in Frieda's affair with Angie, had in some sense now come full circle. The Dial Press had decided that *The First Lady Chatterley*, as it was entitled, differed sufficiently from the final manuscript to warrant separate publication. (The second version has never been issued in book form.) Published early in 1944, it was a resounding critical success.

However, the publication led to huge trouble for Frieda and Angie. On May 5, 1944, the New York Society for the Suppression of Vice, during the war a powerful, semi-autonomous law-enforcement body and something of an FBI service organization, seized 398 of the 7,500 printed copies from Dial offices in Staten Island, New York, and the publisher was informed of a possible violation of a federal statute controlling "interstate transportation of obscene matter." At a Special Sessions Court hearing, a local magistrate and Assistant U.S. Attorney Thomas F. Murphy, of the Southern District of New York, reserved opinion pending a reading of the novel. On May 30 the book was ruled obscene.

In June the FBI paid several visits to the Lobo; a "Security Matter investigation" into Frieda's alleged subversive activities, political and personal, lasted through the summer. The investigation, classified under the "White Slave Traffic Act" and possibly given added momentum by Harold Hawk, was instigated by John S. Sumner, the executive secretary of the Vice Society. Sumner claimed to have received an anonymous letter from the distraught parent of a runaway; it was signed "An admirer," and represented the entire basis for the FBI's suspicions:

> A very good thing you will prosecute those people. . . . I can't afford to get mixed up and help sending the whole bunch where they should be—away from decent society—and I have good reasons. My own daughter is ruined by reading such trash and is crazy about the bunch of them I mean to say the woman Lawrence, the German widow of that author and the other bunch out there in New Mexico the one name Huxley and the wife of that man I don't know the name. Do you know those people have a place where debaucheries of sex go on all the time under the name of some ancient religion or occult studies? Daughter has left her home to be near them and I hear practices free love as they all do. Also I have my suspicions those people are German spies because the woman widow Lawrence is a sister of a German Head of Aviation my daughter boasts about. Also in letter I took from my daughter I read the German woman widow Lawrence writing about living with an Italian young man as her lover. I know the German widow is an old woman. My daughter boasted the lover was a young man. All is too horrible and it should have investigation. Because the people know prominent people they can do anything it seems. Why is that German woman who hates our country and spies for her brother is allowed to live free and in sin. You just find out . . . and find also a woman who has had five husbands the last one a Mexican Indian and my daughter said she wanted now to have a Chinaman. The name of that woman I don't know well but is a writer also and the first name is Mabel—an old woman with painted red hair I understand. Hope you investigate this people. In three years my daughter has come home once. She writes poetry and those people have made her think herself a genius and flatter her she is very

> good looking and only 26 years old but has lost all her good morals. . . . Mabel . . . is the rich one and perhaps her last name is Dodge or Podge Mabel Dodge and daughter has received money from her many times to pay for trips out there I would be so happy to read they are in jail all of them. But I hope they never find out I wrote to you as they are bad people and they be sure to make trouble for me.
>
> Hoping you put them all in jail and the F.B.I. gets after the German widow Lawrence.[78]

Despite Sumner's persistence, the FBI, as in 1939, could find no reason to prosecute Frieda. The case was declared closed on November 10, 1944, in an internal memo noting Frieda's use of an "alias"—"Freiin Von [*sic*] Richthofen"—but citing her "good reputation in town from a security standpoint": "Subject has [n]ever transported anyone in interstate commerce for immoral purposes."[79]

A series of unexplained cancellations of citizenship hearings by the INS followed, dragging on for more than a year and a half, well beyond the surrender of Germany to the Allies in May 1945. Frieda had been forced in the late 1930s to hire a lawyer, Judge Henry A. Kiker, to deal with such eventualities; in late 1946 she angrily told him she wanted to revoke her application, and he carried out her wishes in a letter of January 14, 1947.[80] To the end of her life she remained, as her passport stated, a "British subject by marriage."

All told the FBI and INS investigations lasted, intermittently, more than a decade, and Frieda grew wary of neighbors and even some longtime friends: One woman she suspected of having turned her in to the FBI had herself been turned in by Harold Hawk. It also made her a bit more scrupulous in her choice of local business associates. Henry J. Hughes, a Santa Fe lawyer who had built a thriving practice representing elderly, moneyed women, briefly managed some of her interests; she fired him before he had done too much damage, and subsequently made a point of warning others. Among them was Helene Wurlitzer, a German American heiress to the piano and organ fortune, who had built an artists' retreat at the edge of Taos in the 1940s and, unwittingly, hired Hughes in 1955. Over lunch one day Frieda invoked Thomas Mann's *Confessions of Felix Krull, Confidence Man*, published the year before. A "*Hochstapler*," she cautioned of Hughes. "Watch it, Helena, watch it."[81]

Her own financial interests soon spread into Texas: On January 31, 1947, she bought a small house in Laguna Vista, a township of some six or seven families in Port Isabel, not far from Brownsville.[82] A trip to Carmel the previous winter, their first after the war's end, had convinced them that California was no longer for them; though the Jefferses had welcomed her into their circle (which included, among others, Henry Miller), she had spent much of each day cooking for their numerous housemates, "a kind of early commune."[83] She longed for more privacy than even the upper ranch provided, and, with some five notebooks and assorted typescripts of "And the Fullness Thereof," set off in a new car with Angie.

The temptation to divest herself of Kiowa altogether had in fact grown strong: Now sixty-eight, she found the burden of caring for the property more than she cared to assume. Plans to give it to the University of New Mexico had been tentatively under way since 1944; when they foundered, she offered it to a painter, Joe Glasco, and the novelist William Goyen, to whom she had also given a valuable piece of real estate adjacent to the lower ranch, where the two men had built their own house. Brett, installed in and then evicted by Mabel from a Los Gallos guesthouse, likewise received a plot and built a house, as did Max and Bertha Ilfeld, owners of the Taos hardware store.[84] Glasco and Goyen eventually realized ownership would require them to play host to visitors to the Lawrence grave, and refused her offer, leading to a renewal of negotiations with the University of New Mexico. Frieda left the property to the university in 1955 with explicit instructions for its use as a mecca for young, unpublished writers.

8

The approach to Port Isabel, a tropical desert town warmed by Gulf breezes, was an unremittingly flat highway that sliced through acres of cornfields, cotton, cactus, palm trees, bougainvillea, bright orange poinciana, and nineteenth-century bungalows. Inhabited more than a hundred years ago by itinerant Indian tuna fisherman from Upper Texas, the town's once-thriving shrimp industry is today evidenced by an idle fleet of eighty-foot red-and-black boats that gives Port Isabel its passed-over look. Frieda, there in the town's heyday, loved the lights from the shrimp boats; their house faced the Gulf, and at dawn she sat at the edge of the water in her nightgown, watching the seagulls, ducks, pelicans, and geese dive and forage. "We never buy any fish," she wrote, in a short article for the *Dallas Morning News*, praising, among other virtues, the cleanliness of the state. "The fishermen bring us beautiful pompano and trout and red snapper right out of the water. Grapefruit and papaya and wild duck the neighbors give us."[85] Angie, she wrote Bynner, "is happy too, fishing and painting. He painted some fish, really good."[86]

She made some of her staunchest friends in Port Isabel, and each winter came loaded down with books for them: copies, in Spanish, of Lawrence's *Apocalypse*, the Trollope novels she loved in her old age, spare Bibles, and works by George Santayana and Lewis Mumford. One woman received a bottle of perfume Angie brought back from a second trip to Buenos Aires. In his absence she treated her friends to oysters and tortillas at the Carlos Café, a bayside, picnic-style restaurant. Occasionally she spoke about Lawrence over the Brownsville radio station, but for the most part Laguna Vista provided only the anonymity and rest she had hoped for. She hired a "typist," Louise Leslie, a former Dallas attorney and self-styled beachcomber. Like Else, Leslie edited Frieda's free-ranging prose at her own discretion.[87]

Hausner asked Frieda's next-door neighbor, Bunny Goldtrap, a young nurse, to monitor her low-sugar diet, which, he explained, Mrs. Lawrence might "be apt to forget purposely."[88] Goldtrap could do nothing to discourage her from the sweets she loved, however, and was soon joining her for babas, her favorite accompaniment to tea. Frieda liked the wry humor of "the Cottontail," as she called Bunny; one winter she arrived to find that the nurse had dyed her hair jet black: Charley, Bunny's husband, a burly, garrulous, notoriously unfaithful man with whom Angie was soon hunting duck and philandering, had developed a taste for a local, dark-haired woman with whom Bunny intended to compete. Dietary management of Frieda's disease failed, and she was taught to give herself insulin injections.

Cold War headlines prompted Frieda to invite Nusch from Austria—"I could not bear it if she disappeared behind the iron curtain"[89]—and she arrived for an extended stay, bringing firsthand accounts of World War II's devastation of Europe. (The twenty-five von Richthofen estates in Silesia had been torched by the Russians or sold off.)[90] Nusch, whose sense of style had not changed since Frieda had last seen her, at the baroness's deathbed, gave a detailed account of personal misfortune as well. She found a willing listener in Spud Johnson, who, also visiting Laguna Vistà, began a long interview that appeared in *El Crepusculo*: Nearly her entire wardrobe, including lingerie, had been stolen by "camp followers" (prostitutes), Nusch explained to Johnson: "I put on my last good dress when the Americans entered the city. And though I was very frightened, I opened the doors wide and invited them in. . . . You see I am never discouraged."[91]

Nusch was the first of Frieda's family not to disapprove of Angie, and despite a chronic lack of funds—Frieda had paid her nine-hundred-dollar round-trip air fare from Vienna—returned to Laguna Vista and Taos several times over the next several years, always at Frieda's expense. Frieda kept her supplied with regular checks, a radio, and a new wardrobe. "[O]ur Nusch always needed a lot of money," she wrote to Else, whom she also saw, in 1951, in Albuquerque, heart trouble prohibiting Else's ascent to Taos; it would be their last visit, despite Frieda's hope that "we'll see each other again as real old hags!"[92] Though she occasionally balked at Nusch's large requests (Nusch once asked for a car), she was immensely proud of her younger sister's grace and charm, which wartime privations had done nothing to diminish. In her will she would provide for $100 monthly to be given her in perpetuity.

9

Frieda resolved, probably sometime in the late 1940s, to leave Angie half her total assets, which included the estate; the other half was to be divided equally among her children. The decision posed a potential inheritance problem: Angie's Italian passport, a positive liability during the war, was hardly an asset even in postwar America. With the experience of fighting for the Lawrence estate behind her, Frieda did not want to take any chances. She decided to assure Angie's future by marrying him, a solution apparently devised by Mabel, whose attitude to Angie had continued to mellow with old age; she had bowed to the earnestness of his artistic efforts by including the painting begun in Hollywood in 1936, *Arizona Mining Town* (albeit with his first name misspelled), in her 1947 book *Taos and Its Artists*.[93]

Marriage would also allow Angie the luxury of trips to Italy again, without the anxiety of possibly being denied reentry on his return.

Frieda, too, could consider a trip abroad: Monty, she learned from Bynner, who had paid her son a visit on his return to Santa Fe from a six-month sojourn in North Africa and Europe, wanted her to move back to England. Frieda was eager to see Monty, who had contracted tuberculosis during the war. Cured by a year's stay in a sanatorium on the Isle of Wight, he was now keeper of the Bethnal Green Museum, a branch of the Victoria and Albert some ten miles outside central London, which specialized in antique toys, Spitalfields silk designs, home furnishings, and costumes. Monty evidently suggested to Bynner the possibility of Frieda's moving in with him and his family, now living in Netteswell House, a small mansion with a Queen Anne facade on museum grounds, traditionally set aside for the keeper; the invitation did not appear to extend to Angie. Barby still harbored a vision of Frieda's returning to Ernest Weekley, whom the war and old age had displaced from Harvard Road to residences in Surrey and North Wales. He was now living with Elsa, Teddy, and their two children; their second son, Richard, had been born in 1941.

Frieda had no intention of retiring to London, and her children's expectations unnerved her—"I would only be a queer creature to them," she wrote Bynner. "But I felt pleased that they want me—a coffin would be the same thing!"[94] She was yearning to meet her five grandchildren, however, and the prospect of a short stay became a distinct possibility when she found someone with whom to share part of the journey, Miranda Speranza Masocco, a young, stylish friend of Bynner's. Orphaned at the age of two or three by the sudden death of her mother aboard a train on their first visit to the United States from Venice, Masocco had remained in Santa Fe and been taken under wing by Bynner, much later often ferrying him to the Lobo in her Studebaker convertible; like Frieda, Bynner never learned to drive. A music aficionado whose friends included Igor and Vera Stravinsky, Masocco was also a student of Lawrence's novels. Frieda was soon calling her "the Mirendi," an approximation of the name of the villa outside Florence where Lawrence had written *Lady Chatterley's Lover*. Like many friends of Frieda's old age, she was half a century younger; one of her enduring memories is of sitting front and center with Frieda under the music tent in Aspen, Colorado, whose newfound resort status and outdoor summer festival drew crowds from all over the world. As a performance of a Norman Dello Joio sonata was getting under way,

Frieda loudly stage-whispered her appreciation of the good looks and muscular physique of flutist Albert Tipton, whom she likened to Tarzan, bringing a laugh from Tipton and applause from the audience for Frieda, whose name was murmured appreciatively.[95]

Frieda and Angie were informed by Judge Kiker that no marriage between them would be legally binding unless the Ravagli marriage was dissolved by a U.S. court, and Angie brought a divorce suit in Taos County against Serafina on grounds of irreconcilable differences. In mid-July 1950, Serafina, then living in Viareggio, was served a complaint and summons and agreed to an American divorce—not valid in Italy—without a hearing. A decree absolute was granted on August 12.

Two and a half months later, on Halloween, Frieda and Angie were married in a civil ceremony in Taos conducted by Justice of the Peace Alex A. Valdez. Joe Fulton, a cub reporter for *El Crepusculo*, put the news on the wire to Santa Fe, noting Angie's skill as a "ceramist," mistakenly changed to "chemist" in the *New York Times* the following day. On the application for their marriage license, the *Times* noted, "Mrs. Lawrence gave her age as 71. Mr. Ravagli said he was 59."[96] That night, Fulton recalls, Angie went dancing.[97]

21

The Art of Dying

I

Frieda departed from tradition for her last trip to England, flying rather than sailing. The Taos–New York leg was by train with Masocco, who would be flying through to the Riviera. The Stravinskys, then staying at the Hotel Lexington, booked some rather dark rooms for them, and Carl Van Vechten, whom Frieda had met at Mabel's, looked after them for several days, spent mostly in search of a smoked ham to present to Monty and Vera. She finally found one at a Gristede's; wrapped in fishnet, its odor filled her room at the Lexington. For their last dinner, Van Vechten took them to Sardi's, and in the morning he drove them to the airport. Dressed for her first flight in a floor-length, thousand-pleat Navajo broomstick skirt, frilled Mexican blouse, ballet slippers, and a brightly colored beanie with earflaps that draped her ears like a World War I pilot's cap, she hoisted the ham on her shoulder as she waved goodbye to Van Vechten; its fumes, by now clinging to her clothes, pervaded the cabin of the prop plane even before takeoff.

Frieda was nervous about this return. It is conspicuously absent from her memoirs, and she seems never to have spoken of it, though the trip was happy enough. Unlike the United States, where she had found acceptance, England held memories of loss, ostracism, Lawrence, and, strangely enough, of Ernest Weekley, and she could not shake an irrational fear of being pulled back into a society that had kept such a strong, unhappy hold on her for so many years. She finally stopped trying, and slept for much of the nine hours over the Atlantic, secure that, uncharacterstically, she had left nothing to chance. Masocco later saw Angie at the Villa Bernarda, and he threw himself at her. "Don't make passes at girls wearing glasses," she said, slightly misquoting Dorothy Parker. Surveying the property from Lawrence's old bedroom, which he gave her for the night, she found herself unable, no matter how she squinted or how far she leaned out the window, to determine the quadrant of arbor or trellis in which "Constance Chatterley" and the "gamekeeper" could have made love and been seen by Lawrence from his sickbed.[1]

Ida Wilhelmy, the children's former nanny, now a nurse, was waiting with Monty to take her to the Kingsley Hotel. It was a letter from Wilhelmy that had clinched Frieda's decision to make the trip: Having heard from Else that Frieda was considering a return to England, she had offered to stay with her at the Kingsley, and otherwise to ease the transition to London. Frieda, it was clear to all, was getting old. Despite the forty-year silence between them, Wilhelmy's loyalty had survived the disintegration of the Weekley family; her first job after leaving Cowley was as assistant to a German surgeon whose wife avidly followed the divorce columns, and she had refused to speak with the woman about Frieda's divorce and remarriage, "in case she said something bad of her."[2]

In the first days she arranged visits from Frere Reeves, Murry (who had retired to the country to farm tobacco), and Pollinger, who had long been handling Frieda's publishing affairs worldwide. Frieda had come to consider him a trusted friend, and had relegated to him much of the work previously done by Zeitlin, who had gone deeply into debt in 1942, bringing an end to their contract. Though her original intention to keep the major manuscripts together had not been fulfilled, most had been bought directly from her by Ed Hanley, whose collection effectively remained both the largest Lawrence repository and a source of steady income; checks arrived regularly from Pennsylvania. She had kept only the three *Lady Chatterley's Lover*s, which had been removed from Bynner's safe and were now in a cardboard box under her bed at home.

She moved to Netteswell House when Ida left, and for the next week and a half "held court in eighteenth-century style" from the bedroom Vera relinquinshed to her.[3] "Propped up on pillows, a wild blonde-grey and resplendent figure in shawl and nightdress," she rarely emerged before noon, chain-smoking and receiving her grandchildren.[4] They had gradually been told the full details of the Lawrence scandal, now all but stripped of the taint of divorce and child abandonment. Elsa's youngest, Richard, now eleven, was enrolled at Saint Paul's. "Oh, they know all about Lawrence and you at the school!" he informed Frieda.[5] She told the children long stories about the southwestern desert, which, she explained, soothed and sustained her; a look of enchantment played over her face whenever she described bathing in the hot springs, looking at the stars at night, or watching bears prowl Kiowa. Each day, another elaborately worked Indian bracelet made its appearance on her wrists. The hope Monty had broached to Bynner that Frieda might spend her last years with them in London was never spoken of.

Though she remained for only a fortnight, her impact on the family was huge. With the exception of Ian, the eldest, they were true Weekleys, reserved and habituated, their routines dictated to some degree by the developmental and emotional problems suffered by Julia, now seventeen and working in hotel management. Monty, who was "inordinately fond" of his daughter, set great store by the rigor of his household but found companionability largely outside—among his passions were the Rotary and the Press Club; Vera, who was often ill, retreated into privacy and solitude. Except for museum functions and family dinners, they spent little time together, and she took her vacations apart from Monty.[6] Despite her tenure at the Slade, her adherence to bourgeois convention was as legendary in the family as Frieda's disregard for it, and they found common ground only in the shopping. Frieda, who believed the heart of a city was in its outdoor market stalls, accompanied her to Roman and Bethnal Green Roads, her dirndl skirts, eyelet blouses, and white knit tights drawing stares. Monty brought her, similarly dressed, to work: Told that smoking was not allowed in the galleries, she did not stay long, however.[7]

Despite the museum's proximity to their house, Monty rarely came home for lunch, but throughout Frieda's stay tea was accorded a respect it normally lacked in Netteswell House. It was served in the back yard, which overlooked museum grounds. One guest particularly impressed Frieda: Sir Allen Lane, the founder of Penguin Books, which had begun reprinting the novels in huge quantities—"a million cheap Lawrence books," she proudly wrote Bynner—though he was still unable to publish *Lady Chatterley's Lover*, in any version.[8] Frieda liked his ironic good humor and self-made composure—he had left school at sixteen—and her laughter reverberated off the brick walls of the surrounding houses, bringing pigeons from the plane trees.[9] Recently knighted for service to literature (*Ulysses*, for example, was already on his backlist), in 1960 Lane would marshal a mammoth team of literary witnesses at Old Bailey for the defense of *Lady Chatterley's Lover*, perhaps the most famous obscenity trial of the second half of the twentieth century.[10] Within five minutes of the verdict in his favor, he marched to a phone booth and ordered the distribution of two hundred thousand copies, which had been printed in anticipation of the victory.

Monty, Elsa and Barby and their husbands, and Frieda's five grandchildren convened in the garden one afternoon, conferring enormous "matriarchal glory" on Frieda, who sat "beaming."[11] Only Elsa—whose loyalties were by now entirely with her father—fulfilled her obligations to her mother with almost palpable distance, perhaps even displeasure. Frieda could not be invited to her home because of Ernest's presence there, but asked to see the garden; Elsa relegated the job to Teddy, with explicit instructions that her mother be shown the flowers from a considerable distance, from a moving car.

As they glided past, Frieda spotted the back of Ernest's head through the window of his study. Eighty-nine and nearly blind, he sat at his desk, apparently peering at a book. She was moved, enough to propose a meeting "if her three children approved." Elsa and Monty turned her down without mentioning the request to Barby, who remembered her great disappointment when Frieda later related the incident. She believed that Ernest had felt more generous toward Frieda as he aged:

> [M]y father had hinted, it seemed to me, of a slight relaxation of his unforgiving attitude: he had said to me once . . . "I am not so rigid,

> you know, about morality as I used to be." Also, when I ventured a remark about the Richthofen family—a disparaging one—he said "Ah, but she was the best."[12]

Two years later Ernest was dead. "[H]e was a learned man inalienably opposed to all merely anecdotal and popular etymology," wrote the London *Times*, "and time-honoured legends went down like card-castles before his gay assault." A picture of him and Frieda, taken in Littenweiler during her first pregnancy, was found in his desk.[13]

2

Frieda's sense of mortality was heightened, after her return to Taos, when a large chunk of the town's old guard—and several other friends besides—began succumbing to illness. Only Brett, now sixty-nine and still riding, fishing, painting, and, of late, snooping avidly through a telescope aimed at Los Pinos, was in perfect health; she would live until 1976. Bynner had undergone an operation for glaucoma that had left him blind in one eye, and he was preparing for his death (still fifteen years hence)[14] by sorting old correspondence. His sense of his own place in literary history was rather aggrandized: For the past several decades he had engaged a secretary to type in triplicate every letter that left his house, though it was primarily his missives from others that later enriched the coffers of several institutions.[15] A cache from Edna St. Vincent Millay detailed a triangle involving their mutual friend Arthur Ficke, with whom both had been in love. Bynner lent the letters to Frieda, who was intrigued. Like many in Taos, she had long since given up pigeonholing her friends' love interests: "Why did'nt you marry her?" she wrote Bynner. ". . . She must have been a thrilling person—And a fighter, and courageous!"[16] Millicent Rogers, who for years had been treated for rheumatic fever and an enlarged heart, died at the age of fifty on January 1, 1953. Mabel would soon suffer advanced senility: "Who is that Indian?" she often asked visitors, pointing to Tony. "Get him out of here." Tony's reply never varied. "That don't matter. I take care of her."[17] On the Luhans' increasingly rare visits, Frieda watched sadly as Mabel repeated, in the voice of a small girl and with a guilty smile on her face, "I was *naughty* about Lawrence."[18] Maria Huxley's death from cancer in 1955 brought a lengthy description of the final hours from Aldous; its humanity, classicism, and accuracy so impressed Frieda she transcribed it for Else and Dudley Nichols: "No slop; he writes . . . 'It is so difficult to know what one can do for someone who is dying, incidentally for oneself. . . . The men of the Middle Ages used to talk of the *Ars Moriendi*—the art of dying.'" She bought a book on the subject, and referred to it often in conversations with friends.[19]

Frieda had developed asthma, though her vigor and magnetism, given greater luster by the fame of the flourishing Lawrence industry, were undiminished. "When she entered a room," recalled Amalia de Schulthess, a Swiss sculptor from Beverly Hills, who visited in the summer of 1953, "the atmosphere changed, became charged, electric. She was very powerful and intensely female."[20] Amalia, a strikingly beautiful woman, was immediately taken up by Angie; invited back by Frieda, she brought her husband, Hans, the nephew of an extravagant book collector. Frieda pulled "the three Lady Cs," as she called them, from under the bed, and Hans, given to grand gestures and no doubt aware of Angie's eyes on his wife, offered to buy them for her. A flirtatious, four-way correspondence ensued, given added momentum by the couple's frequent visits to the Lobo, which unfailingly ended in passes from Angie and a display of the manuscripts. Frieda never missed a chance to alert other prospective buyers to such competition, particularly the University of Texas at Austin, which sent a graduate student named Warren Roberts to appraise the three manuscripts: "[T]hey are my 'pièce de résistance,'" she wrote Roberts, "and I want a lot for them."[21] She was well aware her attachment to the manuscripts made them more attractive: "I enjoy looking at them and reading them in the raw as it were."[22]

Austin finally upped the ante by unveiling plans for a million-dollar Lawrence repository (another was in the making in Eastwood). The purchase of the balance of Frieda's collection was mentioned as a strong likelihood, and Roberts and Harry Ransom, the future dean of the university, invited her to solicit a third-party appraisal of its worth. Zeitlin, with whom she and Angie had maintained a friendship, was called in, and he came up with a figure just under $25,000, remarkably close to what Frieda had quoted Harvard two decades before—though now far fewer primary materials were offered. This new lot included the odd, discarded typescript, letters, even first editions.[23] In fact, the demand had become so great that everything Lawrencian commanded a price. The de Schulthesses, who had offered $10,000 for the three *Lady Chatterleys*, called in their accountant, but Frieda kept him politely at bay.

She received an invitation to meet Ransom and tour Austin, which, with the two offers coming in, she had taken to calling "great," "the richest in the world."[24] With the manuscripts in the back seat, she set out with Angie in November 1954, en route to Laguna Vista. The visit was a disaster. Ransom, who felt that a handshake was sufficient to seal the university's intention to buy the manuscripts, was not prepared to write a check, and Angie angrily insisted that they were being taken advantage of, a sentiment expanded upon in a strangely punctuated, vituperative letter to Roberts, sent from Laguna Vista. Frieda was left to smooth the ruffled feathers: "Now we never in the world suspected your integrity. But we had had our own ideas and they were not the same as yours. That's all. . . . Angelino got worked up and wrote more harshly than he ever meant to. . . . You see Angelino wants to be businesslike and American!"[25] The de Schulthesses bought the three manuscripts and deposited them in a Los Angeles bank vault. They divorced several years afterward, the manuscripts remaining in Amalia's possession, sealed in a Beverly Hills bank vault.

Several years after Frieda's death Texas acquired the three *Lady Chatterleys* for $50,000, as well as the bulk of Hanley's Lawrence trove, enriched by his earlier purchase of *The Rainbow* for $3,500: It had increased almost five times in value since Frieda's original plan to sell it for Else's passage. Hanley paid, as usual, in ten installments of $350. A judicious mania for acquisition had catapulted his worth to some eight million dollars, and after a long bachelorhood he had settled down with an Egyptian belly dancer. They often went on buying sprees in Hollywood and New York, where Hanley, whose love of collecting was rivaled only by a love of show business, was on a first-name basis with the roustabouts, clowns, and acrobats of every three-ring circus that passed through. Despite his marriage, his parsimony remained: In Hollywood he stayed at the Roosevelt Hotel, which offered a reduced rate for a room whose walls abutted the shaft housing the elevator machinery. When he dined out, he never ordered anything but a steak and a glass of milk. On such trips their Victorian home, a considerable fire hazard, went unwatched; eventually Hanley's insurance adjusters stipulated that coverage would be continued only if he sold the paintings or the manuscripts. It was only after Frieda died, however, that he was willing to part with them.

3

Angie left for Buenos Aires to see his sister not long after sending the letter to Roberts. Frieda sent for Wilhelmy, who arrived in Brownsville aboard a banana boat from Bremen. Frieda paid the fare—it was half the cost of flying—and had been anticipating the visit since the trip to London. The two spent long afternoons on Padre Island, a deserted beach whose capture by pirates several centuries before was spoken of by locals in the same breath as more recent history. The setting and Wilhelmy's conversation made Frieda feel her Americanness as she never had before. "She tells me much about Germany which is not so easy for me to understand," she wrote to Else.[26]

Her Germanness was noticed by some more than others. Suzette Hausner, the French wife of her Santa Fe doctor, saw her as quintessentially European, interpreting even her fidelity to Angie as "typically German."[27] Other friends noted her assimilation, and her concerns and interests were, without a doubt, American: She spoke admiringly of Eisenhower, went to the San Antonio stock show, complained about income tax—"alas . . . the more you have the less you get"[28]—and was grateful for her monthly social security check of seventy dollars.

Wilhelmy tried to monitor her diet, but Frieda invited two German restaurateurs from Taos, who restored a full measure of fat and sugar to her meals.[29] Angie's postcards from "the must populated street city in the world" arrived regularly, and Frieda immersed herself in *Barnaby Rudge*, the letters of Goethe, B. H. Tawney's *Religion and the Rise of Capitalism*, and, like her dying mother, Shakespeare.[30] "[T]hose tame heroines," she wrote Bynner, "I am glad no man ever said to me: 'Get thee to a nunnery!' "[31]

The sense that her creative powers had begun to ebb was reinforced in thousands of small ways. Frieda, with her great belief in destiny, took them as positive signs of her approaching death. Promotion of Lawrence's reputation had been given over largely to "Professors," she wrote Bynner, whose "short appearances" on the Lobo "with wives and families" made her "feel like a calf with 6 legs!"[32] The first major biography of Lawrence appeared, as well as what for Frieda was the first entirely satisfactory book on his erotic and spiritual ethos.[33] The unfinished state of "And the Fullness Thereof," which would remain incomplete at her death, did not concern her. (It was compiled and edited by E. W. Tedlock, Jr., a friend and University of New Mexico professor of English, and published in 1964 as *Frieda Lawrence: The Memoirs and Correspondence*, the now very free-ranging autobiography fleshed out with 258 letters from and to Frieda.) Her chief interest was in settling the estate, and it was around this time that the upper ranch was finally deeded to the University of New Mexico. Negotiations for the property were completed shortly before what would be her last trip to Laguna Vista.

On their return, in April 1956, she and Angie took a wrong turn at Clines Corners, one of the windiest, most godforsaken trading posts in the state, a mistake that put them in Las Vegas, New Mexico. Frieda's good friend Rudolph Kieve still worked there, but rather than calling on him, or retracing their steps, they continued. An icy switchback over the lower Sangre de Cristo range brought them to an elevation of about eleven thousand feet, and they emerged onto what looked like a snowy moonscape. If it had not been pitch black and the snow falling so thickly, Frieda probably would have appreciated the scenery, but her age, the hour, and Angie's exhaustion—they had been on the road for several days and were some ten hours behind schedule—made her "nightmarishly frightened," and she thought of little but becoming stranded.[34] When they reached the lower ranch it was well past daylight. They both fell asleep, and that night Frieda lost consciousness; when she came to she was on the bathroom floor and could not remember how she had gotten there. She struggled to get up, reluctant to wake Angie. Illnesses, she knew, produced in him an agitation bordering on hysteria. When half an hour had gone by and she was still immobilized, she gave up and summoned him. He found her still on the floor. "Funny," she said. "I can't get up."[35]

He called Dr. Martha Elizabeth Howe, a transplanted New Yorker with a local practice. Frieda, now running a high fever, was brought by ambulance to Santa Fe, where Hausner diagnosed a viral infection. (Angie later believed she had suffered a mild stroke.) She was released eight days later and preferred not to speak much of the incident, though word of its seriousness and of her weakened condition traveled quickly. Barby made plans to come, and Frieda spent a couple of weeks on a daybed in the "sunroom" at Los Pinos, a glassed-in porch Angie had added to the house several years before. She had filled it with massive potted plants and liked to read and sleep there, watching shooting stars through the ivy that clung to the panes, growing to like the heat of the broiling midday sun, which baked the glass and made the room fifteen or twenty degrees hotter than the rest of the house.

Barby arrived in mid-May, bringing Isadora Duncan's autobiography, which Frieda, who had seen her perform in Munich, devoured. She had made a more or less complete recovery by the time Angie set off for "a kind of business trip, and a successful one," as he later wrote an old friend of Frieda's: "I visit her children and grand children, plus all the Agent in New York, England, and Italy," before continuing on to spend several weeks with Serafina.[36] Frieda and Barby made trips to the hot springs to fill water bottles and "soak," as Frieda liked to say; her mornings were spent in her bedroom, smoking and reading. An advance copy of F. R. Leavis's *D. H. Lawrence, Novelist*, a book largely responsible for the postwar reassessment of Lawrence by British academics, occasioned a rereading of George Eliot, to whom Leavis compared Lawrence; complaints to Barby (Eliot had made the "pretty heroine" of *Adam Bede* "suffer because the writer herself was such a plain woman");[37] and finally a letter to Leavis:

> From the *Rainbow* on Lawrence is no longer a British writer, but a universal one. If you read again about the child Ursula's relation with her father, you will see it is not a mother and son relationship, but a father-daughter one. It happened to be mine with my father. Only instead of potatoes it was asparagus. . . . You say I was not maternal, I think I was, and not intellectual, but I was not dumb either and thought things out for myself.[38]

Frieda's approach to literature had remained essentially unchanged since her marriage to Ernest. Her anti-intellectualism, before almost universally regarded as stupidity, had come, strangely enough, into a sort of vogue; her more recent articles, in the *New Republic*, the *New Statesman*, and elsewhere—chiefly defenses and explications of Lawrence's intentions and mission—made her a figure to contend with even among former "detractors," as she said to Barby, who "gave me nothing but *lip*."[39] Occasional pieces on former literary friends were strictly and intentionally "human interest": a short profile of Mansfield dwelled on the writer's favorite soap (Cuticura), impeccable grooming, and beauty regimen, and concluded with her recipe for a Knox gelatin dessert.

Barby timed her departure to correspond with Angie's return in late July. Though her children had decided to treat and speak of Angie as "something approximating to a stepfather"—as Monty wrote his mother shortly after Ernest's death—they still did not particularly like him.[40]

At the end of Angie's first week back Frieda invited Dorothy Horgan to the lower ranch for the afternoon. She was by now part of both their lives, and Frieda's upset over being supplanted had long been relegated to the past. Her own role in the Taos community was now paramount. To a younger generation of writers, artists, and musicians, many of whose careers she had helped cultivate and finance, she was something of a retired diva, a role that imposed the grace of abdication, as William Hughes, a friend introduced either by Horgan or Helene Wurlitzer, recalled:

> When people came to see or interview Frieda, she would put on a little act for ten minutes and then she was back, saying, "What are we going to do for dinner?" It reminded me of [the diva] Lucrezia Bori, in Cleveland with her dog Fifi, done up to the nines in her leopard coat. Then, later, it was like, "I'm through with that glamour role now. Tonight is the young singers' night. You're going to hear some young voices, they're beautiful." I have the feeling something similar was going on with Frieda.[41]

Horgan arrived, expecting cocktails, but found Frieda in the kitchen, deep-frying doughnuts. At ninety-two degrees, it was not the hottest day of the summer, but the heat and smell of the oil made the air in the house seem viscous. The doughnuts were served in the "greenhouse," as most friends now called the sunroom, with the mercury hovering around 110 degrees. No drinks were forthcoming, and Horgan left as soon as she politely could.

4

For a party across the road that night at Glasco and Goyen's, Frieda dressed in a pink-and-blue dress, fashioned from a length of intricately patterned Italian silk Angie had brought back from his latest "business trip." She presided, "very much the Queen of the evening," as Glasco later recalled, at the head of a table of some of her oldest friends, Brett, Mabel, Rebecca James, Ruth Swayne, and Johnnie Griffin among them.[42] The property Frieda had given "the boys," as she called Glasco and Goyen, had a more commanding view of the mesa than her own, with a picture window spanning 180 degrees. The party was a huge success, running late into the night. Frieda awoke at five the next morning, a Saturday, to do the wash. A pain across her stomach and heart made her double over, and Dr. Howe was called in and prescribed a sedative and bed rest. She slept off and on but could not obey Howe's order to avoid the exertion of washing herself, and rose several times on Sunday for long baths, in whose curative powers she had a strong belief. Angie left early Monday morning for a fishing date and returned to find her better. Her strength came back on Tuesday, and she wrote a letter to Bynner, at whose house they were expected three days later for the joint birthday party that had become a fixture in both their lives, but by Wednesday night she was exhausted. She moved a nightgown, her books, and a fountain pen to the sunroom, and told Angie that if she became ill, she did not want to be taken back to the hospital, and that she wanted to be buried on the Lobo, a "rude wooden cross" placed over her grave. He stayed home that evening, and at ten o'clock she called out to him with an endearment acquired from Ernest Weekley: "It's late—go to sleep, blighter."[43]

He was awakened an hour later by a thud and what sounded like radio static. Frieda was on the floor next to the daybed, crippled by a massive stroke. Her right side was paralyzed, her mouth twisted into an unrecognizable shape and making strange noises. Fighting an urge to faint, he lifted her to the bed and summoned Howe, who gave Frieda two injections to help her sleep. She was sure Frieda would not last the night but said nothing to Angie. Frieda woke in the middle of the night, however, and Angie opened a window and described the constellations to her. "*Ja*," she said, trying to smile, and lost consciousness.[44]

At 8:00 the next morning, August 9, Howe, who had stayed the night, was relieved by Rachel Hawk, who made the trip down from the Lobo. A hospital bed was found at Mabel's, and at noon Glasco went into Taos for an oxygen tank. Frieda had come to, but her breathing was labored, and Howe advised oxygen treatments every twenty minutes. Consciousness came and went during the day, but she "was still able to wisper 'Thank you,'" Angie later wrote, "any time I, or someone else, was doing something to make Her confortable."[45] Two nurses were summoned and began intravenous feeding. Angie, upset that "the house is transform in Hospital," had to be given a sedative.[46] Frieda went into a coma the following evening, August 10. Glasco and Goyen, who were taking turns with the oxygen tank, began to feel the futility of keeping her alive and reduced her treatments. Angie was awakened from a deep sleep induced by the sedative, and just before dawn wrote Ed Hanley, from whom a couple of $350 *Rainbow* installments were still due: "Even if she should rigain conscienceness she will not be able to write or speak. So will you please send your check in my name only, because—unfortunately we have no [joint] Bank account and that is the time I need lots of money."[47]

Frieda died an hour and a half later, on the morning of her seventy-seventh birthday, August 11, 1956, leaving her letter to Bynner on one of the side tables in the sunroom:

> This is your seventy-fifth birthday. How long have we known each other? It seems to me always. So on this day I want to tell you how much your friendship had meant to me. I won't be the only one who feels like this, with your rich, generous nature you have given so much to so many. Sometimes you found me a nuisance and sometimes you did not approve of me and told me so, but always your friendship was there as a support and a joy.
>
> These are my loving thanks to you on this day.
>
> Frieda Lawrence Ravagli[48]

Epilogue

Frieda's death was celebrated in strict medieval fashion, though Angie, at the last minute, forsook the plain cross she had wanted—for fear of looking cheap.[1] At 4:00 P.M. on Monday a long procession began the ascent to the Lobo in a northern New Mexico sirocco. Most of the residents of Taos over the age of seventy were in the line, including Helene Wurlitzer, fortified with brandy, a supply of oxygen, and sandwiches. Frieda was buried outside Lawrence's tomb, and the sound of her voice soon filled the air: Several years before, John Candelario, a local painter and manufacturer of 78s, had recorded her recitations of several Lawrence poems and Psalm 121; the latter was played at full blast on her gramophone. The wind subsided, a hummingbird flew into the tomb, Frieda's friends spread out their suppers on blankets, and Angie lit the *tricolore* paper lanterns.

He was convinced that her ghost visited the lower ranch for a few weeks. "She is around the house in her nighty," he wrote a friend ten days later, "I am non scared or paniky, as I though, but only peace and tranquillity. I feel so proud of myself for it. That is what is a grate love, after much time, peace and tranquillity. . . . She brake my heart."[2]

Efforts to get Dorothy Horgan to marry him failed, though they took several trips together, including at least one to Laguna Vista. Otherwise he found little acceptance in Taos, and in 1959, three years after Frieda's death, he returned to his family in Savona, having sold off both remaining houses and Frieda's papers.[3] As Frieda had long promised, he was left half the estate—initially valued at just over two hundred thousand dollars, not including the Laguna Vista property; the other half went to Monty, Elsa, and Barby. Also missing from the figure were future royalties, which, with the 1960 *Lady Chatterley* obscenity trial in London and one the previous year in New York, became almost incalculably huge.

NOTES

All interviews were conducted by the author, with the exception of those indicated as being housed in the Nottingham County Library and those with Montague Weekley and Barbara Barr, July 13, 1978, and June 17, 1978, respectively, which are in the collection of the British Library.

Prologue

1. Mabel Dodge Luhan, *Lorenzo in Taos* (New York: Alfred A. Knopf, 1932), p. 36; letter of May 14, 1990, from Arthur L. Lloyd, director of public affairs, Amtrak.

2. Most who knew her during this period described her eyes as green; on later passports the color was recorded variously as blue and gray.

3. The yearning had been set in motion before they arrived. See, e.g., D. H. Lawrence (hereafter DHL) to Else Jaffe, September 27, 1922, *The Letters of D. H. Lawrence*, vol. 4 (Cambridge, Eng.: Cambridge University Press, 1987), p. 310 ("Frieda . . . hankered after America"; hereafter the Cambridge edition of the Lawrence letters, ed. J. T. Boulton et al., published 1979–93, will be abbreviated *DHL Letters*, followed by volume and page numbers); Frieda Lawrence, *"Not I, but the Wind . . . "* (New York: Viking, 1934; hereafter *NIBTW*), p. 135 ("travelled . . . to Taos in great expectation"). The abstraction, Frieda's customary response in moments of great passion or anger and to newness, was reinforced by the change in altitude—see, e.g., DHL to Thomas Seltzer and to Robert Mountsier, September 12, 1922, *DHL Letters*, 4, p. 295 ("we are quite overwhelmed"; "we are chiefly . . . dazed").

4. Knud Merrild, *With D. H. Lawrence in New Mexico* (London: Routledge & Kegan Paul, 1964), p. 252; Witter Bynner, *Journey with Genius* (New York: John Day, 1951), pp. 1–2; *NIBTW*, p. 116; DHL to Anna von Richthofen, February 19, 1922, *DHL Letters*, 4, pp. 198–199.

5. Luhan, *Lorenzo in Taos*, p. 38.

6. I am indebted to Ray Taylor, of Santa Fe, and the Harwood Foundation, Taos, for photographs and other archival material relating to Lamy in the 1920s.

7. Originally spelled *Lujan.* Sterne changed the spelling later; I have used Luhan throughout to avoid confusion. In citing letters from and publications by Mabel, who was born Dodge and took, successively, the surnames Evans, Sterne, and Luhan during the period covered by this book, I use the surname she preferred at the time.

8. Merrild, *With D. H. Lawrence in New Mexico*, p. 252.

9. Luhan, *Lorenzo in Taos*, p. 36.

10. Frieda Lawrence to Mabel Dodge Sterne, January 26, 1922: "In my mind I have already lived in Taos. . . ," *Lorenzo in Taos*, p. 15.

11. Luhan, *Lorenzo in Taos*, pp. 38–39.

Chapter 1 Mismatches

1. Address of the von Richthofens and occupation of Friedrich von Richthofen: Archives Municipales, Metz; Direction des Services d'Archives, Départment du Bas-Rhin, Strasbourg (hereafter Dépt. Bas-Rhin). Description of countryside and of garden of Friedrich von Richthofen: *NIBTW*, pp. 32–33 and *Frieda Lawrence: The Memoirs and Correspondence*, ed. E. W. Tedlock, Jr. (New York: Alfred A. Knopf, 1964; hereafter *M&C*), p. 53. Anna von Richthofen described their house as a "country-house" (Reminiscence by Anna von Richthofen supplied by Frederick R. Jeffrey, trans. Helen Diets; hereafter AvR), and its outbuildings, etc., are enumerated in *M&C*, p. 44. Transplanting flowers: Letter from Frieda von Richthofen to Else von Richthofen, May 27, 1895, Harry Ransom Humanities Research Center, University of Texas at Austin (hereafter HRC). Also see DHL, "The Thorn in the Flesh," p. 118 (all page references to Lawrence short stories are from the Penguin paperback editions, 1986).

2. *M&C*, p. 53.

3. Frieda Lawrence to Richard Aldington, March 21, 1949, as quoted in *Frieda Lawrence and Her Circle*, ed. Harry T. Moore and Dale B. Montague (Hamden, Conn.: Archon Books, 1981), p. 92.

4. *M&C*, p. 49.

5. Ibid., p. 469.

6. Information in the following paragraphs on the von Richthofen family, coat of arms, genealogy: conversations with Patrick Mansur Freiherr Praetorius von Richthofen, summer, 1988, Munich, and family tree supplied by him; *Genealogisches Handbuch des Adels*, Freiherrliche Häuser B VII (Limburg an der Lahn: C. A. Starke Verlag, 1978), pp. 300, 372–374, 1224; Robert Ehrenzweig (Lucas), *Frieda Lawrence: The Story of Frieda von Richthofen and D. H. Lawrence* (hereafter Lucas, *Frieda Lawrence*), trans. Geoffrey Skelton (New York: Viking, 1973), pp. 4–7.

7. Ferdinand von Richthofen, *Baron von Richthofen's Letters, 1870–1872*

(Shanghai, 1872); Bailey Willis, "Ferdinand, Freiherr von Richthofen," *Journal of Geology* 13 (October–November 1905), pp. 561–567.

8. John Quincy Adams, *Letters on Silesia* (London: J. Budd, 1804), p. 45.

9. Adams, *Letters on Silesia*, p. 28.

10. Reminiscence by Friedrich von Richthofen, trans. Frieda Lawrence, HRC.

11. Lucas, *Frieda Lawrence*, p. 291.

12. Political background on Upper Silesia: Alojzy Targ, comp., *German Testimonies*, pamphlet no. 5, "Cardinal Bertram and the Polishness of Opole Silesia" (Warsaw: Wydawnictwo Zachodnie, April 1960), pp. 4–10; Józef Kokot, ed., *The Miseries of the Prussian Eastern Provinces*, pamphlet no. 3 (Poland, Western Press Agency), p. 4; Józef Borowik and Roman Lutman, eds., *Baltic and Scandinavian Countries* 3, no. 2 (Gdynia, Poland: Baltic Institute, May 1937); Władysław Semkowicz, *Silesia: Its Name, Territory and Boundaries: A Study in Historical Geography* (n.p.), trans. B. W. A. Massey; Lawrence Schofer, *The Formation of a Modern Labor Force: Upper Silesia, 1865–1914* (Berkeley: University of California Press), 1975.

13. Reminiscence by Friedrich von Richthofen, trans. Frieda Lawrence, HRC.

14. Houston Peterson, ed., *A Treasury of the World's Greatest Speeches* (New York: Simon & Schuster, 1965), p. 528.

15. There are two different English-language versions: "My fathers [*sic*] Diary," "Papa's Tagebuch," trans. Frieda Lawrence; HRC.

16. John Macdonald, *Great Battlefields of the War* (London: Michael Joseph, 1984), pp. 102–105; Michael Howard, *The Franco-Prussian War: The German Invasion of France, 1870–1871* (New York: Macmillan, 1962), pp. 4–8, 16, 36, 59, 61–62, 82 ff., 127, 447.

17. "My fathers Diary," "Papa's Tagebuch."

18. "Papa's Tagebuch."

19. Phone interview with Frederick R. Jeffrey, February 27, 1991. Other family members maintain that he was wounded at Sedan, but the facts do not seem to bear this out.

20. AvR.

21. Offenburg Kirchenbücher, Adressbücher, Einwohnermeldekartei, Verlassenschaftsakten (Testamente), Ratsprotokollen (no. 249, 8 July 1776 [application for residence permit of Franz Josef Marquier], for the years 1778, 1783, 1784, 1788, 1789); family tree and death, birth, and marriage certificates; Ratsprotokollen nos. 1382 and 1419 for the year 1817; Ratsprotokoll no. 41 for the year 1818. Additional information and documents provided by Oberarchivrat, Generallandesarchiv Karlsruhe.

22. Background on Donaueschingen here and in the following paragraphs: AvR; Georg Goerlipp et al. and (visual information) Kurt Grill, *Donaueschingen* (Freiburg: Verlag Karl Schillinger, 1978); Rudi Schlatter, *Narren-Chronik der Stadt Donaueschingen* (Donaueschingen, n.p., 1975). I am grateful to Claudia Schmidt, of Donaueschingen, for showing me the town in the summer of 1988.

23. AvR.

24. Ibid.

25. For various literary references to the river and disputes over its source, see Claudio Magris, *Danube* (New York: Farrar, Straus & Giroux, 1990), trans. Patrick Creagh.

26. AvR.

27. Ibid.

28. Generallandesarchiv Karlsruhe.

29. Information and background on Freiburg: Wilhelm Schlang, *Freiburg im Breisgau Together with its Environs in the Black Forest* (Freiburg: Publishing Department of the Freiburg and Black Forest Travellers' Society, 1911).

30. For information on the Institute Blas: Waldhof Volksbildungsheim E.V., Freiburg; letter of April 29, 1990, from Fritz Schaffer; letter of July 3, 1990, from Fritz Schaffer's sister, Marianne Pitsch; advertisements, "Das Pensionat & Töchter-Institut der Fräulein Blas und [Victorine] Peter . . . " and "Töchter-Institut. . . ," announcing the school's opening on May 8, 1864, and listing the names of teachers, etc.; "Julie Blas—A Eulogy," *Freiburger Zeitung*, March 1920; "Life Rules for Girls," a statement of school policy; letter of December 20, 1872, to Julie Blas from the Grand-Duchess of Baden, Karlsruhe; pages from the Blas guest register; a sample report card.

Other sources: Staatsarchiv Freiburg, Stadt Freiburg im Breisgau for death certificates and Julie Blas's will.

31. Biographical and family information, dates, and events here and in the following paragraphs: AvR.

32. Generallandesarchiv Karlsruhe.

33. The story of the kaiser's reception, the first meeting between Friedrich von Richthofen and Anna Marquier, and the Constance fresco here and in the following paragraphs was related to me by Frederick R. Jeffrey, interview, March 16, 1989, Greenwich.

34. Two conflicting documents in the Archives Municipales, Metz, list her as both Catholic and Protestant but clearly indicate she was born Catholic.

35. The image is from DHL, "The Prussian Officer," p. 133.

36. AvR.

37. Archivist, Stadt Konstanz; Konzil Gaststätten; Pressebildbüro.

38. Dépt. Bas-Rhin. I am grateful to Elisabeth Pyroth, Goethe House, New York City, for translations of this and other diplomatic titles of Friedrich von Richthofen.

39. AvR.

40. Ibid.

41. Ibid.

42. Dépt. Bas-Rhin.

43. Intact today but with a different number, and with its street name restored: 18 Rempart St. Thiébault.

44. AvR.

Chapter 2 The Smell of Invasion

1. Guy de Maupassant, "Boule de Suif," *Selected Short Stories*, trans. Roger Colet (London: Penguin, 1987), p. 23.

2. Dépt. Bas-Rhin.

3. AvR.

4. James Elery Holland, *The Memoirs of Frieda Lawrence*, doctoral diss., University of Texas, Austin, 1976 (hereafter Holland), p. 105.

5. *M&C*, p. 53.

6. Ibid., pp. 55, 470.

7. Holland, p. 328.

8. *M&C*, pp. 43, 44, 51, 52, 470.

9. Ibid., p. 55.

10. Ibid., p. 43.

11. Ibid., p. 54.

12. Ibid., p. 44.

13. Ibid., p. 53.

14. She adapted this story of a paralyzed baron to her own purposes (*M&C*, p. 44). See also Holland, p. 80.

15. *M&C*, p. 45.

16. Holland, p. 81. Anna von Richthofen and Baron Podewils conducted a long correspondence during Frieda's childhood; their letters are housed in the HRC.

17. (*Note:* Throughout, I use the words "occupation" and "annexation" interchangeably to refer to the period in Metz following the Franco-Prussian War and extending through World War I.)

Notebook 5, HRC. Cf. Lucas, *Frieda Lawrence*, p. 14: "Frieda saw nothing of the hatred beneath the smooth and orderly surface of affairs. . . . she never showed any awareness that all was not well between the Germans and the French. Nowhere in any of her reminiscences, in her surviving letters or in recorded conversations, is there any acknowledgment of it. National problems meant nothing to her. She ignored all the symptoms—until the First World War came to teach her better."

18. *M&C*, p. 48. The name was presumably fictitious; Frieda's school records have not survived; she probably attended first an *école protestante* (as they were known even during the annexation) in Sablon and, later, one of Metz's many *Mädchenschulen*.

19. Holland, p. 100.

20. *NIBTW*, p. 38.

21. Dépt. Bas-Rhin.

22. Holland, p. 264.

23. Ibid., p. 265.

24. *M&C*, p. 55.

25. Ibid., p. 469.

26. *NIBTW*, p. 38.

27. *M&C*, p. 50.

28. Ibid., p. 55.

29. Max Weber to Marianne Weber, as quoted in Martin Green, *The von Richthofen Sisters: The Triumphant and the Tragic Modes of Love* (New York: Basic Books, 1974), p. 118.

30. *M&C*, pp. 469–470.

31. Ibid., p. 468.

32. Holland, p. 105.

33. Phone interview with Barbara Barr, October 6, 1994. *Mädchen in Uniform*, directed by Leontine Sagan and based on the play *Gestern und Heute*, by Christa Winsloe (who also wrote the screenplay, with F. D. Andam), was originally released in 1931. The U.S. ban was eventually lifted with the help of Eleanor Roosevelt. The first reference to Frieda's lesbian affair appeared in Rosie Jackson, *Frieda Lawrence* (London: Pandora, 1994), pp. 61–62.

34. *M&C*, p. 63.

35. *NIBTW*, p. 38.

36. "town girls": *M&C*, p. 65; "behind her rose the cathedral on its hill, a crouching, spreading cathedral with one tower, lifting its finger"; "You entered the cathedral like the hollow skeleton of an enormous prehistoric animal": *M&C*, pp. 47, 65.

37. *M&C*, p. 63.

38. Ibid., p. 68.

39. Ibid., p. 64.

40. Various letters from Frieda to Else, n.d. (autumn 1913), refer to Friedrich's mistress and, apparently, a sixteen-year-old illegitimate son, which would place the date of the boy's conception at 1897, when Frieda was eighteen. "I think Papa misses the warmth of Selma—he needs so much love, and that Mama spoils him with warmth one cannot say"; "So clearly I perceived again that this empty, inwardly hollow living together is mortifying for people. If Papa were with Selma, he would have *something*, it is *mortifying* for a sensitive person—Mama's bad treatment"; "He also told me about Selma—it is *awful* about the money, he says another 1000 M." HRC. See also chapter 8.

DHL's play *The Fight for Barbara* (see chapter 7) and his semi-autobiographical novel *Mr. Noon* (London: Cambridge University Press, 1985, p. 180) also used the facts of Friedrich von Richthofen's affair.

The amounts of money Selma demanded perhaps increased later, around 1907, when a federation of German women's associations began publicly demanding changes in Prussian illegitimacy laws. See Richard J. Evans, *Rethinking German History: Nineteenth-Century Germany and the Origins of the Third Reich* (London: Unwin Hyman), p. 226.

41. Frieda von Richthofen to Else von Richthofen, May 25, 1896, HRC.

42. Archives Municipales, Metz.

43. Green, *The von Richthofen Sisters*, p. 15. There the haircuts seem to have been perpetrated on all three girls, at a much earlier date (after only one servant was dismissed). Frieda's letter to Else, however, as well as other internal evidence, would seem to place these events in 1896—when Else no longer effectively lived at home. The photo mentioned in Green perhaps dates from another incident.

44. *NIBTW*, p. 37.

45. Frieda is often said (at the age of seventeen) to have attended a finishing school run by Moravian Brothers in the Black Forest (see, e.g., *M&C*, p. 41). No evidence has been found for this claim; furthermore, a finishing school for girls is unlikely to have been run by men.

46. Letter from Marianne Pitsch, July 3, 1990.

47. Frieda von Richthofen to Else von Richthofen, May 25, 1896, HRC.

48. Karl von Marbahr to Frieda Lawrence, n.d. (1940s or 1950s), *M&C*, p. 297.

49. *Portrait of Frieda Lawrence*, comp. and narr. A. Alvarez, prod. Sasha Moorsom, BBC broadcast November 14, 1961; hereafter BBC.

50. Karl von Marbahr to Frieda Lawrence, n.d., *M&C*, p. 297.

51. Only about one in thirty Berlin residences had telephones. Berliner Adressbuch of 1898, provided by Landesarchiv Berlin.

52. Information supplied by Patrick von Richthofen; *Genealogisches Handbuch des Adels*; *M&C*, p. 74; Lucas, *Frieda Lawrence*, p. 17.

53. *Genealogisches Handbuch des Adels*, p. 375.

54. Friedrich von Richthofen to Else von Richthofen, October 24, 1900, trans. Frieda Lawrence, HRC; Prince Bernhard von Bülow, *Memoirs*, vol. 1 (Boston: Little, Brown, 1931–32), p. 454.

55. *M&C*, p. 42.

56. Ibid., p. 73.

57. Anne Topham, *Memories of the Kaiser's Court* (London: Methuen, 1914), p. 76.

58. Maurice Leudet, *The Emperor of Germany at Home*, trans. Virginia Taylour (London: Hutchinson, 1898), p. 269.

59. Lucas, *Frieda Lawrence*, p. 19.

60. Ibid.

61. Leudet, *The Emperor of Germany at Home*, p. 271.

62. *M&C*, p. 75.

63. Ibid.

64. Frieda von Richthofen to Else von Richthofen, February 21, 1898, *M&C*, pp. 143–144.

Chapter 3 Ernest Weekley

1. In 1901, for example, she wrote:

> The body decays
> The stone disintegrates
> But *Eichberg* will hold!

Pages from the Blas guest register supplied by Marianne Pitsch, July 3, 1990.

2. For background and walking trips I have relied principally on Schlang, *Freiburg im Breisgau*, pp. 32, 34, 35, 39.

3. Weekley's appointment as French lecturer commenced January 10, 1898. Details of his studies and work from Montague Weekley, "Ernest Weekley, 1865–1954," in Ernest Weekley, *An Etymological Dictionary of Modern English* (New York: Dover Publications, 1967).

4. Ernest Weekley's salary here and throughout provided in letter of July 18, 1988, from Linda Shaw, University of Nottingham Library; desire for a chair at Oxford or Cambridge: interview with Montague Weekley, July 13, 1978.

5. The publisher, in London, was W. B. Clive.

6. Interview with Veronica Murphy, July 16, 1988, London.

7. *M&C*, p. 80.

8. Frieda von Richthofen to Else von Richthofen, n.d., HRC. The misspelling of "Carissima" was Frieda's.

9. David Garnett, *Great Friends: Portraits of Seventeen Writers* (London: Macmillan, 1979), p. 78.

10. *M&C*, pp. 80–81.

11. Ernest Weekley to Else von Richthofen, August 18, 1898. I am grateful to Martin Green for providing a copy of the letter.

12. *M&C*, p. 80.

13. Montague Weekley, "Ernest Weekley, 1865–1954."

14. From an archival source in the collection of the British Library; hereafter this particular material is referred to as BL.

15. *M&C*, pp. 80, 81.

16. Ibid., p. 81.

17. In *Mr. Noon*, pp. 195 ff., Lawrence suggests that Else had never liked Weekley.

18. July 30, 1898, guest register, courtesy Marianne Pitsch.

19. Dates of the von Richthofens' arrivals and departures from Blas guest register pages supplied by Marianne Pitsch; letter from Ernest Weekley to Else von Richthofen, August 18, 1898 ("My dear Elsa [*sic*], Lovers are. . . ").

20. *M&C*, p. 474.

21. Ibid., pp. 474–475.

22. BL.

23. *M&C*, pp. 81, 474–475.

24. Ibid., pp. 81, 475.

25. Holland, p. 316.

26. *M&C*, p. 81.

27. Barbara Barr, "I Look Back," *Twentieth Century* 165 (March 1959), p. 254.

28. BL.

29. Ibid.

30. Interview with Montague Weekley, July 13, 1978; BL.

31. Ibid.

32. *M&C*, p. 81.

33. Interview with Montague Weekley, July 13, 1978.

34. Interview with Veronica Murphy, July 16, 1988, London.

35. *M&C*, p. 82.

36. Ibid., p. 80.

37. Ibid.

38. Holland, p. 317.

39. Holland, p. 141.

40. Ibid., p. 146.

41. *M&C*, p. 80; Frieda von Richthofen to Else von Richthofen, April 26, 1899, indicates that Frieda and Ernest visited Cambridge together on this trip and that Ernest was actively contemplating a translation from the German of a geographical work written by Frieda's uncle Ferdinand von Richthofen. The translation never came to pass.

42. Marriage certificate, Trevelyan House (Weekley divorce file), London.

43. *M&C*, p. 79.

44. Ibid., p. 83.

45. Ibid.

46. J. C. Heer, *Guide to Lucerne, The Lake, and Its Environs* (Lucerne: H. Keller, 1899), pp. 7, 10, 19, 31–32, 129–130, 134, 142–143, 156–165.

47. John Worthen, *D. H. Lawrence: The Early Years, 1885–1912* (Cambridge: Cambridge University Press, 1991), p. 375.

48. Holland, p. 318.

49. *M&C*, pp. 83–85; see also Garnett, *Great Friends*, p. 78.

Chapter 4 Simmering in Nottingham

(*Note:* The chapter title is from Claire Tomalin, *Katherine Mansfield: A Secret Life* [New York: Alfred A. Knopf, 1988], and is used with permission.)

1. *M&C*, p. 85.

2. J. D. Chambers et al., *A Century of Nottingham History, 1851–1951* (Nottingham: Univeristy of Nottingham, 1952), p. 8.

3. Background information on Nottingham, here and below: Chambers et al., *A Century of Nottingham History*; Duncan Gray, *Nottingham Through 500 Years: A History of Town Government*, 2nd ed. (Nottingham: City of Nottingham, 1960), pp. 192, 195, 232; Roy A. Church, *Economic and Social Change in a Midland Town: Victorian Nottingham, 1815–1900* (London: Frank Cass & Co., 1966), p. 339; *The Stranger's Guide Through Nottingham* (Nottingham: B. S. Oliver, 1848), p. 67; *Wright's Directory of Nottingham*, various years.

4. Interview with Montague Weekley, July 13, 1978.

5. Addresses of Frieda and Ernest Weekley here and throughout from documents dated February 8, 1913, in Trevelyan House (Weekley divorce file), London; *Wright's Directory*, various years.

6. Wallace Reyburn, *Flushed with Pride* (London: Macdonald, 1969).

7. Gray, *Nottingham Through 500 Years*, p. 228.

8. Goldswong Terrace fits the description of typical terraced housing developments of the time found in Church, *Economic and Social Change in a Midland Town*, p. 343.

9. Wedding presents: *M&C*, p. 90. Gas: *M&C*, pp. 85–86, and see Gray, *Nottingham Through 500 Years*, p. 234.

10. Holland, p. 147.

11. *M&C*, p. 86.

12. Interview with Montague Weekley, July 13, 1978.

13. As, for example, the British Liberal party leader, Sir Henry Campbell-

Bannerman, learned when the popular press accused him of treason for denouncing the camps (see Robert K. Massie, *Dreadnought: Britain, Germany, and the Coming of the Great War* [New York: Random House, 1991], pp. 554–555). Frieda's opinion of the war: Holland, p. 150.

14. Frieda Weekley to Else von Richthofen, March 3, 1902, *M&C*, p. 154.

15. Interview with Veronica Murphy, July 16, 1988, London.

16. BL.

17. Holland, p. 152; *M&C*, p. 88.

18. *Wright's Directory*, 1901.

19. *M&C*, p. 85.

20. Interview with Barbara Barr, June 17, 1978.

21. In the course of his career he completed at least four: *French Prose Composition*, *School French Grammar*, *Exercises in the French Subjunctive*, and *A Higher French Reader*—all, as previously cited, for University Tutorial.

22. Frieda Weekley to Else von Richthofen, December 15, 1899, *M&C*, p. 144.

23. Frieda Weekley to Else von Richthofen, n.d., ibid., p. 146.

24. *M&C*, p. 91.

25. Letter from Barbara Barr, July 12, 1988.

26. Montague Weekley, "Ernest Weekley, 1865–1954."

27. BL; Barr, "I Look Back," p. 254.

28. BL.

29. Ibid.

30. See Ernest Weekley to Anna von Richthofen, September 13, 1902, *M&C*, p. 157.

31. "[H]e soon got rid of his pacifier and holds it with disdain!" Frieda Weekley to Else von Richthofen, n.d., HRC.

32. Archives Municipales, Metz; Green, *The von Richthofen Sisters*, p. 22.

33. See Frieda Weekley to Edward Garnett, November 19, 1912, *DHL Letters* 1, p. 479: "I have heard so much about 'form' with Ernst."

34. Maude Weekley to Frieda Weekley, May 14, 1912, *M&C*, p. 166.

35. Frieda Weekley to Else von Richthofen, n.d., ibid., p. 151.

36. Frieda Weekley to Else von Richthofen, n.d., ibid., p. 155.

37. See Frieda Weekley to Else von Richthofen, June 18, 1901(?), ibid., p. 148.

38. Frieda Weekley to Else von Richthofen, October 5, 1901, ibid., p. 149.

39. Johann Christoph Friedrich von Schiller, *Select Ballads*, ed. Frieda Weekley (London: Blackie's Little German Classics, 1902).

40. Frieda Weekley to Else von Richthofen, November 25, 1901, *M&C*, p. 150.

41. As she did every year: interview with Montague Weekley, July 13, 1978.

42. See Evans, *Rethinking German History*, p. 232.

43. Ernest Weekley to Friedrich von Richthofen, August 5, 1900, collection of Martin Green.

44. Green, *The von Richthofen Sisters*, pp. 23, 184.

45. Friedrich von Richthofen to Else von Richthofen, October 24, 1900, trans. Frieda Lawrence, HRC.

46. Frieda Weekley to Else von Richthofen, July 4, 1900, HRC.

47. Friedrich von Richthofen to Else von Richthofen, October 24, 1900.

48. They were married in Karlsruhe on November 18, 1902.

49. Green, *The von Richthofen Sisters*, p. 25.

50. Ibid.

51. She called her feelings for Edgar "*freundschaftlich*"—friendly. Ibid.

52. BBC.

53. Ernest Weekley to Friedrich von Richthofen, September 16, 1902, *M&C*, p. 158.

54. Ernest Weekley to Else von Richthofen, September 15, 1902, ibid.

55. Letter from Barbara Barr, July 8, 1989.

56. Frieda Lawrence to Else Jaffe, February 26, 1955, *M&C*, p. 394.

57. Frieda Lawrence to Else Jaffe, June 25, 1955, ibid., p. 398.

58. BL.

59. See Frieda Weekley to Else Jaffe, n.d. (ca. Christmas 1902), HRC.

60. Frieda Weekley to Anna von Richthofen, n.d., *M&C*, p. 160.

61. *M&C*, p. 87.

62. Cf. ibid., p. 86.

63. BL.

64. Interview with Veronica Murphy, July 16, 1988, London.

65. Gray notes a great increase in the number of motor cars as early as 1901. See *Nottingham Through 500 Years*, p. 231.

66. For information on the Nottingham suffragists I have relied on Elisabeth Kirkham's thesis "Suffragettes in Nottingham: The Origins and Development of the Women's Suffrage Society in Nottingham" (n.d., copy in Nottingham County Library [hereafter NCL]), which contains relevant newspaper clippings.

67. Dowson address: *Wright's Directory*, 1903. Suffragette meeting: see, e.g., Nottingham *Evening Post*, April 19, 1895, for an account of a meeting held in Friends' Schoolroom, Friarlane, which the Dowsons attended. Mrs. Dowson was named honorary secretary. Will Dowson's name disappears from the attendance records as the years go by.

68. *M&C*, p. 93.

69. Interview with Montague Weekley, July 13, 1978.

70. BL.

71. BBC.

72. *M&C*, p. 86.

73. BL; cf. *Mr. Noon*, p. 192.

74. BL.

75. BL; *M&C*, p. 81; cf. *Mr. Noon*, p. 125.

76. Edward Nehls, ed., *D. H. Lawrence: A Composite Biography*, vol. 3 (Madison: University of Wisconsin Press, 1961), p. 162. Vols. 1 and 2 were published in 1958 and 1959, respectively. Hereafter Nehls, followed by volume and page numbers.

77. *M&C*, p. 92.

78. BL.

79. Green, *The von Richthofen Sisters*, p. 27.

80. Ludwig Bechstein, *Bechstein's Märchen*, ed. Frieda Weekley, Blackie's Little German Classics (London: Blackie's, 1906).

81. Interview with Montague Weekley, July 13, 1978.

82. *M&C*, p. 85.

83. *Wright's Directory*, 1905, 1906.

84. BL.

85. Ibid.

86. Ibid.

Chapter 5 "Our Old Mother's Skin"

1. Address: Zurich police document no. 129453 VI, November 25, 1909.

2. *D. H. Lawrence Review* (hereafter *DHL Review*) 22, no. 2 (Summer 1990), p. 197. The issue contains translations of a large body of correspondence between Frieda Weekley and Otto Gross (HRC), translated by John Turner with Cornelia Rumpf-Worthen and Ruth Jenkins. Most of the letters are undated; I refer to them here by the page numbers in the *Review* on which the translation appears.

3. *M&C*, p. 93.

4. Wolfgang Leppmann, *Rilke: A Life*, trans. Russell M. Stockman (New York: Fromm International, 1984), p. 61.

5. See introductory note to Ernst Scheyer, *Albert Bloch, 1882–1961: An Exhibition of Watercolors, Drawings, and Drypoints* (Lawrence: University of Kansas Museum of Art, n.d.), unpaged: The term combined "the ethnic-Slavic with the geographical, that is the region still east of Vienna."

6. Holland, pp. 276, 280; Martin Esslin, ed., *The Genius of the German Theater* (New York: Mentor/NAL, 1958), pp. 460–461.

7. *M&C*, pp. 93-94. I am indebted to J. Zweifel of the Staatsarchiv des Kantons Zürich for providing police-blotter records, internal departmental memos, and newspaper clippings relating to Frick and others discussed in this chapter; and to Martin Green for the letters from Frieda Weekley, Otto Gross, Ernst Frick, Else Jaffe, and Frieda Gross that provide the background to much of the narrative.

8. *M&C*, p. 93; Holland, p. 275.

9. "Better people," usually a term used self-deprecatingly (and often with some self-mockery) by the lower middle class to describe their betters. Frieda also used it to describe Ida Wilhelmy.

10. Staatsarchiv des Kantons Zürich.

11. Background on Reventlow from Franziska Gräfin zu Reventlow, *Tagebücher, 1895–1910* (Hamburg: Luchterhand, 1992); *M&C*, p. 93; Martin Green, *Mountain of Truth* (Hanover, N.H.: University Press of New England, 1986), pp. 135–136, 160 ff. I am grateful to Brigitte McNamara, of Taos, for help with translation of the Reventlow diary.

12. Holland, p. 171.

13. Reventlow, *Tagebücher*, p. 428.

14. Holland, p. 160. Gross lived on the corner of Georgen- and Schleisheimerstrassen (Zurich police document no. 129453 VI, November 25, 1909).

15. Emanuel Hurwitz, *Otto Gross: Paradies-Sucher zwischen Freud und Jung: Leben und Werk* (Zurich: Suhrkamp Verlag, 1979), p. 216.

16. Leonhard Frank, *Links wo das Herz ist* (Munich: Nymphenburger Verlag, 1952), as quoted in Lucas, *Frieda Lawrence*, p. 36. The book was translated by Cyrus Brooks as *Heart on the Left* (London: Arthur Barker, 1954).

17. See Green, *The von Richthofen Sisters*, pp. 43, 56, and *Mountain of Truth*, pp. 150–151.

18. *M&C*, p. 94; Holland, p. 276; cf. *Mr. Noon*, p. 127.

19. Holland, p. 276.

20. See Jennifer E. Michaels, *Anarchy and Eros* (New York: Peter Lang, 1983; orig. *Utah Studies in Literature and Linguistics* 24), p. 25.

21. *NIBTW*, p. 5.

22. Holland, pp. 158–159, 171–172.

23. *NIBTW*, p. 1.

24. Green, *The von Richthofen Sisters*, pp. 39, 43, 49; *DHL Review* 22, pp. 171, 172.

25. See Green, *The von Richthofen Sisters* and *Mountain of Truth*, from which much of the background on Hans and Otto Gross and others in this chapter—on pages too numerous to cite—is drawn.

Other sources of which I have made use throughout the chapter include Emanuel Hurwitz, "*Otto Gross: Von der Psychoanalyse zum Paradies*," in *Monte Verità: Berg der Wahrheit* (Milan: Electa, 1978) and *Otto Gross: Paradies-Sucher zwischen Freud und Jung*; Michaels, *Anarchy and Eros*; *Compte Rendu des Travaux du 1er Congrès International de Psychiatrie, de Neurologie, de Psychologie et de l'Assistance des aliénés* (Amsterdam: J. H. Bussy, 1908), hereafter *Compte Rendu*; *Het Nieuws van den Dag*, September 3, 1907, pp. 1–2.

Also see Arthur Mitzman, "Anarchism, Expressionism and Psychoanalysis," in *New German Critique*, 1977, and *The Iron Cage: An Historical Interpretation of Max Weber* (New York: Knopf, 1970), p. 280; Franz Kafka, *Letters to Friends, Family, and Editors* (New York: Schocken, 1958), pp. 153, 167, 455 (n. 65), 458 (n. 115); Eva Brabant, Ernst Falzeder, and Patrizia Giampieri-Deutsch, eds., *The Correspondence of Sigmund Freud and Sandor Ferenczi*, vol. 1, 1908–1914, trans. Peter T. Hoffer (Cambridge: Belknap/Harvard University Press, 1993), pp. 142, 154; R. Andrew Paskauskas, ed., *The Complete Correspondence of Sigmund Freud and Ernest Jones, 1908–1939* (Cambridge: Belknap/Harvard University Press, 1993), pp. 1–2, 3–4, 62; *The Freud/Jung Letters*, ed. William McGuire, trans. Ralph Manheim and R. F. C. Hull (Cambridge: Harvard University Press, 1988), hereafter *Freud/Jung*.

26. I am indebted to Herr Doktor Klaus Krainz, the director of the present Kriminalmuseum, for background information, and to Jamie James, of New York, for visiting the premises for me on a trip to Graz.

27. *Mr. Noon*, p. 126.

28. Green, *The von Richthofen Sisters*, p. 40.

29. A remark Otto retained and reported to Freud as his first memory of his father. *Freud/Jung*, p. 152.

30. Translations and spinoffs include *Criminal Psychology: A Manual for Judges, Practitioners, and Students* (Boston: Little, Brown, and Co., 1911; trans.

from 4th ed. by Horace M. Kallen) and *Criminal Investigation: A Practical Textbook for Magistrates, Police Officers and Lawyers*, 4th ed., by J. Adam and J. Adam; ed. R. M. Howe (London: Sweet & Maxwell, 1949).

31. Kallen, *Criminal Psychology*, p. 27.
32. Adam, *Criminal Investigation*, pp. 160–161.
33. As he later told his wife—see Green, *Mountain of Truth*, p. 26.
34. Green, *The von Richthofen Sisters*, p. 40.
35. "Café Stefanie, 1912," in *Johannes R. Becher*, vol. 2 (Berlin: Aufbau-Verlag, 1960), pp. 227–228.
36. Green, *The von Richthofen Sisters*, p. 37.
37. *Freud/Jung*, p. 90.
38. Published in 1902, place of publication unknown.
39. Green, *Mountain of Truth*, p. 26.
40. *DHL Review* 22, p. 188.
41. Ibid., p. 169.
42. Ibid.
43. Ibid., pp. 188–189.
44. Ibid., p. 190.
45. *Mr. Noon*, p. 127.
46. *DHL Review* 22, p. 165.
47. Ibid., p. 167.
48. Published in 1907 in Leipzig.
49. *DHL Review* 22, p. 197.
50. These, at least, were her thoughts as later filtered through Lawrence. DHL, *Mr. Noon*, p. 126.
51. Green, *The von Richthofen Sisters*, p. 53.
52. *Mr. Noon*, p. 127.
53. Background from Green, *Mountain of Truth*.
54. Green, *Mountain of Truth*, pp. 120, 125–126.
55. *DHL Review* 22, p. 196.
56. Ibid., p. 197.
57. Ibid., pp. 168–169.
58. Ibid., pp. 191, 192.
59. Ibid., p. 167.
60. Ibid., p. 168.
61. *M&C*, p. 90.
62. Holland, pp. 156–157.
63. *M&C*, p. 95.
64. Ibid., p. 161.
65. *DHL Review* 22, p. 166.
66. Ibid., p. 172; Green, *The von Richthofen Sisters*, p. 52.
67. *DHL Review* 22, p. 195.
68. *M&C*, p. 87.
69. Interview with Montague Weekley, July 13, 1978.
70. Ibid.
71. *NIBTW*, p. 5.

72. *DHL Review* 22, p. 194.
73. Reventlow, *Tagebücher*, p. 428.
74. *DHL Review* 22, p. 170.
75. Ibid., p. 194.
76. Ibid., p. 195—she was quoting, as the translators note, *Hamlet.*
77. *DHL Review* 22, pp. 196–197.
78. Ibid., p. 197.
79. BL.
80. *Compte Rendu*, pp. 298–299, 593–597, 598, 917; *Het Nieuws van den Dag*, September 3, 1907, pp. 1–2.
81. Green, *The von Richthofen Sisters*, p. 55.
82. *DHL Review* 22, pp. 174–175.
83. Green, *Mountain of Truth*, p. 51.
84. *DHL Review* 22, p. 176.
85. Phone conversation with Frederick R. Jeffrey, February 4, 1992.
86. *DHL Review* 22, p. 179.
87. Ibid., p. 187.
88. Ibid., p. 190.
89. Freud, who knew Jones's penchant for seduction, wrote to Jung on May 3, 1908, recommending that Frieda Gross *not* be treated by his colleague. See *Freud/Jung*, p. 146.
90. *Freud/Jung*, p. 142.
91. Ibid., p. 151.
92. Ibid., p. 153.
93. Ibid., pp. 155–156.
94. Green, *The von Richthofen Sisters*, pp. 57, 90.
95. Ibid., p. 57.
96. Ibid., p. 53.
97. *Freud/Jung*, p. 174, n. 4.
98. *Mr. Noon*, p. 192.
99. Ernst Leopold Stahl, *Das Land der Sehnsucht*, published in Düsseldorf in 1911, as noted in Worthen, *D. H. Lawrence: The Early Years*, pp. 377 and 565, n. 23.
100. *Tages-Anzeiger für Stadt und Canton Zürich*, March 8, 1911 (no. 57), supplement 1.
101. Archiv des Kantons Zürich; Green, *Mountain of Truth*, p. 132.

Chapter 6 Simple Men, Giantesses, and Rabbits

1. The date is conjectural (accounts place it variously at from two to six weeks before or a week or two after); I have accepted the chronology offered in Worthen, *D. H. Lawrence: The Early Years*, from which much background on Lawrence in this chapter is drawn. I have also relied throughout the chapter on Jessie Chambers, *D. H. Lawrence: A Personal Record* (Cambridge University Press, 1980); Nehls, 1–3; *M&C*; *NIBTW*; Émile Delavenay, *D. H. Lawrence: The Man and His Work*, trans. Katharine M. Delavenay (London: Heinemann, 1972) and abridged from the original French; and vol. 2 of the original French edition

of Delavenay (*D. H. Lawrence: L'Homme et la Genèse de son Oeuvre. Les Années de Formation, 1885–1919* (Paris: Libraire C. Klincksieck, 1969), hereafter Delavenay 2. I am indebted to Monsieur Delavenay for several long letters throughout the early years of the writing of this book.

2. Interview with Montague Weekley, July 13, 1978.

3. *NIBTW*, p. 4.

4. Barr, "I Look Back," p. 255.

5. Frieda Lawrence, taped recollection of meeting and conversation. BBC tape as recorded in studio of Prof. Alberto Pisani, Lungarno Corsini, Florence, Italy, September, 3, 1957, HRC.

6. Jessie Chambers was considered Lawrence's fiancée; Louisa Burrows was actually his fiancée—for both, see below, in text. For "possible fiancée," see DHL to Agnes Holt, November 27, 1909, *DHL Letters*, 1, p. 146; for "maîtresse," see Delavenay 2, p. 705.

7. *NIBTW*, p. 4.

8. David Gerard, interview with Barbara Barr, NCL.

9. *NIBTW*, p. 4.

10. Ibid., pp. 4, 5.

11. Frieda missed or was late with a menstrual period and believed she may have been pregnant; see DHL to Frieda Weekley, May 15, 1912 (*DHL Letters*, 1, pp. 402–403: "Never mind about the infant. If it should come, we will be glad"). Claims that she and Lawrence made love almost immediately—at Cowley, presumably before lunch—are probably apocryphal.

Mr. Noon, begun nine to ten years later, contains a passage (see pp. 118–130) occasionally used to support a quick first coitus, though there the circumstances are different: no Ernest Weekley–like character is present; instead, an Edgar Jaffe–like one is. Some of the novel's sexual detail tends to farce (for example, a Lawrence-like character, Gilbert Noon, is congratulated by a Frieda-like character, Johanna Keighley, for coming to orgasm three times in forty-five minutes).

Other sources occasionally cited as proof of Frieda and Lawrence's having had sex right away include: (1) Luhan, *Lorenzo in Taos*, p. 103 (written twenty years after the fact); and (2) notes (based on the recollection of one Lewis Richmond, and housed in the Nottingham Record Office) of a comment that William Hopkin, an Eastwood journalist and friend of Lawrence's, may or may not have made to the effect. According to Richmond's secondhand account, Lawrence and Frieda had sex before twenty minutes had elapsed (see Worthen, *D. H. Lawrence: The Early Years*, pp. 382 and 566, n. 40; Worthen does not accept the theory). Hopkin is also the source of the rather fanciful story of Lawrence's first encounter with Alice Dax (see below, in text, and note 54).

Lawrence himself, not long after his first meeting with Frieda, rejected out of hand the offer to go to bed with her at Cowley (see below, in text). Furthermore, the availability of Gladys Bradley's London apartment, Edward Garnett's house (see below, in text), and, for that matter, the Forest (in Nottingham) and Sherwood Forest would have made searching for a convenient spot to make love unnecessary.

12. DHL to Rachel Annand Taylor, December 3, 1910, *DHL Letters*, 1, p. 190.

13. Chambers, *D. H. Lawrence*, p. 32.
14. Ibid., p. 37.
15. *NIBTW*, p. 37.
16. Chambers, *D. H. Lawrence*, p. 47.
17. Ibid., p. 15.
18. "Never despair," ibid., p. 29.
19. Ibid., p. 26.
20. As quoted in Worthen, *D. H. Lawrence: The Early Years*, p. 98.
21. Nehls, 3, p. 583.
22. Ibid., p. 603.
23. Chambers, *D. H. Lawrence*, p. 57.
24. Worthen, *D. H. Lawrence: The Early Years*, p. 288.
25. See DHL to Blanche Jennings, July 30, 1908, *DHL Letters*, 1, p. 68.
26. Chambers, *D. H. Lawrence*, p. 103.
27. Ibid., p. 189.
28. Ibid.
29. Ibid., p. 117.
30. See Worthen, *D. H. Lawrence: The Early Years*, p. 154.
31. Chambers, *D. H. Lawrence*, p. 135.
32. Ibid., p. 127.
33. Ibid., p. 134.
34. Ibid., p. 133.
35. DHL to Louie Burrows, n.d. (ca. September 1906), *DHL Letters*, 1, p. 29.
36. Chambers, *D. H. Lawrence*, p. 76.
37. As quoted in Worthen, *D. H. Lawrence: The Early Years*, p. 196.
38. DHL to Louie Burrows, November 20, 1909, *DHL Letters*, 1, p. 145.
39. Lucas, *Frieda Lawrence*, p. 61.
40. DHL to Louie Burrows, November 20, 1909, *DHL Letters*, 1, p. 145.
41. Chambers, *D. H. Lawrence*, p. 170.
42. Ibid., p. 171.
43. Ibid., p. 174.
44. Ibid., p. 172.
45. *The White Peacock* (Carbondale and Edwardsville: Southern Illinois University Press, 1966), p. 245.
46. Delavenay 2, p. 702.
47. See *Sons and Lovers* (New York: Modern Library, 1962), p. 374; cf. Nehls, 3, p. 619.
48. DHL to Rachel Annand Taylor, December 3, 1910, *DHL Letters*, 1, pp. 190–191.
49. As quoted in Worthen, *D. H. Lawrence: The Early Years*, p. 144.
50. As quoted in ibid., p. 412.
51. Ibid., p. 270.
52. *Morning Post*, February 9, 1911. Among the other British reviews were those in *Times Literary Supplement*, January 26, 1911; *Observer*, January 29, 1911; *Daily Chronicle*, February 10, 1911; *Standard*, February 3, 1911; *Daily Mail*, February 3, 1911; *Daily News*, February 14, 1911; *English Review*, May 1911. For

a complete listing, see R. P. Draper, ed., *D. H. Lawrence: The Critical Heritage* (London: Routledge & Kegan Paul, 1970), pp. 33 ff.

53. Alice Dax to Frieda Lawrence, January 23, 1935, *M&C*, p. 248.

54. Harry T. Moore, *The Priest of Love* (London: Heinemann, 1974), p. 112; cf. *M&C*, p. 461.

55. Chambers, *D. H. Lawrence*, p. 196.

56. Interview with Montague Weekley, July 13, 1978.

57. The first volume of *The Forsyte Saga* (1906) was Galsworthy's most popular novel to date, but *The Patrician* (1911) was the most recently published. Most of Galsworthy's earlier novels were published under the pseudonym John Sinjohn; *The Island Pharisees* (1904) and *The Country House* (1907), published under his own name, were not widely sold, according to his biographer, Dudley Barker (*The Man of Principle* [New York: Stein and Day, 1969]). *Fraternity*, another of his class novels, was published in 1909.

58. David Gerard, interview with Barbara Barr, NCL.

59. Frieda Weekley to Edward Garnett, September 7, 1912, *DHL Letters*, 1, p. 449.

60. *NIBTW*, p. 56.

61. David Gerard, interview with Barbara Barr, NCL.

62. *NIBTW*, p. 294.

63. It was a term he used often: See, e.g., DHL to Edward Garnett, May 17, 1913, *DHL Letters*, 1, p. 550.

64. DHL to Edward Garnett, April 19, 1912, *DHL Letters*, 1, p. 384.

65. BBC.

66. Ibid.

67. Ibid.

68. *NIBTW*, p. 7.

69. Ernest Weekley to Anna von Richthofen, September 26, 1912, HRC.

70. Ernest Weekley to Friedrich von Richthofen, May 11, 1912, HRC.

71. *Phoenix*, vol. 1, ed. Edward D. McDonald (London: Viking, 1936), pp. 71–75.

72. *Mr. Noon*, p. 169.

73. *NIBTW*, p. 7.

74. DHL to Ernest Weekley, May 7, 1912, *DHL Letters*, 1, p. 392.

75. DHL to Frieda Weekley, May 9, 1912, *DHL Letters*, 1, p. 396.

76. Maupassant, *Selected Short Stories*, pp. 259–264.

77. Cf. DHL to Edward Garnett, May 21, 1912, *DHL Letters*, 1, p. 409.

78. *Mr. Noon*, p. 177.

79. Ibid., pp. 177–178.

80. DHL to Edward Garnett, May 21, 1912, *DHL Letters*, 1, p. 409.

81. BL.

82. Ernest Weekley to Frieda Weekley, May 10, 1912, *M&C*, p. 162.

83. DHL to Frieda Weekley, May 15, 1912, *DHL Letters*, 1, pp. 402–403.

84. *Mr. Noon*, p. 191.

85. "First Morning," from *Poems*, selected and introduced by Keith Sagar (London: Penguin, 1986), p. 60.

86. *NIBTW*, p. 40.

87. Ibid.

88. BL.

89. Maude Weekley to Frieda Weekley, May 14, 1912, *M&C*, pp. 165–166.

90. Lily Kipping to Frieda Weekley, n.d., *M&C*, p. 167.

91. *NIBTW*, pp. 40–41.

92. Ibid., p. 39.

93. Ibid.

94. DHL to Edward Garnett, June 29, 1912, *DHL Letters*, 1, p. 419.

95. As quoted in Worthen, *D. H. Lawrence: The Early Years*, pp. 411–412; see also plate 42.

96. Garnett, *Great Friends*, p. 80. The story is considered apocryphal by some, despite its immortalization in verse by the British poet Anna Wickham (who was told the story by Garnett):

> Am I pleasant?
> Tell me that, old Wise!
> Let me look into your eyes
> To see if you can comprehend my beauty,
> That is a lover's duty.
> I look at you to see
> If you can think of anything but me.
> Ah, you remember praise and your philosophy!
> My love shall be a sphere of silence and of light,
> Where Love is all alone with Love's delight.—
> Here is a woodcutter who is so weak
> With love of me, he cannot speak.
> Tell me, dumb man, am I pleasant, am I pleasant?
> Farewell, philosopher! I love a peasant.

("Imperatrix," from *The Contemplative Quarry* and *The Man with a Hammer* [New York: Harcourt, Brace and Company, 1921], p. 86.)

97. *NIBTW*, p. 36.

98. *Poems* (Sagar), p. 64; also see *NIBTW*, p. 49.

99. DHL to Edward Garnett, June 2, 1912, *DHL Letters*, 1, p. 415.

100. Cf. *Mr. Noon*, p. 237.

101. *Mr. Noon*, p. 186.

102. *Daily News*, June 21, 1912. The other, mostly favorable reviews included: *Athenaeum*, June 1, 1912; *Manchester Guardian*, June 5, 1912; *Westminster Gazette*, June 8, 1912; *Morning Post*, June 17, 1912; *Standard*, June 21, 1912; *Saturday Review*, June 22, 1912.

The *Nottinghamshire Guardian* (July 2, 1912) headlined its review "Reprehensible Jaunt" and more or less panned the book, though Lawrence's "cleverness in putting all sorts of strange emotions into words and discriminating the slightest shades of sensation" was noted.

103. DHL to Edward Garnett, June 29, 1912, *DHL Letters*, 1, p. 419.

Chapter 7 Over the Alps

1. DHL to Edward Garnett, August 4, 1912, *DHL Letters*, 1, pp. 429–430; cf. *Mr. Noon*, p. 218.

2. Cf. *Mr. Noon*, p. 224. Lawrence's description is entirely in keeping with Monty's later memory of the manner in which Frieda customarily gave vent to her derision: interview with Montague Weekley, July 13, 1978.

3. DHL to Edward Garnett, August 4, 1912, *DHL Letters*, 1, pp. 429–430.

4. *NIBTW*, p. 48.

5. Ibid., p. 53.

6. Interview with Montague Weekley, July 13, 1978.

7. Ibid.

8. DHL to Edward Garnett, September 7, 1912, *DHL Letters*, 1, p. 448; cf. *Mr. Noon*, p. 234.

9. BL.

10. *Mr. Noon*, pp. 191–194.

11. Background on English marriage law from Joan Perkin, *Women and Marriage in Nineteenth-Century England* (London: Routledge, 1989), pp. 1, 7–8, 23, 56–57, 59, 69–70, 93–95, 118 (table), 137, 139, 207, 214, 224–225, 235, 253, 275–276, 283–285, 311; O. R. McGregor, *Divorce in England: A Centenary Study* (London: Heinemann, 1957), pp. 17–19, 23–24, 29–31, 36, 63, 65–67; Leonard Shelford, *A Practical Treatise of the Law of Marriage and Divorce* (Philadelphia: n.p., 1841); E. S. P. Haynes, *Divorce Problems of To-Day* (Cambridge: W. Heffer & Sons, 1912), pp. 1, 30, 37, 43–45, 47, 92, 94, 96.

12. BL.

13. Interview with Montague Weekley, July 13, 1978.

14. Ernest did not dismiss her in a rage over Frieda's having left him, as has occasionally been written elsewhere; Wilhelmy's plans to become a nurse had long been under way, and she left voluntarily, probably at the end of March. Interview with Montague Weekley, July 13, 1978.

15. BL.

16. Interview with Veronica Murphy, July 16, 1988, London.

17. BL.

18. Interview with Montague Weekley, July 13, 1978.

19. BL. In 1912, there was a tram between Camden and the Hampstead Heath Underground Station at the foot of the long hill up to Well Walk.

20. BL.

21. Ibid.

22. Ibid., from which all information and quotations in the paragraph are drawn.

23. Ibid., from which all information and quotations in the paragraph are drawn.

24. Ibid., from which all information and quotations in the paragraph are drawn. Ernest later sent other pictures: Frieda Weekley to Edward Garnett, October 30–November 2, 1912, *DHL Letters*, 1, p. 467.

25. See, e.g., Witter Bynner, *Journey with Genius*, p. 3; Knud Merrild, *With D. H. Lawrence in New Mexico*, p. 35; "She Said as Well to Me," in *Poems* (Sagar), pp. 73–74.

26. Cf. DHL to David Garnett, September 11, 1912, *DHL Letters*, 1, p. 451.
27. David Garnett, *Great Friends*, p. 80.
28. Frieda Weekley to Edward Garnett, September 7, 1912, *DHL Letters*, 1, p. 449.
29. DHL to Edward Garnett, May 21, 1912, ibid., p. 409.
30. DHL to Edward Garnett, April 21, 1913, ibid., p. 542.
31. Frieda Weekley to David Garnett, November 19, 1912, ibid., p. 476.
32. Frieda Weekley to Edward Garnett, September 7, 1912, ibid., p. 449.
33. Worthen, *D. H. Lawrence: The Early Years*, p. 446.
34. *NIBTW*, p. 56.
35. Worthen, *D. H. Lawrence: The Early Years*, p. 442.
36. Frieda Lawrence to F. R. Leavis, May 22, 1956, *M&C*, p. 412.
37. BL.
38. BL. Cf. DHL to Frieda Weekley, May 14, 1912, *DHL Letters*, 1, p. 400.
39. Frieda Weekley to Edward Garnett, November 19, 1912, ibid., p. 479.
40. *NIBTW*, p. 56.
41. Brigit Patmore, "A Memoir of Frieda Lawrence," in *A D. H. Lawrence Miscellany*, ed. Harry T. Moore (Carbondale: Southern Illinois University Press, 1959), p. 138.
42. Frieda Weekley to Edward Garnett, September 7, 1912, *DHL Letters*, 1, p. 449.
43. *The Fight for Barbara*, from *The Complete Plays of D. H. Lawrence* (New York: Viking, 1965), p. 276.
44. *NIBTW*, p. 56.
45. Frieda Weekley to Edward Garnett, November 19, 1912, *DHL Letters*, 1, p. 479.
46. The uncut book was published in 1992 by Cambridge University Press.

Chapter 8 "Mrs. Lawrence"

1. DHL to Arthur McLeod, January 17, 1913, *DHL Letters*, 1, p. 506.
2. DHL to Ernest Collings, November 7, 1912, ibid., p. 468.
3. DHL to Edward Garnett, January 20, 1913, ibid., p. 507.
4. The complete text of the foreword is in Aldous Huxley, ed., *The Letters of D. H. Lawrence* (New York: Viking, 1932), pp. 97–102.
5. DHL to Edward Garnett, February 1, 1913, and March 11, 1913, *DHL Letters*, 1, pp. 510, 526.
6. *Rhythm*, March 1913.
7. *NIBTW*, p. 69.
8. DHL to Ernest Collings, January 13, 1913, *DHL Letters*, 1, p. 503.
9. DHL to Sallie Hopkin, December 23, 1912, ibid., p. 490.
10. For opening sentence of "Elsa Culverwell," see ibid., p. 496, n. 5.
11. DHL to Edward Garnett, January 12, 1913, *DHL Letters*, 1, p. 501.
12. DHL to Edward Garnett, May 2(?), 1913, ibid., p. 545.
13. *The Complete Poems*, p. 86.
14. *Poems* (Sagar), pp. 71–72.
15. Frieda Weekley to Edward Garnett, May 17, 1913, *DHL Letters*, 1, p. 549.

16. *NIBTW*, pp. 68–69.

17. Barbara Weekley Barr, "Memoir of D. H. Lawrence," *D. H. Lawrence: Novelist, Poet, Prophet*, ed. Stephen Spender (New York: Harper & Row, 1973), p. 9; *Chiswick and Turnham Green: The Official Publication of the Urban District Council*, 1913–14, Chiswick Public Library.

18. DHL to Edgar Jaffe, February 10, 1913, *DHL Letters*, 1, p. 514.

19. Ibid.

20. It was the Probate, Divorce and Admiralty Division of the High Court. See DHL to Edward Garnett, February 18, 1913, ibid., pp. 516–517.

21. Haynes, *Divorce Problems of To-Day*, title page epigraph.

22. McGregor, *Divorce in England*, p. 67.

23. For her attitude, see, e.g., *M&C*, p. 108.

24. Frieda Weekley to David Garnett, February 27, 1913, *DHL Letters*, 1, p. 521.

25. Text of affidavit sworn February 8, 1913, by Ernest Weekley. Trevelyan House (Weekley divorce file); DHL to Arthur McLeod, March 5, 1913, *DHL Letters*, 1, p. 524.

26. March 3 is the presumed date, based on DHL to Edward Garnett, March 3, 1913, *DHL Letters*, 1, p. 522.

27. See ibid., p. 527, n. 2.

28. DHL to Jessie Chambers, ca. March 13, 1913, ibid., pp. 527–528.

29. Ibid., p. 531, n. 1.

30. *M&C*, pp. 107–109. Frieda dates receipt of the letter as a Saturday after she and Lawrence "had been together for nearly a year," the reference presumably being to their May departure from England for Metz; she goes on to say that Lawrence "developed a bad cold" three days after the letter came; he was sick from about March 20 to March 22 (see DHL to Edward Garnett, March 22, 1913, *DHL Letters*, 1, pp. 529–531).

31. *M&C*, pp. 108–109.

32. DHL to David Garnett, April 5, 1913, *DHL Letters*, 1, p. 536.

33. DHL to Edward Garnett, May 17, 1913, ibid., p. 550; DHL to Henry Savage, January 19, 1914, ibid., 2, pp. 137–138.

34. DHL to Edward Garnett, March 22, 1913, ibid., 1, p. 530.

35. DHL to Arthur McLeod, March 5, 1913, ibid., pp. 524–525. Her husband's full name was Per Johan Hugo Almgren, his patron Prince Carl of Sweden. See Tony Cyriax, *Among Italian Peasants* (London: William Collins, 1919).

36. Frieda Weekley to David Garnett, March 25, 1913, ibid., pp. 533–534.

37. DHL to Katharine Clayton, October 21, 1915, ibid., 2, pp. 413–414; as noted on p. 414, n. 1, the sketch was included in *Twilight in Italy*, published in England on June 15, 1916, by Duckworth.

38. DHL to Edward Garnett, May 2(?), 1913, and DHL to David Garnett, April 5, 1913, ibid., 1, pp. 546, 536.

39. DHL to Edward Garnett, June 10, 1913, ibid., 2, p. 22.

40. DHL to Cynthia Asquith, August 20, 1913, ibid., p. 63.

41. DHL to Ada Lawrence, April 19, 1913, and DHL to Arthur McLeod, April 23, 1913, ibid., 1, pp. 541, 543; DHL to William Hopkin, August 11,

1913, DHL to Cynthia Asquith, August 20, 1913, DHL to Edward Garnett, August 24, 1913, ibid., 2, pp. 57, 63, 65.

42. DHL to Edward Garnett, April 22, 1914, ibid., p. 164.

43. DHL to Edward Garnett, March 22, 1913, ibid., 1, p. 530.

44. DHL to Else Jaffe, February 10, 1913, ibid., pp. 513–514.

45. See, e.g., DHL to Arthur McLeod, April 23, 1913, ibid., p. 544.

46. AvR.

47. Frieda Weekley to Edward Garnett, May 17, 1913, and DHL to Edward Garnett, May 19, 1913, *DHL Letters*, 1, pp. 550, 551.

48. *NIBTW*, p. 67; the baron's condition is described in AvR.

49. *M&C*, p. 12.

50. *NIBTW*, p. 69.

51. Frieda Weekley to Edward Garnett, May 17, 1913, *DHL Letters*, 1, pp. 549–550.

52. Frieda Weekley to Edward Garnett, May 27, 1913, Berg Collection, New York Public Library; Frieda Lawrence to Harry T. Moore, January 14, 1955, *M&C*, p. 390; ibid., p. 429.

53. Frieda Weekley to Edward Garnett, May 27, 1913, Berg Collection.

54. *NIBTW*, pp. 68–69.

55. Frieda Weekley to Edward Garnett, June 16, 1913, *DHL Letters*, 2, p. 23.

56. *M&C*, p. 111.

57. Interview with Montague Weekley, July 13, 1978.

58. Foregoing anecdote and dialogue from *M&C*, pp. 111–112.

59. *Chiswick and Turnham Green*.

60. *NIBTW*, p. 67. For another version of the story, see BBC.

61. Affidavit sworn by Maude Weekley before a commissioner for oaths at 357 High Road, Chiswick, July 24, 1913. Trevelyan House (Weekley divorce file).

62. DHL to Constance Garnett, July 13, 1913, *DHL Letters*, 2, p. 37.

63. Seduction attempt, "no gentleman," arterial blood: Garnett, *Great Friends*, p. 81.

64. *Standard*, May 30, 1913; *Westminster Gazette*, June 14, 1913; *Daily Chronicle*, June 17, 1913; *Saturday Review*, June 21, 1913. For the text of the reviews, see Draper, ed., *D. H. Lawrence: The Critical Heritage*, pp. 58–66.

65. *NIBTW*, pp. 67–68.

66. Most of the foregoing material on the life of Mansfield is drawn from Tomalin, *Katherine Mansfield*, and Antony Alpers, *The Life of Katherine Mansfield* (London: Penguin, 1982).

67. See Katherine Mansfield to Dorothy Brett, June 6, 1922, *The Letters of Katherine Mansfield*, ed. John Middleton Murry (London: Constable, 1928), vol. 2, p. 216.

68. DHL to Constance Garnett, July 10(?), 1913, *DHL Letters*, 2, pp. 31–32.

69. DHL to Katharine Clayton, July 13, 1913, ibid., p. 37.

70. *The Nation*, July 12, 1913. For text of review, see Draper, *D. H. Lawrence: The Critical Heritage*, p. 72.

71. As quoted in Perkin, *Women and Marriage in Nineteenth-Century England*, p. 95.

72. Edward Marsh to Rupert Brooke, July 20, 1913, in Marsh, *A Number of People* (London: Heinemann, 1939), p. 288.

73. DHL to John Middleton Murry, July 22, 1913, *DHL Letters*, 2, p. 45.

74. Frieda Weekley to Else Jaffe, July 22(?), 1913, ibid., pp. 49–50. Ernest's letter, which may have been written to Anna von Richthofen rather than Frieda, was probably forwarded by Anna; it has not survived.

75. Patmore, "A Memoir of Frieda Lawrence," p. 139.

76. Tomalin, *Katherine Mansfield*, p. 119. The book, entitled *Maata*, was never completed.

77. DHL to Edward Garnett, July 28, 1913, *DHL Letters*, 2, p. 51.

78. Trevelyan House (Weekley divorce file).

79. He sold two sketches to the *Westminster Gazette*, which had published eight poems in May 1912 and his sketch "Christs in the Tirol" in March 1913.

80. DHL to William Hopkin, August 11, 1913, *DHL Letters*, 2, pp. 57–58.

81. "The Return Journey," *Twilight in Italy*, in *D. H. Lawrence and Italy* (New York: Penguin, 1985), p. 147.

82. As quoted in Green, *The von Richthofen Sisters*, p. 70. Much of the account of Gross's last years is drawn from this source.

83. As quoted in Green, *Mountain of Truth*, p. 141.

84. Green, *The von Richthofen Sisters*, p. 70.

85. *M&C*, p. 102.

86. Frieda Weekley to Else Jaffe, n.d., HRC.

87. DHL to Arthur McLeod, October 17, 1913, *DHL Letters*, 2, p. 86.

88. *NIBTW*, p. 69.

89. *New York Times Book Review*, September 21, 1913.

90. *News of the World*, October 19, 1913, p. 1.

91. Sunday *Times*, October 19, 1913, p. 15.

92. *Daily Mail*, October 20, 1913, p. 4.

93. Lack of books: DHL to Ernest Collings, July 22, 1913, *DHL Letters*, 2, p. 47; "B." H. Lawrence: the wording is from the *Times*; the other two papers omitted the word "being."

94. Trevelyan House (Weekley divorce file).

95. Frieda Weekley to Cynthia Asquith, October 23, 1913, *M&C*, p. 187.

96. DHL to Arthur McLeod, December 2, 1913, *DHL Letters*, 2, p. 118.

97. DHL to Cynthia Asquith, November 25, 1913, ibid., p. 109.

98. Horsehair, Frieda's outfit, and all quotations in foregoing paragraph: Lina Waterfield, *Castle in Italy: An Autobiography* (London: John Murray, 1961), p. 138.

99. *NIBTW*, pp. 72–73.

100. BBC.

101. DHL to Edward Garnett, January 29, 1914, *DHL Letters*, 2, p. 143.

102. Frieda Weekley to Edward Garnett, March(?) 1914, ibid., pp. 150–151.

103. Frieda, as quoted in DHL to Edward Garnett, July 16, 1913, ibid., p. 40.

104. Frieda Weekley to Edward Garnett, March(?) 1914, ibid., p. 150.

105. See DHL to Edward Garnett, May 9, 1914, ibid., p. 173; possible reference: "It was the Rainbow gave thee birth/and left thee all her lovely hues" (W. H. Davies, "Kingfisher" [1910], in Allan Bloom, ed., *The Oxford Dictionary of Quotations* New York: Oxford University Press, 1992. Much later, DHL offered other explanations of the title: see, e.g., DHL to Waldo Frank, July 27, 1917, *DHL Letters*, 3, p. 142 ("I . . . called it *The Rainbow*—in reference to the Flood").

106. Trevelyan House (Weekley divorce file).

107. DHL to John Middleton Murry, April 3, 1914, *DHL Letters*, 2, p. 162.

108. See, e.g., DHL to Constance Garnett, May 6, 1914, ibid., p. 167.

109. Ivy Litvinov, "A Visit to D. H. Lawrence," *Harper's Bazaar*, October 1946. *Times Literary Supplement*, March 19, April 2, 1914.

110. DHL to Ivy Low, April 1914, *DHL Letters*, 2, p. 160.

111. Ivy Litvinov, "A Visit to D. H. Lawrence."

112. DHL to David Garnett, June 13, 1914, *DHL Letters*, 2, p. 186.

113. BBC.

114. Lucas, *Frieda Lawrence*, p. 100, but the book gives the wrong year.

115. BBC.

116. *NIBTW*, p. 77.

117. Barbara Weekley Barr, "Memoir of D. H. Lawrence," p. 9.

Chapter 9 "Don't You Know Me? I'm Frieda"

1. Catherine Carswell, *The Savage Pilgrimage: A Narrative of D. H. Lawrence* (London: Secker & Warburg, 1951), pp. 18–19.

2. Tomalin, *Katherine Mansfield*, p. 127.

3. Also present were a young, independently wealthy poet and Harvard undergraduate from Arkansas named John Gould Fletcher; the Russian-born poet-journalist John Cournos, who had recently worked as an art critic on the Philadelphia *Record*; and a poet named F. S. Flint, who had been published in the *English Review*. Biographies of Amy Lowell, Lawrence, and others cite Frieda's presence at the party, but there is no evidence that she was there.

4. DHL to Harriet Monroe, July 31, 1914, *DHL Letters*, 2, pp. 202–203.

5. H. D., *Bid Me to Live* (1949; reprint, New York: Dial Press, 1960), p. 141.

6. DHL to Arthur McLeod, July 8, 1914, *DHL Letters*, 2, p. 193.

7. DHL to Arthur McLeod, June 2, 1914, ibid., pp. 180–181.

8. Or, as Kot once transcribed it, "*Ranani Zadikim Zadikim l'Adonoi*" (see *DHL Letters*, 2, p. 252, n. 3).

9. DHL to Cynthia Asquith, January 31, 1915, *DHL Letters*, 2, p. 268.

10. DHL to Edward Marsh, September 13, 1914, ibid., p. 213.

11. Green, *The von Richthofen Sisters*, p. 98.

12. *NIBTW*, p. 92.

13. Garnett, *Great Friends*, p. 83.

14. I have relied primarily on Miranda Seymour, *Ottoline Morrell: Life on the Grand Scale* (London: Hodder and Stoughton, 1992), for background and incident.

15. Bertrand Russell, *The Autobiography of Bertrand Russell, 1914–1944* (New York: Bantam, 1969), p. 3.

16. *NIBTW*, p. 77.

17. Ibid., p. 79.

18. DHL to J. B. Pinker, September 5, 1914, *DHL Letters*, 2, p. 212.

19. Gilbert Cannan, *Mendel* (New York: George H. Doran Co., 1916), p. 227.

20. Interview with Montague Weekley, July 13, 1978.

21. Frieda Lawrence to Edward Marsh, September 13(?), 1914, *DHL Letters*, 2, pp. 214–215.

22. The play had been published by Mitchell Kennerley six months before in the United States.

23. *NIBTW*, p. 292.

24. John Middleton Murry, *Reminiscences of D. H. Lawrence* (London: Cape, 1933), p. 40.

25. John Middleton Murry, journal entry, November 18, 1914, as quoted in Alpers, *The Life of Katherine Mansfield*, p. 170.

26. Alpers, *The Life of Katherine Mansfield*, p. 171.

27. *DHL Letters*, 2, pp. 224–225, n. 4.

28. DHL to Amy Lowell, October 16, 1914, ibid., p. 223.

29. Nehls, 1, p. 258.

30. John Middleton Murry, journal entry, November 18, 1914, as quoted in Alpers, *The Life of Katherine Mansfield*, p. 170.

31. Beatrice Lady Glenavy, *Today We Will Only Gossip* (London: Constable, 1964), p. 78.

32. See DHL to Amy Lowell, December 18, 1914, *DHL Letters*, 2, p. 244.

33. Frieda Lawrence to Ottoline Morrell, May 19, 1915, ibid., p. 344. Italics added to "were."

34. DHL, *The Rainbow* (London: Penguin, 1981), p. 101.

35. *The Rainbow*, pp. 225–226. As indicated, quotations are drawn from the published book. Not all of Lawrence's early drafts of the book—indeed, few pieces of them—have survived, and it would be difficult both to pinpoint when these particular visions of Frieda's childhood were created and to venture a guess about whether Lawrence had completed either of the passages, here or above, by the winter of 1915. In that sense, I have taken some liberty here in suggesting that the passages were completed then.

36. Ibid., p. 187.

37. As quoted in Lucas, *Frieda Lawrence*, p. 121.

38. DHL to S. S. Koteliansky, January 24, 1915, *DHL Letters*, 2, p. 261.

39. See, e.g., ibid., p. 372, n. 1.

40. *NIBTW*, p. 82.

41. See David Garnett, *The Flowers of the Forest* (London: Chatto & Windus, 1955), pp. 50–52.

42. AvR.

43. P. N. Furbank, *E. M. Forster: A Life* (New York: Harcourt Brace Jovanovich, 1978), vol. 2, p. 5.

44. DHL to E. M. Forster, January 28, 1915, *DHL Letters*, 2, p. 266.

45. Furbank, *Forster*, vol. 2, p. 7.

46. Frieda Lawrence to E. M. Forster, February 5–6, 1915, *DHL Letters*, 2, p. 277.

47. Ibid., p. 257, n. 3.

48. Furbank, *Forster*, vol. 2, p. 11.

49. Frieda Lawrence to Ottoline Morrell, after May 19, 1915, *DHL Letters*, 2, p. 345; see DHL postscript.

50. *DHL Letters*, 2, pp. 273–274, n. 2.

51. DHL to Bertrand Russell, February 12, 1915, ibid., pp. 282–286.

52. DHL to Ottoline Morrell, February 11(?), 1915, ibid., p. 281.

53. DHL to Ottoline Morrell, February 22, 1915, ibid., p. 291.

54. *NIBTW*, p. 82.

55. Ibid., p. 83.

56. John Middleton Murry to Katherine Mansfield, May 11, 1915, *The Letters of John Middleton Murry to Katherine Mansfield*, ed. C. A. Hankin (London: Constable, 1983), p. 62.

57. Katherine Mansfield to John Middleton Murry, May 11, 1915, *The Collected Letters of Katherine Mansfield*, vol. 1, 1903–1917, ed. Vincent O'Sullivan and Margaret Scott (Oxford: Oxford University Press, 1984), p. 183.

58. John Middleton Murry to Katherine Mansfield, May 11, 1915, *Letters of John Middleton Murry to Katherine Mansfield*, p. 63.

59. Katherine Mansfield to John Middleton Murry, May 14, 1915, *Collected Letters of Katherine Mansfield*, vol. 1, p. 187.

60. Frieda Lawrence to Harry T. Moore, January 14, 1955, *M&C*, p. 389; Violet Hunt, *I Have This to Say* (New York: Boni and Liveright, 1926), pp. 259–260; Ford Madox Ford, *Portraits from Life* (Boston and New York: Houghton Mifflin, 1937), p. 89; Moore, *The Priest of Love*, p. 232; Delavenay, *D. H. Lawrence: The Man and His Work*, pp. 232–233.

Chapter 10 "She Actually Seemed a Lady"

1. DHL to J. B. Pinker, April 23, 1915, *DHL Letters*, 2, p. 327.

2. DHL to Bertrand Russell, April 29, 1915, ibid., p. 327.

3. DHL to J. B. Pinker, May 29, 1915, ibid., p. 349.

4. DHL to Ottoline Morrell, May 14, 1915, ibid., p. 340.

5. Frieda Lawrence to Ottoline Morrell, May 19, 1915, ibid., pp. 344–345.

6. DHL to E. M. Forster, June 2, 1915, ibid., p. 351.

7. Sybille Bedford, *Aldous Huxley* (London: Chatto & Windus, 1973), vol. 1, p. 80; see also David King Dunaway, *Huxley in Hollywood* (New York: Harper & Row, 1989), p. 72, and Seymour, *Ottoline Morrell*, p. 219.

8. Lady Ottoline Morrell, *Ottoline at Garsington: Memoirs of Lady Ottoline Morrell, 1915–1918*, ed. Robert Gathorne-Hardy (London: Faber & Faber, 1974), p. 36.

9. See Garnett, *Flowers of the Forest*, pp. 108 ff.

10. As quoted in Lucas, *Frieda Lawrence*, p. 130.

11. *NIBTW*, p. 82.

12. Morrell, *Ottoline at Garsington*, p. 37.

13. Ottoline Morrell to Bertrand Russell, June 18, 1915, as quoted in Paul Delany, *D. H. Lawrence's Nightmare* (New York: Basic Books, 1978), p. 114.

14. Bertrand Russell to Ottoline Morrell, June 20, 1915, as quoted in ibid., p. 114.

15. Cynthia Asquith, *Lady Cynthia Asquith: Diaries: 1915–1918*, ed. E. M. Horsley (New York: Alfred A. Knopf, 1969), p. 75, and *Remember and Be Glad* (London: James Barrie, 1952), pp. 139–140.

16. See, e.g., DHL to Ottoline Morrell, July 12, 1915, DHL *Letters*, 2, p. 363.

17. Bertrand Russell to Ottoline Morrell, July 1915, *Autobiography of Bertrand Russell, 1914–1944*, p. 59.

18. *M&C*, p. 463.

19. Russell, *Autobiography of Bertrand Russell, 1914–1944*, p. 14.

20. See Delany, *D. H. Lawrence's Nightmare*, pp. 118–119; Delavenay, *D. H. Lawrence: The Man and His Work*, p. 275.

21. DHL to Ottoline Morrell, July 19, 1915, *DHL Letters*, 2, p. 367.

22. DHL to Bertrand Russell, July 26, 1915, ibid., p. 371.

23. All St. Paul's School records courtesy Jacqueline Childs and Christopher Dean, archivists, respectively, of the Girls' and Boys' sections. I am grateful to Deborah Baker for her researches into the Girls' School archives in 1990.

24. Barr, "Memoir of D. H. Lawrence," p. 9.

25. BL.

26. Interview with Montague Weekley, July 13, 1978.

27. BL.

28. Interview with Montague Weekley, July 13, 1978.

29. DHL to Cynthia Asquith, August 16, 1915, *DHL Letters*, 2, p. 379.

30. Asquith, *Remember and Be Glad*, pp. 148–149.

31. *NIBTW*, p. 80.

32. Manfred von Richthofen, *The Red Baron* (*Der Rote Kampfflieger*), trans. Peter Kilduff, ed. Stanley M. Ulanoff (London: Sphere, 1976), p. 59.

33. *NIBTW*, p. 80.

34. Barbara Guest, *Herself Defined: The Poet H. D. and Her World* (New York: Quill, 1984), p. 73.

35. Ernest Jones, *Free Associations* (London: Hogarth, 1959), pp. 251–252; Vincent Brome, *Ernest Jones: Freud's Alter Ego* (London: Caliban, 1982), p. 103.

36. DHL to Bertrand Russell, September 14, 1915, *DHL Letters*, 2, p. 392.

37. Phone interview with Barbara Barr (October 6, 1994), who believes that the chapter is a closer approximation of Frieda's experience than Else's or Mansfield's.

38. Ottoline Morrell to Bertrand Russell, April 27, May 7, 1915, as quoted in Delany, *D. H. Lawrence's Nightmare*, p. 106.

39. Asquith, *Diaries 1915–1918*, p. 86; Frieda Lawrence to Cynthia Asquith, n.d. (late winter or spring 1916), *M&C*, p. 200.

40. Frieda Lawrence to Cynthia Asquith, n.d. (late winter or spring 1916), ibid.

41. Patmore, "A Memoir of Frieda Lawrence," p. 138.

42. Ibid.

43. DHL to J. B. Pinker, October 31, 1916, *DHL Letters*, 2, p. 669. "The Mortal Coil" was first published in the journal *Seven Arts* (July 1917). See *The Mortal Coil and Other Stories* (London: Penguin, 1988), pp. 210–236.

44. Nehls, 3, pp. 96–97.

45. DHL to Catherine Carswell, July 16, 1916, *DHL Letters*, 2, p. 635.

46. AvR.

47. Garnett, *Great Friends*, p. 91.

48. DHL to John Middleton Murry and Katherine Mansfield, November 25, 1915, *DHL Letters*, 2, p. 452.

49. DHL to Bertrand Russell, December 8, 1915, ibid., p. 470.

50. Huebsch eventually merged with Viking.

51. DHL to S. S. Koteliansky, December 30, 1915, *DHL Letters*, 2, p. 491.

52. *NIBTW*, p. 83.

Chapter 11 *Dies Irae*

1. See, e.g., DHL to: Catherine Carswell, December 31, 1915, and January 11, 1916; J. D. Beresford, January 5, 1916; S. S. Koteliansky, January 6, 1916; John Middleton Murry and Katherine Mansfield, January 17, 1916, *DHL Letters*, 2, pp. 493, 502, 495, 499, 507.

DHL to: Cynthia Asquith, December 30, 1915; Edith Eder, December 30, 1915; Ottoline Morrell, December 31, 1915; Dollie Radford, December 31, 1915; Katherine Mansfield, January 7, 1916; William and Sallie Hopkin, January 25, 1916; Katharine Clayton, February 2, 1916, ibid., pp. 491, 492, 493, 499, 514, 524.

2. Frieda Lawrence to S. S. Koteliansky, February 13, 1916, *M&C*, p. 198; also see Frieda Lawrence to S. S. Koteliansky, February 19, 1916, *DHL Letters*, 2, p. 545.

3. Frieda Lawrence to Bertrand Russell, ca. January 13, 1916, *M&C*, p. 198.

4. See Delany, *D. H. Lawrence's Nightmare*, pp. 189–190.

5. See Bertrand Russell to Ottoline Morrell, January 30, 1916, *Autobiography of Bertrand Russell, 1914–1944*, p. 69.

6. DHL to Ottoline Morrell, February 15, 1916, *DHL Letters*, 2, p. 538.

7. Frieda Lawrence to Bertrand Russell, February 24, 1916, ibid., p. 553.

8. Frieda Lawrence to Ottoline Morrell, January 22(?), 1916, HRC.

9. Ottoline Morrell to Bertrand Russell, January 1916, as quoted in Delany, *D. H. Lawrence's Nightmare*, p. 200.

10. See DHL to Ottoline Morrell, January 24, 1916, *DHL Letters*, 2, pp. 511–512; DHL to S. S. Koteliansky, February 9, 1916, ibid., p. 530.

11. DHL to Mark Gertler, February 10, 1916, ibid., p. 531.

12. Delany, *D. H. Lawrence's Nightmare*, pp. 190–191.

13. *Times Literary Supplement*, June 15, 1916.

14. DHL to Ottoline Morrell, February 25, 1916, *DHL Letters*, 2, p. 556.

15. See DHL to J. B. Pinker, February 25, 1916, ibid., p. 558.

16. DHL to: Beatrice Beresford, February 28, 1916, and J. D. Beresford, February 24, 1916, *DHL Letters*, 2, pp. 559, 552.

17. C. J. Stevens, *Lawrence at Tregerthen* (Troy, N.Y.: Whitston, 1988), p. 11.

18. *NIBTW*, p. 84.

19. DHL to John Middleton Murry and Katherine Mansfield, March 8, 1916, *DHL Letters*, 2, p. 570.

20. Eventually retitled *Prelude*.

21. Frieda Lawrence to Katherine Mansfield, early March 1916, *DHL Letters*, 2, p. 571.

22. *NIBTW*, p. 85.

23. *M&C*, p. 425; John Middleton Murry, *The Autobiography of John Middleton Murry: Between Two Worlds* (New York: Messner, 1936), p. 405.

24. Frieda Lawrence to Ottoline Morrell, ca. April 1916, HRC.

25. John Middleton Murry to Ottoline Morrell, April 12, 1916, HRC.

26. John Middleton Murry to Ottoline Morrell, April 12, 1916, as quoted in Delany, *D. H. Lawrence's Nightmare*, pp. 222 and 405, n. 14; the translation is Delany's.

27. Murry, *Autobiography*, pp. 403, 404.

28. Ibid., p. 409.

29. Katherine Mansfield to S. S. Koteliansky, May 11, 1916, *Collected Letters of Katherine Mansfield*, vol. 1, p. 263.

30. BL.

31. *Phoenix*, vol. 2, pp. 103–104.

32. Ibid., pp. 106–107.

33. Katherine Mansfield to S. S. Koteliansky, May 11, 1916, *Collected Letters of Katherine Mansfield*, vol. 1, pp. 263, 264.

34. Katherine Mansfield to Ottoline Morrell, May 17, 1916, ibid., p. 268.

35. Murry, *Reminiscences of D. H. Lawrence*, p. 78; for another version, see Murry, *Autobiography*, p. 416.

36. DHL to Catherine Carswell, June 19, 1916, *DHL Letters*, 2, p. 617.

37. See, e.g., DHL to J. B. Pinker, October 31, 1916, ibid., p. 669.

38. See Frieda Lawrence to John Middleton Murry, August 6, 1953, *M&C*, p. 360.

39. Stevens, *Tregerthen*, p. 49.

40. Ibid., pp. 76–77.

41. Ibid., p. 82.

42. *Kangaroo* (New York: Viking, 1970), p. 236.

43. Stevens, *Tregerthen*, pp. 50–51.

44. DHL to Barbara Low, September 1, 1916, *DHL Letters*, 2, p. 649.

45. *Women in Love*, p. 284.

46. Huebsch, first American edition, 1916.

47. See DHL to Ottoline Morrell, May 24, 1916, *DHL Letters*, 2, p. 610.

48. During the war years, the terms had begun to start later than the usual date of September 15 (Jacqueline Childs, archivist, Saint Paul's Girls' School).

49. DHL to S. S. Koteliansky, September 4, 1916, *DHL Letters*, 2, p. 650.

50. DHL to Dollie Radford, September 5, 1916, ibid., p. 651. Also see DHL to: Catherine Carswell, August 14, 1916; Cynthia Asquith, September 1, 1916; Barbara Low, September 8, 1916, ibid., pp. 639–640, 649, 653.

51. DHL to Dollie Radford, September 5, 1916, ibid., p. 651.

52. Interview with Montague Weekley, July 13, 1978. He misremembered the venue as Covent Garden (to which the Beecham Company moved in 1919); its 1917 season was at the Aldwych.

53. BBC.

54. Carswell, *The Savage Pilgrimage*, pp. 76–77.

55. DHL to Katherine Mansfield, September 27, 1916, *DHL Letters*, 2, p. 658.

56. DHL to John Middleton Murry, October 11, 1916, ibid., p. 662.

57. Carswell, *The Savage Pilgrimage*, p. 78.

58. *Women in Love*, pp. 472–473.

59. Ottoline Morrell to Bertrand Russell, January 2, 1917, as quoted in Delany, *D. H. Lawrence's Nightmare*, p. 273.

60. Stevens, *Tregerthen*, p. 99.

61. *NIBTW*, p. 87.

62. DHL to Robert Mountsier, January 9, 1917, *DHL Letters*, 3, p. 72.

63. Frieda Lawrence to S. S. Koteliansky, April 1, 1917, ibid., p. 109.

64. There are two conflicting versions of the story: see Carswell, *Savage Pilgrimage*, p. 92, and Mabel Dodge Luhan, *Lorenzo in Taos*, pp. 40, 51.

65. DHL to S. S. Koteliansky, May 11, 1917, *DHL Letters*, 3, p. 124.

66. *Poems* (Sagar), pp. 73–74.

67. Ibid., pp. 61–62.

68. Ibid., p. 72.

69. Stevens, *Tregerthen*, p. 85; also see John Middleton Murry to Frieda Lawrence, January 3, 1954, *M&C*, p. 367.

70. Stevens, *Tregerthen*, p. 84.

71. Anthony Powell, *Messengers of the Day* (New York: Holt, Rinehart & Winston, 1978), as quoted in Guest, *Herself Defined*, p. 97.

72. Interview with Bertha Ilfeld, October 22, 1988, Albuquerque.

73. Cecil Gray, *Peter Warlock: A Memoir of Philip Heseltine* (London: Cape, 1934), p. 114.

74. Cecil Gray, *Musical Chairs, or Between Two Stools* (London: Hogarth, 1985), p. 138.

75. *NIBTW*, p. 90.

76. H. D., *Bid Me to Live*, p. 89.

77. Ibid., pp. 77–78.

78. DHL to Cecil Gray, November 7, 1917, *DHL Letters*, 3, p. 180.

79. H. D., *Tribute to Freud* (Boston: David Godine, 1974), p. xiv.

80. Moore, *The Priest of Love*, p. 289.

Chapter 12 *Heimweh*

1. By Secker in England (June 1924) and in the United States by Seltzer (August 1923).

2. Frieda Lawrence to Mark Gertler, n.d. (late 1916), Harvard University Library.

3. Nehls, 1, p. 487.

4. Ibid., p. 505; *Sea and Sardinia*, in *D. H. Lawrence in Italy* (London: Penguin, 1985), p. 60.

5. Delany, *D. H. Lawrence's Nightmare*, p. 348.

6. *NIBTW*, p. 92.

7. Nehls, 1, p. 464.

8. Ibid., p. 461.

9. As quoted in Delany, *D. H. Lawrence's Nightmare*, p. 383, and Tomalin, *Katherine Mansfield*, p. 185. It is Tomalin's supposition that Mansfield may have been infected with tuberculosis by Lawrence.

10. DHL to Cynthia Asquith, September 26, 1918, *DHL Letters*, 3, p. 287.

11. Garnett, *Flowers of the Forest*, pp. 190–191.

12. Katherine Mansfield to Ottoline Morrell, November 14(?), 1918, as quoted in Delany, *D. H. Lawrence's Nightmare*, p. 386.

13. Ibid.

14. DHL to Katherine Mansfield, December 5, 1918, *DHL Letters*, 3, pp. 301–302.

15. AvR.

16. Lawrence also used "*Heimweh*," as well as other, similar terms in foreign languages, to describe his *own* conflicting feelings of homesickness and nostalgia (for him, almost always combined with disgust) for places he had been and left; later, Capri was one such place. See, for example, DHL to Compton Mackenzie, March 8, 1920, and to John Ellingham Brooks, March 8, 1920, *DHL Letters*, 3, pp. 480, 481. Cf. "I feel a Sehnsucht nach Italien," DHL to Anna von Richthofen, August 17, 1921, ibid., 4, p. 72.

17. DHL to S. S. Koteliansky, March 14, 1919, ibid., 3, p. 337.

18. DHL to Godwin Baynes, n.d., ibid., p. 478.

19. Godwin Baynes's father, Helton Baynes, noted "Godwin's free and easy ways with both sexes"; see Rosalind Thornycroft and Chloë Baynes, *Time Which Spaces Us Apart* (privately printed, Batcombe, Somerset, 1991), p. 61. I am grateful to Chloë Green for making me aware of the existence of the book and providing a copy.

20. DHL to Godwin Baynes, n.d., *DHL Letters*, 3, p. 478.

21. Thornycroft and Baynes, *Time Which Spaces Us Apart*, pp. 26 ff., 55 ff., 60 ff.

22. Nehls, 2, p. 5.

23. DHL to Cynthia Asquith, September 16, 1919, *DHL Letters*, 3, p. 395.

24. Nehls, 1, p. 465.

25. Ibid., p. 503.

26. DHL to Thomas Moult, September 4 or 5, 1919, *DHL Letters*, 3, p. 389.

27. *Kangaroo*, p. 264.

Chapter 13 The Queen Bee

1. Carswell, *The Savage Pilgrimage*, p. 120.

2. Nehls, 1, p. 507.

3. See Havelock Ellis, *The Fountain of Life* (Boston: Houghton Mifflin,

1930), and Phyllis Grosskurth, *Havelock Ellis: A Biography* (New York: Alfred A. Knopf, 1980).

4. DHL to Cynthia Asquith, November 18, 1919, *DHL Letters*, 3, p. 417.

5. Introduction to Maurice Magnus, *Memoirs of the Foreign Legion*, reprinted in *Phoenix*, vol. 2, p. 304.

6. *NIBTW*, p. 93.

7. Ibid., p. 93.

8. Ibid., p. 95.

9. DHL to: Emily King, December 4, 1919; Ada Clarke, December 4, 1919; Cynthia Asquith, December 6, 1919; Irene Whittley, December 18, 1919; Sallie and William Hopkin, January 9, 1920; Amy Lowell, February 13, 1920, *DHL Letters*, 3, pp. 427, 429, 435, 450, 474.

10. *NIBTW*, p. 98.

11. The novel, by Elizabeth Gaskell, began appearing in *Household Words* in December 1851 and ran through May 1853. "Although the ladies of Cranford know all each other's proceedings, they are exceedingly indifferent to each other's opinions. . . . each has her own individuality, not to say eccentricity, pretty strongly developed"; "It was impossible to live a month at Cranford, and not know the daily habits of each resident" (Oxford University Press [London, 1972], ed. Elizabeth Porges Watson). "Cranford" became a catchword for the Lawrences, who later used it to describe Capri.

12. DHL to Benjamin Huebsch, January 29, 1920, *DHL Letters*, 3, p. 466.

13. DHL to Waldo Frank, July 27, 1917, ibid., p. 144.

14. See Frieda Lawrence to Richard Aldington, January 7, 1948, and May 4, 1950, quoted in Moore and Montague, *Frieda Lawrence and Her Circle*, pp. 87, 101.

15. Frieda Lawrence to Cecily Lambert, December 17, 1919, *M&C*, p. 215.

16. DHL to Rosalind Baynes, December 16, 1919, *DHL Letters*, 3, p. 431.

17. Compton Mackenzie, *My Life and Times*, Octave 5, 1915–1923 (London: Chatto & Windus, 1966), pp. 164 ff.

18. DHL to Cynthia Asquith, January 25, 1920, *DHL Letters*, 3, pp. 462–463.

19. DHL to John Middleton Murry, January 30, 1920, ibid., pp. 467–468.

20. DHL to Katherine Mansfield, February 6, 1920, ibid., p. 470.

21. Rings: See DHL to Compton Mackenzie, March 8, 1920, ibid., p. 480. Checks from America: He received one hundred dollars from admirers Louis Untermeyer, Jeanette Starr Untermeyer, and Emile Tas (see DHL to Benjamin Huebsch, January 4, 1920, *DHL Letters*, 3, p. 445). There was also a royalty check for five hundred dollars from J. B. Pinker; ninety dollars for an introduction, for magazine publicaton, to his own *New Poems*; and one hundred dollars from Amy Lowell, which, however, came in the form of a check (for 1,315 lire) that he could not cash till June. For details of these three latter checks see John Worthen, *D. H. Lawrence: A Literary Life* (New York: St. Martin's, 1989) and DHL to Amy Lowell, February 13, 1920, *DHL Letters*, 3, pp. 474–475. See also Carswell, *The Savage Pilgrimage*, p. 131.

22. *NIBTW*, p. 100.

23. DHL to Jan Juta, June 13, 1920, *DHL Letters*, 3, p. 551.

24. *NIBTW*, p. 112.

25. See Gaetano Saglimbeni, *I Peccati e gli Amori di Taormina* (Messina: Edizioni P&M Associati, 1990), pp. 63–74. I am grateful to Abigail Asher for the translation.

26. Frieda Lawrence to Else Jaffe, November 2, 1921, HRC.

27. Interview with Anthea Goldsmith, June 28, 1988, London; letter from Ian Weekley, September 26, 1994.

28. See, e.g., DHL to Amy Lowell, June 26, 1920, *DHL Letters*, 3, p. 557.

29. *NIBTW*, p. 99.

30. Ibid.

31. Nehls, 2, p. 84.

32. Ibid., p. 88.

33. DHL to Catherine Carswell, May 28, 1920, *DHL Letters*, 3, p. 533.

34. Magnus "a jewel": DHL to Jan Juta, May 29, 1920, ibid., p. 535; bisexuality: Maurice Magnus to Norman Douglas, July 18, 1920, as quoted in Brenda Maddox, *The Married Man: A Life of D. H. Lawrence* (London: Sinclair-Stevenson, 1994), p. 26. The latter letter was first brought to light and cited by Maddox.

35. BL.

36. Barbara Weekley to Frieda Lawrence, circa April 4, 1920, *M&C*, pp. 216–218.

37. His maternal grandfather was apparently King Friedrich Wilhelm IV, and his uncle, Wilhelm II; see Introduction to *Memoirs of the Foreign Legion*, *Phoenix*, vol. 2, pp. 360–361.

38. DHL to Irene Whittley, September 8, 1920, *DHL Letters*, 3, p. 592.

39. Thornycroft and Baynes, *Time Which Spaces Us Apart*, pp. 78–79. Lawrence's thirty-fifth birthday was September 11, 1920.

40. They appeared on January 6 and 19, 1921.

41. DHL to Amy Lowell, September 12, 1920, *DHL Letters*, 3, p. 593.

42. DHL to Anna von Richthofen, September 26, 1920, ibid., p. 601.

43. DHL to Rosalind Baynes, September 29, 1920, ibid., p. 604.

44. Green, *The von Richthofen Sisters*, pp. 165, 226.

45. DHL to Compton Mackenzie, September 12, 1920, *DHL Letters*, 3, p. 594.

46. Frieda Lawrence to Irene and Percy Whittley, October 23, 1920, ibid., p. 615.

47. DHL to Edward Marsh, October 13, 1920, ibid., p. 611.

48. DHL to Amy Lowell, November 30, 1920, ibid., p. 629.

49. Frieda Lawrence to Else Jaffe, November 1920, HRC.

50. Nehls, 1, p. 461.

51. *Sea and Sardinia*, in *D. H. Lawrence and Italy*, pp. 19–20.

52. *Sea and Sardinia*, p. 134.

53. Frieda Lawrence to John Middleton Murry, December 19, 1951, *M&C*, p. 341.

54. DHL to Robert Mountsier, March 15, 1921, *DHL Letters*, 3, p. 684.

55. DHL to Anna von Richthofen, March 16, 1921, ibid., p. 685.

56. See Nehls, 3, p. 163, where Barbara Barr describes him as a "dishevelled wreck."

57. DHL to Robert Mountsier, February 28, 1921, *DHL Letters*, 3, p. 673.

58. DHL to Else Jaffe, May 9, 1921, ibid., p. 717.

59. DHL to S. S. Koteliansky, May 27, 1921, ibid., p. 728.

60. *NIBTW*, p. 94.

61. Ibid., p. 96.

62. If they met again, it was the following September. Letter of July 11, 1994, from Chloë Green; Thornycroft and Baynes, *Time Which Spaces Us Apart*, p. 83.

63. Frieda Lawrence to Mabel Dodge Sterne, April 19, 1922, *Lorenzo in Taos*, p. 22.

64. *John Bull*, September 12, 1921.

65. *New Statesman*, July 6, 1921.

66. Virginia Woolf to Molly McCarthy, June 20, 1921, *The Letters of Virginia Woolf*, vol. 2, 1919–1922, ed. Nigel Nicolson and Joanne Trautmann (New York: Harcourt Brace Jovanovich, 1976), p. 474.

67. DHL to Martin Secker, November 10, 1921, *DHL Letters*, 4, p. 116.

68. DHL to Anton Kippenberg, November 12, 1921, ibid., p. 117.

69. *The Captain's Doll* was entitled *The Ladybird* in England.

70. DHL to Thomas Seltzer, October 8, 1921, *DHL Letters*, 4, p. 93.

71. DHL to Violet Monk, October 12, 1921, ibid., p. 98.

72. Frieda Lawrence to Else Jaffe, November 2, 1921, HRC.

73. DHL to Mabel Dodge Sterne, November 5, 1921, *DHL Letters*, 4, p. 111.

74. Lois Palken Rudnick, *Mabel Dodge Luhan* (Albuquerque: University of New Mexico Press, 1987), p. 195.

75. Frieda Lawrence to Mabel Dodge Sterne, ca. November 8, 1921, *Lorenzo in Taos*, p. 7.

76. As quoted in Rudnick, *Mabel Dodge Luhan*, p. 195.

77. DHL to Anna von Richthofen, November 15, 1921, *DHL Letters*, 4, p. 122.

78. DHL to Norman Douglas, March 4, 1922, ibid., p. 207.

79. Frieda Lawrence to Mabel Dodge Sterne, January 26, 1922, *Lorenzo in Taos*, p. 15.

Chapter 14 Around the World

1. Nehls, 2, pp. 118, 126.

2. Ibid., p. 125.

3. DHL to Mary Cannan, April 3, 1922, *DHL Letters*, 4, p. 221.

4. Ibid.

5. DHL to Mary Cannan, April 5, 1922, ibid., p. 224.

6. Frieda Lawrence to Mabel Dodge Sterne, April 19, 1922, *Lorenzo in Taos*, p. 22.

7. Nehls, 2, p. 136.

8. Ibid., p. 134.

9. Preface to M. L. Skinner, *Black Swans*, reprinted in *Phoenix*, vol. 2, p. 294.

10. Apparently Captain Bertie Scrivener. All information relating to Scott and, in the paragraphs below, the King and Empire Alliance, Sir Charles Rosenthal, etc., is from Robert Darroch, *D. H. Lawrence in Australia* (South Melbourne: Macmillan, 1981).

11. *DHL Letters*, 4, p. 14; also see Worthen, *D. H. Lawrence*, pp. 114 ff.

12. DHL to Anna von Richthofen, May 30, 1922, *DHL Letters*, 4, p. 250.

13. DHL to Anna Jenkins, May 30, 1922, ibid., p. 250.

14. DHL to Mabel Dodge Sterne, June 3, 1922, ibid., p. 251.

15. *Kangaroo*, pp. 16–17.

16. DHL to Else Jaffe, June 13, 1922, *DHL Letters*, 4, p. 263.

17. See DHL to Mabel Dodge Sterne, October 6, 1922, ibid., p. 318.

18. Frieda Lawrence to Else Jaffe, July 31, 1922, HRC.

19. Louis Berman, *The Glands Regulating Personality Type: A Study of the Glands of Internal Secretion in Relation to the Types of Human Nature* (New York: Macmillan, 1922).

20. Frieda Lawrence to Mabel Dodge Sterne, June 21(?), 1922, *DHL Letters*, 4, p. 268.

21. Frieda Lawrence to Mabel Dodge Sterne, May 19, 1922, *Lorenzo in Taos*, p. 22.

22. Frieda Lawrence to Mabel Dodge Sterne, June 21(?), 1922, *DHL Letters*, 4, pp. 268–269.

23. The Returned Servicemen's League was also called the Returned Soldiers' Politic League.

24. *Kangaroo*, pp. 326, 333.

25. Ibid., pp. 64–66, 94, 176.

26. Nehls, 2, p. 158.

27. DHL to Achsah Brewster, July 24, 1922, *DHL Letters*, 4, p. 280.

28. Frieda Lawrence to Else Jaffe, July 31, 1922, HRC; DHL to Robert Mountsier, July 17, 1922, *DHL Letters*, 4, p. 277 (Lawrence related Frieda's desire for a farm to him).

29. See ibid., p. 283.

30. *NIBTW*, p. 133.

31. DHL to Mary Cannan, August 31, 1922, *DHL Letters*, 4, p. 287; DHL to Compton Mackenzie, August 22, 1922, ibid., p. 286.

32. *NIBTW*, p. 133.

33. DHL to Anna von Richthofen, September 5, 1922, *DHL Letters*, 4, p. 289.

Chapter 15 The Lobo

1. Luhan, *Lorenzo in Taos*, p. 36.

2. DHL to Robert Mountsier, July 17, 1922, *DHL Letters*, 4, p. 277.

3. Luhan, *Lorenzo in Taos*, p. 36.

4. *NIBTW*, p. 135.

5. Rudnick, *Mabel Dodge Luhan*, p. 182. Much of the material on Mabel in the chapter is drawn from this source.

6. Reprinted in Gertrude Stein, *Selected Writings of Gertrude Stein*, ed. Carl Van Vechten (New York: Vintage, 1990), pp. 525 ff.

7. In his autobiography, *Money Writes!* (New York: Charles Boni, 1927), as related in Rudnick, *Mabel Dodge Luhan*, p. 85.

8. Partially because of the similarity of this and her previous address. But see *The Spectator*, October 1917 (vol. 1, no. 7). The move apparently occurred not long after her marriage to Maurice Sterne. I am grateful to Jan Seidler Ramirez, curator of Paintings and Sculpture, Museum of the City of New York, for furnishing this information.

9. As quoted in Rudnick, *Mabel Dodge Luhan*, p. 141.

10. Ibid., pp. 149, 176.

11. Ibid., p. 156.

12. Bynner, *Journey with Genius*, pp. 4–6, 69.

13. Ibid., p. 2.

14. Ibid., p. 6.

15. Ibid., p. 5.

16. Interview with Paul and Rowena Keith, October 16, 1988, Taos.

17. Bynner, *Journey with Genius*, p. 6.

18. *NIBTW*, p. 135.

19. Frieda Lawrence to Witter Bynner, September 10, 1942, Harvard University Library.

20. Luhan, *Lorenzo in Taos*, pp. 43–46.

21. Rudnick, *Mabel Dodge Luhan*, p. 155.

22. Luhan, *Lorenzo in Taos*, pp. 47–50.

23. DHL to Thomas Seltzer, September 12, 1922, *DHL Letters*, 4, p. 295.

24. DHL to Anna von Richthofen, September 12, 1922, ibid., pp. 293–294.

25. Luhan, *Lorenzo in Taos*, pp. 47–50, 51.

26. Ibid., pp. 47–50.

27. *NIBTW*, p. 136.

28. Luhan, *Lorenzo in Taos*, pp. 59–60.

29. Rudnick, *Mabel Dodge Luhan*, p. 195.

30. Luhan, *Lorenzo in Taos*, p. 61.

31. *NIBTW*, p. 136.

32. Nehls, 3, p. 104.

33. *Phoenix*, vol. 1, p. 146.

34. Luhan, *Lorenzo in Taos*, pp. 71–72.

35. Ibid., p. 88.

36. Ibid., p. 72.

37. *NIBTW*, p. 34.

38. DHL to Mabel Dodge Sterne, October 6, 1922, *DHL Letters*, 4, p. 318.

39. DHL to Else Jaffe, September 27, 1922, ibid., pp. 310–311.

40. DHL to Mabel Dodge Sterne, October 6, 1922, ibid., p. 318.

41. Frieda Lawrence to Robert Mountsier, October 6, 1922, ibid., p. 319.

42. *Kangaroo*, p. 356.

43. *NIBTW*, p. 137.

44. Frieda Lawrence to Mabel Dodge Sterne, 1922, as quoted in Rudnick, *Mabel Dodge Luhan*, p. 198.

45. *NIBTW*, p. 136.

46. Luhan, *Lorenzo in Taos*, p. 74.

47. Ibid., p. 67.

48. Mabel Dodge Sterne to Leo Stein, n.d., as quoted in Rudnick, *Mabel Dodge Luhan*, p. 199.

49. Nehls, 2, p. 197.

50. *NIBTW*, p. 136.

51. DHL to Mabel Dodge Sterne, December 1, 1922, *DHL Letters*, 4, p. 346.

52. Frieda Lawrence to Anna von Richthofen, December 8, 1922, ibid., pp. 356–357.

53. Merrild, *With D. H. Lawrence in New Mexico*, p. 209.

54. Frieda Lawrence to Anna von Richthofen, December 8, 1922, *DHL Letters*, 4, pp. 356–357.

55. Bynner, *Journey with Genius*, p. 16.

56. Interview with Dorothy Brandenburg, October 25, 1988, Taos.

57. *Taos Valley News and El Crepusculo*, December 12, 1922.

58. DHL to Bessie Freeman, January 24, 1923, *DHL Letters*, 4, p. 372.

59. DHL to John Middleton Murry, February 2, 1923, ibid., p. 375.

60. Frieda Lawrence to Adele Seltzer, February 10, 1923, ibid., pp. 384–385.

61. Merrild, *With D. H. Lawrence in New Mexico*, p. 139.

62. Interview with Rachel Hawk, October 15, 1988, Lobo Mountain; conversation with Albert Bearce, October 15, 1988, Lobo Mountain; letter from Rachel Hawk, November(?) 1990 or 1991.

63. *Phoenix*, vol. 1, p. 92.

64. Bynner, *Journey with Genius*, p. 18.

Chapter 16 Golden and Tin Calves

1. Bynner, *Journey with Genius*, p. 46. The lyrics to "Three O'Clock in the Morning" were written in 1921 by Dorothy Terris; music by Julian Robledo. It was used in the revue *Greenwich Village Folies* by Richard Bold in the same year. Paul Whiteman and His Orchestra made it a hit in 1922. (It was also used in the 1943 Judy Garland movie *Presenting Lily Mars*.)

2. Bynner, *Journey with Genius*, p. 47.

3. Ibid., p. 46.

4. See "Walk to Huayapa," *Mornings in Mexico* (London: Secker, 1927).

5. Nehls, 2, p. 228; Bynner, *Journey with Genius*, p. 61.

6. Bynner, *Journey with Genius*, pp. 61–62.

7. DHL to Anna von Richthofen, April 27, 1923, *DHL Letters*, 4, pp. 433–434.

8. For a summary of this view, see Simon Leys, "Lawrence of Australia," in *New York Review of Books*, April 21, 1994, pp. 29–35.

9. DHL to Frieda Lawrence, May 1, 1923, *DHL Letters*, 4, p. 435.

10. DHL to Thomas Seltzer, May 2, 1923, and John Middleton Murry, May 3, 1923, ibid., p. 437.

11. DHL to John Middleton Murry, May 3, 1923, ibid., p. 437.

12. John Middleton Murry to Katherine Mansfield, ca. December 10, 1920, *Letters of John Middleton Murry to Katherine Mansfield*, p. 319.

13. Alpers, *Katherine Mansfield*, p. 388.

14. DHL to Thomas Seltzer, June 15, 1923, *DHL Letters*, 4, p. 458.

15. *St: Mawr*, in *St. Mawr and the Man Who Died* (New York: Vintage, 1953), p. 6.

16. Nehls, 2, p. 239.

17. Bynner, *Journey with Genius*, p. 150; cf. Frieda Lawrence to Witter Bynner, n.d., Harvard University Library.

18. Nehls, 2, p. 239.

19. Bynner, *Journey with Genius*, p. 61.

20. Ibid., p. 100; Frieda Lawrence to Adele Seltzer, June 10, 1923, *DHL Letters*, 4, p. 455.

21. Bynner, *Journey with Genius*, p. 62.

22. DHL to Witter Bynner, August 14, 1923, *DHL Letters*, 4, p. 484.

23. DHL to John Middleton Murry, August 7, 1923, ibid., p. 480.

24. Frieda Lawrence to Witter Bynner, ca. August 18, 1923, *M&C*, p. 220.

25. Mark Gertler to Ottoline Morrell, September 11, 1923, HRC, as quoted in Sean Hignett, *Brett: From Bloomsbury to New Mexico* (New York: Franklin Watts, 1983), p. 138.

26. Frieda Lawrence to Adele Seltzer, September 6 or 13(?), 1923, *D. H. Lawrence: Letters to Thomas and Adele Seltzer*, ed. Gerald M. Lacy (Santa Barbara: Black Sparrow Press, 1976), p. 108.

27. BL.

28. Frieda Lawrence to Adele Seltzer, September 1923, in *Letters to Thomas and Adele Seltzer*, p. 109.

29. Cf. Frieda Lawrence to S. S. Koteliansky, October 30, 1923, *M&C*, p. 222: "I am supposed to be impressed by your chastities: I am not, it's male conceit."

30. Kai Götzsche to Knud Merrild, October 25, 1923, as quoted in Merrild, *With D. H. Lawrence in New Mexico*, p. 343.

31. Frieda Lawrence to S. S. Koteliansky, October 30, 1923, *M&C*, pp. 221–222.

32. Frieda Lawrence to DHL, November 1, 1923; see DHL to Thomas Seltzer, November 3, 1923, *DHL Letters*, 4, p. 526.

33. DHL to Anna von Richthofen, November 10, 1923, ibid., pp. 531–532.

34. DHL to Frieda Lawrence, November 10, 1923, ibid., p. 529.

35. DHL to Anna von Richthofen, November 10, 1923, ibid., pp. 531–532.

36. Frieda Lawrence to S. S. Koteliansky, December 4, 1923, *M&C*, p. 223.

37. Murry, *Reminiscences of D. H. Lawrence*, p. 110.

38. Carswell, *The Savage Pilgrimage*, p. 202.

39. Ibid., p. 202.

40. Interview with Montague Weekley, July 13, 1978.

41. Nehls, 3, p. 21.

42. Ibid., 2, p. 294.

43. Ibid., p. 295.

44. BL.

45. Dorothy Brett, *Lawrence and Brett* (Philadelphia: Lippincott, 1933), p. 21;

Lawrence's story "The Last Laugh" contains a sketchy description of the device Brett used to pick up on group repartee (see also Hignett, *Brett*, p. 64 ["instruments for general conversation," in Dorothy Brett to Ottoline Morrell, n.d.]).

46. Brett, *Lawrence and Brett*, p. 21.

47. For an explication and summary of the charge of plagiarism, see Maddox, *The Married Man*, pp. 165–171, 537–542; "so like a schoolmaster": DHL to Thomas Seltzer, November 28, 1922, *DHL Letters*, 4, p. 345.

48. DHL to Thomas Seltzer, February 4, 1924, ibid., p. 569.

49. DHL to John Middleton Murry, February 7, 1924, ibid., pp. 572–573.

50. Brett, *Lawrence and Brett*, pp. 30–32.

Chapter 17 Angelino Ravagli

1. Brett, *Lawrence and Brett*, p. 39.

2. DHL to John Middleton Murry, March 14, 1924, *DHL Letters*, 5, p. 17.

3. For Lawrence's 1923–24 earnings, see Worthen, *D. H. Lawrence: A Literary Life*, pp. 124 ff.

4. Joseph Foster, *D. H. Lawrence in Taos* (Albuquerque: University of New Mexico Press, 1972), p. 28; cf. DHL to Anna von Richthofen, December 5, 1922, *DHL Letters*, 4, p. 352 ("a little buffalo").

5. See Michael Squires, ed., *D. H. Lawrence's Manuscripts: The Correspondence of Frieda Lawrence, Jake Zeitlin and Others* (New York: St. Martin's, 1991), p. 276.

6. *St. Mawr*, pp. 145–146.

7. More precisely, $462.65; *DHL Letters*, 5, p. 45, n. 2.

8. Brett, *Lawrence and Brett*, p. 104. There are similar passages in several of Lawrence's books—e.g., DHL and M. L. Skinner, *The Boy in the Bush* (New York: Viking, 1972), p. 361.

9. Luhan, *Lorenzo in Taos*, p. 227, and, for a different version, Brett, *Lawrence and Brett*, p. 109.

10. DHL to Willard Johnson, June 21, 1924, *DHL Letters*, 5, p. 60.

11. DHL to Clarence Thompson, August 27, 1924, ibid., p. 106.

12. E.g., "Indians and Entertainment," *New York Times Magazine* (October 26, 1924), *Adelphi* (November 1924); "The Hopi Snake Dance," *Theatre Arts Monthly* (December 1924), *Adelphi* (January–February, 1925).

13. He was born on June 18, 1846, and died on September 10, 1924.

14. David Gerard, interview with William Lawrence, NCL.

15. Brett, *Lawrence and Brett*, pp. 128–129.

16. *NIBTW*, p. 147.

17. DHL to Robert Mountsier, July 12, 1920, *DHL Letters*, 3, p. 566.

18. *NIBTW*, p. 147.

19. DHL to Curtis Brown, November 14, 1924, *DHL Letters*, 5, p. 166.

20. For the most celebrated, see Kate Millett, *Sexual Politics* (London: Abacus/Sphere, 1972), pp. 238, 240, 245, 281, 283–285.

21. Ibid.; Ross Parmenter, *Lawrence in Oaxaca* (Salt Lake City: Peregrine Smith, 1984), pp. 313–314.

22. Frieda Lawrence to Witter Bynner, n.d., Harvard University Library.

23. *NIBTW*, p. 152.

24. Brett, *Lawrence and Brett*, p. 208.
25. *NIBTW*, p. 149.
26. Ibid., p. 149.
27. Ibid., pp. 150–151.
28. Ibid., p. 151.
29. DHL to Ida Rauh, July 13, 1925, *DHL Letters*, 5, p. 276.
30. Frieda Lawrence to Kathryn Herbig, April 26, 1938, *D. H. Lawrence's Manuscripts*, p. 174.
31. *NIBTW*, p. 152.
32. Nehls, 3, pp. 8–9.
33. Willam Gerhardie, *Memoirs of a Polyglot* (London: Macdonald, 1973), pp. 279–281, 289.
34. Frieda Lawrence to Dorothy Brett, November 25, 1925, *DHL Letters*, 5, p. 344.
35. DHL to Dorothy Brett, November 4, 1925, ibid., pp. 332–333.
36. *NIBTW*, p. 179.
37. The birthdate of Queen Elena (née Princess Elena Petrovich-Niegosh, daughter of the first and last king of Montenegro) is variously given as January 8, 1873, or June 13, 1871. The Lawrences probably met Ravagli on November 19, 1925; his birthday was November 27.
38. Nehls, 3, p. 17.
39. Ibid., p. 18.
40. Letter from Stefano Ravagli, August 12, 1990.
41. Nehls, 3, p. 18.
42. New Mexico state divorce file, no. 4754; letter from Stefano Ravagli, August 12, 1990; Holland, pp. 231–236, 243.
43. *M&C*, pp. 25, 26.
44. Frieda Lawrence to Dorothy Brett, December 8, 1925, *DHL Letters*, 5, p. 350.
45. Ibid., p. 349.
46. Ibid.
47. Nehls, 3, p. 21.
48. BL.
49. *NIBTW*, p. 179.
50. Nehls, 3, p. 21; *NIBTW*, pp. 179–180.

Chapter 18 Vence

1. Nehls, 3, p. 22.
2. *The Virgin and the Gipsy* (New York: Vintage, 1984), p. 17.
3. BL; *Virgin and Gipsy*, p. 70.
4. Nehls, 3, p. 25.
5. *NIBTW*, p. 180.
6. Ibid.
7. *M&C*, pp. 20–21.
8. Lady Cynthia Asquith, ed., *The Ghost-Book* (London: Hutchinson, 1926).
9. Hignett, *Brett*, p. 191.

10. Hignett, *Brett*, pp. 190–192; in another version, Lawrence said not "pubes" but "boobs": see Dorothy Brett, *Lawrence and Brett* (Santa Fe: Sunstone, 1974), epilogue.

11. Nehls, 3, p. 27.

12. DHL to Dorothy Brett, March 18, 1926, *DHL Letters*, 5, p. 406.

13. *NIBTW*, p. 181.

14. DHL to Anna von Richthofen, April 4, 1926, *DHL Letters*, 5, p. 411.

15. DHL to Else Jaffe, April 7, 1926, ibid., p. 416.

16. DHL to S. S. Koteliansky, April 10, 1926, ibid., p. 419.

17. Nehls, 3, p. 26.

18. Ibid., pp. 57–58.

19. Richard Aldington, *Pinorman* (London: Heinemann, 1954), p. 28.

20. Nehls, 3, p. 187.

21. Ibid., p. 23.

22. *NIBTW*, p. 189.

23. DHL to Giuseppe Orioli, October 6, 1926, *DHL Letters*, 5, p. 549.

24. DHL to Aldous Huxley, November 14, 1927, *DHL Letters*, 6, p. 214.

25. *NIBTW*, p. 194.

26. Martin Secker to Frieda Lawrence, June 9, 1926, Rarebook & Special Collections Library, University of Illinois, Urbana-Champaign. I am grateful to Michael Squires for calling this letter to my attention.

"Lied des . . . ": "The Lay of the Imprisoned Huntsman," lyrics by W. Scott. See Minnie Earl Sears, *Song Index* (New York: H. W. Wilson Co., 1926).

27. Nehls, 3, p. 138.

28. Ibid., p. 70.

29. Frieda Lawrence to S. S. Koteliansky, August 9, 1926, *M&C*, p. 225.

30. Carswell, *The Savage Pilgrimage*, p. 255.

31. Frieda Lawrence to Mabel Dodge Luhan, October 30, 1926, *DHL Letters*, 5, p. 568; BBC; Frieda Lawrence to Witter Bynner, November 10, 1929, *M&C*, p. 233.

32. See, e.g., Alister Kershaw and Frédéric-Jacques Temple, eds., *Richard Aldington: An Intimate Portrait* (Carbondale: Southern Illinois University Press, 1965), p. 85.

33. Nehls, 3, p. 83.

34. *M&C*, p. 459.

35. Aldous Huxley, *Eyeless in Gaza* (New York: Harper & Brothers, 1936), p. 616, and *The Genius and the Goddess* (New York: Bantam, 1969).

36. Nehls, 3, p. 58.

37. DHL to Earl Brewster, February 27, 1927, *DHL Letters*, 5, p. 648.

38. *NIBTW*, p. 193.

39. Brigit Patmore, "A Memoir of Frieda Lawrence," p. 140.

40. DHL to Achsah Brewster, January 19, 1927, *DHL Letters*, 5, p. 627.

41. Frieda Lawrence to Montague Weekley, October 31, 1926, ibid., p. 569.

42. Nehls, 3, p. 143.

43. DHL to Martin Secker, November 15, 1926, *DHL Letters*, 5, p. 576.

44. Foreword to *The First Lady Chatterley*, as reprinted in *M&C*, p. 449.

45. *NIBTW*, p. 193.

46. Frieda Lawrence to Anna von Richthofen, April 14, 1927, *DHL Letters*, 6, p. 35.

47. Partially reproduced in *Laughing Horse* 21 (Winter 1939), n.p.

48. See Osbert Sitwell, *Penny Foolish* (London: Macmillan, 1935), pp. 295–297, and *Laughter in the Next Room* (London: Macmillan, 1949), pp. 310–311.

49. Seymour, *Ottoline Morrell*, pp. 316–318; Nehls, 2, p. 461; Michael Squires, *The Creation of Lady Chatterley's Lover* (Baltimore: Johns Hopkins University Press, 1983), p. 63; letter from Eric Quayle to Leo Hamalian, April 16, 1975 (I am grateful to Leo Hamalian for supplying a photocopy).

50. For Frieda as Bertha Coutts, the gamekeeper's wife, see, e.g., H. M. Daleski, *The Forked Flame* (London: Faber and Faber, 1965), p. 290, and Squires, *The Creation of Lady Chatterley's Lover*, p. 63. Frieda's "feeble": as quoted in Green, *The von Richthofen Sisters*, pp. 52, 135.

51. Mabel Dodge Luhan to Una Jeffers, July 2, 1931, Bancroft Library, University of California, Berkeley (hereafter Bancroft).

52. *NIBTW*, p. 195.

53. Nehls, 3, p. 160.

54. *Lady Chatterley's Lover* (New York: Grove Weidenfeld, 1982), p. 93.

55. DHL to Beatrice Campbell, February 3, 1928, *DHL Letters*, 6, p. 282; Juliette Huxley, *Leaves of the Tulip Tree* (London: Murray, 1986), p. 118.

56. Interview with Lady Juliette Huxley, London, July 4, 1988.

57. They also printed two hundred paperbacks.

58. See, e.g., DHL to Ada Clarke and to Martin Secker, July 9, 1928, *DHL Letters*, 6, p. 455.

59. DHL to Aldous and Maria Huxley and to Nancy Pearn, December 15, 1928, ibid., 7, pp. 64 and 65; Nehls, 3, p. 274.

60. Nehls, 3, p. 272.

61. Ibid., p. 275.

62. *Rasputin, the Holy Devil* (London: G. P. Putnam's Sons, 1928), trans. F. S. Flint and D. F. Tait.

In December 1944, the Rydal Press in Santa Fe published 100 copies of Frieda's translation of a letter (dated 1700) from Emperor K'ang Hsi to Pope Clement XI. The letter was from Fülöp-Miller, *Macht und Geheimnis der Jesuiten* (The power and secret of the Jesuits [New York: Viking, 1930], trans. Flint and Tait). Frieda was apparently unaware of the existing translation. Willard Hougland financed the printing; Frieda distributed some of her copies to friends as Christmas gifts. I am grateful to William Hughes for showing me his copy.

63. Geoffrey Wolff, *Black Sun: The Life of Harry Crosby* (New York: Random House, 1974), p. 234; Frieda Lawrence to Harry T. Moore, January 14, 1955, *M&C*, p. 390.

64. *NIBTW*, p. 198.

65. Nehls, 3, p. 343.

66. Frieda Lawrence to Hilda Huelin, July 15, 1929, *DHL Letters*, 7, p. 373.

67. DHL to Else Jaffe, October 28, 1927, ibid., 6, pp. 198–199.

68. Nehls, 3, p. 343.

69. Ibid., p. 345.
70. *NIBTW*, p. 199.
71. Ibid., p. 289.
72. Nehls, 3, p. 435.
73. *NIBTW*, p. 293.
74. Interview with Barbara Barr, June 17, 1978.
75. *NIBTW*, p. 295.
76. Ibid.
77. Nehls, 3, p. 435.
78. Ibid., p. 436.

Chapter 19 *"Not I, but the Wind . . ."*

1. Date, time, and place of ship's arrival: *New York Times*, May 18, 1931, p. 37.

2. Frieda Lawrence to Martha Gordon Crotch, May 17, 1931, quoted in Moore and Montague, *Frieda Lawrence and Her Circle*, pp. 44–45 (where it is misdated May 19).

3. Frieda Lawrence to Witter Bynner, April 20, 1931, Harvard University Library; Frieda Lawrence to Martha Gordon Crotch, May 17, 1931, and "Sunday" (May 24, 1931), quoted in Moore and Montague, *Frieda Lawrence and Her Circle*, pp. 44–45.

4. Mabel Dodge Luhan to Una Jeffers, June 3, 1931, Bancroft.

5. Frieda also was acquainted with Robert Hobart Davis, a *Sun* executive and columnist who had met and photographed Lawrence in Florence in May 1928.

6. New York *Sun*, May 20, 1931, p. 23; New York *Evening Post*, May 20, 1931, p. 7 ("BOOK ON LAWRENCE ASSAILED BY WIDOW; Letters She Is Helping Huxley Edit Will Refute 'Woman Hater' Idea, She Says; See Biography Appalling"); George Britt, New York *World-Telegram*, May 21, 1931, p. 3 ("LAWRENCE LIVING TO WIDOW, BARING 'OTHER SIDE'"); Lewis Gannett, New York *Herald Tribune*, May 23, 1931, p. 13 ("Books and Things"; see subhead "Lawrence's Flowered Chest"). For other mention of the interviews (and proposals), see Martha Gordon Crotch, *Memories of Frieda Lawrence* (Edinburgh: Tragara, 1975), p. 25, where the context would indicate Frieda's letter to her is dated 1933; but it is clearly 1931. Also see Mabel Dodge Luhan to Una Jeffers, n.d. (but probably June 4 or 5, 1931), Bancroft.

The Prince George achieved notoriety decades later as a welfare hotel, and was closed in 1993 after a fire.

7. See "that *bullying* Pollinger," Frieda Lawrence to Martha Gordon Crotch, May 24, 1931, quoted in Moore and Montague, *Frieda Lawrence and Her Circle*, p. 45.

8. *M&C*, p. 25.

9. Frieda Lawrence to Martha Gordon Crotch, July 22, 1931, quoted in Moore and Montague, *Frieda Lawrence and Her Circle*, p. 50.

10. Mabel Dodge Luhan to Una Jeffers, June 3, 1931, Bancroft.

11. The name of the telegraph operator, who served as stationmaster at

Embudo—between Santa Fe and Taos, and the terminus of the train line—also occasionally is spelled Patchum.

12. Mabel Dodge Luhan to Una Jeffers, June 3, 1931, Bancroft.

13. Ibid.

14. Dorothy Brett to Alfred Stieglitz, June 2, 1931, Beinecke Library, Yale (hereafter Beinecke).

15. Frieda Lawrence to Martha Gordon Crotch, July 22, 1931, quoted in Moore and Montague, *Frieda Lawrence and Her Circle*, p. 50.

16. Mabel Dodge Luhan to Una Jeffers, n.d., Bancroft.

17. Mabel Dodge Luhan to Una Jeffers, July 2, 1931, ibid.

18. Ibid. The mistaking of nut ("*noce*") for night (*notte*) was probably Mabel's.

19. Mabel Dodge Luhan to Una Jeffers, July 2, 1931, Bancroft.

20. Nehls, 3, p. 448.

21. Mabel Dodge Luhan to Una Jeffers, June 3, 1931, Bancroft.

22. Letter from Barbara Barr, July 5, 1994; Crotch, *Memories*, pp. 1, 5.

23. Frieda Lawrence to Witter Bynner, July 23, 1930, *M&C*, p. 240, and n.d., 1931, Harvard University Library.

24. *NIBTW*, p. 296.

25. Frieda Lawrence to Witter Bynner, March 12, 1930, *M&C*, p. 235.

26. London *Times* June 12, 1930, p. 16D.

27. Crotch, *Memories*, p. 12.

28. See Frieda Lawrence to Caresse Crosby, n.d.; Crosby to Lawrence, May 26, 1930; Lawrence to Crosby, June 6, 1930, Crosby to Lawrence, June 26, 1930, quoted in Moore and Montague, *Frieda Lawrence and Her Circle*, pp. 39–41.

29. Barbara Weekley to Francis Hackett and Signe Toksvig, n.d., HRC. Hackett (1883–1962), a journalist born in Ireland, had been an associate editor of the *New Republic*; among his books are *Ireland: A Study in Nationalism* (New York: Huebsch, 1918), *Henry the Eighth* (New York: Liveright, 1929), and *What "Mein Kampf" Means to America* (New York: Reynal & Hitchcock, 1941). Toksvig, born and raised in Nyköburg, on the Danish island of Sjaelland, met and married Hackett while on the *New Republic* staff. Among her books are *The Life of Hans Christian Andersen* (London: Macmillan, 1933), *Emanuel Swedenborg: Scientist and Mystic* (New Haven: Yale University Press, 1948), and *Swan on a Black Sea* (London: Routledge & Kegan Paul, 1965), a study in automatic writing.

30. Frieda Lawrence to A. S. Frere Reeves, n.d., courtesy Camellia Investments, London.

31. Frieda Lawrence to Edward Titus, April 30, 1930, quoted in Moore and Montague, *Frieda Lawrence and Her Circle*, p. 11.

32. *Il Corriere della Sera*, March 4, 1930, p. 8. I am grateful to Abigail Asher for the translation.

33. Nehls, 3, p. 449.

34. See Crotch, *Memories*, p. 13, and Mabel Dodge Luhan to Una Jeffers, July 2, 1931, Bancroft.

35. *M&C*, p. 25.

36. Nehls, 3, p. 450.

37. Crotch, *Memories*, p. 16.

38. Interview with Barbara Barr, June 17, 1978.

39. *M&C*, p. 21.

40. *Times Literary Supplement*, March 13, 1930, p. 208. Murry's name did not appear; the obituary was signed "A Correspondent."

41. *The Last Devil* (New York: John Day, 1927).

42. BL.

43. Lucas, *Frieda Lawrence*, p. 255.

44. Ibid., p. 256.

45. Frieda Lawrence to A. S. Frere Reeves, n.d. (sent from Château Brun [the Brewsters' Provençal farmhouse], St. Cyr-sur-Mer, Var, France). Courtesy Camellia Investments.

46. Frieda Lawrence to A. S. Frere Reeves, n.d. (sent from Heidelberg), courtesy Camellia Investments.

47. Frieda Lawrence to A. S. Frere Reeves, n.d. (sent from Sanavy, France[?]), courtesy Camellia Investments.

48. Nehls, 3, p. 466.

49. Lucas, *Frieda Lawrence*, p. 256.

50. Ibid., p. 257.

51. Frieda Lawrence to Witter Bynner, n.d., Harvard University Library.

52. Mabel Dodge Luhan to Una Jeffers, June 3, 1931, and July 15, 1931, Bancroft.

53. Letter from Barbara Barr, July 5, 1994.

54. Interview with Veronica Murphy, July 16, 1988, London.

55. Mabel Dodge Luhan to Una Jeffers, July 15, 1931, Bancroft.

56. Barbara Barr to Francis Hackett and Signe Toksvig, June 11, 1931, HRC.

57. They were married May 17, 1934; Ernest Weekley hosted a champagne party at 49 Harvard Road. Stuart Barr also stood for Parliament twice as a Labour candidate (phone interview with Barbara Barr, October 6, 1994).

58. Crotch, *Memories*, pp. 5, 6.

59. Ibid., p. 6.

60. Frieda Lawrence to Edward Titus, December 5(?), 1930, quoted in Moore and Montague, *Frieda Lawrence and Her Circle*, p. 24.

61. Frieda Lawrence to Richard Aldington, May 27, 1954, ibid., p. 105.

62. Letter from Barbara Barr, July 5, 1994.

Though there is no evidence of the precise nature of Frieda and Frere Reeves's relations, her letters to him are uncharacteristically wistful and confidential—"Frere, am I as fond of you as I think I am, or is it not true? One is afraid," she wrote from the Kingsley Hotel, and, later, from New Mexico, "Do you remember, dear Frere, how we both were so miserable, wandering like lost souls on the embankment and now we are happy and weren't we nice with each other, *you* did me the world of good" (n.d., courtesy Camellia Investments).

63. Frieda Lawrence to Jake Zeitlin, November 21, 1937, *D. H. Lawrence's Manuscripts*, p. 134.

64. The date of the marriage was October 4, 1930; letter from Ian Weekley, June 15, 1994.

65. Crotch, *Memories*, p. 15.

66. Ibid., p. 16.

67. Frieda Lawrence to Mabel Dodge Luhan, April 1, 1930, *M&C*, p. 237.

68. Dorothy Brett to Alfred Stieglitz, February 1933, Beinecke, as quoted in Hignett, *Brett*, p. 219.

69. Crotch, *Memories*, p. 6.

70. David Gerard, interview with William Lawrence, NCL. She wore folk dress.

71. Aldous Huxley to Flora Strousse, October 15, 1932, *Letters of Aldous Huxley*, ed. Grover Smith (London: Chatto & Windus, 1969), p. 364.

72. From an entry in Forster's commonplace book, as quoted in Furbank, *E. M. Forster*, p. 165.

73. Glenavy, *Today We Will Only Gossip*, p. 165.

74. Frieda Lawrence to Martha Gordon Crotch, November 7(?), 1932, quoted in Moore and Montague, *Frieda Lawrence and Her Circle*, p. 62.

75. Bynner, *Journey with Genius*, p. 347.

76. London *Times*, November 4, 1932, p. 4.

77. Letter from Stefano Ravagli, August 12, 1990.

78. HRC.

79. Luhan, *Lorenzo in Taos*; Brett, *Lawrence and Brett*.

80. Henry Seidel Canby, *Saturday Review of Literature*, October 13, 1934, p. 203.

81. Interview with Dorothy Horgan, May 30, 1993, Talpa/Ranchos de Taos.

82. Crotch, *Memories*, p. 33.

83. Angelo Ravagli to Martha Gordon Crotch, March 16, 1935, quoted in ibid., p. 35.

84. Interview with Eya Fechin Branham, October 13, 1988, Taos. For variations on the story, see Cecil Smith, "Frieda Lawrence—A Personal Memoir," *Los Angeles Times*, November 8, 1981 (Smith recounts that the ashes disappeared for ten years, were found, and finally "enshrined"), and Hignett, *Brett*, pp. 224–228, 269–270.

85. Margaret Lefranc, "Auden in the Southwest," in *El Palacio* 98 (Winter 1992–1993); phone interview with Margaret Lefranc, February 2, 1993.

86. See Dorothy Brett to Alfred Stieglitz, July 5, 1935, Beinecke, as quoted in Hignett, *Brett*, p. 226.

87. Interview with Eya Fechin Branham, October 13, 1988, Taos.

88. Dorothy Brett to Alfred Stieglitz, May 30, 1939, Beinecke, as quoted in Hignett, *Brett*, p. 233.

89. Dorothy Brett to Una Jeffers, May 4, 1935, Beinecke, as quoted in Hignett, *Brett*, p. 226.

90. Nehls, 3, p. 485.

Chapter 20 From Hollywood to Laguna Vista

1. Else's own, one-sentence message sends "greetings" and "love." December 10, 1934, Beinecke. If one assumes that Else sent the postcard because she supported Hitler, it becomes difficult to see why Frieda would later have kept it; it could serve only to implicate them both.

Frieda made her reason for wanting Else to leave Germany clear to Jake Zeitlin. See Zeitlin to Frank J. Hogan, April 3, 1936, *D. H. Lawrence's Manuscripts*, p. 34. (The letter, however, gives the mistaken impression that Edgar Jaffe was still alive; he had died in 1921. The mistake is repeated in the introduction to *D. H. Lawrence's Manuscripts*, p. 4.)

2. Here and throughout, I have drawn on *D. H. Lawrence's Manuscripts* for background on Zeitlin.

3. Frieda Lawrence to Witter Bynner, n.d., Harvard University Library.

4. *D. H. Lawrence's Manuscripts*, p. 4.

5. "Galka Scheyer's Bequest to Pasadena," *Art News* 52 (September 1953), p. 48; "Pasadena's Blue Four Bequest," *Art Digest* 27 (September 1953), p. 15. Phone interview with Elfriede Fischinger, November 2, 1994; letter from Marcy Guzman, December 2, 1994. The Pasadena Art Institute is now the Norton Simon Museum.

6. Interviews with Genevieve Janssen, October 9, 1988; Helen Kentnor, October 17, 1988; Lucille Pond, October 26, 1988 (all, Taos).

7. *M&C*, p. 476.

8. Angelino Ravagli to Jake Zeitlin, April 1, 1937, *D. H. Lawrence's Manuscripts*, p. 78.

9. Angelino Ravagli to Elsa Seaman, December 1935, University of New Mexico Library, Folder I–L; the text is from a draft in Ravagli's notebook (hereafter this source is referred to as UNM).

10. BL.

11. Angelino Ravagli to Friedrich Jaffe, December 1935, UNM.

12. Christopher Miles, interview with Joe Glasco, summer 1988, London.

13. *M&C*, p. 478; interview with Eya Fechin Branham, October 13, 1988, Taos.

14. Frieda Lawrence to Witter Bynner, January 6, 1943, *M&C*, p. 288.

15. Frieda Lawrence to Jake Zeitlin, n.d., *D. H. Lawrence's Manuscripts*, p. 42.

16. Lois Hoffmann, "Altering the Text: A Study of the Discrepancies between *Not I, but the Wind* and Its German Translation, *Nur der Wind*," HRC.

17. Interview with Helen Kentnor, October 17, 1988, Taos.

18. Frieda Lawrence to Jake Zeitlin, January 29, 1938, *D. H. Lawrence's Manuscripts*, p. 167.

19. Frieda Lawrence to William York Tindall, September 16, 1939, *M&C*, pp. 277–278.

20. Ibid., pp. 293–294.

21. Frieda Lawrence to Edward Gilbert, September 17, 1944, *M&C*, pp. 294–295 (where *Bejahung* is misprinted as *Bejaung*).

22. *M&C*, p. 294.

23. Ibid., pp. 437, 439.

24. Dunaway, *Huxley in Hollywood*, p. 30.

25. Interview with Arturo Montoya, September 19, 1988, El Prado.

26. Maria Huxley to Baron Edward Sackville-West, June 23, 1937, as quoted in Bedford, *Aldous Huxley*, vol. 1, pp. 346–347.

27. Frieda Lawrence to Jake Zeitlin, November 5, 1937, *D. H. Lawrence's Manuscripts*, p. 125.

28. The transaction occurred, according to Brill, "long before Lawrence died" (see A. A. Brill to Jake Zeitlin, January 18, 1938, *D. H. Lawrence's Manuscripts*, p. 164). The belief that Mabel paid her own treatment bill with the manuscript is, according to a letter from Frieda Lawrence to Witter Bynner (September 14, 1951, Harvard University Library), a misconception perpetuated by a misstatement in Bynner's *Journey with Genius*.

29. Stefano Manara to Frieda Lawrence, October 20, 1937, *D. H. Lawrence's Manuscripts*, p. 122.

30. *M&C*, p. 35.

31. A later letter from Angelo Ravagli to T. E. Hanley (August 11, 1956, HRC) places him in Bradford; and see *D. H. Lawrence's Manuscripts*, pp. 14–16.

32. Frieda Lawrence to Angelo Ravagli, December 3, 1937, *M&C*, pp. 255–256.

33. Conversations with Henry A. Sauerwein, fall 1988 and fall 1989, Taos; Frieda Lawrence to Witter Bynner, n.d. (Summer 1937). Bynner hand-corrected the spelling of the baron's name to Maltzan, but I have retained Frieda's spelling.

34. Frieda Lawrence to John Middleton Murry, September 9, 1952, *M&C*, p. 347.

35. Frieda Lawrence to Witter Bynner, March 28, 1938, Harvard University Library.

36. Interviews with Saki Karavas, October 12, 1988, September 28, 1990, Taos.

37. Frieda Lawrence to Angelo Ravagli, March 5, 1938, *M&C*, p. 266.

38. Interview with Lillian Montoya, September 14, 1988, El Prado.

39. Interview with J. J. and Juanita Montoya, September 5, 1988, El Prado.

40. One of O'Keeffe's visits was recorded by *El Crepusculo*, September 20, 1951; she was accompanied by Doris Bry.

41. Rogers-Luhan affair: interview with Suzette Hausner, October 2, 1990, Santa Fe; Miranda Levy (phone conversations, October 1, 1993, and July 13, 1994) disputes the notion that they were lovers. The O'Keeffe-Luhan affair is widely acknowledged in Taos.

42. Calvin Tompkins, "The Rose in the Eye Looked Pretty Fine," *The New Yorker*, March 4, 1974, p. 54.

43. *El Crepusculo*, November 29, 1951; Rudnick, *Mabel Dodge Luhan*, p. 328.

44. Frieda Lawrence to Witter Bynner, 1938, Harvard University Library.

45. See, e.g., *El Crepusculo*, social columns, August 9, October 25, November 8, 1951; restaurant menu courtesy Alexander Böker.

46. Interview with Veronica Murphy, July 16, 1988, London.

47. Interview with Montague Weekley, July 13, 1978.

48. Frieda Lawrence to Montague Weekley, August 22, 1939, *M&C*, p. 275.

49. Ian Weekley, "Frieda Lawrence: A Memoir" (a joint publication of the Luton School of Art and Dunstable College of Further Education, March 1962), unpaged; Frieda Lawrence to Montague Weekley, August 22, 1939, *M&C*, p. 275.

50. W. H. Auden to A. E. Dodds, n.d., Manuscripts Division, Bodleian Library, Oxford, England.

51. Chester Kallman to Harold Albaum, July 13, 1939, Manuscripts Division, Lilly Library, University of Indiana, Bloomington. I am grateful to Nicholas Jenkins for providing the texts of this and the above letter.

52. Tennessee Williams, *Memoirs* (New York: Doubleday, 1975), p. 104.

53. Frieda Lawrence to Ernest Tedlock, Jr., September 11, 1948, *M&C*, p. 315; Humphrey Burton, *Leonard Bernstein* (New York: Doubleday, 1994).

54. Interview with Dorothy Horgan, May 30, 1993, Talpa/Ranchos de Taos.

55. Letter from Enid C. Hilton, September 19, 1990. Hilton, the daughter of Lawrence's Eastwood friend William Hopkin, was a friend of Frieda's and, like Frieda, was turned in to the FBI by Harold Hawk.

Possible later evidence of Hawk's role as an informer is found in an FBI file (no. 10-387), made available to the author under the Freedom of Information Act. It states, in part: "on February 24, 1941, a letter was received from the Special Agent in Charge of the Buffalo Field Division furnishing information submitted by"—the name is blacked out.

56. See Frieda Lawrence to Dudley Nichols, n.d., *M&C*, p. 274.

57. Phone interview with Joe Fulton, October 22, 1988; Frieda Lawrence to Witter Bynner, July 25, 1939, *M&C*, p. 273.

58. Frieda Lawrence to Witter Bynner, September 15, 1940, Harvard University Library.

59. See Witter Bynner to Frieda Lawrence, August 28, 1942, ibid.

60. *New York Times*, "Munich Bans Dreiser Books," February 9, 1935, p. 6.

61. Conversations with Henry A. Sauerwein, Jr., 1988–1993, Taos, and interview, May 27, 1993. He includes Auden, Jung, and countless other visitors to Taos in a list of those who were of a similar "mindset."

62. See. e.g., Mabel Dodge Luhan to Una Jeffers, June 3, 1931; Frieda Lawrence to Witter Bynner, n.d. (summer 1937), Harvard University Library. See also Frieda Lawrence to: Montague Weekley, August 22, 1939, and September 3, 1939; Dudley Nichols, November 4, 1939; Else Jaffe, November 8, 1955, *M&C*, pp. 275, 276, 279, 403.

As is clear from the complete Luhan-Jeffers correspondence dating from the summer of 1931, Frieda had no taste (despite Ravagli's esteem for Mussolini, and despite her praise for the literary value of *Mein Kampf* [see below, in text]) for totalitarian rule.

63. Interview with Frank Waters, October 11, 1988, Arroyo Seco.

64. For the complete text see *Virginia Quarterly Review* 16 (Winter 1940), pp. 127–129.

65. HRC.

66. See note 62, above.

67. Witter Bynner to Frieda Lawrence, August 28, 1942, Harvard University Library; Russell, "Portraits from Memory 3: D. H. Lawrence," *Harper's*, February 1953, p. 94. Comparison with the quotation from *The Autobiography of Bertrand Russell, 1914–1944* in chapter 10 of this book shows the progression of Russell's thought, toward putting the onus on Frieda.

68. In 1919.

69. BL.

70. Interview with Dorothy Horgan, May 30, 1993, Talpa/Ranchos de Taos; I am grateful to Barbara Horgan for allowing me to interview her on the phone (October 1, 1991).

71. *M&C*, p. 20.

72. Interview with Barbara Chavez, September 13, 1988, Arroyo Hondo.

73. Interview with Suzette Hausner, October 2, 1990, Santa Fe.

74. Letters from and conversations with Frederick R. Jeffrey, 1988–1991, and interview with Frederick R. and Marianne Jeffrey, March 15, 1989, Greenwich, Connecticut.

75. Barr, "I Look Back," p. 254.

76. Frieda Lawrence to Frederick R. Jeffrey, September 12, 1945. Courtesy Frederick R. Jeffrey.

77. Interview with William Hughes, April 7, 1992, New York.

78. Unsigned letter (postmarked New York) to John S. Sumner, n.d. Obtained from the FBI through the Freedom of Information Act.

79. Memo obtained under the Freedom of Information Act.

80. HRC.

81. Interview with Henry A. Sauerwein, Jr., May 27, 1993, Taos.

82. The property was then called Block 443; it is now 443 Beach Boulevard; the house (enlarged) is still standing.

83. Cecil Smith, "Frieda Lawrence—A Personal Memoir," *Los Angeles Times*, November 8, 1981.

84. Interview with Bertha Ilfeld, October 22, 1988, Albuquerque.

85. *Dallas Morning News*, February 7, 1954, part 7, p. 7; reprinted in *M&C*, p. 435.

86. Frieda Lawrence to Witter Bynner, February 17, 1947, ibid., p. 309.

87. Interview with Louise Leslie, November 17, 1990, Port Isabel.

88. Letter from Eric P. Hausner, M.D., to Bunny Goldtrap, November 18, 1949, in the possession of the author (courtesy the late Bunny Smirch).

89. Frieda Lawrence to E. W. Tedlock, Jr., March 23, 1948, *M&C*, p. 311.

90. Frieda Lawrence to Rolf Gardiner, June 21, 1947, as quoted in Lucas, *Frieda Lawrence*, p. 278.

91. Spud Johnson, "Von Richthofen Sisters, Nusch & Frieda, Are Reunited," *El Crepusculo*, May 12, 1949, p. 4.

92. Frieda Lawrence to Else Jaffe, May 18, 1954, and March 24, 1954, *M&C*, pp. 377, 373.

93. Published in New York by Duell, Sloan and Pearce.

94. Frieda Lawrence to Witter Bynner, August 13, 1950, Harvard University Library.

95. See Paul Horgan, *Tracings* (New York: Farrar, Straus & Giroux, 1993), pp. 93–95.

96. "Widow of D. H. Lawrence Wed," *New York Times*, November 1, 1950, p. 40; phone interview with Joe Fulton, October 22, 1988.

97. Phone interview with Joe Fulton, October 22, 1988.

Chapter 21 The Art of Dying

1. Phone interviews with Miranda Levy, October 1, 1993, July 13, 1994.

2. BL.

3. Interview with Veronica Murphy, July 16, 1988, London.

4. Ian Weekley, "Frieda Lawrence: A Memoir."

5. Frieda Lawrence to Harry T. Moore, October 1, 1988, *M&C*, p. 349.

6. "[I]nordinately fond": letter from Ian Weekley, October 4, 1994; interview with Anthea Goldsmith, June 28, 1988, London.

7. Interview with Jim Fordham, June 26, 1988, Essex.

8. Frieda Lawrence to Witter Bynner, December 6, 1949, *M&C*, p. 317.

9. Ian Weekley, "Frieda Lawrence: A Memoir."

10. The book was prosecuted in 1960 under the 1959 Obscene Publications Bill.

11. Ian Weekley, "Frieda Lawrence: A Memoir."

12. BL.

13. He died on May 7; see London *Times*, May 8, 1954, p. 8. The photograph of Frieda, often incorrectly described as one taken on their honeymoon, was dated spring 1900 by the Blases; Frieda's pregnancy is well concealed, in the manner of the times.

14. He died on June 1, 1968, having survived Frieda by twelve years.

15. Among them Harvard University Library and New Mexico State University at Las Cruces.

16. Frieda Lawrence to Witter Bynner, January 2, 1953, Harvard University Library.

17. Rudnick, *Mabel Dodge Luhan*, p. 329.

18. Barr, "I Look Back," p. 259.

19. Frieda Lawrence to Dudley Nichols, February 26, 1955, *M&C*, p. 393. The volume Frieda had may have been *The Book of the Craft of Dying and Other English Tracts Concerning Death* (ed. Frances M. M. Comper [New York, Bombay, and Calcutta: Longmans, Green & Co., 1917]), a reprint of a popular medieval work, *De arte Moriendi*.

20. *D. H. Lawrence's Manuscripts*, p. 22.

21. Frieda Lawrence to Warren Roberts, January 5, 1953, HRC.

22. Frieda Lawrence to Warren Roberts, n.d., as quoted in *D. H. Lawrence's Manuscripts*, p. 21.

23. For the appraisal, see ibid., pp. 17, 207–208, 210–211, 293–311.

24. Frieda Lawrence to Warren Roberts, May 12, 1954, and to Alan C. Collins, October 12, 1954; ibid., pp. 206, 209.

25. Frieda Lawrence to Warren Roberts, November 30, 1954, ibid., p. 212.

26. Frieda Lawrence to Else Jaffe, February 26, 1955, *M&C*, p. 394.

27. Interview with Suzette Hausner, October 2, 1990, Santa Fe.

28. Frieda Lawrence to Witter Bynner, February 13, 1956, *M&C*, p. 409.

29. They were the proprietors of Frenchy's.

30. Angelo Ravagli to Bunny and Charley Goldtrap, March 8, 1955. In the possession of the author. I am grateful to the late Bunny Smirch for providing this and other letters.

31. Frieda Lawrence to Witter Bynner, February 13, 1956, *M&C*, p. 409.

32. Frieda Lawrence to Witter Bynner, July 3, 1955, Harvard University Library.

33. Harry T. Moore, *The Intelligent Heart: The Story of D. H. Lawrence* (New York: Farrar, Straus & Young, 1954)—the book was later retitled *A Priest of Love*; Mark Spilka, *The Love Ethic of D. H. Lawrence* (Bloomington: Indiana University Press, 1955).

34. Frieda Lawrence to John Middleton Murry, May 18, 1956, *M&C*, p. 411.

35. Lucas, *Frieda Lawrence*, p. 283.

36. Angelo Ravagli to Enid Hilton, August 23, 1956, HRC.

37. Barr, "I Look Back," p. 258.

38. Frieda Lawrence to F. R. Leavis, May 22, 1956, *M&C*, pp. 412–413. Leavis's book was published in England by Chatto & Windus the following year.

39. The *New Republic* (February 28, 1955) and the *New Statesman* (August 13, 1955) published her response (in two slightly different versions) to Moore, *The Intelligent Heart*; Barr, "I Look Back," p. 259.

40. Montague Weekley to Frieda Lawrence, June 2, 1956, HRC.

41. Interview with William Hughes, April 7, 1992, New York.

42. Joe Glasco to Barbara Barr, August 16, 1956, *M&C*, p. 418.

43. Angelo Ravagli to Montague Weekley, Elsa Seaman, and Barbara Barr, August 17, 1956, *M&C*, p. 416.

44. Joe Glasco to Barbara Barr, August 16, 1956, *M&C*, p. 419.

45. Angelo Ravagli to John Middleton Murry, September 24, 1956, HRC.

46. Angelo Ravagli to T. E. Hanley, August 11, 1956, HRC.

47. Reduction of oxygen treatments: Christopher Miles, interview with Joe Glasco, summer 1988, London; "need lots of money": Angelo Ravagli to T. E. Hanley, August 11, 1956, HRC.

48. Frieda Lawrence to Witter Bynner, August 10, 1956, *M&C*, p. 415; she had postdated the letter.

Epilogue

1. Paul Keith, the sculptor whose phoenix adorns the Lawrence memorial, transported a several-ton block of granite from Colorado for use as the headstone Angie wished Frieda to have; it rests just outside the memorial. On it are carved Frieda's coat of arms (which, according to Keith, differs slightly from the von Richthofens' [interview with Paul and Rowena Keith, May 15, 1993, Taos]) and an inscription celebrating the twenty-five-year "companionship" with Angie. A small glass globe sunk in the stone displays a photograph of Frieda in old age.

2. Angelo Ravagli to Enid Hilton, August 23, 1956, HRC.

3. The latter to the HRC.

SELECTED BIBLIOGRAPHY

Except for works by Frieda Lawrence, I have listed below only books to which full references are not given at first mention in the notes.

Works of Frieda Lawrence

Bechstein, Ludwig. *Bechstein's Märchen.* Selected and edited by Frieda Weekley. London: Blackie's Little German Classics, 1906.

Frieda Lawrence: The Memoirs and Correspondence. Edited by E. W. Tedlock, Jr. New York: Alfred A. Knopf, 1964.

Fülöp-Miller, Rene. From *Macht und Geheimnis der Jesuiten* [The power and secret of the Jesuits]. Partial translation by Frieda Lawrence. Santa Fe: Rydal, 1944.

"Not I, but the Wind . . . ". Santa Fe: Rydal, and New York: Viking, 1934.

Schiller, Johann Christoph Friedrich von. *Select Ballads.* Edited by Frieda Weekley. London: Blackie's Little German Classics, 1902.

Yeats, W. B. *Das Land der Sehnsucht* [The land of heart's desire]. Translated by Frieda Weekley and Ernst Leopold Stahl. Düsseldorf: Englisches Theater in deutscher Ubertragung, no. 1, 1911.

Articles, Letters

"About D. H. Lawrence." *New Mexico Quarterly* 21, Summer 1951.

"Becky's Embroideries." *El Crepusculo*, March 15, 1951.

"The Bigger Heart of D. H. Lawrence." *New Republic*, February 28, 1955.

D. H. Lawrence's Manuscripts. The Correspondence of Frieda Lawrence, Jake Zeitlin, and Others. Edited by Michael Squires. New York: St. Martin's, 1991.

Freida Lawrence and her Circle. Edited by Harry T. Moore and Dale B. Montague. Hamden, Conn.: Archon, 1981.

"Frieda Lawrence Likes Texas." *Morning News* (Dallas), February 7, 1954; the article appeared, with editorial changes, as "D. H. Lawrence as I Knew Him" in the *New Statesman*, August 13, 1955.

Letter to the editors of *Harper's* regarding Bertrand Russell's "Portrait from Memory" of D. H. Lawrence. April 1953.

"Life with Lawrence: His Wife Recalls Their Tempestuous Marriage." In *Seven Arts* 4(2), September 1960.

"A Small View of D. H. Lawrence." In *Virginia Quarterly Review* 10, February 1940.

Introductions, Prefaces, Forewords

D. H. Lawrence and the Way of the Dandelion: A Tributary Essay. Cornwall, England: Ark Press, 1975.

Lawrence, D. H. *The First Lady Chatterley*. New York: Dial, 1944.

———. *Lady Chatterley's Lover*. Abridged ed. London: Secker, 1932.

———. *Look! We Have Come Through!* Cornwall, England: Ark Press, 1959 (2nd ed.).

Nehls, Edward. *D. H. Lawrence: A Composite Biography*. Vol. 1, 1885–1919. Madison: University of Wisconsin Press, 1957.

Spilka, Mark. *The Love Ethic of D. H. Lawrence*. London: Dennis Dobson, 1958.

Tedlock, E. W., Jr. *The Frieda Lawrence Collection of D. H. Lawrence Manuscripts: A Descriptive Bibliography*. Albuquerque: University of New Mexico Press, 1948.

Williams, Tennessee. *I Rise in Flames, Cried the Phoenix*. In *New World Writing*. New York: NAL/Mentor, 1952.

Interviews

"BOOK ON LAWRENCE ASSAILED BY WIDOW; Letters She Is Helping Huxley Edit Will Refute 'Woman Hater' Idea, She Says; See Biography Appalling." New York *Evening Post*, May 20, 1931.

Britt, George. "LAWRENCE LIVING TO WIDOW, BARING 'OTHER SIDE.'" New York *World-Telegram*, May 21, 1931.

Gannett, Lewis. "Books and Things." New York *Herald Tribune*, May 23, 1931.

"Wife to Defend Memory of Poet; Mrs. D. H. Lawrence to Write Answer to Murry's Story." New York *Sun*, May 20, 1931.

General

(*Note: Dates are those of the edition consulted and are not necessarily the original dates of publication.*)

About, Edmond François Valentin. *Le Roi des Montagnes, par Edmond François Valentin About*. Adapted and edited by Ernest Weekley. New York: Macmillan (Siepmann's Advanced French Series), 1917.

Aldington, Richard. *D. H. Lawrence: Portrait of a Genius But . . . .* New York: Collier, 1967.

Alvarez, A. *Life After Marriage: Scenes from Divorce*. London: Macmillan, 1982.

Ambrosi, Marietta. *When I Was a Girl in Italy*. Boston: Lothrop, Lee & Shepard, 1906.

Angulo, Jaime de. *Jaime in Taos: The Taos Papers of Jaime de Angulo*. Compiled, and with a biographical introduction, by Gui de Angulo. San Francisco: City Lights, 1985.

Asquith, Margot. *The Autobiography of Margot Asquith*. Edited, and with an introduction, by Mark Bonham Carter. London: Eyre & Spottiswoode, 1962.

Baker, Paul G. *A Reassessment of D. H. Lawrence's* Aaron's Rod. Ann Arbor: University Microfilms Research Press, 1983.

Bedford, Sybille. "The Last Trial of Lady Chatterley." *Esquire*, April 1961.

Belloc, Hilaire. *Richelieu*. Philadelphia: Lippincott, 1929.

Bellows, John. *The Track of the War around Metz*, 2nd. ed. London: Trübner and Co., 1871.

Bewick, Thomas. *A Memoir of Thomas Bewick, Written by Himself.* Edited, and with an introduction, by Montague Weekley. London: Cresset, 1961.

———. *Bewick to Dovaston: Letters, 1824–1828*. Edited by Gordon Williams. Introduction by Montague Weekley. London: Nattali & Maurice, 1968.

Blumenschein, Helen G. *Sights and Sounds of Taos Valley*. Taos: Deckerhoff, 1983.

Bodine, John J. "A Tri-Ethnic Trap: The Spanish Americans in Taos." In "Spanish-Speaking People in the United States." Proceedings of the 1968 Annual Spring Meeting of the American Ethnological Society. Edited by June Heim. Seattle and London: University of Washington Press, 1968.

Bout, Roger. *Practical Guide to Metz*. N.p., 1953.

Brewster, Earl, and Achsah Brewster. *D. H. Lawrence: Reminiscences and Correspondence*. London: Secker, 1934.

Brooke, H. H. the Hon. Sylvia Lady (née Sylvia Brett). *Queen of the Head-Hunters*. London: Sidgwick & Jackson, 1970.

Bruccoli, Matthew. *The Fortunes of Mitchell Kennerley, Bookman*. San Diego: Harcourt Brace Jovanovich, 1986.

Burnham, John C. *Jelliffe: American Psychoanalyst and Physician & His Correspondence with Sigmund Freud and C. G. Jung*. Edited by William McGuire. Foreword by Arcangelo R. T. D'Amore. Chicago and London: University of Chicago Press, 1983.

Bynner, Witter. *Eden Tree*. New York: Alfred A. Knopf, 1931.

———. *Prose Pieces*. Edited by James Kraft. New York: Farrar, Straus & Giroux, 1979.

———. *Selected Letters*. Edited by James Kraft. Farrar, Straus & Giroux, 1981.

———. *Selected Poems*. Edited by Robert Hunt. New York: Alfred A. Knopf, 1936.

Callow, Philip. *Son and Lover: The Young D. H. Lawrence*. New York: Stein and Day, 1975.

Cellini, Benvenuto. *The Autobiography of Benvenuto Cellini*. Translated by John Addington Symonds. New York: Modern Library, n.d.

Corke, Helen. *D. H. Lawrence: The Croydon Years*. Austin: University of Texas Press, 1965.

Crane, Frances Kirkwood. *The Polkadot Murder*. New York: Random House, 1951.

———. *The Turquoise Shop*. New York: Random House, n.d.

Crosby, Caresse. *The Passionate Years*. London: Alvin Redman, 1955.

Cunard, Nancy. *Grand Man: Memories of Norman Douglas*. London: Secker & Warburg, 1954.

Cushman, Keith. *D. H. Lawrence at Work: The Emergence of the* Prussian Officer *Stories*. Hassocks, England: Harvester, 1978.

Daudet, Alphonse. *Selected Stories*. Emmaus, Pa.: J. I. Rodale, 1951.
de Grazia, Edward. *Girls Lean Back Everywhere: The Law of Obscenity and the Assault on Genius*. New York: Random House, 1992.
Dierick, Augustus P. *German Expressionist Prose*. Toronto: University of Toronto Press, 1987.
Eggert, Gertude H. *Wernicke's Works on Aphasia: A Sourcebook and Review*. The Hague, Paris, and New York: Mouton, 1977.
Fechin, Eya. "Teenage Memories of Taos." In *American West*, November/December 1984.
Fedder, Norman J. *The Influence of D. H. Lawrence on Tennessee Williams*. The Hague: Mouton, 1966.
Ford, Ford Madox. *Mightier Than the Sword*. London: Allen & Unwin, 1938.
Foster, Joseph. *D. H. Lawrence in Taos*. Albuquerque: University of New Mexico Press, 1972.
Frank, Leonhard. *Dream Mates*. New York: The Philosophical Library, 1946.
Friedman, Alice T. *House and Household in Elizabethan England*. Chicago: University of Chicago Press, 1989.
Gide, André. *Corydon*. New York: Farrar, Straus and Co., 1950.
Goerlipp, Georg, et al. *Donaueschingen*. Freiburg: Schillinger, 1978.
Grant, Blanche C. *Taos Indians*. Taos: Santa Fe New Mexican Publishing Corp., 1925.
Grattan, Virginia L. *Mary Colter: Builder Upon the Red Earth*. Flagstaff, Ariz.: Northland, 1980.
Grazzini, Antonio Francesco. *The Story of Doctor Manente*. Translated, and with a foreword, by D. H. Lawrence. Florence: Orioli, 1929.
Gregorovius, Ferdinand. *Latian Summers and an Excursion in Umbria*. Vol. 2 of *Wander Jähre* [sic] *in Italien*. Translated by Dorothea Roberts. London: Junior Army & Navy Stores, 1902.
———. *The Roman Journals of Ferdinand Gregorovius, 1852–1974*. Edited by F. Althaus and translated from 2nd German ed. by G. W. Hamilton. London: G. Bell & Sons, 1911.
Hall, Ruth. "Angelino." London *Observer*, Sunday color magazine. December 13, 1970.
Haxthausen, Charles, and Heidrun Suhr, eds. *Berlin: Culture and Metropolis*. Minneapolis and Oxford: University of Minnesota Press, 1990.
Highet, Gilbert. *Poets in a Landscape*. New York: Alfred A. Knopf, 1957.
Huxley, Juliette. *Leaves of the Tulip Tree*. London: Murray, 1986.
Jeffers, Robinson. *The Selected Letters of Robinson Jeffers, 1897–1962*. Edited by Ann N. Ridgeway. Foreword by Mark Van Doren. Baltimore: Johns Hopkins University Press, 1968.
Juta, Jan. *Background in Sunshine*. New York: Charles Scribner's Sons, 1972.
King, Leonard. *Port of Drifting Men*. San Antonio, Tex.: Naylor, 1945.
Krutch, Joseph Wood. *The Voice of the Desert: A Naturalist's Interpretation*. New York: William Sloane, 1956.
Lavrin, Nora. *D. H. Lawrence: Nottingham Connections*. Preface by Monica Partridge. Nottingham: Astra, 1986.
Luhan, Mabel Dodge. *Winter in Taos*. Taos: Las Palomas de Taos, 1982.
May, Karl. *Mein Leben und Streben*. Freiburg: Friedrich Ernst Fehsenseld, n.d.

———. *Unter Geiern*. Bamberg: Karl May Verlag, 1953.

Metz en 64 images a pleine page par 37 artistes avec texte explicatif et 115 biographies de peintres, dessinateurs et sculpteurs. Metz: Librairie Mutelet, 1951.

Mizener. Arthur. *The Saddest Story: A Biography of Ford Madox Ford*. New York: Carroll & Graf, 1985.

Mommsen, Wolfgang. *Max Weber and German Politics, 1890–1920*. Translated by Michael S. Steinberg. Chicago and London: University of Chicago Press, 1984.

Murry, Colin Middleton. *Shadows on the Grass*. London: Gollancz, 1977.

Murry, John Middleton. *Son of Woman: The Story of D. H. Lawrence*. London: Cape, 1931.

Nabokov, Peter. *Indian Running*. Santa Fe: Ancient City Press, 1981.

Natan, Alex, ed. *German Men of Letters*. Vol. 3. London: Oswald Wolff, 1972.

Nauck, E. T. *Die Privatdozenten der Universität Freiburg im Breisgau*. Freiburg: Eberhard Albert Universitätsbuchhandlung, 1956.

Nicolson, Harold. *Diaries and Letters, 1930–1939*. Vol. 1. Edited by Nigel Nicolson. London: Collins, 1966.

Nin, Anaïs. *Journals*, 1944–47. London: Peter Owen, 1971.

Parker, Patricia. *Literary Fat Ladies: Rhetoric, Gender, Property*. New York: Methuen, 1987.

Peattie, Donald Culross. *Vence: Immortal Village*. Chicago: University of Chicago Press/Phoenix, 1963.

Peltre, Christine. *L'Ecole de Metz, 1834–1870*. Nancy: Editions Serpenoise, Presses Universitaires, 1988.

Reeve, Frank D. *History of New Mexico*. Vol. 1. New York: Lewis Historical, 1961.

Richthofen, Bolko Freiherr von. *Schlesien und die Schlesier*. Wolfenbüttel: Grenzland Verlag Rock & Co., 1967.

Robinson, Janice S. *H. D.: The Life and Work of an American Poet*. Boston: Houghton Mifflin, 1982.

Rolf, C. H., ed. *The Trial of Lady Chatterley: Regina* v. *Penguin Books Limited*. London: Penguin, 1990.

Rose, William J. "Upper Silesia: A Glance Down the Years." In Józef Kokot, ed., *The Miseries of the Prussian Eastern Provinces*. Warsaw: Western Press Agency, 1958.

Russell, Bertrand. *Portraits from Memory*. London: Allen and Unwin, 1956.

Ruvigny, Marquis of, ed. and compiler. *The Titled Nobility of Europe*. Malta: Interprint, 1980.

Schlatter, Rudi. *Narren-Chronik der Stadt Donaueschingen*. Donaueschingen: n.p., 1975.

Sitwell, Osbert. *Left Hand, Right Hand!* New York: Little, Brown, 1964.

———. *Penny Foolish: A Book of Tirades and Panegyrics*. London: Macmillan, 1935.

Sloss, Radha Rajagopal. *Lives in the Shadow with J. Krishnamurti*. London: Bloomsbury, 1991.

Smylie, Vernon. *The Secrets of Padre Island*. Corpus Christi: Texas News Syndicate Press, n.d.

Spender, Stephen. *World within World: The Autobiography of Stephen Spender*. London: Faber, 1977.

Stanley, F. *The Lamy, New Mexico Story*. Pep, Tex.: n.p., 1966.

The Story of Alsace & Lorraine and How They Were Lost by Germany. London: John Camden Hotten, 1981.

The Stranger's Guide through Nottingham. Nottingham: B. S. Oliver, 1848.

Teuber, Alfons. *Silesia in Pictures*. Translated by Margaret D. Senft. Munich: Christ Unterwegs, 1951.

Toklas, Alice B. *Staying on Alone: Letters of Alice B. Toklas*. Edited by Edward Burns. New York: Vintage, 1975.

Van Vechten, Carl. *Peter Whiffle: His Life and Works*. New York: Alfred A. Knopf, 1922.

Verlaine, Paul. *Confessions of a Poet*. Introduction by Peter Quennell. Translated by Joanna Richardson. London: Thames and Hudson, 1950.

Vinke, Johannes. *Freiburger Professoren des 19. und 20. Jahrhunderts*. Freiburg: Eberhard Albert Universitätsbuchhandlung, 1957.

Weber, Max. *The City*. Translated by Don Martindale and Gertrude Neuwirth. New York: Free Press, 1966.

Wedekind, Frank. *Diary of an Erotic Life*. Edited by Gerhard Hary. Translated by W. E. Yuill. Oxford: Basil Blackwell, 1990.

Weekley, Ernest. *Adjectives—and Other Words*. New York: Dutton, 1930.

———. *A Concise Etymological Dictionary of Modern English*. London: Murray, 1924.

———. *The English Language*. New York: Cape and Smith, 1929.

———. *Jack and Jill: A Study in Our Christian Names*. New York: Dutton, 1940.

———. *More Words Ancient and Modern*. New York: Dutton, 1927.

———. *The Romance of Names*. London: Murray, 1914.

———. *The Romance of Words*. London: Murray, 1912.

———. *Saxo Grammaticus; or, First Aid for the Best-Seller*. London: K. Paul, Trench, Trübner, 1930. Published in the United States as *Cruelty to Words; or, First Aid for the Best-Seller*. New York: Dutton, 1931.

———. *Something About Words*. New York: Dutton, 1936.

———. *Surnames*. London: Murray, 1916.

———. *Words Ancient and Modern*. New York: Dutton, 1926.

———. *Words and Names*. New York: Dutton, 1933.

Weekley, Montague. *Thomas Bewick*. London and New York: Oxford University Press, 1953.

———. *William Morris*. London: Duckworth (Great Lives Series), 1934.

Weigle, Marta, and Kyle Fiore. *Santa Fe and Taos: The Writer's Era, 1916–1941*. Santa Fe: Ancient City Press, 1982.

Weinstein, J. *Upper Silesia: A Country of Contrasts*. Paris: Gebethner & Wolff, 1931.

Werfel, Franz. *Class Reunion*. Translated by Whittaker Chambers. New York: Simon & Schuster, 1929.

———. *Embezzled Heaven*. Translated by Moray Firth. New York: Viking, 1940.

Wood, A. C. *A History of University College, Nottingham, 1881–1948*. Oxford: Blackwell, 1953.

Zipes, Jack. *The Brothers Grimm*. New York: Routledge, 1988.

ACKNOWLEDGMENTS

The archives of Alsace-Lorraine are complicated, with records in French and German. I am indebted to Jocelyne Barthel, of the Archives Municipales, Metz, who answered questions and accommodated my visits over six and a half years of research and writing. For documentation of the career of the Baron Friedrich von Richthofen: Christian Wolff and Jacques d'Orléans, Départment du Bas-Rhin, Direction des Services d'Archives, Strasbourg; Lucie Roux, Départment de la Moselle, Metz; Direction du Patrimoine Historique, Metz. I also wish to thank the staffs of the Metz City Library and of the Musée de Metz; and Mireille Pette, Sister Jeanne Fortin, Sister General Superior Françoise Berteaux, and Anne Marie Robion, of Ste.-Chrétienne.

Frederick R. Jeffrey provided the text of a memoir by the Baroness Anna von Richthofen-Marquier, and answered numerous letters and phone calls on matters ranging from the von Richthofen courtship to Frieda Lawrence's relationship with her sister Nusch; he and his wife, Marianne, showed great hospitality in Connecticut, where I was permitted to read a sheaf of unpublished letters from the 1940s and 1950s. Helen Diets translated the baroness's memoir and all other material written in a German script no longer decipherable to most, and I am grateful to her and her sister, the late Ena Diets. Josef Hohmann did extensive genealogical research on the Marquier family, through Latin church books, council records, address books, and resident registration cards of the cities of Offenburg, Freiburg, and Donaueschingen that would otherwise have been inaccessible. Herbert Ebersold, parson, Saint Sixtus, Offenburg, and other clerics passed along my search letters to Mr. Hohmann. I wish to thank Georg Goerlipp, of the Fürstlich Fürstenbergisches Archiv, and Claudia Schmidt, both of Donaueschingen, and Dr. John, of the Generallandesarchiv,

Karlsruhe. In Constance: Konzil-Gaststätten-Betrieb; Kulturamt der Stadt; A. Kuthe, Stadtarchiv; Heinz Finke, Pressebildbüro. In Baden-Baden: Ingrid Lauck, of the Stadtarchiv im Baldreit; officials at the DRK-Ludwig-Wilhelm-Stift (Deutsches Rotes Kreuz); Hartmann Freiherr von Richthofen. In Bonn: Oswald Freiherr von Richthofen; in Munich: Patrick Mansur Freiherr Praetorious von Richthofen and Alexander Böker. In Wrocław (Breslau): Bruno Weber, Generalkonsul der Bundesrepublik Deutschland. In Berlin: Sabine Preuss, of the Landesarchiv, Subrata Ghosh, Gary Finder.

In Freiburg: Marianne Pitsch and Fritz Schaffer, of Freiburg, who supplied material from an archive chronicling the development of the Pensionat & Töchter-Institut (Boarding and High School for Girls) run by Julie and Camilla Blas, as well as biographical and other background on the Blases; K. Schäfer and R. Frank, Waldhof Volksbildungsheim; the Vereinigung Deutscher Landerziehungsheime; Dr. Ecker, Stadtarchiv; Ulrike Petzold, Universitätsbibliotek; E. Krieg, Staatsarchiv.

In Graz: Dr. Klaus Krainz and Professor Karlheinz Probst, of the Institut für Strafrecht, Strafprozessrecht und Kriminologie, University of Graz, who graciously answered my letters about the institute founded by Hans Gross.

In the Netherlands, for searching ships' passenger lists and researching other matters relating to the 1907 First International Congress of Psychiatry, Neurology, Psychology, and the Assistance to the Insane; D. van Wingerden, Archiefdienst, Gemeente Rotterdam; F. van Anrooij, Algemeen Rijksarchief, Rijksarchief voor de Centrale Regeringsarchieven Vanaf; S. A. J. van Faassen, Nederlands Letterkundig Museum en Documentatiecentrum; W.Chr. Pieterse, Gemeentearchief, Amsterdam; J. P. van Loon, Koninklijke Bibliotheek, Gravenhage; Rd. Bekendam, Universiteits–Bibliotheek, Amsterdam; Ron Brand, Maritime Museum, Rotterdam.

In Zurich: J. Zweifel, of the Staatsarchiv des Kantons Zürich, for kindly supplying police–blotter sheets, dossiers, newspaper clippings, arrest records, and other details of the anarchist careers of Otto Gross and Ernst Frick.

In the United States: Henry A. Sauerwein, Jr., of the Helene Wurlitzer Foundation of New Mexico (Taos), who made countless introductions; Tracy McCallum and the staff of the Harwood Library and David Witt, of the Harwood Foundation, both of Taos; the University of New Mexico Library, Albuquerque; Vicente Martinez and Patrick T. Houlihan, Millicent Rogers Museum, Taos; Orlando Romero, Palace of the Governors History Library, Santa Fe; New Mexico Vital Records Office; the offices of the county clerk and district court, Taos; County Court, Brownsville, Texas; Cathy Henderson, Andrea Inselmann, and the staff of the Harry Ransom Humanities Research Center, University of Texas at Austin, the largest repository of Frieda Lawrence material; Jennie Rathbun, Harvard University Library (Houghton); Berg Collection, Rare Books and Manuscripts Division, periodicals division, genealogy division, general reading room, and Music Research Division, New York Public Library; Nicole L. Bouché, Manuscripts Division, The Bancroft Library, University of California, Berkeley; Anne Caiger, Department of Special Collections, University of California, Los Angeles; Margaret Kimball, Department of Special Collections and University Archives, Stanford University Libraries; Ellen M. Murphy, University of Wisconsin-Milwaukee; Patricia Willis, Collection of American Literature, Beinecke Rare Book and Manuscript Library, Yale University; Rarebook & Special Collections Library, University of Illinois, Urbana-Champaign; Richard J. Wolfe, Francis A. Countway Library of Medicine, Boston; Jung Library, New York; German Information Center, New York; German Consulate, New York; Goethe House, New York; Italian Heritage and Culture Committee, New York; Consulate General of Italy, New York; Italian Cultural Institute, New York; Federal Bureau of Investigation; Immigration and Naturalization Service.

In England: Jermy & Westerman Antiquarian & Second-Hand Booksellers, Nottingham, whose owners offered books, background information, and hospitality; Dorothy Ritchie and Sheila M. Cooke, Nottingham County Library; Linda Shaw and Dr. Dorothy Johnston, University of Nottingham Library; Reg Brocklesby, Nottingham Archive Office; Sally Brown and Michael J. Boggan, Manuscripts Collection of the British Library, as well as the staffs of the General Reading Room and various other rooms, which house, among other material, well-preserved copies of Frieda Weekley's editions of Schiller and Bechstein; Carolyn Hammond, Chiswick Public Library; Terri Elliot, Leisure Services, Borough of Hounslow; Sarah C. Woodcock, Theatre Museum, London; Elizabeth Esteve-Coll and Alicia Robinson, Victoria and Albert Museum; Christopher Dean and Jacqueline Childs, St. Paul's School, London; John Saumarez-Smith and Kate Hedworth, Christie's, London; D. M. Bacon, Camellia Investments, London; Hermann Freiherr von Richthofen.

Gerald J. Pollinger, of Laurence Pollinger Ltd, extended permission to quote from works protected by the estate of Frieda Lawrence Ravagli. Permission was also granted by the following to quote from copyright and other material: Witter Bynner Foundation for Poetry; the estate of Mabel Dodge Luhan; Alfred A. Knopf, Inc. (*Frieda Lawrence: The Memoirs and Correspondence*, by Frieda Lawrence, ed. E. W. Tedlock, Jr., copyright © 1961, 1964 by the Estate of Frieda Lawrence); Penguin Books Ltd. (*Selected Short Stories*, Guy de Maupassant, translated by Roger Colet, copyright © Roger Colet, 1970); New Directions Publishing Corp. (H. D., *Bid Me to Live*, copyright © by Norman Holmes Pearson); University of Wisconsin Press (Edward Nehls, ed., *D. H. Lawrence, a Composite Biography*, vols. 1–3, copyright © 1957–1959); Oxford University Press and Cambridge Univerisity Press (*The Collected Letters of Katherine Mansfield* and *The Letters of D. H. Lawrence*, as cited in notes).

Several people associated with Cambridge University Press offered hospitality, answered letters, and otherwise facilitated my research; I am especially grateful to J. T. Boulton, David Ellis, Mara Kalnins, Michael Squires, Lindeth Vasey, and John Worthen.

Martin Green permitted me to read letters passed back and forth on the Munich-Ascona-Nottingham circuit in the period 1907–1912 and thereafter; John Turner, Cornelia Rumpf-Worthen, and Ruth Jenkins allowed me to quote from their translations of the Otto Gross–Frieda Weekley correspondence.

• • •

Attempting a biography without the cooperation or assistance of immediate family is difficult, and while this is by no means an "authorized" biography, I am particularly indebted to Frieda Lawrence's daughter Barbara Barr for her extended correspondence. Stefano Ravagli provided facts of his father's life and career. Ian Weekley answered questions at a late stage.

Among those who agreed to be interviewed in London, I am grateful to Veronica Murphy, Montague Weekley's close companion and colleague of long standing; Mr. Weekley's former colleague Jim Fordham, and his wife, Mabel; Annemarie Edwards, Anthea Goldsmith, and Lady Juliette Huxley.

Many who knew Frieda Lawrence in New Mexico and Texas also consented to interviews; a few have since passed away. I am grateful to Ruth H. Alegre, Ernestina B. Barrera, Eya Fechin Branham, Helen Blumenschein, Mrs. Howard (Elspeth) Bobbs, Dorothy Brandenburg, Howard Brandenburg, Maria Chabot, Barbara Chavez, Kay Dicus, Bonnie Evans, Joe Fulton, Ruth Hatcher, Suzette Hausner, Rachel Hawk, Walton Hawk, Barbara Horgan, Dorothy Horgan, William Hughes, Bertha Ilfeld, Genevieve Janssen, Saki Karavas, Paul and Rowena Keith, Helen Kentnor, Barbara Latham, Margaret Lefranc, Louise Leslie, Miranda Levy, Rowena Martínez, Ila McAfee, Tom Merlan, Wilma Merlan, Arturo Montoya, J. J. and Juanita Montoya, Lillian Montoya, Ruth Mras, Lucille Pond, Martha Reed, Deborah Sherman, J. J. ("Bunny") Smirch (who provided a cache of unpublished correspondence from Frieda Lawrence's later years), Carrie May Varnam, Jenny Wells Vincent, and Frank Waters.

Others whose replies, conversation, friendship, hospitality, and help I appreciate include Richard Abramowitz, Gillon Aitken, Brian Aldiss, A. Alvarez, Michael Arlen, Marilyn Atkins, Coleman Barks, Ruth Bartell, Albert Bearce, Carol Bemis, Mary Benson, Mitzi Brunsdale, Stephen Calia, Christine Carswell, Fritz Caspari, Sarah Chalfant, Emily Concha, Chandler Crawford, Keith Cushman, Pat d'Andrea, Pia Davis, Émile Delavenay, Stella Dong, Wolfgang Ebert, Teresa Ebie, David Ellis, John Ermisch, Traut Felgentreff, James Fitzgerald, Marlen Gabriel, Brewster Ghiselin, Amitav Ghosh, Joe Glasco, Doris Roberts Goyen, Russell Graham, Chloë Green, Renée Gregorio, Leo Hamalian, Antony Harwood, Enid C. Hilton, James Elery Holland, Joel Honig, Paul Horgan, Lawrence Hornstein, Dennis Jackson, Nicholas Jenkins, Gendron Jensen, Joy Johannessen, Lisa Jones, Frederick and Dolores Karl, Rebecca Karl, Deirdre Katz, Clark Kimball, John Kirkpatrick, Ken Kleinpeter, Jane Kornbluh, James Lasdun, Carol Leach, Stan Leavitt, Lynda Lee-Potter, Josette Lefebvre, Kim Lewis, Ulrich Linse, Bridget Love, Ida Lucas, Charles David Lucas, Tal Luther, Brenda Maddox, James L. Mairs, Robert K. Massie, Colleen McCarthy, Bob McCracken, William McGuire, Delilah McKavish, Roberta Courtney Meyers, Christopher Miles, Kathy Toy Miller, Albert Mobilio, Barbara Moss, Diane Munti, Lee Nichols, Geoffrey O'Brien, Arthur Olivas, Leslie Parr, Monica Partridge, Christine Taylor Patten, Mike Petty, Reginald Phelps, James Polster, Mag Porcelli, Lawrence Clark Powell, David Rakoff, Tally Richards, Sally Riley, Charles Rossman, Richard Rudisill, Lois Rudnick, François Samuelson, Lucille Santiesteban, Peter Seligman, 'Annah Sobelman, Sarah Stroud, Sister Franziska

Sucharipa, Janet Suzman, Edward Swift, Harald Szeeman, Lois A. Theobald, Sister Agnes Therrien, Claire Tomalin, Mary Tomlinson, Diana Trilling, Martin Tucker, Tom Verlaine, Michael Wallis, Harvey Wang, Bryan and Carolyn Welch, Alan Wells, Ed Wood, Andrew Wylie, Joseph Zavadil.

Abigail Asher, Jutta Koether, Brigitte McNamara, Judy Smith, Rashmini Yogaratnum, and Rene Yogaratnum provided occasional translations from the Italian, German, and Sinhalese.

At HarperCollins, Terry Karten read the manuscript closely, twice. At each stage, she offered invaluable suggestions; much earlier, Aaron Asher's reading resulted in an entirely new draft. I am also grateful to Sue Llewellyn, the copy (and production) editor, whose considerable expertise—and fluency in German—saved me from many errors; Maureen Clark, the proofreader; Ashley Chase; and, at Bloomsbury, Liz Calder and Ruth Logan. Ann Rittenberg and Katrina Kenison (whom I never met) were the original impetus for the biography, and John Herman its first editor.

Listing the names of those who reviewed early drafts and talked me through later ones hardly conveys their contributions, which, in some cases, went beyond simple commentary: Deborah Baker, Celesta T. Byrne, Susan Byrne, Thomas Byrne, Jamie James, Deborah Karl (my agent), Jamie Pilkington, and Lisa Ross.

Much of the manuscript was written at the home of Alicia Whitaker, and I am grateful to her and to her sister, Linda, of Glorieta, New Mexico, for their friendship, and to Vincent Calenda for his forbearance.

My family and family-in-law know how much I have relied on them.

Without Ivan Solotaroff, my husband, it probably would not have been possible for me to complete this book. His work on the manuscript was unstinting and good humored, and at times I felt he knew, if not the subject, at least the material and its potential better than I did.

INDEX

Aaron's Rod, 219, 226, 232, 247, 249, 250, 259
Academic Society for Literature and Music, Vienna, 148
Acton, Harold, 320
Adam Bede (Eliot), 411
Adams, John Quincy, 10, 11
Adelphi, 286, 288, 290, 294
Aga Khan, 337, 339
Age of Anxiety, The (Bernstein), 386
Akademischer Verband für Literatur and Musik. *See* Academic Society for Literature and Music
Alassio, Italy, 309, 312
Albergo Ligure, Spotorno, 309, 315
Albert and Charles Boni, publishers, 344, 345
Albert Street Schools, Eastwood, 93
Albuquerque, New Mexico, 365, 379, 380, 386, 388, 399
Aldington, Hilda Doolittle. *See* H. D.
Aldington, Richard, 159, 185, 323, 333, 359
Alexandria, Egypt, 35
Allgemeines Militär Casino, 8
Almgren, Antonia, 133, 134
Almgren, John, 133–134
"Aloe, The" (Mansfield), 199, 202
American Agricultural Chemical Company, 363
American Telephone and Telegraph Company, 363
Amores, 198, 207, 236
Andrews, Esther, 210, 211, 212
"And the Fullness Thereof," 379, 392, 397, 410
Anglican Church of Saints George and Boniface, 47
Angulo, Jaime de, 300
Anna Karenina (Tolstoy), 124, 325
Ansell, Mary. *See* Cannan, Mary
anti-German sentiment: in Lorraine, 20–21, 22, 23, 24, 27; in Cornwall during World War I, 210–211, 216, 220; in New Mexico during World War II, 386–387, 395–396
Anton, Gabriel, 71, 74
Antwerp (Hueffer), 177
Apocalypse, 352, 360, 398
Apollinaire, Guillaume, 148
Appenzell, Switzerland, 17
Aquitania, 297
Archiv für Kriminalanthropologie und Kriminalistik, 71

Archiv für Sozialwissenschaft und Sozialpolitik, 62
Arlen, Michael, 191, 196, 331
Armistice, World War I, 223
Ars Morendi, 407
Artillerie Offiziers Casino, 8
Ascona, Switzerland, 74–76, 84, 112, 147, 182, 245
Aspen, Colorado, 400
Asquith, Cynthia, 144, 184–185, 222, 287, 316, 329
Asquith, Herbert, 144, 181
Asquith, John, 144
astrology, 267
As You Like It (Shakespeare), 170
Athenaeum, 225, 238, 251, 287
Atlixco, Mexico, 285
Auden, Wystan, 385
Austin, Mary, 300
Aztec mythology, 288, 290
Azzarini, Ezechiele, 151

Baden-Baden, Germany, 136, 149, 161,174, 224, 230, 233–234, 238, 243, 245, 293, 308, 311, 328, 330, 333, 335, 338, 356, 359
Bad Wörishofen, 143
Baker, Ida, 144
Bakunin, Mikhail, 74
Bandol, 333, 338
Barnaby Rudge (Dickens), 409
Barr, Stuart, 358, 463n57
Barr, Ursula, 384
Barrie, Sir James Matthew, 164, 185
"Bavarian Gentians," 338
Bay, 220
Baynes, Godwin, 226, 227
Baynes, Rosalind, 226–227, 241; liaison with D. H. Lawrence, 243–244; model for Lady Chatterley, 247, 329
Beach, Sylvia, 298, 332
Beardsall, Lydia. *See* Lawrence, Lydia
Beaverbrook, Lord, 308
Becher, Johannes R., 71
Bechstein, Ludwig, 63
Becker, Lady Delphine Therese, 231
Becker, Sir Walter Frederick, 231
Beecham, Sir Thomas, 208
Beggar's Opera, 208
Behrendt, Ryker (Ernest Weekley's landlady), 118, 169
Bell, Vanessa, 251
Belt, Elmer, 370, 378
Bennett, Arnold, 154
Benz, Sophie, 83
Beresford, Beatrice, 193, 194, 198
Beresford, J. D., 193, 194, 198
Berkeley Hotel, London, 159
Berkshire, 219, 220, 226
Berlin, 34–38
Berliner Tageblatt, 211
Bernhardt, Sarah, 26–27
Bernstein, Burton, 386
Bernstein, Leonard, 386
Bersaglieri, 123, 309, 310, 311, 312, 343, 346
Bethlehem, Pennsylvania, 159
Bethnal Green Museum, 400, 404
Beuerberg, Germany, 109–110
Bibesco, Prince Antoine, 196
Bible, Frieda's interest in, 127, 301–302, 339, 398
Bid Me to Live (H. D.), 159–160
Biddle, Francis, 387
Biddle, George, 387
Big Venture, The (Brod), 68
Birds, Beasts and Flowers, 244, 246, 290, 299
Bismarck, Otto von, 12, 36
Black Forest, 14–15, 34, 233
Blackie's publishers, 56, 62
Blackmore, R. D., 98
Black Sun Press, 335
Blake, William, 93
Blast, 160
Blas, Camilla, 18, 34, 39, 42, 46, 62
Blas, Julie, 18, 28, 39, 42, 46, 62
Blätter zur Bekämpfung Machtwillens. See Journal for the Suppression of the Will to Power
Bloomsbury, 162
Blue Hussars, 22
Blue Review, 142, 143, 145
Blutbruderschaft, 181–182, 199, 201
Boccaccio Story, 326, 337
Bodensee. *See* Lake Constance
Boer War, 51–52
Böhmfeldt, Ursula Böhm von, 10
Böker, Alexander, 383

Bolsover, Lady, 162, 329
Boni and Liveright publishers, 236
Booklovers bookshop, 257
Book of Revelation, 128, 352
Booth, Lizzie, 315, 316
Boots Cash Chemists, 52
Bori, Lucrezia, 412
"Boule de Suif" (Maupassant), 22
Bowden, George, 143
Boy in the Bush, The, 258, 297, 303
Bradford, Pennsylvania, 380
Bradley, Frederick James, 63
Bradley, Gladys, 63, 80, 104, 117, 212
Bradley, Madge, 63, 80
Brahms, Johannes, 59, 208
Brandenburg, Germany, 10
Brave New World (Huxley), 377
Brenner Pass, Switzerland, 121
Brett, Dorothy Eugenie, 303, 304, 306, 308, 322; on Angelino Ravagli, 347–348; as artist, 190, 302, 317, 347; described, 297; and D. H. Lawrence, 312, 317–318, 458n10; Lady Chatterley model, 329; meets Lawrences, 190; and Murry, 287; in New Mexico, 297, 301, 307, 322, 346–348, 349, 350, 367, 397, 406, 413; rift with Lawrences, 298, 305; writes memoir of D. H. Lawrence, 361, 365
Brett, Reginald Baliol, 190
Brewster, Achsah, 251, 256, 263, 264, 299, 316–317, 333, 350
Brewster, Earl, 251, 255, 256, 316–317, 328, 333, 339
Brewster, Harwood, 256
Brill, A. A., 267, 268, 378
British Museum, 346, 366
British press, 350. *See also* individual publications
British School, Eastwood, 93
Broadstairs, England, 142
Brod, Max, 57, 68, 148
Brontë, Charlotte, 92
Brontë, Emily, 92
Brown, Albert Curtis, 249
Brownsville, Texas, 390, 392, 398, 409
Bryher, 231
Buber, Martin, 76
Buddenbrooks (Mann), 147, 170
Bülow, Prince Bernhard von, 36
Burghölzli asylum, 72, 82
Burnet, John, 183
Burns, Robert, 129
Burrows, Louie, 94, 95, 101, 153, 198
Bursum Land Bill, 278
Bynner, Harold Witter "Hal," 271, 272, 275, 276, 302, 304, 319, 350, 357, 370, 374, 381, 383, 387, 393, 398, 400, 404, 405, 406, 409, 413, 414; and D. H. Lawrence ashes, 366; on D. H. Lawrence's putative fascism, 389; deteriorating health of, 406; on Frieda Lawrence, 270, 290; as homosexual, 390; on Lawrence marriage, 280, 281; meets Lawrences, 269; in Mexico, 283, 284, 289–290

Cacopardo, Carmelo, 240
Cacopardo, Francisco "Ciccio," 239
Cacopardo, Grazia, 240
Café Bett, Munich, 67
Café Grössenwahn, Munich, 65
Café Royal, London, 297
Café Stephanie, Munich, 65, 67, 71
Cain, 65
"Calamus: A Song" (Whitman), 227
Callcott, Alfred, 259
Callcott, Lucy, 259
Cambridge University, 40, 50, 56
Cameron, Jo, 383
Campbell-Bannerman, Sir Henry, 426n13
Campbell, Beatrice, 161, 168, 362
Campbell, Gordon, 145, 155, 156, 168, 179
Candelario, John, 415
Cannan, Gilbert, 164, 167, 171, 172
Cannan, Mary, 164, 172, 237, 242, 257
Capri, 172, 237–239, 251, 316
Captain's Doll, The, 252, 263, 299
Carco, Francis, 176
Carl Alexander, Grand Duke of Saxe-Weimar, 38
Carlos Café, Laguna Vista, 398
Carlyle, Thomas, 97
Carossa, Dr. Hans, 330
Carswell, Catherine, 208, 222, 230, 297, 323, 331. *See also* Jackson, Catherine

Cather, Willa, 299
Cavalleria Rusticana (Verga), 330
Cavendish-Bentinck, Arthur, 162
Cearne, the, 101, 104, 140, 142, 197
Cendrars, Blaise, 148
Centaur bookshop, 307
Century magazine, 101
Cervi, Orazio, 227, 237, 241
Ceylon, 251, 253, 255–257, 272
Chambers, Alan, 91
Chambers, Jessie, 91–92, 94–95, 97, 98–99, 132, 136
Chambers, Mary, 93
Chanslor, Ray, 278
Chapala, Lake, 286
Chapala, Mexico, 286
Chaplin, Charlie, 375
Charleroi, battle of, 185
Château-Salins, Lorraine, 21
Chatto and Windus publishers, 212
Chekhov, Anton, 143
Chesham, Buckinghamshire, 164
Chexbres-sur-Vevey, 333
"Child-Who-Was-Tired, The-" (Mansfield), 143
Chiswick, 118. *See also* 49 Harvard Road
Cholulo, Mexico, 285
Christian, Bertram, 166
Christian Science, 267
Christmas celebrations, 23, 50, 56, 152, 172, 280, 313
Churchill, Winston, 128, 159
Clarke, William, 146
Clayton, Katharine, 142
Colet House, 140
Collier's Friday Night, A, 97
Collings, Ernest, 129
Collins, Alan, 364
Confessions of Felix Krull, Confidence Man (Mann), 396
Conrad, Joseph, 96, 154
Constable, John, 44
Constance, Germany, 16, 17
Constance, Lake, 17, 19, 147
Contadini, 337
Cooper, James Fenimore, 92
Corbin, Alice, 270
Corke, Helen, 99, 101, 111, 129, 198, 227
Cornwall, 193, 194–216, 220, 260, 273
Corriere della Sera, Milan, 262, 353, 383
Corydon (Gide), 331
Cosimo, Piero de, 280
Côte d'Azur, 333
Council Hall, Constance, 19, 20
Cournos, John, 442n3
coverture, 117
Cowley, Nottingham, 83, 87, 88, 116, 117, 118, 155, 403
Cranford (Gaskell), 235
Crapper, Sir Thomas, 51
Crosby, Caresse, 335, 351
Crosby, Harry, 335
Crotch, Martha Gordon, 343, 358, 365
Crowley, Aleister, 75
Crowninshield, Frank, 299
Cuernavaca, Mexico, 285
Curtis Brown, 345, 360, 364
Czernowitz University, 71

Daily Chronicle, London, 142
Daily Express, London, 332
Daily Mail, London, 151
Daily News, London, 113
Dallas Morning News, 398
d'Allura, Pepina, 240
Darley, Cumberland and Company, 132
Dasburg, Andrew, 268, 279
Das Freudsche Ideogenitätsmoment und seine Bedeutung im manisch-depressiven Irresein Kraepelins. See The Freudian Factor of Ideogeneity and Its Significance in Kraepelin's Manic-Depressive Illness
Das grosse Wagnis. See The Big Venture
David, 306, 307
Davidson Road School, Croydon, 96
Davies, Rhys, 334
Davies, W. H., 154
Dax, Alice, 101, 126, 365, 432n11
De Acosta, Mercedes, 324
Death in Venice (Mann), 142, 145
Death of Procris (Cosimo), 280
Decameron, The (Boccaccio), 326
Defence of the Realm regulations, 216
Degen, Mabel, 383
Dehmel, Richard, 135
Delius, Frederick, 191
Dello Joio, Norman, 400

Del Monte ranch, 280
dementia praecox, 72
Dennis, Louisa "Gipsy," 90
Denver Post, 271
De Quincey, Thomas, 230
Der Berg der Wahrheit Monte Veritá. *See* Mountain of Truth
Des Imagistes, 159
D. H. Lawrence & Susan His Cow (Tindall), 375
D. H. Lawrence, Novelist (Leavis), 411
"D. H. Lawrence, the Failure," 376
Dial, 253
Dial Press, 394
Dickens, Charles, 92
divorce law, England, 131
Dodge, Edwin, 267
Dodge, Mabel. *See* Luhan, Mabel Dodge; Sterne, Mabel Dodge
Doheny, Edward L., 370
Donaueschingen, Germany, 14–17, 39, 75
Dostoyevsky, Fyodor, 195, 200, 334
Douglas, Norman, 142, 232, 235, 319, 320, 356, 359
Dove's Nest and Other Stories, The (Mansfield), 287
Dowson, Helena B., 60, 427n67
Dowson, William Enfield, 60–61, 102, 124, 209
Duckworth and Company publishers, 101, 109, 125, 142, 153
Duckworth, Gerald, 101, 142
Duncan, Isadora, 75, 232, 334, 411
Duse, Eleonora, 267
DuTant, Charles, 381

"Eagle in New Mexico," 278
Eastman, Max, 268
Eastwood, Nottinghamshire, 88–91, 93, 129, 241, 323
Eckardt, Marianne von, 378. *See also* Jaffe, Marianne
École des Beaux-Arts, 267
Eddy, Mary Baker, 267
Eder, David, 223, 262
Egoist, The, 179
Eichberghaus, Littenweiler, 34, 39, 42, 46–47, 59, 62
8 Vickers Street, Nottingham, 59
Elbe, Anna von, 36, 37, 38
El Crepusculo, Taos, 381, 399, 401
Elena (queen of Italy), 310
"Elephant," 257
Eliot, George, 53, 92, 411
Eliot, Thomas Stearns, 195
Eliot, Vivienne, 195, 293
Elise (servant), 20, 21, 24
Ellinger, Désirée, 208
Ellis, Havelock, 195, 231
El Ortiz Hotel, Lamy, New Mexico, 2, 3
Emanuel Swedenborg: Scientist and Mystic (Toksvig), 462n29
"Empty Bed Blues," 335
Ends and Means (Huxley), 377
England, My England, 252
English Review: Austin Harrison edits, 101; D. H. Lawrence article on German poetry, 135; Ford Madox Hueffer edits, 96, 98; Norman Douglas assistant editor of, 142, 232; publishes D. H. Lawrence, 97, 98, 189, 214, 220; publishes F. S. Flint, 442n3
Escaped Cock, The, 328, 335, 351, 366
Etruscan Essays, 328
Etruscan tombs, Lawrence visits, 328
Evans, John, 266, 276, 279
Evans, Sir Samuel Thomas, 150
Evening News, London, 332
Evening Post, New York, 344
Eve: The Ladies Pictorial, 317
Eyeless in Gaza (Huxley), 324

Fantasia of the Unconscious, 252, 278, 286
Fantazius Mallare (Hecht), 278
Farjeon, Herbert, 222, 227
Farjeon, Joan, 221, 226
Fechin, Nikolai, 366
Fechin, Tinka, 366
Federal Bureau of Investigation (FBI), 386, 395, 396
Feininger, Lyonel, 369
Fergusson, Erna, 379
Fiascherino, Italy, 149
Ficke, Arthur, 406
57 Chancery Lane, 142
Fight for Barbara, The, 125

First International Congress of Psychiatry, Neurology, Psychology and the Assistance to the Insane, Amsterdam, 80
First Lady Chatterley, The, 325–327, 394
Fish, Ruth, 383
Flaubert, Gustave, 215
Flersheim, Mrs. (Weekley neighbor), 55, 58, 61
Fletcher, John Gould, 442n3
Flight Back into Paradise, 326
Flint, F. S., 442n3
Florence, Italy, 230–231, 232, 251, 319–321
Florida, 191–192
Fontana Vecchia, Sicily, 246
Ford, Ford Madox. *See* Hueffer, Ford Madox
Ford, John, 372
Forster, Edward Morgan, 174–175, 362
49 Bischofstrasse, Metz, 33, 45, 57
49 Harvard Road, Chiswick, 141, 155, 168, 314
40 Well Walk, Hampstead, 44, 55, 117
Forum magazine, 335
"Fox, The," 222, 252
Franco-Prussian War, 7, 12–13, 173
Frank family, 16–17
Frankfurt an der Oder, 10
Frank, Leonhard, 65, 83
Franz Ferdinand (Archduke, Austria), 159
Frazer, James, 192
Frederick the Great, 10
French Foreign Legion, 232
Freiburg, Germany, 14, 17, 30, 34, 39
Freiburg University, 39, 40
Frere Reeves, A. S., 359, 403, 462n30, 463n45, 46, 47, 62
Freudian Factor of Ideogeneity and Its Significance in Kraepelin's Manic-Depressive Illness, The, 74
Freud, Sigmund, 69, 73, 74, 81, 82
Frick, Ernst, 66, 75, 81, 84
Frieda Lawrence: The Memoirs and Correspondence, 410. *See also* "And the Fullness Thereof"
Frühlings Erwachen (Wedekind), 65
Fülöp-Miller, Rene, 334, 460n62
Fulton, Joe, 401
Galsworthy, John, 83, 102, 154, 434n57
Garbo, Greta, 324, 372
Garda, Lake, 122, 135
Gardiner, Rolf, 323
Gargnano, Italy, 122, 123, 135
Garnett, Constance, 101, 141, 142
Garnett, David, 101, 121, 122, 142, 163
Garnett, Edward, 113, 127, 128, 134, 135, 139, 141, 142; as friend, 101–102, 104, 124, 140, 162, 197; as editor, 109, 126, 147, 153, 169
Garnett, Robert, 132, 140, 178
Garsington, Oxford, 179, 180, 220, 329
Gaudier-Brzeska, Henri, 159
Gauguin, Paul, 304
General Motors Corporation, 363
Genius and the Goddess, The (Huxley), 324
Genoa, Italy, 309
Gentlemen Prefer Blondes (Loos), 320
George, W. L., 190
Georgian Poetry, 1911–1912, 128, 144
Gerhardie, William, 308
Gering, Josef, 14
Germany, unification of, 12
Gertler, Mark, 165, 172, 184, 190, 199, 222, 292, 298
Gide, André, 267, 331
Gilbert, Edward, 375
Gish, Lillian, 375
Glands Regulating Personality, The (Berman), 261
Glasco, Joe, 397, 412–413
Glasgow Herald, 157, 187
"Goats and Compasses," 197
Goethe, Johann Wolfgang von, 37, 138, 330, 409
Goldberg, Barrett and Newell, 131, 178
Golden, Miriam, 367
Golden Treasury (Palgrave), 93
Goldman, Emma, 268
Goldring, Douglas, 242
Goldtrap, Bunny, 398
Goldtrap, Charley, 398
Gong, The magazine, 95
gonorrhea, 143
"Goose Fair," 98
Gordon Home for Waifs and Strays, 96
Götzsche, Kai, 280, 281, 293
Goyen, William, 397, 412, 413

Gradisca, Italy, 333
Grand Canyon Limited, 265
Gravelotte, battle of, 12
Gray, Cecil, 214–216, 231
Graz Kriminalmuseum, 70
Graz University, 70
Grenoble, 333
Griffin, Johnnie, 390, 413
Griggs, Mrs.: model for Lady Chatterley, 329
Gristede's, 402
Gross, Hans, 69–71, 81, 82, 147–148
Gross, Frieda "Friedel": affair with Ernst Frick, 66, 84; analyzed by Freud and Jung, 73; at Ascona, 75, 161; Frieda visits, 63, 64, 109; marries Otto Gross, 58; radical Munich circle of, 62; separates from Otto Gross, 63. *See also* Schloffer, Frieda
Gross, Otto: affair with Frieda, 73, 76, 77–80, 109, 149; and cocaine, 71, 73, 76, 102; correspondence with Frieda, 76–80, 109, 112, 122; description of, 68; dies, 149; disinherited, 147; father of Peter Jaffe, 81, 139; final years, 147–149; on Frieda, 69, 112; incarceration of, 72, 148, 149; marries Schloffer, 58; radical Munich circle of, 62; on Reventlow, 67; on transference, 70
Gross, Peter, 66
Gstaad, Switzerland, 333
Gsteig, Switzerland, 333
Guadalahara, Mexico, 286
Gurdjieff, George, 282

Hackett, Francis, 352, 389, 462n29
Haggs Farm, 91, 98
Hale, Swinburne, 300
Hampstead, London, 41, 43. *See also* 40 Well Walk, New End House
Hampstead Board of Governors, 44
Handbook for Examining Magistrates (Handbuch für Untersuchungsrichter), 70
Hanley, T. E. "Ed," 379, 403, 408–409, 414
Harris, Frank, 359
Harrison, Austin, 101
Hardy, Thomas, 96, 158, 164, 191
Hartmann, Caroline "Lilly" von, 35
Harvard University, 368, 378
Harwood Foundation, Taos, 382, 383
Hattemer, Lotte, 75–76
Haulleville, Baron Prosper de, 366
Hauptmann, Gerhart, 37
Hausner, Eric Peter, 393, 398, 410
Hausner, Suzette, 393, 409
Hawk, Alfred, 280
Hawk, Harold, 386, 395
Hawk, Lucy, 280
Hawk, Rachel, 280, 281, 283, 413
Hawk, William, 280, 281
Haywood, William "Big Bill," 268
H. D., 159, 185, 216, 217, 219, 231, 308, 323
Hearst's International, 263
Hearst syndicate, 268, 344
Hecht, Ben, 278
Heidelberg, Germany, 63, 155, 369
Heidelberg University, 57
Heinemann publishers, 98, 102, 359
Henderson, Alice (daughter), 270, 276
Henderson, Alice (mother), 270
Henderson, William Penhallow, 270
Henning, Udo von, 108, 185
Henry the Eighth (Hackett), 462n29
Heraclitus, 188
Heseltine, Philip, 191, 196, 214, 251
Hesse, Herman, 75
High Court of Justice, Divorce, Probate and Admiralty Division, 150, 178, 362
Hindenburg, Paul von, 161
History of the Conquest of Mexico (Prescott), 9, 290
Hitler, Adolf, 369, 388–389
Hobson, Harold, 121, 126, 142
Hocking, Stanley, 199, 203, 205, 214
Hocking, William Henry, 203, 205–206, 215, 263
Hoffmansthal, Hugo von, 321
Hogan, Frank J., 370, 374
Hogarth Press, 198
Holy Family, 325
Hopkin, William, 101, 432n11
Hopkins, Emma Curtis, 267
Horgan, Barbara, 391, 392
Horgan, Dorothy, 390–392, 394, 412, 415

Horgan, Paul, 379
Horgan, Ralph, 391, 392, 394
Hôtel Krone, Munich, 249
Hotel Schweitzerhof, Lucerne, 47
Hotel zum Schützen, Donaueschingen, 16
Hougland, Willard, 383, 460n62
Howe, Dr. Martha Elizabeth, 410, 413
Huebsch, Benjamin, 192, 236, 259
Hueffer, Ford Madox, 96–98, 159, 177
Hughes, Henry J., 396
Hughes, William, 412
Huitzilopochtli, 9, 288
Hunt, Violet, 96, 97, 177
Husum, Germany, 66
Huxley, Aldous: antipathy to Frieda, 362; anti-World War II, 377; edits Lawrence's letters, 360; friendship with Lawrences, 324–325, 331, 334; and Lawrence's death, 340, 350; meets Lawrences, 191; in New Mexico, 376; use of Frieda as model, 324
Huxley, Julian, 331
Huxley, Juliette, 331
Huxley, Maria, 324–325, 331, 340, 366, 376, 406. *See also*, Nys, Maria
Huxley, Matthew, 376

Ibsen, Henrik, 37
Icking, Germany, 111, 114
"Il Capitano," 346. *See also* Ravagli, Angelino
Ilfeld, Bertha, 397
Ilfeld, Max, 397
Ilkeston, 93, 94
Immigration and Naturalization Service (INS), 386–387, 396
Imperial Institute, Vienna, 10
In a German Pension (Mansfield), 143
Incorporated Society of Authors, Playwrights, and Composers, The, 191
Industrial Workers of the World, 267
Informer, The film, 372
Insel-Verlag publishers, 242, 243, 245, 252
Institute Blas, Freiburg, 17–18, 28, 34, 72
Institute for the Harmonious Development of Man, 282
"*Insurrection of Miss Houghton, The,*" 129, 241. *See also The Lost Girl*
Ireland: A Study in Nationalism (Hackett), 462n29
Iron Cross, 13, 19, 29, 185
Irschenhausen, Germany, 134, 138, 330
Isar River, 111
Isherwood, Christopher, 385
Isle of Wight, 96
Istituto Magistrale Superiore, Savona, 309

Jackson, Catherine, 157, 173, 187, 208. *See also* Carswell, Catherine
Jaffe, Edgar: owner of Irschenhausen cottage, 134, 135; edits *Archiv für Sozialwissenschaft und Sozialpolitik*, 62; failing health and death of, 234, 249; finds Italian house for Lawrences, 149; Frieda visits, 63; marries Else, 57; as Reventlow's lover, 67; in World War I, 161
Jaffe, Else, 58, 62, 63, 68, 82, 84, 104, 105, 107, 115, 133, 136, 138–139, 145, 149, 161, 189–190, 245, 249, 250, 254, 260, 277, 330, 333, 374; and Alfred Weber, 57, 111, 333; and D. H. Lawrence, 105, 135, 186, 333; and Hitler, 369–370; marriage to Edgar Jaffe, 57, 234; and Otto Gross, 76, 80–81, 82; and Max Weber, 57, 234, 245; on Weekley marriage, 42, 46; and World War I, 161, 163. *See also* Richthofen, Else von
Jaffe, Friedel, 58, 139, 302, 306
Jaffe, Hans, 83, 139
Jaffe, Marianne, 62, 139, 333. *See also* Eckardt, Marianne von
Jaffe, Peter, 81, 139, 189–190
James, Henry, 96, 154, 164, 320–321
James Nisbet and Company publishers, 158, 166
James, Rebecca, 382, 413
James Tait Memorial Prize, 246
Jane Eyre (Brontë), 46, 90
Japanese internment, World War II, 390
Jawlensky, Alexei, 369
Jeffers, Robinson, 346, 370, 397
Jeffers, Una, 346, 397
Jeffrey, Friedel, 393–394. *See also* Jaffe, Friedel

Jeffrey, Marianne Riezler, 393
Jelliffe, Smith Ely, 253, 273
Jenkins, Anna, 255, 257
Jicarilla reservation, 272–273, 274
John Pflueger's General Merchandise, 2
Johnson, Willard "Spud," 278, 281; edits *El Crepusculo*, 381, 399; meets Lawrences, 271; in Mexico, 284, 289
Jones, Ernest, 68, 72, 81, 186
Journal for the Suppression of the Will to Power, 148
Joyce, James, 179, 298, 332
Jugend, 330
Jung, Carl, 68, 73, 75, 81–83, 223–224, 300
Jung, Franz, 148
Junkers, 8, 11, 157
Juta, Jan, 241–242

Kafka, Franz, 57, 148
Kallman, Chester, 385
Kandy, Ceylon, 255–257
Kandinsky, Wassily, 369
Kangaroo, 228, 260–263, 277–278, 281, 290, 299, 387
Karavas, Saki, 381
Karlsruhe, Germany, 57
Kavan, Anna, 334
Keith, Paul, 367, 470n1
Keller, Model von, 149
Kennerly, Mitchell, 147, 150
Kensington Registry Office, 155
Keynes, John Maynard, 177
Kibbo Kift, the Woodcraft Kindred, 323
Kiev University, 160
Kieve, Rudolph, 385, 410
Kiker, Henry A., 396
King and Empire Alliance, 259, 262
King, Samuel, 99
Kingsley Hotel, London, 361, 362, 403
Kiowa ranch, 301, 328, 354, 371, 382, 397, 404
Kippenberg, Anton, 245, 246
Kipping, Frederick Stanley, 54, 83
Kipping, Lily, 54, 55, 83, 108, 131, 141
Kissel, Eleanora, 383
Klages, Ludwig, 67
Klee, Paul, 369
Knopf, Alfred A., 307
Knopf, Blanche, 307
Knopf publishers, 332, 346
Kokoschka, Oscar, 371
Koller, Baroness von, 15
Kosel district, Upper Silesia, 10, 11
Koteliansky, Samuel Solomonovich "Kot": *Adelphi* business manager, 286; denigrates Frieda, 167, 188, 292, 362; description of, 160; and D. H. Lawrence, 160, 186, 226, 227, 262; dunned by Lawrences, 195, 220; as Lawrences' guest, 167, 172, 297, 298
Kouyoumdjian, Dikran. *See* Arlen, Michael
Kraepelin, Emil, 72, 74
Krafft-Ebing, Richard von, 70
Krug, Emil, 250, 330
Kuh, Anton, 148
Kulturgeschichte als Kultursoziologie (Weber), 356, 369–370

Labour party, 259, 463n57
Lace Market, Nottingham, 52
"Ladybird, The," 252
Lady Chatterley's Lover, 416; disposition of manuscripts of, 352, 378, 405, 407–408; drafting of, 247, 327–328, 330–331; reception of, 331–332, 387
La Doña Luz restaurant, Taos, 383
"Laetitia." *See The White Peacock*
La Fonda Hotel, Taos, 381
Laguna Vista, Texas, 397, 398, 408, 409–410, 415
Lambert, Cecily, 221, 222, 226, 227–228
Lamy, New Mexico, 1–2, 264
Ländli, Baden-Baden, 136
Land of Heart's Desire, The (Yeats), 83
Land's End, Cornwall, 211
Lane, Sir Allen, 405
Laschowski, Amalie Louise von (Frieda's grandmother), 11, 52, 169
La Spezia, Italy, 232
Last Devil, The (Toksvig), 355
Last Poems, 352, 360
Las Vegas, New Mexico, 385, 410
La Tentation de Saint Antoine (Flaubert), 215

Lawrence, Ada (sister): childhood of, 89, 91; conflict with Frieda, 315, 316, 363; finds Lawrence housing, 222; marries William Clarke, 146; meets Frieda, 168; nurses Lawrence, 132, 225, 226, 308; supports Frieda, 337, 351, 358
Lawrence, Arthur (father), 89, 100, 303
Lawrences, D. H. and Frieda: ill with flu, 305; passport renewal refused, 211; relationship, 180–181, 215, 220, 246, 275, 339; social activities of, 151, 179, 322; travels of, 242, 247, 255–264, 265, 271, 285, 332, 335. *See also* Lawrence, David Herbert; Lawrence, Frieda
Lawrence, David Herbert:
childhood and youth of: born, 88; childhood, 89, 90, 92; and Jessie Chambers, 93, 99, 132; and Louie Burrows, 94, 95, 101; and mother, 92–93, 99–100, 103, 186
death of and aftermath: death, 340; burial, 350; reburial, 363, 365–368
homoerotic attractions of: Hocking, 203, 205–206, 215; Magnus, 233, 241–242; Murry, 201, 202–203, 205, 376; Thompson, 302
possible homosexuality of: 88, 98, 205, 209–210, 215; sexual ambivalence of, 175, 177, 187
marriage to Frieda: domesticity of, 121, 199–200, 214, 220, 230, 270–271, 326; and Frieda's children, 135, 136, 283, 291, 314, 318–319; marriage, 155–156; negative attitude to Frieda, 166, 225–226, 280, 285, 295; positive attitude to Frieda, 104, 107, 112–113, 128, 279, 290, 432n11; violence in, 204, 226, 275, 298, 312, 335
and money: 178–179, 214, 246–247, 259, 299, 332
other relationships: and Amy Lowell, 159; and Anna von Richthofen-Marquier, 243, 245, 250, 295; and Antonia Almgren, 133–134; and Rosalind Baynes, 244; and Bertrand Russell, 186, 196, 308; and Brett, 317–318; and Forster, 174–175; and H. D., 217; and Mabel Dodge Sterne, 274, 277, 279; and Maugham, 304; and Murrys, 201, 202–203, 223, 225, 287
as painter, 325–326, 336–338, 371
philosophy of: putative fascist politics of, 183, 184, 236, 324; muddled philosophy of, 127–128, 128–129, 192, 223, 224, 288
personal characteristics of: description of, 1, 87, 220, 274; ill health of, 102, 166, 194, 197, 219, 225, 238, 306, 308, 315, 321, 323, 329–330, 339, 438n30; mental instability of, 179, 188, 207, 225, 236, 252, 286, 291; reactions to travel, 115–116, 120–122, 164, 189, 212, 257–258, 283–286
reliance on Frieda for critique and development of manuscripts, 123–126, 128, 133, 135, 136, 138, 139, 142, 146–147, 153–154, 186–188, 247–248
and World War I: 171–172, 181, 207, 222, 223
See also Lawrences, D. H. and Frieda
Lawrence, Emily (sister), 91, 146, 308, 333, 358
Lawrence, Ernest (brother), 90, 92
Lawrence, Frieda von Richthofen:
affairs, possible and reputed affairs, and romances of: with d'Allura, Pepina, 240; with Dowson, Will, 60–61; with Frick, Ernst, 84; with Gray, Cecil, 215–216; with Gross, Otto, 73, 76, 77–80; with Henning, Udo von, 108; with Hobson, Harold, 121, 122; with Marbahr, Karl von, 34, 396; with Murry, John Middleton, 355; with Ravagli, Angelino, 310–311, 343–399 passim; with Richthofen, Curt von, 32–33; with unnamed schoolmistress, 31–32, 187
and Angelo Ravagli: early affair, 310–311, 334, 343, 345; in New Mexico, 346, 354, 363, 373, 393, 394; marriage to, 399–401

anti-Frieda sentiment, 157, 164, 176, 188, 270, 292, 411–412
anti-intellectualism of, 126, 127, 128, 411–412
childhood: adolescence, 23, 28, 31–38; born, 7, 21; early childhood, 7, 9–10, 24–28, 422n43; education, 27, 421n18, 423n45; relationship with father, 8–9, 28, 29
and D. H. Lawrence: competition for, 196–197, 200, 203, 211–212, 241, 274, 278, 315–316; early relationship with, 87–88, 104, 115–116, 120–122; emotional triangles with, 319; on homosexual tendencies of, 205, 218; marriage with, 155–156, 316; relationship with, 130, 146, 152, 248, 294, 305; violence in marriage with, 138, 188, 204, 208, 276; and works of, 112, 154, 169–170, 187, 209, 219, 262–263; on works of, 103, 123–126, 138, 153, 304, 306–307, 327, 371
and Ernest Weekley: courtship, 42–43; divorce from, 131–132; marriage with, 46, 48, 50, 53, 54–55, 58, 63, 104; in old age, 405; visitation battle with, 116–117, 130–131, 132–133, 145, 168–169, 252
family history: father, 10–12; mother, 14–18
as a German: alleged fascism of, 182, 236, 467n62; and Boer War, 52; and World War I, 161–162, 164, 165, 177, 181, 185; and World War II, 386–390
as money manager: as businesswoman, 352, 359, 363, 369–371; and D. H. Lawrence's estate, 344–345, 362–363; duns friends, 194–195, 196; Frieda's estate, 399
in old age: 370, 390, 397, 399, 401; death of, 413, 414, 415, 470n1
other relationships of: and Bynner, 270, 290; and Horgan, 392; on John Almgren, 133–134; on Mansfield, 412; and Orioli, 319; and Rhys Davies, 334; and Sterne, 273–274
personal characteristics of: abstraction and guardedness of, 1, 110, 133, 138, 417n3; appearance, 67, 121, 122, 265, 306, 337; appetite, 33, 45, 285, 306; belief in self as instrument of fate, 316, 354; description of, 1, 229, 306, 323, 382; health of, 215, 305, 336, 365, 393, 398, 407, 410; hospitality of, 334, 349–350, 380, 382–383, 412; libido/atavism of, 73, 112, 137, 329; love of literature, 127, 301, 339, 352, 409, 411; nesting talents of, 215, 228, 257, 259–260, 284, 326, 377, 412; support and patronage of young artists, 165, 334, 349, 397, 412; Pascalian wager with the world, 348; wardrobe of, 122, 220, 281, 368, 374, 402
relationship with children: as adults, 233, 318–319, 400, 404, 411; in childhood, 172, 184, 207–208, 291
relationship with family: with Else, 62, 63, 136, 234, 245, 333, 356, 374, 399; with father, 104–107, 111, 136; homesickness, 225–226; with mother, 114–115, 136, 137, 234, 250, 333, 356; with Nusch, 56, 61, 62, 234, 245, 250, 398
sense of self as brought out by Lawrence, 88, 103, 112, 146
travels without Lawrence: Baden-Baden, 136, 230, 293, 332, 333, 356; England, 291; Florence, 235, 359; Germany, 228, 245, 356; Hollywood, 369–374; U.S., 343–344
works of, 125, 328, 360–361, 364, 368, 376, 379, 392, 397, 411–412, 460n62.
See also Christmas celebrations; Lawrences, D. H. and Frieda
Lawrence, George (brother), 90, 358, 362
"Lawrence H. Davison" (pseudonym), 225
Lawrence, Lydia Beardsall (mother), 88, 89, 99, 100, 375
Lawrence memorial, New Mexico, 366
Lawrence Tree, The (O'Keeffe), 383
Laughing Horse magazine, 271, 278
Lausanne, Switzerland, 333
Lavrin, Janko, 54
Leavis, F. R., 411

Leen, River, 49
Lefranc, Margaret, 385
Lenin, 66
Lenz, Elly, 75
Lerici, Bay of, 149
Les Aspras, Vence, 358, 360
Les Diablerets, Switzerland, 331
Leslie, Louise, 398
Lewis, Edith, 299
Lewis, Wyndham, 160
Liberal party, 63, 162
Lied des Gefangenen Jägers (Scott/Schubert), 321
Life of Hans Christian Andersen, The (Hackett), 462n29
Lincolnshire, coast of, 61, 95
Lippmann, Walter, 268
Little German Classics, 56
Littlehampton, 181
Little Novels of Sicily (Verga), 307
Littenweiler, Germany, 34, 39, 42, 46–47, 59, 62
Lobo, the, 271, 279, 301, 347, 350, 360, 363–364, 413. *See also* Kiowa ranch
Loeffler, Gisella, 383
London Psycho-Analytical Society, 186
London University, 40
Look! We Have Come Through!, 212, 218, 236
Loos, Anita, 320
Lorenzo in Taos (Luhan), 346
Lorna Doone (Blackmore), 98
Los Angeles Public Library, 378
Los Gallos, Taos, 272, 280
Los Pinos, 380–382, 406, 410–414
Lost and Found on a South Sea Island film, 264
Lost Girl, The, 241, 246
Love Poems and Others, 129–130, 167
Low, Barbara, 154, 223
Lowell, Amy, 159, 165–166, 167, 194, 244
Low, Ivy, 154, 157
Lucas, Percy, 189
Lucerne, Switzerland, 47
Luciani, Nick, 379
Ludwig-Wilhelm-Stift, 233, 245, 249, 250, 280, 357, 359
Luhan, Antonio "Tony," 2, 261, 266, 269, 272, 320, 346, 382, 383
Luhan, Candelaria, 261, 269, 272, 363
Luhan, Mabel Dodge, 301, 320, 348–349, 350, 357, 361, 363, 367, 371, 377, 378, 387, 391, 395–396, 397, 399, 402, 413; adoration of D. H. Lawrence, 297, 300, 322; on Angelino Ravagli, 347, 349, 372, 399; memoir of D. H. Lawrence, 346, 365; in old age, 367, 382, 406; relationship with Frieda, 302, 322, 345–346. *See also* Sterne, Mabel Dodge
lunettes, 8, 13, 106
Lusitania, 179, 185
Luxemburg, Rosa, 66
Lyon's, London, 208

Mablethorpe, Lincolnshire, 95
McCowen, George, 42
McCowen sisters (Hannah and two unnamed), 55
Macht und Geheimnis der Jesuiten. See The Power and Secret of the Jesuits
Mackenzie, Compton, 171, 237–238
MacMillan publishers, 379
Mädchen in Uniform film, 31–32
Maestracci, Dr., 339, 340, 357
Maggiore, Lake, 75
Magnus, Hedwigis Rosamunda Liebeträu, 239
Magnus, Maurice, 232, 233, 235, 239, 241–242, 243
Mahaweli River, Ceylon, 256
Maillot, Aristide, 137
Maistre, Violet de, 293
Malleson, Lady Constance, 196
Maltzahn, Baron von, 380–381, 388
Manara, Stefano, 378
Manby, Arthur, 268
Manby Hot Springs, New Mexico, 275–276
Manchester Guardian, 179
manic-depressive disorder, 72, 267
Man and Superman (Shaw), 103
Man Who Died, The, 367. *See also The Escaped Cock*
"Man Who Loved Islands, The," 238
Mann, Thomas, 142, 147, 396
Mansfield, Katherine, 146, 186, 187, 188,

189, 199, 208, 209, 216, 225, 264, 351, 371, 412; affair with Carco, 175–176; in Cornwall, 164, 166, 172, 200, 202–205; description of, 143–144; dies, 282; editor of *Rhythm*, 128; ill health of, 143, 222, 239; at Lawrence wedding, 155; and Murry, 158, 220, 223, 287; on *Sons and Lovers*, 146; supports Frieda, 145, 167, 168, 184, 223–224; on *Touch and Go*, 222
Marquier, Adolf (Anna's brother), 16, 18, 20
Marquier, Anna. *See* Richthofen-Marquier, Baroness Anna von
Marquier, Franz (Anna's brother), 16, 17, 18
Marquier, Franz Joseph (Anna's great-grandfather), 14
Marquier, Josef (Anna's grandfather), 14
Marquier, Josef Adolph (Anna's father), 14, 15
Marquier, Josefa Octavia (Anna's aunt), 14
Marbahr, Karl von, 34, 392
Marinetti, Emilio, 160
Marriage of Figaro, The (Mozart), 208
Mars la Tour, battle of, 12
Marsh, Edward, 128, 144–145, 159, 165, 167, 246
Martindale, Elsie, 96
Masocco, Miranda Speranza, 400, 402, 403
Massachusetts Guaranteed Housing, 363
Masses, The, 268
Mastro-don Gesualdo (Verga), 255, 256, 290, 299
Maugham, Somerset, 304
Maupassant, Guy de, 22, 26
Mayrhofen, Austria, 116, 1a, 10–121
Meadows, the, Nottingham, 50
Mechanics' Institute Library, 92
Medley, C. D., 358
Meinhardis, Manuela von, 32
Mein Kampf (Hitler), 389
Memoirs of the Foreign Legion (Magnus), 243, 307
Mendel (Cannan), 164–165, 237
menopause, 274, 278
Menzingerstrasse, Munich, 64
Mercure de France, 148
Merrild, Knud, 280, 281, 283, 364
Metaphysics of Love (Schopenhauer), 95
Methuen publishers, 158, 161, 178, 183
Metz, Lorraine, 7, 13, 21, 27, 34, 35, 38, 39, 43, 45, 55, 56, 104–108, 109, 379
Mexico, 284, 303. *See also* Chapala, Oaxaca
Meynell, Alice, 173
Meynell, Viola, 173, 177, 178, 189
Meynell, Wilfred, 173
Mikado Café, Nottingham, 52, 61–62, 116
Mike's Night Club, Taos, 381
Milan, Italy, 149
Millay, Edna St. Vincent, 390, 406
Miller, Henry, 397
Miss Dollman's School, 130, 156
Mr. Noon, 106, 108, 110, 247, 253–254, 432n11
Molybdenum Corporation of America, 363
Monk, Violet, 221, 222, 226, 227–228
Monroe, Harriet, 159
Montaigne, Michel, 372
Montaner Dance Hall, Taos, 381
Monte Cassino, Italy, 233, 239, 243
Montoya, J. J., 381–382
Montoya, Juanita, 381–382
Montoya, Lillian, 381–382
Moon and Sixpence (Maugham), 304
Moore, Merrill, 368
Morgan, William de, 98
Morrell, Julian, 180
Morrell, Lady Ottoline, 176, 179–181, 187, 200, 201, 204, 206–207, 218, 224, 251, 253, 292, 324; *Amores* dedicated to, 207; and Bertrand Russell, 162–163; description of, 162, 163; and D. H. Lawrence, 175, 191, 196, 329; on Frieda, 181, 187, 190, 196–197, 210; as hostess, 163, 179, 180, 220, 329; model for Lady Chatterley, 329
Morrell, Philip, 162, 180, 191, 336
Morris Plains, New Jersey, 291
"Mortal Coil, The," 188
Moselle River, 7, 29, 106
Motta, Emma, 241
Mountain of Truth, 74
Mountsier, Robert, 210, 211, 238, 244, 263, 277–278, 281–282
Movements in European History, 225

Mozart, Wolfgang Amadeus, 208
Mühsam, Erich, 65, 75
Mumford, Lewis, 398
Munich, 62, 63–65, 134
Munich University, Technical College of, 135
Münsingen, Germany, 39
Murphy, Thomas F., 394
Murry, John Middleton, 145, 154, 189, 206, 208, 209, 210, 223, 225, 231, 248, 251, 253, 271, 279, 282, 324, 344, 349, 351, 371, 375, 376; *Adelphi* publisher, 286; affair with Brett, 292–293; in Cornwall, 164, 166, 172–173, 200–205; and D. H. Lawrence, 176, 186, 193, 238, 297, 298; on D. H. Lawrence, 201–202, 251, 344; editor of *Athenaeum*, 225; editor of *Rhythm*, 128; and Frieda Lawrence, 166–167, 176, 188, 201, 355, 403; and Katherine Mansfield, 158, 175–176, 192, 199, 220, 223, 287; at Lawrence wedding, 155; meets Lawrences, 142–144; reputation of, 158; second marriage of, 293; *Still Life* published, 198; testifies on Lawrence will, 362
Murry, John Middleton, II, 293
Murry, Katherine, 293
Mussolini, Benito, 323, 346

Nairobi Herald, 238
Napoleon III, 12
Napoleonic wars, 11
Nation, The, 144, 291
National Association for the Advancement of Colored People (NAACP), 268
National Union of Women's Suffrage Societies (NUWSS), 60
Nervenklinik der Ludwig-Maximilians-Universität, Munich, 72
"Nethermere." *See The White Peacock*
Netteswell House, 400, 404
Nettles, 338, 351
Neue Freie Presse, Vienna, 148
Neustadt, Germany, 14
New Age weekly, 143
New End House, Hampstead, 41, 43
New Mexico Quarterly, 387
New Poems, 220
New Republic magazine, 244, 331, 411, 462n29
News of the World, London, 150
New Statesman, 251, 411
Newstead Abbey, 61
Newsweek magazine, 365
Newth, H. G., 162
New York City, 211, 290, 343–344
New Yorker, The, 271
New York Society for the Suppression of Vice, 192, 259, 394
New York Sun, 344
New York Times, 278, 401
New York Times Book Review, 150
New York Times Magazine, 303
Nichols, Dudley, 372
Nichols, Robert, 191
Nietzsche, Friedrich, 59, 73, 96, 99, 267
9 Goldswong Terrace, Nottingham, 51, 59
92 Nottingham Road, New Basford, 50
Nohl, Johann, 76
Nottingham, 49–63, 77, 83, 90, 92, 95, 103, 116, 117, 118, 168–169
Nottingham Boat Club, 60
Nottingham High School, 90, 92, 116, 117
Nottingham Royal Theatre, 104
"Not I, but the Wind . . . ", 361, 364, 374, 379
Nouvelle Revue Francaise, 331
Nüble, Walbürga, 14
Nur der Wind. See "Not I, but the Wind . . . "
Nusch. *See* Richthofen, Helene Johanna Matilde von
Nuttall, Zelia, 288, 304
NUWSS. *See* National Union of Women's Suffrage Societies
Nymphenburg Park, Munich, 64
Nys, Maria, 179–180. *See also* Huxley, Maria

Oaxaca, Mexico, 304
Obscene Publications Act of 1857, 190, 337
Oder River, 26, 52, 170
"Ode to a Skylark" (Shelley), 204
"Odour of Chrysanthemums," 97, 101
Oehring, Richard, 148

Offenburg, Germany, 14
Office of Strategic Services (OSS), 387
Officers Training Corps, 221
O'Keeffe, Georgia, 382–383
Orbita, 291
Orioli, Giuseppe "Pino": as D. H. Lawrence publisher, 330, 351, 360; as friend of D. H. Lawrence, 320; as friend of Frieda, 319, 355, 356; and *Lady Chatterley's Lover* manuscripts, 352, 378
Orizaba, Mexico, 285
Ormea, Italy, 353
Otis, Raymond, 383
Oxford University, 50, 296
Oxford University Press, 222

Palace Hotel, San Francisco, 264
Palance, Jack, 368
Pankhurst, Emmeline, 60
Pankow sanatorium, 149
Pansies, 333
Papeete, Tahiti, 264
Paris, 297
Parker, Dorothy, 403
Pasadena Art Institute, 371
Passion of Christ, The film, 284
Patagonia, 71, 76
Patchen, "Ole Cap'," 346
Paterson Strike Pageant, 1913, 267
Patmore, Brigit, 185, 188
Patmore, Coventry, 185
Patrician, The (Galsworthy), 102
"Paul Morel," 99, 101, 102, 120. *See also Sons and Lovers*
Paul Morel, or His Mother's Darling, 125
Peccati e gli Amori di Taormina, I (Saglimbeni), 240
PEN, 304
Penguin Books, 405
Pension Balestra, Florence, 232
Perkins, Frances, 387
Perth, Australia, 257–258
Phillips, Harry Irving "Hi," 343–344, 345
Picasso, Pablo, 371
Pieve di Teco, Italy, 353
Pilgrimage (Richardson), 308
Pinker, J. B., 142, 158, 169, 210, 236, 238
Pink House, Taos, 272, 275, 276
Piovine, Count and Countess Guido di, 383
Plato, 78, 154
Plessen, Elisabeth von, 36, 37, 38
Plumed Serpent, The, 288, 290, 294, 304, 307, 387
Podewils, Baron, 27
Poe, Edgar Allan, 129
Poetry, 159
Pointed Roofs (Richardson), 308
Pollinger, Laurence, 345, 351, 359, 403
Port Cros, France, 333
Port Isabel, Texas, 397, 398, 399, 408, 409–410, 415
"Portrait of Mabel Dodge at the Villa Curonia" (Stein), 267
Possessed, The (Dostoyevsky), 195
Pound, Ezra, 97, 159
Powell, Lawrence Clark, 370
Power and Secret of the Jesuits, The (Fülöp-Miller), 460n62
Prague University, 57
Prescott, William Hickling, 9, 290
Prichard, Katharine Susannah, 258
Prince George Hotel, New York, 344, 461n6
"Princess, The," 303
Principles of Social Reconstruction, 196
Prussian Officer and Other Stories, The, 139, 142, 174, 236
Psalm 121, 415
Psalm 33, 160
Psychiatrisch-Neurologische Klinik, Graz, 70
Psychoanalysis and the Unconscious, 2, 250, 253, 268
Puebla, Mexico, 285
Putnam publishers, 379

Quarant'Otto, 320
Queen's College, London, 143
Quetzalcoatl, 285, 288

Radford, Maitland, 197
Rainbow, The, 355; drafting of, 128, 154, 160, 169–171, 176, 232; publication of, 158, 161, 186, 196, 236, 245; ruled obscene, 190, 191; sale of manuscript of, 370, 371, 374

Rainbow Books and Music, 198
Ranalow, Frederic, 208
Rananim, 160–161, 172, 174, 185, 190–191, 205, 211, 225
Ransom, Harry, 407, 408
Raschowa, Upper Silesia, 10–12
Rasputin, the Holy Devil (Fülöp-Miller), 334
Ratcliffe-on-the-Wreake school, 99
Ravagli, Angelo Nunzio Gaspero "Angelino," "Angie": description, of, 309–310, 343; early affair with Frieda, 310–311, 315, 321–322, 326, 327, 353; as factotum to Frieda, 363, 372, 380, 381–382; and Frieda's death, 414, 416; limitations of, 345, 346, 371, 381; marries Frieda, 401; and New Mexico, 347, 348, 354, 355–356; opinions on, 318, 347, 349, 371, 372, 399; peccadillos of, 371–373, 381, 390–392, 393, 412, 415; returns Lawrence remains to Taos, 365–366; travel, 387, 409; World War I experiences of, 310, 311
Ravagli, Federico, 353, 354
Ravagli, Frieda. *See* Lawrence, Frieda
Ravagli, Ina Serafina, 309–311, 320, 354, 360, 371
Ravagli, Magda, 310
Ravagli, Stefanino, 310
Ravello, Italy, 317
Record, Philadelphia, 442n3
Reed, John, 268
Reflections on the Death of a Porcupine and Other Essays, 307
Religion and the Rise of Capitalism (Tawney), 409
Religionssoziologie (Weber), 245
Returned Servicemen's League, 262
Reventlow, Franziska zu "Fanny," 66–67, 75, 79, 149
Revolution, Munich, 148
Rhys, Ernest, 97
Rhys, Grace, 97
Rhythm, 128
Richardson, Dorothy, 308
Rich, Edwin, 345
Richthofen-Marquier, Baroness Anna Elise Lydia von (mother): and D. H. Lawrence, 114–115, 123, 356; death of, 359; family history of, 13–18; flawed marriage of, 20, 23, 30–31, 136; heart attack of, 249; as hostess, 105; love of literature, 23, 356, 357; in old age, 233, 234, 357; parental ineptitude of, 24, 56; sees Frieda through Lawrence's heroines, 137, 234; on Weekley, 43, 56; and World War I, 161, 224; youth of, 8–9, 10, 19–20
Richthofen, General-Lieutenant Bernhard von, 37
Richthofen, Curt von (cousin), 32–33, 170
Richthofen, Dieprand von (Oswald's son), 35
Richthofen, Elisabeth Helene Amalie Sophie von "Else" (sister), 9, 23, 28, 33, 38, 41, 46, 50, 53; born, 21; childhood, 8, 27; as de facto head of household, 29; engagement, 57; Heidelberg doctorate, 57; meets Webers, 57; relationship with father, 29; as teacher, 29–30. *See also* Jaffe, Else
Richthofen, Emil von (great-uncle), 10, 11, 20
Richthofen, Emma Maria Frieda Johanna Baroness (Freiin) von. *See* Lawrence, Frieda
Richthofen, Baron Friedrich Ernst Emil Ludwig von (father): career of, 12, 13, 20, 21, 22, 28; courtship and marriage, 19–20; degenerative neurological disease suffered by, 136; description of, 8, 19; dies, 173–174; drinking, gambling and other vices of, 13, 33, 149–150, 422n40; family history of, 10–12; flawed marriage of, 24, 30–31, 169–170;, and Frieda, 54, 104–105, 106–107, 111; as parent, 24, 56
Richthofen, Hartmann von (Oswald's son), 35
Richthofen, Helene von (aunt), 11
Richthofen, Johann Karl Christian Friedrich Ludwig August Praetorius von (grandfather), 10–11, 12
Richthofen, Louis von (uncle), 11

Richthofen, Baron Manfred von, 10, 185, 211, 221, 305
Richthofen, Ferdinand von, 10
Richthofen, Helene Johanna Matilde von "Nusch" (sister), 9, 25, 28, 29, 34, 37, 39, 46, 47, 58, 107, 133, 234; born, 23; childhood, 8, 24, 30; children of, 56, 62; description of, 56, 250; and D. H. Lawrence, 105, 250; engagement and marriage to Schreibershofen, 54, 55, 56; and Frieda, 61–62, 250, 398, 399; relationship with mother, 234; relationship with and marriage to Krug, 250, 330; and World War I, 161; and World War II, 398
Richthofen, Oswald von, 10, 35, 36
Richthofen, Oswald von, Jr., 35
Richthofen, Paul von (uncle), 11
Richthofen sisters, development of personalities of, 24–25
Rickards, Edward Arden, 304
Rilke, Rainer Maria, 67, 82
Rio Grande Gorge, 275
"Ripley's Believe It or Not" television show, 368
Riva, Italy, 122
Rivera, Diego, 371
RMS Orsova, 257
RMS Osterley, 253, 254
RMS Tahiti, 264
Roberts, Warren, 407
"Rocking Horse Winner, The," 316
Rogers, Millicent, 382, 406
Romance of Words, The (Weekley), 84, 103, 116
Rosenbach, Abraham Simon Wolfe "Abe," 352, 370
Rosenthal, Sir Charles, 262
Ross, Vera Edith, 360. *See also* Weekley, Vera
Rossi, Giovanni, 309
Rothschild, Baron Phillipe de, 383
Rottach-am-Tegernsee, Germany, 338
Rousseau, Henri, 335
Royal Literary Fund, 167, 222
Rubenstein, Helena, 332
Ruskin, John, 97
Russell, Alys, 162, 163
Russell, Bertrand, 178, 181, 183, 185, 186, 192, 195, 196, 197, 210, 218; and D. H. Lawrence, 175, 177, 181–183, 308; on D. H. Lawrence, 182, 218, 323, 390; on Frieda Lawrence, 182, 389–390; and Ottoline Morrell, 162–163
Rydal Press, Santa Fe, 364, 460n62

Saarburg, Germany, 21
Sablon (Metz suburb), 7, 23, 379
Sackville-West, Baron Edward, 377
"Saga of Siegmund." *See The Trespasser*
Saint Christiana (Sainte-Chrétienne) school, Metz, 34
Saint Geneviève, 1, 254
Saint Ives, Cornwall, 198, 211
St. Mawr, 288, 301, 303, 307
Saint-Nizier-de-Pariset, 333
Saint Paul's Girls' school, 183
Saint Paul's Boys' school, 118, 130, 140, 141, 404
Samuelli, Maria, 122
San Cristobal, New Mexico, 283, 301
San Francisco, 1, 264
Sanger, Margaret, 268
San Geronimo festival, 274–275
San Gervasio, Italy, 243
Sangre de Cristo mountains, 2, 3, 271, 410
San Juan, Mexico, 285
Santa Fe, New Mexico, 3, 269, 270, 271, 277, 284, 381, 383, 410
Santayana, George, 398
Sardinia, 247–248
Sargent, John Singer, 322
Saturday Review magazine, 142
Sauerwein, Henry A., Jr., 387
Savona, Italy, 353, 409, 416
Schaffhausen, Switzerland, 147
Schaffner, Perdita (daughter of H. D. and Cecil Gray), 231
Scheyer, Galka, 369, 371
Schiller, Friedrich von, 34, 37
Schloffer, Frieda "Friedel," 58, 62, 72. *See also* Gross, Frieda
Schlosser, Josefa Theresia Walburga (Frieda's grandmother), 14
Schmidt, Samuel, 10
Schmidt, Tobias, 10

Schnitger, Marianne. *See* Weber, Marianne
Schoenberner, Franz, 330
Schopenhauer, Arthur, 95
Schreibershofen, Anita von, 56
Schreibershofen, Hadubrand von, 62
Schreibershofen, Max von, 54
Schreibershofen, Nusch von. *See* Richthofen, Helene Johanna Matilde von
Schröer, Professor and Mrs., 39, 40, 41
Schubert, Franz, 59, 208, 321
Schultheiss, Paul, 10
Schulthess, Amalia de, 407, 408
Schulthess, Hans de, 407, 408
Schwabing, Munich, 64, 65, 66, 73, 109
Science of Life, The (Huxley/Wells), 331
Scilly Islands, 231
Scotland Yard, 70
Scott, Major William Rendal, 258, 262
Scott-Moncrieff, Charles, 320
Sea and Sardinia, 247–248, 253, 322
Seaman, Bernal Edward De Martelly "Teddy," 315, 335
Seaman, Eileen, 315, 316
Seaman, Geoffrey, 373
Seaman, Richard, 400, 404
Secker, Martin, publisher, 220, 238, 252, 332
Secker, Rina, 309
Seidel, Frau (servant) 24, 25, 33
Selma (Friedrich von Richthofen's mistress) 33, 149, 422n40
Seltzer, Adele, 290
Seltzer, Thomas, 236, 237, 238, 257, 259, 281–282, 299, 344
Settignano, Italy, 232
17 Friedrich Wilhelmstrasse, Berlin, 35
sexual license in Taos, 390–391
"Shades of Spring," 143
"Shadow in the Rose Garden, The," 298
Shakespeare, William, 37, 53, 356, 409
Shakespeare and Company, 298
Shaw, George Bernard, 103
Shelley, Percy Bysshe, 150, 182, 200, 204
Sherwood Forest, 61, 209
Shestov, Leo, 227
Shultis, Velma, 383
Sicily, 239–242, 246, 251–254
Sidgwick and Jackson publishers, 198
Siebenhaar, William, 258
Signature, The, 186, 188
Sigyn, 147
Silesia, Upper, 19, 26
Simenon, Georges, 69
Sinclair, Upton, 268
Sinister Street (Mackenzie), 171
"The Sisters," 133, 134, 135, 136, 138, 146. *See also*, "The Wedding Ring," *Women in Love*
Sitwell, Edith, 328
Sitwell, Sir George, 329
Sitwell, Lady Ida, 329
Sitwell, Osbert, 328
Skinner, Mollie, 258, 293–294
Slade School of Art, London, 165, 190, 296, 360
Smith, Bessie, 335
"Snap Dragon," 128
Sobieniowski, Floryan, 143
Social Darwinism, 73
Society for the Suppression of Vice. *See* New York Society for the Suppression of Vice
Songs of Experience (Blake), 93
Songs of Innocence (Blake), 93
Sons and Lovers: disposition of manuscript of, 378; foreword to, 127–128; Frieda on, 125–126, 153; published, 150, 245; reception of, 142, 143, 154, 167, 387; Sterne and, 2, 253, 273, 300–301; writing of, 125, 132, 140. *See also* "Paul Morel"
Son of Woman (Murry), 344, 349
Sorbonne, Paris, 40
Spender, Stephen, 386
Spicheren, battle of, 12
Spotorno, Italy, 309, 315, 316, 333, 354
SS Conte Grande, 343
Stahl, Ernst, 83
Standard, London, 142
Standard Oil, 363
Stanford University, 374, 377
Staten Island, New York, 394
Steffens, Lincoln, 268
Stein, Gertrude, 233, 267
Stein, Leo, 233, 253, 279
Stekel, Wilhelm, 148
Stendhal, 53

Stendhal Gallery, Los Angeles, 371
Stern, Benjamin, 344, 345
Sterne, Mabel Dodge, 254, 257, 264, 271, 272, 273–279, 280; biography, 266–269, description of, 2; on Frieda, 266, 273; and Gertrude Stein, 267; gossips about Lawrences, 270; health problems of, 267; meets Lawrences, 2–3, 265–266; as salonist, 267–268; wealth of, 267; woos D. H. Lawrence, 253, 260–261. *See also* Luhan, Mabel Dodge
Sterne, Maurice, 266, 269
Stevens, Annette, 385
Stevenson, Robert Louis, 92
Stieglitz, Alfred, 268, 332, 347, 366
Still Life (Murry), 158, 175, 176, 198
Stokowski, Leopold, 372
Strachey, Lytton, 190
Stranski, Barbara, 14
Strasbourg, France, 12
Stravinsky, Igor, 400, 402
Stravinsky, Vera, 400, 402
Strauss, Richard, 321
Studies in Classic American Literature, 219, 299
"Study," 95, 198
Suchocki, Bogdan von, 67
Sudermann, Hermann, 37
Sumner, John S., 395
"Sun," 335
Sunday Dispatch, London, 332
Sussex, 172, 173
Swan on a Black Sea (Toksvig), 462n29
Swayne, Ruth, 383, 413
Swinburne, Algernon, 93
Sydney Bulletin, 262
syphilis in Taos pueblo, 269

Tages-Anzeiger, Zurich, 83–84
Taormina, Sicily, 239–242, 244, 246, 251–254
Taos, New Mexico, 2, 233, 253, 268–269, 270, 271–280, 300, 345, 380, 381, 382, 387, 392, 399, 401, 402, 406, 409, 412, 413, 415
Taos and Its Artists (Luhan), 399
Taos Chamber of Commerce, 383
Taos Star, 381
Taos Valley, 271–272
Taos Valley News and El Crepusculo, 281. *See also El Crepusculo*
Tawney, Richard Henry, 409
Taylor, Geraldine, 305
Taylor, Norman, 305
Teapot Dome scandal, 370
Tedlock, E. W., Jr., 410
Tehuacán, Mexico, 285
Tempest, The (Shakespeare), 91
Temple of Quetzalcoatl, Mexico, 285
Temple of the Tooth, Ceylon, 256
Tennyson, Alfred Lord, 41, 45
10 Theobaldswall, Metz, 21
Teotihuacán, Mexico, 285
Texcatlipoca, Mexico, 288
Thackeray, William Makepeace, 53, 92
Theocritus, 239
theosophy, 267
Thirroul, Australia, 259, 263
Thompson, Clarence, 300
"Thorn in the Flesh, The," 139
Thornycroft, Sir Hamo, 221, 247
"Three O'Clock in the Morning," 284
Thus Spake Zarathustra (Nietzsche), 59, 72
Tilley, Gertrude (Ernest Weekley's sister), 45, 118, 120
Tilley, John, 44, 118, 120
Times, The, London, 151, 355, 363, 406
Times Literary Supplement, The, 154, 197, 218, 321
Tindall, William York, 375
Tipografia Giuntina, 331
Tipton, Albert, 401
Titanic, 111
Titus, Edward, 332, 352
Tiwa Indians, 268–269, 274, 288
Toksvig, Signe, 352, 389, 462n29
Tolstoy, Leo, 96, 124
Toomer, Jean, 372
Touch and Go, 222
Tower Beyond Tragedy, 307, 348
Treaty of Versailles, 226
Tredozio, Italy, 311, 318
Tregerthen, Cornwall, 199–200, 206
Trench, Frederic, 232
Trench, Lilian, 232
Trent, River, 49

Trespasser, The, 109, 111, 113, 122, 227, 236
Trial, The (Kafka), 148
Trient (Trento), Italy, 121
Trinity College, Cambridge University, 40
Trollope, Anthony, 398
Troppau asylum, 148
Trotter, Philip, 336–338
tuberculosis: D. H. Lawrence and, 194, 197, 207, 306, 321, 329–330, 339; Katherine Mansfield and, 282; in Weekley family, 42
Turner, Reginald, 319, 320
Turnham Green, Chiswick, 140, 141, 155
Twentieth Century Limited, 345
23 Fifth Avenue, New York, 268
23 Washington Square, New York, 268
Twilight of the Idols (Nietzsche), 73
Twilight in Italy, 197, 236
208 Augny West, Sablon, 7
2 West Street, Finsbury Circus, 184
typhoid fever, 12

U-boats, 210
Ullman, Regina, 82, 245
Ulysses (Joyce), 298, 405
Unconscious, The (Jung), 223
Underwood National school, 92
U.S. Rubber Company, 363
Untermeyer, Louis, 368
University of Bern, 40
University of California, 271, 278, 378
University of California at Los Angeles, 370
University College, Nottingham, 40, 51, 56, 63, 198
University of Dijon, 370
University of Edinburgh, 50
University of Liverpool, 50
University of Munich, 71
University of New Mexico, Albuquerque, 388, 397, 410
University of Texas at Austin, 407
Upper Darby, Pennsylvania, 159
Uxbridge, Middlesex, 42, 45, 55

Valdez, Alex A., 401
Van Dine, S. S., 70
Vale of Health, 183, 193
Vanity Fair magazine, 299
Van Vechten, Carl, 268, 402
Vence, France, 339–340, 343, 350, 355, 357–360
Venice, Italy, 246
Verga, Giovanni, 255, 256, 307
Verlaine, Paul, 94
Verona, Italy, 134
Victoria and Albert Museum, 296, 308, 384
Viking publishers, 360, 364, 379
Villa Beau-Soliel, Bandol, 338
Villa Bernarda, Spotorno, 309, 315, 316, 333, 354
Villa Curonia, Florence, 267
Villa Igea, Gargnano, 122, 127, 131
Villa Mirenda, Florence, 320, 326, 327, 333
Villa Robermond, Vence, 338–339, 350, 358
Villingen, Germany, 17
Vinkovci, Yugoslavia, 148
Virgil, 91
Virgin and the Gipsy, The, 314, 351, 360, 373
"Virgin Mother, The," 100, 198
Virginia Quarterly Review, 388
Visconti, Marco, 254
Vittorio Emmanuele II (king of Italy), 310
Voghera, Italy, 353

Wagner, Richard, 37, 99
Wake-up Call, 66
Walling, William Ernest, 268
Walsh, Raoul, 264
Warlock, Peter. *See* Heseltine, Philip
Warren, Dorothy, 191, 336
wartime harassment. *See* anti-German sentiment
Waterfield, Aubrey, 151, 152
Waterfield, Lina, 151, 152
Waters, Frank, 388
Weaver, Harriet Shaw, 179
Weber, Alfred: affair with Else Jaffe, 57, 234, 333, 356; befriends Lawrences, 111, 115, 155; Max Weber on, 234, 245; in World War I, 161
Weber, Marianne, 30, 57, 245
Weber, Max, 30, 57, 62, 68, 234, 245
Weckruf. *See Wake-up Call*

"Wedding Ring, The," 153. *See also* "The Sisters," *Women in Love*
Wedekind, Frank, 65, 66, 67
Weekley, Agnes (Ernest's mother): children of, 41–43; description of, 43; evicts Frieda, 155; Frieda meets, 44–45; as grandmother, 314; manages Chiswick ménage, 119; on religious education, 118
Weekley, Barbara Joy "Barby" (third child of Ernest and Frieda): as art student, 184, 242–243; born, 60;, childhood of, 183, 184, 242–243; Christmas visit of, 308, 309, 312, 316; and D. H. Lawrence, 296, 314; as family advocate for Frieda, 242–243, 393, 405–406; on Frieda's divorce, 373, 393; ill health of, 355, 357–358; marriage of, 358, 384, 463n57; relationship with mother, 104, 137, 141, 411
Weekley, Bruce Edward "Ted" (Ernest's brother), 44, 120, 358
Weekley, Charles (Ernest's brother), 44
Weekley, Charles (Ernest's father), 41, 42, 43
Weekley, Elsa Agnes Frieda (second child of Ernest and Frieda): born, 58; childhood of, 120, 130, 156, 183; on D. H. Lawrence, 296; on Frieda, 77; Italian visit, 309, 315, 316; marriage, 373; nurses Barby, 358; relationship with mother, 104, 141, 233, 405; on Weekleys, 120
Weekley, Ernest: background of, 40, 41–42; at Barby's wedding, 463n57; battle over visitation rights, 131, 132, 141, 146, 154; career of, 56, 62, 84, 103, 116, 426n21; courtship and marriage, 41–43, 46–47; as D. H. Lawrence's professor, 95; model for Huxley novel, 324; moves to Hampstead, 117–118; old age and death of, 400, 405, 406; reaction to Frieda's desertion, 105, 108, 116, 126
Weekley, Frieda. *See* Lawrence, Frieda
Weekley, George (Ernest's brother), 44, 120
Weekley, Gertrude. *See* Tilley, Gertrude
Weekley, Ian (Monty's son) 360, 404
Weekley, Julia (Monty's daughter), 384, 404
Weekley, Julia (sister of Agnes), 44
Weekley, Kit (Ernest's sister), 44, 155, 156
Weekley, Lucy (Ted's wife), 44–45, 358
Weekley, Maude (Ernest's sister): description of, 44; in charge of Frieda's children, 119, 155, 314; disapproves of Frieda, 55, 79–80, 141, 155; on religious education of children, 55–58
Weekley, Montague (Ernest's brother), 42
Weekley, Montague Karl Richthofen "Monty" (first child of Ernest and Frieda): adult life and career of, 296, 308, 358, 360, 384, 400; born, 54; early childhood of, 56, 58, 59–60, 118, 119; and Frieda's departure from Nottingham, 116, 137, 140–141; meets D. H. Lawrence, 322–323; relationship with daughter, 404; talent for mimicry, 59, 119, 184, 322; visits Taos, 383–384; as youth, 208, 221, 240–241, 296
Weekley, Vera (Monty's wife), 404. *See also* Ross, Vera
Weeks, Carl, 383
Weiner Reichsanstalt. *See* Imperial Institute, Vienna
Weininger, Otto, 188
Welbeck Abbey, 162, 329
Wells, Cady, 383
Wells, G. P., 331
Wells, Harry K., 368, 378
Wells, H. G., 96, 97, 154, 158, 331, 339
Wells, Jane, 177
Wells, Jenny, 368, 378
Wellington House, 177
Wellington, New Zealand, 264
Wernicke, Carl, 74
West, Rebecca, 251
Westminster Gazette, London, 142, 158
Wemyss, earl of, 144, 181
What "Mein Kampf" Means to America (Hackett), 389, 462n29
"What's the Big Idea." *See* "And the Fullness Thereof."
Wheelock, Ruth, 253

Where Angels Fear to Tread (Forster), 174
Whiteman, Paul, 284
White Peacock, The, 97, 98, 99, 100, 157. *See also* "Laetitia," "Nethermere"
White Slave Traffic Act, 395
Whitman, Walt, 227, 268
Widowing of Mrs. Holroyd, The, 165, 167
Wickham, Anna, 435n96
Wiehre (Freiburg suburb), 47
Wilde, Oscar, 319
Wilder, Thornton, 372
"Wilful Woman, The," 276
Wilhelmy, Ida, 58, 62, 117, 403, 409, 436n14
Willenstein, Franziska, 14
Williams, Tennessee, 385–386
Wilhelm (manservant), 24, 25, 30, 33
Wilhelm I (kaiser), 12, 18–19
Wilhelm II (kaiser), 36–37, 239
Wilson, Edmund, 331
Wolfratshausen, 107, 109, 135
"Woman Who Rode Away, The," 302, 303
Women in Love, 375; drafting of, 128, 202–203, 206–207, 209–210; publication of, 236, 238, 247, 251; "suppressed" Prologue of, 202–203, 206. *See also* "The Sisters," "The Wedding Ring"
Women's Social and Political Union (WSPU), 60
women's suffrage, 101, 129
Woolf, Leonard, 162, 198
Woolf, Virginia, 162, 198, 251, 308
World War I, 161, 268. *See also* anti-German sentiment, Armistice, Treaty of Versailles
World War II, 385, 390, 398. *See also* anti-German sentiment, Japanese internment
Worth, battle of, 12
WSPU. *See* Women's Social and Political Union
Wurlitzer, Helene, 396, 412, 415
Wyewurk, Thirroul, 259, 262

Xochimilco, Mexico, 285

Yardley's Cosmetics, 296
Yeats, William Butler, 83, 97
Yorke, Dorothy (Arabella), 323
Young, Francis Brett, 237, 239
Young, Jessica Brett, 237, 239
Young-Hunter, Eve, 383
Young-Hunter, John, 383
Young, Jessica, 237

Zeitlin, Jacob Israel, 369–371, 403
Zeitlin, Jean, 370
Zell-am-See, Austria, 250
Zennor, Cornwall, 198, 200
Zurich Polizeikommando, 65
Zurich, Switzerland, 66